Telecommunications, Broadcasting, and Information

Law, Policy, and Regulation

Edited by

Dr. Amit M. Schejter and Sangyong Han

Pennsylvania State University

cognella

San Diego, CA

First published in the United States of America in 2010 by Cognella, a division of University Readers, Inc.

Trademark Notice: Product or corporate names may be trademarks or registered trademarks, and are used only for identification and explanation without intent to infringe.

14 13 12 11 10   1 2 3 4 5

Printed in the United States of America

ISBN: 978-1609279-93-6

www.cognella.com 800.200.3908

CONTENTS

CHAPTER 3: REGULATING THE
TELECOMMUNICATIONS INFRASTRUCTURE

CHAPTER 1

PRINCIPLES, INSTITUTIONS, AND VALUES

The first chapter in this course introduces you to the basic concepts of communications policy and regulation. It is important to understand that all the rules and regulations you will encounter in the course of your study emanate from a structured system that developed principles justifying them and means to implement them. Thus, this first chapter discusses the structure of the system, the organs that make the decisions and the justification for making regulatory policies. It also differentiates between the different types of policies that exist and highlights the fact that one of the unique aspects of communications policy is that it encompasses regulations aimed at reaching both economic and social goals. The two principles that underlie telecommunications policy in the United States—freedom of expression and serving the public interest—are presented in this chapter as well. It concludes with a discussion of spectrum policy, the cornerstone of telecommunications policy in the United States.

UNIT 1

Chaos or Order?
The U.S. Legal System

In this reading, journalism professors Kent R. Middleton and William E. Lee provide an overview of the American legal system. Understanding the structure of the legal system and the principles that guide it is of fundamental importance to any understanding of the regulatory system. Following the lecture and the reading you should expect to retain the following principles:

a. The need for laws

b. The sources of law

c. The hierarchy of certain rules over others

d. The distinction between the different branches of government

e. The distinction between the federal and state systems

f. The hierarchy within the court system

g. The role of the courts in determining the law

h. The difference between criminal, civil, and administrative law.

Public Communication
and the Law

William E. Lee and Kent R. Middleton

The jailing of a journalist is an extraordinary event in the United States. On July 6, 2005, *New York Times* reporter Judith Miller was jailed, not for anything she wrote, but because she refused to testify before a grand jury investigating the leaking of a CIA agent's name. Miller claimed that the First Amendment protects reporters who, as part of their newsgathering activities, promise confidentiality to sources. Miller's claims were unsuccessful; a federal district court and appellate court ruled that reporters, like other citizens, must answer questions posed during legitimate law enforcement investigations. Miller's need to protect the confidentiality of her sources was outweighed by the government's need to investigate crimes.

The *Miller* case highlights many of the complex issues that will be discussed in this book. Should journalists have special status in our society, or should journalists be treated like other citizens? If journalists are entitled to special status, would the category of journalists be narrowly confined to reporters for newspapers and broadcast stations, or would it also include web bloggers? Is newsgathering by journalists entitled to the same level of constitutional protection as publishing? How should courts analyze the competing interests of journalists and other segments of society?

This book is concerned with law that affects journalists, as well as law affecting other public communicators such as advertising and public relations professionals. This book will discuss not only the law governing reporter–source relationships but also the law of libel, privacy, political communication, copyright, obscenity, coverage of court proceedings, and access to government-held information. The book focuses on the law affecting the content of public communication, including printed publications, electronic media, advertising, and public relations.

This chapter will examine legal concepts and procedures that are important to an understanding of the law of public communication. It will talk about the purpose and organization of law. It will also describe court procedures and discuss how communicators work with lawyers.

THE SOURCES OF LAW

Law can be defined in many ways, but for our purposes, law is the system of rules that govern society. The system of rules serves many functions in our society, including regulating the behavior of citizens and corporations. Law prohibits murder and restricts what advertisers can say about their products. It provides a vehicle to settle disputes, such as when a reporter refuses to testify in court. Furthermore, law limits the government's power to interfere with individual rights, such as the right to speak and publish.

The law in the United States comes primarily from six sources: constitutions, statutes, administrative rules and regulations, executive actions, the **common law**,[1] and the law of **equity**.

Constitutional Law

Constitutions are the supreme source of law in the United States and are the most direct reflection of the kind of government desired by the people. Constitutions of both the federal and state governments supersede all other declarations of public policy. The Constitution of the federal government and the constitutions of the fifty states establish the framework for governing. They outline the structure of government and define governmental authority and responsibilities.

Frequently, a constitution limits the powers of government, as in the case of the Bill of Rights, the first ten amendments to the U.S. Constitution. The Bill of Rights, printed in Appendix B of this book, protects the rights and liberties of U.S. citizens against infringement by government. The First Amendment, particularly its prohibition against laws abridging freedom of speech and the press, provides the foundation for communication law.

The federal constitution is the country's ultimate legal authority. Any federal law, state law, or state constitution that contradicts the U.S. Constitution cannot be implemented; the U.S. Constitution prevails. Similarly, a state constitution prevails in conflicts with either the **statutory law** or the common law in the same state. However, federal and state laws that do not conflict with the federal constitution can provide more protection for communicators than is available under the First Amendment alone. For example, the majority of states shield journalists from revealing confidential news sources in more circumstances than the First Amendment as interpreted by the U.S. Supreme Court.

The Supreme Court, the nation's supreme judicial body, has the last word on the meaning of the federal constitution. Each state's supreme court is the interpreter of that state's constitution. Only the U.S. Supreme Court can resolve conflicts between the federal and state constitutions. The courts make constitutional law when they decide a case or controversy by interpreting a constitution. In 1980, the U.S. Supreme Court said the First Amendment requires that the public and press ordinarily be permitted to attend trials.[2] Constitutional law can be understood only by reading the opinions of the courts.

The U.S. Constitution is hard to amend and therefore is changed infrequently. Amendments to the U.S. Constitution can be proposed only by two-thirds of the members of both houses of Congress or by a convention called by two-thirds of the state legislatures. Amendments must be ratified by three-fourths of the state legislatures or by state constitutional conventions in three-fourths of the states.

Statutory Law

A major source of law in the United States is the collection of statutes and ordinances written by legislative bodies—the U.S. Congress, the fifty state legislatures, county commissions, city councils, and countless other lawmaking bodies. Statutes set forth enforceable rules to govern social behavior. Areas of communication law controlled by statutes include advertising, copyright, electronic media, obscenity, and access to government-held information.

Almost all of this country's criminal law, including a prohibition against the mailing of obscenity, is statutory. Statutes not only prohibit antisocial acts but also frequently provide for the oversight of acceptable behavior. For example, the federal Communications Act of 1934 was adopted so that the broadcast spectrum would be used for the public good.

The process of adopting statutes allows lawmakers to study carefully a complicated issue—such as how to regulate the use of the electromagnetic spectrum—and write an appropriate law. The process permits anyone or any group to make suggestions through letters, personal contacts, and hearings. In practice, well-organized special interests such as broadcasters, cable television system operators, and telephone companies substantially influence the legislative process. As shown in Chapter 7, highly regulated industries have the largest lobbying expenditures.

The adoption of a statute does not conclude the lawmaking process. Executive branch officials often have to interpret statutes through administrative rules. Judges add meaning when either the statutes themselves or their application are challenged in court. Judges explain how statutes apply in specific cases, as when the U.S. Supreme Court ruled in 1984 that the Copyright Act allows homeowners to tape television programs on their VCRs.[3] In 1989, the Court said a provision in the federal Freedom of Information Act allows the FBI to withhold from the public a compilation of an individual's criminal records stored in a computer database. The Court said that giving the records to a reporter would constitute an "unwarranted" invasion of privacy.[4]

The courts can invalidate state and local laws that conflict with federal laws or the U.S. Constitution, including the First Amendment. In 1974, the U.S. Supreme Court declared unconstitutional a Florida statute that required newspapers to print replies to published attacks on political candidates.[5] In 2006, the Court struck down a Vermont law limiting both the amounts candidates for state office could spend on their campaigns and the amounts individuals and political parties could contribute to those campaigns.[6]

Sometimes federal laws **preempt** state regulation, thereby monopolizing governmental control over a specific subject. Article VI of the U.S. Constitution, known as the "supremacy clause," provides that state law cannot supersede federal law. In addition, under the Constitution, congressional regulation of the economy supersedes state law. In 1984, the U.S. Supreme Court nullified an Oklahoma statute banning the advertising of wine on cable television because it conflicted with federal law prohibiting the editing of national and regional television programming carried by cable systems.[7]

Administrative Law

Federal agencies such as the Federal Communications Commission (FCC) and the Federal Trade Commission (FTC) develop rules and decisions known as **administrative law**. These agencies dominate several areas of communication law. The FCC regulates the broadcast, cable, satellite, and telephone industries. The FTC regulates advertising and telemarketing. Other agencies overseeing communication include the Securities and Exchange Commission (SEC), which controls communication related to the securities industry, the Federal Election Commission (FEC), which regulates political campaign contributions and expenditures, and the Food and Drug Administration (FDA), which regulates

prescription drug and medical product advertising. Table 1.1 lists these agencies, their areas of regulation, and key regulations.

Administrative agencies are often founded on the premise that they would be independent bodies of experts who set policy solely by analyzing facts. However, regulation by administrative agencies is an intensely political process involving complex interactions among the regulatory agency, the regulated industry, Congress, the President, and public interest groups. The President influences an agency by naming commissioners, subject to approval by the Senate, and designating an agency's chair. Through the Office of Management and Budget, the executive branch reviews proposed regulations to determine consistency with the President's policies. Congress shapes regulation by telling agencies what industries or practices they can regulate. Moreover, Congress controls the budget of agencies, and Congressional committees closely monitor the actions of agencies. Regulated industries, such as telecommunications, are among the largest contributors to political campaigns. These industries use their ties to elected officials to influence regulatory agencies.

Successful nominees for agency positions have close ties to powerful political leaders. Michael Powell, chair of the FCC from 2001 to March 2005, is the son of former Secretary of State Colin Powell; Julius Genachowski, President Obama's choice for FCC chair, was Obama's law school classmate, basketball teammate, and advisor during the 2008 presidential campaign. The nominating process, like other aspects of agency regulation, involves the tug and pull of political factions. For example, because of a political stalemate, the position of FDA commissioner was vacant for nearly two years after President George W. Bush took office.[8] Senate Democrats insisted that the nominee not be tied to the pharmaceutical industry. The drug industry spent heavily on advertising in favor of Republican candidates in the 2000 and 2002 elections.[9] In return for its support of Republicans, the drug industry expected to influence President Bush's selection of a nominee. In July 2001, Senate Democrats rejected a nominee as being too closely tied to the industry; in February 2002, the drug industry complained to the Bush administration that a potential nominee would be too aggressive

TABLE 1.1 Federal Regulatory Agencies

Agency	Areas of Regulation	Key Regulations
Federal Communications Commission (FCC)	Radio, television, cable, satellite, telephone	Political broadcasting rules, indecency regulations, children's television regulations
Federal Election Commission (FEC)	Federal elections	Contribution limits and prohibitions, disclosure of campaign finances, campaign expenditures
Federal Trade Commission (FTC)	Advertising (except prescription drugs and medical devices), telemarketing	Deceptive advertising, product labeling, unfair consumer practices, children's online privacy, tobacco health warnings
Food and Drug Administration (FDA)	Food, drugs, medical devices, cosmetics	Prescription drug advertising, medical device advertising, food, drug, cosmetic labels
Securities and Exchange Commission (SEC)	Securities brokers, investment advisors, stock exchanges	Insider trading, false/misleading information

a regulator. Finally, the Bush administration found a nominee who was acceptable to both sides.[10] In October 2002, the Senate approved Mark McClellan as FDA Commissioner. McClellan, whose brother was President Bush's press secretary, comes from a prominent Texas political family.

McClellan left the FDA in 2004 to become the administrator of the Centers for Medicare and Medicaid Services. Because the FDA regulates one quarter of the nation's economy, and addresses controversial topics, such as the availability of the "morning-after" emergency contraception pill, the agency draws intense scrutiny from politicians. Politicians, upset over the agency's handling of the "morning-after" pill, fought over McClellan's successor for more than a year before confirming Lester Crawford as head of the FDA in July 2005.[11] Crawford suddenly resigned in September 2005 and joined a lobbying firm. Shortly after his resignation, it was disclosed that he was under investigation for conflict-of-interest due to his ownership of shares in companies regulated by the FDA. (Employees of regulatory agencies are barred from owning shares in companies regulated by the agency.) In October 2006, Crawford pleaded guilty to lying and conflict-of-interest charges in connection with stock ownership.[12]

Congress creates administrative agencies to supervise activities or industries that require more attention than legislators can provide. Administrative agencies serve a variety of functions, unique in the American system of government. First, agencies engage in **rule making**, a process that is similar to the legislative function. For example, the FCC developed a rule prohibiting a company from owning a television station and a newspaper in the same city. Second, agencies **adjudicate** disputes, resolving complaints initiated by business competitors, the public, or the agency itself. Administrative law judges conduct hearings resembling judicial proceedings at which evidence is submitted and witnesses are examined and cross-examined. After a hearing, an FTC administrative law judge found that advertisements for Extra Strength Doan's pills were deceptive because they contained an unsubstantiated claim that Doan's pills relieved pain more effectively than competing brands such as Tylenol. Third, agencies perform executive branch functions when they enforce rules against a firm or individual. In recent years, the FCC has fined broadcasters for violating indecency regulations by broadcasting sexual language. Before making its ruling, the agency reviewed the complaints of listeners and responses of broadcast licensees.

Regulatory agencies are bound by the requirements of the Administrative Procedure Act (APA).[13] This statute specifies the procedures that must be employed when an agency enacts rules or enforces regulations. For example, the APA requires that parties have the opportunity to comment on proposed rules. Parties may also petition an agency to issue, amend, or repeal a rule. And the APA establishes the procedures governing a hearing conducted by an administrative law judge, such as a party's right to cross-examine witnesses. Finally, under the APA, a party may seek judicial review of an agency action on a number of grounds, such as the agency has exceeded its statutory authority. Federal judges reviewing agency actions ensure that administrative agencies act within the boundaries set by the Constitution and statutory law.

An administrative action may be challenged on the ground that the agency has exceeded its statutory authority. For example, the Supreme Court agreed with tobacco manufacturers that the FDA exceeded its authority when the agency banned outdoor tobacco advertisements near schools and playgrounds. Although the Supreme Court agreed that tobacco poses a serious health threat, the Court found Congress excluded tobacco products from the FDA's jurisdiction. The Court stated, "an administrative agency's power to regulate in the public interest must always be grounded in a valid grant of authority from Congress."[14]

An agency's action may be challenged on the ground that it is arbitrary and capricious. A federal appeals court recently ruled that the FCC was arbitrary and capricious when it decreed that one company could own two television stations in the same market but not a television station and a cable system.[15] The court said it was illogical for the FCC to conclude that television station and cable system ownership was harmful when the agency found that multiple television station ownership was in the public interest.

An agency's action may also be challenged as unconstitutional. The Supreme Court ruled that the FCC acted unconstitutionally when it sought to punish the Colorado Republican Party for purchasing radio advertising in a political campaign.[16] The Supreme Court ruled that a political party's advertising expenditures, like those of other individuals or groups, are constitutionally protected speech that cannot be limited as long as the expenditures are not coordinated with any candidate. "The independent expression of a political party's views is 'core' First Amendment activity no less than is the independent expression of individuals, candidates, or other political committees," the Court stated.

Executive Actions

The President and other governmental executive officers can also make law. The President exercises power by appointing regulators, issuing executive orders and proclamations, and forging executive agreements with foreign countries. Much of the President's authority derives from Article 2 of the U.S. Constitution, requiring the President to "take Care that the Laws be faithfully executed." The Supreme Court has allowed the chief executive broad regulatory powers under the clause. In addition, Congress often grants the President the authority to administer statutes.

Perhaps the President's greatest influence on communication law comes from the power to nominate judges to the federal courts, including the U.S. Supreme Court. The political and judicial philosophies of the judges, and particularly their interpretation of the First Amendment, determine the boundaries of freedom for communicators. The President also nominates the members of several administrative agencies, including the FCC, the FTC, and the SEC. The President seldom issues executive orders that directly affect the law of public communication. An exception is the order that determines the documents that should be "classified" and thereby withheld from public disclosure to protect national security.

Common Law

The common law, often called judge-made law, was the most important source of law during the early development of this country. Unlike the general rules adopted as statutes by legislatures, the common law is the accumulation of rulings made by the courts in individual disputes. Judges, not legislatures, largely created the law of privacy, which allows individuals to collect damage awards for media disclosure of highly offensive personal information.

Common law in the United States grew out of the English common law. For centuries, judges in England, under the authority of the king, decided controversies on the basis of tradition and custom. These rulings established **precedents** that, together, became the law of the land. When the English colonized America, they brought the common law, including the precedents, with them.

The common law recognizes the importance of stability and predictability in the law. The common law is based on the judicial policy of **stare decisis**, which roughly means "let past decisions stand." In the common law, a judge decides a case by applying the law established by other judges in earlier, similar cases. The reliance on precedent not only provides continuity but also restricts judicial abuse of discretion. Thus, editors can use previous case law to help them determine whether a picture they want to publish is likely to be considered a violation of someone's privacy.

Although the common law promotes stability, it also allows for flexibility. The common law can adjust to fit changing circumstances because each judge can interpret and modify the law. Judges have five options when considering a case. They can (1) apply a precedent directly, (2) modify a precedent to fit new facts, (3) establish a new precedent by distinguishing the new case from previous cases, (4) overrule a previous precedent as no longer appropriate, or (5) ignore precedent. In most cases, precedent is either followed or adjusted to meet the facts at hand. Judges only rarely overrule previous precedents directly. Ignoring precedents greatly increases the risks of an opinion being overturned by a higher court.

Constitutional law and statutory law have a higher legal status than the common law, and therefore, the common law is relied on only when a statute or constitutional provision is not applicable. In a representative democracy, the people and their representatives in the legislatures, and not the courts, have the task of lawmaking. Sometimes legislatures incorporate portions of the common law into a statute, a process called *codification.* For example, in 1976, Congress rewrote the federal copyright statute to reflect a judicially created exception to a copyright owner's absolute control of a book, film, or musical score.

Sometimes, people confuse the common law with constitutional law. Both are created in part by judicial opinions based on precedent. However, constitutional law is based on judicial interpretation of a constitution, whereas common law is based on custom and practice.

The common law is not written down in one book. It can be understood only by reading recorded court decisions in hundreds of different volumes. Although the 1976 copyright statute is located in one volume of the *United States Code,* the common law of privacy can be discovered only by synthesizing numerous state and federal judicial opinions.

Common law is primarily state law. Each state has its own judicial traditions. However, as shown in Chapter 11, the Federal Rules of Evidence now allow federal judges to create common law testimonial privileges. In 1996, the U.S. Supreme Court ruled that a federal common law privilege covered confidential communications between therapists and patients.[17] Recently, journalists have argued that a federal common law privilege should also protect journalist–source relations. These claims have largely been rejected.

Law of Equity

The sixth source of law, equity, is historically related to the common law. Although *equity* is a legal term, it means what it sounds like. The law of equity allows courts to take action that is fair or just.

The law of equity developed because English common law allowed individuals to collect only monetary compensation after an injury had occurred. Under the law of equity, a **litigant** could petition the king to "do right for the love of God and by way of charity."[18] The law of equity allowed for preventive action and for remedial action other than monetary compensation. Although judges sitting in equity must consider precedent, they have substantial discretion to order a remedy they believe fair and appropriate.

Unlike England, the United States and most of the fifty states have never had separate courts of equity. Equity developed in the same courts that decided common law cases. However, juries are never used in equity suits.

Equity is significant in communication law primarily because of its preventive possibilities. Judges, for example, might use equity to halt the publication of a story considered a danger to national security. Punishment after publication would not protect national security.

Summary

Law in the United States comes from constitutions, statutes, administrative agencies, executive orders, common law, and equity. Constitutions outline the structure of government and define governmental authority and responsibilities. In the United States, the First Amendment to the federal Constitution protects the right to free speech and to a free press. Statutes are enforceable rules written by legislative bodies to govern social behavior. Administrative agencies make law as they adopt rules and adjudicate disputes, as authorized by statute. Executive orders are issued by the top officer in the executive branch of government. The common law is a collection of judicial decisions based on custom and tradition. Equity provides alternatives to the legal remedies available through the common law.

THE COURTS

Although agencies in all three branches of government in the United States make law, the judiciary is particularly important to a student of the law of public communication. There are fifty-two court systems in the country: the federal system, a system for each state, and another in the District of Columbia. The structures of the fifty-two systems are similar, but the state systems operate independently of the federal system under the authority of the state constitutions and laws.

Most court systems consist of three layers (see Figure 1.1). At the lowest level are the trial courts, where the facts of each case are evaluated in light of the applicable law. The middle layer for both the federal system and many states is an intermediate **appellate court**. Finally, all court systems include a court of ultimate appeal, usually called a supreme court. The federal court system is the most important for the law of public communication.

The Federal System

The U.S. Constitution mandates only one federal court, the U.S. Supreme Court, but provides for "such inferior courts as the Congress may from time to time ordain and establish."[19] The Constitution also spells out the **jurisdiction**, or areas of responsibility, of the federal courts. The federal courts exercise ultimate

FIGURE 1.1 Comparative Examples of State and Federal Court Structures

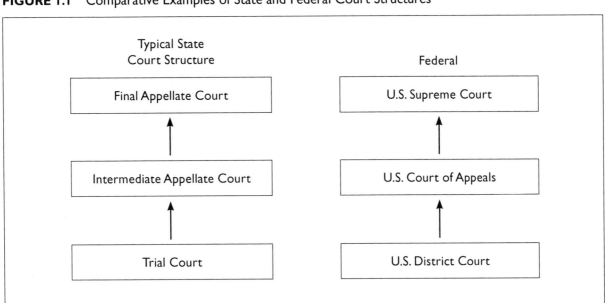

authority over the meaning of the Constitution, including the constitutionality of statutes that impinge on the First Amendment. The federal courts also resolve conflicts in the interpretation of federal statutory law. The federal courts hear controversies involving the United States, such as when the U.S. Department of Justice seeks a court order to obtain the name of a confidential news source. The federal courts can hear controversies between citizens or corporations of different states. Frequently, for example, the two parties in a libel suit—the person suing and the publisher or broadcaster being sued—live in different states. Matters not specifically assigned to the federal courts by the Constitution are tried in state courts.

Congress created the federal judicial system in 1789 with the adoption of the Federal Judiciary Act. The federal system includes ninety-four trial courts, the U.S. district courts; thirteen intermediate appellate courts, the judicial circuits of the U.S. Courts of Appeals; and the highest appellate court, the U.S. Supreme Court. Courts with special jurisdiction, such as the U.S. Tax Court, are not generally important to the law of public communication.

Trial Courts

Almost all court cases begin in the trial courts, the U.S. district courts. These are also called courts of **original jurisdiction**. Trial courts examine the facts, or evidence, in a case and then apply the appropriate law. Only trial courts employ juries.

There are ninety-four U.S. district courts. There is at least one federal district court in every state. Some states, such as Alaska, have only one district court. Other states, such as New York, have multiple districts. District courts also exist in the District of Columbia and in territories such as Guam. Many districts have more than one judge. By 2009, Congress had authorized 678 district court judgeships.

Intermediate Appellate Courts

Every person who loses in a trial court has the right to at least one **appeal**. In the federal system, that appeal is made to an intermediate appellate court. Appellate courts do not hold new trials and generally do not re-evaluate the facts of cases. Rather, their responsibility is to ensure that trial courts use the proper procedures and apply the law correctly.

Appellate court judges decide cases primarily on the basis of lower court records and lawyers' written arguments, called *briefs*. The judges also hear a short oral argument by attorneys for both sides. If an appellate court discovers that a trial court has erred, the higher court may reverse, or overturn, the lower court and **remand** the case or send it back to a lower court for a new trial

An appeal of a federal district court decision will ordinarily be considered in one of the thirteen circuits of the U.S. Courts of Appeals (see Figure 1.2). The jurisdictions of twelve of these courts are defined geographically. The thirteenth, the U.S. Court of Appeals for the Federal Circuit, handles only specialized appeals.

By 2009, Congress had authorized 179 appellate court judgeships. The Ninth Circuit, with twenty-eight judges, has the largest number of judges; the First Circuit, with six judges, has the smallest number. Most cases are heard by a panel of three judges. Particularly important cases will be heard **en banc**, that is, by all the judges of the court. For example, in 1993, the U.S. Court of Appeals for the Eighth Circuit affirmed en banc an FCC ruling that television stations are not required to provide balanced coverage of referenda, initiatives, or other ballot issues.[20]

The decisions of the U.S. Courts of Appeals must be followed by the federal district courts under their jurisdiction. Opinions of the Courts of Appeals may be persuasive authority but are not binding on state courts in the same jurisdiction deciding similar issues. Although federal appeals court decisions are not binding outside their jurisdiction, they are frequently influential.

Three circuits of the U.S. Courts of Appeals are particularly important to communication law. The Second Circuit, which hears appeals from federal courts in New York, decides a large number of media cases because New York City is the center of commercial telecommunications and the headquarters for many magazines, book publishers, advertising and public relations agencies, and newspapers. The Court of Appeals for the D.C. Circuit hears most of the appeals of decisions by the FCC and the FTC and many of the cases involving the federal Freedom

FIGURE 1.2 The Thirteen Circuits of the U.S. Courts of Appeals

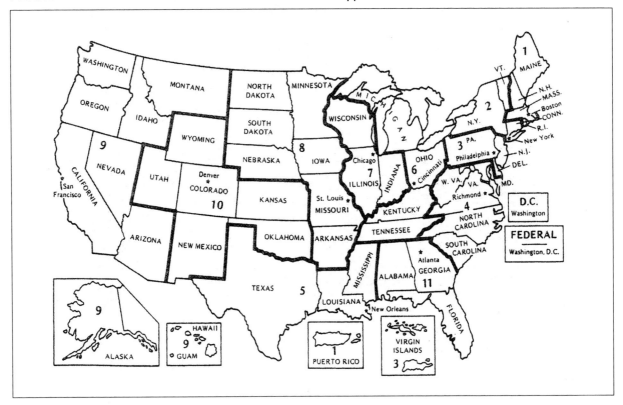

of Information Act. The Ninth Circuit, with jurisdiction over the West Coast, frequently decides film, television, and copyright cases.

The U.S. Supreme Court

Although the U.S. Supreme Court can exercise both original and appellate jurisdiction, it is primarily an appellate court. The Constitution specifically limits the occasions when the Supreme Court can be the first court to consider a legal controversy, and the Court has decided cases in that capacity fewer than 250 times in the history of the country.[21] However, because the Court has the last word in the interpretation of federal law, the Court's appellate duties make it one of the most powerful institutions in the world. Appellate cases reach the Court from all other federal courts, federal regulatory agencies, and state supreme courts.

The nine Supreme Court justices, like all federal judges, are appointed by the President and confirmed by the Senate. Since 1789, the Senate has refused to confirm twelve Supreme Court nominees. Eleven nominations have been withdrawn when strong opposition was apparent. Most recently, Harriet Miers's nomination was withdrawn in 2005 when Senators questioned her qualifications. Justices are appointed for life, or as long as they choose to remain on the Court. They can be removed only by impeachment.[22] Of the nine justices on the Court in the October 2008 Term, seven were appointed by Republican presidents. President Bush appointed two new conservatives in 2005, Chief Justice John Roberts Jr. and Justice Samuel Alito, replacing the conservative Chief Justice William Rehnquist and Justice Sandra Day O'Connor, a moderate (see Photo 1.1). In May 2009, President Obama nominated federal appeals judge Sonia Sotomayor to replace retiring Justice David Souter, a move not expected to shift the Court's ideological makeup.

The Court is substantially more conservative than it was in the 1960s, when a majority of the justices had been appointed by Democrats. Conservative justices tend to interpret constitutional rights more narrowly than liberals. Conservatives also tend to favor states rights over central government regulations and to support individual property rights. Liberal justices are more concerned about protecting individual civil rights, including free speech and press. Liberal justices are also usually more willing

PHOTO 1.1 **The Roberts Court, 2009**
Front row: Associate Justices Anthony M. Kennedy, John Paul Stevens,
Chief Justice John G. Roberts, Antonin G. Scalia, and Clarence Thomas.
Back row: Associate Justices Samuel A. Alito, Ruth Bader Ginsburg,
Stephen G. Breyer, and Sonia Sotomayor.

to recognize new constitutional rights—such as a right of privacy—not explicitly stated in the Bill of Rights, and to increase access to government information. None of the justices on the Court in 2009 are considered as protective of civil liberties as former justices William Brennan Jr., Thurgood Marshall, and William Douglas.

During the period from 1994 to 2005, the Court had stable membership, and two distinct voting blocs emerged. The conservative bloc featured Rehnquist, Antonin Scalia, Clarence Thomas, and Anthony Kennedy. The liberal bloc featured Stevens, Ruth Bader Ginsburg, Stephen Breyer, and David Souter. Justice O'Connor, poised between the two blocs, was frequently the critical swing vote. With the replacement of Rehnquist and O'Connor by Roberts and Alito, the Court is in a period of transition. However, the early terms of the Roberts Court show the Court is becoming more conservative. Justice Alito, O'Connor's replacement, voted with the conservative bloc 15 percent more often than O'Connor had.[23] Justice Kennedy votes more often with the conservative bloc than with the liberal bloc, but has abandoned

the conservatives in several 5–4 cases. Most recently Kennedy voted with Stevens, Breyer, Ginsburg, and Souter in prohibiting the death penalty for the rape of a child and finding that enemy combatants may challenge their detention in federal court.[24] Thus, Kennedy is emerging as the new swing vote.[25] Although the Court may be more liberal or conservative at any given time, it seldom follows a prolonged extreme ideological course. As legal scholar Nelson Lund observes, "Our courts rarely make a lot of big lurches." If they do move in significant new directions, they are then apt to pull back toward the center.[26]

The justices who are considered "conservative" and those who are considered "liberal" do not always vote as blocs, nor do conservatives or liberals always have predictable votes in free expression cases. Many of the conservative justices have joined their more liberal colleagues to support freedom of expression. For example, Kennedy and Scalia joined Brennan, Marshall, Harry Blackmun, and Stevens in ruling unconstitutional damages assessed against a newspaper for publishing the name of a rape victim.[27] Kennedy and Scalia also voted with Brennan, Marshall, and

Blackmun to hold that flag burning is protected by the First Amendment.[28] In a recent case in which the Court upheld a restriction on expressive activities occurring near health clinics, Scalia, Thomas, and Kennedy claimed in dissenting opinions that the Court's decision was harmful to freedom of expression.[29] Conversely, Justice Breyer dissented in two recent cases in which the Court struck down restrictions on sexual material on cable and the World Wide Web; Breyer believed the restrictions were necessary to protect children.[30]

As shown in Table 1.2, the number of cases filed with the Supreme Court has dramatically increased since 1954. While the number of cases accepted for oral argument and disposed of with a full opinion increased during the tenure of Chief Justices Warren (1953–69) and Burger (1969–86), Chief Justice Rehnquist (1986–2005) sought to reduce the number during his tenure. In the later part of Rehnquist's tenure, the Court usually received nearly 8,000 petitions annually and agreed to hear arguments in fewer that 100 cases a term. Although Chief Justice Roberts stated during his confirmation hearings he thought the Court could "contribute more to the clarity and uniformity of the law by taking more cases," the Court has yet to increase its caseload under Roberts. In the 2005 Term, the Court's first with Roberts as Chief Justice, the Court heard oral arguments in 87 cases; it heard arguments in 78 and 75 cases respectively in its 2006 and 2007 terms. In 1988, Congress passed legislation giving the Supreme Court nearly total discretion in selecting the cases it will hear.[31] Until then, the Court was required to hear several kinds of appeals accounting for 20 percent of its caseload. Now, even more than before, most cases reach the Court by a writ of **certiorari**, a Latin term indicating the Court is willing to review a case. As the Office of the Clerk of the Supreme Court explains, "review by this Court by means of a writ of certiorari is not a matter of right, but of judicial discretion. The primary concern of the Supreme Court is not to correct errors in lower court decisions, but to decide cases presenting issues of national importance beyond the particular facts and parties involved."[32]

The process of submitting a case to the Supreme Court for review begins when an attorney files a written argument, called a petition for certiorari, asking the Court to review a decision by a federal court or state supreme court. Four Supreme Court justices must vote yes if the Court is to grant a writ of certiorari and put the case onto its calendar. The Court rejects about 99 percent of the petitions for certiorari, usually with no explanation. When a petition for certiorari is denied, the lower court decision stands. The Supreme Court's refusal to accept a case does not affirm a lower court's opinion. Denial of certiorari "signifies only that the Court has chosen not to accept the case for review and does not express the Court's view of the merits of the case."[33] The Court denies certiorari for many reasons, perhaps because a case lacks legal significance or because there is no significant conflict in the lower courts to resolve.

TABLE 1.2   United States Supreme Court Caseload 1954–2004 Terms

	1954 Term (Warren, C.J.)	1964 Term (Warren, C.J.)	1974 Term (Burger, C.J.)	1984 Term (Burger, CJ.)	1994 Term (Rehnquist, CJ.)	2004 Term (Rehnquist, CJ.)
Cases filed	1,397	2,288	3,661	4,046	6,996	7,496
Cases disposed of by full opinions	86	103	144	159	90	87
Disposed of by per curiam opinions	16	17	20	11	3	2

Sources: Administrative Office of the United States Courts, *Judicial Business of the United States Courts: 2005 Annual Report of the Director;* United States Supreme Court, *Chief Justice's Year-End Reports on the Federal Judiciary,* 2005; Lee Epstein et. al, *The Supreme Court Compendium: Data, Decisions & Developments* (2003).

If the Supreme Court accepts a case, the review process is much the same as for other appellate courts. The attorneys file briefs arguing their position. The briefs generally present the facts of the case, the issues involved, a review of the actions of the lower courts, and legal arguments. The Supreme Court justices review the written arguments and then listen to what is usually a half hour of oral argument from each attorney. The justices often interrupt attorneys to ask questions or challenge the arguments being presented. The time limit is precise. An attorney arguing before the Court is expected to stop in the middle of a sentence if the light in front of the lectern signals that time has expired.

Following oral arguments, the justices meet in chambers to discuss the case. No one except the justices is permitted in chambers. Once the justices have voted, a justice voting with the majority will be designated to write the Court's opinion. If the chief justice is part of the majority, he or she decides who will write the opinion of the Court. If the chief justice votes in the minority, the most senior justice in the majority decides who will write the Court's opinion. The choice of author for an opinion is significant because the author of the Court's opinion can weave in his or her political philosophy, view of the role of the Court, and interpretation of law.

After a justice drafts an opinion for the Court, the draft is circulated to the other justices for editing and comment. Drafts of dissenting opinions may be shared as well. The justices may bargain over the language in the drafts. Votes may shift. Ordinarily, at least a few justices will join the opinion of the Court without adding their own comments. However, justices often write their own **concurring** or **dissenting opinions** to explain their votes. They can also join, or sign onto, opinions written by other justices.

Sometimes none of the draft opinions presented to the Court attracts the five votes necessary for a majority. In such a situation, the draft with the most support becomes the **plurality** opinion of the Court, as occurred in *Richmond Newspapers v. Virginia*. Although the justices in *Richmond Newspapers* voted 7–1 that the First Amendment requires trials to be open to the public, no more than three justices agreed to any one opinion explaining why courtrooms should remain open during trials.[34] If many

of the justices write their own opinions rather than joining an opinion of the Court, the high court offers little guidance to lower courts facing similar circumstances. A majority of the justices deciding a case, usually five, must agree to any point of law for the Court's opinion to become binding precedent.

In what is known as the Pentagon Papers case, discussed in Chapter 3, each of the nine justices wrote his own opinion. Although the Court voted 6–3 that the *New York Times* and the *Washington Post* could report a secret Defense Department study, the only opinion issued on behalf of the six-justice majority was an unsigned, three-paragraph **per curiam** opinion. A per curiam opinion is "by the court" rather than an opinion attributed to any one justice. The Court's opinion in the Pentagon Papers case said only that the government had not sufficiently justified barring news stories based on the Defense Department study.[35] The justices could not agree on the reasons a **prior restraint** was unjustified.

Technically, the Supreme Court's decisions apply only to the case being decided. The Supreme Court's opinions do not establish statutelike law. However, lower courts assume the Supreme Court will decide similar cases in similar ways, so they adjudicate conflicts before them accordingly. Otherwise lower court judges risk having their decisions overturned.

The Supreme Court, in its role as interpreter of the U.S. Constitution, can review the constitutionality of all legislation. This means that the Supreme Court can invalidate an act of Congress that violates the Constitution. The Court has declared all or part of a federal statute unconstitutional about 160 times in the history of the country. The Court has also declared provisions of about 1,250 state laws and constitutions to be unconstitutional.[36] The Supreme Court has frequently expanded freedom of expression by invalidating state and federal statutes found to conflict with the First Amendment.

Neither the Supreme Court nor any other court can enforce its own decisions. The courts have no troops or police to force compliance. The executive branch enforces court decisions. Law enforcement officers ensure that fines are paid and sentences are served. When the Supreme Court rules against the executive branch, it relies on tradition and its own prestige to achieve compliance. In 1974, public respect for the Court forced President Nixon to obey an order to release secret White House tapes to a special prosecutor who was investigating the Watergate scandal.[37]

The State Systems

Most state court systems are organized much like the federal courts. Each state has trial courts, similar to the federal district courts, which handle nearly every kind of civil or criminal case. These courts, often called county courts, are ordinarily the first state courts to consider libel or privacy cases. These trial courts also handle appeals for a number of subordinate trial courts responsible for minor civil matters, traffic violations, and criminal misdemeanors. Most state court judges are elected, usually in nonpartisan elections.

State court systems provide either one or two levels of appellate courts. In some states, appeals go directly from the county courts to what is usually called the state supreme court. However, many states have intermediate appellate courts to moderate the workload of the supreme court. State courts of appeals, like the federal circuit courts, often use small panels of judges. State appellate court decisions interpreting state law are binding on both lower state courts and federal courts in the same jurisdiction.

The decisions of state supreme courts, usually made up of seven to nine justices, constitute the law of the state and are binding on all of the state's courts. Each state supreme court is the final arbiter of its own state constitution, provided there is no conflict with the federal constitution. A losing **party** in a state supreme court case may have recourse before the U.S. Supreme Court only if a substantial federal question is involved.

Summary

There are fifty-two court systems: one for the federal government, one for the District of Columbia, and one for each state. Most court cases originate in the trial courts, where the law is applied to the facts of each case. Appeals courts ensure that the trial courts use the proper procedures and apply the law correctly. The federal court system consists of federal district courts, the thirteen circuits of the U.S. Courts of Appeals, and the U.S. Supreme Court.

THE LITIGATION PROCESS: CIVIL AND CRIMINAL

In criminal law, the government punishes individuals who commit illegal acts such as murder, arson, and theft. Civil law ordinarily resolves disputes between two private parties. The dispute can be over a dog bite or a news story. Most communication cases are brought in civil court rather than criminal court.

A crime is an antisocial act defined by law, usually a statute adopted by a state legislature. State criminal statutes forbid behavior such as murder and rape and specify punishment, usually a jail sentence, a fine, or both. Criminal law is enforced by government law enforcement officers. Once suspects are arrested, they are prosecuted by government attorneys. The state must prove its case beyond a reasonable doubt, a heavy **burden of proof** demanding that jurors be all but certain that the government's version of events is correct. One example of criminal law discussed in this book is obscenity. Both the federal and state governments prosecute individuals who distribute obscene publications.

Understanding criminal law is important to journalists who report news of the criminal courts. Several issues discussed in this book—access to courtrooms, pretrial publicity, and cameras in the courtroom—relate directly to criminal court proceedings.

In contrast to criminal cases intended to punish illegal behavior, civil cases often involve claims by individuals or organizations seeking legal redress for a violation of their interests. A person or organization filing a civil suit usually seeks compensation for harm suffered because of the actions of another. A woman may sue a neighbor for medical costs after being bitten by the neighbor's dog. Or a man may sue a newspaper for defamation if the paper inaccurately reports that he is an adulterer. A legal wrong committed by one person against another is often called a **tort**. Civil law provides the opportunity for a "peaceful" resolution when one person accuses another of committing a tort.

Litigants in civil cases can win by proving their cases by a preponderance of the evidence. Unlike criminal prosecutors, lawyers representing civil plaintiffs do not have to prove wrong beyond a reasonable doubt. Preponderance of the evidence means that litigants must convince jurors that their version of events is more probable—if by a narrow margin—than that of the opposing party. If the person suing wins a civil case, he or she often recovers monetary **damages**. If the person being sued wins, frequently no money changes hands except to pay the lawyers' fees. In civil law, there are no jail terms and usually no fines.

Civil law, including libel and privacy, is a significant part of the law of public communication. Civil suits are more likely to be based on common law than on statutory law. In media law, in particular, the government is not ordinarily involved except to provide neutral facilities—the judge, the jury, and the courthouse—to help settle the dispute. However, a civil suit can be based on a statute, and a person or group can sue, or be sued by, the government. Some states' open meetings and open records laws allow private citizens to sue officials to secure public access.

A Civil Suit

A civil case begins when the person suing, called the **plaintiff**, files a legal complaint against the person being sued, the **defendant**. In April 1976, Dr. Ronald Hutchinson, then the research director at a Michigan state mental hospital, filed a civil complaint against Senator William Proxmire of Wisconsin in the U.S. District Court for the Western District of Wisconsin. Hutchinson complained that Proxmire had libeled him by giving a "Golden Fleece" award to his research on monkeys. Proxmire had said that the American public was being "fleeced" by the nearly half-million dollars spent for Hutchinson's research by the National Science Foundation, the National Aeronautics and Space Administration, and the Office of Naval Research. The agencies were examining the problems faced by monkeys and humans confined in close quarters for long periods of time, as in space or underwater exploration. Proxmire said, however, that the federal government ought to get out of the "monkey business." He said the "transparent worthlessness" of Hutchinson's research was taking a bite out of the American taxpayer. Hutchinson's civil complaint asked for $8 million in damages because, he said, Proxmire had humiliated him and held him up to public scorn, damaged his professional and academic standing, and damaged his ability to attract research grants.[38]

Once a complaint has been filed at the courthouse, a defendant, in this case Senator Proxmire, is served with a summons, a notice to appear in court. If defendants fail to appear, courts may hold them in contempt and require them to forfeit their cases. Defendants often respond to complaints by denying the accusations. Senator Proxmire "answered" the complaint, in part, by filing a motion for **summary judgment**, a common defense tactic in communication cases. A judge can grant a summary judgment to either a defendant or a plaintiff if the judge believes that the two sides in a case agree on the facts of the dispute and that one side should win as a matter of law. A summary judgment terminates a suit in its early stages, saving attorney fees and avoiding the often unpredictable outcome of a jury trial. Summary judgments are discussed more thoroughly in Chapter 4.

Hutchinson's complaint, Proxmire's answer, and a reply by Hutchinson are called the *pleadings,* documents stating the nature of a case. Sometimes the two sides in a dispute file a series of documents in an attempt to narrow the issues and thereby limit the length and expense of a trial. Frequently, the two sides will ask a judge for a pretrial conference in another attempt to narrow the issues or even to settle the case.

Meanwhile, the parties, sometimes called litigants, begin what is called **discovery**. Discovery is the information-gathering process. During discovery—which in major cases can take several years—each side finds out as much as possible about the evidence possessed by the other party. The lawyers often prepare interrogatories, written questions that must be answered under oath by people who might have relevant information. Then lawyers frequently take depositions, that is, ask questions in person that also must be answered under oath.

During discovery, lawyers may request that the judge issue a **subpoena** requiring a journalist or someone else to testify or bring documents or other evidence to court. A subpoena must be served to the person named in it. Failure to comply with a subpoena can result in a contempt of court ruling. Journalists frequently fight subpoenas on the grounds that revealing sources or evidence will limit their ability to gather news, a subject discussed in Chapter 11.

In the *Hutchinson* case, the judge granted time for discovery after receiving Senator Proxmire's motion for summary judgment. The two parties exchanged interrogatories and subsequently the answers. Hutchinson requested a jury trial. He also asked to amend his complaint, a motion that was granted over the objection of Senator Proxmire. In the amended complaint, Hutchinson said the Golden Fleece announcement not only libeled him but also infringed on his rights of privacy and peace and tranquillity. Both Hutchinson, the plaintiff, and Proxmire, the defendant, filed the results of depositions. Shortly thereafter, Hutchinson filed a brief, along with five volumes of exhibits, arguing against Proxmire's motion for summary judgment. Senator Proxmire filed a reply brief with exhibits.

About a year after Hutchinson filed his complaint, the district court judge granted Senator Proxmire's motion for summary judgment.[39] If the summary judgment had not been granted, the case would have gone to trial.

A jury trial is required if the two parties disagree on the facts of a case and one of the parties insists on a jury. After both sides present their cases, the judge explains the relevant law to the jurors. The jury is asked to apply the law to the facts, and it may set monetary damages as part of the verdict. If a judge believes the jury verdict is contrary to law or that the damage award is excessive, he or she can overturn the jury's decision. This occurred early in the 1980s when a judge decided that a jury verdict in favor of Mobil Oil president William Tavoulareas and against the *Washington Post* was contrary to libel law.[40]

Once a judgment has been recorded in a case, either party can appeal. The person who appeals is known as the **petitioner**; the person fighting the appeal is called the **respondent**. The petitioner in one appeal may be the respondent in another appeal. In Hutchinson's suit, Hutchinson became a petitioner when he appealed the grant of summary judgment to the U.S. Court of Appeals for the Seventh Circuit, where it was upheld. Hutchinson's petition for certiorari to the U.S. Supreme Court was granted. Proxmire was the respondent before both the Seventh Circuit and the Supreme Court. The Supreme Court reversed the decision of the Seventh Circuit and remanded the case to the lower courts for disposition consistent with the Supreme Court's opinion. Hutchinson and Proxmire eventually settled out of court. Hutchinson received $10,000 in damages and an apology from Senator Proxmire. The Supreme Court opinion, *Hutchinson v. Proxmire,* is discussed in Chapter 4.

A Criminal Case

The key steps in a criminal prosecution are substantially the same in most states. The procedures may be labeled differently or occur in a different sequence.

A criminal action begins with a law enforcement investigation. The government's case against an individual begins with the arrest, or apprehension, of the person suspected of committing a crime. The case of Dr. Sam Sheppard, important to communication law, began with his arrest in July 1954. Sheppard, a Cleveland, Ohio, osteopath, was arrested on a charge of murdering his wife, Marilyn. (Fictionalized accounts were presented in the 1960s television series *The Fugitive* and a 1990s movie of the same name.) The one-month investigation prior to the arrest established that Mrs. Sheppard had been killed with a blunt instrument, that Dr. Sheppard was in the house at the time, that no money was missing from the home, and that no readable fingerprints could be found.[41] The investigation included an inquest ordered by the coroner to determine whether a murder had been committed. Extensive, sensational publicity, discussed in Chapter 10, began immediately.

After an arrest, the person accused of a crime appears before a magistrate for a preliminary hearing. At the hearing, the person is advised of the nature of the crime and reminded of his or her right to counsel and the right to remain silent. The primary purpose of a preliminary hearing is to determine if there is sufficient evidence, or **probable cause**, to justify further detention or a trial. Sheppard appeared before a magistrate, was informed of the murder charge, and was bound over to the grand jury.

If the magistrate decides that there is probable cause, he or she will set the bail, that is, announce the amount of money that must be posted before the accused can be released from jail. The bail is intended to ensure that the accused appears in court. Sheppard was denied bail.

The next step, depending on the state, could be the filing by the prosecutor of a criminal information, a document formally accusing the person of a crime. Or the prosecutor may take the evidence to a grand jury to seek an **indictment**, a formal accusation by a grand jury. Not all states have grand juries, and their role in the criminal justice system varies. On August 17, 1954, a grand jury in Ohio indicted Sheppard for first-degree murder.[42]

An arraignment usually follows the formal accusation. The arraignment is the official, formal reading of the indictment or information to the accused. The accused is asked to plead guilty or not guilty.

If the defendant pleads not guilty, the focus turns to pretrial preparation and negotiation. Both the prosecution and defense engage in discovery, the pretrial fact-finding. Both sides may submit a variety of motions to the judge. The defense may move for an adjustment or dismissal of the charges. Or as in Sam Sheppard's case, a defense attorney may ask that a trial be relocated or delayed because of extensive pretrial publicity. The judge in the Sheppard trial denied both motions.

During the pretrial maneuvers, the prosecution and defense may agree to resolve the case through a plea bargain. In plea bargaining, a trial is avoided because the defendant is willing to plead guilty, often to reduced charges. Roughly 90 percent of criminal defendants plead guilty, thereby avoiding a trial.[43] Plea bargains not only save time and money but also avoid the uncertainty inherent in a trial.

A trial can take place before a judge or a jury. Criminal defendants can waive their right to a jury trial. After the jury announces the verdict of guilty or not guilty, a judge pronounces the sentence. A jury in the Common Pleas Court of Cuyahoga County, Ohio, decided that Sheppard "purposely and maliciously" killed his wife, the requirement for second-degree murder in Ohio. The judge sentenced Sheppard to life in prison, the mandatory penalty in Ohio for the crime of second-degree murder.

Sheppard appealed to the Court of Appeals of Ohio for Cuyahoga County, an intermediate appellate court. He argued that there were nearly forty errors in the conduct of the trial, including the denial of motions to move the trial and to postpone the trial. He also argued that the jury had been improperly selected and prejudicial evidence had been improperly allowed during the trial. The three-judge panel decided that Sheppard "has been afforded a fair trial by an impartial jury and … substantial justice has been done."[44] Sheppard also lost a 1956 appeal in the Ohio Supreme Court. The U.S. Supreme Court denied certiorari the same year.[45] Nine years later, the U.S. Supreme Court agreed to consider Sheppard's contention that he was denied a fair trial because of sensational media coverage. That story is told in Chapter 10.

Summary

Criminal law prohibits antisocial behavior as defined by statute. Violations are punishable by jail sentences and fines. Criminal law is enforced by the government. A criminal action begins with an investigation and an arrest. A preliminary hearing is held to determine if there is sufficient evidence to justify a trial. Then either a prosecutor or a grand jury formally accuses a person of a crime. After the accused responds to the charge during an arraignment, the prosecution and the defense engage in pretrial fact-finding, known as discovery. Civil law ordinarily involves disputes between two private parties. A plaintiff sues a defendant for damages. After the plaintiff files a civil complaint and the defendant responds, the two parties engage in discovery. Civil and criminal cases can be dismissed or otherwise resolved before trial.

WORKING WITH THE LAW
Finding and Reading the Law

Many professional communicators value the ability to locate and understand the law by themselves. Communicators do not have to have legal training to find statutes and court opinions. Law libraries have knowledgeable personnel ready to help. Information in Appendix A in this book provides background to enable students to find court cases and other material. Although a nonlawyer can find the law with a little assistance, reading and understanding the law take time and practice. A few tips are offered in the appendix. Also in the appendix are explanations of the legal citations in this book. However, journalists should not try to be their own lawyers, even if they have law degrees.

Working with Lawyers

Because public communication often raises questions of law, professional communicators frequently need lawyers. Communicators should not fear or avoid lawyers; rather, communicators should use lawyers intelligently.

Most communicators will not have direct access to a lawyer in their first job. Newspapers, for example, generally prefer journalists to take legal questions to a supervisor. In newsrooms, city editors and managing editors ordinarily can answer routine legal questions and usually decide when a lawyer should be consulted. Some major daily newspapers and large advertising and public relations firms hire staff lawyers, known as in-house attorneys. Other media companies engage a law firm they can call as needed. Even the smallest communications organization should have experienced legal counsel to call when questions arise.

Lawyers, whose hourly fees are usually high, should be used when possible to prevent a legal conflict rather than to resolve one. A lawyer should be consulted in the following cases:

- When a communicator is served with a subpoena, a summons, or an arrest warrant. Communicators need the advice of a lawyer before responding to a legal document.

- When there is a concern that a story being considered for publication could lead to a libel or privacy suit. Attorneys can assess the risks of stories and suggest modifications.

- When a news medium is asked to print retractions or corrections. Some well-intentioned corrections can increase, rather than decrease, the risk of a suit if a lawyer is not consulted.

- When a communicator is approached by a lawyer hired by someone else. A layperson should not respond to the legal moves of a legal adversary.

- When a communicator is considering an action that may be illegal. Reporters pursuing a story sometimes consider trespassing, tape recording, or obtaining stolen documents. Sometimes it is obvious when an act is illegal; often it is not. Reporters need to understand the legal consequences of their actions. A lawyer may help.

Lawyers can do more than help limit the legal jeopardy of communication professionals. They can also help communicators do their jobs. For example, lawyers can help journalists obtain access to closed records or meetings by explaining to officials the rights of the public and press. Lawyers also help public relations specialists and broadcasters complete forms required by the Securities and Exchange Commission, the Federal Communications Commission, and other administrative agencies.

When communicators work with lawyers, they should remember that lawyers, like other professionals, are trained to do some tasks and not others. Lawyers can help resolve a legal conflict, but they cannot eliminate the sloppy writing or editing that may have caused a suit. Attorneys can explain the probable risks and consequences of a story or an ad. They can discuss the factors that ought to be considered in deciding how to avoid **liability**. An attorney should know the questions an opposing attorney will ask about a story and what arguments are likely to be made in a libel trial.

Lawyers are not usually qualified to tell a communicator what to write or how to edit. Some lawyers are insensitive to the problems, values, and commitments of journalists. Some attorneys regularly advise cutting stories to avoid trouble. They sometimes suggest eliminating the defamatory portions of stories without regard to the public importance of the information. The job of a lawyer, according to James Goodale, a prominent media attorney, should be "to figure out how to get the story published," not trimmed or killed.[46] The lawyer should explain legal risks; the communicator should make the editorial decisions after weighing those risks.

Public communicators may sometimes need a personal attorney. An employer might refuse to represent an employee in court, especially if the employee acts contrary to instructions or without consulting a supervisor. In the early 1970s, the *New York Times* refused to defend one of its reporters, Earl Caldwell, when he declined to testify before a grand jury. The *Times* wanted Caldwell to respond to a grand jury subpoena by entering the grand jury room, even if he refused to answer questions. However, Caldwell refused even to enter the grand jury room, which is closed to the public and the press. Caldwell believed that once he went behind closed doors, his sources would no longer trust his commitment to keep what he knew confidential. When Caldwell was found in contempt of court for refusing to testify, the *Times* did not provide him with a company attorney. Caldwell's case was considered by the Supreme Court in *Branzburg v. Hayes,* a case discussed in Chapter 11.

An attorney needs to know all of the facts that pertain to a legal issue. Communicators should hold nothing back. Although it is embarrassing for journalists to confess careless reporting or writing, the failure to tell a lawyer everything can be legally damaging, particularly if the errors are first revealed by an opposing lawyer in front of a jury. Attorneys need to know the worst in order to present the best case.

Summary

Legal advice can be an expensive but necessary part of modern communication. Lawyers should be called when a communicator must respond to an official document or someone else's attorney. Lawyers should be consulted when a communicator is considering an act that may be illegal. Lawyers should review stories that could lead to libel or privacy suits. Lawyers can explain the risks of publishing a story, but they should not be allowed to act as editors. Information about doing legal research is in Appendix A of this book.

LIMITATIONS OF LAW

This book focuses on the law. Professional communicators need to know the law in order to do their jobs effectively and without unnecessary risk. However, the law does not resolve all questions that may arise in public communication.

For one thing, the law does not necessarily protect every action that a professional communicator believes to be in the public interest. Libel law does not always protect a newspaper that wants to report an allegation of government corruption. In addition, reporters who refuse to reveal the names of sources for a story about government corruption could go to jail. At times, communicators have to decide whether the public benefit of a story is worth a jail sentence or a libel suit. The fact that journalists might not be protected by

law is not the only factor to be considered when they are deciding whether to publish a story.

Conversely, the law may allow behavior that exceeds personal or professional ethics. Ethics is the consideration of moral rights and wrongs. Ethics involves honesty, fairness, and motivation. It also involves respect for the emotional well-being, dignity, and physical safety of others. The law, as reflected in statutes and court decisions, does not always parallel personal and professional codes of conduct. The First Amendment frequently permits expression, such as the publication of the names of rape victims, which many journalists consider unethical. Ethical questions are raised not only by the publication of highly personal information but also by pretrial publication of information about criminal defendants and by the refusal of journalists to reveal their news sources, all of which are sometimes permitted by law. Communicators base decisions to publish on whether behavior is morally "right" or "wrong" as well as on its legality. However, a discussion of ethics is left for another book. The purpose of this book is to help professional communicators understand the law that affects their performance.

Notes

1. Definitions for the terms printed in boldface can be found in the glossary at the end of the book.
2. Richmond Newspapers v. Virginia, 448 U.S. 555 (1980).
3. Sony Corp. v. Universal City Studios, 464 U.S. 417 (1984).
4. Department of Justice v. Reporters Comm. for Freedom of the Press, 489 U.S. 749 (1989).
5. Miami Herald Publishing Co. v. Tornillo, 418 U.S. 241 (1974).
6. Randall v. Sorrell, 126 S. Ct. 2479 (2006).
7. Capital Cities Cable, Inc. v. Crisp, 467 U.S. 691 (1984).
8. Alan Murray, "Partisanship Leaves FDA Leaderless at Crucial Juncture," *Wall Street Journal,* June 18, 2002, at A4.
9. Tom Hamburger, "Drug Industry Ads Aid GOP," *Wall Street Journal,* June 18, 2002, at A4.
10. Sheryl Gay Stolberg, "After Impasse, F.D.A. May Fill Top Job," *Washington Post,* Sept. 25, 2002, at A18.

11. Marc Kaufman, "Crawford Confirmed As Head of FDA," *Washington Post,* July 19, 2005, at A19.

12. David Stout, "Ex-F.D.A. Chief Pleads Guilty in Stock Case," *N.Y. Times,* Oct. 18, 2006, at A21.

13. 5 U.S.C. §§ 551 et seq.

14. FDA v. Brown & Williamson Tobacco Co., 529 U.S. 120, 161 (2000).

15. Fox Television Stations, Inc. v. FCC, 280 F.3d 1027 (D.C. Cir. 2002).

16. Colorado Republican Campaign Committee v. FEC, 518 U.S. 604 (1996).

17. Jaffee v. Redmond, 518 U.S. 1 (1996).

18. Henry Abraham, *The Judicial Process* 14 (1986).

19. U.S. Const, art. III, § 1.

20. Arkansas AFL-CIO v. FCC, 11 F.3d 1430 (8th Cir. 1993).

21. Lee Epstein et al., *The Supreme Court Compendium: Data, Decisions, and Developments* 63–65 (1994).

22. U.S. Const, art. III, § 1; *see also* Samuel Mermin, *Law and the Legal System* 327 (2d ed. 1982).

23. Linda Greenhouse, "Roberts Is at Court's Helm, But He Isn't Yet in Control," *N.Y. Times,* July 1, 2006, § 1, at 1.

24. Kennedy v. Louisiana, 128 S. Ct. 2641 (2008); Boumediene v. Bush, 128 S. Ct. 2229 (2008).

25. Jess Bravin, "Lawyers Swing for Kennedy Vote," *Wall Street Journal,* Oct. 3, 2006, at A2.

26. Linda Greenhouse, "Court in Transition: The 2004–2005 Session," *N.Y. Times,* July 4, 2005.

27. Florida Star v. B.J.F., 491 U.S. 524 (1989).

28. Texas v. Johnson, 491 U.S. 397 (1989).

29. Hill v. Colorado, 530 U.S. 703 (2000).

30. Ashcroft v. ACLU 542 U.S. 656 (2004); United States v. Playboy Enter. Group, Inc., 529 U.S. 803 (2000).

31. Supreme Court Case Selections, Pub. L. No. 100-352, 102 Stat. 662 (1988) (amending 28 U.S.C. §§ 1254, 1257 & 1258).

32. Office of Clerk, United States Supreme Court, *Guide for Prospective Indigent Petitioners for Writs of Certiorari* at 1, Oct. 2005.

33. *Id.*

34. 448 U.S. 555 (1980).

35. N.Y. Times Co. v. United States, 403 U.S. 713 (1971).

36. Lee Epstein et.al., *The Supreme Court Compendium: Data, Decisions, and Developments,* 163–93 (2003).

37. United States v. Nixon, 418 U.S. 683 (1974).

38. Hutchinson v. Proxmire, 443 U.S. 111 (1979).

39. 431 F. Supp. 1311 (W.D. Wis. 1977).

40. Tavoulareas v. Washington Post Co., 567 F. Supp. 651 (D.D.C. 1983), *aff'd,* 817 F.2d 762 (D.C. 1987) (en banc).

41. State v. Sheppard, 128 N.E.2d 471 (Ohio Ct App. 1955).

42. *Id;* Sheppard v. Maxwell, 384 U.S. 333 (1966).

43. American Bar Association, *Law and the Courts: A Handbook of Courtroom Procedures* 44 (1995).

44. State v. Sheppard, 128 N.E.2d at 504.

45. State v. Sheppard, 128 N.E.2d 471 (Ohio Ct. App. 1955), *aff'd,* 135 N.E.2d 340 (Ohio 1956), *cert. denied,* 352 U.S. 910 (1956).

46. Ann Rambo, "Litigious Age Gives Rise to Media Law," *presstime,* Nov. 1981, at 7.

UNIT 2

Distributing or Regulating?
The Role of the State

The rationales for regulating lead to different types of policies. But communication policies are not only a result of market failures and economic considerations. In this unit you will be introduced to the economic and legal bases for regulation in general, not specifically in the field of media and telecommunications. This unit in particular outlines the role taken by the state in this process. When you engage in the readings in this and the two subsequent units you should be aware of two things: First, the communications industry is subject to two types of regulations (generally speaking): Economic regulations and "social regulatory" policies. Second, that the communications industry is subject to general policies of competition, which in the United States are known as "antitrust rules," and to specific rules that apply only to the communications industry. Under the question "distributing or regulating" class discussions and lectures will cover the following topics:

a. The process of policy making

b. Theories of policy making

c. Types of policy: distributive, constituent, redistributive, and regulatory

d. The emergence of regulation as the preferred form of policy making

e. The nature and need for regulation

f. The legal basis for regulation

The Policy Process

"Policy" is an outcome of a political process in which government makes use of its authority in order to take action aimed at resolving what it perceives as a "problem." Beyond the formal structure of law we discussed in the first unit, and which may affect the form of the policy enacted, there is a plethora of activities that affect the content of the decisions made. Political scientist Larry Gerston defines in this reading what public policy is and how it emerges out of the political process. He describes the components and institutions of, and the trends in, public policy and he differentiates among social, economic, and technological issues that are at the base of policymaking.

The Context of Public Policy

Larry N. Gerston

Every few years, Congress approves a farm subsidy package to many of the nation's growers. Historically, the program has generated controversy over whether government should be in the business of providing financial assistance to a segment of the private sector. In 2002, the 107th Congress once again tackled this issue. It was a narrowly divided body, with Senate Democrats holding a one-seat advantage over Republicans and House Republicans maintaining a dozen seats more than the Democrats. Did such division auger gridlock over the farm support question? Hardly. With what observers commonly call "bipartisanship," the bill passed by decisive majorities in both houses.[1] In a country whose leaders routinely espouse "free market" competition, the bill provided more than $180 billion in farm subsidies over the next six years, with three-quarters of the payments going to 10 percent of the nation's largest farmers. Even more surprising, the bill was more than double the $73 billion originally sought by President George W. Bush, who was quickly losing his fight to provide a balanced budget. Nevertheless, the president, champion of competition and opponent of subsidies, signed the bill. Out of character? Perhaps. Nevertheless, this strange twist of events illustrates the erratic turns of the public policy–making process.

The public policy–making arena is fraught with confusion, contradictions, and consternation. In order to make policy, decision makers often merge conflicting objectives into acceptable outcomes. It's not pretty, but it works. Yet, whatever difficulties the student or practitioner may have in understanding the concept of policy making, it is a process that must be reckoned with.

Public policy is a relatively new subfield in political science. Its development as an area of study emerged out of the recognition that traditional analyses of government decisions were incomplete descriptions of political activities. As the relationships between society and its various public institutions have become more complex and more interdependent, the need has developed for more comprehensive assessments of what governments do, how they put their decisions into practice, and why they pursue some policy alternatives over others.

Focus on the public policy process has developed with the emergence of modern society and industrialization. Prior to the seventeenth and eighteenth centuries, most polities were consumed with self-survival and potential threats from foreign enemies. Political organization and infrastructure were largely irrelevant for obvious reasons: there were few decisions to make, and those who made them were dictators, monarchs, small bands of rulers, or unrepresentative legislative bodies. During the nineteenth century, representative government began to evolve in some parts of the world. With increased political participation by larger portions of the public, government decisions assumed greater importance and legitimacy. Clashing values with respect to social, economic, and political questions had profound implications for politics and government. With these changes, governments began to focus on the problems of their citizens.

These changes did not go unnoticed by those who studied political phenomena in the United States. As this young country matured, so did the approaches to the study of government and politics. Earlier in this century, American political scientists were content to analyze government in the context of its three major branches: the executive, the legislative, and the judicial.[2] While such studies were instructive about the powers of institutions, they were less than complete descriptions of the political process.

Fifty years later, political scientists expanded their perspectives of government activities. Some examinations centered on the informal relationship between interest groups and government, leading one scholar to conclude that political institutions "operate to order the relationships among various groups in society."[3] Other studies focused on the interdependence between government activities and diverse forces such as political parties or public opinion. Out of this evolution came the recognition of the symbiotic association between government and politics.[4]

Recent assessments in political science offer yet another slant on the powers and abilities of government bodies. Some contemporary scholars now argue that government is not designed to be merely responsive; nor, they assert, is government even neutral or benign. Instead, these writers contend that government institutions and officeholders possess powerful tools for altering social, economic, and technological arrangements. In light of the effects that policy makers have on society, we have come to appreciate that what comes out of government is as important as what goes in.[5] This thinking brings us to the concept of public policy. Viewed as a multifaceted approach to the study of politics, public policy making shows

the workings of modern government and the flow of political life.

IN SEARCH OF A FRAMEWORK

As an approach to understanding political change, public policy has almost as many definitions as there are policy issues. *Institutionalists*, those who concern themselves with the formal, observable building blocks of government, view public policy as a benign component of identified rules and procedures. As Lawrence Friedman writes, "in societies like ours … there arises an enormous demand—a need—for formal controls which have to come from some sort of organized government."[6] *Behaviorists*, scholars consumed with what people actually do, interpret public policy as the result of the interaction of powerful forces, some of which may be far removed from the halls of government. To that end, Calvin MacKenzie concludes, "law is a guide to public policy, a statement of what policy makers hope policy will be; but it is not necessarily public policy."[7]

The debate over parameters is more than an exercise or game, for it is the word *process* that differentiates public policy from other approaches to government and politics. A process is dynamic and ongoing and, as such, is constantly subject to reevaluation, cessation, expedition, or even erratic movement. Conceptually speaking, then, policy making exists in an open environment with neither a beginning nor an end, and with virtually no boundaries. What seems inconceivable as a policy issue one day may well be the focal point of heated debate the next. Within this nomadic context, our task is to examine public policy making as a concept, as a process, and as a mechanism of political change.

While there is little concurrence among scholars on the framework of the public policy–making arena, they tend to agree on a core of basic assumptions. Most obviously, government activities and commitments are crucial to the meaning of public policy. Defense, welfare, transportation, education, and agriculture are but a few major areas of historical concern to government. Other areas of interest, such as space exploration, the environment, biotechnology, and homeland security, are relatively new government concerns. However, the history of government fascination with a policy area is not as important as the attention itself. Without government involvement and direction, there is no public policy.

Another point upon which analysts agree is that sizable portions of society and its resources are affected by public policies. Whether we speak of consumers, the disabled, automobile drivers, handgun owners, or acquired immune deficiency syndrome (AIDS) victims, each of these constituencies and countless others are likely to be affected by many public policies. Some policies, such as defense, taxation, or public education, affect almost everyone. In fact, most people's lives are directly influenced by many public policies simultaneously. However, only a few public policy commitments consciously concern people at any one time.

Finally, virtually all students and practitioners of public policy concur that policy making is a process. The search for, debate about, development of, application of, and evaluation of a given policy spring from a continuum of events, with a beginning that is almost impossible to pinpoint and an end that is rarely permanent. As Deborah Stone writes, "policy is more like an endless game of Monopoly than a bicycle repair."[8] Whatever the issue in question, scholars agree that public policy making has a perpetual, dynamic, and evolutionary quality.

A WORKING DEFINITION OF PUBLIC POLICY

Aside from these basic areas of consensus, policy analysts differ greatly on the basis and limits of the public policy field. Consider the following definitions from three leading political scientists: Thomas Dye characterizes public policy as the study of "what governments do, why they do it, and what difference it makes."[9] Seeking to extend linkage, B. Guy Peters adds that public policy is the "sum of government activities, whether acting directly or through agents, as it has an influence on the lives of citizens."[10] Conversely, David Robertson and Dennis Judd take a more restrained course by casting government as the independent variable—that is, the crucial intersection of change—not only in terms of crafting current policies but with respect to future demands for different policies.[11]

These approaches and others all have merit and individually address key components of the policy-making process. However, for our purposes, we seek a definition that responds to the actions and exchanges of both people and governments in a dynamic, interdependent manner. Thus, *public policy* is defined here as *the combination of basic decisions, commitments, and actions made by those who hold or affect government positions of authority*. In most instances, these arrangements result from interactions among those who demand change, those who make decisions, and those who are affected by the policy in question. The determinations made by those in positions of legitimate authority—most commonly, one or more public offices in government—are subject to possible redirection in response to pressures from those outside government as well as from others within government.

The linkage between policy makers and policy receivers is vital to understanding the meaning and power of public policy. In a very direct sense, society benefits or suffers because of government activity. Sometimes, both experiences may occur simultaneously. At a minimum, the more controversial a proposed policy or policy area, the more likely it is that one part of society will benefit at the expense of another segment. Furthermore, the variety of potential public policy questions is so great that some government decisions emerging from the political process have greater impacts on society than others. The simple fact is that each public policy question has its own unique impact on those who lie in its path.

Public policies result from the blend of politics and government. David Easton defines politics as "the authoritative allocation of values."[12] Public policy, then, is as important in defining prevailing values (politics) as it is in defining solutions to prevailing problems (through government). In a very real sense, values predetermine public policies, although the values of some parts of society will often be more influential on a policy than the values of others.

COMPONENTS OF THE PUBLIC POLICY PROCESS

The methods of public policy analysis differ from those used in the "hard" sciences. Social science revolves around needs, emotions, unanticipated events, and a good deal of irrationality. These characteristics are extremely difficult to quantify or duplicate, and they rarely produce consensus regarding any order of importance or rank. Such is not the case in other disciplines.

Although the formulas themselves may be complicated or esoteric, the laws of physics, mathematics, and other sciences have a predictability that captures a certain respect from social scientists. In these fields, the hypothetical problem of 2 + 2 will always yield 4 regardless of inflation, war, unemployment, terrorism, disease, or any number of factors that may affect society. Such accuracy does not occur in the study of public policy. However, some components are constant in the public policy universe. They are:

- Issues that appear on the public agenda
- Actors who present, interpret, and respond to those issues
- Resources affected by those issues
- Institutions that deal with issues
- The levels of government that address issues.

Perhaps the most critical of these components is the determination of which policy issues will be resolved in the public sector, although the ability to respond to them may often be defined by the desire to do something and the resources available. In addition to describing public policy areas and their costs, it is necessary to identify the actors and the formal structures of government that may be the drivers of resolution.

Finally, it is important to determine which levels of government are best equipped to make policy. Public policy may be developed *horizontally*, with several agencies coordinating efforts at the national, state, or local level. Policy may also be developed *vertically*; in this approach, the decisions made at one level—commonly the national—are carried out on behalf of all parties or perhaps assigned to another level—often the states—for execution. As we will see below, these five ingredients highlight the complexities of making public policy.

Policy Issues

We can compare commonly discussed areas of public policy to a revolving ferris wheel at an amusement park. The wheel operates with a consistent pattern; it travels for a fixed period of time, stops, then proceeds again. While the wheel's movement is predictable, the entries, departures, and combinations of the passengers are not. Sometimes the wheel is almost full, but at other times it is nearly empty. A few passengers may opt to ride the wheel for several turns, while a single cycle will suffice for others. Public policy issues are the "passengers" that move off and on the "wheels" of government. Some, such as the debate over abortion, have incredible staying power; others, such the proposal by President Bush in 2003 to develop hydrogen fuel as a replacement for gasoline, disappear quickly after their emergence.

Although policy areas include a range of ever-changing public needs, the types of issues can be divided into two broad categories: *substantive* and *symbolic*. Substantive issues are those areas of controversy that have a major impact on society. Regulation of the economy, welfare reform, civil rights legislation, environmental protection, and homeland security are examples of substantive public policy issues. Because of their comprehensive impact, substantive issues are usually quite difficult to resolve and may linger on the public agenda for long periods of time, and sometimes without any resolution.

Symbolic issues center on irritating public problems and "quick fixes" to get them off the public agenda. Responses to these issue areas tend to provide more psychological relief than actual change in the political system. Outcomes are generally uncontroversial because the policy commitment does not threaten major shifts of social, economic, or political capital. For example, after a string of corporate corruption issues became public in 2002, then Securities and Exchange Commission Chairman Harvey Pitt ordered the chief executive officers of the nation's 1,000 largest companies to sign sworn statements as to the accuracy of their financial reports.[13]

Sometimes, substantive issues are addressed by symbolic responses, generating a good deal of resentment as a consequence. For example, in 1994 many congressional candidates rode the illegal immigration issue to victory. The suddenly explosive issue led the

Clinton administration to respond by increasing the number of U.S. border patrol guards, leading many critics to cry "tokenism," or a symbolic response to a substantive issue. The issue lingered longer than many had expected, and in 1996 there was a more substantive response, with provisions in the Welfare Reform Act that denied welfare benefits to illegal and legal immigrants. Both substantive and symbolic policy agendas are discussed in chapter 3.

Actors

How do policy issues get their "tickets" to the public policy "ride"? Unlike matters that remain solely private or as individual problems, public policy issues gain their status when they reach the eyes and ears of government actors. These individuals are catalysts for change; they are found at all levels of the policy-making process, from the national arena to a school board—in short, in any environment where someone in authority has the capability to manage the issue under discussion. As we will see in chapter 2, *triggering mechanisms* catapult once-private matters into the public forum of discussion. From this point on, policy makers may seize various public issues and try to formulate appropriate responses.

Issues are generated from a variety of sources. Sometimes problems are presented by individuals who are outside government altogether; for example, a celebrity who falls victim to a terrible disease or accident may, because of his or her notoriety, raise public consciousness. At other times, an investigation or exposé by a prominent media representative may serve as the conduit to government leaders. Then again, the people who are in government and closest to the policy-making process may advance an issue and generate support for resolution.

Resources

Recognizing problems is one part of the policy-making process; deciding how to pay the price to solve them is another. Sometimes, policy makers target those responsible for a problem to pay for it. For example, when Congress passed the 1990 Clean Air Act, the legislation committed the United States to a massive antipollution program—but at a significant cost to polluters. Compliance with the law's new standards forced producers and users of pollution-controlling materials to pick up much of the tab. Thus, within three years, the price of a new automobile increased by an average of $225, gasoline edged up between 3 and 5 cents per gallon, and the costs of products ranging from dry-cleaning services to refrigerators went up to meet the requirements of the new law.[14] On other occasions, public policy makers elect to use national revenues to pay for a program. Nowhere is this more evident than in our foreign policy commitments. Thus, when presidents have committed troops and weapons to such places as Afghanistan or Iraq, the tab has been picked up by the taxpayers. Most of the time, the public is deferential on such issues. Nevertheless, the fact that such commitments are sometimes made without a thorough national airing may backfire on leaders, as was the case when President Lyndon Johnson's pursuit of the Vietnam War during the mid-1960s ultimately cost him his office.[15]

What makes policy makers commit resources for some policies and not for others? Values, the extent of a crisis, awareness, and other factors enter into the equation that determines the answer. But the availability of resources plays a large part as well.

Public Institutions

Public institutions are the vehicles through which public policies are formulated and carried out. The word *institution* rings of formality and organization, but it also suggests the routes for traffic traveling through the policy process. Aside from occasional policies mandated by the electorate at the state and local levels, the basic policy-making institutions are the executive, legislative, and judicial branches of government. Bureaucracies and regulatory agencies are also prominent in the creation and implementation of public policies.

The Executive Branch

Numerous examples highlight the roles of institutions and their strategists in the development of public policy. More often than not, the "checks and balances" organization of government requires the various branches to act in complementary fashion. However, there are occasions when a single element of government can frame, if not dominate, the policy process. Presidents, governors, and mayors are among those who place issues on the public agenda by their positions of executive authority. Sometimes, they can even make policy. When presidents, for example, sign executive orders to prevent abortion funding to international agencies or when governors sign executive orders to speed up construction of power plants, they wield their power to make policy. Likewise, when presidents send weapons or U.S. troops to other countries in crisis situations, they direct public policy in the arena of foreign affairs. A very large portion of any president's leadership stems from his ability to establish priorities and define policy commitments.

The Legislative Branch

Legislative bodies, collective decision-making units of many individuals elected by voters in districts or states, have prominent roles in the public policy–making process. Nowhere is this more visible than with the workings of the U.S. Congress. As the nation's chief legislative body, Congress makes policy with the hundreds of statutes or laws it enacts each year. The ability to reach these decisions gives Congress a major role in guiding the nation, even if it means opposing the president. One recent example of legislative independence occurred in 2003, when the Senate decided not to permit oil exploration in the Arctic National Wildlife Refuge. Opposed by environmentalists, the idea of such exploration was a cornerstone of President Bush's environmental agenda. Nevertheless, the Republican-controlled Senate decided to protect the wilderness area, demonstrating considerable independence from the president.[16]

The Judiciary

Although courts are not active in the legislative process, they play an important role in policy making. Courts establish policy through interpretation of the law as it pertains to guarantees in the Constitution, sometimes to the chagrin of Congress and the president. One such example occurred over the constitutionality of late-term or "partial birth" abortions, a procedure that had been outlawed in Nebraska and thirty other states. By a 5:4 vote in 2000 the Court ruled that the Nebraska law was so vague that it would keep physicians from performing first- or second-trimester abortions.[17] But the issue didn't end there. In 2003, Congress passed and the president signed a federal law prohibiting late-term abortions. Proponents of the concept sued, citing the 2000 case. Given the time required for cases to work their way up the judicial ladder, a showdown in the U.S. Supreme Court is expected toward the end of the decade.

The Bureaucracy

The three branches mentioned above are recognized staples of American government. Yet, the policy-making process includes a number of other, less obvious governmental actors. The bureaucracy, a collection of agencies designed to carry out relatively specific tasks, has become so vital in modern society that it is commonly described as the "fourth branch" of government. Officially, most bureaucratic agencies administer policies created by Congress and the White House; others operate at the state and local levels. But it is often difficult to determine where the administration ends and policy making begins. For example, the Immigration and Naturalization Service periodically changed the circumstances under which illegal immigrants could remain in the United States, causing confusion among immigrants and elected policy makers alike.[18] Absorption of the agency into the new Department of Homeland Security in 2003 ended its erratic behavior, although the larger questions related to immigration persisted.

Regulatory Agencies

Regulatory agencies constitute yet another element in the policy-making process. For the better part of the twentieth century, the Security and Exchange Commission (SEC), the Federal Trade Commission (FTC), and dozens of other boards and commissions have been active partners in making the decisions of government. These bodies have been created in waves, first to deal with economic issues such as trade and commerce, and more recently on social problems.[19] Although there appears to be consensus regarding the value of most economic regulatory units, considerable disagreement has emerged in recent years over the wisdom of regulatory bodies dealing with social issues such as environmental protection and worker safety.[20]

We have noted how policy making institutions and their authorities execute several valuable functions. They organize issues for the public agenda and, under the right circumstances, convert them into public commitments. But once a policy has been created, its success or failure depends upon the extent to which it is carried out. This is implementation, an activity that turns official policy commitments into reality. Many of the policy actors cited above share responsibility for this function, as discussed more fully in chapter 5.

Federalism—The Sharing of Power among Governments

The fifth component of the public policy–making process centers on the participant levels of government. Just as the roles of government have grown throughout the twentieth century, the numbers of governments responding to issues have also increased. More than ever, governments share policy-making functions and responsibilities. This evolution suggests major changes in *federalism*, defined here as the political and legal framework within which different levels of governments interact.

The extent to which intergovernmental relations have changed is the subject of some debate. Using the 1930s as a watershed mark, Michael Reagan and John Sanzone find substantial differences in the ways governments make policies. The chief change has been in the shift of policy making responsibility primarily to the national level: "If we compare the reach of the federal government today with that which existed prior to World War II, … the range of public sector decisions subject to national government influence is immeasurably greater now."[21] Others are not so convinced that such sweeping changes remain in place. Thus, Virginia Gray and her colleagues conclude, the national government has grown "increasingly reluctant to undertake new domestic policy initiatives, especially expensive ones."[22] While these two conclusions do not show federalism in the same light, their authors acknowledge the struggle for and distribution of power at multiple levels of government.

Until now, we have focused on the levels of *formal* governments that take part in the public policy process. Yet, some citizens may also initiate policy from outside traditional government structures. About half of the state governments—mostly in the West—and virtually all local governments have referenda and/or initiatives as policy-making tools.

In most cases, a referendum allows the electorate to vote on a policy proposal drafted by a legislature or a local government body; an initiative permits voters to propose modifications in the constitution, charter, or ordinance, which are then approved or rejected at the next election.[23] Many initiative and referendum questions cover extremely complex questions. Nevertheless, in recent years voters in various states have decided on policy questions on topics such as euthanasia, legalized gambling, immigration, and capital punishment. This method of participation not only brings citizens directly into the public policy–making process, but also awakens national leaders to emergent issues.

Sometimes, state or national public officials make policy decisions that conflict with another level of government. When such clashes occur, they are usually settled by the federal courts. Thus, in 1996 when California voters passed a first-of-its-kind initiative to allow seriously ill people to obtain marijuana for "medical purposes," opponents took the question to the federal courts. In 2001, the U.S. Supreme Court ruled by an 8:0 vote that existing federal laws clearly prohibit the distribution of marijuana even for medical purposes.[24] Such are the uncertainties of the policy-making process because of federalism.

Federalism has emerged as a crucial policy making element. Although the pressure points of the political process extend in both vertical directions (among levels) and horizontal directions (among branches) of government, most of the discussion in the following chapters will focus on the national government's responses to policy issues. It is at this level that questions with the widest application are presented, debated, and resolved, often with profound implications for policy makers and citizens at lower levels of government.

CONTEMPORARY TRENDS IN PUBLIC POLICY

Between the late 1930s and the 1980s, American government expanded its role in society. During this period, the proportion of public expenditures to the nation's income increased dramatically. One study of federal activity shows that, between 1951 and 1976, the national government's budget outlays alone grew

FIGURE 1.1 Federal Budget Outlays, 1950–2002 (as a percent of GDP)

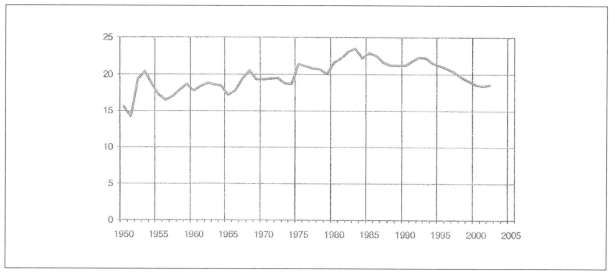

Source: Executive Office of the President.

from 14.7 percent to 22.8 percent of the gross domestic product (GDP).[25] Federal commitments reached 24 percent of the GDP in 1990, but recent statistics suggest a possible long-term retrenchment, or at least a slowdown of the government's public spending. In 1991, federal spending as a percentage of the GDP began to decrease to about the 20 percent level, marking a reversal in the role of government. The expenditure percentages have hovered at or slightly below this level for the past several years and into the twenty-first century (see Figure 1.1). Uncertain at this time is whether the nation's recent concern with homeland security and terrorism, sparked by the attacks on September 11, 2001, and the U.S. invasion of Iraq in 2003 will produce long-term increases in government spending.

Why the general downward redirection in government spending at the national level? Some speculate that the end of the Cold War and massive defense spending are responsible for the new direction. Others note the generally negative perception of unnecessary, if not bloated, federal government, many commitments from which go to questionable domestic spending areas of activity. In fact, both themes have emerged on the public agenda.

Prior to 9/11, annual defense expenditures by the federal governments dropped precipitously from $328 billion in 1990 to $280 billion in 2000, a decrease of nearly 15 percent over the decade. All that

changed however, after the terrorist attacks and the U.S.-led invasion of Afghanistan, followed by a war with Iraq. As a result of these commitments, defense spending soared to $380 billion by 2004, plus more than $100 billion to fund the Iraq War.

A more consistent pattern has been seen in the domestic arena. On the one hand, "entitlement" programs such as Social Security, Medicare, Medicaid, and federal civil service pensions have soared with the aging of America. However, on the other hand, virtually all other domestic areas have received considerably less attention from the federal government, particularly with the George W. Bush administration and a Republican Congress in power. Among the losers: housing, labor, interior, health, and environment programs, relative to the defense-related winners.[26]

Much of the current debate over policy objectives centers on the ability of the national government to meet society's needs at a time when resources are no longer as endless as they once seemed. During the 1990s, for example, the economy grew at a robust rate, allowing for both new programs and the accumulation of modest budget surpluses toward the decade. All that changed with a stubborn recession in 2001 and 2002, coupled with a series of tax cuts promoted by the Bush administration, resulting in a sea of budget deficits during the first half of the first decade of the new century. Conventional wisdom once suggested that American ingenuity and technology would enhance our lives on a regular basis. Indeed, the mere possibility of slowed growth has been heretical to a society where, for most, fulfillment of the "American dream" has been a routine expectation and accomplishment. Increasingly, futurists fear a future with a series of built-in scarcities and broken dreams. Lester Thurow, for one, rattles off a list of social and economic problems that have escalated in size and seriousness, and that are spiked by the inability of government to solve them.[27] Others, such as David Osborne and Ted Gaebler, view the crisis as an opportunity for governments to "reinvent" themselves, with market-driven programs and decentralized management.[28] Either way, the possible allocation of fewer public benefits for society only underscores the importance of understanding the public policy process.

As the nation embraces a new century, the most controversial elements of American public policy seem to be in three broad areas: social issues, economic issues, and technological issues. Each of these has a decidedly domestic tone, although none is completely without influence from foreign factors. Nevertheless, these issues share a common bond: They draw attention to defining the "proper" extent of government commitments. In this regard, they reflect the contemporary concerns of American politics.

Social Issues

While social issues are hardly new to the American political mosaic, government response to them is largely a recent phenomenon. For most of this country's two centuries, governments tended to minimize their roles in any activities that involved social change or assistance. Even in such areas as welfare relief and care for the elderly, compelling questions by today's standards, public policies were conspicuously absent. The lack of government attention was not based on economics so much as on a political tradition steeped in the virtues of individualism.

Attitudes toward welfare and other social questions underwent reassessment during the Great Depression of the 1930s. Until that time, a few states and local governments dealt with relief on a minimal basis. But after President Franklin Roosevelt urged, and the Congress passed, the Social Security Act of 1935, governments became immersed in social issues that had previously been viewed as private matters. Aid to the poor, medical research, and health care are but a few of the social issue offshoots that have received government attention as a result of the seeds sown during Roosevelt's "New Deal." Further attention was generated during the 1960s, when U.S. social policies included urban renewal, abortion funding, and federal aid for education, largely inspired by President Lyndon Johnson's "Great Society."

Despite the debate over government involvement in social issues, some responses have garnered more consensus than others. Social Security, for example, has generally been taken off the agenda as a controversial issue. Medicaid, a program providing medical assistance for the elderly indigent population, has been susceptible to some debate. And federally funded abortions have become so controversial that Congress has eliminated financial support in most instances. Still other issues, such as capital punishment, gun control, and federal funding for private schools, have found so little agreement that the national government has steered away from any significant policy commitments.

Economic Issues

Governments respond to economic problems because of the widely held sentiment that society should operate with some sense of security. However, whether the benefits accrue in the form of wage guarantees, subsidies, or safety, the costs for providing such protection are ultimately passed on to the public. Debates over the necessity of a given economic policy, weighing both costs and benefits, may be divisive. Nevertheless, government leaders are responsible for developing policies and services to match public needs.

Economic policies tend to be controversial because they have uneven impacts on society's members. The most serious economic issue areas involve two major themes: the appropriate extent of government involvement in the economy and income redistribution through taxation. Both areas have received a "walking-on-eggshells" treatment in American politics. As the economy has become more complex and more interdependent, some critics have called for government to referee the disputes between private business interests; others have been equally adamant in demanding that the private and public sectors be kept as far apart as possible. Income redistribution issues have been controversial because of the tension between the "haves" and the "have-nots," and because of the debate over what, if anything, government should do to alter such disparities through progressive taxation.

Several government bodies create economic policies for Americans. They are particularly powerful at the national level, where policy decisions also influence lower government structures. The Federal Reserve Board and the president's Council of Economic Advisers are just two of several agencies concerned with economic issues. The Federal Reserve Board has substantial control over credit, interest rates, and other important facets of the economy. The Council of Economic Advisers guides the president on long-term economic problems such as inflation, recessions, employment cycles, and balance-of-payments difficulties. Although these institutions contribute much to the resolution of thorny economic questions, their work is not widely followed or understood.

Economic public policy issues are predicated to a large extent upon the political values held by individuals, society, and government. Moreover, often the resolution of an economic issue is tied closely to the resolution of a social issue. If, for example, the national government commits to a balanced budget, reduced expenditures for low-income families might foster social disruption. Conversely, if the national government commits to a spending format that ignores the balanced budget imperative, repeated deficits may cause inflation, leaving unhappy citizens with less purchasing power. Thus, the management of economic questions can have broad implications for all sectors of American society.

Technological Issues

From a philosophical perspective, technology has always represented a challenge to society. Ever since the Industrial Revolution, scholars have written about the drawbacks and improvements that technology seems to provide for the political order.[29] In their research on comparative politics, Gabriel Almond and G. Bingham Powell note the direct impact of technological growth on urbanization, education, communication, and countless other forms of political, economic, and social activity. Several consequences of technological change—notably, weak family structures, psychological alienation, and uncertain economic conditions—present formidable problems for the political system.[30] Given our long history of technological evolution, American society is particularly susceptible to these difficulties.

With the emergence of the postindustrial age, the tendency has been to let technology take its own course, independent of government oversight. Yet developments have moved faster than society's ability to cope with them. With respect to life issues, artificial respirators and other mechanical life-support systems have led to new problems in defining life and death. Automation has eliminated millions of low-tech jobs, while creating millions of high-tech opportunities. The global reliance upon fossil fuels has increased global prosperity as well as "global warming," a condition that threatens to choke the earth in its own, normally beneficial natural atmosphere. Cloning has created opportunities for efficient food reproduction, while causing great concerns in the area of human reproduction. The ironies are almost daunting.

It now appears that reliance on technology cannot continue without adequate safeguards for society. As technologist Rudi Volti notes, the proliferation of knowledge has produced a dizzying pace of change. "But for technology to be truly beneficial, … [o]ur challenge will be to develop and apply many different kinds of knowledge—ethical, philosophical, sociological, political and economic, so that we can do a better job of defining our real needs and creating the technologies that serve them."[31] To this, Theodore Lowi responds, "The increased pace of technological change in our epoch seems only to make the need for administration more intense" in the name of sound, well-thought-out public policies.[32] Indeed, the debate now centers on which issues require government oversight and to what extent such management should take place—tough questions for a society that regularly debates the role of government.

In summary, public policy authorities deal with many social, economic, and technological issues. The public agenda—the list of questions awaiting governmental disposition—is carved from these areas of concern. Given the multitude of issues and the large number of policy-making agencies, the agenda is perpetually full and ripe for action.

A LOOK AHEAD

The creation of public policy is a dynamic process. Events, actors, and political institutions combine and conflict in a wide array of unpredictable ways. Yet there is a general method through which basic questions are raised, considered, and perhaps decided.

The concepts and tools provided in this book should help with the analysis of virtually any policy issue, whether national or local in significance. Why? Because policy making is a process filled with never-ending issues, competing approaches to their solutions, and conflict over their implementation.

SUGGESTED READING

Abraham, Henry J., *The Judiciary: The Supreme Court in the Governmental Process,* 9th ed. (Dubuque, IA: Brown and Benchmark, 1991).

Anderson, James E., *Public Policymaking,* 3d ed. (Boston: Houghton Mifflin, 1997).

Bonser, Charles F., Eugene B. McGregor, Jr., and Clinton V. Oster, Jr., *American Public Policy Problems,* 2d ed. (Upper Saddle River, NJ: Prentice Hall, 2000).

Cochran, Clarke, Lawrence C. Mayer, T.R. Carr, and N. Joseph Cayer, *American Public Policy,* 6th ed. (New York: Bedford/St. Martin's Press, 1999).

Dye, Thomas R., *American Federalism* (Lexington, MA: Lexington, 1990).

Hird, John A., and Michael Reese, *Controversies in American Public Policy,* 2d ed. (New York: St. Martin's/Worth, 1999).

Koven, Steven G., Mack C. Shelley II, and Bert E. Swanson, *American Public Policy* (Boston: Houghton Mifflin, 1998).

Naisbitt, John, *Megatrends* (New York: Warner, 1982).

Ripley, Randall B., and Grace A. Franklin, *Congress, the Bureaucracy and Public Policy,* 5th ed. (Pacific Grove, CA: Brooks/Cole, 1991).

Stone, Deborah, *Policy Paradox: The Art of Political Decision Making* (New York: W.W. Norton, 1997).

Thobaben, Robert G., Donna M. Schlagheck, and Charles Funderburk, *Issues in American Political Life: Money, Violence, and Biology,* 4th ed. (Upper Saddle River, NJ: Prentice Hall, 2002).

Tolchin, Susan J., and Martin Tolchin, *Dismantling America* (New York: Oxford University Press, 1985).

NOTES

1. The bill, HR 2646, the Farm Security and Rural Investment Act, passed by a vote of 280:141 in the House and 58:40 in the Senate. President Bush signed the bill into law on May 13, 2002.

2. For an example of early-twentieth-century emphasis on institutions, see Woodrow Wilson, *Constitutional Government in the United States* (New York: Columbia University Press, 1908).

3. David B. Truman, *The Governmental Process* (New York: Alfred A. Knopf, 1951); p. 52.

4. Among the many works taking this approach, see V.O. Key, *Public Opinion and American Democracy* (New York: Alfred A. Knopf, 1965).

5. David Easton was one of the first political scientists to write with such a framework. See his *The Political System* (New York: Alfred A. Knopf, 1953).

6. Lawrence Friedman, *American Law* (New York: W.W. Norton, 1984), p. 32.

7. Calvin MacKenzie, *American Government: Politics and Policy* (New York: Random House, 1986), p. 4.

8. Deborah Stone, *Policy Paradox: The Art of Political Decision Making* (New York: W.W. Norton, 1997), p. 259.

9. Thomas Dye, *Understanding Public Policy,* 10th ed. (Upper Saddle River, NJ: Prentice Hall, 2002), p. 1.

10. B. Guy Peters, *American Public Policy: Promise and Performance,* 4th ed. (Chatham, NJ: Chatham House, 1996), p. 4.

11. David Robertson and Dennis Judd, *The Development of American Public Policy: The Structure of Policy Restraint* (Glenview, IL: Scott, Foresman, 1989), p. 7.

12. Easton, *The Political System,* p. 129.

13. "Can Trust Be Rebuilt?" *Business Week,* July 8, 2002, pp. 31–37.

14. "Clear Benefits of Clean Air Act Come at a Cost," *Wall Street Journal,* November 11, 1993, pp. B1, B5.

15. Historian Arthur M. Schlesinger, Jr., makes this point in *The Imperial Presidency* (Boston: Houghton Mifflin, 1973), pp. 178–87.

16. "Oil-Drilling Defeat Angers Alaskan," *Washington Times,* March 20, 2003, p. 1.

17. The case was *Stenberg vs. Carhart,* 99–830. For an analysis of the case and its consequences, see "Court Rules That Governments Can't Outlaw Type of Abortion," *New York Times,* June 29, 2000, pp. A1, A20.

18. "Ambivalence Prevails in Immigration Policy," *New York Times,* May 27, 2001, p. 12.

19. For a brief history of the regulatory movement, see Larry N. Gerston, Cynthia Fraleigh, and Robert Schwab, *The Deregulated Society* (Pacific Grove, CA: Brooks/Cole, 1988), pp. 7–17.

20. For two distinctly different approaches to the question of social regulation, see Eugene Bardach and Robert A. Kagan, *Going by the Book: The Problem of Regulatory Unreasonableness* (Philadelphia: Temple University Press, 1982); and Michael D. Reagan, *Regulation: The Politics of Policy* (New York: Little, Brown, 1987).

21. Michael D. Reagan and John Sanzone, *The New Federalism,* 2d ed. (New York: Oxford University Press, 1981), p. 158.

22. Virginia Gray, Russell L. Hanson, and Herbert Jacob, eds., *Politics in the American States,* 7th ed. (Washington, DC: CQ Press, 1999), p. 60.

23. For a summary of these tools of citizen government, see Ann O'M. Bowman and Richard C. Kearney, *State and Local Government,* 5th ed. (Boston: Houghton Mifflin, 2002), pp. 95–100.

24. The case was *U.S. v. Oakland Cannabis Buyers' Cooperative,* 00–151. See "Top Court Says No to Medical Marijuana Use," *Los Angeles Times,* May 15, 2001, pp. A1, A13.

25. Dennis S. Ippolito, *The Budget and National Politics* (San Francisco: Freeman, 1978), p. 27.

26. "Bush's Tradeoffs: Budget for Harder Times Offers New Plans but Lots of Cutbacks," *Wall Street Journal,* February 4, 2003, pp. A1, A9.

27. See Lester Thurow, *The Zero-Sum Society* (New York: Penguin, 1981), pp. 9–11.

28. David Osborne and Ted Gaebler, *Reinventing America* (New York: Penguin, 1992).

29. For two classical treatments on the impact of technological change, see Emile Durkheim, *The Division of Labor in Society,* 1933 (New York: Free Press, 1964); and Ferdinand Tonnies, *Fundamental Concepts of Sociology* (New York: American, 1940).

30. Gabriel Almond and G. Bingham Powell, *Comparative Politics* (Boston: Little, Brown, 1966), p. 95.

31. Rudi Volti, *Society and Technological Change,* 3d ed. (New York: St. Martin's Press, 1995), p. 293.

32. Theodore Lowi, *The End of Liberalism,* 2d ed. (New York: W.W. Norton, 1979), p. 23.

Why Regulate?

The legal scholar Robert Baldwin and economist Martin Cave uncover in this reading the motivation for regulation. They provide an inconclusive list of 12 rationales for economic regulation and illustrative examples. Incorporating the lecture with this reading will provide you, in addition to understanding the list, also with the relevant communication policies that fall under the same headings. Some are more apparent—such as the need to regulate monopolies, as you should be acquainted with the fact that the telecommunications industry emerged from a monopoly-controlled status—others will be studied in the next few months, such as dealing with externalities (indecency regulation), availability of service (universal service), public goods (public broadcasting), unequal bargaining power (interconnection), and scarcity (spectrum management).

Why Regulate?

Robert Baldwin and Martin Cave

Motives for regulating can be distinguished from technical justifications for regulating. Governments may regulate for a number of motives—for example they may be influenced by the economically powerful and may act in the interests of the regulated industry or they may see a particular regulatory stance as a means to re-election. Different commentators may analyse such motives in different ways and a variety of approaches to such analysis will be discussed in Chapter 3. To begin, though, we should consider the technical justifications for regulating that may be given by a government that is assumed to be acting in pursuit of the public interest.[1]

Many of the rationales for regulating can be described as instances of 'market failure'. Regulation in such cases is argued to be justified because the uncontrolled market place will, for some reason, fail to produce behaviour or results in accordance with the public interest.[2] In some sectors or circumstances there may also be 'market absence'—there may be no effective market—because, for example, households cannot buy clean air or peace and quiet in their localities.

I. MONOPOLIES AND NATURAL MONOPOLIES

Monopoly describes the position in which one seller produces for the entire industry or market. Monopoly pricing and output is likely to occur and be sustained where three factors obtain:[3]

- a single seller occupies the entire market;
- the product sold is unique in the sense that there is no substitute sufficiently close for consumers to turn to;
- substantial barriers restrict entry by other firms into the industry and exit is difficult.

Where monopoly occurs, the market 'fails' because competition is deficient. From the public interest perspective, the problem with a firm occupying a monopolistic position is that in maximizing profits it will restrict its output and set price above marginal cost. It will do this because if it charges a single price for its product, additional sales will only be achieved by lowering the price on the entire output. The monopolist will forgo sales to the extent that lost revenue from fewer sales will be compensated for by higher revenue derived from increased price on the units still sold. The effects of monopoly, as compared to perfect competition, are reduced output, higher prices, and transfer of income from consumers to producers.

One response to potential monopolies is to use competition (or antitrust) laws so as to create a business environment conducive to competition. Where a 'natural monopoly' exists, however, the use of competition law may be undesirable.[4] A natural monopoly occurs when economies of scale available in the production process are so large that the relevant market can be served at the least cost by a single firm. It is accordingly less costly to society to have production carried out by one firm than by many. Thus, rather than have three railway or electricity companies laying separate networks of rails or cables where one would do, it may be more efficient to give one firm a monopoly subject to regulation of such matters as prices and access to the network. Determining whether a natural monopoly exists requires a comparison of demand for the product with the extent of the economies of scale available in production. If a firm is in a position of natural monopoly then, like any monopoly, it will present problems of reduced output, higher prices, and transfers of wealth from consumers to the firm. Restoration of competition by use of competition law is not, however, an appropriate response since competition may be socially costly and thus regulation of prices, quality, and output as well as access may be called for. The regulator will try to set price near incremental cost (the cost of producing an additional unit) in order to encourage the natural monopolist to expand its output to the level that competitive conditions would have induced.

Not all aspects of a supply process may be naturally monopolistic. As Ogus points out,[5] the economies of scale phenomenon may affect only one part of a given process—for instance the *transmission* of, say, electricity, rather than its *generation*.[6] The task of many governments and regulators (at least those committed to minimalist regulation) is to identify those parts of a process that are naturally monopolistic so that these can be regulated while other aspects are left to the influence of competitive forces.[7]

2. WINDFALL PROFITS

A firm will earn a windfall profit (sometimes called an 'economic rent' or excess profit) where it finds a source of supply significantly cheaper than that available in the market place.[8] It may do so by, say, locating a rich seam of an easily extracted mineral; by coming upon a material efficiency in a production process; or by possessing an asset that suddenly escalates in value—for example a boat in a desert town that has been flooded. Regulation may be called for when it is desired either to transfer profits to taxpayers or to allow consumers or the public to benefit from the windfall.

The rationale for regulating is strongest where the windfall is due to accident rather than planned investments of money, effort, or research. Where such investments have taken place or where society might want to create incentives to search for new efficiencies, products, or areas of demand, there is a case for allowing windfall or 'excess' profits to be retained. Even in the desert town it may be desirable to encourage some individuals to store boats in order to cope with periodic floods.

3. EXTERNALITIES

The reason for regulating externalities (or 'spillovers') is that the price of a product does not reflect the true cost to society of producing that good and excessive consumption accordingly results.[9] Thus, a manufacturer of car tyres might keep costs to consumers down by dumping pollutants arising from the manufacturing process into a river. The price of the tyres will not represent the true costs that production imposes on society if clean-up costs are left out of account. The resultant process is wasteful because too many resources are attracted into polluting activities (too many tyres are made and sold) and too few resources are devoted by the manufacturer to pollution avoidance or adopting pollution-free production methods. The rationale for regulation is to eliminate this waste—and to protect society or third parties suffering from externalities—by compelling the internalization of spillover costs—on 'polluter pays' principles.

4. INFORMATION INADEQUACIES

Competitive markets can only function properly if consumers are sufficiently well informed to evaluate competing products.[10] The market may, however, fail to produce adequate information and may fail for a number of reasons: information may cost money to produce (e.g. because researching the effects of a product, such as a drug, may prove expensive). The producer of information, however, may not be compensated by others who use that information (e.g. other manufacturers of the drug). The incentive to produce information may accordingly be low. There may also be incentives to falsify information—where, for example, consumers of the product are ill-positioned to challenge the falsification and seek remedies for damages suffered or where they face high costs in doing so. Areas in which consumers purchase a type of product very infrequently may give rise to this problem. The information produced may, in addition, not be of sufficient assistance to the consumer—for instance because the consumer lacks the expertise required to render technical data useful. Finally, collusion in the market place, or insufficient competition, may reduce the flow of information below the levels consumers might want. Producers, as a group, may thus fail to warn consumers about the general hazards or deficiencies associated with a product. Breyer notes that until the US Government required disclosure, accurate information was unavailable to most buyers in that country concerning the durability of light bulbs, nicotine content of cigarettes, fuel economy for cars, or care requirements for textiles.[11]

Regulation, by making information more extensively accessible, accurate, and affordable, may protect consumers against information inadequacies and the consequences thereof and may encourage the operation of healthy, competitive markets.

5. CONTINUITY AND AVAILABILITY OF SERVICE

In some circumstances the market may not provide the socially desired levels of continuity and availability of service. Thus, where demand is cyclical (for example, as with passenger air transport to a holiday island) waste may occur as firms go through the processes of closing and reopening operations.[12] Regulation may be used to sustain services through troughs—for example by setting minimum prices at levels allowing the covering of fixed costs through lean periods. This would be justified where the extra costs imposed on consumers by pricing rules are less than those caused

by the processes of closing and opening services in response to the business cycle. The subsidizing of off-peak by peak travellers will, however, raise issues of equity to be considered alongside questions of social policy. In the case of some products or services—for example water services—it may be considered, as a matter of social policy, that these should be generally available at least to a certain minimum standard. In the unregulated market, however, competition may lead to 'cream-skimming'—the process in which the producer chooses to supply only the most profitable customers—and services may be withdrawn from poorer or more geographically disperse groupings of customers. Regulation may be justified in order to produce socially desirable results even though the cross-subsidizations effected may be criticizable as inefficient and unfair.

6. ANTI-COMPETITIVE BEHAVIOUR AND PREDATORY PRICING

Markets may be deficient not merely because competition is lacking; they may produce undesirable effects because firms behave in a manner not conducive to healthy competition. A principal manifestation of such behaviour is predatory pricing. This occurs when a firm prices below costs, in the hope of driving competitors from the market, achieving a degree of domination, and then using its position to recover the costs of predation and increase profits at the expense of consumers. Preconditions for a rational firm to engage in predatory pricing are: that it must be able to outlast its competitors once prices are cut below variable costs and it must be able to maintain prices well above costs for long enough to recover its prior losses. The costs of entry to and exit from the market must, accordingly, allow it this period of comfort before new competition arises. The aim for regulators is to sustain competition and protect consumers from the ill-effects of market domination by outlawing predatory or other forms of anti-competitive behaviour.

7. PUBLIC GOODS AND MORAL HAZARD

Some commodities, e.g. security and defence services, may bring shared benefits and be generally desired. It may, however, be very costly for those paying for such services to prevent non-payers ('free-riders') from enjoying the benefits of those services. As a result, the market may fail to encourage the production of such commodities and regulation may be required—often to overcome the free-rider problem by imposing taxes.

Similarly, where there is an instance of moral hazard—where someone other than the consumer pays for a service[13]—there may be excessive consumption without regard to the resource costs being imposed on society. If, for example, medical costs are not met by the patient, but by the state or an insurer, regulatory constraints may be required if excessive consumption of medical services is to be avoided.

8. UNEQUAL BARGAINING POWER

One precondition for the efficient or fair allocation of resources in a market is equal bargaining power. If bargaining power is unequal, regulation may be justified in order to protect certain interests. Thus, if unemployment is prevalent it cannot be assumed that workers will be able to negotiate effectively to protect their interests (even leaving aside informational issues) and regulation may be required to safeguard such matters as the health and safety of those workers.

9. SCARCITY AND RATIONING

Regulatory rather than market mechanisms may be justified in order to allocate certain commodities when these are in short supply. In a petrol shortage, for example, public interest objectives may take precedence over efficiency so that, instead of using pricing as an allocative instrument, the petrol is allocated with reference to democratically generated lists of priorities.

10. DISTRIBUTIONAL JUSTICE AND SOCIAL POLICY

Allocative efficiency attempts to maximize welfare but is not concerned with the distribution of that welfare amongst individuals or groups within society. Regulation may be used to redistribute wealth or to transfer resources to victims of misfortune (e.g. injured parties).[14]

Distrust of individuals' rationality or wisdom may also underpin another rationale for regulation—paternalism. As a matter of policy society may decide to overrule individuals' preferences on some issues and regulate—for example by demanding that seat belts be worn in motor vehicles. In the strongest form of such paternalism, the decision is taken to regulate even where it is assumed that the citizens involved are possessed of full information concerning products.[15] On a series of other issues, governments may regulate simply in order to further social policies such as the prevention of discrimination based on race, sex, or age.

11. RATIONALIZATION AND COORDINATION

In many situations it is extremely expensive for individuals to negotiate private contracts so as to organize behaviour or industries in an efficient manner—the transaction costs would be excessive.[16] The firms in an industry may be too small and geographically dispersed to bring themselves together to produce efficiently. (This might happen when small fishing concerns in a sparsely populated area fail to make collective marketing arrangements.) Enterprises may, moreover, have developed different and incompatible modes of production. In these circumstances regulation may be justified as a means of rationalizing production processes (perhaps standardizing equipment in order to create effective networks) and in order to coordinate the market. Centralized regulation holds the advantage over individual private law arrangements where information can be more efficiently communicated through public channels and economies of scale can be achieved by having one public agency responsible for upholding standards.[17]

It is noteworthy that this rationale for regulation is based more on the desire to *enable* effective action to take place than on the need to prohibit undesirable behaviour.

12. PLANNING

Markets may ensure reasonably well that individuals' consumer preferences are met but they are less able to meet the demands of future generations or to satisfy altruistic concerns (e.g. the quality of an environment

TABLE I Rationales for Regulating

Rationale	Main Aims of Regulation	Example
Monopolies and natural monpolies	• Counter tendency to raise prices and lower output. • Harness benefits of scale economies. • Identify areas genuinely monopolistic.	Utilities.
Windfall profits	Transfer benefits of windfalls from firms to consumers or taxpayers.	Firm discovers unusually cheap source of supply.
Externalities	Compel producer or consumer to bear full costs of production rather than pass on to third parties or society.	Pollution of river by factory.
Information inadequacies	Inform consumers to allow market to operate.	Pharmaceuticals. Food and drinks labelling.
Continuity and availability of service	Ensure socially desired (or protect minimal) level of 'essential' service.	Transport service to remote region.
Anti-competitive and behaviour predatory pricing	Prevent anti-competitive behaviour.	Below-cost pricing in transport.
Public goods and moral hazard	Share costs where benefits of activity are shared but free-rider problems exist.	Defence and security services. Health services.
Unequal bargaining power	Protect vulnerable interests where market fails to do so.	Health and safety at work.
Scarcity and rationing	Public interest allocation of scarce commodities.	Petrol shortage.
Distribution justice and social policy	• Distribute according to public interest. • Prevent undesirable behaviour or results.	Victim protection. Discrimination.
Rationalization and coordination	• Secure efficient production where transaction costs prevent market from obtaining network gains or efficiencies of scale. • Standardization.	Disparate production in agriculture and fisheries.
Planning	• Protect interests of future generations. • Coordinate altruistic intentions.	Environment.

not personally enjoyed).[18] There is also, as far as altruism is concerned, a potential free-rider problem. Many people may be prepared to give up some of their assets for altruistic purposes only if they can be assured that a large number of others will do the same. The problems and costs of coordination mean that regulation may be required in order to satisfy such desires.[19]

CONCLUSIONS: CHOOSING TO REGULATE

There are, as seen above, a number of well-recognized reasons commonly given for regulating. It should be stressed, however, that in any one sector or industry the case for regulating may well be based not on a single but on a combination of rationales. As Breyer points out,[20] health and safety regulation, for example, can be justified with reference to a number of rationales—for example externalities, information defects, unequal bargaining, and paternalism.

A second point, to be borne in mind in considering whether to regulate, is that the market and all its failings should be compared with regulation and all its failings. Any analysis of the need to regulate will be skewed if it is assumed that regulatory techniques will operate perfectly. We will see during this book that all regulatory strategies have strengths and weaknesses in relation to their implementation as well as their design. Regulatory and market solutions to problems should be considered in all their varieties and with all likely deficiencies and side-effects if true comparisons are to be effected.

NOTES

1. For detailed reviews of public interest reasons for regulating see S. Breyer, *Regulation and Its Reform* (Cambridge, Mass., 1982), ch. 1; A. Ogus, *Regulation: Legal Form and Economic Theory* (Oxford, 1994), ch. 3; E. Gellhorn and R. J. Pierce, *Regulated Industries* (St Paul, Minn., 1982), ch. 2; J. Kay and J. Vickers, 'Regulatory Reform: An Appraisal', in G. Majone (ed.), *De-Regulation or Re-Regulation?* (London, 1989); B. Mitnick, *The Political Economy of Regulation* (New York, 1980), ch. 5; C. Sunstein, *After the Rights Revolution* (Cambridge, Mass., 1990), ch.

2; C. Hood, *Explaining Economic Policy Reversals* (Buckingham, 1995).

2. See also J. Francis, *The Politics of Regulation* (Oxford, 1993), ch. 1.

3. See Gellhorn and Pierce, *Regulated Industries*, 36–7 and Chapter 15 below. On regulating monopolies generally see C. Foster, *Privatisation, Public Ownership and the Regulation of Natural Monopoly* (Oxford, 1992), ch. 6; Ogus, *Regulation*, 30–3; Breyer, *Regulation and Its Reform*, 15–19; Francis, *Politics of Regulation*, ch. 3; E. Gellhorn and W. Kovacic, *Antitrust Law and Economics* (St Paul, Minn., 1994), chs. 3 and 4.

4. On natural monopolies see M. Waterson, *Regulation of the Firm and Natural Monopoly* (Oxford, 1988), ch. 2; Foster, *Privatisation*, ch. 6.2.

5. Ogus, *Regulation*, 31.

6. G. Yarrow, 'Regulation and Competition in the Electricity Supply Industry', in J. Kay, C. Mayer, and D. Thompson, *Privatisation and Regulation* (Oxford, 1986).

7. See Chapter 16 below, and the White Paper, *Privatising Electricity*, Cm. 322 (London, 1988).

8. See Breyer, *Regulation and Its Reform*, 21. On the 'windfall tax' see below, pp. 233–5.

9. See Breyer, *Regulation and Its Reform*, 23–6; Ogus, *Regulation*, 35–8.

10. See F. Hayek, "The Use of Knowledge in Society," (1945) 35 *Am. Econ. Rev.* 519; Breyer, *Regulation and Its Reform*, 26–8; Ogus, *Regulation*, 38–41.

11. Breyer, *Regulation and Its Reform*, 28.

12. Ogus, *Regulation*, 43–6.

13. See generally G. Calabresi, *The Cost of Accidents: A Legal and Economic Analysis* (New Haven, 1970).

14. See Ogus, *Regulation*, 46–51.

15. Ibid. 51–4.

16. See Ogus, *Regulation*, 41–2; S. Breyer and P. MacAvoy, 'The Federal Power Commission and the Coordination Problem in the Electrical Power Industry' (1973) 46 *S. Cal. LR* 661.

17. In the transportation sector coordination and regulation by a central agency may be needed in order to organize a route network—see S. Glaister, *Deregulation and Privatisation: British*

Experience (World Bank, Washington DC, 1998).

18. See Ogus, *Regulation,* 54; R. B. Stewart, 'Regulation in a Liberal State: The Role of Non-Commodity Values' (1983) 92 *Yale LJ* 1537; Sunstein, *After the Rights Revolution,* 57–61

19. Ogus, *Regulation,* 54.

20. Breyer, *Regulation and Its Reform,* 34.

Legal Bases of Regulation

Regulation does not sprout in a vacuum. And now that you are acquainted both with the structure of the legal system and with the reasoning for regulatory intervention, this reading written by Christopher Sterling, Phyllis Bernt, and Martin Weiss, all communication and information science scholars, describes the legal basis for regulation, its constitutional justification and different theories as to its nature. This reading and the lecture accompanying it are the first opportunity, very early in this course, for you to incorporate knowledge acquired in previous lessons and build upon it. Now that you understand how laws are made and why regulation is needed, you should be able to understand the challenge of creating a regulated environment that is legally sound.

Legal Bases of Regulation

Christopher H. Sterling, Phyllis W. Bernt,
and Martin B.H. Weiss

There are many industries that appear to be "affected with a public interest," such as meat packing or drugstores, that are not regulated as public utilities, while other industries, such as grain elevators and electricity, are deemed to be of such a high degree of public interest that they warrant close regulation. According to one observer, there is no "definite way of foretelling the necessary characteristics for distinguishing an industry affected with a public interest from one that is not sufficiently affected to require detailed public regulation." Industries are treated as public utilities because (a) the public has demanded that they be regulated, (b) a legislature has found it necessary to regulate the industry in the interests of the public, and (c) the courts have recognized a need for regulation.[1]

Efforts in the United States to regulate private enterprises in the public interest have fallen in and out of favor.[2] The Colonial period witnessed efforts to control the price of food and tobacco, and the early 19th century saw the granting of exclusive charters to corporations building canals, bridges, turnpikes, and railroads. The price controls of the Colonial period were soon rescinded, and, as the 19th century progressed, the courts refused to recognize the exclusivity of the charters. The emphasis during the middle of the 19th century was on private rights and on the benefits of competition, not on regulation.

During the later part of the century, the courts and the public changed their views about the need for government regulation. Economic recessions, the development of large monopolies, the growing number of mergers, the decline in business competition, and pricing discrimination by the railroads made regulation an attractive prospect. Perhaps the loudest voices advocating government action were those of the Grangers (the Patrons of Husbandry), who called for the regulation of the railroads.

Congress and state legislatures responded to public sentiment by creating regulatory bodies and passing laws with the purpose of protecting the public interest. Congress created the Interstate Commerce Commission; state legislatures established railroad advisory boards; and, as will be discussed more fully, state legislatures passed laws to regulate the prices charged by grain elevator operators, insurance companies, and even grocers. These legislative actions did not go unchallenged, however. Companies, facing regulation, challenged the government's right to interfere with the actions of private businesses. The courts, through a series of landmark cases, established a web of legal precedent that supported the government's right to regulate private enterprises in order to protect the public interest.

In the first landmark case, *Munn v. Illinois* (1877),[3] the Supreme Court found that the presence of a monopoly justified government regulation. Acting on the authority granted to it by the 1870 revision of the Illinois State Constitution, the Illinois legislature passed a law requiring grain elevator operators in Chicago to obtain a license, file their rates, and charge no more than a legally established maximum rate. The operators of one grain elevator, Munn and Scott, were sued for failure to comply with the law. Munn and Scott contested the Illinois law, claiming that it violated Article I of the Constitution because it interfered with the U.S. Congress's right to regulate interstate commerce and violated the Fourteenth Amendment to the Constitution by denying Munn and Scott due process of law.[4] The majority opinion, expressed by Chief Justice Waite, found against Munn and Scott. In his opinion, Justice Waite relied heavily on the precedent of English common law, stating that "when the people of the United Colonies separated from Great Britain, they changed the form, but not the substance, of their government."[5] Quoting heavily from the words of a 17th-century English chief justice, Justice Waite articulated the basis for government regulation of certain types of businesses:

> This brings us to inquire as to the principles upon which this power of regulation rests, in order that we may determine what is within and what without its operative effect. ... We find that when private property is "affected with a public interest, it ceases to be *juris privati* only." This was said by Lord Chief Justice Hale more than two hundred years ago ... and has been accepted without objection as an essential element in the law of property ever since. Property does become clothed with a public interest when used in a manner to make it of public consequence, and affect the community at large. When, therefore, one devotes his property to a use in which the public has an interest, he, in effect, grants to the public an interest in that use, and must submit to be controlled by the public for the common good, to the extent of the interest he has thus created.[6]

Noting that the grain elevators in Chicago were controlled by nine businesses and that these met annually to set their rates, Justice Waite found

these elevators to be a "virtual" monopoly standing in the "very 'gateway of commerce,' and take[ing] toll from all who pass."[7] As such, the grain elevators were invested with a public interest and so subject to regulation.

The *Munn v. Illinois* case established the precedent that the existence of a monopoly could justify regulation; future court cases expanded the basis for regulation beyond the existence of a monopoly. In *German Alliance Insurance Company v. Lewis* (1914), the courts found that the necessity of a service could trigger the need to regulate its provider. Under Kansas law, the superintendent of insurance could require the posting of insurance schedules and could mandate changes in insurance premiums; in 1909 the superintendent ordered a 12 percent reduction in fire insurance premiums. German Alliance Insurance Company, though complying with the order, asked the Supreme Court to declare the Kansas law unconstitutional. Arguing that the fire insurance business was not a monopoly and that fire insurance companies received no special privileges or immunities from the State of Kansas, the German Alliance Insurance Company argued there was no basis for state regulation of fire insurance. The court disagreed with German Alliance Insurance. Writing for the majority, Justice McKenna found that

> the business of insurance has very definite characteristics, with a reach of influence and consequence beyond and different from that of the ordinary business of the commercial world. ... To the insured, insurance is an asset, a basis of credit. It is practically a necessity to business activity and enterprise. It is, therefore, essentially different from ordinary commercial transactions, and, ... is of the greatest public concern.[8]

The *German Alliance v. Lewis* case expanded the reach of regulation beyond monopoly. *Nebbia v. New York* (1934) established the precedent that virtually *any* enterprise could be regulated. The State of New York had established a milk control board to regulate the price of milk in order to "remedy conditions of oversupply and destructive competition or curtailment of the dairy industry, a paramount industry of the state."[9] A grocer sold milk for less than the minimum price and was convicted of violating the Milk Control Board's order. The grocer (Nebbia) appealed his conviction to the Supreme Court. In a sweeping opinion, the court found against him, stating:

> If the law-making body within its sphere of government concludes that the conditions or practices in an industry make unrestricted competition an inadequate safeguard of the consumer's interests, produce waste harmful to the public, threaten ultimately to cut off the supply of a commodity needed by the public, or portend the destruction of the industry itself, appropriate statutes passed in an honest effort to correct the threatened consequences may not be set aside because the regulation adopted fixes prices reasonably deemed by the legislature to be fair to those engaged in the industry and to the consuming public. And this is especially so where, as here, the economic maladjustment is one of price, which threatens harm to the producer at one end of the series and the consumer at the other. The Constitution does not secure to anyone liberty to conduct his business in such fashion as to inflict injury upon the public at large, or upon any substantial group of the people. Price control, like any other form of regulation, is unconstitutional only if arbitrary, discriminatory, or demonstrably irrelevant to the policy the legislature is free to adopt.[10]

According to *Nebbia. v. New York*, any enterprise, not just a monopoly or a virtual necessity, could be regulated if the legislature determined a need for regulation in order to protect the public.

CONSTITUTIONAL BASES OF REGULATION

While the courts may have established legal precedent to support the government's right to regulate the activities of private businesses, the government's ultimate authority to regulate private enterprises rests in the Constitution of the United States. The federal government's power to regulate businesses arises from Article I, Section 8. This article, known as the "interstate commerce clause," states that the Congress shall have the power "to regulate commerce with foreign nations, and among the several states." Moreover, Section 8 of Article I also gives Congress the power to "make all laws which shall be necessary and proper for carrying into execution the foregoing powers, and all other powers vested by this Constitution in the government of the United States."

The Constitution thus gives the government the broad power to make all laws necessary to regulate interstate business. This power is not absolute, however. Limitations on governmental power are found in the Fifth Amendment which requires that private property not be taken without due process of law and just compensation. Specifically, the language of the Fifth Amendment states that no person shall be "deprived of life, liberty, or property, without due process of law; nor shall private property be taken for public use, without just compensation." This amendment is also referred to as the "takings clause." Telecommunications companies have invoked this amendment when contesting FCC decisions the companies believed to be confiscatory, that is, depriving them of their property. In particular, telephone companies have used the takings clause when arguing against FCC limitations on the amount of earnings companies are allowed to realize, or against rates a telephone company believes to be inadequate to cover costs and provide an adequate profit.

States derive their power to regulate private entities from the Tenth Amendment to the Constitution, which simply says that "the powers not delegated to the United States by the Constitution, nor prohibited by it to the states, are reserved to the states respectively, or to the people." The Tenth Amendment is the source of what are called the "police powers" of the states; that is, the "broad powers of the states to protect the health, safety, morals, and general welfare of their citizenry."[11] As with the federal power to regulate business, the states' powers are also limited by requirements for the due process of law. According to the Fourteenth Amendment, no state shall "deprive any person of life, liberty, or property, without due process of law; nor deny to any person within its jurisdiction the equal protection of the laws."

In considering the effects of both the Fifth and the Tenth Amendments, it is important to remember that corporations have the legal status of persons. The due process, just compensation, and equal protection provisions outlined in both of these Constitutional amendments apply, therefore, to corporations as well as to individuals.

REGULATORY THEORIES

Many theories have been proposed to explain both why regulatory bodies have developed and why they function as they do.[12] While no one theory seems to explain all of the actions taken by regulatory bodies, such theories do provide possible ways to understand regulatory behavior and possible measures by which to gauge the effectiveness of state and federal regulatory commissions. Although the various theories of regulation are presented here in four seemingly neat categories, there is actually much overlap among the various theories. The concern in analyzing the theories of regulation is not into which category the theory seems to fit, but rather the underlying assumptions about the role of regulation that each theory presents.

Public Interest Theory

This is the oldest, and perhaps the most obvious, theory of regulation. Its basic premise is that the primary goal of the regulator, and the primary motive underlying regulatory activity is, or should be, the protection of the public from potential abuses in the marketplace. Public interest theory developed in the early years of regulation, during which some industries (notably utilities) were regarded as natural monopolies. The assumption underlying the concept of a natural monopoly is that, in some industries, because of the high costs of market entry or because of economies of scale and scope, one company can provide service more cheaply and efficiently than can two or more. However, even though a monopoly may be efficient, the monopoly provider can, if unchecked, abuse its power by refusing to provide service, pricing unfairly or providing substandard service quality. The role of the regulator, according to the public interest theory, is to prevent these abuses of monopoly power by regulating price, service

provision, and service quality. Some authors discuss several variants of the public interest theory which they also call the "consumer protection theory." They list several goals or rationales for regulation in the public interest, including correcting economic, social and political failures.[13] They also note that the public interest theory is normative; that is, it is a theory that explains what regulators *should do*, rather than explaining why regulators actually act as they do. Another researcher agrees with this assessment, calling this theory the "yardstick by which regulation is measured."[14]

Private Interest or Interest Group Theory

Students of regulation became disenchanted with the public interest theory, regarding it as naive and incapable of explaining the actual behavior of regulatory bodies. Several variants of private interest or interest group theories have been developed that claim to be more realistic and better able to explain why regulatory bodies do not always seem to regulate purely in the interest of the public. At the core of these theories is the idea that individuals and groups use the regulatory process to serve their own private needs and interests, rather than to advance the public good. In this view, everyone from stockholders to managers of companies, to interveners in regulatory proceedings, to employees of the regulated companies, to the regulators themselves seek to use the regulatory process to further their own ends. One observer presents an interesting variation called "Coalition-Building Theory."[15] According to this notion, regulators regulate by building political coalitions; in other words, for regulation to be possible at all, consensus must be reached. It is the role of the regulator to build this consensus; in the process, the regulator amasses political power, thus using regulation to serve his or her own interests.

Regulatory Capture Theory

While there are many parties with an interest in the regulatory process, Regulatory Capture Theory focuses on the concerns of the regulated industry itself. This theory claims that the regulatory body is captured by the industry it regulates. Arguments in support of this theory often point to the revolving door that exists between the regulatory body and the industry it regulates, noting the frequency with which former regulators move into jobs with the regulated firms; regulators hoping to gain more financially rewarding positions with the regulated firm will be less likely to act in a way that will harm the firm's interests. Other arguments offered in support of this theory cite the much stronger lobbying presence that the regulated industry can maintain compared to the lobbying power of consumer interests. For whatever specific reason, according to the capture theory, the regulatory body comes to serve, and even identify with, the interests of the regulated industry rather than the public interest. An interesting variant of the capture theory is the "Life Cycle Theory" which sees regulatory bodies passing through various life stages.[16] As the regulatory body is formed and in its very first years, it is filled with a sense of mission and vigor; the emphasis during this period is very much on serving the public interest. In its youth, the regulatory body is still effective in fulfilling its role as protector of the public good; however, as the regulatory body progresses into maturity and then old age, it comes to identify more and more with the industry it regulates. Finally, in its old age, the regulatory body serves the interests of the regulated firm. The life cycle theory suggests that the regulatory body is initially formed to serve the public interest, and that, over time, it becomes the captive of the regulated industry. A more sinister variation, the "Conspiracy Theory" claims that, from its very inception, the regulatory body was created to serve industry interests rather than the public interest.[17]

Equity-Stability Theory

This theory claims that regulation exists because of legislators' desire to further social equity and fairness. Legislators create administrative bodies like regulatory commissions in order to "protect society from the unimpeded operation of the market forces."[18] If left to the marketplace, society's resources would not be distributed in a socially equitable manner; the role of regulation is to act as a corrective and to assure equity and fairness. Whereas this theory emphasizes social equity for its own sake, one variation, the Capitalist State Theory, suggests a less altruistic rationale for regulation. This theory holds that regulation exists "due to the inability of the market

to regulate capitalist behavior."[19] In effect, it is the role of regulation to assure the continuation of the capitalist system by controlling its excesses.

There are other theories of regulation in addition to the four major categories listed above. For example, there are theories that focus on the regulatory body as an organization, and explain that regulators operate out of a sort of organizational imperative. They are regulators, so given the opportunity, they will regulate. All of these theories have shortcomings. Focusing on the life cycle of a regulatory body does not explain why some regulatory bodies have gone through periods of resurgence and rededication to serving the public interest. Capture theories do not adequately explain why regulatory bodies often require firms to act in ways that are counter to the firms' interests. Though these theories may not be totally accurate in explaining regulatory behavior, they do point to the varying interests and stakeholders affected by the regulatory process, and they do provide a framework for analyzing regulatory activity.

NOTES

1. Ibid., pp. 93–94.
2. For detailed discussions of the following historical developments, see Robert Britt Horwitz, 1989. *The Irony of Regulatory Reform* (New York: Oxford University Press), pp. 48–65; Glaeser, pp. 14–78; and Phillips, pp. 91–93.
3. According to Glaeser, this case has "by common consent, been placed at the threshold of our modern treatment of the public utility problem," p. 206.
4. Munn v. Illinois, 94 US 113 (1877).
5. Ibid.
6. Ibid.
7. Ibid.
8. German Alliance Insurance Company v. Lewis, 233 US 389 (1914).
9. *Nebbia v. New York*, 291 US 502 (1934).
10. Ibid.
11. Howe and Rasmussen, pp. 43–44.
12. This overview of the theories of regulation owes much to the discussions found in Bonbright et al., pp. 33–66; Horwitz, pp. 22–45; Barry M. Mitnick, 1980. *The Political Economy of*

Regulation: Creating, Designing, and Removing Regulatory Forms (New York: Columbia University Press), pp. 79–241; Phillips, pp. 182–187; and Harry M. Trebing, 1981. "Equity, Efficiency, and the Viability of Public Utility Regulation," in *Applications of Economic Principles in Public Utility Industries*, edited by Werner Sichel and Thomas G. Gies (Ann Arbor: University of Michigan Press), pp. 17–52.

13. Bonbright et al, p. 33.

14. Horwitz, p. 27.

15. Trebing, pp. 25–28.

16. Howe and Rasmussen refer to these stages as "incipiency, youth, maturity, and old age" (p. 169). Horwitz discusses the life cycle theory as described by Bernstein; according to Bernstein, the stages are gestation, youth, maturity, and old age.

17. Horwitz, pp. 31–38.

18. Trebing, p. 28.

19. Horwitz, p. 41.

UNIT 3

Competition Law or Telecommunication Law I? Antitrust Regulation Basics

Antitrust Economics

Since the telecommunications industry emerged out of a decades-long monopoly, understanding the rules that regulate monopolies and why we need them is extremely important. In this reading, law professor Herbert Hovenkamp explains succinctly the basic economic principles behind monopoly regulation: Price theory and industrial organization. Once you have read this chapter and attended the lecture you should be familiar with the economics vocabulary and the bases of antitrust policy: the concepts of supply and demand and how they relate to competition, the challenges monopolies pose in a market, and the relationship between monopoly control and consumer behavior.

Antitrust Economics

Price Theory and Industrial Organization

Herbert Hovenkamp

In order to understand modern antitrust policy, you need at least a nodding acquaintance with two basic areas of economics: price theory and industrial organization. Price theory is the theory of firm decisionmaking about how much to produce and what price to charge. Industrial organization is the theory of how the structure of the business firm and the market are determined.

A. AN OVERVIEW OF BASIC PRICE THEORY FOR ANTITRUST

1. Supply and Price Under Perfect Competition

A perfectly competitive market has the following characteristics:

a. All sellers make an absolutely homogeneous product, so that customers do not care which seller they purchase from, provided that price is the same;

b. Each seller in the market is so small in proportion to the entire market that the seller's increase or decrease in output, or even its exit from the market, will not noticeably affect the decisions of other sellers in the market;

c. All participants in the market have perfect knowledge of price, output and other information about the market.

The perfect competition model also generally assumes "constant returns to scale"—that is, that it costs the same amount per unit to purchase a product, no matter how many the producer makes. "Economies of scale," which are efficiencies that obtain only when production reaches a certain volume, can undermine the perfect competition model, particularly in extreme cases; they are discussed below in B.1.

a. *The Value of the Perfect Competition Model*
Perfect competition exists nowhere in the real world. Nevertheless, the perfect competition model is useful because it predicts the behavior that we would expect to see in real world competitive markets, even though that behavior may be manifested only imperfectly. For example, in the perfect competition model, price equals marginal cost (see § 1.c. below). In the real world price may often be higher than marginal cost; however, as real world markets become more competitive, price tends to approach marginal cost.

b. *Supply and Demand in Perfect Competition*
For every product there are different customers willing to pay different amounts. For example, both artificial hearts and whiffle balls are made from plastic. However, the manufacturers of artificial hearts place a much higher value on the plastic than the whiffle ball makers do, because the cost of the plastic is such an

insignificant part of the cost of producing an artificial heart. If whiffle balls and artificial hearts both use one unit of plastic and the price of one unit rises by $100, the price of a whiffle ball would rise from 89¢ to $100.89. Demand for whiffle balls would drop precipitously. However, the price of artificial hearts would rise from $175,000.00 to $175,100.00, and demand would change very little.

1) The "Reservation Price"

If only a small amount of plastic were produced in a given year, the artificial heart manufacturers would bid the price of it up very high, with the result that no whiffle balls would be manufactured. This is so because the price of plastic would be higher than the "reservation price" of the whiffle ball manufacturers. *A reservation price is the highest price a particular customer is willing to pay for a product.* As more and more plastic is manufactured, however, the markets for people with very high reservation prices (such as artificial heart manufacturers) will become saturated. Then the plastic will have to be sold to people whose reservation prices are lower. In order to reach the whiffle ball manufacturers, the price of one unit of plastic may have to drop to 50¢.

Importantly, when the price drops all buyers in the market—even those with very high reservation prices—will be able to purchase the product at the lower price. This is generally true because the seller will not be able to segregate different groups of customers and will not be able to prevent "arbitrage." Arbitrage occurs when purchasers who pay a low price resell the product to purchasers asked to pay a higher price.

Example: Assume that the plastic supplier asked whiffle ball manufacturers to pay 50¢ per unit for plastic, and artificial heart manufacturers $1000 per unit. The whiffle ball manufacturers would respond by purchasing more plastic than they needed and re-selling it to the artificial heart manufacturers at some price between 50¢ per unit and $1000 per unit.

2) The Supply Curve

Manufacturers and other sellers have costs. "Cost," in economic terms always includes competitive profits (which are enough profits to maintain investment in the industry). *As a general rule, costs rise when output increases.* This is so because the first production in a market will take advantage of the cheapest and best raw materials. As production increases, increasingly marginal materials will be used.

Example: A farmer who has 1000 acres and intends to plant 100 will choose the 100 most fertile, where the cost of production per unit is lowest. If the farmer decides to plant a second 100 acres, she will choose the 100 most fertile of the 900 remaining acres, etc.

3) Equilibrium

Figure One illustrates how a market arrives at "equilibrium"—the point where supply of a good and demand for it are perfectly balanced. Figure One illustrates the demand curve (D) and the supply curve (S) facing an entire market for a single product. The vertical axis represents price, which increases from zero as one moves upward. The horizontal axis represents output (or quantity), which increases from zero as one moves to the right.

At low levels of output the cost of production, indicated by the supply curve (S), is quite low. Demand, illustrated by the demand curve (D) is very high, for the good will be sold only to buyers with very high reservation prices. At such price and cost levels, sellers will be earning enormous profits on their output. *Remember, "cost" includes normal, or competitive profits. Since the supply curve represents costs, a price equal to the supply curve gives the firm a competitive rate of profit, which is defined as a rate of profit sufficient to maintain investment in the industry. Any vertical distance between the supply curve and the demand curve represents "excessive" or "monopoly" profits.*

Monopoly profits naturally attract increased output. As long as the profits earned in a market are very high, two things will happen:

a. Firms already in the market will produce more, so they can earn more of the large profits;

b. New firms will enter the market.

This will continue to happen until output reaches a level where the supply curve and demand curve intersect. From that point any further increase in production would generate higher additional costs (shown by the

FIGURE ONE

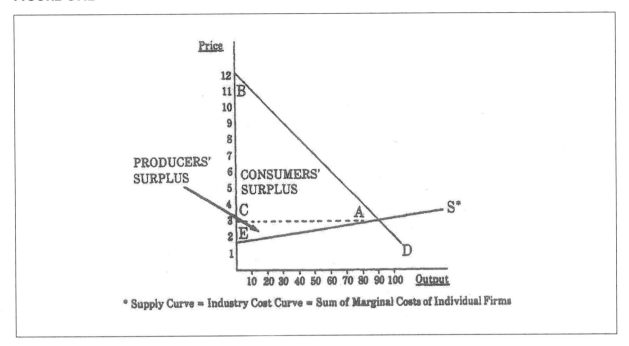

* Supply Curve = Industry Cost Curve = Sum of Marginal Costs of Individual Firms

supply curve) than it would produce additional revenues (shown by the demand curve). The competitive market reaches "equilibrium" at the point where the supply curve and demand curve intersect.

Two things are important to know about competitive equilibrium:

a. When a market is in equilibrium supply and demand will not change unless the market is shocked by some kind of *external* change, such as a war, famine, weather, a new invention that creates new competition or decreases production costs, new entry by a large firm, changes in customer taste, etc.;

b. Competitive equilibrium is determined by the "marginal" buyer and the "marginal" seller in the market. That is, the buyer located at the intersection of the supply and demand curves in Figure One is the buyer who has the *lowest reservation price and is still able to purchase in the market.* Anyone with a lower reservation price will be unwilling to purchase at the competitive price. Likewise, the seller located on the supply curve at the same intersection is the seller *with the highest costs who is still capable of staying in the market.* Any seller with higher costs would lose money at the competitive price.

4) Consumers' Surplus and Producers' Surplus

As noted above, in a competitive market all buyers pay the "market price," determined by the intersection of the supply and demand curves, even though their individual reservation prices may be much higher. Triangle ABC in Figure One represents "consumers' surplus," or the difference between what customers were willing to pay and what they were required to pay in a competitive market. At the same time, some firms in the market will have lower costs than others, perhaps because they have better access to resources, or perhaps because they are more efficient. They are also able to sell at the market price, even though they have lower costs. For them, the competitive price yields high profits in the form of "producers' surplus." Producers' surplus is the difference between a firm's costs and the price it obtains for a product.

5) Market Elasticities of Supply and Demand

The supply and demand "curves" illustrated in Figure One are generally *not* linear in the real world. They can assume a wide variety of shapes. The shapes generally reflect the responsiveness of buyers and sellers to changes in price.

Elasticity of Demand is a relationship between the change in the price of a product and the amount of consumer demand for it. As a fraction, it is equal to the percentage change in demand for a product, divided by the percentage change in price necessary to cause that change in demand. This fraction is generally a negative number (demand goes down as price goes up, and vice-versa), but it is expressed positively.

Example: At a price of $1.00 per unit, demand for a product equals 1000 units. When the price rises to $1.25, demand falls to 800. In this case a 25% price increase caused a 20% demand decrease. The elasticity of demand in the market is 20/25 or .8.

When customers are highly sensitive to changes in price, we say demand in that market is "elastic." As a general rule, elasticities of demand greater than one are considered elastic. Elasticities of demand less than one are considered inelastic.

Elasticity of supply is a ratio between the change in the amount of a product produced and the corresponding price change. It is expressed as a fraction, with the change in the amount produced as the numerator and the corresponding price change as the denominator. For example, if a 10% increase in price causes a 30% increase in the amount produced, the elasticity of supply is 30/10 or 3. Elasticity of supply is a positive number.

c. *The Output Decision of the Individual Firm in Perfect Competition: Marginal Cost*

1) The Perfect Competitor's Price Decision

The individual firm in perfect competition is a "price taker"—that is, it has no price decision to make. It can sell all it pleases at the market price, but it will sell nothing if it attempts to charge more, for some other firm will always be there to make the sale. We say, therefore, that *the firm in perfect competition faces a horizontal* individual *demand curve.* This is sometimes called the "residual" demand curve, to distinguish it from the demand curve of the market as a whole. The curve is said to be "residual" because it describes the demand that is left over for the firm after all other firms have made their sales at the going price.

2) The Perfect Competitor's Output Decision

Although the perfect competitor accepts the market price as given, it *does* have to decide how much to produce. Even a perfectly competitive market contains firms of different sizes, and each one makes its own output decisions.

The individual firm in perfect competition always produces at that level of output at which the market price equals its marginal costs. Marginal cost is the additional cost that a firm incurs in the production of one additional unit of output. A firm's marginal costs usually rise as output increases in the relevant range because, just as the market as a whole, the individual firm must use its best resources first, its second best resources second, etc. As a result the relationship between the horizontal demand curve and the marginal cost (MC) curve of the individual firm in perfect competition looks like Figure 2.

Note that in the perfectly competitive market the *individual firm* faces a horizontal demand curve, D, which is equal to the market, or competitive price, P_c. For the individual perfect competitor that price cannot be varied.

Suppose that price is $1.00, and that at the lowest point on the marginal cost curve, MC equals about 60. From that point, if the firm produced one additional unit of output, the MC curve tells us that it would incur 60 in additional costs. Since the market price is $1.00, this unit could be sold for a 40 profit. The firm will increase output. How long will the increases continue? Once the firm has reached output level Q_c on the curve in Figure Two, it will no longer make additional money by increasing output, but will begin losing money. For example, if output is to the right of Q_c, an additional increase in output of one unit will generate additional revenues of $1.00, the market price, but it will generate additional costs of more than $1.00. The firm will maximize its profits if it can control its production at precisely the rate at which its marginal costs equal the market price. From that point it will make less money if it produces one unit more, or one unit less. Thus we can say that price under competition equals marginal cost.

2. Monopoly

The monopolist, which is the *only* firm selling in a particular market, makes different price and output

FIGURE TWO

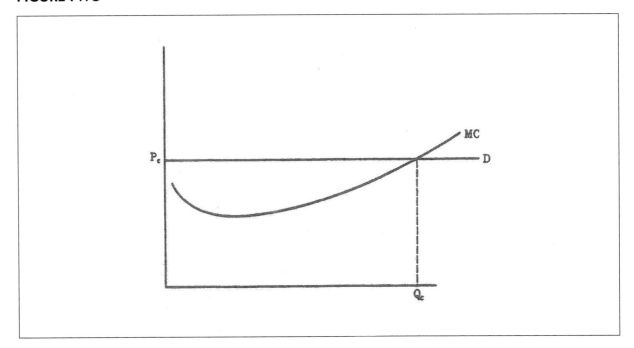

decisions than those made by the perfect competitor. The analysis that follows makes two assumptions about the monopolist that generally do not apply to the *de facto* monopolist in the real world. (The *de facto* monopolist is a monopolist that achieved its position by its own doing, and does not have statutory monopoly protection.) The assumptions are:

1. The monopolist is the only firm in the market;

2. The monopolist does not need to be concerned about new entry from a competitor.

In the real world we often consider firms to be "monopolists" for antitrust purposes even though they control only 90% or perhaps even only 70%–80% of their markets. Furthermore, in the real world the de facto *monopolist generally faces the threat that another firm will come in and challenge its monopoly position.*

a. *The Monopolist's Price and Output Decisions*
Because our monopolist is the only firm in its market, it faces the same demand curve as the *market* demand curve illustrated in Figure One above. However, we have redrawn that curve, together with some others, in Figure Three below.

Even the monopolist cannot charge an infinite price for its product, because the monopolist's customers have reservation prices, and they will not pay

more. On the other hand, the monopolist is not a price taker. *Unlike the perfect competitor, the monopolist has the power to obtain a higher price for its product by reducing output.* As Figure Three reveals, the less the monopolist produces, the higher will be the "market clearing price" (i.e., a price sufficiently low to sell all units produced).

1) The Marginal Revenue Curve
Note the marginal revenue (MR) curve in Figure Three. *The MR curve represents the additional revenue that the monopolist obtains when it increases output.* For the perfect competitor the MR curve is horizontal and identical with the demand curve that the perfect competitor faces, because the market price remains constant. However, the monopolist's MR curve slopes downward more sharply than the monopolist's demand curve, because when the monopolist increases output it must reduce the price of every unit that it sells. For example, suppose that at an output of one unit the monopolist's price is $20. When output increases to two units, the market price drops to $18. However, the monopolist must sell both the first and second units for $18.00, so its total revenue increases to $36.00. This is an increase of $16.00 over the revenue that was obtained when output was one unit. In short, when the price fell $2, from $20.00 to $18.00,

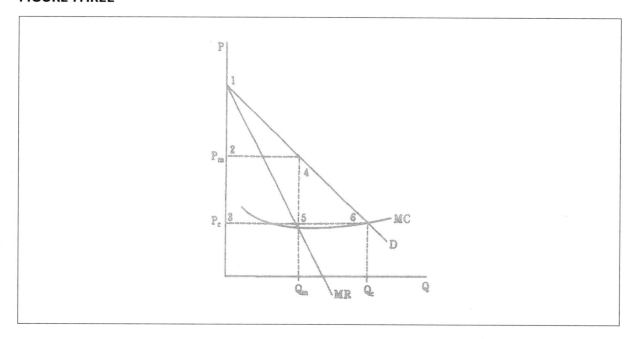

marginal revenue (the *additional* revenue earned) fell $4, from $20.00 at an output of one unit, to $16.00 at an output of two units.

2) The Monopolist's Profit-Maximizing Price

The monopolist will produce and set a price at the point at which its marginal revenue (MR) curve intersects its marginal cost (MC) curve. As long as the monopolist is producing less than this amount, an output increase will result in more additional revenues than additional costs. As soon as the monopolist increases output to the right of the intersection of MR and MC, however, the additional costs will increase more rapidly than the additional revenues. *For this reason the intersection of the MR and MC curves determine the monopolist's "profit-maximizing price" and profit-maximizing rate of output.* Output at that point is designated by Q_m in Figure Three and price at that point by P_m. This is sometimes called the "monopoly price."

Note 1: The difference between a monopolist's profit-maximizing price and its marginal cost (which would be the price in a competitive market) tells us something about the amount of market power that a firm has. If a firm's profit-maximizing price is $1.02 and its marginal cost at that point is $1.00, the firm

has a small amount of market power. However, if the firm's profit-maximizing price is $2.00 and its marginal cost at that point is $1.00, then the firm has a substantial amount of market power.

Note 2: A "monopsonist" is a monopoly buyer rather than a seller. Just as a monopolist reduces output and raises the price of the goods that it sells, a monopsony buyer reduces output and *lowers* the price of the things that it purchases.

b. *The De Facto Monopolist in the Real World*

In the preceding discussion we assumed that the monopolist controlled 100% of its market and was unconcerned about new entry by competitors. When those two assumptions are relaxed, the monopolist may not charge the price dictated by the intersection of its MR and MC curves. *Rather, the real world monopolist may behave "strategically"—i.e., it may set a somewhat lower price designed to make output increases by competitors, or potential entry by new firms, somewhat less attractive.* The effect of such a price decrease will be to reduce the monopoly price for a single unit of the monopolist's product; however, it may greatly increase the *duration* of the monopoly.

c. *The Social Cost of Monopoly*

The social cost of monopoly is the *net loss to society* caused by the existence of monopoly in the economy. *You should distinguish a social cost from a wealth transfer. For antitrust purposes, a transfer of wealth—the mere payment of money from one person to another—is assumed to make society no richer or poorer than it was before: one person is wealthier but another person is poorer by exactly the same amount.*

Reconsider Figure Three above. In a competitive market, where price equals P_c and output equals Q_c, purchasers would enjoy a consumers' surplus equal to triangle 1–3–6. The monopolist, however, will reduce output to Q_m and increase price to P_m. In that case two things will happen:

1. Buyers located along the demand curve between points 1 and 4 will pay a higher price;

2. Buyers located along the demand curve between points 4 and 6 will not purchase the monopolized product at all, for the monopoly price is higher than their reservation price.

1) The Monopoly Wealth Transfer

Under monopoly consumers' surplus has been reduced to triangle 1–2–4. Rectangle 2–3–5–4 represents a "wealth transfer" to the monopolist—that is, the monopolist has "robbed" consumers of this amount of consumers' surplus. Because it is merely a wealth transfer it does not make society as a whole worse off—the monopolist is merely richer and the customers poorer by the same amount

2) The Deadweight Loss Triangle

Triangle 4–5–6 is a different story. It represents people who would have purchased the product at the competitive price, but substitute away at the monopoly price. As a result, the consumers' surplus is lost to consumers; however, the monopolist gains nothing from this area either, for it makes no profit on unmade sales. *As a result, triangle 4–5–6 is a net social loss. Because of this monopoly society as a whole is poorer by the area of triangle 4–5–6. This triangle is called the "deadweight loss" of monopoly, or the "social cost" of monopoly.*

Note: It seems clear today that triangle 4–5–6 in the above illustration *under*states the true social cost of monopoly. That is, although the triangle represents the social cost of monopoly *pricing* it does not measure the social cost of monopoly *conduct*. The *de facto* monopolist may spend a great amount of money in various "exclusionary" practices in order to preserve its monopoly position. Chapter III.A.3. below is concerned with such practices. Many of these practices, such as predatory pricing and raising the costs of rivals may be inefficient and thus increase the social cost of monopoly. At the extreme, the monopolist may spend most of the anticipated profits from its monopoly position (i.e., rectangle 2–3–5–4) in maintaining its monopoly. In that case a substantial part of rectangle 2–3–5–4 should not be considered a wealth transfer at all, but part of the social cost of monopoly.

B. INDUSTRIAL ORGANIZATION: ECONOMIES OF SCALE AND THE DILEMMA OF ANTITRUST POLICY

Industrial organization is the study of firm structure. A knowledge of industrial organization can be important to antitrust analysis for two reasons:

a. It can help us distinguish markets in which the perfect competition model has some application from those in which it does not;

b. It can help us understand why firms engage in certain practices, such as vertical integration or mergers, and what are the consequences of such practices for competition,

1. Economies of Scale

An economy of scale exists whenever the cost of some input declines as volume increases. *The result of economies of scale is that the cost of production decreases on a per unit basis as the amount being produced increases.* Economies of scale are widespread in most markets. Consider the following examples:

a. To drive a truck from point A to point B costs $100, whether the truck is full or half empty As a result the full truck carries its cargo at a lower cost per pound.

b. To set up a metal lathe to turn out a particular machine part costs $100 in labor. Once the lathe is set up, the costs of turning out the parts is $1.00 each.

If the lathe is set up to turn out a single part, the cost of that part will be $101.00. If the lathe turns out 10,000 parts, their cost will be $1.01 each.

c. A manufacturer of essential medical supplies must always keep one production machine in reserve, so that a breakdown will not interrupt production. If he produces with a single machine operating at a time, he must therefore maintain capacity equal to twice his actual output. If he produces with eight machines, however, he needs to maintain only nine machines, a capacity equal to 12% more than his output,

d. A thirty-second television commercial advertising automobiles costs $100,000, whether the manufacturer produces 10,000,000 automobiles per year, or 90,000 automobiles per year. As a result, advertising costs are far lower per unit for the larger manufacturer.

a. *Economies of Scale and Technology*

Economies of scale are largely a function of technology, which both creates and destroys economies of scale. Scale economies can generally be divided into economies of scale that can be attained by a single plant and multi-plant economies that make it cheaper to operate multiple plants than it is to operate only one.

b. *Minimum Optimal Scale*

The term Minimum Optimal Scale (MOS) or Minimum Efficient Scale (MES) refers to the smallest production unit capable of achieving all relevant economies of scale. If a firm or plant operates at MOS, no other firm or plant can be more efficient because of its scale of operation. (Keep in mind, however, that firms can be inefficient for reasons that have nothing to do with economies of scale; for example, even the very large firm may be poorly managed.)

2. Natural Monopoly

At the extreme, economies of scale in a market may be so substantial that the market will operate most cheaply if a single firm controls the entire market. Such markets are called natural monopolies. *Technically, a market is a natural monopoly if costs decrease as output increases all the way to the point that the market is saturated.*

Unfortunately a natural monopolist, just as any other monopolist, maximizes its profit by engaging in monopoly pricing. This creates a problem for those concerned with efficient market behavior: "competition" among multiple firms will require that the market operate inefficiently because the relatively small firms will have higher costs. By contrast, the monopoly will operate inefficiently because the monopolist will charge a monopoly price. *The traditional solution in cases involving recognized natural monopoly is to establish a regulatory agency that will permit a single firm to occupy the market, but regulate its prices in order to maintain them at the competitive level.* See Hovenkamp § 1.4b.

3. The Dilemma of Antitrust Policy: Coping with Bigness

The existence of economies of scale can create extraordinary dilemmas for antitrust policy On the one hand, antitrust policy has traditionally expressed a concern with bigness in business. Furthermore, bigness can incline businesses toward anticompetitive behavior. For example, price fixing is much more likely to occur in "concentrated" markets—i.e., markets that contain only a few large firms (see chapter II.A. below). On the other hand, any *unqualified* attack on bigness or high business concentration can produce higher consumer prices because the antitrust laws will prevent firms from attaining Minimum Optimal Scale.

If antitrust policy is to be guided by the "consumer welfare principle"—that is, if its overriding goal should be to maximize output and minimize consumer prices—then a certain tolerance of large firms is necessary. *Finding the proper balance between the efficiencies that result from scale economies on the one hand, and our distrust of bigness and some of its anticompetitive consequences on the other, is a problem that is pervasive in antitrust policy today.*

C. THE ECONOMIC MODEL AND REAL WORLD MARKETS

The economic models presented in the preceding discussion are somewhat simplistic in comparison with the situation that exists in the real world. It is a good idea to be aware of the most important differences between the models and the markets that can be found in antitrust litigation. Antitrust policy must deal with each of these real world deviations from the basic economic models:

1. Product Differentiation

In the perfect competition model, you will recall, the products sold by all sellers were fungible. As a result, customers were sensitive only to price. In the real world, however, many products, particularly manufactured products, are differentiated from one another. For example, although IBMs and Apples are both computers and both compete in the same market, some customers prefer one to the other, and may even be willing to pay a higher price in order to have their preference. The result of product differentiation is that many firms face a slightly downward sloping demand curve and may charge a price somewhat higher than their marginal cost. *More importantly for antitrust analysis, product differentiation may explain why many firms employ various restrictions on distribution, such as those discussed in chapters V and VI.*

2. Price Discrimination

In the perfect competition model price discrimination never occurs and all buyers pay exactly the same price for a product. In the real world, however, price discrimination occurs daily. The topic of price discrimination will come up frequently in this discussion of antitrust law, but it is discussed systematically in chapter X. below.

3. Transaction Costs

Transaction costs are the costs of using the marketplace. The perfect competition model outlined above assumes that transaction costs are nonexistent. In the real world, however, transaction costs can be substantial, and they can explain many aspects of business behavior, particularly vertical mergers, tying arrangements, exclusive dealing, and restrictions on distribution.

4. Barriers to Entry

In economic models of competitive behavior we generally assume that entry by competitors will occur instantly when price rises above marginal cost. In the real world, however, various barriers to entry may prevent or delay such entry. In general, an entry barrier is some factor that makes the cost of doing business higher for the newcomer than for the incumbents. Certain parts of antitrust analysis, particular of mergers and monopolization by predatory pricing, begin with the premise that anticompetitive results are likely only if entry barriers into the market at issue are high.

The Analytical Framework

But how do we know whether or not the market we are analyzing is competitive? In this reading, John Shenefield, the former head of the Antitrust Division in the U.S. Department of Justice, and Irwin Stelzer, a prominent economist, describe the analytical framework of market analysis. Once you read their chapter you should be able to understand how markets are defined. The definition of the market and the eventual calculation of the market share are the bases for developing the Herfindahl-Hirschman score for that market.

The lecture to which these readings serve as an illustration covers the history of antitrust legislation. At this stage you should be acquainted with the significance of the Interstate Commerce Act of 1887, the Sherman Act of 1890, the Mann-Elkins Act of 1910, the Clayton Act of 1914, and the Willis-Graham Act of 1921 to the regulation of the telecommunications industry.

The Analytical Framework

Markets and Market Power

John H. Shenefield and Irwin M. Stelzer

With the exception of a few of the per se restraints, suspicious conduct is analyzed under the antitrust laws to determine whether it will produce injury to competition. Such a determination necessarily involves delineating the arena in which competition is occurring, known in the trade as defining the relevant market. After all, if the point of the exercise is to determine the effect of some business practice on competition, then the competitive reality must be isolated and analyzed. Firms compete to sell goods to a buyer; the buyer decides which mix of product, price, and quality best suits it. A restraint that is said to affect that interaction among buyers and sellers can be assessed only when all relevant buyers and sellers are identified. A relevant market consists of all buyers and sellers of all products that are actual or potential competitors with one another.

The objective of defining a relevant market is to determine the boundaries within which effective competition occurs, or, conversely, market power is exercised. Put slightly differently, the aim of market definition is to determine what group of competitors could jointly effect a substantial, durable price increase. For such a determination to be made, several dimensions of the competitive arena must be delineated.

First, the product involved in the competitive battle must be identified: is it tin can versus tin can or tin can versus all containers? Is the fight between natural gas from different fields or among all fuels? Do championship boxing matches compete for paying fans and television viewers only with other championship fights or with routine boxing matches or with other sporting events? Second, we must locate the boundaries of the arena, its geographic dimension: is the fight between domestic contestants only, or are foreigners battling for the consumer's favor?

THE PRODUCT MARKET

Courts attempt to include in the relevant market all goods that consumers view as realistic substitutes, one for the other. All goods or services that consumers actually substitute for one another are, of course, in the market. So, too, are products to which consumers can readily switch, if the price of the product they are using begins to rise sharply. A rise in transcontinental air fares is unlikely to cause people to switch to trains; a rise in New York–Washington shuttle fares well might. So the market for transportation services would in the first instance exclude rail, but in the latter case include it. The test is at what point consumers react to price rises by switching from one good or service to another. Of course, not *every* customer will be willing to switch brands or find alternatives when prices are raised. It is sufficient that enough customers be willing to make such substitutions to affect the conduct of sellers in the market. The courts are, in other words, interested in competition at the margin, in the presence of a significant number of customers for whom there are realistic substitutes for any firm's product.

THE GEOGRAPHIC MARKET

In addition to defining the product dimension of the market, it is necessary to determine its geographic limit. A bakery in Manhattan produces the same bread as a bakery in San Francisco, but there is no sense in which they are competitive—transportation costs are prohibitive. By contrast, a manufacturer of jumbo jets in the United States is competitive with another manufacturer in Europe.

Market definition must take account of both realities. In the first case, the geographic markets are extremely local, perhaps occupying a small portion of Manhattan or San Francisco, respectively. In the case of jumbo jets, the geographic market is very likely worldwide. Again, the focus is on what alternatives are realistically available to the buyer.

THE COMPETITORS

After defining the product and geographic markets, we can identify the firms competing in those markets: all firms that supply that product or that could do so with relative ease. In the short run that would include all firms with the ability to supply that product by using the same personnel and equipment. In the longer term it would include all firms with the ultimate ability to shift from the supply of one good to another by adding some new equipment or new personnel.

That, then, is the hypothetical market within which the competitive effect of the conduct at issue can most realistically be analyzed—the analytical tool that best enables antitrust analysts to answer the crucial question: does the practice injure competition?

MARKET POWER

Following the definition of the market, the next analytical step is to determine whether the conduct in question is carried out by a firm or group of firms with market power. Since the basic inquiry concerns competitive injury, which is usually defined as an artificial increase in price, restriction of output, or exclusion of competition, the sensible question is whether the firm or firms could possibly produce such an effect. In the absence of direct evidence of actual control over price or output, antitrust analysis tests for market power, which is viewed as the "surrogate for detrimental effects" (*Federal Trade Commission v. Indiana Federation of Dentists*, 476 U.S. 447 (1986)).

A shorthand way of assessing market power is to examine the market shares of the firms engaged in the suspect conduct. Market share is sometimes reckoned in simple percentage terms and at other times in somewhat more complicated ways. The effort, however, remains the same: to find out how much of all the business done by firms in the market is controlled by those said to be involved in the restraint of trade. Below some point, the firms' efforts even in the pursuit of nefarious purposes are viewed as harmless; above that point, as market share increases, the conduct takes on an ever more sinister significance.

For instance, mergers between two competitors, assessed within the defined market, begin to raise questions in the minds of antitrust enforcers when the combination obtains a significant market share, say, 20 percent of a market comprising many competitors. Two firms that agree to boycott a third may be guilty of an antitrust violation if together they constitute 70 percent of the relevant market. If their share is trivial, though, and the buyer has dozens of other sources, the agreement is of no competitive effect and cannot satisfy the competitive injury requirement of the antitrust laws. In that way, market share helps to reveal the potential for competitive injury.

Market share is, however, only one aspect of the analysis of market structure, albeit the most important one. Courts consider, too, whether high market shares have persisted over time or are tending to erode; whether the small group dominating the market has a constant or changing membership; whether a significant group of potential entrants is poised to move, should prices rise; and whether the producers with large market shares face powerful or dispersed buyers.

In short, while market power and market share are often closely related—the former deriving from the latter—they are not necessarily opposite sides of the same coin. A firm might produce a preponderant portion of some product but trigger a wave of new entrants by raising price. That firm has no market power. The same firm, were it able to wall out potential competition deliberately by frequent and indiscriminate patent infringement litigation, would have market power. The ability to earn very high profits that persist over many years may also be evidence of market power.

Some market power determinations examine whether customers of a particular branded product are a market by themselves and are thus subject to the market power of the product manufacturer. Are owners of Ford cars "locked in" to Ford-manufactured replacement parts, and does Ford therefore have market power in the replacement part market, even though Ford is confronted with brutal competition to sell its automobiles? The answer depends upon further examination of the factual record, but the point is that nothing may be assumed.

However determined, the existence of market power can be an extremely important clue in the search for competitive impact. In the absence of market power, certain business practices, no matter how objectionable on other legal grounds, cannot adversely affect competition and are therefore beyond the concern of the antitrust authorities.

NOTES

United States v E. I. duPont de Nemours & Co., 351 U.S. 377 (1956).

Brown Shoe Co. v. United States, 370 U.S. 294 (1962).

Federal Trade Commission v. Indiana Federation of Dentists, 476 U.S. 447 (1986).

Northwest Wholesale Stationers, Inc. v. Pacific Stationery & Printing Co., 472 U.S. 284 (1985).

United States v. General Dynamics Corp., 415 U.S. 486 (1974).

United States v. Baker Hughes, Inc., 908 F.2d 981 (D.C. Cir. 1990).

Eastman Kodak Co. v. Image Technical Services, 504 U.S. 451 (1992).

United States v. E. I. duPont de Nemours & Co., 351 U.S. 377 (1956).

Economic Regulation: Rate-of-Return and Price Caps

Among the regulatory policies used to oversee monopolies, which as you have learned has been a major sticking point in the development of telecommunications and media markets, regulating the intake of the monopolies and their motivation to grow has been a major concern. To illustrate this point, excerpts from books by Sterling, Bernt, and Weiss and by legal scholars Jonathan Nuechterlein and Phillip Weiser discuss the difference between regulating a monopoly's rate-of-return and capping its prices.

Rate-of-Return Regulation

Christopher H. Sterling, Phyllis W. Bernt,
and Martin B.H. Weiss

Rate-of-return regulation (RoR) appears to be a relatively uncomplicated approach to controlling business activity. A regulatory body establishes, through a rate hearing, the amount of revenue a company needs to generate in order to cover its service costs, pay its debts, provide earnings for its stockholders, and maintain its credit rating so it can continue to attract investors. This amount of revenue, the revenue requirement, is the amount of money the company is allowed to target when it sets its rates. While the basic concepts appear to be simple, the implementation of this form of regulation has often been a contentious process, with regulators and the regulated company arguing over each step in the process.[1]

The RoR method provides regulators with a method for balancing the interests of the subscriber with those of the service provider. On the one hand, it is the regulator's duty to assure that the prices charged by the monopoly provider are "just and reasonable." On the other hand, the regulator has to assure that the prices charged are not "confiscatory"; in other words, the prices charged must be sufficient to cover the provider's costs so that the provider continues to be a viable company. A revenue requirement that exceeds the provider's valid needs results in prices that are too high to be "just and reasonable." A revenue requirement that does not meet the provider's valid needs

results in prices that are "confiscatory." Obviously, the key is to establish exactly what constitutes "valid needs."

The RoR formula is:

$$RRQ = E + (RB - D) \times R$$

Where:	RRQ =	Revenue Requirement
	E =	Allowable Expenses
	RB =	Rate Base
	D =	Accumulated Depreciation
	R =	Allowed Return

The values assigned to each of these elements have been the subject of much debate. In a RoR hearing, the regulated firm presents its figures for E, RB, and D in the above formula. The figures presented are usually based on the actual transactions that took place during a previous 12-month period, the "historic test year." Since the purpose of the rate hearing is to identify the amount of revenue a provider will attempt to achieve through future service prices, it is in the interests of the regulated firm to try to include in its formula any known and expected changes, such as planned salary increases. It is up to the regulator to determine how valid such changes are and whether they should be included. The calculation of revenue requirement on historical figures has led to a phenomenon called "regulatory lag." As an example, assume a firm's revenue requirement is calculated on the expenses and rate base incurred in year one, and that the revenue requirement is targeted to be recovered through prices billed in year two. Assume further that the firm greatly expanded its staff and added significant equipment during year two, none of which was included in the revenue requirement calculation and therefore not in the service prices charged during year two. These increases in staffing and equipment will not be included in the firm's revenue requirement calculation, and therefore its prices, until a later rate hearing. It is this timing difference that is called regulatory lag.[2]

It is the responsibility of the regulator to determine the levels of E, RB, and D that are allowable in calculating RRQ. Any expenses or investment disallowed in calculating RRQ are considered "below the line." They are not recovered through the prices charged to ratepayers and so are, in effect, charged to the stockholders. Expenses and investment deemed to be appropriate for inclusion in the RRQ calculation are "above the line" and so are built into service prices to be recovered from the ratepayer.

The major concern regarding expenses has been which expenses are "allowable." The regulated firm can include everything from employees' wages to taxes to utility costs to country club memberships; however, the regulator can determine that some of these expenses should not be covered by the rates charged to subscribers. For example, regulators often found that advertising costs were not valid expenses to be incurred by the ratepayers of a monopoly service. Such expenses were then considered "below the line."

The rate base consists of the buildings, equipment, land, and other facilities that have been used in providing regulated service. It is an extremely important element in the rate-of-return equation because it is the basis upon which the regulated firm can generate revenues to provide earnings for its shareholders, to build retained earnings to be used for future plans, and to generate a profit. Determining the proper rate base has been a major concern for both the regulator and the regulated firm. Perhaps the most important aspect of the rate base is the valuation basis used. For all practical purposes, the rate base can be valued in one of two ways: (1) on the basis of historical costs (the actual dollars expended at purchase), or (2) reproduction costs

(the dollars it would cost to replace the items at current prices). Prior to World War I, regulators tended to use reproduction costs because they seemed to be more reliable; the lack of standardized accounting practices made it difficult to determine exactly what historical costs had been. However, when construction costs rose sharply after World War I, regulators began to adopt historical costs as a valuation base. The regulated firm, as is to be expected, advocated whichever method would result in a larger rate base.

Court involvement was, therefore, inevitable. Until the early part of the 1940s, the courts were actively involved in trying to determine how best to value the rate base, with judges split between reproduction costs and historical costs as the method more likely to yield a return that would be fair to the ratepayer and also fair, that is, not confiscatory, to the regulated firm. In 1944, in a case involving natural gas, the Supreme Court adopted the "end result" doctrine. Rather than the courts attempting to determine what constituted the "fair value" of the rate base, the courts determined that the regulatory commissions could use whatever valuation method they desired so long as the end result was just and reasonable to both the ratepayers and the firm. The FCC and the majority of state commissions were then free to enforce historical cost as the required valuation method.[3]

In addition to valuation base, another major concern regarding rate base is that only those facilities that are "used and useful" are to be included. Only those buildings, equipment, and facilities that are used in the provision of service are to be included in calculating the revenue requirement that will result in the prices charged for those services. A major issue involved in the "used and useful" standard is the treatment of plant under construction. Regulators must determine at what point, and how, to reflect the costs of constructing new facilities that are not yet in use at the time of the rate hearing.

While the issue of rate base valuation may have dominated the regulatory landscape during the early part of this period, the issue of the allowed return has been a dominant point of controversy ever since. The allowed return is the amount that the regulated firm is permitted to earn on its investment. Just one or two percentage points make a significant difference: "Given the rate base, earnings are 25 percent higher under a 10 percent return than under an 8 percent return."[4] The larger the rate base, the greater the impact of even a fraction of a percentage in allowed return. Determining the appropriate allowed return is an important regulatory challenge.

Regulators in setting the allowed return have tended to use the "cost of capital" approach. The cost of capital "may be defined as the annual percentage that a utility must receive to maintain its credit, to pay a return to the owners of the enterprise, and to ensure the attraction of capital in amounts adequate to meet future needs."[5] In implementing the cost of capital approach, regulators first identify the firm's capital structure, and then determine the costs of debt and equity.

A firm's capital structure is its proportion of debt and equity. As an example, a firm's capitalization may consist of 40 percent long-term debt and 60 percent common stock. The cost of debt is usually fixed; however, the cost of equity is difficult to determine. Regulators must decide the level of return on equity that is required to make the firm's common stock attractive to investors. While several methods have been used to determine the cost of equity, the most often used methods have been a market-determined standard and a comparable earnings standard.[6] The market-determined standard attempts to capture the level of earnings and dividends an investor expects before investing in a firm; the comparable earnings standard looks at what an investor can earn by investing in other firms with a comparable level of risk.

Once the capital structure and the costs of debt and capital are determined, the allowed return is calculated by summing the weighted costs of debt and capital. Returning to the earlier example of a firm with 40 percent debt and 60 percent equity capitalization, if the cost of debt is assumed to be 10 percent and the appropriate cost of equity is determined to be 15 percent, the resulting allowed return is calculated as 13 percent, as follows:

	Capital Structure		Cost		Weighted Cost
Long-Term Debt	40%	×	10%	=	4%
Common Stock	60%	×	15%	=	9%
Cost of Capital (Allowed Return)					13%

It is important to remember that the RoR method did not guarantee the regulated firm that it would achieve the allowed return. Instead, RoR regulation provided the firm with the opportunity to earn the allowed return. Fluctuations in service demand, changes in investment or expense levels, or changes in the cost of debt could result in earnings below, or above, the allowed level.

The RoR method was refined during the period of regulated monopoly from 1921 to 1956. The fine points of valuating the rate base and calculating cost of capital were developed, and the RoR methodology became the dominant form of telecommunications regulation until the 1980s when commissions began to examine alternative, incentive-based regulatory models.[7]

NOTES

1. While new incentive forms of regulation have been developed during the past 10 to 15 years, rate-of-return regulation is still the method (at the time of this writing) that is applied to many small telephone companies at both federal and state levels.

2. Regulators and the regulated have long been aware of this aspect of rate-of-return regulation. The alternative to the historical approach to rate-of-return is to calculate the revenue requirement based on forecasted expenses and rate base and to then perform a true-up calculation after the resulting rates have been charged for a period of time to determine whether the firm over- or underearned. This approach was adopted when access charges were established at the onset of long distance competition. (See section 7.3.)

3. Phillips, pp. 321–331. This discussion of valuation of rate base, as well as the following one regarding allowed return relies heavily on chapters 8 and 9 of Phillips.

4. Ibid., p. 375.

5. Ibid., p. 388.

6. Ibid., pp. 394–400.

7. Policymakers came to regard RoR regulation as providing the regulated firm with the wrong set of incentives. Regulators feared that the cost-plus nature of this method led to "gold plating" and inefficiencies. This aspect of the RoR method

will be discussed more fully in section 4.3. Train also explores in some depth the potentially adverse effects of RoR regulation, pp. 19–113.

Price Caps

Jonathan E. Nuechterlein and Philip J. Weiser

Up to this point, our discussion of telephone company cost recovery has presupposed the use of rate-of-return regulation, in which federal and state policymakers set their respective retail rates and access charges at levels designed to guarantee each local telephone company an opportunity to earn, overall, a reasonable return on the prudently incurred costs attributable to its regulated activities. But traditional rate-of-return regulation tends to give any public utility perverse incentives to "gold plate" its assets: that is, incentives to spend more than is efficient or necessary simply to increase the rate base on which it earns its profits. Rate-of-return regulation also can make it easier for firms to engage in monopoly leveraging by over-assigning joint and common costs to its monopoly markets and thereby *cross-subsidize* its operations in competitive markets—a phenomenon we discuss in part III of this chapter. In the 1980s and 1990s, federal and most state regulators sought to address these incentive problems by adopting a *price cap* scheme for retail rate regulation of the largest local telephone companies.

A price cap analysis starts with the retail rates produced in a given year under traditional rate-of-return regulation. In succeeding years, however, retail rates will be determined on the basis not of new rate-of-return proceedings, but of mathematical adjustments designed principally to reflect (a) expected industry-wide increases in efficiency (known as the "X-factor") due to technological and other innovation and (b) fluctuations in inflation and other macroeconomic variables.[1] A price cap approach, unlike a traditional rate-of-return regime, rewards the incumbents for their efficiency over time by entitling them to keep much of the extra profit they generate as the result of cutting unnecessary costs.[2]

Although the size of the X-factor is a source of lively debate and often successful litigation,[3] price caps have proven quite effective in balancing the financial needs of the incumbents against the consumer welfare interest in lower retail rates.[4] The retail rates of the largest incumbent telephone companies, as well as their access charges, are now generally subject to price cap rules. Smaller incumbents are often still subject to rate-of-return regulation.

NOTES

1. *See* United States Tel. Ass'n v. FCC, 188 F.3d 521 (D.C. Cir. 1999).

2. *See, e.g.,* W. Kip Viscusi, Et Al., Economics Of Regulation And Antitrust 369–70 (MIT Press, 3d ed. 2000); Nat'l Rural Telecom. Ass'n v. FCC, 988 F.2d 174 (D.C. Cir. 1993).

3. *See United States Tel Ass'n, supra* (invalidating FCC's rationales for imposing 6.0% X-factor).

4. The federal price cap regime contains a "low-end adjustment" mechanism that carriers may theoretically invoke to raise their rates if their rate of return falls below a prescribed level. *See* Southwestern Bell Tel. Co. v. FCC, 10 F.3d 892, 894–95 (D.C. Cir. 1993). That mechanism is unavailable, however, to price cap carriers that have availed themselves of the FCC's pricing flexibility rules. *See* 47 C.F.R. § 69.731.

UNIT 4

Competition Law or Telecommunication Law II? Network Regulation Basics

Any attempt to understand communications and information policy needs to begin by first understanding the nature of communication and information processes. Indeed, if the policy designed is aimed at preserving the integrity of the communication process and the free flow of information, one needs to first understand the communication process and its elements.

Information Theory

In the first reading in this unit, P.H. Longstaff, a professor of television, radio, and film, breaks down the communication process and the flow of information into their most basic building blocks. Understanding Claude Shannon and Warren Weaver's model of communication, how its different elements are defined, and how they are applied to the communications sector is at the center of this reading. When done, you should be able to recognize where within the communication process a particular information activity is taking place.

Information Theory

P.H. Longstaff

INFORMATION THEORY: THE BUILDING BLOCKS OF ALL COMMUNICATIONS

The perspective of information theory is the most important tool in our new toolkit. It enables us to use all the other tools because it gives us the basic building blocks of all communication. One can think of these building blocks as the pieces of a simple set of children's blocks—there are only a few types of pieces (several sizes and shapes) with which one can build many different things. The basic building blocks of any communication are sender, receiver, coding and decoding, sending and receiving devices, channel, message, and noise (see figure 2.1). All communications industries are made up of companies that contribute one or more of these functions.

The information theory tool has been used to analyze subjects as diverse as weapons delivery, cybernetics, psychology, and art. It is useful in so many areas because it describes every communication process, from the intracellular to the interstellar. Every communication can be broken down into these basic building blocks, all of which may be present on many levels or at many stages of the process. Table 2.1 gives examples from the communications sector.

Communication often has two other attributes.

- *Storage.* The message may be stored during or between communication transactions. For example, messages are stored in books, on computer disks, and, of course, in the human brain.

- *Feedback.* A message is sent by the receiver (who is now the sender) in response to the original message from the sender (who is now the receiver). This creates a communication loop that is sometimes called interactivity. This loop can be synchronous, as in a phone conversation, or asynchronous, as in an e-mail exchange.

In the widely used Harvard Information Business Map (see figure 2.2) communication has also been analyzed into "substance, process, and format." These concepts are consistent with the information theory tool. They describe ways in which the building blocks of communication work together. For example, *format* describes how coding and decoding work together with the channel (a book is coded into a written language, then printed on paper as its channel). All complex modern systems of communication—radio, television, satellite communication, cable, and wireless phones and computers—are refinements or elaborations of these building blocks (see figure 2.2).

The birth of information theory cannot be traced to any one place in any one country or one discipline.

FIGURE 2.1 Model of Communication

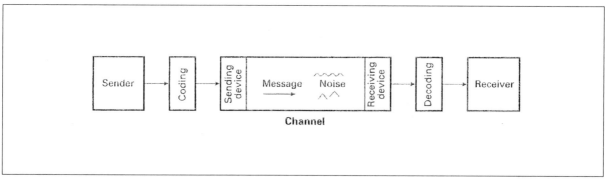

Its intellectual roots are in many areas, but primarily in physics and mathematics. Like most scientific theories, it did not come to the attention of those outside academic circles until it could be put to practical use to make something work or work better.

During World War II it became important to predict the position of moving enemy airplanes and ships in order to aim the bombs that would destroy them. This required that the messages received by radar devices—the "ping" that was bounced off the moving target—be used to predict the *future* position of the detected enemy craft. This computational problem was solved independently in Russia, by A. N. Kolmogoroff, and in the United States, by Norbert Wiener (1948). In both efforts, a system was devised to separate out any unwanted *noise* from the signal made by the movement of the vessel in order to plot the vessel's likely course. At about the same time, mathematician Claude E. Shannon (1948) was developing mathematical theories that became the foundation for the computer language of binary digits (1s and 0s) and the basis of modern digital communication. These two bodies of work have been used to build communication systems that can encode messages and transmit them accurately and swiftly in the presence of noise. Accuracy and speed allow more messages to be sent in the same amount of time, increasing the efficiency of the communication process.

Information theory has been used for many years in mathematics and engineering—places where some business executives and government policymakers do not eagerly go. But here there are no formulas to decipher and no complex schematics to learn. They are not necessary for what we want to do. What we are looking for must be elegantly simple because it must be applicable to past,

present, and future communications in every country. This gives us the broader view we need of how things work in a world where technological lines are blurring and communication flows more easily across national borders.

As more communication systems become digital, the basic similarities among communication technologies become apparent. This makes it increasingly difficult to posit any relevant difference between messages delivered by coaxial cable, fiber-optic cable, or satellite. A byte is a byte is a byte.

The term *information theory* should not be confused with *information policy.* The latter is often applied to a broad range of issues, including privacy and intellectual property rights. Nor should information theory be confused with the social science known as communications theory, although they are tangentially related in subject matter. The more complex models of communication developed by social scientists may be helpful for policymakers in analyzing particular issues with regard to the *effects* of messages on certain receivers.

Next, it is important to define what is meant in this book by *regulation.* The term is used here to mean any limitation on the choices of persons (individual or corporate) who control any of the components of a communication process. It could apply to government restrictions or to restrictions that are imposed by companies on themselves, sometimes with the agreement of government or via an agreement among themselves. For government restrictions, the term *regulation* applies equally to limitations imposed by the judicial, legislative, and administrative branches

TABLE 2.1   Building Blocks of the Information Theory Tool

Building Block	Definition	Examples from the Communication Sector
Sender	The one attempting to send a message to one or more receivers	Radio producer, e-mail sender
Receiver	Anyone—whether an intended recipient or not—who perceives the message	Radio listener, e-mail recipient
Encoding	The process that puts the message into appropriate form for sending on the channel	Changing to analog signal, digital signal
Sending device	A machine that puts the coded message into the channel	Radio transmitter, computer
Receiving device	A machine that takes the coded message out of the channel	Car radio, computer
Decoding	The process that puts the message into into a form that is understandable by the receiver	Analog signal becomes audible as music, digital signal becomes readable as text
Channel	The route through which the message travels. A message can go through several layers of channels in a networked system or through several channels before it reaches the receiver(s)	Air (using variations in electromagnetic waves), phone or cable lines
Message	Intended changes or variations in what goes over the channel	Variations in wave frequency or length, variations in digits (1s and 0s)
Noise	Other signals in the channel that make it difficult for the receiver to perceive the message	Electromagnetic signals caused by sunspots or storms, temporary interruptions in the signal

of government at any level, from international regulatory bodies to the government of the smallest village.

It is not always immediately clear which part of the communication process is being regulated. In some cases, governments have attempted to classify restrictions on senders as regulation of channels in order to make the regulations more politically or constitutionally palatable. In many cases, one individual or company acts in several capacities in the process.

By using the information theory tool, one can in all cases determine what is being regulated by asking which of the elements or building blocks of the communication process is being limited. For example, the regulation of violence on television might be characterized as regulation of the airwaves (the channel), but instead it is regulation of the sender because the channel itself is not limited by the regulation—only the sender's activities and choices are circumscribed.

FIGURE 2.2 Information Business Map

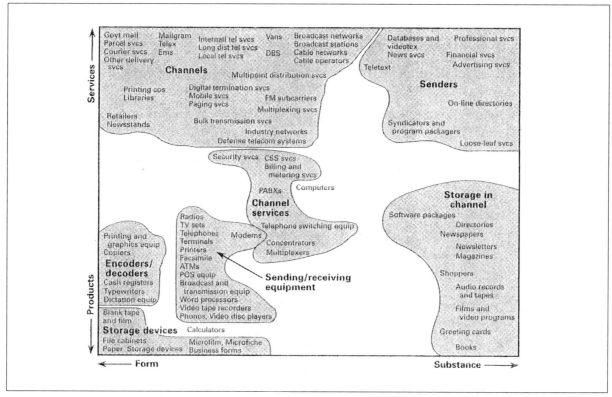

There are several other issues of definition. First, the terms *media* and *medium* are avoided in this discussion where possible. In communications regulatory circles, these terms are generally applied to businesses that both are senders of messages and have some control of the channels through which messages are sent. For example, print, broadcast, and cable companies all control access to a channel, send their own messages in that channel, and make choices about coding of the messages. Thus, in order to keep these various elements of communication separate, the terms *media* and *medium* are not used. Similarly, terms that have specific meaning with regard to particular technologies are avoided, such as *user*, *application*, *carrier*, *programmer*, and *transmitter*. The boundaries between communication and computation have become virtually impossible to draw. Computers are used for many purposes in the communication process, including encoding and decoding, sending and receiving, and storage. Computation can be used to increase the speed or efficiency of any part of the communication process,

except (at least for now) the human beings who are the ultimate senders and receivers. Because communication and computation have become so closely intertwined, separating communication geese and computation ducks has become a task even engineers find vexing. There are a lot of deese and gucks. The only reason anyone has tried to solve this taxonomic riddle is because most countries regulate communication but not computation. We will assume that, at this point in the evolutionary process, communication and computation are inextricably intertwined.

IS IT A DUCK?

In any time of pervasive change, new wards creep into conversations to express ideas and things not experienced before, and this seems especially true in areas of changing technology. For example, the merger of computers with various communication technologies has spawned words like *multimedia*, *compunications*, *telematics*, and *mediamatics*. If a telephone company offers something that looks like a cable television service, is that a cablephone service? If a broadcaster uses part of its spectrum allocation to offer data services, does that make it a datacaster? What if a cablephone company retransmits the signal of a datacaster?

These questions are neither frivolous nor far-fetched, and their meaning goes beyond linguistics. As noted in chapter 1, new products and services defy old distinctions and national borders. A newly adopted faith in the marketplace to allocate scarce communications resources has also changed the regulatory landscape in many countries. Companies that once cooperated are now competing, and companies that were once competitors are now cooperating via mergers and joint ventures in order to get better competitive positions. Failure to understand exactly what part of the process a company now operates in has caused many failed business plans because the business of being a sender is different from the business of being a channel.

Even worse, many legal and policy questions arise about where a service falls with regard to the regulatory definitions established in the twentieth century—back when industries such as telephony and broadcasting seemed to be separate industrial species that ought to have separate regulatory systems. The first question in any public policy analysis has been equivalent to, Is it a duck or is it a goose?

Consider a business that wants to put a color printer in homes and offices to be used with a cable TV service to print out color coupons, advertisements, news articles, or even whole books. Is this a cable service? A publishing service? Will this business be subject to the laws regulating cable TV or the laws, or absence of laws, applicable to publishing? Which level of government should have jurisdiction: local, national, or international? Or should these hybrid technologies remain outside the regulatory process?

In many countries, governments have supported new roles for existing communications industries in order to provide competition for similar services that have operated as monopolies. For example, in some countries cable companies were allowed to offer telephone service in addition to their standard video fare in order to bring more competition to telephone companies. Electric companies were also allowed to offer both telephone service and video programming to their customers to compete with cable and telephone companies. In one case, a duck took on a second job as a goose, and in the other, a seagull also works as both a duck and a goose. Everyone was supposed to look like ducks, geese, seagulls, and even hawks. Unfortunately, just calling yourself a duck or a sender and installing the appropriate technology doesn't mean you are good enough at this business to be a successful competitor. "If it walks like a duck and quacks like a duck, it *is* a duck." No longer.

APPLYING INFORMATION THEORY TO THE COMMUNICATIONS SECTOR

The following discussion of the elements of communication is intended to be illustrative, not exhaustive. It is a rough guide to how the perspective of information theory with regard to the building blocks of communication can be used to build business and regulatory strategies that apply to the entire communications sector.

Senders

Human beings are not the only senders of messages. For example, a neutron star sends a signal that announces its presence and the type of star it is. A dog barks at the door to announce its desire to go out. But for our purposes, senders are assumed to be persons, either individuals or groups such as corporations or government agencies. A sender is the original source of a message, the one whose actions started the communication. These actions do not need to be purposeful. Indeed, everyone sends thousands of unintended messages every day by the way they dress and walk, and by their facial expressions. All these messages allow others to perceive important information. In most cases, however, senders exercise some choice.

If a sender has no choice, the message would convey no meaning, because the message would be absolutely predictable. For example, if I always send only one message ("Wolf!"), receivers will soon perceive no new information coming from me because they are certain of what I will say. Similarly, if I am required to wear the same clothes as everyone around me, I do not send any messages about myself by my choice of clothing. Any restriction on the choices of the sender increases the certainty and decreases the uncertainty of the receiver. This diminishes the amount of possible information sent by the actions of the sender. This is called entropy, and it is a useful concept for the discussion of regulating the message choices of senders or their choices for coding. Entropy indicates that limiting the choices of senders will decrease the amount of information available in the system. This has implications for business strategy and discussions of free speech. For example, any message that is perceived as predictable—giving no new or unknown information—will not be perceived as valuable, and consumers are unlikely to be willing to pay for it or even tolerate it. Banner ads on Web pages that are predictable or unchanging are not likely to be effective. In many countries governments force companies to send certain messages. For example, some products are required to carry a health warning—surely a laudable goal—but when consumers see the same message every time they pick up the product it becomes predictable and loses much of its power to convey information.

Other government restrictions on the choices of senders include regulation of the following:

Access
Few channels are big enough to accommodate all messages and efficient enough to move them at little or no cost. Channel capacity must be allocated by the market or by government. In addition, all countries have regulations that restrict the ability of senders to put their messages in particular channels. For example, in virtually every country a sender who wants to use the broadcast spectrum must get a license from government because that spectrum is said to be scarce: there are a limited number of frequencies, and two senders cannot use the same frequency at the same time. Cable TV companies are also required to get a license or franchise, even though they do not use the broadcast spectrum, on the theory that cable customers are a scarce resource and only one company can survive on their patronage. This function of government as allocator of scarce channel resources has come under attack on several fronts. Some opponents of these policies claim that the marketplace would be more efficient at channel allocation, and others challenge the idea that these resources are scarce at all in the light of new technological advances and new channels.

Timing
Market mechanisms and government regulations sometimes reduce a sender's choices about the time periods when a message can enter a channel. For example, a city might specify times for protest marches or a national government could restrict the time of day when adult (pornographic) programming may be aired. An Internet access provider might charge more for access during periods of heavy traffic.

Coding
Companies that control channel access usually control how the sender codes the message that goes into the channel. This also gives channels at least some control (and the sender fewer choices) over the *coding/decoding devices* that move messages into and out of the channel. Telephone companies have some control over the coding of messages that go into their channel, and this gives them some control over the consumers' telephone devices. Cable companies get a big say in the coding for their customers' set-top boxes.

Most governments have some restrictions on senders' choices about how they will encode their messages. Some require that the messages be in a certain language. Others have restrictions on the use of cryptography (secret codes) that cannot be decoded by government agents involved in national security or criminal investigations.

Messages
Communications companies that are channels often reduce the choices of senders as to the messages the channel will allow to be sent because some messages make more money than others. Since most channels can not send all potential messages, they prefer those that will bring the highest return. These may be messages that many people will pay a small amount for or that a few people will pay a lot for.

All governments prohibit senders from sending messages that are thought to have undesirable effects on those who receive them. For example, some messages are thought to be harmful to children. Other messages are thought to have undesirable effects on the social order; it is feared that certain information will destabilize the local political or economic system and hurt all citizens. This type of restriction on senders might include their ability to send messages that show political leaders or certain cultural groups in a bad light.

Senders often assert unfettered choice of access, coding, timing, and message as their right, but this has never been the case in any country. Even in countries that have allowed senders many choices, there is a responsibility for the consequences of those choices, including punishment for defamation and copyright infringement. Interestingly, countries that allow the most choice to senders also have the most stringent enforcement of copyright, while countries that allow senders very few choices often fail to provide for copyright enforcement. Where government is the only authorized sender, it does not often restrict its own choices. The restrictions on senders may vary according to the channel they choose to use. Senders may find that their messages are legal in one channel (the Internet) but illegal in another (broadcast).

Receivers

A receiver is an identifiable entity that becomes aware of a message. As in the case of senders, receivers need not be human. A dog becomes aware of a message when scolded by its owner and may learn from the message to change its behavior. But, as with the definition of senders, we assume that receivers are individuals or groups such as corporations or government agencies. Like sending, the act of receiving need not be purposeful. Human beings and corporations become aware of messages not intended for them and which they had no intention of receiving. For example, overhearing a conversation in a café is receiving a message, even if the receiver were to take steps not to hear it by moving away from the speakers.

Direct regulation of receivers by government is rare because it would require laws that would place physical limits on the ability to perceive messages. For example, it would make it illegal to *listen to* certain messages or certain senders. In addition to being difficult to enforce, the restriction of choices for receivers, just like the regulation of senders, strikes directly at the heart of freedom of expression. Government regulation restricting choice for the equipment required to receive messages (satellite dishes) is more common.

Companies, on the other hand, have a critical interest in restricting the choices of receivers. If a consumer has only three radio stations to choose from, the number of receivers for each will be much higher, and the value of advertising much greater, than if there were ten stations to choose from.

Sometimes governments restrict the choices of senders in order to protect the receivers. These restrictions include regulation of junk fax (where the receiver often must pay for the unwanted message), junk cellular messages (unsolicited messages sent to cell phones), and spam (unsolicited e-mail).

The rights of receivers are also debated with regard to their access to a given channel or certain kinds of information. For example, some countries force senders to send certain information, thus restricting their choices, because it is "good for" receivers. Other laws mandate that certain channels or messages be available to all receivers regardless of their ability to pay for the access. Many of these regulations restrict the choices of senders, channels, and encoders in the short term in order to give receivers more choices. In the longer term these policies may actually reduce the choices available to receivers if they discourage economic activity by senders and channels.

Encoding and Decoding

A code is a set of agreements made in advance between potential communicators that establishes significance for certain words, gestures, electronic signals, or other ways in which messages are sent. Language is a code whereby two or more people agree in advance that particular sounds (or letters representing those sounds) signify a specific thing or concept. A code thus restricts the choices of senders and receivers. It can also affect the choices of those who control the coding equipment, sending/receiving equipment, or access to the channel. An e-mail message is encoded before it is put into the telecommunications channel, so it is important that the receiver has equipment that will use the same code to display it.

Mass communications channels require coordination in advance between senders and receivers on a large scale. This coordination can be accomplished through market competition, when only one company survives to become the available coder. But code regulation has customarily fallen to government. In complex technological systems, the coding is closely linked to the sending, receiving, and channel equipment used. Coding of a broadcast signal, for example, depends on the equipment used by the broadcast stations and the receiving devices used by consumers. It would not be profitable to code a signal in digital form if most consumers' receiving devices understand only analog code. Any change in coding requires all communicators to agree to change, and government is often the mediator in reaching these agreements.

In many cases, messages are coded to deny access to them. Only those who know the code can decode them. This is important for national security and the maintenance of a business's trade secrets. Security is also critical for selling access to information. Information, like all other economic goods and services, has no value unless it is a scarce resource. If you can't keep everyone away from your information, you can't charge for access. Who would pay for what they can receive for free? For example, information sent to subscribers by cable for "premium" channels is encoded so that only those with the appropriate decoders can receive it. Similar coding techniques are used for messages sent by the many new satellite and telephone-based services. In all these businesses the commercial value of what they have to sell depends on the sender's or channel's control over distribution of the code or, more often, of the decoding devices. For the sake of security, governments are often asked to make receiving coded messages, and selling codes or devices that allow decoding, a crime.

These coding issues are addressed with diminishing regard for traditional concepts of which channel they occur in and with increasing consideration for what kinds of regulations by companies and governments are realistically enforceable. Companies may find that they have limited powers to restrict the choices of others in a world where digital coding allows messages to move with great speed within and between channels. For example, a movie can be downloaded onto the Internet from a disk and made available to a worldwide audience instantly. This creates difficult problems for the enforcement of copyright. The time may not be far away when electronic message theft can only be effectively dealt with across all channels and across all national borders.

Devices for Sending and Receiving

People come into contact with communication systems through the systems' devices for sending and receiving messages. These include telephones, computers, and TV sets. The primary function of sending and receiving devices is to put messages into a channel or take them out. These devices often do the encoding and decoding as well. As with other elements of the communication process, the equipment employed for sending and receiving must use the same operating specifications and the same coding and decoding (codec) system. In other words, they must be compatible with the rest of the system. While the devices themselves do not make choices and are thus not "regulated" under our definition, the companies who make them do make choices about what to sell. These decisions are often restricted by government standards. Since all the devices that must work together are not always distributed by the same company, someone needs to decide what the standards will be for the entire system.

When should government impose standards for codec systems or sending and receiving equipment, thereby limiting the choices of the marketplace and giving a potential windfall to one of the competing standards? Many governments enforce standards in order to ensure the ubiquitous availability of the technology. In some cases this is thought to be necessary to promote consumer confidence in the equipment's continued viability (Will parts and service become unavailable when standards change?). Consumers may also be unwilling to invest in new equipment if it will be incompatible with ancillary products (Will I be able to record the messages I receive with my current equipment?).

Standards set by the government, not by competition in the marketplace, also reduce the waste of resources that can never be recovered by the companies who tried to sell the losing technology. When governments set standards, new technologies, and those from countries with different standards, will not be allowed to compete. Government standards setting allows technologies with access to political power to promote their own products and keep competitors at bay.

Messages and Substance

In information theory, a message is a coded token—something that stands for something else—that moves through the channel and has no meaning for anyone until decoded. The messages in a channel using a binary digital system are a meaningless series of 1s and 0s unless the receiver knows how they were coded.

What the receiver actually perceives has been called meaning or content, but here the term *substance* is used to avoid any suggestion that messages might contain anything separate from the coding and the information already possessed by the receiver. Thus, substance = coded message + information already possessed by the receiver. If I code a message into French and attempt to convey something about snow to someone who does not know French and lives near the equator, the substance received will be quite different from the same message sent to a person in Paris. Thus, no two people will perceive a message in exactly the same way.

Unfortunately, many communications business plans and most public policymakers continue to act as if messages are like bullets: whoever they are aimed at will perceive the same messages and accept them as truth regardless of their previous knowledge and experience. A more informed view of the communication process might result in greater success for attempts to market products and mold public opinion or public morals.

Because neither a message nor substance is a person whose choices can be limited, neither can be regulated directly. However, as described, both can be affected by restrictions on the choices of persons in other parts of the communication process.

Noise

Noise can be defined as unwanted signals in the channel that are not part of the sender's message. Radio and telephone receivers hiss or crackle in certain atmospheric conditions, when natural electromagnetic fluctuations join messages of human origin in the channel. When broadcasting video images, this electromagnetic noise takes the form of "snow" in the picture. Similarly, when two radio programs or telephone conversations are sent in the same channel, the receiver may have difficulty separating the message from the noise. Messages encoded using digital rather than analog technology are somewhat less affected by electronic noise in the channel, but noise is present in all channels.

Noise can lessen the clarity of the message or even distort it. In this context, the accuracy of the message has nothing to do with its "truth." A message is accurately received if the coded tokens (words, bytes) are received in the same way they were transmitted. The problem of a noisy channel is easy to visualize. Think of trying to talk to someone right next to you in the midst of a very exciting football game. The channel (the surrounding air) is so filled with messages (shouts, cheers, boos, songs) that people must talk louder than the ambient noise level in order for a message to reach the intended receiver. Talking where there is less noise requires less energy and results in more accurate transmission of the message.

Noise in the channel can also cause errors in the communication. Too much noise or the wrong kind of noise in the channel can result in the receiver's getting a message different from the one that was sent. These errors may be merely irritating (missed letters in the transmission of text) or may create big problems (errors in the numbers received in a banking transaction).

Regulation of noise sometimes restricts messages that may interfere with the ones intended by those who operate the channel. These regulations are restrictions on the choices of other senders. Broadcast frequencies are licensed to one sender, and any one else sending in that channel would be violating the law. Regulations that result in the ejection of a disruptive audience member might also be seen as a regulation of noise. Ejecting the disruptive person clearly restricts the sending choices of that person while it increases the sending choices of the speaker on the podium. Other company or government regulations of noise include technical specifications for sending/receiving devices that screen out distortions in the message caused by atmospheric disruptions. These regulations restrict the choices of those who make the equipment.

Channels

Channels can be divided into four types, depending on the number of senders and receivers of a particular message:

- *Point-to-point.* One sender to one receiver, for instance, the postal service and plain old telephone service—POTS
- *Point-to-multipoint.* One to many, such as broadcast, cable, print
- *Multipoint-to-point.* Many to one, for instance, credit card verification systems
- *Multipoint-to-multipoint.* Many to many, such as videoconferencing and computer bulletin boards

Some channels like postal and, more recently, telecommunications channels can be used for both point-to-point and point-to-multipoint communication.

All types of channels can be interactive on a synchronous or asynchronous basis. Both wired and wireless technologies can be used for all these types of channels and will, in many places, compete directly for customers. Different business plans or regulatory treatment for channels that essentially do the same thing in every way that matters will become increasingly unsuccessful. But distinctions based on the type of channel can clarify goals and make regulations applicable to all appropriate channels. The implications of forming communication channels into networks is explored in more detail in chapter 3.

Channels as Senders

Those who own or control channels are often also senders in those channels. Broadcasters and cable systems send their own shows to their viewers as well as ones they receive for retransmission from syndicators or networks. Newspapers send their own stories to readers as well as those from syndicators or news services. Regulation of the channels' own messages by government or by the channels' corporate headquarters would be restrictions on the choices of the channel owners *as senders,* not on the channels.

In many countries the type of channel will determine how many restrictions are placed on a channel company when it acts as sender. Often, broadcasters who also own print channels (magazines) and distribute one or both over the Internet will have different rights and responsibilities for the same information in all three channels.

Access to Channels

Should some channels be required to offer universal, low-cost access for senders or receivers while others are allowed to distribute the same messages on an ability-to-pay basis? As noted, such policies can increase the choices for senders and receivers but often decrease the choices for channels.

Many government policymakers continue to think of channels as quasi-public property. In many countries most channels were owned by the government until the end of the twentieth century. They continue to be seen as a public resource where choices of the owners must be limited if they conflict with the choices of other participants in the communication process, especially senders and receivers. This has led to debates on who should have access, and at what price, to phone and cable channels that are capable of the high-speed, broadband service required for advanced interactive services. As discussed in chapter 3, communication channels are not the only or the first to face this question. The experience of channels in networks for energy and transportation can give us new tools for debating these issues productively.

Government Promotion of Certain Channels

Should the government prefer one channel to another by offering it special protection from competitors, subsidizing research and development, or giving it special tax incentives? That has been the history of each new communication channel, from the postal service to the Internet. In countries where the government owned the new channels and in countries where they were privately owned, those with an interest in the new channels have relied on the taxpayers to reduce the tremendous risks associated with building them. This has generally assumed that the new channels would not kill the old ones, giving senders or receivers more choices. Even if the new channels were seen to pose a danger to the existing ones, government subsidies were justified as necessary to give senders and receivers faster, cheaper, or better service.

SUMMARY

Information theory gives everyone a better tool for understanding how communication works. It meets all the specifications for new tools that we set out in chapter 1. It is flexible and can be applied to many different kinds of communication. It can be applied to large and small businesses and to all levels of government. It does not make assumptions about the existence of scarce resources or who should allocate them. It can be applied to both private and public entities. It can be applied to any technology, even ones we don't know of yet. It can help avoid dual regulation of the same service. It does not dictate any particular outcome and can be used by people who must work together but who make different choices about their goals, their strategies, or their tactics.

The important things to remember are the basic building blocks of communication: senders, receivers, coding and decoding, sending and receiving devices, channels, messages, and noise. The concepts of feedback and storage are also important in specific strategy-building problems.

REFERENCES

Abeshouse, Jill, Erwin G. Krasnow, and Michael R. Senkowski. 1983. "The New Video Marketplace and the Search for a Coherent Regulatory Philosophy." *Catholic University Law Review* 32 (3): 529–602.

Brand, Stewart. 1987. *The Media Lab: Inventing the Future at M.I.T.* New York: Viking Penguin.

Compaine, Benjamin M. 1988. "Information Gaps: Myth or Reality." In *Issues in New Information Technology.* Norwood, N.J.: Ablex.

Crevier, Daniel. 1993. *AI: The Tumultuous History of the Search for Artificial Intelligence.* New York: Basic Books.

Crichton, Michael. 1990. *Jurassic Park.* New York: Knopf.

Ferris, Timothy. 1999. "The Last Bit: Information Theory Is the Answer to Everything." *Forbes ASAP* (Oct. 4): 258–260.

Friedman, Thomas L. 1999. *The Lexus and the Olive Tree.* New York: Farrar, Straus, Giroux.

Hardt, Hanno. 1992. *Communication History and Theory in America.* New York: Routledge.

Jackson, Sally. 1992. *Message Effects Research: Principles of Design and Analysis.* New York: Guilford Press.

Johnson, David R., and Kevin A. Marks. 1993. "Mapping Electronic Data Communications onto Existing Legal Metaphors: Should We Let Our Conscience (And Our Contracts) Be Our Guide?" *Villanova Law Review* 38 (2): 487–515.

Liversidge, Anthony. 1990. "Interview with Claude Shannon." *Scientific American* (January): 22–22B.

McManus, Thomas E. 1990. Telephone Transaction-Generated Information: Rights and Restrictions. Cambridge, Mass.: Center for Information Policy Research, Harvard University.

NCTP (National Critical Technologies Panel). 1993. *Second Biennial Report.* Washington, D.C.: Government Printing Office.

NTIA (National Telecommunications and Information Administration). 1993. *The National Information Infrastructure: Agenda for Action.* Report #PB93-231272. Washington, D.C.

Oettinger, Anthony G. 1993. "The Abundant and Versatile Digital Way." In *Mastering the Changing Information World,* ed. Martin L. Ernst, 85–168. Norwood, N.J.: Ablex.

Pierce, John R. 1980. *An Introduction to Communication Theory, Symbols, Signals and Noise.* New York: Dover.

Schramm, Wilbur. 1983. "The Unique Perspective of Communication: A Retrospective View." *Journal of Communication* 33 (3): 6–17.

Shannon, Claude E. 1948. "A Mathematical Theory of Information." *Bell System Technical Journal* 27: 379–423, 623–656.

Wiener, Norbert. 1948. *Cybernetics.* Cambridge, Mass.: Technology Press.

Understanding Networks

The communications model described in the previous reading is but one such process of which there are endless taking place concurrently in the context of the networks that make up the communications industry. In this reading, Professor Longstaff describes the relevant components of networks, which one needs to be acquainted with in order to understand the design of communications policy. The description of the components is complemented by a description of common challenges to the regulation of networks and a discussion of the different measures, including competition, that need to be taken in order to ensure the network operates smoothly. Following this reading you should be acquainted with the different parts of networks and with the different means to overcome the challenges network management faces.

The third reading in this unit, derived from the work of Nuechterlein and Weiser, focuses on the role of network effects and interconnection regulation. Once you have been introduced to the **components** of networks, it is important to be aware of their unique **nature**, in particular the positive effect their growth has on all their members. Connectivity is a unique goal of communications policy, which contributes to the need to differentiate network regulation from general competition and antitrust policy.

The readings in this unit are supplemented by a lecture, which provides a historical review of communication legislation. Students should be acquainted with this history and the justification to the emergence of the Radio Act of 1912, the Radio Act of 1927, and the Communications Act of 1934.

A Tool for Networks

P.H. Longstaff

A new tool for networks? Doesn't everybody already have a pretty good idea of how things work for networks? After all, they've been around for a long time. We have a lot of experience with telephones, railroads, electric grids, postal systems, roads, and many more. Unfortunately, it looks like we don't know as much as we thought we did.

When networks for communication, transportation, and energy were opened up to competition in the last years of the twentieth century, a lot of things happened that nobody anticipated. Everyone knew things would change, but almost no one forecast the landscape that would develop. Everyone predicted more providers of services and lower prices for consumers, but few predicted a decrease in the quality of service (indeed, most predicted an increase) or the wave of consolidation and bankruptcies that swept each industry. The strategic tool we have used for how things work in networks and how networked industries respond to market forces apparently needs to be revised. It is time, once again, to recall the lesson of those faster-swimming frogs and jump out of this hot water. We need a new view of how things work, one that lets us see networks from a broader perspective.

All networks have a lot in common: their operational principles, their problems, the history of their development and (we now know) their response to competition. This means it is possible to design tools that will work for all of them. Such tools may be even more important if, as predicted, the networked industries all become even more closely linked. We assume that a worldwide system linked by computers will require a dependable and affordable energy network. If e-commerce ever meets the expectations of its advocates, it will require a dependable and affordable transportation network to get goods and services delivered.

At the same time, it is important to keep in mind that each networked industry is also unique in some ways, and those unique characteristics will require some specialized tools for dealing with them. Many of these specialized tools already exist in the operating knowledge of the people who run these networks, but even more specialized tools will undoubtedly be developed as technology and other forces change each network.

The networks tool presented in this chapter is a new synthesis of the basic principles of network operation, setting out the things that all networks have in common. This tool will be a starting place for business decisions and regulation for networks. Then the specialized tools for each industry can be applied to fine-tune the strategy. The networks tool offered here includes a new, comprehensive nomenclature to facilitate the discussion of networks between people in the different industries. Often they don't know how much they have in common because they use different terms to mean the same thing. At the end of this chapter this tool is applied to a problem they are all facing: increasing competition.

AN OVERVIEW OF NETWORKS AND NETWORKING

Networks are collections of smaller entities connected with one another in order to function at least part of the time as a larger entity. In our bodies, the network we call the nervous system allows cells to communicate with the brain. The network we call the circulatory system allows individual cells to receive energy and dispose of wastes. In human societies, networks allow individual people and businesses to combine their resources in order to communicate with one another and deliver goods over very long distances. As networks grow larger and more efficient, they break down the need for some localized services (such as retailing), allowing such services to be concentrated in hubs where they can get the benefits of increased economies of scope and scale.

Networks operate as sets of connections built for the benefit of those connected. Economists have identified what they call network externalities, or things about the network that accrue to each person connected. Generally, people talk about positive network externalities such as the fact that as new people or businesses, sometimes called agents or nodes, are added to the network, the benefit of being connected to the network increases for everyone on the network. The more people who have telephones, the more people you can call. Negative externalities are also possible. If too many people are connected to the network, it can exceed its capacity and the system will slow down for everyone on the network. People who try to use the Internet at peak times or experience "brownouts" of their electric service on hot days will be familiar with this phenomenon. After the network reaches its capacity, the value of the network for each node will decrease as more nodes are added. Positive and negative externalities in a network are difficult to deal with by using typical economic models because the network does not charge customers more money every time a new node is added, even though the

service is now arguably worth more to them. Nor do they charge customers less when new nodes are added after capacity is reached, when the service is now worth less to them. This means that the value of cooperation and competition for network resources is often difficult to price and regulate.

By their nature, networks are cooperative systems. Organisms and economic units do not cooperate unless cooperation will allow them to obtain more of a scarce resource than they could obtain on their own through competitive interaction. So, when some people connected to a network perceive that they can get what they want without cooperating with the rest of the people on the network, they are likely to strike out on their own and perhaps compete with the old network for the scarce resources. For example, large customers or large concentrations of customers, or both, for a resource (air transport, computation, electricity) may have enough demand to start their own network. They can then abandon smaller or more dispersed customers on the old network. Those who remain will often find the network worth less to them, because they are connected to fewer people, even as the cost of continuing to participate goes up, because fewer people are sharing the costs of operating the system.

Cooperation in networks is also necessary at the organizational level. Central coordination usually is necessary to keep everything moving in the system, including the coordination of security, signaling, and scheduling. The persons connected to the system, sometimes called the nodes, can't perform coordinating functions alone, and they don't have any incentive to do so because such activities theoretically will not get them more of the resources available within the system.

Networks may be organized in a variety of ways, depending on their purpose. Networked industries are most commonly either point-to-point networks and point-to-multipoint networks. Each works better in particular situations.

Point-to-point networks allow all nodes to connect with one another so that traffic can move from any one node to any other. Examples include air travel and telephones. They allow traffic (people, goods, information) to move up and down the network hierarchy, so that resources can be sent from anywhere to anywhere else in the network. This type of network is

FIGURE 3.1 Point-to-Point Network

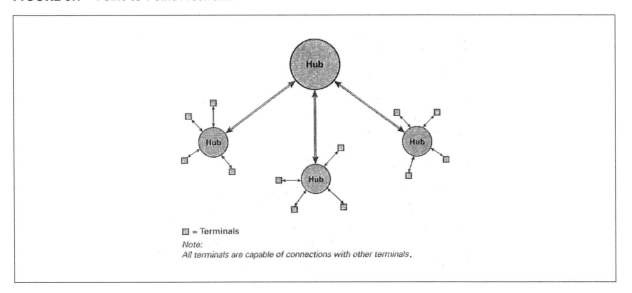

= Terminals
Note:
All terminals are capable of connections with other terminals.

useful where resources are located in many places and must be moved to many different places.

In a simple point-to-point network all the nodes are connected directly to one another, but this can mean a lot of connections once there are more than a few nodes.

When more than a few nodes are connected, the network is likely to develop hubs that act as collection points for traffic. Hubs become critical to the operation of the system, because they switch traffic from one node to another within the local hub or from one layer of hubs to another for traffic moving between local hubs. Hubs can become bottlenecks in the network if traffic backs up there. The ability of the hubs to move traffic quickly and efficiently can thus determine the capacity of the entire network. (See figure 3.1.)

Point-to-multipoint, or one-to-many, networks only require nodes to connect with a central source that acts as the system's central supplier of resources (see figure 3.2). Examples include broadcast and cable networks, energy networks (gas, electric), and computer systems that have a central processing unit (CPU). This kind of organization is sometimes referred to as a command-and-control network because its nodes are not directly connected with one another, although they may develop connections outside the network. They send information about local needs to a central supplier or controller, which then sends them resources or commands. This kind of network

works best where a centrally located resource must be distributed to many places at the same time.

Figures 3.1 and 3.2 represent necessarily simplified pictures of point-to-point and point-to-multipoint networks. Modern networks usually have many types of connections at many levels. Some of these connections are within the network and others connect the network with other networks. For example, two lower-level hubs of the network will often have direct connections to each other, such as an airline with direct service between two hub airports. Other connections will be between two service providers in the same industry, such as two airlines serving the same airport that connect their terminals via bus or train service. Some connections are to the hubs of other networks, such as airline terminals connected to train terminals.

NETWORKED INDUSTRIES

What distinguishes a networked industry? As suppliers to and customers of other firms, all firms are parts of commercial networks. They have all been urged to consider these networks crucial to their success and to think of themselves as part of a larger, interdependent whole. But in some industries, firms cannot exist unless they have direct connections with other firms that offer the same services as they do. In the past, such firms had a territory that they called their own or that they shared with a few others, and most were

FIGURE 3.2 Point-to-Multipoint Network

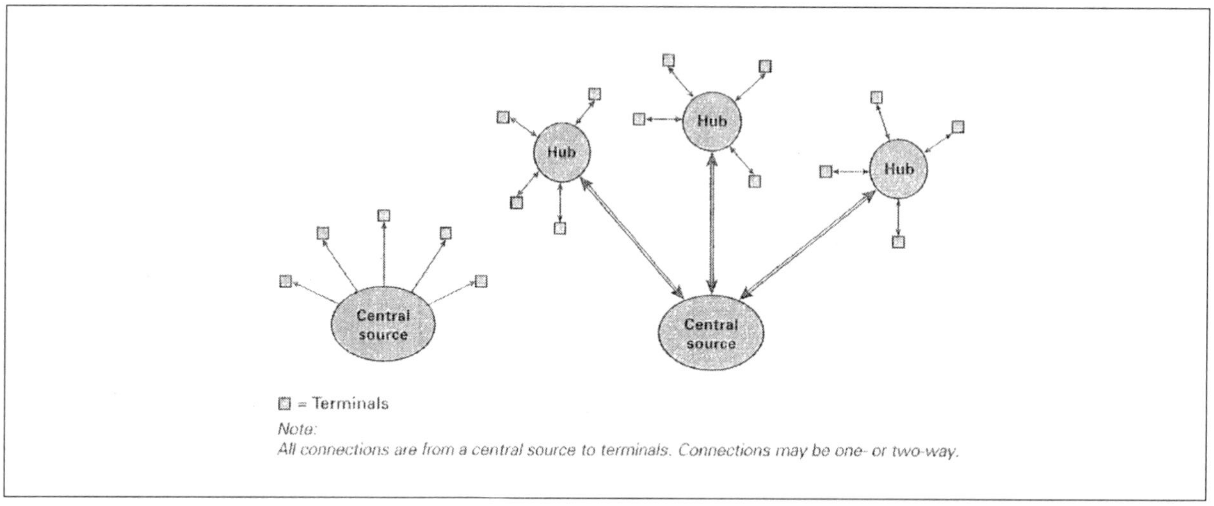

☐ = Terminals
Note:
All connections are from a central source to terminals. Connections may be one- or two-way.

once considered natural monopolies. Firms such as local rail and telephone companies need to move their traffic outside their own territory and move traffic from other territories to customers in theirs. The local networks generally have high fixed costs, including infrastructure and acquiring the right-of-way for that infrastructure. Local networks also have low marginal costs, that is, the cost of each additional phone call or kilowatt sent in the system. These high fixed costs act as a barrier to the entry of competitors, and the low marginal costs can attract competitors if they don't have to share too much of the high fixed costs or if they can develop a technology to get around the fixed costs. Networked industries include energy (gas, electric), transportation (roads, rail, canals, air travel), and communications (postal, telephone). Garbage removal, water service, broadcasting, and cable TV networks share some characteristics of networked industries but tend to have less need for connections with local networks outside their own territories.

New networks in transportation, communication, and energy often are developed because they can increase the speed of traffic in the channel. Increases in speed are no accident, because often the initial research and development (R&D) for these new networks are conducted or financed by military authorities seeking strategic advantages over opponents through faster access to information and other important resources. Increasing the rate at which traffic moves through, enters, or leaves the channel

can also enhance the efficiency of the channel. For example, flying from one city to another may take less time in the channel as compared with travel by automobile or bus, but it may take the same or even more time because of the process of loading or unloading at airport terminals.

As technology made it possible for communications traffic to move through airwaves and various forms of wires, large segments of the communications sector were physically divorced from the transportation network for the first time. In the past, written communication traveled in transportation channels such as waterways or roads. But communication and transportation networks continue to have a profound impact on one another. Many commentators and scholars have predicted that improved communication (via digital broadband services) will allow firms and other institutions to depend less on travel while they conduct more business through videoconferencing and computer networks. In other words, they think communication will substitute for transportation. Historically, transportation and communication complement each other in that the more people communicate, the more they want to meet, and vice versa.

Both communication and transportation networks have large effects on all economic activity because they extend each individual's or institution's range of activities. Large transportation and communication networks allow businesses to enter new markets far from their home territories. This increases competition for customers in these new territories, often bringing economic and political turbulence as the "invaders" compete with local providers of those goods and services. Both communication and transportation networks can change the structure of local social institutions, such as the family, because they bring new ideas along with the new goods and services, and they often encourage people to move away from the local area to the network hubs.

Because services such as communication and transportation are often regarded as public goods, most countries have not allowed network facilities to be owned by foreign nationals. This barrier has begun to break down as foreign investment has come to be seen as necessary for growth or even survival in the new competitive environments. The twentieth century was a period of relative world peace, so that the ownership of public goods by foreigners or multinational corporations came to be seen as less dangerous than before. It was often regarded as worth the risk in return for the improved services made possible by foreign investment, and was deemed critical for world competitiveness. This calculation may change and perceptions about security may change.

In the late 1990s the business and political worlds were full of calls for the deregulation of the industries that provided transportation, communication, and energy. Most of the advocates of deregulation wanted governments to sell the networks they owned to the private sector (privatization) and introduce competition into these services (liberalization). Each time deregulation happens, many of the same problems have been observed. And each case seems to repeat episodes in the history of other networks. For example, many economic and political realities of the postal service and the telegraph network reappeared with the Internet.

These repeating patterns are not limited to networks in the same industry. Some things that appear first in transportation networks appear later in communication networks. Many similarities between the history of railroads, electric power, and the Internet have been noted, including each industry's promotion by government and its promise of a better society. So it is not a waste of time to look at the history of established networks to get an idea about the future of new ones. Since deregulation came first to the transportation sector, we might look to transportation networks for a glimpse of what may happen to communication. When we take this broader view, we see that when new technology or other forms of competition have been introduced into networked systems, at least one result always seems to follow: a spurt of mergers and acquisitions. Unfortunately, it is unlikely that any tool could give precise predictions for these systems, given the enormous and growing complexity of each network. But there are directions or movements of these systems that seem to be predictable. Regulation or business planning of any kind requires at least some preliminary assumptions about how networked industries are likely to respond to a new economic or regulatory stimulus. Assumptions are, by their nature, dangerous unless they can be tested frequently against what is actually happening. As we have noted, feedback from the tactical level is critical to any successful strategy.

Although people working in and regulating what used to be called the public utility networks (phone, electric, gas, water) always noted that these networks had some things in common, they tended to concentrate on the physical characteristics and missions that made the networks unique. The differences often became more important than the similarities. But there is a lot of evidence that they are more alike than has been thought. For example, the terms used to describe them were originally borrowed from other industries. Over the years these borrowings were forgotten and the industries came to see these terms and the processes they denote as uniquely theirs. Governments have often seen the similarities and have borrowed heavily from the regulation of existing networks in order to write rules for new ones. For example, in the United States the regulatory structure of the telephone system was taken from existing regulation of the railroads.

NETWORK COMPONENTS

All networks have essential components in common. They cannot operate as networks if one of these pieces is missing. The history of networks shows that these components influence the nature of the network to which they belong, and that a change in any one has consequences for the others as well as for the network as a whole. Thus, these components are interdependent parts of the system. Like the heart, lungs, and brain of the system called the human body, these pieces cannot exist without the others.

The names used here for these components are drawn from a variety of networked industries. These names were selected on the basis of their use by nonspecialists or their use in more than one industry. Specialists in one industry may find a familiar function called by another name. The selection of names may seem somewhat arbitrary, but finding a common language that crosses old boundaries is critical for a tool that will work for many kinds of networks. The examples in table 3.1 illustrate the many ways in which these networks exhibit the same components.

Senders and Receivers

Senders are the people or entities that put traffic into the network. In point-to-point networks (postal service, telephony, railroads), they may also be receivers. They may or may not pay a fee to put traffic into the system. As a general rule, receivers ultimately pay this cost, directly or indirectly, as part of the cost of the goods or services received. Senders may continue to own the traffic while it's in the channel, unless it is already owned by the receiver, but they have little control over how traffic gets to its destination, that is, they cannot control how traffic is routed in the network. Their main concerns are speed, reliability, and price, any one of which can become a trade-off against the others. For example, they might be willing to pay more for more reliable or faster service. But unless these senders are high-volume customers they have little economic power over any of these concerns.

Receivers take traffic out of the network. In point-to-point networks, they can also be senders. For example, receivers of phone messages can also send them. Like senders, receivers are concerned about speed, reliability, and price. And, like senders, they have little economic control unless they can aggregate large amounts of demand.

When senders and receivers are citizens of democratic regimes, they sometimes use their political power to compensate for a lack of economic power. They demand service at "reasonable" rates. Those not served by the particular network, perhaps because the price they are willing to pay for use will not cover the costs of providing the infrastructure, are likely to demand that government ensure universal service. This usually means that senders and receivers in other parts of the network—or taxpayers, who may or may not be a part of it—pay extra for the service in order to extend the network to unprofitable customers or areas.

Channels

Channels are routes along which traffic travels. Individual portions of those routes are sometimes called edges or lines in network analysis literature. Channels may involve substantial terrestrial infrastructure, such as pipelines and railroads, or they may be allocations of air space (for air travel) or of the electromagnetic spectrum (for broadcasting). New channels often are larger—usually many times larger—than existing ones, because they compete with established channels by offering more links to potential senders or receivers. For example, since 1800 each new transportation infrastructure (from canals to railroads to airlines) has expanded into a network ten times larger than the previous infrastructure (Grubler 1990).

Channels are often expensive to build, because the owner must acquire rights-of-way (the right to cross property owned by others). For example, no electric power network can be built without erecting poles and lines over both private and government-owned property. Often this cannot be done without government's forcing private property owners to allow this construction. In return for this exercise of power, governments often insist that the channel be used in the public interest. Because rights-of-way and channel infrastructure are so expensive, two or more networks often use them and new networks are often built on top of old ones. For example, electric and telephone, and, more recently, cable TV, networks all share the same rights-of-way and sometimes even the same poles. These rights-of-way may be public streets, which also act as channels of transportation. Many of the networks discussed here are arranging new uses for these valuable rights-of-way. In some countries gas and electric companies have used their infrastructure to build fiber-optic networks for telecommunications.

Traffic and Payload

The "stuff" that moves in the channel is the traffic. Traffic may be moved by itself through the channel,

TABLE 3.1 Network Components and Functions

Network Component/ Function	Description	Examples
Sender	Puts the traffic into system	Manufacturers, call placers, electricity and oil producers
Receiver	Takes the traffic out of system	Retailers, consumers, postal recipients, electricity customers
Channel	A route through which traffic moves	Roads, waterways, railroads, airwaves, telephone lines, electric lines, pipelines
Traffic/Payload	What moves through the channel	Commodities, finished goods, electrons, oil, gas, signals (bytes, waves)
Transport	Movement of traffic through the channel	Movement of trains, trucks, communication signals, gas flow
Terminal	Where traffic is put into and taken out of the channel (traffic may be temporarily stored)	Railroad depots, train terminals, telephone customer equipment, gas or oil storage depot
Ancillary	Any other component necessary for the network to develop or function, including energy to move traffic through system	Fueling stations, tugboats, electric power (for phones and computers)
Scheduling	Routing or switching capacity: routes traffic within the channel or from one part of the channel to another or from one mode of transport to another (traffic may be temporarily stored)	Routing or switching between rail, telephone, or electric trunk lines, or between satellite and cable or trucks and rail cars, or scheduling capacity in the channel for transponder or rail time
Signaling	Communication within the system to ensure system safety and security	Railroad crossing signs, "addressing" digital signals, flow meters in energy lines
Security	Keeps traffic safe from theft and keeps network safe from disruption	Security procedures at airports, guards at cargo terminals, fences around pipeline terminals

such as gas in a pipeline or pedestrians on a road. Traffic can also move as payload in some sort of vehicle, such as a document in an envelope or passengers in an automobile.

When traffic moves as a payload, the vehicle that carries it becomes ancillary (or connected) to the system, and it must be compatible with the channel. The wheels of train cars, for example, must be the same gauge (or width) as the tracks. One way to keep traffic out of a channel is to set standards that make the channel incompatible with or inhospitable to particular traffic or vehicles. Setting up incompatible standards will permit a network to exclude traffic from competitors or from other countries. Some rail interests tried to use their influence to ensure that roads were inhospitable (that is, very bumpy) to the automobile in order to suppress that new form of competition (Beasley 1988).

Transport

The network component that we have called transport should not be confused with transportation networks, even though both perform the function of moving things around. The network component of transport refers to the movement of anything from sender to receiver within any network. In some networks, this function has been unbundled from ownership of the channel so that firms other than the channel owner can provide it. For example, trucking companies move things on the network of roads but don't own or control the roadways.

Transport often involves several classes of service that are priced according to the priority assigned to the traffic. In a network operating near capacity, higher classes of traffic, such as first-class mail, will move more quickly than lower classes. First-class transport may also include a higher level of service, such as the extra services given to first-class airline passengers.

Terminals

The point where traffic enters or leaves the network is here called a terminal. Terminals are generally located at the network's nodes. Terminals may be used both to send and receive (as in airports or telephones) or for one or the other (as in broadcasting, where a transmitter is used to send a program to a TV set). Terminals may also temporarily store traffic while it is out of the network (as in oil depots and parking garages).

Like ancillaries, terminals must be compatible with the channel and sometimes with several channels. A grain terminal may need to be located on a waterway, a railroad, and a highway in order to schedule its traffic efficiently, so its facilities must accommodate barges, rail cars, and trucks. In this kind of situation the terminal becomes a hub where traffic is switched between several different networks.

In the communications sector the development of new terminals has become a critical factor in the development or convergence of new networks. As discussed in chapter 5, there is some debate about which terminal—the computer or the TV set—will ultimately bring digital information and entertainment into the home. Makers of set-top converter boxes hope to supply the means to make any terminal compatible with several channels.

Ancillaries

A network's parts are interdependent, and no network is independent of the world in which it operates. Building a network at any particular time and in any particular place depends on the existence of many things outside the network itself. Gas networks need gas, and they also need things that are ancillary to their business: the right regulatory and financial environment, potential customers who are not locked in to using another energy source, technical and managerial talent, and terminal equipment that customers find easy to use and economical to convert to. All networks have the following ancillaries:

- *Power sources.* Electricity for computer networks and gasoline stations near roads are examples.

- *Production inputs.* These are used for one or more functions, such as paper for mail, lightweight metal alloys for airplanes, and low-resistance wires for electric transmission.

- *Other networks to transport critical inputs.* An electric utility, for example, might depend on railroads to bring it coal or on a gas network to bring it natural gas that it will use to generate power. The same electric utility will need telecommunications networks to keep the system load even and report outages, the postal network to send bills to customers, and road systems for trucks to maintain the system.

Ancillaries must be available at a cost that keeps the network competitive with substitute products or services. A sharp rise in the price of paper would hurt the mail service and make it less competitive with substitute communication networks such as telecommunications. On the other hand, if the price of postal service were similarly to increase, the price of paper would go down because there would be lower demand. Thus, network managers and regulators are well advised to pay close attention to their network's ancillaries and to the ancillaries of competing networks. The need for control over ancillaries often leads to the vertical integration of networked industries, even to the point of acquiring a resource outside the scope of the network, such as when an electric company buys a coal mine.

NETWORK FUNCTIONS

Now that we have described the components of all networks, we can look at how they work together. This will give us the broader picture of networks that we need. Because all these components are connected, they must work together to keep the network operating. The cooperative functions of any network fall into three categories: scheduling, signaling, and security.

Scheduling

No network can move an unlimited amount of traffic at all times. Networks must allocate their limited capacity by scheduling how traffic moves in the network's channels. Scheduling includes routing (a determination of the most efficient route within the network), switching (transferring traffic from one part of a channel to another or from one channel to another), and capacity planning. Traffic may be stored temporarily as part of its scheduling.

The most efficient routing is often, but not always, the shortest path between two points. A longer route may be more desirable if the shorter one contains a potential bottleneck, such as insufficient capacity at a natural barrier (a bridge), a switch (a road interchange), or damage to the channel (a burst pipeline). Computer simulations have created new opportunities to model networks and to develop routing solutions to congestion problems.

An efficient switch moves incoming traffic to a new level of the network hierarchy in a minimum amount of time and with a minimum number of errors. This is a sorting function. The telecommunications switch directs calls from the level of one local line to the other local line or, for long-distance calls, the appropriate long-line service. A regional postal processing center takes mail from the many post offices of the region and routes it to the next level of sorting or to another local post office. Technology

has changed many switching operations, making them faster and more error-free, and changing the level at which those operations can take place, usually moving them higher in the network hierarchy (postal sorting, which used to be done by postal carriers, is now largely automated at certain hubs).

Networks also need good capacity planning in order to keep the system running efficiently. This means forecasting both peak and average traffic loads. Peak capacity planning involves predicting traffic at peak times and making sure that the channel can handle it. To handle heavy traffic the network will establish procedures that either add temporary capacity or that reschedule, store, or turn away any excess traffic. If traffic levels are allowed to exceed the network's capacity, all traffic in the system will slow down.

Peak capacity planning can be seen in the procedures of telephone companies and the traffic control systems on urban freeways. The telephone network assumes that demand will spike on holidays, when people call their families. When a certain capacity is reached, the system keeps all additional callers out in order to avoid using resources to find paths for all the calls because this would slow the entire system. Some cities keep automobile traffic off freeways with traffic lights at entrance ramps when a certain capacity is reached (rush hour) in order to keep the freeway network moving at an acceptable pace.

If keeping traffic out of the network at peak times is not acceptable, the network may need to increase its infrastructure (add fiber-optic lines, more highway lanes) to handle peak loads, leaving them underused during off-peak times. Another alternative would be to divert traffic to the channels of other networks at peak times (encouraging people to use alternative transportation or communication networks during peak traffic times). Increasing the amount of infrastructure may prove difficult if it must be done in large chunks (adding another power-generating station).

Sometimes traffic must be stored at a network hub if there is a difference in the amount of traffic coming in and going out. For example, if rail cars come into a rail hub faster than they can be sent out on trains, they will need to be stored while they wait their turn to go out. Higher capacity may reduce these storage costs, but it may be more expensive than occasional storage at peak periods (the cost of a new rail-switching yard may be higher than that of storing rail cars during a backlog).

Average capacity planning involves predicting how much traffic the network will carry, on average, in the future. This involves assumptions about new uses that consumers will find for the network and potential changes in usage patterns and demographics. This might require capacity planners to make assumptions about the usage patterns of a population with an average age that is getting higher. Do older people use as many communication, energy, and transportation services as young people? Technology can also affect average usage patterns. Many telephone switches were designed for three- to four-minute calls and may be ill equipped to handle the large amounts of "bursty" (coming in irregular bursts, not in a steady stream) data signals of Internet traffic.

Since the costs for building any new capacity must be added to the price of network services, the assumptions made in capacity planning can be critical and controversial. Capacity assumptions can be used to justify more investment in controversial power plants, airport facilities, and telephone switches. The costs of these investments are then passed on to customers for electricity, air travel, and telephony.

Pricing is an important tool in capacity planning because it can affect who uses the network, how much they use it, and when they use it. Many of the networks discussed here use or have used one or more of the following practices.

Peak and Off-Peak Pricing

This practice is especially powerful because it can be used to even out system loads and reduce the highest levels of peak demand by encouraging a shift to off-peak times in exchange for lower prices. Some peaks are predictable—they occur at certain times of the day, seasons of the year, or points in the business cycle—whereas others like abnormal weather conditions are not. Variable rates applied to unpredictable peaks can be unpopular because they mean that customers must assume the risk of higher prices at times that they can't predict and don't control.

Interruptible/Noninterruptible Pricing

These distinctions allow customers to make decisions about risks for unpredictable peaks and about their own willingness to forgo service during peaks, when prices can rise dramatically. So, for example, a business could choose to do without electric service—shut down its operation or switch to another energy source—when the charge per kilowatt-hour exceeds a certain amount. If no customers are willing to be interrupted, the network with a capacity shortage has the option of reducing service to everyone, which would mean a slowdown of the entire system. Electric customers experience such a service reduction as a "brown-out," and Internet users experience these service reductions as a slowing down of the rate at which data arrive at their computer.

Distance Pricing

The distance between senders and receivers or between hubs is usually a cost factor because the cost of distribution increases with each mile owing to the costs of rights-of-way or energy consumed, although these costs may still be lower than short-haul. This is politically sensitive in rural areas, where customers are farther from the network hubs. Rural residences and industries in small communities would pay more for their service.

Volume Discount Pricing

Heavy-traffic customers are often given volume discounts because they are less expensive to serve and are more likely to bypass the network by building their own infrastructure. Volume discounts also allow resellers (those competing for retail sales but who do not have their own local distribution infrastructure) to get lower wholesale rates by combining the demand of many low-traffic retail customers.

Long-Term Contracts

Long-term relationships with senders and receivers allow channels to plan for capacity needs and to make a sufficient investment in the network to develop strong cooperative ties. Such contracts become a negative factor when cooperation begins to look like collusion to defeat the interests of other parties peripheral to the transactions, such as suppliers or other customers.

Signaling

Signaling is the network's own internal communication function. It lets the parts of a network communicate with one another about scheduling traffic, including determining the traffic's final destination, sometimes called addressing. Signaling systems also alert the network about matters of safety or security. A train may be signaled to pull onto a side track in order to avoid a collision or to allow a train with a higher priority to go through on the main track. A freight train can signal the exact cars it carries by the markings on those cars. The contents of each car are known to the system so that the right goods get to the right terminal.

Unlike energy networks, where traffic is usually a commodity (nobody cares which gas molecules or electrons they get), in communication and transportation networks the traffic is specific and the particular parcels, people, or messages must get to a specific place. Specific traffic must include the address of the receiver. In many cases, the address or at least the identity of the sender is required to punish people who put dangerous or illegal traffic into the system.

Advances in communication technology and communication networks have improved the signaling capacity of other kinds of networks. This is important because the rate at which the network can signal will determine the upper limit of its speed. A disruption in or corruption of the system's signaling can bring the entire network to a halt. So access to signaling systems is subject to strict security.

The meaning assigned to the network's signals must be agreed upon in advance by all parts of the network. If the international air traffic control system uses English to communicate with planes, all airlines must agree in advance to use English and to employ English-speaking pilots. The switches that route calls must understand the signals used by all parts of a telecommunications network. All train employees must know how to interpret emergency signals.

Security

The security of a network is critical because the whole network can be slowed or stopped by many things, including the creation of a bottleneck or a signaling failure. Damage to part of the network, either directly or indirectly by putting a contaminant into the system, can cut off local service or require that traffic be rerouted. The capacity of the air transportation system could be brought to zero in a local area by jamming the radio frequencies (inserting noise into the channel) air traffic controllers use to guide planes. In wartime, the capacity of an enemy's transportation network is reduced by blowing up bridges or airport terminal facilities, creating bottlenecks that require extensive rerouting. Security procedures for all networks involve stopping unauthorized access to network facilities that might intentionally or unintentionally cause damage to the network or to traffic. Security measures are often heaviest at terminals where traffic enters and exits the network, such as airports. Governments are often asked to provide security for networks that operate within their territory, but this can be a problem when those networks are connected to terminals and networks outside their jurisdiction. Intergovernmental cooperation is necessary for the security of airports with international flights and for Internet services that can be accessed from many countries.

Security procedures are also undertaken by private or public organizations to avoid damage to or theft of the traffic or the vehicles while they are in the channel. This often requires cooperation between the channel and the terminal. For example, special systems ensure that air cargo is stored in secure terminal facilities and that passengers are asked if anyone unknown to them has given them anything to take with them that might be an explosive device. The meters on energy networks measure flow in order to detect thefts of traffic. If the levels of damage or theft are unacceptable, the senders and receivers may look to another network for delivery of their traffic.

Communication and transportation networks have an additional security concern: privacy. Airlines protect passengers who do not wish to draw attention to themselves or to have their identities revealed. Many communication networks are required by law not to disclose the identities of senders and receivers or the nature of their traffic in the system. For example, in some countries, cable TV systems cannot disclose which services their customers subscribe to or which movies they order. The Internet has created many new opportunities for the collection of information about senders and receivers, and a new level of interest in the concept of privacy in networks. This is complicated by uncertainty about whether senders, receivers, or the channel own the information constructed for the signaling function, for instance, street address, phone number, and e-mail address (Branscomb 1994). The privacy of senders, receivers, and traffic may sometimes be incompatible with the network's security functions.

COMMON NETWORK PROBLEMS

Networked industries share not only components and functions but also common problems (see table 3.2). Since each industry has evolved similar answers to these problems, we can assume that it is possible to build a tool that works on all of them.

Bottlenecks

Bottlenecks occur when one part of a network has lower capacity than the other parts. It may be a temporary problem caused by a natural disaster, for example. Or it may be an ongoing problem caused by a failure to build or maintain the same level of capacity in all parts of the system. Building a bridge big enough to handle all the flow at peak capacity may be too expensive, so when traffic comes to the bridge, it slows, even to the point of backing up and waiting in line for access, with priority in the line given to certain classes of traffic. If a flood washes out the bridge, traffic must be routed around it and its effective capacity drops to zero. Bottlenecks can also be caused by failures in the network's signaling, scheduling, or security systems. Scheduling or signaling problems may mean that a railroad bridge may be able to handle less traffic per hour than the rail lines that connect with it. Failure of all parts of a network to cooperate for equipment upgrades, including upgrades to ancillaries, such as recording devices for TVs, will also cause bottlenecks because traffic must be rerouted around incompatible equipment.

If bottlenecks become too costly, the network will need to find a way to build capacity at the bottlenecks. Building involves the investment by, or cooperation of, many parts of the network, and some parts may benefit more than others. Those who had to pay a premium to be at the front of the line will benefit the most. Working out the interests of all stakeholders can be a complex problem, and often government is called in to arbitrate. The introduction of competition into the network only increases the difficulty. Players who can use bottlenecks

(or their ability to get around them) as a competitive advantage have no incentive to cooperate.

The term *bottleneck* has also been used to describe the difficulty faced by new competitors for channel services. Often they can't build competing infrastructure, especially at the local level, and must utilize the incumbent channel's infrastructure. However, these issues are not, strictly speaking, bottlenecks because improving capacity, either by adding channel capacity or by improving signaling, scheduling, and security, does not address the real problem.

Access

When government does not own a network, it must often mandate access to privately owned network channels for various public purposes, including defense activities and relief from bottlenecks or scheduling problems in other networks. Mandated access for competitors is used also to ensure the maintenance or creation of competition in the network.

In countries where there is more than one railroad company, governments often mandate access to railroad channels. In the United States this is accomplished through Directed Service Orders, which are issued by the federal government. These orders require one line to accept the traffic of another in case of damage to a right-of-way owing to a natural disaster or an emergency that has snarled traffic. They have been used also when a line has become insolvent to assure continuity until new management takes over. A Directed Service Order can also require one line to use the cars or engines of other lines to keep traffic moving. U.S. cable TV networks must give broadcasters access to their networks under "must carry" provisions of the law. Congress apparently felt that access to the cable networks is necessary for anyone trying to reach television receivers. These lawmakers were apparently convinced that cable systems must carry the signals of local broadcasters (their competitors for advertising dollars and viewers) in order to ensure that consumers had many choices of senders.

The price charged for access to a company's infrastructure can be the most controversial part of these public policies, and government is usually forced to act as a referee in deciding on a price that is "fair" and not designed to keep competitors out of "essential facilities." Certain network facilities or functions are

TABLE 3.2 Problems Common to Networked Industries

Problem	Description	Examples
Bottleneck	Where traffic stacks because capacity is limited or temporarily blocked	An airport that is too small, a telephone switch with insufficient capacity, a damaged railroad bridge
Access	Physical: inability to connect; economic: inability to pay for connection or use	Physical: people in an area without phone service; economic: people unable to afford phone service
Small vs. Large Customers	Costs to haul many small units of traffic to many receivers are higher because there are fewer opportunities for economies of scale (marginal costs high) and more signals and scheduling are required.	Aggregated shipments of many small freight customers can be handled at lower cost. One large customer for electric service can be served at lower cost per kilowatt hour than many small ones.
Short vs. Long Haul	Cost of short haul is greater per mile because more signals and scheduling are needed than for long haul.	Delivering a package within a city is more expensive per mile than sending the same package between cities.

assumed to be so expensive to construct or operate that they act as barriers to the entry of new product or service providers. Discussions of essential facilities often ignore the existence of alternative channels in which the traffic in question could flow. For example, rail cargo can also move in highway and air transport channels. Video messages in cable channels can also move in broadcast, satellite, and broadband telephone channels. In many networks the only parts of the network that are too expensive to build and operate are those for short hauls (local delivery from hubs, such as the local loop of the telephone network) or small loads (those that go to small customers, such as residences or small businesses).

Small vs. Large Loads

Small loads of traffic are more expensive to handle per unit than large ones because they require more scheduling. A carload of books is cheaper to handle per book than a carton of books. Delivering 10,000 megawatts of electric power to one customer is cheaper than delivering the same amount to many small customers.

Theoretically, e-commerce on the Internet allows anyone to sell to anyone anywhere in the world. This kind of small commerce on a global scale would increase the traffic in transportation networks for small loads over long hauls for delivery to Internet customers and require a massive reorganization and growth in the capacity of transportation, postal, and parcel networks. Since small businesses would not have as much traffic as their larger competitors, they would undoubtedly pay more for the transportation of their goods.

Consolidators or forwarders put together, or aggregate, traffic to take advantage of the lower rates offered to large customers or for large loads. Traffic can be stored until the optimum amount is ready for transport or until capacity in the channel can be purchased at a reduced cost and resold at a profit, though often at a rate lower than that charged by the channel owner. This occurs in telecommunications, freight shipping, and passenger traffic for railroads and airlines.

Short vs. Long Haul

Most networks begin as a collection of disconnected short hauls that later connect with one another to form a larger system. The first railroads were built to connect a quarry or mine with a river or barge canal and only later to connect several cities. At first, interconnection was actively discouraged by the competing railroads, so passengers and freight that transferred to another railroad had to use local roads in order to move from one terminal to another. Similarly, the first telephone systems connected only local businesses and local residents. Gas was distributed first only locally, from the facilities where it was processed from coal. The value of being connected with a network rises with the number of people connected, so interconnection is important for wide adoption and in some cases has become an important competitive tool.

But the economics of short haul and long haul turn out to be quite different. Long-haul routes typically are cheaper per traffic mile to build, and they meet less local political resistance because they usually go through less populated areas. The costs of acquiring right-of-way for interstate highways and long-distance telephone lines usually are less than those to acquire right-of-way in metropolitan areas, where the price of real estate may be much higher. Long-haul routes are thought to have more or less constant returns to scale and can often maximize efficiency by scheduling traffic for higher capacity use (sending fewer but larger batches of traffic). In some cases, long hauls are more efficient per mile than short hauls because the cost of frequent starts and stops is high. For example, airplanes use more fuel on takeoff and landing than in flight, so frequent stops are more expensive than long flights. Many long-haul operators are less adversely affected than local or short-haul operators are by increases in their production costs or ancillary services.

Since short-haul routes have different economic realities than long-haul routes, they are often separately owned parts of a network. Many of them are owned by local companies or local branches of large companies that deliver local traffic and traffic coming in or going to locations outside their region. Short-haul routes require more costly, individualized scheduling and signaling, and are generally less efficient to operate and more expensive to build than long-haul routes. Some believe that these high costs may make short hauls a natural monopoly because no one would invest the money necessary to set them up without the assurance of the returns made possible by monopoly rents (the extra money that a monopoly can charge because customers have no other choices).

The impact of competition on the short-haul and long-haul levels of a network may be very different. This is especially true for economic development. If competition reduces long-haul rates to something near cost, then the price for service on heavy-traffic lines may well go down, and activity sensitive to this change in price may concentrate at points where a competitor can get access to those high-traffic routes. That concentration would then affect the economics of switching and other bottlenecks on those routes, further lowering the cost of service at certain locations. These cost considerations have a profound impact on business location patterns.

REGULATING NETWORKS

Networks have been regulated by governments in three ways, as common roads, common carriers, or private carriers. Common roads are channels that accommodate traffic of many sizes and shapes, and the owner of the channel does not control the vehicles that carry traffic through the network. Common roads are generally but not necessarily owned by government, which may charge when traffic is put into the network (toll roads) and for the use of bottleneck facilities (bridges, canal locks). These charges enable the channel owner to recover the costs of building and maintaining the channel and to control capacity. Common roads are not responsible for the safety of traffic in the system, except insofar as they keep the channel free from obvious hazards. Senders choose their routes within the common road network. Highways and canals are often regulated as common roads, as are public-access channels on local cable TV networks. Digitization of information may make it possible for more communication channels to become common roads.

Common carriers carry the traffic brought to them over a channel that they utilize or control. They are required to take all traffic that meets certain requirements and pays the appropriate fee. In some countries the trucking industry, railroads, telephone service, and leased-access channels in local cable systems all have been treated as common carriers. They control all aspects of the traffic flow in the channel—routing, switching, transport, and occasionally terminals. They do not own the traffic while it is in the channel, and they are not responsible for damage the traffic may cause to others. So, for example, telephone companies are not responsible for any violations of copyright laws that may be committed by their customers. Common carriers are generally responsible for the safety of the traffic while it is in their channel—they see that it is not stolen or damaged in transit. Common carriers have sometimes been given a monopoly to serve a part of a network in order to recover risky up-front investments. Most of them were at one time owned by government or heavily regulated as to their level of service, duty to accept all traffic brought to them, and the rates they charge.

Private carriers own or control the channel and often own the traffic they carry through it. Private carriers control all aspects of their network, although they may use part of government-owned or government-regulated channels, such as common roads or common carriers. They choose which traffic they will carry, and their rates are not regulated. Private carriers exist for natural gas, certain telecommunications services (including corporate networks), and package delivery (DHL, United Parcel Service).

EFFECTS OF INTRODUCING COMPETITION

During the twentieth century, communication, transportation, and energy networks saw new technologies make possible the invasion of their territories by other networks that offered a substitute for the original service. For example, the Internet competes for text communication with the postal services. This is internetwork competition. Networks were also invaded by similar companies from other territories. For example, phone companies invaded the markets of other telephone companies in search of new customers after the government implemented policies for liberalization and privatization. This is intranetwork competition. Internetwork and intranetwork competitors from other countries also appeared in networked industries with the advent of new rules for free trade, such as the General Agreement on Tariffs and Trade (GATT).

Intranetwork competition generally occurs when two or more firms try to sell the same services (air transport, access to a telecommunications channel, electric generation) to the same customers. As discussed in chapter 4, intense intraindustry competition results in a weeding out of the weakest players. In the late 1990s there was an explosion of competitive access providers for telephone and Internet services, but only a few were expected to survive the inevitable cut-throat price competition.

Internetwork competition occurs when one network seeks the customers of another network by offering a substitute service, for example, where airlines try to take traffic away from railroads or satellite services try to take customers away from cable networks.

Competition may result in the displacement of one network by another, because introducing a new competitor may not widen the market for the service and there may not be enough demand to keep both networks in business. For example there is almost certainly a limit on the amount of time that people will spend on communication and entertainment. If households spend no more than a certain percentage of their income or time on a particular activity (transportation, energy, information, communication), then that percentage is a limited resource for which all providers of the service and substitute services must compete. Services sold by a new competitor will decrease the services that can be sold by incumbents. Thus, introducing competition does not guarantee that all the players will stay in the field to compete in a way that will benefit consumers. A number of individual businesses or industries will almost certainly fail. But old networks do not die inevitably or immediately. They may instead abandon some of their markets to new entrants, conceding the battle for traffic of higher value (passengers, information) or lower cost (long haul) in order to concentrate on commodities that are more cost-sensitive (mineral ores, grains) and other traffic that is less time-sensitive (entertainment).

The introduction of competition has had many of the same effects on all networked industries. Where once there was a system of impermeable local monopolies, usually protected from invasion by government, that cooperated to form a larger system (The Network), there are now several large competing networks, often engaged in providing many more services.

When competition was introduced, companies often cooperated with each other in an attempt to grow by capturing more of each customer's business. This led to interindustry cooperation (vertical integration of related businesses) and intraindustry cooperation (horizontal integration of similar companies) to build large, highly integrated networks with lower costs. Existing networks that were challenged by new networks often tried to retain some of their business by becoming feeders to the new networks, creating a larger, bimodal system. Rail cars became compatible with trucks to facilitate moving traffic in both networks. Some believe that television and radio stations may become feeders to the Internet.

Other factors in internetwork competition include the range of the services offered (how many possible connections can be made) and the quality (how dependable is delivery and what shape will the traffic be in when it arrives). These factors and the availability of substitute services all affect the success of the network. The consumers' final choice of a particular network will reflect a complex mixture of these factors.

Introducing Competition Is Not Deregulation

Although political debates often call the introduction of competition into networked industries deregulation, the relative level of regulation does not always go down. Instead, the regulation shifts focus. Networked industries are still regarded as critical to industrial economies, and no one, including new competitors, really trusts the marketplace to deliver a system that will please all stakeholders. Competition seems to mandate new regulations to establish rules of fair play, either through specific rules in each sector or by application of a country's general competition laws.

As long as individual companies saw themselves as part of The Network, they cooperated to achieve efficiency by moving one another's traffic and by jointly administering scheduling, terminals, and security measures. Given that providers no longer cooperate, some other form of coordination becomes necessary. Usually, the coordination of things like scheduling, terminals, and security is done by government or voluntary private-sector coordinating bodies set up for this purpose.

Competition often brings both the expected reductions in consumer prices, although large customers and long-haul customers benefit far more than small ones. Competition also spurs the deployment of new technologies. But it can also bring unexpected problems.

With the introduction of competition, beginning in the 1970s for airlines, the networks for air transportation, energy, and telecommunications each fragmented into competing hub systems that offered full service in the attempt to keep their customers away from other players. In air transportation, hubbing meant several plane changes for travel between two points at the outskirts of two systems, often with flights many miles out of the way to reach connecting hubs.

While competition brought down the price of airline tickets to major hubs, which have high traffic and lower costs per passenger, the price of tickets to small cities, which have low traffic and higher costs per passenger, went up, and service was either curtailed or turned over to smaller carriers. This new pricing pattern seemed to come as a surprise to regulators, but given what we now know about the economics of long and short haul, it was absolutely predictable. By the end of the twentieth century, similar scheduling and pricing patterns were developing in telecommunications, where large companies began spinning off rural services, which have low traffic and short haul. At the same time, these companies sought to bundle all the communications services that large customers in urban areas would need (local, long-distance, wireless, cable, Internet access), thus making them high-traffic customers. Internet portals seeking high traffic put together connections to other sites and became known as hubs.

Tough competition for these high-traffic, high-profit customers means that the players must develop economies of scope and scale that allow them to keep their prices low in order to increase and hold their market share. So perhaps the wave of mergers and acquisitions that hits networks after competition is introduced occurs is predictable. Introducing competition into the system causes players to do things that may earn them the perceived competitive advantage of being the biggest kid on the block. And many of them were already pretty big kids.

Effects of Competition on Rates and Service

In networks that do not allow competition (those in which government establishes territories and keeps out competitors), rates are heavily regulated to keep the monopoly service provider from receiving monopoly rents and to ensure customers "fair" prices. Political considerations might require that all customers in the network be charged roughly the same price, or they might dictate that large users of the service pay less per unit of service. Political considerations can also come into play when networks cover large areas and serve all customers in those areas. The economic problems of short haul and small loads must be compensated for by spreading the costs for serving these less profitable or unprofitable customers over all the customers in the entire network. Low-cost customers (urban, industrial) can end up paying far than more than the cost of their service in order to subsidize high-cost customers (rural, residential). Interestingly, consumers often prefer flat rates—unlimited access to the network for a set rate per month—even though these rates mean that statistically half the usage, although not necessarily half the users, carries more than its share of the costs. People seem to feel they are getting a better deal by having unlimited access to capacity. But this deal may have a down side and may be related to what is known in economics as the tragedy of the commons. When use of a scarce resource is not related to the price (people can use as much as they want for one price), the demand for that resource quickly outstrips the capacity of the system to deliver it. This is particularly true if demand is concentrated at certain times of the day or year.

A system of regulated monopolies requires regulators to approximate costs for operating the network and to oversee the allocation of those costs to various classes of customers at two levels: wholesale (sale to those who will resell it to retail customers) and retail (sale to the ultimate consumers of the service). Allocation is necessary to favor politically important customers, perhaps residential customers or large industries that are important to the local economy. Regulation of cost allocations is also necessary to avoid internal subsidies not approved by regulators. A vertically integrated monopoly provider could allocate more of its costs to one class of service, making it less profitable, at least on paper, in order to lower the allocated costs for another service, thus allowing the provider to become more price-competitive in that service. This can also be a problem where the provider's own subsidiary is one of its biggest customers. A gas company could thus give lower rates to electric utilities in order to favor its subsidiary electric company.

Even when competition is introduced into a network, the need to supervise rates does not seem to disappear entirely. Regulation is often considered necessary, at least during a transition period, in order to protect retail customers and keep the competitive playing field fair for new entrants. Regulation of cost allocations becomes particularly controversial during such a transition, because regulators need to make sure that rates do not increase dramatically for those previously subsidized, which might prove uncomfortable for some incumbent providers and elected officials. The political power for subsidies for rural areas has faded to some extent, however, as voters increasingly move to urban areas.

The introduction of competition into networks has seldom resulted in building redundant channel infrastructure for short-haul or local traffic, and few envision two telephone or cable lines going by each house except in densely populated urban areas. Instead, competition at the local level usually takes place in the provision of local services using existing infrastructure that belongs to the incumbent provider of local service. Competition for local services requires the owners of the local channel infrastructure to provide their new competitors with access to their infrastructure. Regulators continue reviewing the incumbent's cost allocations because they may need to make sure that the local infrastructure owner does not charge competitors, who are also the incumbent's wholesale customers, more than their share of the costs for operating the channel. To do so would mean that the incumbent operator could charge its own retail customers lower prices than the new competitors, and this would soon put the competition out of business.

Regulators hope that the new competitors in the networks will compete both on price and service, but telecommunications, transportation, and energy services are essentially commodities, and the real competition tends to be on price. Reducing prices in order to compete means cutting costs, which sometimes results in a lower quality of service. Dependability suffers, for example, when backup systems become too costly, as does the maintenance of facilities to handle unexpectedly high traffic loads. By breaking up the network to encourage competition, the resources that once paid for upgrades and maintenance are often lost. Instead, the local infrastructure owner will be tempted to use those resources to reduce retail prices in search of market share. The quality of service has not gone up in railroad, airline, telecommunications, or electric services after the introduction of competition. What is rising in each of these networks is the level of customers' complaints about poor service, confusing price options, and even fraud.

SUMMARY

Strategists in networked industries will do well to take into account the many similarities that we have identified in the development and operation of transportation, communication, and energy networks. While no two networks operate in exactly the same way, when their experiences show a repeating pattern we need to pay attention. Our broader view of networks has identified repeating patterns that will be immediately relevant for business planning and policymaking. Perhaps the most important are those that surface with the introduction or reintroduction of intraindustry or interindustry competition into a networked industry. Starting with the "deregulated" airlines, newly competitive networks, including the Internet, underwent the following experiences:

- New entrants who successfully aggregated demand for long hauls and large loads were later mostly absorbed by incumbents or went out of business owing to economies of scale and scope enjoyed by incumbents.

- A vast wave of mergers and acquisitions occurred as players attempted to develop further economies of scope and scale.

- Foreign direct investment increased as players looked for resources to upgrade infrastructure in order to fend off competition.

- There was less cooperation among parts of the network, which resulted in problems of scheduling and security.

- Separate networks (hub-and-spoke configurations) developed by each competing network to keep customers out of competing networks.

- "Feeders" developed from existing networks or from short-haul and low-traffic hubs.

- Prices decreased in price-elastic segments of the market and price increased in inelastic segments.

- More competition and lower consumer prices came about for long-haul routes and high-density areas in the network, but less competition and higher consumer prices and investment existed in short-haul and low-density portions.

- Quality or dependability of service decreased.

This pattern may not appear in all networks, but the possibility cannot be ignored. For builders of the newest networks, such as computers, these experiences are worth noting, particularly in such areas as interconnection, capacity planning, cooperation for security, and the impact of ancillaries.

Network Effects
and Interconnection

Jonathan E. Nuechterlein and Philip J. Weiser

Flash back about 100 years to the infancy of the U.S. telephone industry. Different telephone companies often refused to interconnect with one another, and each had its own set of subscribers. Few consumers, of course, wanted to buy several telephones—and pay subscription charges to several telephone companies—simply to make sure they could reach anyone else they wished to call. Unfortunately, this was the choice many consumers faced in the early 1900s.

Such arrangements are quite wasteful in that they misallocate society's scarce resources away from their most productive uses. To be sure, the prospect of extra profits from the successful deployment of a closed (non-interconnected) telephone network may well have encouraged some entrepreneurs to build a better product and reach customers more quickly than they otherwise would.[1] Apart from those incentive effects, however, consumers typically received little added value from multiple subscriptions that they would not have received from one subscription to a single carrier if the various networks were interconnected and exchanged traffic at reasonable rates. For the most part, consumers simply paid more money for the same thing, which meant that they had less money to spend on purchasing things of value in other markets.

In the absence of any interconnection obligation, virtually every telephone market in early twentieth century America reached a "tipping point," in which the largest network—the one with the greatest number of subscribers—became perceived as the single network that everyone had to join, and the rest withered away. The potential for certain industries to slide into monopoly in this manner illustrates an economic phenomenon known as *network effects*. In many markets, individual consumers care very little how many *other* consumers purchase the same products that they buy. For example, the bottle of shampoo you just bought does not become significantly more or less valuable to you as the number of other purchasers of the brand increases or falls. The telecommunications industry, like several other "network industries," is different: the value of the network to *each* user increases or decreases, respectively, with every addition or subtraction of *other* users to the network.

Suppose, for example, that you lived in a midwestern American city in 1900, and there were two non-interconnecting telephone companies offering you service. You would be much more inclined (all else being equal) to select the company operating 80% of the lines rather than the one operating 20% because the odds would be much greater that the people you wished to call would be on the larger network. The absence of interconnection arrangements among rival networks thus creates a cut-throat race to build the largest customer base in the shortest time frame—and then put all rivals out of business by pointing out the dwindling value of their shrinking networks. Economies of scale—a carrier's ability to reduce its per-customer costs by increasing its total number of customers—further accelerates this process by permitting larger carriers to undersell smaller ones in the market.

By the early twentieth century, the U.S. telephone market had "tipped." In most population centers, the victor was the mammoth Bell System: a collection of very large "operating companies" that provided local exchange services and were eventually bound together by a long distance network known as Long Lines. All of the far-flung operations of the Bell System were owned by American Telephone & Telegraph (AT&T), which maintained its own equipment manufacturing arm (Western Electric) and also, for a time, held the rights to patented technologies developed by the Bell System's creator and namesake.

In the areas AT&T did not control, which typically were the less populous ones, the so-called "independent" local telephone companies vied for market share. In many cases, AT&T sought to coerce these independent companies into joining the Bell System by refusing to interconnect them to AT&T Long Lines, which was then the only long distance network in the United States. The independent companies were in no position to build a rival long distance network. Even if they could have cooperated to construct the needed transcontinental facilities (and done so without infringing any remaining AT&T patents), they still could not have used that shared network to send calls through to the increasing majority of Americans who were served by local exchanges owned by the non-interconnecting Bell System. As a result, without interconnection rights, these independent companies could not provide their customers with satisfactory telephone service—i.e., service extending beyond the local serving area—unless they could somehow duplicate the nationwide physical infrastructure the Bell System had built up over several decades of sharp dealing and self-reinforcing good fortune. That was an economic impossibility.

AT&T's coercion of the independent companies ultimately aroused the attention of the Justice Department's antitrust authorities. In the Kingsbury Commitment of 1913, AT&T resolved the dispute by agreeing to interconnect its Long Lines division with these independent local companies and to curb its practice of buying up independent rivals.[2] In exchange, the government placed its effective imprimatur on AT&T's monopoly control over all U.S. telecommunications markets in which it was already dominant. This incident is noteworthy not just because it illustrates the monopolistic tendencies of an unregulated telephone industry, but also because it provides an instructive contrast to the anticompetitive conduct that ultimately led to the breakup of the Bell System 70 years later into its local and long distance components. In 1913, AT&T used its control of the *long distance* market to suppress other *local* carriers. As explained below, AT&T would later leverage its control of most *local* markets to suppress the *long distance* competition that technological advances had made possible by the 1960s.

The network effects phenomenon presents different competitive questions in different industries, and reasonable people can disagree about when the government should require a firm to share access to its customer base. But when such intervention is deemed necessary, the usual solution is an interconnection requirement. Suppose you own a telephone network and one of your subscribers wants to place a call to someone who subscribes to Provider X's network. If Provider X's network is larger than yours, it may have the incentives just described to refuse to interconnect, in which event your subscriber learns that the call has failed—and considers defecting to Provider X. But if the government forces Provider X to take the call onto its network and route it to the intended recipient, your customer remains satisfied, and you stay in business. Interconnection obligations work the other way as well: Provider X cannot preclude its subscribers from reaching yours.

If dealing with network effects were as simple as decreeing that all competing carriers "must interconnect," telecommunications regulation would not be so complex. But many critical details need to be worked out to ensure that two networks cooperate efficiently. For example, when you, the owner of the smaller network, hand off calls for completion by the larger network, how much—if anything—should that larger network be able to charge you for this task? That may seem like a simple question, but it is theoretically quite complex, and answering it incorrectly can have debilitating consequences, as chapter 9 explains.

The physical details of interconnection arrangements can also raise a number of thorny issues. There are many subtle ways in which a larger network operator can disadvantage a smaller one through shoddy interconnection arrangements, such as providing only limited capacity within its interconnection facilities for the receipt of calls from you, the smaller carrier. Your subscribers might then receive an "all circuits busy" signal when they try to call the larger carrier's subscribers during peak calling periods—leaving them, once more, dissatisfied and tempted by the prospect of defection. To prevent such problems, regulators often need to develop rules to govern the operational details of interconnection arrangements and penalize non-compliance.

Although we have focused so far on the telephone industry, network effects are endemic to information technology industries generally, and there are ongoing debates about when, if ever, the government should step in to address any anticompetitive consequences. Consider the market for instant messaging. The key to instant messaging technology is a centralized database, known as a "names and presence directory," which allows a service provider to tell its subscribers when their designated "buddies" have logged on to the same provider's network and are available for a kind of e-mail exchange in real time. So long as each such directory is proprietary to a particular firm and unshared with others, subscribers are likely to value an instant messaging service in direct proportion to the number of their "buddies" who are also subscribers to the same service. This dynamic tends to favor the service provider with the largest customer base, which, in the United States, has traditionally been America Online (AOL).

When it approved AOL's merger with Time Warner in 2001, the FCC expressed concern that the instant messaging market was tipping and that AOL's instant messaging systems—and particularly, in the U.S., "AOL Instant Messenger"—had accumulated such a large subscriber base that users of instant messaging would feel compelled to choose AOL as their provider. The FCC was particularly alarmed that AOL had dragged its feet in designing an interconnection mechanism that would enable the subscribers of other services to make use of AOL's proprietary names and presence directory and communicate with AOL's subscribers as freely as with each other. Some people cited AOL's reluctance to interconnect as conclusive evidence that the company itself perceived the instant messaging market as likely to tip and produce a lucrative AOL monopoly. As the FCC's then-chief economist later explained: "If it is a more competitive market, the incentive is for all the players to interoperate. There is a mathematical proof on that one."[3]

In the end, the FCC stopped short of ordering AOL to interconnect with its rivals for the generation of instant messaging services that had become familiar to many American consumers. Controversially, however, the FCC did impose an "interoperability" condition for any "advanced," video-oriented applications of instant messaging using high speed Internet services.[4] Instant messaging programs, the FCC reasoned, can be modified to serve as "information platforms" for all sorts of communications applications, including video conferencing; indeed, some people believed that instant messaging would gradually supplant the telephone as the dominant means of person-to-person communication. The FCC feared that, unrestrained by interconnection obligations, AOL's proprietary systems would become *de facto* standards and would become indispensable to residential and business users over time. The FCC thus worried that AOL would end up monopolizing portions of the telecommunications market much as AT&T's Bell System had done almost one hundred years before and would raise consumer prices dramatically once it had succeeded. As AOL's share of instant messaging users steadily declined in the early 2000s, these concerns began to seem overblown and the FCC lifted the interoperability requirement.[5] But such concerns reveal the unusual sensitivity of regulators to the monopolization threat posed by network effects in the communications industry.

One of AOL's fiercest opponents in the instant messaging debate was Microsoft, which offered its own proprietary brand ("MSN Messenger") and had repeatedly tried and failed to interconnect with AOL's instant messaging network. There was no small irony here, for Microsoft was simultaneously defending itself in court against the Justice Department's claims that, in subtly similar ways, it had abused its dominance in the market for personal computer operating systems.

The dominance of Microsoft Windows in today's personal computer market arises from network effects and, specifically, from what antitrust courts have called the *applications barrier to entry*.[6] At some point in the 1980s, software designers realized that more users were choosing Microsoft's operating systems than the alternatives, a choice cemented by Microsoft's eventual development of the Windows "graphical user interface." In response, more and more applications developers created programs only for Windows, leaving would-be rivals (like IBM) to sell operating systems that did not have as many programs designed for them and were therefore less popular. As a result, Microsoft won an increasing share of the operating system market. That, in turn, reinforced the software designers' predictions about the dominance of Windows and their desire to produce applications for it, often to the exclusion of applications for rival operating systems.[7]

In these and other contexts, reasonable people can disagree about whether network effects create any problems for which the government should offer a solution. The proponents of government intervention argue that monopolization is virtually always an evil to be avoided, reasoning that monopolization of any industry necessarily produces higher consumer prices, less product variety, and lower quality. Opponents of government intervention, by contrast, point to a theory of competition, first developed by economist Joseph Schumpeter, that focuses on the "creative destruction" of old incumbents by new insurgents, who are rewarded with monopolies of their own until knocked off their perch by the next round of insurgents.[8] Under this theory, the most significant competition takes place not *within* a market—in the form of price wars or incremental increases in quality—but *for the market itself*: i.e., in establishing the next great invention that will displace the old monopoly with a new one.[9]

The first key premise of the modern-day Schumpeterian perspective is that, in high-tech industries, the next industry-transforming technology could arise at any moment to eclipse the products of today's monopolists.[10] This threat is said to give current monopolists powerful incentives to keep their products as efficient and consumer-friendly as possible. The second key Schumpeterian premise is that the best way to induce entrepreneurs to risk enormous sums in developing revolutionary technologies is to welcome the prospect of a temporary monopoly when those technologies succeed. Because they view temporary monopolies favorably, modern-day Schumpeterians argue for strong intellectual property protection and freedom from both competition-oriented regulation and aggressive antitrust enforcement.[11] As Richard Posner has put it: "The gale of creative destruction that Schumpeter described, in which a sequence of temporary monopolies operates to maximize innovation that confers social benefits far in excess of the social costs of the short-lived monopoly prices that the process also gives rise to, may be the reality of the new economy."[12]

Although network effects can dramatically influence the course of competition in information industries, the arguments for and against government intervention to counteract that influence are subtle and specific to each individual market. Nonetheless, today there is broad consensus that the government should impose interconnection obligations on ordinary telephone networks. One reason for this is that the telephone market, with its high fixed costs, is characterized not just by network effects, but also by enormous *economies of scale and density* (which we discuss below). Without interconnection rights, a new provider could not offer its customers effective telephone service—i.e., service capable of reaching all the people those customers wish to call—unless the provider first builds a new, ubiquitous physical network whose geographic scope rivals that of the dominant network, and then finds some way of underwriting that network without passing on its unusually high per-customer costs to its initially small customer base. To articulate this challenge is to reveal the economic near-impossibility of meeting it.

NOTES

1. One renowned study of these early years concludes that, before AT&T's Bell System cemented its lock on most major markets, the competition for market dominance prompted rival telephone

companies to build out infrastructure throughout population centers as quickly as possible, with quite significant consumer benefits. See Milton Mueller, Universal Service: Competition, Interconnection, and Monopoly in the Making of the American Telephone System (AEI Press, 1997). That may well be so, but there is broad consensus that, left to its own devices, such competition was bound in the end to produce a single dominant provider in any given market.

2. See generally Gerald W. Brock, Telecommunication Policy for the Information Age 65–66 (Harv. Univ. Press, 1994).

3. David D. Kirkpatrick, *As Instant Messaging Comes of Age, AOL Says F.C.C. Rule Holds It Back*, N.Y. Times, May 26, 2003, at C1 (quoting Wharton professor Gerald Faulhaber).

4. Memorandum Opinion and Order, *Applications for Consent to the Transfer of Control of Licenses and Section 214 Authorizations by Time Warner Inc. and America Online, Inc., Transferors, to AOL Time Warner Inc., Transferee*, 16 FCC Rcd 6547, ¶¶ 191–200 (2001). For a critical evaluation of the decision, see Philip J. Weiser, *Internet Governance, Standard Setting, and Self-Regulation*, 28 N. Ky. L. Rev. 822, 844 (2001).

5. Memorandum Opinion and Order, *Time Warner Inc.*, 18 FCC Rcd 16,835 (2003) (lifting condition). The major IM providers have reportedly made progress on a negotiated solution to interoperability. See Jim Hu & David Becker, *IM Giants Drop Some Barriers to Peace*, cnetnews.com (July 15, 2004) (http://news.com./2100-1032_3-5270067.html) (reporting on settlement of issue).

6. *See* United States v. Microsoft Corp., 84 F. Supp. 2d 9, 18–23 (D.D.C. 1999), *aff'd in relevant part*, 253 F.3d 34, 55–56 (D.C. Cir 2001).

7. An analogous dynamic explains the victory of the VHS standard over Betamax in the market for video cassette recorders (VCRs). After a period of direct competition, the market tipped to VHS. At first glance, one might think that a Betamax user should have been indifferent to the choice of most other viewers to buy VHS recorders, so long as her own Betamax recorder continued to work. The problem was that her Betamax recorder was valuable to her largely to the extent that she could go to the store and rent videos to play in it. Once it became clear that the market was tipping, fewer firms manufactured Betamax videos and fewer retail outlets reserved shelf space for them. This process fed on itself, and users began switching in droves to VHS, which became the established standard in part because of these indirect network effects. For a classic exposition of such network effects phenomena throughout the economy, see Carl Shapiro & Hal Varian, Information Rules: A Strategic Guide to the Network Economy 173–225 (Harv. Bus. School Press, 1998).

8. Joseph A. Schumpeter, Capitalism, Socialism, and Democracy 81–90 (Harper & Bros., 2d ed. 1947). For a discussion of the Schumpeterian perspective, see Philip J. Weiser, *The Internet, Innovation, and Intellectual Property Policy*, 103 Colum. L. Rev. 534, 576–583 (2003).

9. *See* Howard A. Shelanski & J. Gregory Sidak, *Antitrust Divestiture in Network Industries*, 68 U. Chi. L. Rev. 1, 10–11 (2001).

10. *See* Clayton M. Christensen, The Innovator's Dilemma (Harv. Bus. School Press, 1997) (discussing related concept of "disruptive technology").

11. *See*, e.g., Richard Schmalensee, *Antitrust Issues in Schumpeterian Industries*, 90 Am. Econ Rev. 192, 194 (2000).

12. Richard A. Posner, *Antitrust in the New Economy*, 68 Antitrust L.J. 925, 930 (2001).

UNIT 5

The State or an Independent Regulator? Types of Regulators

Once the basic principles have been comprehended, and the basic structure has been described, we move on to understand what are the institutions that govern communications policy and regulate the industry. Communications scholars Kimberly Zarkin and Michael Zarkin provide us with an overview of the Federal Communications Commission, its history, authority, organization and procedures.

The Federal Communications Commission

Front Line in the Culture and Regulation Wars

Kimberly A. Zarkin and Michael J. Zarkin

THE FCC'S STATUTORY AUTHORITY

The FCC's regulatory authority over the communications industry today is drawn from a variety of statutes. While the Communications Act of 1934 (P.L. 73-416) still provides the basic framework for federal communications regulation, it has been amended over the years, with the most recent and important additions provided by the Cable Acts of 1984 and 1992, and the Telecommunications Act of 1996. The Telecom Act, discussed at greater length in subsequent chapters, generally directed the FCC to move further in the direction of competition in virtually all areas of the communications industry. The following is a summary of the major provisions of the Communications Act as amended.

Title I: General Provisions

Title I, section 1 of the Communications Act begins by stating the purposes of the law, which include:

> [R]egulating interstate and foreign commerce in communication by wire and radio so as to make available, so far as possible, to all the people of the United States, without discrimination on the basis of race, color, religion, national origin, or sex, a rapid, efficient, nationwide and world-wide wire and radio communication service with adequate facilities at reasonable charges, for the purpose of the national defense, for the purpose of promoting safety of life and property through the use of wire and radio communication, and for the purpose of securing a more effective execution of this policy by centralizing authority heretofore granted by law to several agencies and by granting additional authority with respect to interstate and foreign commerce to wire and radio communication, there is hereby created a commission to be known as the "Federal Communications Commission," which shall be constituted as hereinafter provided, and which shall execute and enforce the provisions of this Act.

Following the purposes stated in section 1:

- Section 2 provides for the general geographical jurisdiction of the FCC.
- Section 3 provides definitions for important statutory terms.
- Section 4 contains provisions relating to the Commission, including the number of commissioners and the qualifications and compensation for commissioners.

- Section 5 deals with the organization of the Commission. This section specifies the duties of the chairman of the FCC and mandates that the agency staff be organized around a series of bureaus structured around the Commission's "principal work load operations." This section also details the procedures for judicial review of a Commission action.

- Section 6 deals with the authorization of appropriations to the Commission.

- Section 7 states that "[i]t shall be the policy of the United States to encourage the provision of new technologies and services to the public" and authorizes the Commission to determine whether any new proposed technology or service is in the public interest.

- Section 8 sets application fees for those seeking spectrum licenses and authorizes the Commission to adjust them from time to time in response to inflation.

- Section 9 sets regulatory fees for the recovery of costs incurred by the Commission in the conduct of its enforcement, policy and rulemaking, and other regulatory activities. The Commission is authorized to adjust the schedule of fees from time to time.

- Section 10, added by the passage of the Telecommunications Act of 1996, is intended to reinforce the general policy of encouraging competition in the communications industry. It specifies that the Commission "shall forebear from applying any regulation or any provision of this Act" if it determines that it is not necessary to ensure that the charges and practices of telecommunications carriers are just and reasonable, protect consumers, or otherwise serve the public interest. The Commission is also generally required to consider the impact of new regulations on competition.

- Section 11 requires the Commission to conduct a biennial review of each of its regulations to determine whether or not they continue to serve the public interest.

Title II: Common Carriers

Title II of the Communications Act as amended by the Telecommunications Act of 1996 is generally divided up into three parts: common carrier regulation (sections 101–231), provisions pertaining to competition (sections 251–261), and provisions pertaining to the Bell Operating Companies (sections 271–276). Key portions of title II, particularly those added by the Telecommunications Act, are discussed in more detail in Chapter 4.

- Section 201 deals with common carrier services and charges. All common carriers engaged in interstate or foreign communication must provide their services upon reasonable request in accordance with rules established by the Commission. This section also authorizes the Commission to determine whether the "charges, practices, classifications, or regulations for and in connection with such communications services" are just and reasonable.

- Section 202 outlaws any unjust or unreasonable discrimination in "charges, practices, classifications, regulations, facilities, or services for or in connection with" common carrier offerings. The Commission is authorized to collect fines for the violation of this provision.

- Section 203 requires common carriers to file with the Commission and make available to the public a schedule of the rates and charges for its services. This section also requires carriers to file changes in their rate schedules, service offerings, and policies 120 days before they go into effect.

- Section 204 authorizes the FCC to call a hearing on proposed new rate schedules or services to determine their lawfulness. With the passage of the Telecommunications Act of 1996, the FCC now has only seven days to review a rate reduction and fifteen days to review a rate increase if it intends to call a hearing.

- Section 205 authorizes the Commission to prescribe "just and reasonable" rates for common carriers following an appropriate hearing and investigation.

- Section 206 states the liability of carriers for monetary injuries caused by unlawful actions. Section 207 allows for the recovery of damages through a complaint to the Commission.

- Section 208 outlines the process by which individuals and governments can file complaints against common carriers with the FCC. Legally, the Commission is required to investigate complaints and issue an order in the matter within five months. Section 209 states that the Commission may issue an order directing a carrier to pay damages to the complainant if indicated by the investigation.

- Section 210 states that carriers are free to exchange franks and passes for use by their officers, agents, employees, and their families. This section also allows common carriers to provide free service to the government for purposes relating to national defense.

- Section 211 requires carriers subject to the Act to file copies of all contracts, agreements, or arrangements with other carriers with the Commission.

- Section 212 prohibits individuals from serving as an officer or director of more than one carrier subject to the Act under most circumstances.

- Section 213 authorizes the Commission to conduct valuations of carrier property and to require carriers to file inventories of all owned property and its original cost.

- Section 214 deals with the extension of new common carrier lines. No carrier may build a new interstate line or extend a line without first obtaining a certificate of "public convenience and necessity" from the Commission. Amendments to this section by the Telecom Act authorize state public utility commissions to designate "eligible telecommunications carriers" for the extension of lines to unserved rural areas. These carriers are eligible to receive "universal service" support under section 254(c) of the Act and may be ordered to extend lines to unserved areas if the state commission deems it to be in the public interest.

- Section 215 authorizes the Commission to investigate financial transactions made by carriers that might impact rates.

- Section 216 states that the provisions of the Act apply to all receivers and operating trustees of carriers to the same extent that they apply to the carriers themselves.

- Section 217 states that carriers are liable for the actions of their agents and employees.

- Section 218 authorizes the Commission to inquire into the management activities of any carrier subject to the Act.

- Section 219 authorizes the Commission to require all carriers subject to the Act to submit annual reports providing information about their personnel and finances.

- Section 220 authorizes the Commission to prescribe methods of accounting and record keeping for carriers subject to the Act. The Commission retains the right to examine these records and accounts and conduct audits from time to time.

- Section 221 contains special provisions closely limiting the Commission's authority over the telephone industry to only those matters of rate setting and property valuation that clearly relate to interstate operations.

- Section 222, added by the Telecommunications Act, requires carriers to protect the privacy of customer information in their business dealings.

- Section 223, amended by the Telecommunications Act, provides for criminal proceedings against individuals who make obscene, lewd, lascivious, indecent, or harassing communications over interstate lines or within the District of Columbia.

- Section 224 authorizes the Commission to make regulations and hear disputes regarding access to public utility poles by interstate telecommunications carriers.

- Section 225 requires the Commission to make and enforce regulations pertaining to telecommunications services for the hearing and speech impaired.

- Section 226 sets the legal obligations of carriers providing telephone operator services and authorizes the Commission to make and enforce additional regulations pertaining to these provisions.

- Section 227 establishes restrictions on the use of automated telephone equipment, sets technical and procedural standards for the use of fax machines, and authorizes rules pertaining to the protection of telephone customers from unwanted solicitations.

- Section 228 authorizes the Commission to make and enforce rules pertaining to pay telephone services.

- Section 229 authorizes the prescription of rules to implement the Communications Assistance for Law Enforcement Act. These provisions are designed to aid law enforcement officials in the interception of evidence through communications media when legally appropriate.

- Section 230, added with the passage of the Telecommunications Act, is aimed at promoting the development and use of Internet blocking and screening software.

- Section 231 requires that access to commercial communications distributed over the World Wide Web that are deemed "harmful to minors" be restricted to adults.

- Sections 251–261, added by the Telecommunications Act, establish a set of general guidelines for the development of competition in local telephone service markets and new programs for the extension of telecommunications services to rural areas and to healthcare and educational facilities.

- Sections 271–276 provide a set of procedures and requirements for the Bell Operating Companies to move beyond their local telephone monopolies by entering previously restricted markets, such as long distance telephone service, information services, and equipment manufacturing.

Title III: Provisions Relating to Radio

Title III sets the Commission's powers with respect to the licensing and operation of "radio" communications services: services utilizing the electromagnetic spectrum. These include broadcast radio and television, spectrum used by ships and aircrafts, cellular telephone providers, and radio communication by public safety officials. Sections 301–336 relate to general matters, sections 351–386 deal with radio services aboard ships, and sections 390–399 are concerned with public telecommunications facilities. The major provisions of title III can be summarized as follows:

- Section 301 states generally that transmission of communication over the electromagnetic spectrum requires a license issued by the federal government.

- Section 302 authorizes the Commission to regulate devices that interfere with radio communications.

- Section 303 outlines the general powers of the Commission relating to the licensing and regulation of radio services. This includes the power to set up classifications of radio services, establish geographical zones to be served by radio services, assign call letters for broadcasters, and require record keeping by providers of radio services. This section also gives the Commission the authority to suspend the licenses of radio operators for violating treaties, failing to carry out lawful orders, broadcasting profane or obscene language, sending false or deceptive signals or communications, willfully interfering with another operator's frequency, or providing the Commission with fraudulent information. As discussed further in Chapter 2 of this volume, operators who have had their license suspended are entitled to a fair hearing. Provisions added to this section under the Telecommunications Act empower the Commission to regulate direct-to-home satellite services.

- Section 304 requires radio service licensees to waive any claim to ownership of their frequency.

- Section 305 provides that radio stations belonging to and operated by the government are to be licensed by the president of the United States and are not subject to the requirements of sections 301–303. Section 306 states that the requirements of 301 do not apply to communications sent from a foreign ship residing within the jurisdiction of the United States.

- Section 307 sets the terms of licenses for radio services. Amendments to this section added under the Telecommunications Act lengthened the term of a license to a maximum of eight years and reduced the amount of paperwork that had to be submitted at license renewal time.

- Section 308 further elaborates the contents for an application for a radio license.

- Section 309 outlines the procedural requirements the Commission must follow in taking action on a radio license application. For most types of licenses, the Commission must determine within thirty days of providing public notice on an application whether or not to grant the license. The application review process is discussed further in Chapter 2.

- Section 310 places limits on the ability of foreign governments and individuals to hold licenses and provides procedural requirements for the transfer of licenses between parties.

- Section 311 outlines a number of special requirements for the licensing of broadcast stations.

- Section 312 states the circumstances under which the Commission may revoke a license or construction permit. See Chapter 2 for a further discussion of this section.

- Section 313 provides for the revocation of licenses for violations of the antitrust laws.

- Section 314 provides for the preservation of competition by placing limits on the ability of commercial radio operators to enter other areas of the communications business.

- Section 315 requires broadcasters to provide equal time to candidates for public office.

- Section 316 allows the Commission to modify station licenses or construction permits if it determines that it is in the public interest, convenience, and necessity to do so. Broadcasters are entitled to a hearing on the matter if they desire.

- Section 317 provides that broadcasters must announce the names of persons or organizations that have paid for broadcast time.

- Section 318 generally provides that the transmitting apparatus in any radio station may only be operated by the licensee.

- Section 319 states that a construction permit issued by the Commission is a precondition for receiving a radio license. This section also sets out the requirements for obtaining a construction permit.

- Section 320 authorizes the Commission to designate radio stations liable to interfere with the distress signals of ships.

- Section 321 authorizes ships to send high-powered distress signals and requires radio stations to give priority to these signals. Radio stations must also cease operations temporarily if their broadcasts are likely to interfere with distress signals.

- Section 322 states that all land stations open to public service between the coast and vessels or aircraft at sea must exchange radio communications with ships and aircrafts.

- Section 323 states that private or commercial radio stations on land that interfere with government radio stations must cease operations for the first fifteen minutes of each hour.

- Section 324 mandates that, with the exception of vessels sending distress signals, all radio stations must use the minimum amount of power necessary to carry out communications.

- Section 325 prohibits false distress signals, places limits on the ability of a cable system or other multichannel video programming distributor to retransmit the signal of a broadcasting station, and prohibits the sending of radio transmissions to foreign broadcast studios.

- Section 326 states that nothing in the Act gives the Commission the power of censorship over radio communications.

- Section 327 authorizes the reception of commercial and press messages over frequencies operated by the Navy.

- Section 329 authorizes the Commission to designate officers of other federal government departments to administer the Act within U.S. territories and possessions.

- Section 330 prohibits the shipment or importation of televisions with decoding (closed caption) and blocking apparatus that do not comply with FCC standards.

- Section 331 establishes that the Commission must allocate very high frequency (VHF) television stations in such a manner that at least one is present in each state whenever feasible. This section also establishes provisions to promote the development of full-time AM radio stations throughout the country.

- Section 332 sets parameters for the allocation of spectrum to private mobile radio services.

- Section 333 prohibits willful or malicious interference with radio communication.

- Section 334 limits the authority of the Commission to revise regulations concerning equal employment opportunity in television broadcasting.

- Section 335 authorizes the Commission to make rules concerning the rates, facilities, and programming of direct broadcast satellite service providers.

- Section 336, added by the Telecom Act, authorizes the Commission to distribute spectrum for digital broadcasting services to incumbent television broadcasters. In the future, when broadcasters take over the "digital" spectrum, they are required to surrender the analog frequencies on which they were originally licensed to operate.

- Section 337 provides for the allocation and assignment of certain frequencies for commercial and public safety services by the Commission.

- Section 338 requires carriage of local television signals by satellite carriers under regulations issued by the Commission.

- Section 339 places limits on the ability of satellite carriers to carry the signals of network affiliates from outside the viewing area.

- Sections 351–386 deal with radio equipment and radio operators on board ships. Large passenger ships, cargo ships, and ships operated by the government on the open sea must be licensed to operate a radio frequency. Large ships are also required to carry radio officers and a radiotelegraph station. With the passage of the Telecommunications Act, some ships are exempt from this requirement if they carry automated distress and safety systems. Passenger ships for hire are required by these sections to have radio telephone equipment. The Commission has the authority in some instances to set technical standards and operating requirements.

- Sections 390–393 a set up a program of matching grants for the construction, planning, and operation of public telecommunications facilities to be administered by the secretary of commerce. This portion of the Act also creates criteria for the approval of grants by the secretary and obligations for the recipients of the funds, and it requires long-range planning in the use of these appropriations.

- Section 394 sets up a National Endowment for Children's Educational Television to be administered by the secretary of commerce.

- Section 395 authorizes the secretary of commerce to make grants and enter into contracts to carry out demonstrations of nonbroadcast telecommunications facilities and services aimed at assisting communication in the fields of health, education, and public and social services.

- Sections 396–399b create the Corporation for Public Broadcasting and set requirements for the operation of noncommercial educational television stations.

Title IV: Procedural and Administrative Provisions

Title IV deals with questions of due process in Commission decisionmaking.

- Section 401 states that Commission orders and decisions may be enforced by the district courts of the United States through a judicial order.

- Section 402 provides that proceedings to enjoin, set aside, annul, or suspend an order of the Commission must be taken before the U.S. Court of Appeals for the District of Columbia Circuit. Appeals of Commission decisions are further discussed in Chapter 2.

- Section 403 authorizes the Commission to undertake investigations on its own initiative in response to complaints or in enforcement of any of the provisions of the Act. Section 404 provides that the Commission must conclude its investigations with a report stating its findings and any order that follows.

- Section 405 allows aggrieved parties to file a petition for reconsideration of any Commission decision.

- Section 406 gives jurisdiction to the U.S. district courts to issue orders of compliance to carriers who have refused to furnish interstate communications facilities upon petition from a complainant.

- Section 407 allows parties who have won a monetary settlement against a carrier in a Commission proceeding to seek an order of enforcement from a U.S. district court.

- Section 408 states that all orders of the Commission other than those involving payment of money will take effect thirty days following the date of notice of the order.

- Section 409 establishes procedures for presenting evidence in hearings and adjudicatory proceedings before the Commission.

- Section 410 authorizes the Commission to establish joint boards to discuss and resolve regulatory matters that require cooperation between the federal and state governments.

- Section 411 authorizes the inclusion of all persons interested in or affected by a regulatory action as parties to a Commission proceeding or plaintiffs in a court action.

- Section 412 states that documents filed as part of a Commission proceeding must be preserved as public records.

- Section 413 requires that all carriers subject to the Act must designate an agent to formally interact with the Commission in official proceedings and litigation.

- Section 414 states that none of the remedies provided in this section should be understood to abridge or alter those available at common law.

- Section 415 sets some general limitations as to the timeframes and circumstances under which some legal actions may be taken before the Commission.

- Section 416 states that Commission orders affecting a carrier must be served on its agent designated under section 413 of this Act.

Title V: Penal Provisions

Title V of the Act establishes a range of civil and criminal penalties for violation of the Communications Act as amended.

- Section 501 establishes the maximum fines and terms of imprisonment for persons who violate provisions of the Act.

- Section 502 establishes fines for persons who violate the rules and regulations of the Commission.

- Section 503 establishes additional penalties for those who accept unlawful rebates or offsets against scheduled rates and charges.

- Section 504 states that all monetary forfeitures accruing from penalties are to be paid to the U.S. Treasury. The U.S. Attorney General, working through the federal courts, has the duty to prosecute for the recovery of these forfeitures.

- Section 505 states that all prosecutions shall be undertaken in the district in which the offense was committed. Offenses committed on the high seas will be prosecuted in the district in which the individual is found or first brought upon return to land.

- Section 506 establishes maximum civil penalties for violation of the Great Lakes Agreement.

- Section 507 requires the disclosure of sums of money paid to broadcasters for the production and/or broadcast of certain materials and states criminal penalties for the violation of the provisions of this section.

- Section 508 establishes criminal penalties for dishonest or deceptive practices relating to game shows.

- Section 510 authorizes the seizure by the government of any radio device not authorized in accordance with sections 301 and 302 of this Act.

Title VI: Cable Communications

Title VI consists largely of amendments that were added with the passage of the Cable Communications Act of 1984 and the Cable Television Consumer Protection and Competition Act of 1992. The most recent major additions came with the passage of the Telecommunications Act of 1996. Sections 601–602 contain general provisions, sections 611–617 deal with the use of channels and cable ownership, sections 621–629 concern franchising and regulation, sections 631–641 contain miscellaneous provisions, and sections 651–653 relate to video programming services provided by telephone companies.

- Section 601 states the general purposes of the cable provisions and Section 602 provides statutory definitions.

- Section 611 authorizes franchising authorities to require cable providers to supply channels for public, educational, or governmental use as a part of their franchising agreement.

- Section 612 requires larger cable systems to set aside a certain portion of their channels for commercial use by unaffiliated persons. The Commission has the authority to enforce this provision and to set rates for the leasing of these channels.

- Section 613 prohibits cable operators from providing certain other types of video programming services within their cable franchising area unless they are already subject to "effective competition" as determined by the Commission. This section also limits the ability of state franchising authorities to restrict ownership of cable systems within their jurisdictions.

- Section 614 requires cable operators of a certain size to carry the signals of local commercial broadcast television stations and qualified low power stations. The Commission is empowered to determine the "viewing area" of local stations if necessary.

- Section 615 requires cable operators of a certain size to carry any qualified local noncommercial educational television station requesting carriage. The Commission is empowered to enforce these provisions through appropriate remedies.

- Section 616 requires the Commission to maintain regulations governing the carriage agreements between cable operators and other video program distributors and vendors.

- Section 617 states that franchising authorities, when authorized to, may take no more than 120 days to act upon a request for approval of the sale of a cable system. In doing so, the franchising authority must act in accordance with Commission regulations.

- Section 621 reiterates that all cable franchises must be written in accordance with the requirements of the Act as amended, and prohibits franchising authorities from awarding exclusive franchises. Provisions added to this section by the Telecommunications Act also prohibit the franchising authority from regulating telephone or other telecommunications services provided by the cable operator.

- Section 622 authorizes franchising authorities to require cable operators to pay franchising fees not to exceed 5 percent of the operator's gross revenues from providing cable service during a twelve-month period.

- Section 623 authorizes franchising authorities to regulate cable rates if there is not effective competition within its jurisdiction. The Commission is also empowered under this section to regulate the rates of basic tier cable service.

- Section 624 prohibits franchising authorities from regulating the services, facilities, and equipment provided by a cable operator. This section does recognize the exception of obscene communication and also requires cable operators to provide subscribers, upon request, with a device to block programming that is sexually explicit. In addition, this section requires the Commission to maintain regulations regarding the minimum technical standards of operation and signal quality for cable operators.

- Section 624[a] requires the Commission to make and periodically review and modify regulations regarding the compatibility of televisions, video cassette recorders, and cable systems.

- Section 625 states that cable operators may obtain modifications to their franchising agreements with respect to certain matters of programming if they can demonstrate that these requirements are no longer practicable.

- Section 626 sets up standard proceedings for the renewal of franchises that require public notice and participation. This section also provides for a right of appeal in the federal district courts for cable operators whose franchise renewal has been denied.

- Section 627 establishes conditions for the sale or transfer of cable systems in the event that a franchising agreement is not renewed or revoked.

- Section 628 seeks to promote competition and diversity in video programming by requiring the Commission to make and enforce regulations prohibiting unfair methods of competition relating to the prices, terms and conditions of service.

- Section 629, added with the passage of the Telecommunications Act, requires the FCC to adopt regulations to assure that consumers can purchase on a commercial basis cable television converters and types of equipment used to obtain video programming services.

- Section 631 relates to the protection of subscriber privacy. Under this section, cable operators must disclose to consumers their methods of collecting and distributing personal information. This section also states the circumstances under which a cable operator may disclose the personal information of subscribers to third parties and prescribes civil remedies for the failure to comply with these provisions.

- Section 632 pertains to the regulation of customer service requirements for cable operators. The Act, as amended in 1992, requires the commission to establish standards by which cable operators may fulfill their customer service requirements. The matters covered by these standards include cable operator office hours and telephone availability to consumers, service calls, and communications between the cable operator and the subscriber.

- Section 633 outlaws and provides criminal and civil penalties for the unauthorized reception of cable services.

- Section 634 requires cable system operators to maintain an equal employment opportunity program in accordance with regulations established by the Commission.

- Section 635 further spells out the procedures for the judicial appeal of a franchising authority decision.

- Section 635a prohibits the awarding of monetary damages as a part of the judicial proceedings spelled out in section 635.

- Section 636 reiterates the general authority of state governments over cable franchising matters and further states that nothing in this title should be understood to interfere with the sovereign powers

of state governments regarding matters of public health, safety, and welfare.

- Section 637 states that all franchises that are in effect are subject to the provisions of this title at its time of passage.

- Section 638 states that nothing in this title should be construed to alter the criminal or civil liability of cable operators under federal, state, and local laws pertaining to libel, slander, obscenity, incitement, invasion of privacy, or false or misleading advertising.

- Section 639 states specifically that the federal laws pertaining to obscene communication apply to cable operators.

- Section 640 requires cable operators to block or scramble signals for all channels to which an individual customer does not subscribe upon his request.

- Section 641 states that a cable provider must fully scramble or block the signals of sexually explicit adult programming.

- Section 651 exempts telephone companies that provide video programming services from most of the provisions of title VI.

- Section 652 establishes the terms and conditions under which cable television operators and local telephone companies can enter joint ventures or purchase one another.

- Section 653 orders the Commission to make rules and regulations for the provision of cable television service by telephone companies through open video systems.

Title VII: Miscellaneous Provisions

Sections 701–714 contain a host of miscellaneous provisions pertaining to Commission powers and the regulation of the communications industry. Section 701 transfers to the Commission certain duties, powers, and functions under existing law previously held by the ICC and the postmaster general. Section 705 contains provisions relating to the unauthorized publication of communications, and Section 706 grants emergency powers to the president to suspend certain Commission regulations during times of war.

Section 707 establishes July 1, 1934, as the effective date of the Act, Section 708 contains a "separability" clause, and section 709 provides that the Act should be referred to as the Communications Act of 1934. Sections 710–714 contain additional regulatory provisions:

- Section 710 requires the Commission to establish regulations to provide for reasonable access to telephone services by the hearing impaired.

- Section 711 requires closed captioning for public service announcements.

- Section 712 requires the Commission to make syndicated exclusivity rules for the delivery of syndicated programming for transmission by satellite of broadcast station signals.

- Section 713, added by the Telecommunications Act, required the Commission to undertake a study and report to Congress regarding the extent of closed captioning in cable television as well as the availability of video descriptions for the visually impaired.

- Section 714 establishes a telecommunications development fund to promote access to capital for small businesses, promote technological development, and support universal service.

FCC RULES AND REGULATIONS

From the above discussion of the Communications Act, it should be evident that the FCC's statutory delegation of authority is quite far reaching. In carrying out its statutory mandates, the Commission has written a vast range of administrative rules over the years. Administrative rules are quasi-legislative statements of policy written and passed under the authority granted by a statute. In making rules, the FCC generally follows the procedural requirements stated in the federal Administrative Procedures Act of 1946 (discussed in greater detail in Chapter 2). FCC rules, once passed, are codified in title 47 of the Code of Federal Regulations. The following is a general summary of title 47 broken down by parts:

- Part 0 deals with Commission organization. In general, this part spells out the duties of the chairman, the responsibilities of the major offices and

bureaus housed within the Commission, and information about Commission rules, proceedings, and facilities.

- Part 1 covers the formal practices and procedures followed by the Commission as it carries out its statutory authority.

- Part 2 contains rules pertaining to the allocation of spectrum frequencies for different purposes by separating them into "bands." This section also outlines the Commission's table of frequency allocations and states general requirements pertaining to radio stations and radio equipment.

- Part 3 is where the FCC delineates its responsibilities in the certification and monitoring of the accounting authorities that settle accounts due to messages transmitted to foreign administrations at sea by or between maritime mobile radio stations.

- Part 5 rules prescribe the procedures through which frequencies are made available by the Commission for experimental radio services pursuant to title III of the Communications Act.

- Part 6 contains rules intended to ensure that telephones and telecommunications equipment are designed and produced in a manner that makes them accessible to persons with disabilities.

- Part 7 contains rules intended to ensure improved access to voice-mail and interactive menu services and equipment by persons with disabilities.

- Part 11 sets up the technical standards and operating requirements for the Emergency Alert System for AM and FM radio, broadcast television, cable television, and other participating entities.

- Part 13 rules prescribe the manner and conditions for the licensing of commercial radio operators.

- Part 15 contains rules by which an intentional, unintentional, or incidental radiator of a radio signal may operate without a license.

- Part 17 rules provide guidelines for the construction, marking, and lighting of radio antennas.

- Part 18 sets forth the conditions under which industrial, scientific, and medical equipment may be operated without undue interference with authorized radio services.

- Part 19 contains rules prescribing appropriate standards of conduct for Commission employees pursuant to the Uniform Standards of Ethical Conduct contained in the Code of Federal Regulations.

- Part 20 sets out requirements and conditions for providers of commercial mobile radio services.

- Part 21 prescribes procedures for making portions of the spectrum available to common carriers and multipoint distribution service operators who require such transmitting facilities.

- Part 22 sets out the requirements and conditions for licensing common carrier radio stations for the provision of public mobile radio services.

- Part 23 sets out the requirements and conditions for the licensing and operation of international fixed public radio-telecommunications services.

- Part 24 contains rules relating to the licensing and operation of personal communications services.

- Part 25 contains rules relating to the licensing and operation of satellite communications.

- Part 27 contains rules relating to the licensing and operation of miscellaneous wireless communications services.

- Part 32 sets up a uniform system of accounts for telecommunications carriers.

- Part 36 contains the procedures for separating a telecommunications carrier's property costs, revenues, expenses, taxes, and reserves for the purposes of delineating federal and state regulatory jurisdictions.

- Part 42 contains rules pertaining to the preservation of common carrier accounts, records, memoranda, documents, papers and correspondence, including those obtained through mergers and acquisitions.

- Part 43 contains guidelines for the submission of reports by common carriers to the Commission regarding their financial dealings.

- Part 51 rules authorize state regulators to approve agreements between common carriers for the interconnection of their lines and facilities.

- Part 52 rules establish the requirements and conditions for the administration and use of telephone/telecommunications numbers.

- Part 53 rules implement sections 271–272 of the Communications Act pertaining to the entry of the Bell Operating Companies into long distance telecommunications services.

- Part 54 rules implement the universal service provisions of section 254 of the Communications Act, as amended.

- Part 59 rules require local telephone companies to share their infrastructure and facilities with competitors under certain circumstances.

- Part 61 contains rules pertaining to the initial filing and revision of tariffs for the setting of charges and the provision of services.

- Part 63 rules concern the extension of lines by common carriers under section 214 of the Communications Act, as amended.

- Part 64 contains miscellaneous other rules pertaining to common carriers.

- Part 65 rules relate to the regulation of rates for interstate telecommunications services.

- Part 68 rules set standards for the attachment of terminal equipment to telecommunications networks and the compatibility of hearing aids and telephones.

- Part 69 sets up the rules by which access charges are to be paid to local telephone companies by long distance companies to compensate them for the use of their infrastructure.

- Part 73 contains rules relating to the classification, assignment, and operation of AM radio frequencies and stations.

- Part 74 contains rules relating to the licensing and operation of experimental, auxiliary, and special broadcast and other program distribution services.

- Part 76 rules pertain to the operation of multi-channel video and cable television services. These provisions include requirements for the certification of cable television systems as well as rules and standards for their operation pursuant to title VI of the Communications Act, as amended.

- Part 78 rules pertain to the licensing and operation of cable television relay service stations.

- Part 79 contains rules relating to closed captioning and video description in video programming.

- Part 80 rules implement the Commission's authority to license and regulate radio stations in the maritime service.

- Part 87 rules implement the Commission's authority to license and regulate radio stations for aviation service.

- Part 90 rules provide for the licensing and regulation of stations for private land mobile radio services such as public safety services and industrial/business radio pool.

- Part 95 contains rules pertaining to the licensing and operation of general mobile radio services.

- Part 97 contains rules pertaining to the licensing and operation of an amateur radio service.

- Part 101 contains rules pertaining to the allocation and licensing of frequencies for fixed microwave communications services.

THE FCC: PROFILING AN ORGANIZATION

As should be clear by now, the FCC's expansive legislative mandate makes the agency the principal policymaking organization in the realm of federal communications regulation. In spite of its seemingly endless list of provisions and requirements, the Communications Act mainly provides a basic legal framework that authorizes the FCC to use its broad rulemaking powers to regulate the communications industry. Over the decades, the FCC has used this broad delegation of authority to do such far-reaching things as limiting and expanding competition in the telephone industry, constructing and later doing away with public interest requirements for broadcasters, introducing new technologies into the marketplace, and making rules concerning the broadcast of indecent messages over the airwaves.

Like any policymaking organization, the FCC and its policies are shaped by (1) the people that work within the organization, (2) its political environment, and (3) the procedures and institutional arrangements that structure policymaking. The purpose of

this volume is to provide a broad reference to the FCC's major policy initiatives and the people, political environment, and institutional arrangements that have shaped them.

ORGANIZATION AND PROCEDURES

Scholars of public bureaucracy have long noted that the nature of an agency's organization and procedures impacts decision-making outcomes. How an agency organizes the conduct of work through its bureaus and offices as well as its procedures for making rules, issuing administrative orders, and appealing decisions to the federal courts can determine whether or not discretionary authority is carried out in a fair and efficient manner. Furthermore, agency organization and procedures can also have political implications. For example, in writing the Communications Act of 1934, Congress put some thought into determining who would have the right to challenge an FCC broadcast licensing decision and under what circumstances. In making decisions such as these, Congress and administrative agencies may be able to empower some interest groups at the expense of others in the bureaucratic decision-making process.

The purpose of this chapter is to describe in detail the organization and procedures of the Federal Communications Commission. The first part of the chapter provides an in-depth description of the FCC's major administrative components and officers. The second part of the chapter provides a discussion of procedures for rulemaking, broadcast licensing, judicial review of agency decisions, and mechanisms through which the public can obtain information regarding Commission activities.

ORGANIZATION OF THE COMMISSION

Perhaps the most important organizational decision made by Congress in writing the Communications Act of 1934 was to make the FCC an independent regulatory commission. Independent regulatory commissions differ from traditional government agencies in that they do not report directly to the president. While the president does nominate the agency heads—or commissioners, as they are called—they then sit on the Commission for lengthy fixed terms

FIGURE 3.2 Organization Chart of the FCC, August 2005

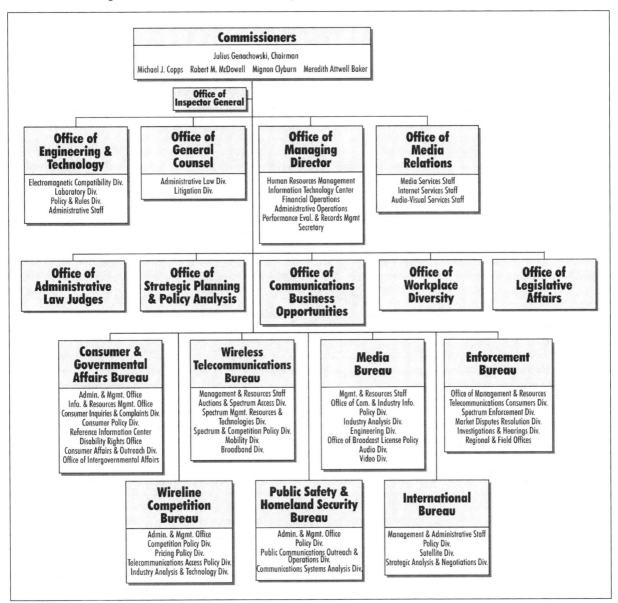

Source: Federal Communications Commission

and cannot be fired for reasons other than corruption or serious misconduct. Furthermore, independent regulatory commissions, unlike most other types of public agencies, have plural chief executives consisting of three to seven commissioners who make policy decisions as a collegial body. Commissions are typically also bipartisan, with no more than a simple majority of their members coming from any single political party. All of these structural considerations are intended to make commissions somewhat independent from traditional electoral politics and enable them to make the most reasoned, technically correct decisions

they possible can. This is not to say, however, that independent regulatory commissions are not highly political entities. Commissioners are appointed by elected officials and bring their own political preferences into the decision-making process. This is just as true of the FCC as any other commission.

From an organizational standpoint, the FCC can be broken down into three major components: (1) the Commission itself, (2) the six policymaking bureaus, and (3) the various staff offices within the agency. The description of Commission organization that follows distinguishes between these major components of the agency.

The Commission

The FCC today consists of five commissioners who are appointed by the president subject to confirmation by the Senate. The normal terms of commissioners are fixed at five years, with one commissioner appointed or re-appointed each year. No more than three of the five commissioners may be members of the same political party. Commissioners are full-time political appointees who are prohibited from retaining any other employment or receiving honoraria for speeches or holding any financial interests in any sector of the communications industry. Beyond these considerations there is no standard career path for becoming a commissioner. The Communications Act does not list any specific qualifications for being a commissioner, though most have been lawyers and many have had prior experience as state-level utility commissioners or at the FCC.

The president holds the authority to designate one member of the Commission to serve as chairman. The chairman serves as the chief executive officer of the agency, which includes such responsibilities as presiding over all meetings and sessions of the Commission, representing the Commission before Congress and other governmental bodies, appointing bureau and office heads subject to the approval of the whole Commission, and generally coordinating the work of the agency. When a new president comes into office, it is his prerogative to designate a new chair from among the sitting commissioners. Technically, dismissal as chair does not mean dismissal as a commissioner, since the appointment is a fixed term. As a practical matter, however, chairmen facing dismissal have traditionally resigned their seat on the Commission and allowed the president to fill the vacancy with a commissioner of his choosing. In the event that the Commission is lacking a chair due to a vacancy, the sitting commissioners may designate from among themselves an acting chairman.

In addition, one commissioner out of the five is designated to serve as the Defense Commissioner. Among other things it is the job of the Defense Commissioner to keep the Commission informed regarding matters relating to emergency preparedness and defense activities and to represent the Commission in national defense matters requiring conferences with other governmental entities. In addition, the Defense Commissioner works with the staff in each of the policy bureaus to develop preparedness programs for the telecommunications industry. Finally, in the event of an enemy attack or imminent threat in which the entire Commission is unable to function at its Washington, D.C., offices, the Defense Commissioner is empowered to temporarily assume the duties and powers of the full Commission and chairman.

The work of the Commission is primarily done as a collegial body. The Commission holds the final say within the agency on all policy matters, though some decision-making authority may be delegated to bureau chiefs and professional staff. Commission decisions are made in weekly meetings, which normally require a quorum of at least three commissioners in order for formal actions to be taken. The agenda for formal meetings is set by the chairman, who provides each commissioner with a list of agenda items at least a week in advance. Commissioners prepare for the meetings with the assistance of their personal staff by gathering information and evaluating the agenda items. The consideration of agenda items in meetings typically involves testimony by staff members in the agency who were involved in preparing the items for Commission consideration. Commissioners are then given the opportunity to question those testifying and to have open discussion among themselves before taking a final vote on the matter. Under the federal Sunshine Act, most formal Commission meetings are open to the public.

Some types of Commission decisions are made through mechanisms other than formal meetings. For instance, in the event that a quorum cannot be obtained, either because of absences or vacancies on the Commission, the chairman may convene a "board of commissioners" consisting of all commissioners present and able to act. A board of commissioners, however, may not act on major policy initiatives. Some fairly routine matters, such as certain types of hearings, may also be handled by individual commissioners acting on behalf of the Commission. On some occasions, Commission business is also done through a process called "circulation" in which a document or agenda item is circulated among the commissioners and approval or rejection is submitted to the chair outside of a formal meeting.

The Policymaking Bureaus

Below the Commission itself are a host of different staff offices, including the six policymaking bureaus. Sometimes functioning like self-contained bureaucracies, each bureau consists of a series of offices and professional staff that work to identify and act upon the major policy matters of the day. The bureau system of organization was started in 1949 as a way to better coordinate staff work relating to specific types of telecommunications policy problems. Prior to that time, staff members were organized around professional affiliations—accounting, engineering, and law. This system of organization posed at least two problems for the Commission. First, staff members were functioning as generalists, never really developing expertise in a specific sector of the telecommunications industry. Second, the three main staff offices largely worked independently of one another. Thus, commissioners could get three very different viewpoints with respect to a policy problem depending on who they asked. In an effort to obtain more unified opinions on policy matters, staff members were organized into bureaus in which professionals from the different fields worked together on specific policy issues.

A major component of the bureau system of organization today is the maintenance of a bureau for each main sector of the telecommunications industry. Thus, there is a Wireline Competition Bureau to regulate the telephone industry, a Media Bureau to regulate broadcasting and cable television, a Wireless Bureau to handle spectrum matters, and an International Bureau to handle international telecommunications issues. In addition, the Commission has established an Enforcement Bureau and a Consumer and Governmental Affairs Bureau. Each bureau is headed by a bureau chief who serves as the principal executive, coordinating the work of the staff. Through authority delegated by the commissioners, the bureaus write rules, undertake adjudicatory proceedings, and take other policy actions on behalf of the Commission, taking what amounts to final action on many matters. The significance of many of these bureaus cannot be understated. Because they are staffed by career civil servants who become technical experts in the matters they deal with, it is frequently the bureaus, rather than the Commission itself, that sets the regulatory agenda for the agency.

Wireline Competition Bureau

Originally called the Common Carrier Bureau, the Wireline Competition Bureau is principally charged with carrying out regulatory responsibilities relating to the telephone industry. As specified in section 47 of the Code of Federal Regulations, the main responsibilities of the Wireline Competition Bureau include:

1. Developing and recommending policy goals, objectives, programs, and plans for the Commission in rulemaking and adjudicatory matters concerning wireline telecommunications. Overall objectives include meeting the present and future wireline telecommunications needs of the nation; fostering economic growth; ensuring choice, opportunity, and fairness in the development of wireline telecommunications; promoting investment in wireline telecommunications infrastructure; promoting the development and widespread availability of wireline telecommunications services; and developing deregulatory initiatives where appropriate.

2. Administering the provisions of the Communications Act requiring that the charges, practices, classifications, and regulations of communications common carriers providing interstate and foreign services are just and reasonable.

3. Acting on applications for the provision of wireline telecommunications services and the construction of wireline telecommunications facilities.

4. Interacting with local, state, and other governmental agencies, the public, and industry groups on wireline telecommunications regulation and related matters.

5. Assisting the Consumer and Governmental Affairs Bureau on issues involving informal consumer complaints and other general inquiries by consumers.

6. Reviewing and coordinating orders, programs, and actions initiated by other bureaus and offices in matters affecting wireline telecommunications

to ensure consistency with overall Commission policy.

Because of the technical nature of the matters it deals with, the Commission has historically given a great deal of deference to this bureau and its staff. Over the course of several decades, this deference has allowed the Wireline Competition Bureau to exert significant influence over the direction of telephone regulation. Under the direction of Chief Bernard Strassburg (1964–1974), the bureau fashioned policies that furthered the development of new technologies such as data communications and gradually opened the door for competition in the long distance telephone industry. This tradition was continued in the 1970s and 1980s under the direction of chiefs such as Phillip Verveer, Albert Halprin, and Gerald Brock, who also took steps to further competition.

The Wireline Competition Bureau is further broken down into several divisions, which include a Competition Policy Division that handles the creation of rules and policies dealing with the local competition and long distance competition provisions of the Telecommunications Act of 1996. The Industry Analysis and Technology Division conducts economic, financial, and technical analyses of telecommunications markets in support of the bureau's activities. The Pricing Policy Division deals with policies and rules pertaining to the rates of long distance telephone service providers. Finally, the Telecommunications Access Policy Division works to advance the universal service goals contained in the various portions of the Telecommunications Act.

Media Bureau

According to section 47 of the U.S. Code of Federal Regulations, the Media Bureau "develops, recommends, and administers the policy and licensing programs for the regulation of media, including cable television, broadcast television, and radio and satellite services in the United States and its territories." Specifically, the Media Bureau's duties include:

1. Processing applications for authorization, assignment, transfer, and renewal of broadcast radio and television station licenses.

2. Conducting comprehensive studies and rulemakings relating to the legal, engineering, and economic aspects of media service.

3. Administering and enforcing rules and policies pertaining to political programming.

4. Administering and enforcing rules pertaining to cable television systems, including those relating to rates, technical standards, and customer service.

5. Assisting the Consumer and Governmental Affairs Bureau on issues involving informal consumer complaints and other general inquiries by consumers.

The Media Bureau is further broken down into eight divisions and offices. The Office of Broadcast License Policy develops, recommends, and administers policies and programs for the regulation of broadcast services. The Audio and Video Divisions handle the licensing of radio and television stations. The Policy Division conducts rulemakings and other proceedings relating to various aspects of broadcasting, cable, and satellite services. The Industry Analysis Division conducts economic research on media ownership and other issues relating to the media industry. The Engineering Division conducts technical analyses of media related matters. Finally, the Office of Communications and Industry Information works with the Office of Legislative Affairs to keep bureau staff apprised of Congressional concerns relating to media regulation.

Wireless Bureau

The Wireless Bureau maintains the authority to make rules and undertake adjudications pertaining to wireless telecommunications services, most prominent among which are cellular telephone, Personal Communications Services, pagers, and two-way radios. A major function of the Wireless Bureau is to manage and license spectrum for these services as well as for use by businesses and state and local governments. The Wireless Bureau is broken down into five major divisions. The Auctions and Spectrum Access Division handles procedural issues relating to spectrum auctions and licensing. The Broadband Division works to facilitate the widespread deployment of wireless broadband services. The Mobility Division makes rules and handles the licensing of various mobile radio services. The Public Safety and Critical Infrastructure Division handles regulatory issues relating to mobile radio services used by public safety authorities. The Spectrum and Competition Policy Division formulates policies aimed at promoting competition and innovation in the use of spectrum and wireless infrastructure. Finally, the Spectrum Management Resources and Technologies Division manages the Bureau's information technology and outreach programs.

International Bureau

The purpose of the International Bureau is to develop and recommend policies and rules pertaining to international telecommunications services. The International Bureau advises the Commission on matters of international telecommunications policy and represents the Commission on international telecommunications matters at conferences and meetings. The bureau also conducts policy analyses and provides advice and technical assistance to U.S. trade officials in the negotiation and implementation of telecommunications trade agreements. It is also charged with interacting with Congress and other executive agencies on international telecommunications matters.

The International Bureau consists of three divisions—Policy, Satellite, and Strategic Analysis and Negotiations. The Policy Division works to formulate international spectrum policy and license international telecommunications facilities. Other important components of the division's work include working to lower rates for international telephone service and providing assistance in trade negotiations. The Satellite Division undertakes policies aimed at developing competitive and innovative telecommunications services through the fast and efficient deployment of satellite services. The Strategic Analysis and Negotiations Division conducts research and participates in international telecommunications conferences and negotiations.

Consumer and Governmental Affairs Bureau

In 2002, the FCC's Consumer Information Bureau was reorganized as the Consumer and Governmental Affairs Bureau. In a press release describing the organization, the Commission stated that a major purpose of the revitalized bureau was to "engage consumers, states, other governmental organizations and the industry in an ongoing discussion, with one objective being to better inform and educate consumers and to enable them to make smart choices in the increasingly competitive telecom marketplace."

More specifically, the jobs of the bureau include advising the Commission on matters pertaining to consumer and governmental affairs, collecting and analyzing data on consumer inquiries and complaints, developing and distributing materials to inform the public, and providing informal mediation and resolution of consumer inquiries and complaints. The Consumer and Governmental Affairs Bureau contains a Policy Division that is responsible for consumer-related rulemakings, orders, and analysis of consumer complaints. The Disability Rights Office handles policy matters pertaining to the impact of telecommunications policy on the disabled community. The Consumer Affairs and Outreach Division works to increase awareness of the FCC as a consumer resource. Consumer centers in Washington, D.C., respond to consumer inquiries and resolve informal complaints, including those pertaining to cable service matters. The Information Access and Privacy Office reviews matters arising under the Freedom of Information Act. Finally, the Consumer and Governmental Affairs Bureau houses the Reference Information Center, which works with anyone wishing to obtain FCC records and documents.

Enforcement Bureau

The Enforcement Bureau holds the responsibility of enforcing the communications laws and Commission rules through the resolution of formal complaints and other actions. The Investigations and Hearings Division handles a wide range of enforcement activities, including those relating to broadcast indecency, telephone company violation of competition and universal service rules, and telephone company auditing. It also enforces rules pertaining to collusion and misrepresentation in nonbroadcast spectrum auctions. The Market Disputes Resolution Division generally investigates and takes action on complaints brought by competitors against dominant telephone carriers. The Office of Homeland Security assists the bureau chief and Defense Commissioner in rulemakings and proceedings relating to the Emergency Alert System and operates the Communication and Crisis Management Center, which handles a variety of secure and nonsecure official communications for the federal government. The Spectrum Enforcement Division enforces a variety of technical rules and requirements pertaining to the provision of radio services. The Telecommunications Consumers Division enforces legal provisions aimed at protecting consumers from fraudulent practices undertaken by telephone companies. Finally, the Enforcement Bureau maintains three regional offices, sixteen district offices, and nine resident agents around the country to conduct on-site inspections, investigations, and audits.

The Staff Offices

In addition to the six bureaus, there are numerous staff offices assisting the Commission in the fulfillment of its policy, procedural, and administrative responsibilities.

Office of the Managing Director

The managing director acts as the FCC's chief operating officer and executive official. The duties of the managing director and his deputies include preparing the FCC's budget, developing and overseeing personnel policies and procedures, and managing a wide range of agency resources, including telecommunications services, physical space, and security. Through the Office of the Secretary, the managing director also coordinates the FCC's meeting schedule and handles the distribution of public documents. The Office of the Managing Director also maintains a special officer to handle public requests for documents and information under the Freedom of Information Act.

Office of the General Counsel

The General Counsel acts as the official legal advisor to the FCC and its staff and represents the agency before the federal courts. The Office of the General Counsel contains three divisions—Administrative Law, Litigation, and the Transactions Team. The Administrative Law Division assists the Commission and the various bureaus in drafting rules and orders and provides procedural advice on matters relating to the Administrative Procedures Act, the Freedom of Information Act, and other federal statutes that frame the agency's regulatory discretion. The Litigation Division represents the Commission before the federal courts. The Transactions Team provides legal analysis of proposed economic transactions such as the transfer of spectrum licenses and telecommunications mergers.

Office of Administrative Law Judges

The Office of Administrative Law Judges conducts adjudicatory proceedings ordered by the Commission in relation to investigations, rulemakings, and orders. All proceedings are presided over by an administrative law judge—a legal professional employed by the agency who conducts the adjudicatory proceeding similar to a trial with sworn testimony and the cross-examination of witnesses. Decisions handed down by the Office of Administrative Law Judges are subject to appeal to the full Commission.

Office of the Inspector General

Since 1989, the FCC has had an inspector general to help prevent waste, fraud, and abuse within the agency. Specifically, the inspector general holds the responsibility of conducting audits and investigations relating to the programs and operations of the agency and its employees. In many instances, these investigations are motivated by allegations brought by FCC employees, citizens, and other interested parties. In addition, the Inspector General reviews proposed and existing programs and makes recommendations regarding how they could more efficiently be administered. The Office of the Inspector General submits semiannual reports to the chairman detailing its activities.

Office of Engineering and Technology

The Office of Engineering and Technology is the principal advisory body to the Commission on scientific matters. It conducts scientific and engineering studies and advises the Commission and bureaus on matters relating to spectrum management and frequency allocations. The Office maintains contacts with other governmental entities and the public on matters relating to communications technology and represents the Commission at national conferences and meetings dealing with technology and standards. Finally, the Office of Engineering and Technology is also actively involved in making legislative recommendations and participating in rulemaking proceedings throughout the FCC administrative structure.

Office of Strategic Planning and Policy Analysis

Originally called the Office of Plans and Policy, the Office of Strategic Planning and Policy Analysis was created in the early 1970s to assist the Commission and its bureaus in the identification of significant communications policy problems and the development of solutions consistent with agency objectives. The Office of Strategic Planning and Policy Analysis presents its ideas through a series of working papers published periodically by the Commission. The working papers are available to the public and the most recent ones have been placed on the FCC web site. Numerous working papers have been cited prominently in Commission proceedings and academic writings, and several have been very influential in shaping major Commission policies. For example, one particularly influential working paper published in 1987 recommended that the FCC replace traditional telephone rate regulation with a method known as price caps implemented in Britain a few years earlier. When Dennis Patrick became Chairman of the FCC later that year, he moved forward with the price caps proposal and it eventually became national policy in 1989. Staff in this office also wrote several influential working papers during the 1980s arguing that spectrum licensing proceedings should be conducted through competitive auctions. Spectrum auctions were eventually authorized by Congress in 1993.

Office of Legislative Affairs

The Office of Legislative Affairs is the FCC's official liaison to Congress. Its responsibilities include advising and making recommendations to the Commission regarding proposed legislation, responding to requests for information on Commission policies by members of Congress, and preparing members of the FCC and its staff to testify.

Office of Media Relations

The Office of Media Relations is responsible for the dissemination of information on FCC policies and procedures to the news media. The Office of Media Relations also manages the FCC web site and audio/visual support services, maintains contacts with outside parties regarding the broadcast of Commission proceedings, and works with the Consumer and Governmental Affairs Bureau on media issues concerning complaints and other consumer issues.

Office of Workplace Diversity

The Office of Workplace Diversity addresses matters relating to equal employment opportunity and affirmative action within the agency. The Office advises the Commission and its various administrative entities regarding their equal employment responsibilities under the federal civil rights laws and conducts independent analyses of FCC policies and practices to make sure they are in line with those goals. The Office also works with the FCC and its staff offices to formulate policies and foster an environment that values diversity.

Office of Communications Business Opportunities

The Office of Communications Business Opportunities works to promote ownership, employment, and other business opportunities for women and minorities. The Office of Communications Business Opportunities acts as the Commission's official advisor in proceedings that impact women and minorities and works to increase awareness of Commission policies and activities among these groups.

FCC DECISIONMAKING PROCESSES

As noted in Chapter 1, the FCC's statutory authority under the Communications Act of 1934 provides it with the ability to make a wide range of discretionary decisions. Two major types of decisions—rulemakings and broadcast licensing proceedings—are discussed below.

Rulemaking

Rulemaking proceedings at the FCC follow the general guidelines provided in the federal Administrative

Procedures Act of 1946 (APA) as amended. Most rulemakings undertaken at the FCC are of the "notice and comment" variety in which there is no formal trial-type proceeding. Rather, the proposed rules are published in the *Federal Register* and the public is given the opportunity to comment on them before they go into effect. Most FCC rulemakings have been initiated at the discretion of the agency within the fairly broad limits of its statutory authority. The impetus for rules, however, may come from a variety of sources. Many of the FCC's most recent rulemakings were mandated by the Telecommunications Act of 1996. The judicial branch can also mandate new rulemakings when it overturns existing rules. Other government agencies, citizens, and other nongovernmental entities can also influence the Commission from time to time by suggesting proposed rules.

The formal process of making a rule is initiated by staff at the FCC within the six major bureaus. A rulemaking is identified by its "docket" number, which contains the abbreviations of the name of the originating bureau, the last two digits of the year, and a specific reference number for the proceeding in question (for instance, a 2004 rulemaking at the Wireline Competition Bureau might be labeled WC #04-132). The rulemaking process generally proceeds with some combination of the following actions by the FCC and the public:

Petition for Rulemaking

While most FCC rulemakings originate with the commissioners and agency staff, members of the public can also initiate a proceeding by submitting a petition for rulemaking. The petition generally contains a discussion of the reasons for the rule as well as the specific wording of the rule that is being requested. Petitions are printed on a weekly basis in the FCC's *Filings* newsletter and the public is given thirty days to comment on their merits. Following the comment period, the FCC may choose to simply dispose of the decision if there is little public interest in the matter. If the agency decides to move forward, however, the next step is either a Notice of Inquiry or a Notice of Proposed Rulemaking.

Notices of Inquiry and Proposed Rulemaking

A Notice of Inquiry (NOI) is issued to solicit comments on some broad topic or issue without formally proposing a rule at that time. By contrast, a Notice of Proposed Rulemaking (NPRM) solicits comments on a specific rule the Commission seeks to adopt. Either an NOI or an NPRM may be used as the first formal step in a rulemaking proceeding. In some instances, however, an NPRM may follow an NOI after a more specific proposal has been generated. In either case, the issuance of an NOI or an NPRM marks the beginning of a formal rulemaking proceeding. Both types of documents are printed in the *Federal Register* as well as in the FCC's weekly newsletter, *Open Proceedings*. Once released, the public is given thirty days or more to comment on NOIs and NPRMs. Following the comment period, written comments are evaluated by the staff in the issuing bureau before further action is taken. Sometimes public comments reveal things that the Commission staff had not originally taken into consideration, such as new facts or possible unintended consequences that might be brought about by the proposed rule. In these instances the FCC will frequently issue a Further Notice of Proposed Rulemaking (FNPRM) in which the rule is amended or further public comment is sought on more specific issues. In some instances, several FNPRMs may be necessary to fully clarify all relevant issues.

Report and Order

After considering the comments submitted in response to the NPRM and FNPRMs, a Report and Order (R&O) is issued in which the Commission publishes its final decision. In the R&O, the Commission might choose to adopt the original rule, adopt an amended rule in response to the public comments, or drop the matter altogether. In any instance, however, the FCC is careful to detail the reasons for its actions. R&Os typically include a description of the adopted regulations and a summary of the major public comments and the FCC's responses to them. If the FCC chooses to side with a particular party or ignore all parties, it explains its reasoning in detail to avoid charges that its decision was "arbitrary and capricious" and, thus, subject to a possible court challenge. A summary of the R&O is published in the *Federal Register* for public review. In many instances, however, the R&O isn't the end of the process. There may still be additional regulatory issues to clarify and the R&O may be accompanied by an additional FNPRM.

Petition for Reconsideration

Parties that are not satisfied with the outcome of the rulemaking process may file a Petition for Reconsideration within thirty days after the appearance of the R&O in the *Federal Register*. Once the Petition for Reconsideration has been fully investigated by the Commission a Memorandum Opinion and Order is issued in which the rules are either amended or the reconsideration is denied. In either case, the FCC once again provides an explanation for its actions.

Judicial Review of FCC Rules

Under the Administrative Procedures Act, interested parties are allowed to challenge FCC orders in the Federal courts unless otherwise precluded by the Communications Act as amended. Challenges to FCC rules go directly to the U.S. Court of Appeals for the District of Columbia Circuit. Parties challenging FCC rules must have standing, meaning that they must in some way have suffered a legal wrong as a result of the rule, although the simple fact that a plaintiff has suffered monetary harm by no means guarantees relief. Parties challenging a rule in court must be able to demonstrate that the agency violated their constitutional rights, did not follow proper procedure, went beyond the authority delegated to it by statute, or acted in an arbitrary and capricious manner by failing to consider all relevant facts, considering facts that were not relevant, or rendering an implausible interpretation of those facts. A judicial decision overturning an FCC rule can force the agency to drop the matter altogether or rewrite the rule to meet court mandates.

NOTES

1. Quoted in Marvin R. Bensman, *The Beginning of Broadcast Regulation in the Twentieth Century* (Jefferson, NC: McFarland, 2000), 50.

2. *In the Matter of Deregulation of Radio,* 73 FCC 2d 457 (1979).

UNIT 6

To Speak or to Be Silenced?
The First Amendment

Philosophical Roots

Telecommunications policy in the United States is founded on two values: preservation of free speech and service to the public interest. Communications scholar Philip Napoli succinctly summarizes in the first reading in this unit more than two centuries of scholarship on the importance of freedom of expression as a basic social value and on the different justifications for its safeguarding. Freedom of expression should be seen in the context of the previous discussion about the communication process and the operation of networks: speech is the "matter" that travels in these networks, thus ensuring the free transit of information is synonymous to keeping the networks open and accessible. Following this reading you should be acquainted with the justifications for free expression and their categorization.

The First Amendment

Philip M. Napoli

The First Amendment is the boundary-setting foundation principle of communications policy. Policies adopted on behalf of any of the other foundation principles must not extend beyond the confines of the First Amendment. At the same time, it is important to recognize that the First Amendment is itself a component of the public interest[1] and in fact permeates each of the other foundation principles to varying degrees. As was illustrated in the previous chapter (and as will become clearer in this chapter and the chapters that follow), within the context of communications regulation concepts such as the marketplace of ideas, diversity, and localism are, to some extent, outgrowths of the First Amendment. Given the relationship between the First Amendment and each of the policy principles that follows, the First Amendment has been positioned as the structure within which all of the other foundation principles reside.

Obviously, a single chapter can hardly do justice to a concept as vast, complex, and important as the First Amendment. Consequently, the focus here is very narrow and emphasizes those aspects of the First Amendment that are of the greatest importance to the design and analysis of communications policies. First, this chapter reviews and discusses the various functions/objectives that have been associated with the First Amendment. From a policy standpoint,

it is essential to understand each of the foundation principles in terms of what they are intended to achieve. Only then can policies instituted on behalf of these principles be effectively evaluated. The First Amendment is particularly challenging in this regard because it has been associated with a broad range of objectives, all of which have been criticized to varying degrees, and some of which can actually conflict with one another.

Stemming from the diverse objectives associated with the First Amendment is the related issue of the differing interpretive approaches. Like all of the other foundation principles discussed in this book, the First Amendment has been subjected to multiple interpretations and applicational approaches. As legal scholar Thomas Emerson (1970) noted 30 years ago, "The outstanding fact about the First Amendment today is that the Supreme Court has never developed any comprehensive theory of what that constitutional guarantee means and how it should be applied in concrete cases" (p. 15). Many would argue that little has changed in this regard today (e.g., Bollinger, 1991; Stern, 1990). This ambiguity has allowed a variety of interpretive conflicts to develop. Arguably one of the central conflicts in First Amendment theory—and certainly one that is vital to the design and analysis of communications policies—revolves around whether the conceptualization of First Amendment freedoms should focus on the individual level or the "collective" level (Post, 1993). That is, should the interpretation and application of the First Amendment prioritize the preservation and enhancement of individual rights of self-expression, or should it prioritize creating a speech environment that maximizes the degree to which the citizenry as a whole is capable of expressing and receiving ideas? On the surface, these two interpretations do not seem contradictory, and in fact in many instances they may not be. However, as this chapter illustrates, in some instances preserving or promoting the First Amendment rights of the individual speaker can reduce the free speech rights of the broader public. Conversely, an emphasis on the First Amendment rights of the collective can infringe on the First Amendment rights of the individual speaker.

From a communications policy perspective, the implications of this unsettled nature of the First Amendment should be clear. Looking back to the model presented in Chapter Two, the boundaries of communications policymaking are essentially indistinct if the First Amendment remains conceptually fuzzy. This interpretive leeway undermines the effectiveness of the First Amendment as an analytical tool for communications policymakers and policy analysts. As is the case with many of the foundation principles discussed in this book, this lack of conceptual clarity contributes to the principle functioning more as a rhetorical tool to justify policy positions than as an analytical tool for evaluating the effectiveness of policies. Absent an agreed-upon meaning, the First Amendment can be employed with equal effectiveness by opposing sides of a policy issue. Compounding this problem is the fact that neither policymakers nor the courts have been particularly consistent in delineating the exact nature and scope of the First Amendment. In sum, the First Amendment provides an appropriate starting point for this discussion of the foundation principles of communications policy in that it embodies all of the conceptual ambiguity and applicational inconsistency that also characterize each of the principles that follows.

FUNCTIONS OF THE FIRST AMENDMENT

Before discussing the debate over individualist versus collectivist interpretations of the First Amendment, it is necessary to review the related debate regarding the functions, objectives, or values[2] served by the First Amendment. That is, what is the First Amendment meant to achieve? Particularly from a policymaking standpoint, the particular functions associated with the First Amendment are inextricably tied to how it is conceptualized and applied. This relationship reflects the necessary connection between ends and means, with the functions of the First Amendment obviously representing the ends, and the conceptualization and application of the First Amendment (e.g., collectivist vs. individualist) representing key components of the means. Indeed, from a policymaking standpoint it may make sense to conceive of the functions of the First Amendment as the policy objectives, the conceptualization of the First Amendment (in terms of the individualist–collectivist dichotomy) as the overall strategy by which the First Amendment objectives are to be pursued, and the specific regulations that are put into place in response to the chosen conceptualization as the tactics utilized to achieve the First Amendment objectives.

Unfortunately, the current First Amendment environment is one in which there is little concrete consensus in terms of objectives, which of course feeds downward to produce a comparable lack of consensus in terms of strategy and tactics. As this section illustrates, constitutional scholars have associated a wide variety of functions with the First Amendment. These separate objectives are not always mutually exclusive. In some instances, the pursuit of one objective can promote the pursuit of others. In other instances, the pursuit of one objective can severely undermine the pursuit of others (see Bloustein, 1981). The primary purpose of this section is not to wade into the debate regarding the supremacy of some objectives over others (e.g., Baker, 1978; Redish, 1982a; Sunstein, 1993). Rather, the primary goal is to outline the full range of objectives that have been associated with the First Amendment and to explore the linkages between these objectives and the competing conceptualizations of the First Amendment.

The framers of the Constitution were ambiguous about what explicit purposes the First Amendment was meant to serve (see Bloustein, 1981). In addition, as mentioned earlier, the Supreme Court has neglected to provide much clarity on this issue (Emerson,

TABLE 3.1   The Functions of Free Speech

Function	Sources	Derivation of Benefits		Conceptualization	
		Transmission	Reception	Individual	Collective
Self-fulfillment-liberty	Baker (1978); Blousein (1981)	X		X	
Development of individual's faculties	Emerson (1970); Whitney v. California (1927)	X	X	X	
Advancing knowledge-discovering truth	Associated Press v. U.S. (1945); Emerson (1970); Wonnell (1986)	X	X	X	X
Enhancing democratic process	Meiklejohn (1960/1972); Fiss(1990, 1996); Sunstein (1993); Bork (1971)	X	X		X
Checking government power	Blasi(1977); Stewart (1975)	X	X		X
Achieving stability in community	Emerson (1970)	X	X		X
Self-realization/ autonomy of consciousness	Redish (1982a); Reed (1997)	X	X	X	X

1970). Consequently, the underlying rationale(s) for the First Amendment has remained contested territory. Legal scholars and political theorists have developed a variety of values associated with the First Amendment, drawing on both constitutional history and the opinions of the Supreme Court, which, as Shiffrin (1983) notes, "has been unwilling to confine the first amendment to a single value or even to a few values" (p. 1251). We are thus faced with a situation in which a variety of First Amendment functions have been proposed, debated, and criticized (see Baker, 1978; Bork, 1971; Redish, 1982a).

Table 3.1 lists the primary functions that historically have been associated with the First Amendment. This list is drawn from the rather extensive literature devoted to this topic (e.g., Baker, 1978; Blasi, 1977; Bloustein, 1981; Bork, 1971; DuVal, 1972; Emerson, 1970; Fiss, 1986, 1996; Meiklejohn, 1948/1960, 1948/1972; Owen, 1975; Redish, 1982a; Sunstein, 1993). This literature, in turn, has drawn primarily from the history and political philosophy surrounding the drafting of the Constitution and the creation of the First Amendment, as well as from the Supreme Court's First Amendment jurisprudence. In some instances, functions that exhibited significant overlap have been collapsed. The table lists each function of the First Amendment, whether the function requires either the transmission or reception of speech (or both), and whether the function is targeted at the individual or the collective level (or both). Finally, the table lists representative sources in which each of these functions has been developed and discussed.

The Liberty/Self-Fulfillment Function

The first function listed in Table 3.1 reflects the collapsing of a number of similar functions. Many First

Amendment analysts have argued that freedom of speech is necessary for self-fulfillment, or, more specifically, it is necessary for individuals to feel a sense of integrity and worth (Baker, 1978; Bloustein, 1981; Emerson, 1970). From this perspective, free speech is an important aspect of the "life, liberty, and pursuit of happiness" values expressed in the Declaration of Independence (Bloustein, 1981, p. 373). The value of free speech in this case extends primarily from respect for individual autonomy, or liberty, and the degree to which speech allows individuals to define, develop, and express themselves (Baker, 1978). Thus, expressions ranging from pronouncements of political positions to the shouting of expletives in anger are of value in the sense that both reflect the exercise of individual autonomy and liberty that are central to this particular valuation of the First Amendment.

It is important to recognize that, within this particular value framework, the benefits of free speech exclusively involve its effects on the speaker, regardless of whether the speech reached, or had any effect on, listeners (Redish, 1982a). Baker (1978) provides a useful example:

A Vietnam war protester may explain that when she chants "Stop This War Now" at a demonstration, she does so without any expectation that her speech will affect the continuance of war or even that it will communicate anything to people in power; rather, she participates and chants in order to define herself publicly in opposition to the war. This war protest provides a dramatic illustration of the importance of this self-expressive use of speech, independent of any effective communication to others, for self-fulfillment or self-realization. (p. 994)

Within this interpretive framework, freedom of speech becomes "a valuable end in itself, an improvement in the human condition" (Owen, 1975, p. 6). The act of speaking is a right to which we are all entitled, given that the act is central to the individual liberties celebrated and valued in both the Declaration of Independence and the Constitution.

This rationale for First Amendment freedoms has been criticized primarily for failing to distinguish speech from other forms of human activity

and therefore failing to explain: (a) why speech receives separate and unique protection under the Constitution; and (b) why the First Amendment protects speech more than nonspeech forms of expression (e.g., Bork, 1971; Schauer, 1983). These critiques note that, although free speech no doubt promotes individual liberty and self-fulfillment, so does a range of other activities. Consequently, the liberty/self-fulfillment rationale suggests that all forms of self-expression—specifically, actions and behaviors that are expressive of an individual's views or perspectives—should receive protection equal to speech. Thus, according to Schauer (1983), "it is impossible to distinguish an argument for self-expression as an argument for freedom of speech from an argument for self-expression as an argument for liberty in general" (p. 1291). The liberty rationale has also been criticized for failing to acknowledge the benefits that can accrue to the individual from the receipt, as well as the dissemination, of communication (Redish, 1982a, 1982b).[3]

The Development of an Individual's Faculties Function

The second major value associated with the First Amendment, the development of an individual's faculties, represents a slight, but important, extension of the self-fulfillment value. This value reflects the notion that, through both the unencumbered sending and receiving of information, an individual's skills, abilities, and talents expand and evolve. Thus, free speech, from both a transmission and reception standpoint, facilitates an individual's engagement in his constitutional right to improve himself (Emerson, 1970). This value is drawn primarily from Justice Brandeis' famous dissent in *Whitney v. California* (1927), in which he argued that "Those who won our independence believed that the final end of the State was to make men free to develop their faculties" (p. 375). Justice Brandeis saw "the power of reason as applied through public discussion" (*Whitney v. California*, 1927, p. 375) as a primary means by which such individual faculties could be developed. It is this recognition of the value of public discussion— and the interactive nature of such discussion—to individual self-development that differentiates this function of the First Amendment from the liberty/

self-fulfillment function, given that the development of an individual's faculties is seen as requiring both the opportunity to develop and express thoughts, as well as the opportunity to receive, analyze, and possibly adopt the thoughts and ideas of others (e.g., by consuming art or literature), thereby allowing the individual to become a better, more developed person.

Like the liberty/fulfillment rationale, the development of individual faculties rationale has been criticized for failing to adequately distinguish between speech and other human activities. In a well-known criticism leveled at both the liberty and development of individual faculties rationales, Bork (1971) noted that:

> An individual may develop his faculties or derive pleasure from trading on the stock market, following his profession as a river port pilot, working as a barmaid, engaging in sexual activity, playing tennis, rigging prices or in any of thousands of other endeavor. ... These functions or benefits of speech are, therefore, to the principled judge, indistinguishable from the functions or benefits of all other human activity. He cannot, on neutral grounds, choose to protect speech that has only these functions more than he protects any other claimed freedom. (p. 25)

Thus, according to Bork (1971), both the liberty and development of individual faculties rationales fail to explain why speech deserves special treatment and consideration.

The Advancement of Knowledge/Discovery of Truth Function

The third major value associated with the First Amendment revolves around the advancement of knowledge and the discovery of truth. In this context, the free and open exchange of ideas facilitated by the First Amendment increases the level of knowledge among citizens, which then allows them to make wise decisions (Emerson, 1970; Wonnell, 1986), both individually and collectively. This First Amendment value is based on the notion that "the free exchange of ideas is a necessary condition for the development of knowledge in all fields of inquiry"

(Bloustein, 1981, p. 375). Under this logic, the greater the volume and diversity of information, the greater the opportunity for increased knowledge and well-informed decision making. This value of the First Amendment owes much to the well-known "marketplace of ideas" concept (see Chapter Five). This metaphor emphasizes the improvements in citizen knowledge and decision making that arise from all individuals having the opportunity to both express their viewpoints and encounter the viewpoints of others (see Wonnell, 1986).

The advancement of knowledge/discovery of truth function has been criticized primarily on the grounds that the notion of an objective and verifiable "truth" is unrealistic (Ingber, 1984; Redish, 1982a). In addition, some scholars have argued that limitations on the free flow of information can actually improve decision making by reducing the burdens and difficulties associated with processing large amounts of information (Fitts, 1990).

The Enhancing the Democratic Process Function

The fourth value frequently associated with the First Amendment focuses explicitly on the political functions of free speech. Specifically, the primary value of free speech is seen as its ability to improve and enhance the democratic process. When the First Amendment is approached primarily in terms of its political value, one can think of free speech as functioning "as a corollary to democratic theory" (Ingber 1984, p. 8). The well-known logic of this relationship between free speech and the democratic process is that, given the democratic system's emphasis on self-determination, democracy only functions effectively when citizens are capable of collectively making decisions that truly serve their best interests. The likelihood of such effective political decision making taking place increases with the degree to which citizens are well-informed about all of the decision options available to them and the pros, cons, and likely effects of each decision option. The likelihood of citizens possessing such knowledge increases with the degree to which ideas representing all sources, perspectives, and viewpoints are available for consideration. Thus, the logic of this perspective dictates that the value of the First Amendment lies within its ability to promote the flow of diverse political ideas and viewpoints to the citizenry.

The origins of this interpretation of the First Amendment, and its increasing prominence in legal scholarship (see Bhagwat, 1995; Bork, 1971; Fiss, 1986, 1996; Lichtenberg, 1990; Sunstein, 1993) and judicial decision making (see Brennan, 1965; Reed, 1997), owe much to the work of Alexander Meiklejohn (1948/1972). Meiklejohn provides a detailed account of the relationship between the First Amendment and the functioning of democracy, arguing that "the citizens of the United States will be fit to govern themselves under their own institutions only if they have faced squarely and fearlessly everything that can be said in favor of those institutions, and everything that can be said against them" (p. 91). This function of the First Amendment is clearly related to the previous function, in that both involve the relationship between knowledge and decision making. However, in this case the context is much more specific, in that the focus is exclusively on knowledge and decision making in the political realm, where collective decision making predominates.

The primary criticism leveled at this rationale for free speech rights is that it takes an unacceptably narrow view of the type of speech that deserves constitutional protection. Under a strict interpretation of the democratic process rationale, a variety of traditionally protected types of speech, such as art, entertainment, and scientific discourse could potentially be excluded (Redish, 1982a; Stern, 1990).[4] In addition, such an approach has been criticized for requiring difficult—and perhaps impossible—content-based judgments as to what constitutes political speech (e.g., Bloustein, 1981; Post, 1993).[5]

Even when the advocates of this democratic process interpretation of the value of free speech have expanded the range of speech types that receive protection, they have been further criticized for providing an insufficient logical framework for such expansions. Meiklejohn (1961), for instance, argues that nonpolitical forms of communication such as science, philosophy, and art are entitled to protection because they promote "the knowledge, intelligence, and sensitivity to human values … which, so far as possible, a ballot should express" (p. 256). Critics

have argued, however, that such an extension is unacceptably broad and undermines the original rationale of a primarily political function of the First Amendment (e.g., Bork, 1971; Stern, 1990; Redish, 1982a).

The Checking Governmental Power Function

The fifth function that has been associated with the First Amendment—the "checking function"—is related to the fourth in terms of its political orientation. The checking function refers to the value of free speech in preventing governmental misconduct. Developed primarily by Blasi (1977), this valuation of the First Amendment focuses on the necessity of free speech for effectively "alerting the polity to the facts or implications of official behavior, presumably triggering responses that will mitigate the ill effects of such behavior" (p. 546). Stewart (1975) argues that the checking function is a primary rationale for the separate "or of the press" clause in the First Amendment, given the drafters' concern with establishing and protecting a "fourth branch" of government (pp. 634–635).[6] This valuation of the First Amendment no doubt reflects important motivating factors for the drafters of the Constitution (Blasi, 1977). When the origination of the First Amendment is placed within its historical context of colonial revolt, it becomes clear that the amendment originated, at least in part, in "reaction to the oppressions of colonial government," and due to an overriding concern with constructing checks on government power (Owen, 1975, p. 6).

The checking value of free speech is perhaps best represented in First Amendment jurisprudence in an opinion written by Justice Hugo Black in *New York Times v. United States* (1971). According to Justice Black:

> The Government's power to censor the press was abolished so that the press would remain forever free to censure the Government. The press was protected so that it could bare the secrets of government and inform the people. Only a free and unrestrained press can effectively expose deception in government. And paramount among the responsibilities of a free press is the duty to prevent any part of

the government from deceiving the people and sending them off to distant lands to die of foreign fevers and foreign shot and shell. (p. 717)

As Blasi (1977) notes, however, such explicit invocations of the checking function of the First Amendment are relatively infrequent in the Supreme Court's decision making.

The primary criticism that has been leveled against the checking function of the First Amendment is that it is indistinguishable from the enhancing democracy function discussed previously (Redish, 1982a). Although Blasi (1977) contends that the checking function is a separate, supplementary function to the democratic process function, Redish (1982a) argues that "the checking function ultimately derives from the principle of democratic self-rule" (pp. 615–616).

The Community Stability Function

The sixth function, achieving stability in the community, grows from the notion that suppression of discussion undermines the possibility for rational judgment and from the idea that "suppression promotes inflexibility and stultification, preventing society from adjusting to changing circumstances or developing new ideas" (Emerson, 1970, p. 7). In contrast, open discussion:

> promotes greater cohesion in society because people are more ready to accept decisions that go against them if they have a part in the decision-making process. ... Freedom of expression thus provides a framework in which the conflict necessary to the progress of a society can take place without destroying the society. It is an essential mechanism for maintaining the balance between stability and change. (Emerson, 1970, p. 7)

Clearly, this viewpoint on the value of freedom of expression extends beyond speech's political function, instead placing speech in the pivotal role of allowing for steady and productive social change, while at the same time ensuring that citizens do not react negatively or hostilely to changes that they oppose.

The community stability rationale has been criticized for focusing only on "issues of expediency or prudence" (Bork, 1971, p. 25) and therefore not falling within the realm of concern of the courts. According to Bork (1971), the community stability rationale

> raises issues to be determined solely by the legislature or, in some cases by the executive. ... These decisions, involving only the issue of the expedient course, are indistinguishable from thousands of other managerial judgments governments must make daily. ... It seems plain that decisions involving only judgments of expediency are for the political branches and not for the judiciary. (pp. 25–26)

Thus, from this perspective, the quest for a stable community is not a concern that generally permeates the question of the appropriate conceptualization and application of the First Amendment.

The Self-Realization–Autonomy of Consciousness Function

Finally, the "self-realization" and "autonomy of consciousness" functions represent efforts to combine each of the functions described earlier into a single, all-encompassing principle. According to Redish (1982a), each of the other First Amendment values discussed previously "are in reality sub-values of self-realization" (p. 596), in that each contributes to an individual's ability to realize his or her full potential or to control his or her own destiny through decision making. A retrospective analysis of the opinions of Justice Thurgood Marshall concluded that his decision making and analysis consistently emphasized the value of self-realization (Wells, 1993), as later articulated by Redish (1982a). Marshall, like Redish (1982a), saw broader social objectives such as effective democracy, governmental restraint, and community stability primarily as a function of individual autonomy and achievement.

The self-realization function of the First Amendment has been criticized for being too broad to establish any meaningful limits on speech. According to Baker (1982), "A value that will justify anything is of little help: an informative theory must describe and defend specific elaborations of such general values" (pp. 667–668).

The "autonomy of consciousness" value is closely related to the self-realization value in that it too attempts to incorporate all of the previously articulated values—including self-realization—into a single, unifying value. Recently articulated by Reed (1997), the autonomy of consciousness value asserts that:

> human consciousness with its strong sense of an individual "self" that both knows and knows that it knows derives specifically from the use of language. In the most direct sense possible, the individual self to which constitutional rights accrue arises from the language in which we are immersed from earliest childhood. "Freedom of speech" becomes, then, the constitutional equivalent of autonomy of consciousness, consciousness that is realized when the government restrains language only in the most exigent circumstances. (p. 2)

Reed (1997) emphasizes that consciousness is both an individual and a social phenomenon, therefore requiring attention to both individual autonomy and community welfare. Although the autonomy of consciousness value of the First Amendment has yet to be subjected to detailed analysis and criticism, its attempt at unifying all First Amendment values under a single umbrella concept would likely make it vulnerable to the same criticisms of overbreadth that have been leveled against the self-realization value.

Observations

A few key points need to be made in regard to this list of First Amendment functions. First, all but the liberty–self-fulfillment function of the First Amendment derive at least part of their value from the reception of information. That is, whereas the liberty function focuses entirely on the benefits that accrue to the speaker via his or her opportunities to express him or herself, the remaining six functions all, to varying to degrees, derive their value from both the transmission and reception of thoughts and ideas. The development of an individual's faculties depends in part on exposure to the ideas and insights of others. The advancement of knowledge can only take place when the relevant information can be obtained,

synthesized, and analyzed. Similarly, the democratic process is strengthened when voters participate with the wisdom and insight that come from the exposure to—and consideration of—a wide range of viewpoints and decision options. Free speech only has the capacity to impose a check on governmental power when the populace becomes aware of government abuses. Stability in the community requires both that citizens participate in the decision-making process and that new ideas and information regarding problems facing society be free to circulate among the citizenry. Finally, the self-realization–autonomy of consciousness function acknowledges the importance of the reception of diverse viewpoints for individual decision making and development (Redish, 1982a; Reed, 1997).

This point regarding the sources of the First Amendment values seems particularly important given that there has been some uncertainty as to whether the First Amendment includes the right to receive information (e.g., Rumble, 1994; Stern, 1990; Wagner, 1998).[7] When this question is informed by the full range of functions associated with the First Amendment, it seems clear that the First Amendment must encompass the reception of information, as well as the dissemination, in order for most of its functions to be effectively carried out. Indeed, an emphasis only on the rights to transmit information would appear to reflect an incomplete application of the First Amendment, one that fails to account for the full range of objectives that the First Amendment is intended to achieve. On this subject, the Supreme Court has noted that "where a speaker exists, ... the protection afforded is to the communication, to its source and to its recipients both" (*Virginia State Board of Pharmacy v. Virginia Citizens Consumer Council, Inc.*, 1976, p. 756).

When we think of the benefits of free speech emanating from both the transmission and reception of information and ideas, another important aspect of the First Amendment's value comes to light. Specifically, as long as benefits are seen in the reception of information, there is a "network externality" component to the First Amendment. Network externalities, in the traditional economic sense, are those benefits that accrue to a user of a particular product or service as a result of the fact that the user is part of a network of users of that product or service. Thus, one of the classic examples of network externalities is the telephone system (see Chapter Eight). As more individuals are connected to the telephone system, the more valuable the system is to the individual user. A telephone is essentially worthless to an individual user until at least one other person, and preferably many more people, also purchases a telephone.

In terms of the First Amendment, the greater the number of people who have and take advantage of their full First Amendment freedoms, the greater the value of these First Amendment freedoms to the individual citizen, given that, for the individual, increased value (as related to the functions of the First Amendment identified earlier) comes from increases in the quantity and diversity of information, viewpoints, and perspectives available for consumption. If we value the First Amendment in terms of its ability to provide a free flow of diverse opinions, viewpoints, ideas, and perspectives to citizens, granting First Amendment freedoms to a select few limits the overall value of the First Amendment to those grantees. In contrast, if the value of the First Amendment resides only in the opportunities it affords for the expression of ideas, then its value for the individual citizen is in no way dependent on the level of First Amendment freedom afforded other citizens. From this perspective, being the only person in the country with free speech rights provides as much value to that individual as a situation in which all citizens have free speech rights.

In addition, once we acknowledge the network externalities aspect of receiving speech, it becomes clear how the possibility that the ideas of some individuals or groups may be very easily accessible or have a very broad range of projection, while the ideas of other individuals or groups may be relatively inaccessible, can itself represent a First Amendment problem. To illustrate with an analogy, the valuation of the reception of information dictates that sending a message out to sea in a bottle—certainly a case of unrestricted expression of an idea—does not serve the values inherent in the First Amendment to the same degree as delivering that same message in a 10,000 seat auditorium, given that the audience that can potentially access the bottled message is much smaller. It seems, then, that maximization of opportunities

for both expression and reception should be a priority for policymakers seeking to uphold the First Amendment.

The second major observation, which ties directly to the discussion that is to follow, is that the values associated with the First Amendment are roughly equally distributed between those targeted primarily at the individual and those targeted at the collective (see Table 3.1). The liberty and development of faculties functions are targeted primarily at the individual, given that they focus on the value of free speech in enabling an individual to achieve happiness and self-worth and become a better, more developed person. In contrast, the democratic process, checking, and community stability functions all focus on the value of the First Amendment for citizens as a collective. These values all focus primarily on the functioning of social institutions, rather than the conduct and quality of individual lives. The remaining values function at both the individual and the collective levels. The advancing knowledge–discovering truth objective functions at both levels, given that a vibrant marketplace of ideas can improve both individual and collective decision making. The self-realization–autonomy of consciousness function also functions at both levels, given that it reflects the idea that an emphasis on the value of individual development is an effective (perhaps the most effective) means of achieving collective-level objectives (Redish, 1982a; Wells, 1993). For instance, the development of individual knowledge and decision-making skills could positively affect collective political decision making (Bloustein, 1981). The self-realization–autonomy of consciousness function therefore falls into both categories, although the direction of the causal relationship asserted within it certainly prioritizes an individual conceptualization of the value of the First Amendment over a collective conceptualization.

The key at this point is to recognize that there is a fairly even distribution between individual and collective values associated with the First Amendment. Given that each of the values previously identified draws at least some support from the historical and intellectual contexts surrounding the development of the Constitution or from Supreme Court jurisprudence, it seems safe to conclude, as many scholars have, that the First Amendment is a multivalued concept (Blasi, 1977; Cohen, 1993; Emerson, 1970; Schauer, 1983; Sunstein, 1993) and that this multi-dimensionality need not be interpreted as a problem requiring solving. As Sunstein (1993) notes, "We should acknowledge that free speech values are likely to be plural and diverse rather than unitary," given that "This is true for most constitutional rights, which serve a range of purposes" (p. 129). Thus, from a policymaking and policy analysis standpoint, the First Amendment represents a wide range of policy objectives to be considered and assessed.

INDIVIDUAL VERSUS COLLECTIVE APPROACHES TO THE FIRST AMENDMENT

These different values associated with free speech figure prominently in the two primary approaches to conceptualizing the First Amendment. One of the central debates in First Amendment theory is the one revolving around whether the First Amendment is primarily intended to protect the speech rights of the individual or the speech rights and well-being of the citizenry as a collective (see Kelly & Donway, 1990). Ingber (1990) notes that these two interpretive positions have typically been regarded as antagonistic. Each conceptualization in this interpretive dichotomy is of course tightly associated with the different sets of values outlined in the previous section. That is, individualist interpretations of the First Amendment draw their strength primarily from the individual-level values identified in Table 3.1 (e.g., liberty, improvement of individual faculties), whereas collectivist interpretations of the First Amendment look to the more community-based values (e.g., stability, democracy, checking governmental power).

This individualist–collectivist tension is particularly important from a communications policy perspective because the conceptual level that is chosen is central to the underlying logic of many policies. Thus, some policies that appear valid and justifiable under a strictly individualistic interpretation of the First Amendment may lose their validity under a strictly collectivist interpretation, and vice versa. Obviously the possibility that a single principle can freely be conceptualized in ways that lead to different policy outcomes undermines the degree to which the principle

can function as a meaningful analytical tool for the design and evaluation of communications policies.

The Individualist Interpretation of the First Amendment

The individualist interpretation of the First Amendment places its highest priority on preserving and enhancing the free speech rights of the individual citizen. Needless to say, this interpretation of the First Amendment draws its underlying logic primarily from the First Amendment functions outlined in the previous section that emphasize individual rights, development, and satisfaction (e.g., Baker, 1978). Individualist interpretations of the First Amendment typically focus on maximizing the autonomy of the individual citizen (e.g., Scanlon, 1979; Strauss, 1991). For instance, Baker's (1978) "liberty" theory of freedom of speech places governmental respect for individual autonomy as a central guiding assumption. This autonomy may be conceptualized primarily in terms of the autonomy to speak or in terms of the autonomy to listen. It is important to recall that both speaker and listener freedoms are central to many of the individual-level values associated with the First Amendment (e.g., decision making, development of individual faculties). As Wells (1997) notes, the Supreme Court has sometimes chosen to emphasize speaker autonomy, while at other times choosing to emphasize listener autonomy.

Such an emphasis on individual autonomy (whether in terms of speaking or listening) grows from the fact that constitutional rights are traditionally perceived as protections of the individual from unjust governmental intrusions (Ingber, 1990). As Fallon (1994) notes, "recognition of autonomy as a First Amendment value promotes coherence between the First Amendment and other constitutional provisions" (p. 902). Ingber (1990) traces the roots of the individualist interpretation of the First Amendment to the Enlightenment era philosophers of the 17th and 18th centuries. He notes that, within this interpretation of free speech, the focus is on:

> the individual as a free, rational, and autonomous agent who serves both as the source of political authority and as the ultimate justification for its exercise. Consequently, most

"rights-based" theories of constitutional law place at their center a concern for upholding individual value preferences and the liberty of individual action. (p. 5)

Within this interpretive framework, with its emphasis on individual autonomy, free speech rights are typically conceived of as a "negative liberty" (see Fallon, 1994); that is, in terms of freedom from external interference in doing what one wants. The key analytical issue in this approach to the First Amendment involves whether or not one individual's exercise of his or her liberties unacceptably intrudes on the liberties (speech or otherwise) of others (Fallon, 1994).

The Supreme Court's prioritization of individual autonomy within the context of the First Amendment is perhaps most vividly illustrated in the Court's opinion in *Buckley v. Valeo* (1976). In this decision, the Court rejected congressional legislation limiting campaign expenditures, viewing such restrictions as a violation of the First Amendment. The Court concluded that "The concept that government may restrict the speech of some … in order to enhance the relative voice of others is wholly foreign to the First Amendment" (pp. 48-49). Clearly, within this interpretation of the First Amendment, under no circumstances can government subjugate the speech rights of an individual to the speech rights of any other individual, organization, or institution. The key aspect of this statement is that, in emphasizing that such subjugation of individual speech rights is "wholly foreign to the First Amendment," the Court is rejecting any notion of a First Amendment conceptualization that extends beyond the level of individual speech autonomy. Other representative examples of an individualistic interpretation of the First Amendment within the Supreme Court include the statement in *Cohen v. California* (1971) that free speech comports "with the premise of individual dignity and choice upon which our political system rests" (p. 24), and Justice Brennan's dissent in *Herbert v. Lando* (1979), in which he stated that free speech is "itself an end" that is "intrinsic to individual dignity" (p. 186).

However, these statements by the Supreme Court do not necessarily suggest that those community-level values associated with the First Amendment, such as

stability and effective democracy, are irrelevant to individualist First Amendment interpretations. In the extreme, this may be the case; however, advocates of individualist interpretations of the First Amendment have often emphasized the capacity of such an interpretive approach to simultaneously advance community-level objectives. Indeed, the concept of individual autonomy certainly has strong theoretical linkages with the effective functioning of democracy (see Fallon, 1994; Wells, 1997). According to this logic, only when citizens are truly and fully autonomous can they effectively carry out their responsibilities for self-rule. Any government-imposed restrictions on this autonomy thereby threaten the process of effective democratic self-governance. As Post (1993) notes, "The protection of individual autonomy prevents the state from violating the central democratic aspiration to create a communicative structure dedicated to 'the mutual respect of autonomous wills'" (p. 1121).

Following this logic, efforts to develop unitary, encompassing values of free speech have generally prioritized individual autonomy as the means by which community-based objectives such as stability and effective self-governance are achieved. Redish's (1982a) "self-realization" approach to the First Amendment is oriented first and foremost (as the label would suggest) toward facilitating the development of the individual. Speech values such as checking government abuses and facilitating effective self-governance are not, however, rejected as irrelevant within this context. Rather, they are placed in the position of "subvalues" of the broader concept of self-realization (Redish, 1982a).

Similarly, Reed's (1997) more recent attempt at unifying the array of values associated with the First Amendment into a single "meta value" begins at the individual level, with an emphasis on the "autonomy of consciousness." Clearly, the autonomy principle, which has traditionally been central to individualist interpretations of the First Amendment, is prominent here. However, Reed then argues for an expanded notion of autonomy that incorporates both the individual and his or her role as part of a larger community (see also Wells, 1997). Thus, as with the self-realization approach, the autonomy of consciousness approach has individual autonomy as its evaluative foundation, but relates the achievement of such autonomy to the achievement of broader, community-based objectives.

In sum, individualist interpretations of the First Amendment focus primarily on how free speech bestows benefits on the individual citizen. Values such as individual liberty, self-development, and autonomy factor heavily in individualist interpretations. Within individualist interpretations, the benefits of the First Amendment may be derived from either the sending or the receiving of speech (or both). In addition, a focus on the individual can lead to the achievement of more community-based First Amendment values, such as effective democracy and community stability. However, such values are generally perceived as secondary to more individualist-oriented goals, or they are perceived as objectives best achieved via the preservation and promotion of individual rights of self-expression, given that within this interpretive approach, individual autonomy is the overriding policy priority.

The Collectivist Interpretation of the First Amendment

The collectivist interpretation of the First Amendment focuses on creating a speech environment in which as many citizens as possible have the means to express their views and to have access to as many other viewpoints as possible. Thus, free speech within the collectivist context refers not to the action of an individual, but to a "social state of affairs" (Fiss, 1986, p. 1411). Adherents to the collectivist perspective tend to emphasize the community-based objectives associated with the First Amendment, such as stability, collective decision making, and, most often, the relationship between free speech and effective democracy. According to Fiss (1996), a well-known advocate of the collectivist interpretation:

> Speech is valued so importantly in the Constitution ... not because it is a form of self-expression or self-actualization but rather because it is essential for collective self-determination. Democracy allows the people to choose the form of life they wish to live and presupposes that this choice is made against a background of public debate that is, to use

the now famous formula of Justice Brennan, "uninhibited, robust, and wide-open." (p. 3)

The First Amendment thus functions as the means to ends that explicitly prioritize the welfare of the collective citizenry over the welfare of the individual speaker. Some scholars have concluded that the logic of providing special protection for speech extends from the fact that the benefits of free speech to the community far outweigh the benefits to the individual (Farber, 1991). Reflecting this assignment of value, a central guiding principle of the collectivist approach is that, "what is essential is not that everyone shall speak, but that everything worth saying shall be said" (Meiklejohn, 1948/1972, p. 25).

From an applicational standpoint, the key point of departure of the collectivist interpretation from the individualist one is that the collectivists reject the absolutist interpretation of the First Amendment's command that Congress make no law abridging freedom of speech or of the press. From the collectivist perspective, the phrasing of the First Amendment clearly grants Congress the authority to make laws that enhance the free speech environment. As Meiklejohn (1948/1972) argues, "by these words, Congress is not debarred from all action upon freedom of speech. Legislation which abridges that freedom is forbidden, but not legislation to enlarge and enrich it" (p. 16). Indeed, many proponents of the collectivist interpretation of the First Amendment advocate the imposition of government regulations (such as campaign spending limits) in order to correct perceived inadequacies in the current system of communicating information to citizens (e.g., Fiss, 1996; Sunstein, 1993), whereas individualist interpretations typically oppose any government regulation of speech as an infringement on individual autonomy.

This difference in applicational approach extends primarily from the fact that legislation designed to enlarge and enrich free speech from a collectivist standpoint can simultaneously impose limitations on the free speech of certain individuals. From a collectivist standpoint such infringements on individual freedoms are generally acceptable, given that the First Amendment's primary responsibility is seen as being to the citizenry as a whole and its key purpose as promoting and maintaining an environment that best ensures a free flow of diverse ideas. Fiss (1990) illustrates this acceptance through a comparison between the individualist interpretation's emphasis on the principle of autonomy and the collectivist interpretation's emphasis on the principle of public debate:

> what the autonomy principle provides, is a very strong presumption against state interference with speech. Under the public-debate principle, there is no such presumption. The state stands on equal footing with other institutions and is allowed, encouraged, and sometimes required to enact measures or issue decrees designed to enrich public debate, even if that action entails an interference with the speech of some and thus a denial of individual or institutional autonomy. (p. 142)

This possibility for infringement on individual freedoms is apparent in Meiklejohn's (1948/1972) well-known illustration of the "town meeting" as the "model by which free political procedures may be measured" (p. 22). Meiklejohn describes the town meeting as a function that all members of the community are free to attend in order to discuss matters of public interest. Within this context, each participant "has a right and a duty to think his own thoughts, to express them, and to listen to the arguments of others. The basic principle is that the freedom of speech shall be unabridged" (p. 22). However, such meetings are presided over by a moderator, whose responsibilities include calling the meeting to order and enforcing rules of order, such as limiting participants' remarks to "questions before the house," and preventing interruptions of a speaker who "has the floor." Clearly, then, there are abridgements of speech within the traditional town meeting format. Without these abridgements, the meeting would be ineffectual in accomplishing the goals for which it was convened. Thus, "The meeting has assembled, not primarily to talk, but primarily by means of talking to get business done. ... It is not a dialectical free-for-all. It is self-government" (p. 23).[8]

In recent years, the collectivist interpretation of the First Amendment seems to have picked up momentum, due in large part to the increasing sense that the development of the means of communications in the United States has followed a path that has diminished the individual citizen's capacity to share in the exchange of ideas and information and has thereby degraded the degree to which the First Amendment promotes effective self-government (e.g., Barron, 1967; Ingber, 1984). The increasing reliance on media technologies for information, the increasing concentration of media ownership, and the inherently commercial orientation of media industries are seen as a combination of factors that undermine the collectivist notion of the First Amendment (e.g., Fiss, 1990; Sunstein, 1993).

The first component of this argument involves the fact that the process of public debate and deliberation has shifted primarily from the interpersonal to the media realm (Page, 1996), thereby allowing a much narrower segment of the population to directly participate in the process. Second, the economic imperatives inherent in what has become the primary realm of public deliberation undermine the expectation of a vibrant exchange of diverse ideas and viewpoints. An early milestone in the development of this argument is the famous report from the Commission on Freedom of the Press (1947), which argued that the increasing influence of economic imperatives on media owners led to a decrease in the diversity and depth of information presented, as owners focused on presenting content that attracted the largest possible audience (see also Barron, 1967). More recently, Fiss (1990), among others (e.g., Bollinger, 1991), has argued that there is an inevitable conflict between the economic imperatives that guide media organizations and the need for citizens to be supplied with a sufficient quantity and diversity of information necessary for effective self-governing decision making.

A key point of these discussions is that it is dangerously myopic to consider the government as the only institution capable of restricting collective-level First Amendment freedoms. Media organizations and other nongovernmental institutions have the capacity to degrade the free speech environment as well (see Ingber, 1984). According to Sullivan (1995):

> Some nominally private entities ... can wield as much power as government (or even more) over the content and distribution of speech. In

this view, for example, corporations, unions, political parties, universities, broadcast media, and organized crime syndicates, to name a few, might have more functional power to shape public discourse than does government. (p. 955)

This point has been explicitly acknowledged by the Supreme Court. In the well-known *Associated Press v. United States* (1945) case, the Court stated that "Freedom of the press from governmental interference under the First Amendment does not sanction repression of that freedom by private interests" (p. 20).

The potential for private institutions to abridge collectively conceptualized First Amendment freedoms, and thereby undermine the democratic process, leads many proponents of the collectivist perspective to advocate that government authority be viewed less as a threat to free speech and more as a means of promoting free speech (Barron, 1967; Fiss, 1990, 1996; Sunstein, 1993). Government's capacity to limit free speech abridgements created by other institutions would thus create an environment that is more conducive to effective self-determination and self-government. From this standpoint, government actions taken against individuals or institutions, such as publishers or broadcasters, who are exercising their capacity to restrict the flow of ideas, may be "examples not of a denial of sovereignty but an exercise of it" (Schauer, 1986, p. 778).

To take this argument one step further, failure to take such action may itself be a dereliction of Congress' responsibility to make no law abridging freedom of speech or of the press. Sunstein (1993) provides perhaps the most thorough articulation of this perspective. He argues that, although private actions are not subject to constitutional constraint, an understanding of the full extent of what constitutes government action reveals that laissez-faire approaches to government involvement in speech themselves represent specific government actions. That is, the opportunities for private entities to favor the expression of some ideas over others are often the result of specific government actions, whether they be common law decisions or the allocation of property rights. Thus, for example, the relative autonomy

granted to broadcasters in their use of the spectrum, and their consequent ability to exclude certain viewpoints while favoring others, is a function of the property rights established by the system of broadcast licensing. The degree to which broadcasters exclude certain viewpoints and thereby degrade the collective conceptualization of the First Amendment is therefore as much a function of government action as if the government directed that certain viewpoints be excluded (Sunstein, 1993).

In the end, the key point of this perspective is that common law rules and property rights represent government-imposed speech regulation in the same way that overt, content-specific regulations do. Any exercise of government-granted exclusionary power over speech should be approached not solely as the exercise of private power, but the exercise of government power as well. When government action is evaluated from this perspective, there is "no such thing as 'no regulation' of speech" (Sunstein, 1993, p. 39),[9] and the analytical framework for examining the relationship between government and the First Amendment broadens considerably (for a critique of this perspective, see Bunker, 2000).

THE FIRST AMENDMENT AND COMMUNICATIONS POLICYMAKING

The preceding sections outlined two distinct, although potentially interrelated, conceptualizations of the First Amendment, each of which draws on a different set of values or objectives that have been associated with the First Amendment. There are a number of key unanswered questions that have allowed these competing interpretations of the First Amendment to exist side by side, absent a clear directive from either constitutional history or the Supreme Court. These questions revolve around possible interrelationships between individualist and collectivist approaches. For instance, is the prioritization of individual freedoms an effective—or even the most effective—means of creating a robust free speech environment? By the same token, what effect does a collective approach to free speech rights have on aggregate individual First Amendment freedoms? Is a collectivist approach to the First Amendment the best means of maximizing individual freedoms (see Bloustein, 1981)? As was discussed previously, theoretical linkages between individualist and collectivist interpretations of the First Amendment have been forged, primarily in terms of assertions that maximizing individual freedoms promotes a vibrant collective speech environment (e.g., Bloustein, 1981; Wells, 1997); however, these central questions may not be effectively transferrable from the theoretical to the empirical realm.

From a policymaking standpoint, an individualist-oriented First Amendment functions primarily as a constraint on policymakers' actions. In contrast, a collectivist-oriented First Amendment functions more as a distinct policy objective to be pursued, rather than as a boundary line to be respected in the pursuit of other policy objectives. Obviously, these two interpretations represent very different roles for the First Amendment in communications policymaking. The Supreme Court has often been characterized as generally favoring the individualist interpretation of the First Amendment over the collectivist interpretation (see Ingber, 1990; Post, 1993). Post (1993) goes so far as to describe the Court as "largely hostile" (p. 1109) to the collectivist interpretation. These observations provide an important indication of which interpretation, as reflected in specific communications policies, is likely to withstand judicial scrutiny.

However, that any one interpretation should predominate in the Court's First Amendment analysis—or in policymakers' analysis, for that matter—is unsettling, given that (a) the values associated with the First Amendment are equally distributed between the individual and the collective interpretations (see Table 3.1); and (b) a positive relationship between individualist and collectivist approaches has not been convincingly demonstrated. It would seem, in fact, that even protecting individual speech autonomy requires significant attention to the broader speech environment.

Recall that six of the seven First Amendment values outlined previously drew at least part of their value from the extent to which audience members had the opportunity to receive a diverse array of information from a diversity of sources. From this standpoint, the protection and promotion of First Amendment rights of listeners seems essential for effectively serving even a reasonable range of First Amendment values. For audience interests to be effectively served, there needs to be at least some emphasis placed on the collectivist interpretation of the First Amendment. Certainly, many individualist values, such as the development of one's faculties and effective decision making, also draw heavily from the reception of information (see Table 3.1); thus, it would be a mistake to associate listener rights with the collectivist interpretation of the First Amendment and speaker rights with the individualist interpretation. However, maximizing an individual's opportunities to receive a diversity of information requires more attention to the environment in which information is transmitted and received than does maximizing an individual's opportunities to speak. If we value the reception aspect of the First Amendment, granting everyone an absolute First Amendment right to speak is meaningless unless they are able to do so in an environment that effectively allows their speech to be accessed by the audience. Only then can the network externalities associated with free speech be realized. This linkage is well-articulated by Scanlon (1979) who notes that, "The central audience interest in expression ... is the interest in having a good *environment* for the formation of one's beliefs and desires" (p. 527; emphasis added). Thus, a free speech interpretation that adequately accounts for the value inherent in audience exposure to speech is most likely also concerned with pursuing the collectivist notion of a vibrant free speech environment (see Stern, 1990).

The Supreme Court offered its most explicit acknowledgment of the value of the collectivist interpretation of the First Amendment in its decision regarding the constitutionality of the Fairness Doctrine *(Red Lion Broadcasting v. Federal Communications Commission,* 1969). The FCC had instituted the Fairness Doctrine under the premise that a primary function of mass communication in a democracy was to develop "an informed public opinion through the dissemination of news and ideas concerning the vital public issues of the day" (Federal Communications Commission, 1949, p. 1249). As this statement suggests, the Fairness Doctrine clearly reflected a collectivist approach to the First Amendment in communications regulation, given its emphasis on free speech's political function (although later reassessment would suggest that the Fairness Doctrine may have undermined this conceptualization of the First Amendment as much as, or more than, it undermined the individualist conceptualization [Federal Communications Commission, 1985a; Hazlett & Sosa, 1997]).[10] This interpretation was largely upheld by the Supreme Court when the Fairness Doctrine came under challenge. According to the Court, the Fairness Doctrine, despite its infringements on the editorial discretion of broadcasters, "enhanced rather than abridged the freedoms of speech and press protected by the First Amendment" (*Red Lion Broadcasting v. Federal Communications Commission*, 1969, p. 375). The Court found that the Fairness Doctrine was not "inconsistent with the First Amendment goal of producing an informed public capable of conducting its own affairs" (*Red Lion Broadcasting v. Federal Communications Commission*, 1969, p. 392). However, in the years following the Red Lion decision, the Court made it clear that its First Amendment analysis in that case was based largely on its perception of the unique "scarcity" of the broadcast spectrum (e.g., *Federal Communications Commission v. League of Women Voters*, 1984). Thus, the Court has offered few other predominantly collectivist interpretations of the First Amendment, and the *Red Lion* decision stands out as something of an anomaly (Post, 1993), particularly given the diminished relevance of the scarcity rationale over the past three decades (see Coase, 1959; Fowler & Brenner, 1982; Spitzer, 1989).[11]

It is important to emphasize that the point here is not to advocate an exclusively collectivist interpretation of the First Amendment. Indeed, such a unidimensional interpretation runs into difficulties similar to those of the purely individualist interpretation when it encounters the extensive history of constitutional thought that has emphasized the primacy of individual rights and a history of Supreme Court jurisprudence that emphasizes individual autonomy (see Ingber, 1990). Rather, the point here is to emphasize that, when we draw from the values associated with the First Amendment, collectivist approaches to free speech have comparable claims to prominence in First Amendment analysis as individualist interpretations. Consequently, it may be that there is a central balancing test inherent in the First Amendment that has gone largely undiscussed.

Toward a New First Amendment Balancing Test

In deciding First Amendment issues, the courts typically balance the First Amendment rights of the speaker against other compelling government interests. This traditional balancing test involves asking whether the gravity of the "evil" sought to be prevented by the government regulation justifies the extent of the infringement on free speech imposed by the regulation. First explicitly articulated by Chief Judge Learned Hand in *United States v. Dennis* (1950), the test was later adopted by the Supreme Court in its decision in the appeal of the *Dennis* decision (*Dennis v. United States*, 1951) and quickly became a prominent component of the Court's First Amendment analysis (see Frantz, 1962; Posner, 1986).

This general First Amendment balancing process has grown more complex over time. Today, different standards of scrutiny have been developed for *content specific* and *content neutral* regulations. Content-specific regulations are based on the content of the material being communicated (e.g., violence or sex). Content-specific regulations must satisfy a "strict scrutiny" standard, which requires that the regulation serve a "compelling" government interest and be the least restrictive means of serving that interest (see *Turner Broadcasting System, Inc. v. Federal Communications Commission*, 1994). Content-neutral regulations, on the other hand, impose speech infringements that are not based on the nature of the content being communicated (e.g., noise restrictions around a hospital). Such regulations are subject to a less stringent "intermediate" scrutiny standard, which requires that the regulation serve a "substantial" government interest, as opposed to a "compelling" government interest, and that the regulation imposes an infringement on First Amendment freedoms that is no greater than is essential to the furtherance of that interest (see Stone, 1987; *United States v. O'Brien*, 1968).

The key point here is that this balancing process may reflect, in some instances, an inaccurate dichotomy between the suppression and nonsuppression of speech. When we consider free speech from both individualist and collectivist perspectives, this traditional dichotomy, which has provided the framework for First Amendment analysis, can break down. This is because the government interest—be it compelling or substantial—that is on the other side of the balancing equation may itself be a fundamentally First Amendment interest. In some instances, the governmental interests that motivate efforts at speech regulation involve issues such as national security, safety, or other types of protections from harms that can arise from speech. In such instances, the traditional balancing approach makes sense. However, in other situations—and particularly in many communications policy contexts—these compelling or substantial government interests involve issues such as diversity and competition, which, as the model presented in Chapter Two illustrated, bear direct relationships to the First Amendment and are particularly vital to its collectivist interpretations. Thus, the balancing test at issue is not always one of the First Amendment versus competing speech-suppressing government interests. Instead, it may be one of individual versus collective First Amendment rights. The distinction can be illustrated in a comparison between two recent policy issues—the regulation of adult content on the Internet and the cable television must-carry rules.

The Internet and Adult Content

Congress has become increasingly concerned with the availability of explicit adult materials over the Internet, and the relative ease with which children are able to access such material. This concern has resulted in two pieces of legislation. The first, the Communications Decency Act (CDA) (1996), made it a felony for any person to use a "telecommunications device" to knowingly transmit obscene or indecent material to minors or to display such materials in a manner that makes them available to any person under 18 years of age. The Act was eventually struck down by the Supreme Court as unconstitutional (*Reno v. ACLU*, 1997).[12] The Court concluded that the Act represented an unacceptable violation of the First Amendment due primarily to the fact that it was not sufficiently narrowly tailored to serve the government interest that motivated it (the motivating government interest in this case was, obviously, to protect minors from adult content). The Court found the language of the statute unacceptably

vague, particularly in terms of providing adequate definitions of the terms "indecent" and "patently offensive," which were central to the main provisions of the CDA (*Reno v. ACLU*, 1997). In addition, the Court found the Act overbroad, in that it threatened to infringe on the constitutional rights of adults in its effort to protect children. Consequently, forms of speech that traditionally received First Amendment protection were threatened under the provisions of the CDA. In sum, the Supreme Court engaged in the traditional process of weighing government interests against individual free speech rights and found that, in this case, although the government's interest was legitimate and compelling, its means of pursuing this interest represented an unacceptable level of infringement on free speech rights.

In response to this decision, Congress passed the Child Online Protection Act (1998). The title change is itself significant in that it more clearly reflects the compelling government interest motivating the legislation. This Act still makes it a crime to knowingly make adult content available to minors, but Congress has attempted to address the Supreme Court's objections to the CDA, primarily by narrowing its definition of relevant content to "material that is harmful to minors" and by providing a detailed definition of material that is harmful to minors.[13] In addition, the Child Online Protection Act limits its restrictions to speech on the World Wide Web, whereas the CDA applied to the entirety of the Internet. The Child Online Protection Act also focuses exclusively on those who make content available for commercial purposes.

Like the CDA, the Child Online Protection Act was immediately subjected to a court challenge (see *ACLU v. Reno*, 1999, 2000; Zick, 1999). Like the CDA, the constitutionality of the Child Online Protection Act will ultimately be decided by the Supreme Court. It remains to be seen how the Court will respond to this revised effort at restricting children's access to Internet content and whether the means employed to achieve the ends are judged to be a sufficiently narrow infringement on free speech in light of the goals being pursued.

These actions by Congress, and their consideration by the Supreme Court, represent the traditional balancing test scenario in First Amendment jurisprudence. In this case, the Court was required (as, theoretically, was Congress, in deciding whether to enact the legislation) to balance the First Amendment rights of citizens against the governmental interest in protecting children from adult content and the emotional and psychological damage that can be associated with exposure to such content.[14] Truly, then, in this case we have a balancing of a free speech interest against another compelling, nonspeech-related, government interest, and thus the traditional balancing analysis accurately reflects the nature of the policy at issue.

Cable Must-Carry

The cable must-carry rules represent an entirely different situation. The must-carry rules require that cable systems carry the signals of local broadcast stations. The must-carry rules have long been a point of contention among Congress, the cable industry, broadcasters, and the FCC (see Geller, 1995). The constitutionality of the must-carry rules was finally decided by the Supreme Court in 1997 (*Turner Broadcasting System, Inc. v. Federal Communications Commission*, 1997). The Court employed the traditional First Amendment weighting analysis. In a prior decision, the Court identified the government interests at issue as: "(1) preserving the benefits of free, over-the-air local broadcast television, (2) promoting the widespread dissemination of information from a multiplicity of sources, and (3) promoting fair competition in the market for television programming" (*Turner Broadcasting System, Inc. v. Federal Communications Commission*, 1994, p. 662). These interests were then weighed against the infringements on the free speech rights of cable systems and programmers. It is important to note that the Court had previously decided that the must-carry provisions represented a content-neutral regulation and were therefore subject only to the intermediate scrutiny standard described previously (*Turner Broadcasting System, Inc. v. Federal Communications Commission*, 1994), although the Court was sharply divided on this issue.[15] As the Court noted, the must-carry rules impose a restraint on cable operators' editorial discretion and reduce the opportunities for cable programmers to receive carriage on the remaining available channels (*Turner Broadcasting System, Inc. v. Federal Communications Commission*, 1997, p. 1198). The Court concluded that the First Amendment impositions placed on cable operators were not sufficient to outweigh the government interests being pursued, and that the must-carry provisions represented a means of pursuing these interests that were not substantially broader than necessary to achieve those interests (the evaluative criteria associated with the "intermediate scrutiny" standard).

The key bit of slippage in this analysis, however, is that the majority decision of the Court focuses on whether or not the pursuit of governmental interests represents an unacceptable level of intrusion on the First Amendment in the name of other government interests, when in fact First Amendment concerns occupy both sides of the analysis. Nowhere in the opinion does the Court acknowledge the First Amendment component of the government's interests (i.e., collectivist First Amendment objectives). From a collectivist standpoint, the promotion of competition among speakers and increasing the diversity of sources of information (the stated objectives of the must-carry rules) are directly related to the First Amendment goals of promoting a vibrant speech environment. This subtle but important point of distinction only emerges in a concurring statement by Justice Breyer. Breyer points out that although must-carry "extracts a serious First Amendment price … there are important First Amendment interests on the other side as well" (*Turner Broadcasting System, Inc. v. Federal Communications Commission*, 1997, p. 1204). Breyer later references earlier Supreme Court decisions, including *United States v. Midwest Video Corp.* (1972) and *Associated Press v. United States* (1945), to point out that the objectives of the must-carry provisions reflect "what 'has long been a basic tenet of national communications policy,' namely that 'the widest possible dissemination of information from diverse and antagonistic sources is essential to the welfare of the public,'" and that the policy "in turn, seeks to facilitate the public discussion and informed deliberation, which, as Justice Brandeis pointed out many years ago, democratic government presupposes and the *First Amendment seeks to achieve*" (*Turner Broadcasting System, Inc. v. Federal Communications Commission*, 1997, p. 1204; citations omitted, emphasis added). Thus, the must-carry policy represents a situation in which, to use

Justice Breyer's words, there are "First Amendment interests on both sides of the equation" (*Turner Broadcasting System, Inc. v. Federal Communications Commission*, 1997, p. 1204).

The difference between the analytical approach reflected in the Court's majority decision and the one reflected in Breyer's concurrence represents the difference between relying primarily on an individualist interpretation of the First Amendment as opposed to integrating both the individualist and the collectivist interpretations into a balancing type of analysis that more accurately reflects the full range of values and functions associated with freedom of speech. In the majority's analytical approach, the only First Amendment rights that are explicitly identified are those of the cable industry. Any community-based rights to the widespread dissemination of information from diverse sources, which have previously been established as an important component of the First Amendment, are excluded from the domain of First Amendment concern. Instead, they are lumped with the concerns for competition and the economic stability of the broadcast industry in the "government interest" category (*Turner Broadcasting System, Inc. v. Federal Communications Commission*, 1997). Clearly, however, the must-carry policy is motivated—or at least potentially justified—by a collective conceptualization of free speech that views expanding the range of voices available to citizens as central to achieving the objectives that underlie the First Amendment (whether they accomplish this objective is another vitally important issue).

Given this discussion, which has suggested that collectivist interpretations of free speech seem to have as much claim to the First Amendment as individualist interpretations, it would seem that the appropriate way to analyze the must-carry issue is not in terms of weighing the First Amendment against another interest, but instead weighing the individualist interpretation and its associated values against the collectivist interpretation and its associated values. The central analytical question in this case then shifts from, "Is this interest compelling enough to override First Amendment concerns?" to "Does this policy sufficiently enhance the speech environment to warrant the level of intrusion on individual speech rights it imposes?" It is within the context of this central balancing question that all of the issues and arguments associated with the must-carry controversy should then be assessed. Similarly, this question should guide policymakers, policy analysts, and judges in any instance in which the government's stated interest involves preserving or enhancing the speech environment.

This analytical reorientation places the individualist and collectivist interpretations of the First Amendment on more equal footing, equal footing that seems wholly justified when we analyze the body of thought devoted to the underlying rationales for having the First Amendment. The current analytical orientation requires that values associated with a collectivist interpretation of the First Amendment be placed in the category of "compelling" or "substantial" government interest, which must then go head-to-head with the First Amendment. This situation places the burden of proof much more heavily on the collectivist side and misrepresents the degree to which policy objectives such as diversity and competition are themselves outgrowths of central values associated with the First Amendment. It is certainly not surprising, therefore, that many observers of the Supreme Court have concluded that the Court has favored individualist interpretations of the First Amendment over collectivist interpretations (Ingber, 1990; Post, 1993). From the Supreme Court's standpoint, the collectivist interpretation and its associated values generally do not exist within the hallowed realm of the First Amendment. Instead, this aspect of the First Amendment is burdened with the much less potent label of "compelling" or "substantial" government interest.

Again, it is worth reemphasizing that the point here is not to advocate the supremacy of the collectivist interpretation of the First Amendment over the individualist. Rather, the point is that, when the First Amendment is examined in terms of the values that have traditionally underlain its development and implementation, collectivist values share comparable prominence with individualist values. Absent compelling evidence that the individualist approach is the best means of achieving collectivist objectives, one is then left with the fact that a thorough and complete application of the First Amendment requires equal consideration of both conceptualizations. Unfortunately, the current approach to First

Amendment analysis tends to misplace collectivist interpretations outside the bounds of the First Amendment when it comes to balancing the interests at stake in a particular policy decision. A correction to this situation would involve the introduction of a new balancing test to First Amendment analysis. This balancing test would focus on weighing individual rights of self-expression against the collective value of a diverse and robust free speech environment, with both sides of the equation falling under the umbrella of the First Amendment. This new balancing test would obviously not be applicable to all communications policy issues, given that in some instances the government interest is not First Amendment–related. Also, this test might not make legal and policy decision making any easier, or bring greater consistency to the process; however, it would assure that the analytical structure in which these decisions were reached better reflected the true scope and breadth of the First Amendment. Ultimately, the balancing test outlined earlier suggests that the First Amendment can simultaneously encourage and restrain communication policymaking. Embracing this somewhat paradoxical situation is essential if the full scope of the social values inherent in the First Amendment are to be reflected in communications policymaking.

NOTES

1. As the Supreme Court has noted, many of the policies instituted on behalf of the public interest "were drawn from the First Amendment itself; the public interest standard necessarily invites reference to First Amendment principles" (*Columbia Broadcasting System v. Democratic National Committee*, 1973, p. 122).

2. The terms "functions," "objectives," and "values," in this discussion, are used interchangeably.

3. For further criticism of Baker's (1978) "liberty" theory, see Shiffrin (1983).

4. See Bork (1971) for a strict political function interpretation of the First Amendment. Bork argues that "Constitutional speech should be accorded only to speech that is explicitly political. There is no basis for judicial intervention to protect any other form of expression, be it

scientific, literary or that variety of expression we call obscene or pornographic" (p. 20).

5. For a discussion of the political/nonpolitical content distinction issue, see Sunstein (1993, pp. 148–154).

6. For counter-arguments to Stewart's (1975) assertion of a logical separation between the speech and press clauses of the First Amendment, see Lange (1975).

7. Rumble (1994) traces how the right to receive information was first associated with the due process clause of the Fourteenth Amendment before becoming explicitly recognized by the Supreme Court in the 1940s.

8. The town meeting analogy has, however, been criticized on a number of grounds (see Massaro, 1993; Post, 1993). The primary criticism is that the analogy offers a somewhat paradoxical situation in which self-determination is seen as central to all aspects of decision making except those decisions relating to the structures within which the decision-making process is located (Post, 1993). Thus, according to Post (1993), the weakness in the Meiklejohn analogy is that "it reflects an insufficiently radical conception of the reach of self-determination, which encompasses not merely the substance of collective decisions, but also the larger framework of function within which such collective decision making is necessarily conceived as taking place" (p. 1117). For a thorough critique of the collectivist approach to the First Amendment, see Powe (1987b).

9. It is worth noting that, from Sunstein's (1993) perspective, there would in fact be no such thing as a First Amendment "absolutist."

10. The FCC concluded that the Fairness Doctrine was having a "chilling effect" on broadcasters, thereby inhibiting them from presenting controversial issues (FCC, 1985a), a conclusion supported in research by Hazlett and Sosa (1997). Thus, the Fairness Doctrine not only infringed on the First Amendment rights of broadcasters, it appears to have also degraded the overall speech environment.

11. As many critics have noted, the notion that the broadcast spectrum is uniquely scarce, and therefore deserving of different regulatory

treatment, buckles under the fact that (a) all resources are essentially scarce; and (b) advances in media technology, such as signal compression and wireline delivery of television signals, have undermined whatever scarcity initially existed (Coase, 1959; FCC, 1985a; Fowler & Brenner. 1982: Spitzer. 1989).

12. For a thorough account of the legislative and judicial activities leading up to the Supreme Court's decision, and a review and discussion of the Court's reasoning, see Jacques (1997).

13. The Child Online Protection Act defines material that is harmful to minors as: Any communication, picture, image, graphic image file, article, recording, writing, or other matter of any kind that is obscene or that: (A) the average person, applying contemporary community standards, would find, taking the material as a whole and with respect to minors, is designed to appeal to, or is designed to pander to, the prurient interest; (B) depicts, describes, or represents, in a manner patently offensive with respect to minors, an actual or simulated sexual act or sexual contact, an actual or simulated normal or perverted sexual act, or a lewd exhibition of the genitals or post-pubescent female breast; and (C) taken as a whole, lacks serious literary, artistic, political, or scientific value for minors. (47 U.S.C. 231(e)(6)).

14. Obviously, all parties involved in this issue, whether they stand for or against the Child Online Protection Act, share the same assumption that minors do not possess a First Amendment right to receive adult content—at least not a right that overcomes the compelling government interest in preventing their exposure to such content.

15. The Court was split 5 to 4 on the issue of whether the must-carry provisions were indeed content neutral. According to Justice Kennedy, in his decision upholding the content-neutrality of the rules, "Congress' overriding objective was not to favor programming of a particular content, but rather to preserve access to free television programming for the 40 percent of Americans without cable" (*Turner Broadcasting System, Inc. v. Federal Communications Commission*, 1994, p. 646). However, Justices O'Connor, Scalia, Ginsburg, and Thomas disagreed with the interpretation of Justice Kennedy and the rest of the Court. In her opinion, Justice O'Connor wrote that "looking at the statute at issue, I can't avoid the conclusion that its preference for broadcasters over cable programmers is justified with reference to content" (*Turner Broadcasting System, Inc. v. Federal Communications Commission*, 1994, p. 676). Justice O'Connor then references a series of statements within the statute that suggest that the must-carry provisions are content motivated. In particular, she cites Congress' statements that the enhancement and preservation of a diversity of viewpoints and local origination of programming (specifically, news and public affairs) justify the must-carry provisions. Consequently, she concludes that the must-carry provisions should be subjected to the strict scrutiny test required of all content-based regulations, not the intermediate scrutiny of the O'Brien test. In sum, this decision illustrates that determining whether a specific policy is content-neutral is far from a straightforward task.

Historical Development and Implementation

The value of "free expression" sounds appealing, but its implementation is complicated, as nothing we attach value to is truly free. Against each free expression of speech a competing value may be affected: reputation, privacy, the freedom of expression of the other, etc. Communications scholars Wayne Overbeck and Genelle Belmas survey in this chapter the history of the legal edict that was created to preserve freedom of expression—the First Amendment to the Constitution. This reading and the lecture that accompanies it further describe the challenges brought against the breadth of the First Amendment and the means by which the Courts have resolved them and serve as a "reality check" to the limitations of the First Amendment and to freedom of expression.

The Legacy of Freedom

Wayne Overbeck and Genelle Belmas

Americans are sometimes accused of taking freedom for granted. It is easy to talk about the First Amendment almost as if it were a universal law of nature, a principle that always existed and always will.

That, of course, is not the case. The kind of freedom of expression that is permitted today in the United States and a few dozen other democracies is unique in world history. Our freedoms were won through centuries of struggle, and they could easily be lost. Even today, fewer than half of the world's people live in countries that fully recognize such basic freedoms as freedom of speech, freedom of the press and freedom of religion. Government leaders in many countries consider "national security" (or their own personal security in office) more important than their people's freedoms. Many leaders see the mass media only as tools of propaganda or national development—weapons to be used against their rivals, both foreign and domestic.

Even in America, the threat of terrorism prompted new restrictions on civil liberties in the aftermath of the events of Sept. 11, 2001. The USA PATRIOT Act, passed shortly after the Sept. 11 attacks, created a new crime of domestic terrorism, broadened the federal government's power to monitor telephone and Internet communications and authorized the attorney general to detain any foreigner believed to threaten national security, among other things. The law's name is an acronym for "Uniting and Strengthening America by Providing Appropriate Tools Required to Intercept and Obstruct Terrorism."

Despite growing concerns about the USA PATRIOT Act's implications for the civil liberties of Americans, Congress acted to renew the law in 2006. The new version made permanent many provisions of the act that had originally been temporary measures with a four-year sunset clause.

The two most controversial provisions were renewed with some modifications and only for another four years. One is the "library provision" that allows government investigators to obtain records from libraries and businesses that would reveal an individual's financial or medical information or even private reading habits. A second controversial provision extends the authorization for "national security letters"—subpoenas issued by a government agency such as the FBI instead of a court.

The renewal of the USA PATRIOT Act does not resolve the questions raised by the *New York Times* in reporting that President George W. Bush had authorized the National Security Agency to conduct secret domestic surveillance without court authorization. A federal criminal investigation was launched to determine how word of that secret program was leaked to the news media, creating the potential for journalists to be subpoenaed to identify their sources. The investigation could also lead to the criminal prosecution of journalists for reporting this story, despite its newsworthiness. Meanwhile, a similar controversy arose when *USA TODAY* reported that several major telephone companies had given the federal government telephone records for millions of Americans.

A federal judge ruled in 2004 that the USA PATRIOT Act violated fundamental constitutional safeguards by allowing federal agencies to gather information about U.S. citizens secretly under national security letters without court approval. The same judge ruled in 2007 that the new version of the PATRIOT Act still gives federal investigators unconstitutionally broad powers to spy on individuals. In 2008, the federal government appealed that decision, contending that the PATRIOT Act's sweeping authorization of domestic surveillance is needed to fight terrorism and does not violate the Constitution. In that case, *Doe v. Mukasey*, No. 07-4943-cv, a three-judge panel of the Second Circuit (including Supreme Court nominee Sonia Sotomayor) upheld the lower court's decision that the "gag order" provisions imposed on recipients of National Security Letters (NSLs), forbidding them to talk to anyone about those letters. A NSL is a subpoena for information such as phone records and Internet activity used by the Federal Bureau of Investigation and other agencies. The burden of proof was also shifted in this case from the recipient of the letter to the government to initiate judicial review of the gag orders.

In 2009, a bill was introduced in the House of Representatives to further extend provisions of the USA PATRIOT Act. This bill, H.R. 1467, would extend some wiretap provisions for 10 years, among other elements.

In much of the world it is still commonplace for governments to censor the mass media directly. And even in some countries where the media are nominally free of censorship, journalists and others who advocate democratic reforms are sometimes arrested, tortured and murdered. Journalists "disappear" so often in some countries that the outside world hardly notices. Short of that, government officials may control the media in more subtle ways, such as by offering lucrative government "advertising" that looks and

sounds just like bona fide news when it is published or broadcast. Without that government subsidy, many news media would quickly go broke—a fact that makes it very difficult for them to maintain any semblance of editorial independence.

It was not long ago that those who advocated basic civil liberties were brutalized in many other countries that now permit free expression and free elections. The story of how earlier generations won the freedoms we enjoy today is an important part of this summary of mass communications law.

CENSORSHIP IN ENGLAND

This summary of the evolution of freedom of expression could begin in the ancient world, were this chapter a survey of the philosophical underpinnings of modern civilization. Powerful arguments for freedom of expression were made thousands of years ago in ancient Greece and several other places around the globe. But our tradition of freedom of expression traces its roots most directly to England about 400 years ago.

In the 1600s, England was caught up in a battle that mixed politics and religion. The monarchy and the government-sponsored Church of England were determined to silence dissenters, many of them Puritans. Moreover, the religious and political struggle was closely linked with an economic battle between the aristocracy and the rising middle class.

Leaders on both sides of this ideological battle understood the importance of the printing press and sometimes resorted to heavy-handed efforts to censor ideas they considered dangerous. In those days more than one Englishman was jailed, tortured and eventually executed for expressing ideas unacceptable to those in power. Brutality that would be shocking to Americans—or Britons—today was fairly commonplace in England in that period.

Official censorship was enforced through a licensing system for printers that had been introduced as early as 1530. The licensing denied access to printing presses to people with unacceptable ideas, but it also enabled government representatives to preview and pre-censor materials before publication. Moreover, by making the possession of a license to print a coveted privilege, the government was often able to control underground printing. The licensed printers themselves helped to ferret out bootleg presses to protect their own self-interests.

Milton and the Puritans

By the early 1600s censorship was being used to suppress all sorts of ideas that threatened the established order. This inspired some of the leading political philosophers of the day to write eloquent appeals for freedom of expression as a vital adjunct to the broader freedom from religious and political oppression they sought. An early apostle of freedom of expression was John Milton, who in 1644 wrote his famous argument against government censorship, *Areopagitica*. Milton's appeal to the Long Parliament for freedom contained this statement:

> Though all the winds of doctrine were let loose to play upon the earth, so Truth be in the field, we do injuriously by licensing and prohibiting to misdoubt her strength. Let her and Falsehood grapple; who ever knew Truth put to the worse in a free and open encounter?

Out of this passage several modern ideas emerged, including the concept that a *self-righting* process would occur through open debate of controversial issues. In effect, Milton said censorship was unnecessary because true ideas would prevail over false ones anyway. Milton advocated something of a *marketplace of ideas*. That was a revolutionary idea: almost no one in Milton's time believed that freedom of expression should be universal. But even to Milton, this freedom had its limits. Although he favored far more freedom than most of his contemporaries, Milton did not think free expression rights should be extended to persons who advocated ideas that he considered dangerously false or subversive. His appeal for freedom specifically excluded "popery (support for the Roman Catholic Church) and open superstition" and ideas that were "impious or evil."

In fact, after the Puritan movement led by Oliver Cromwell gained control of England and executed King Charles I in 1649, Milton accepted a government appointment that required him to act as something of a government censor. One of his duties was to license and oversee the content of an official newssheet,

Mercurius Politicus. By 1651—only seven years after he appealed to the government to allow true and false ideas to struggle for popular acceptance—Milton was engaged in the prior censorship of ideas. And he was serving in a government that imposed strict Puritan beliefs on England and showed little tolerance for the beliefs of other religious groups.

Was Milton's later employment inconsistent with the spirit of *Areopagitica*? Perhaps it was, but even today scholars disagree about the role Milton actually played in Cromwell's government. Some doubt that Milton really did much censoring. Whatever Milton later did—or did not do—to earn a living, his *Areopagitica* was an eloquent appeal for freedom of expression and an important influence on later English political thought.

In fairness to Cromwell's followers, we should also point out that there were some who went further than Milton did in advocating freedom of expression. For instance Roger Williams, a onetime Puritan minister in the Massachusetts Bay colony who was exiled to Rhode Island for his controversial religious ideas, later returned to England and wrote *Bloudy Tenent of Persecution for Cause of Conscience* in the same year as Milton's *Areopagitica*. Williams urged freedom of expression even for Catholics, Jews and Muslims—people Milton would not have included in his marketplace of ideas.

Perhaps even more emphatic in their arguments for freedom from censorship in the 1640s were the Levellers, a radical Puritan group. Their tracts consistently contained passages condemning censorship and the licensing system. In their view, free expression was essential to the religious freedom and limited government authority they so fervently sought.

In a 1648 petition to the Parliament, the Levellers appealed for a free press. When "truth was suppressed" and the people kept ignorant, this ignorance "fitted only to serve the unjust ends of tyrants and oppressors." For a government to be just "in its constitution" and "equal in its distributions," it must "hear all voices and judgments, which they can never do, but by giving freedom to the press."

Despite the rhetoric of the Puritans, England restored the monarchy in 1660 and the licensing of printers continued (although Parliament by then had a much larger say in the process). Although the post-1660 Restoration period was marked by unprecedented freedom—and even bawdiness—in English literature, it was also a time of religious repression. A 1662 act of Parliament, for instance, limited the number of printing presses and prohibited the printing of books contrary to the Christian faith as well as seditious or anti-government works.

John Locke and Natural Rights

As the struggle between the monarchy and Parliament became more intense in the late 1600s, new philosophers of free expression emerged. Perhaps chief among them was John Locke. His ideas were not necessarily original, but he presented them so eloquently that he is remembered as one of the most important political theorists of his time. Locke's famous *social contract theory* said that governments were the servants of the people, not the other way around. Locke believed men were endowed with certain natural rights, among them the right to life, liberty and property ownership. In effect, Locke said the people make a deal with a government, giving it the authority to govern in return for the government's promise to safeguard these natural rights.

Central to these natural rights, Locke felt, was freedom of expression. Thus, when the English licensing system came up for review in 1694, Locke listed 18 reasons why the act should be terminated. The act was allowed to expire, primarily because of "the practical reason arising from the difficulties of administration and the restraints on trade."

Other forces in English society were also providing impetus for freedom of expression. For one, Parliament gained a major victory over the monarchy in the Glorious Revolution of 1688. James II, an avowedly Catholic king so offensive that several warring factions united against him, fled the country that year. Then in 1689 Parliament enacted a Bill of Rights and invited William of Orange and his consort, Mary, James' Protestant daughter, to assume the throne with limited powers. In the Declaration of Rights, William and Mary accepted these conditions, ending England's century-long struggle between Parliament and the monarchy.

In addition, a two-party system was emerging in England; the times were ready for open, robust political debate. The two parties, the Whigs and Tories, both relied extensively on the printing press in taking their views to the people.

Seditious Libel as a Crime

If official censorship by licensing the press was a thing of the past as England moved into the 1700s, the crime of seditious libel (i.e., the crime of criticizing the government or government officials) remained a viable deterrent to those who might publish defamatory tracts.

A good illustration of this problem was the 1704 case of John Tuchin, who was tried for "writing, composing and publishing a certain false, malicious, seditious and scandalous libel, entitled, *The Observator*" (see *Rex v. Tuchin*, 14 Howell's State Trials 1095).

Tuchin was convicted of the crime, and in the process the presiding judge defined the common law on seditious libel:

> To say that corrupt officers are appointed to administer affairs, is certainly a reflection on the government. If people would not be called to account for possessing the people with an ill opinion of the government, no government can subsist. For it is very necessary for all governments that the people should have a good opinion of it. And nothing can be worse to any government, than to endeavor to procure animosities, as to the management of it; this has been always looked upon as a crime, and no government can be safe without it be punished.

This common law rule did not go unchallenged for long. Free press advocates, perhaps strengthened by their success in abolishing licensing, opened the eighteenth century with a flurry of articles and tracts advocating greater freedom. Nevertheless, criticism of the government remained a crime throughout the century, with the truthfulness of the criticism not a defense against the charge. The prevailing legal maxim was "the greater the truth, the greater the libel."

How could this be? The assumption underlying this philosophy was reminiscent of Milton: if a printer publishes a false attack on the government, it will be disregarded by the people; if, on the other hand, a truthful attack is published, the people are likely to lend it credence and perhaps revolt, causing disorder and anarchy.

Parliament itself recognized the abuses possible under the common law of seditious libel, and in 1792 the Fox Libel Act was passed. That act permitted juries, rather than judges, to decide whether a statement was libelous. Prior to that time, the law allowed the jury to determine only whether the defendant was guilty of printing the libelous publication. The judge ruled on the legal question of whether the material was actually libelous.

This legal reform did not eliminate seditious libel prosecutions, but it did make it more difficult for a government to punish its critics because a jury, whose members might well sympathize with the defendant's allegedly libelous statements, could decide if the statements were libelous.

An additional reform came in 1843, further strengthening the rights of those who would criticize the government in England. In that year, Parliament passed Lord Campbell's Act, establishing truth as a defense in all seditious libel cases. Thus, the old maxim, "the greater the truth, the greater the libel," was at last abolished.

While the struggle for freedom of expression was being fought in England, a parallel battle was under way in the American colonies.

FREEDOM IN A NEW NATION

Although many of the early colonists in North America left England or the European continent to escape religious or political oppression, they found (or created) an atmosphere of less than total freedom in some of the colonies here. As the Puritans gained control in New England, they established close church-state ties, and persons with unpopular religious or political ideas were hardly more welcome here than they had been in England.

In fact, the first laws that restricted freedom of the press in North America preceded the first newspaper here by some 30 years. Even without any specific authority, colonial rulers often simply assumed they had the right to censor dissenting publications because the authorities had that right in England. Even after licensing was abolished in England, colonial leaders continued to act as if they had licensing powers, and several colonial newspapers carried the phrase "published by authority" in their mastheads years after the right to publish without government permission was won in England.

Moreover, in North America as in England, seditious libel prosecutions were used as a means of controlling the press, as were laws that placed special tax burdens on newspapers. The Stamp Act of 1765, for instance, taxed newspapers by forcing publishers to purchase revenue stamps and attach one to every copy. The result was such blatant defiance of British authority by colonial publishers that it helped inspire the eventual revolution against the mother country.

The Zenger Libel Trial

Early in the colonial publishing experience there was a seditious libel case that became a *cause célèbre* on both sides of the Atlantic: the trial of John Peter Zenger in 1735 (*Attorney General v. John Peter Zenger*, 17 Howell's State Trials 675).

Zenger, a German immigrant, was the publisher and printer of the *New York Weekly Journal*. His paper became a leading voice for the opposition to a particularly unpopular royal governor, William Cosby. After some legal maneuvering, the governor was able to have Zenger jailed and charged with "printing and publishing a false, scandalous and seditious libel, in which … the governor … is greatly and unjustly scandalized, as a person that has no regard to law nor justice."

Zenger was fortunate enough to have Andrew Hamilton of Philadelphia, one of the most respected lawyers in the colonies, make the trip to New York for his defense. And Hamilton, ignoring the orders of Cosby's hand-picked judge, appealed directly to the jury. He urged the jurors to ignore the maxim of "the greater the truth, the greater the libel" and to decide for themselves whether the statements in question were actually true, finding them libelous only if they were false.

"Nature and the laws of our country have given us a right—and the liberty—both of exposing and opposing arbitrary power … by speaking and writing truth," Hamilton said.

In urging the jurors to ignore the judge's instructions and acquit Zenger if they decided the statements were true, Hamilton was clearly overstepping the bounds of the law. A less prestigious lawyer might have been punished for an action so clearly in contempt of the court's authority. However, Hamilton was not cited, and his eloquent appeal to the jury worked: the jury returned a not-guilty verdict even though there was little question that Zenger was the publisher of the challenged statements.

It would be difficult to overstate the importance of the Zenger trial in terms of its psychological impact on royal governors in America. Still, its direct effect on the common law was minimal in America and England itself. Even in those days, a criminal trial verdict established no binding legal precedent. English courts continued to punish truthful publications that were critical of government authority. For instance, the trial of John Wilkes for publishing a "wicked and seditious libel," a 1763 English case, made it clear that the common law had not been changed by the Zenger trial.

Nevertheless, the argument was made again and again that mere words critical of the government— and especially truthful words—should not be a crime. In 1773 the Rev. Philip Furneaux wrote that only overt acts against a government should be punished:

> The tendency of principles, tho' it be unfavourable, is not prejudicial to society, till it issues in some overt acts against the public peace and order; and when it does, then the magistrate's authority to punish commences; that is, he may punish the overt acts, but not the tendency which is not actually harmful; and therefore his penal laws should be directed against overt acts only.

THE FIRST AMENDMENT

When a series of incidents strained relations between England and the colonies past the breaking point, the colonists declared their independence in 1776. Yet even in breaking with England, the Americans borrowed heavily from the mother country. Thomas Jefferson's ideas and even some of his language in the Declaration of Independence were borrowed from English political philosophers, notably John Locke. Locke's natural rights and social contract ideas appear repeatedly in the declaration.

After independence was won on the battlefield, the new nation briefly experimented with a weak central government under the Articles of Confederation and then became a unified nation under the Constitution, which was ratified by the states in 1788. Despite its ratification, many Americans feared the new federal government, particularly because the Constitution had no guarantees that basic civil liberties would be respected. Although the defenders of the Constitution argued that these civil liberties were firmly entrenched in the common law we had inherited from England, many were wary. Some states ratified the Constitution only after they received assurances that it would be amended quickly to add a Bill of Rights.

That promise was kept. In the first session of Congress, the Bill of Rights was drawn up and submitted to the states to ratify. It was declared in force late in 1791. Of paramount concern to the mass media, of course, is the First Amendment. Taken literally, it is almost everything that a free press advocate might hope for, but phrases such as "Congress shall make no law" have not always been taken literally. In fact, the exact meaning of the First Amendment has been vigorously debated for more than 200 years.

Early First Amendment Questions

The record of the Congressional discussions when the Bill of Rights was drafted is sketchy: it is impossible to be certain what Congress had in mind. Constitutional scholars have advanced various theories, but most doubt that the majority of the framers of the Constitution intended the First Amendment to be an absolute prohibition on all government actions that might in anyway curtail freedom of the press.

The crucial question, then, and the one that is the focus of the rest of this chapter, is this: which restrictions on freedom of expression are constitutionally permissible and which ones are not? Many scholarly works have been published attempting to answer this question; several historians have dedicated much of their lives to examining records, debates and documents of the period in an attempt to find the answers. Some of their conclusions will be presented shortly.

Whatever the first Congress intended in drafting those words, it was only a few years later that Congress passed laws that seemed to be a flagrant violation of the First Amendment. In 1798 Congress hurriedly approved the *Alien and Sedition Acts*, a group of laws designed to silence political dissent in preparation for a war with France, a war that was never declared. The Sedition Act made it a federal crime to speak or publish seditious ideas. The law had one important safeguard: truth was recognized as a defense. Nevertheless, a fine of up to $2,000 or two years' imprisonment was prescribed for any person who dared to:

> … (W)rite, print, utter or publish, or … knowingly and willingly assist or aid in writing, printing, uttering or publishing any false, scandalous and malicious writing or writings against the government of the United States, or either house of the Congress of the United States, or the President of the United States, with intent to defame the said government, or either house of said Congress, or the said President, or to bring them, or either of them, into contempt or disrepute; or to excite against them, or either or any of them, the hatred of the good people of the United States, or to stir up sedition within the United States.

There were about 25 arrests and 15 indictments under the act. All were aimed at opponents of President John Adams and the Federalist Party, which then controlled Congress and had enacted the law over the opposition of Jefferson and his followers. Even though the Federalist press was often guilty of vicious attacks on Thomas Jefferson and other non-Federalist government officials, no Federalist was ever prosecuted under the Sedition Act. A two-party system was emerging, and the Jeffersonian, or anti-Federalist, opposition party was the real target of the Sedition Act.

Jefferson, by then the vice president, strenuously opposed the Alien and Sedition Acts. The Kentucky and Virginia legislatures passed resolutions, backed by Jefferson, that purported to "nullify" these laws, thus raising questions about states' rights that would not be resolved until the Civil War.

James Madison, later to be Jefferson's secretary of state and then the nation's fourth president, made it clear in drafting the Virginia Resolution that he felt the Sedition Act was a violation of the First Amendment. Madison believed the First Amendment was supposed to be an absolute prohibition on all actions of the federal government that restricted freedom of the press.

Jefferson probably agreed. In one letter to a friend, he wrote: "I am … for freedom of the press and against all violations of the Constitution to silence by force and not by reason the complaints or criticisms, just or unjust, of our citizens against the conduct of their agents."

When Jefferson ran for president in 1800, he made the Alien and Sedition Acts a major issue; public discontent over these laws was certainly an important factor in his victory. Immediately after his inauguration, Jefferson ordered the pardon of those who had been convicted under the Sedition Act.

However, Jefferson's record as a champion of a free press was not entirely unblemished. During his presidency he was subjected to harsh personal attacks by some opposition newspapers. Although he usually defended the right of his foes to express their views, he eventually became so annoyed that he encouraged his backers to prosecute some of his critics in state courts.

THE FIRST AMENDMENT: SCHOLARS' VIEWS

The Sedition Act expired in 1801, and it was more than 100 years before Congress again attempted to make criticism of the government a federal crime.

However, this does not prove the First Amendment was intended to eliminate seditious libel as a crime, and the debate over that issue continued well into the twentieth century. Historian Leonard Levy, a leading constitutional scholar, once wrote:

> What is clear is that there exists no evidence to suggest an understanding that a constitutional guarantee of free speech or press meant the impossibility of future prosecutions of seditious utterances. … The security of the state against libelous advocacy or attack was always regarded as outweighing any social interest in open expression, at least through the period of the adoption of the First Amendment.

Levy argued that most likely the framers of the First Amendment weren't certain what its full implications were, but that most of the framers believed future prosecutions for seditious utterances were possible.

However, later in his life Levy rethought that conclusion based on extensive additional research into the content of early American newspapers. He ultimately decided that the framers must have intended for the First Amendment to provide "a right to engage in rasping, corrosive, and offensive discussions on all topics of public interest." His earlier, more narrow view of the First Amendment was presented in a 1960 book, *Legacy of Suppression: Freedom of Speech and Press in Early American History*. In 1985, he published a revised and enlarged edition of the book that he retitled *Emergence of a Free Press*. For those with an interest in such matters, Levy's dramatic reversal of his position—described in his 1985 edition—makes fascinating reading. In the preface to his new edition, Levy wrote:

> I was wrong in asserting that the American experience with freedom of political expression was as slight as the conceptual and legal understanding was narrow. ... Press criticism of government policies and politicians, on both state and national levels, during the war (for independence) and in the peaceful years of the 1780s and 1790s, raged as contemptuously and scorchingly as it had against Great Britain in the period between the Stamp Act and the battle of Lexington. Some states gave written constitutional protection to freedom of the press after Independence; others did not. Whether they did or not, their presses operated as if the law of seditious libel did not exist.

In revising his views, Levy came much closer to agreeing with several other noted legal historians. For example, Harvard Professor Zechariah Chafee wrote that the First Amendment was indeed intended to eliminate the common law crime of seditious libel "and make further prosecutions for criticism of the government, without any incitement to law-breaking, forever impossible in the United States."

Chafee, in his 1941 work, argued that freedom of expression is essential to the emergence of truth and advancement of knowledge. The quest for truth "is possible only through absolutely unlimited discussion," Chafee said. Yet, he noted that there are other purposes of government, such as order, the training

of the young, and protection against external aggression. Those purposes, he said, must be protected too, but when open discussion interferes with those purposes, there must be a balancing against freedom of speech, "but freedom of speech ought to weigh heavily on that scale."

Chafee argued against prior restraint of expression unless it was very clear that such expression imperiled the nation. He wrote:

> The true boundary line of the First Amendment can be fixed only when Congress and the courts realize that the principle on which speech is classified as lawful or unlawful involves the balancing against each other of two very important social interests, in public safety and in the search for truth. Every reasonable attempt should be made to maintain both interests unimpaired, and the great interest in free speech should be sacrificed only when the interest in public safety is really imperiled, and not, as most men believe, when it is barely conceivable that it may be slightly affected. In war time, therefore, speech should be unrestricted by the censorship or by punishment, unless it is clearly liable to cause direct and dangerous interference with the conduct of war.

Chafee's boundary line, then, is that point where words will incite unlawful acts. As we'll see later, that is precisely the point at which the Supreme Court has drawn the line in recent decisions on the meaning of the First Amendment.

A third noted constitutional scholar, Alexander Meiklejohn, agreed for the most part with Chafee's interpretation of the First Amendment. He said that only expression that incites unlawful acts should be punishable. Further, he said, incitement does not occur unless an illegal act is actually performed and the prior words can be directly connected to the act. Then, and only then, can words be punished in spite of the First Amendment.

Meiklejohn said that the First Amendment was written during a time when large sections of the population were hostile to the form of government then being adopted. Thus, the framers knew full well that a program of political freedom was a dangerous thing. Yet, Meiklejohn said, the framers chose to write the First Amendment as it is and not the way the courts have rewritten it during the twentieth century. He said that if the framers had wanted the federal government to control expression, the First Amendment could have read:

> Only when, in the judgment of the legislature, the interests of order and security render such action advisable shall Congress abridge the freedom of speech.

Both Chafee and Meiklejohn felt that the voters must be well informed to make wise decisions. Both endorsed Milton's "marketplace of ideas" concept, and Meiklejohn supported Milton's view that truth will prevail in this clash of ideas:

> No one can deny that the winning of the truth is important for the purposes of self-government. But that is not our deepest need. Far more essential, if men are to be their own rulers, is the demand that whatever truth may become available shall be placed at the disposal of all the citizens of the community. The First Amendment … is a device for the sharing of whatever truth has been won.

Much of what we have just discussed is quite theoretical, but the views of scholars such as Chafee, Meiklejohn and Levy have often influenced the U.S. Supreme Court when it was forced to make difficult decisions about the scope and meaning of the First Amendment in the real world.

NINETEENTH-CENTURY PRESS FREEDOM

Whatever the framers of the Constitution and Bill of Rights intended, the question received little attention in the 1800s. The nineteenth century was a time when Americans were preoccupied with such overriding issues as national expansion and slavery. There was surprisingly little attention given to the meaning of the First Amendment during most of that century. Instead, the country and the courts were looking at other issues for the most part.

The Supreme Court and Judicial Review

In 1803, the Supreme Court gained the power to declare acts of Congress unconstitutional and thereby invalidate them. In the landmark case of *Marbury v. Madison* (1 Cranch 137), what the court really did was simply to declare that it had the power to overturn acts of Congress. Perhaps the court got away with it mainly because President Jefferson and his followers were happy with the outcome of the case.

Just before his term expired, John Adams, the lame-duck Federalist president, had appointed a number of federal judges. Because of their belated appointments, they came to be called "midnight judges." The new judges were Federalists, and the Jeffersonians were anxious to keep them from taking office. James Madison, Jefferson's secretary of state, refused to give William Marbury, one of the would-be judges, his signed commission (the document appointing him to office). Marbury sued to get the commission. The Jeffersonians were not displeased when the high court, under its famous chief justice, John Marshall, dismissed Marbury's claim by overturning the Judicial Act of 1789, on which the would-be judge had based his lawsuit. In the convoluted politics of the day, Marshall—a Federalist—had sided with the Jeffersonians on a small matter (Marbury's commission), but in so doing Marshall had prevailed on the larger issue: the right of the court to review actions of other branches of government for compliance with the Constitution.

Ironically, Chief Justice Marshall had himself been appointed by John Adams during the final year of his presidency. Although the Federalist Party faded away, never winning another national election, Marshall served as chief justice for 34 years, allowing the Federalist philosophy to have an ongoing impact on American law long after the Federalist Party disappeared from the scene.

Marshall's Supreme Court asserted its authority in many other areas, attempting to define the scope and limits of federal power. In 1812, the Supreme Court ruled that the federal courts had no authority to entertain actions involving common law crimes such as criminal libel. In *U.S. v. Hudson and Goodwin* (7 Cranch 32), the high court said this area of law fell within the exclusive domain of the states, a philosophy that has remained largely unchanged ever since. On the other hand, in *McCulloch v. Maryland* (4 Wheat. 316), an 1819 decision that is among Marshall's most famous, the court upheld the right of Congress to create a national bank and regulate the economy even though a narrow, literal reading of the Constitution might not permit it. Having so ruled, Marshall then declared once and for all that the states may not tax agencies of the federal government.

When the Bill of Rights was added to the U.S. Constitution, its authors wanted to be certain that the federal government's powers would be strictly limited so as to avoid usurping the powers of the states. The Tenth Amendment reads, "The powers not delegated to the United States by the Constitution, nor prohibited by it to the states, are reserved to the states respectively, or to the people."

To the amazement of many Americans, the Supreme Court reasserted the principle of a strictly limited federal government in a series of decisions 200 years later. For example, in 2000, the Supreme Court overturned the Violence against Women Act of 1994, holding that Congress had invaded an area of law reserved for the states (i.e., the prosecution of crimes such as rape) by passing this law (*U.S. v. Morrison*, 529 U.S. 598).

While the federal government stayed out of mass communications law during much of the nineteenth century, the states filled that void. Throughout the century, the states were expanding the common law and adopting statutory laws in such areas as libel and slander.

One of the best-known state cases was the 1804 libel trial of Harry Croswell in New York (*People v. Croswell*, 3 Johnson's Cases 336). Croswell attacked President Jefferson in print and was prosecuted for criminal libel. He was convicted, but he appealed to a higher state court. His defense attorney, Federalist leader Alexander Hamilton, argued that truth plus "good motives for justifiable ends" should be a defense in such cases.

Although Croswell lost when the appellate panel of four judges deadlocked 2–2, the concept that truth should be a libel defense was sometimes called the *Hamilton Doctrine* and was adopted in a number of states during that era. For instance, the New York legislature recognized the truth defense by statute in 1805—and added a provision empowering the jury to determine whether the statement in question was actually libelous. Some states had recognized truth as a libel defense even before that time and, of course,

the 1798 Sedition Act had recognized it on the federal level. Nevertheless, what Andrew Hamilton, the distinguished Philadelphia lawyer, had argued for in the Zenger trial 70 years earlier gained general acceptance in American law only after another distinguished lawyer named Hamilton made it his cause as well.

Alexander Hamilton, of course, didn't live long enough to enjoy whatever recognition the Hamilton Doctrine might have brought him: a newspaper account of something he purportedly said during the Croswell trial led to the infamous duel in which he was killed by Aaron Burr, then the vice president of the United States.

Slavery and Free Expression

Aside from the gradual evolution of libel law, probably the most significant conflict over American freedom of expression in the 1800s resulted from the struggle over slavery and the War Between the States.

As the national debate over slavery intensified in the early 1800s, a number of southern states enacted "gag laws" that prohibited the circulation of newspapers and other materials advocating the abolition of slavery. Although these laws were clearly acts of prior censorship and violated the spirit of the First Amendment, the First Amendment had not yet been made applicable to the states, and these laws were never tested for their constitutionality.

Some northern states also attempted to curb abolitionist literature through various laws; these laws too escaped constitutional scrutiny because the Bill of Rights did not yet apply to the states.

Even Congress adopted rules to suppress debate about slavery that violated the spirit and probably the letter of the First Amendment. When anti-slavery groups began submitting petitions to Congress asking that the slave trade in Washington, D.C. be abolished, the House of Representatives adopted internal "gag rules" to prevent these petitions from being introduced and considered. These rules not only censored anti-slavery members of Congress but also took direct aim at the First Amendment's provision guaranteeing the right to petition the government. Rep. John Quincy Adams of Massachusetts, who returned to Congress after serving as the nation's sixth president, led the fight against these gag rules. At one point he arrived in Washington with anti-slavery petitions signed by more than 50,000 persons. When he was barred from presenting them formally, he left the petitions stacked high on his desk in the House of Representatives as a silent protest against the gag rules. In 1844, Adams—by then 77 years old—finally garnered enough support to have the Congressional gag rules eliminated.

During the Civil War itself, a vigorous antiwar movement emerged in the North, and antiwar editors came to be known as Copperheads. Some of them tested freedom of the press in wartime to the limit, openly advocating a southern victory.

The Copperheads' rhetoric often hindered recruiting for the Union Army. On several occasions, military commanders in the North acted against Copperheads, creating a difficult dilemma for President Lincoln, who was deeply committed to the First Amendment but also wanted to end the war quickly. He is generally credited with exercising great restraint in the face of vicious criticism from the Copperhead editors. On one occasion he actually countermanded a general's decision to occupy the offices of the *Chicago Times* to halt that paper's attacks on the war effort.

However, in 1864 Lincoln reached his breaking point when two New York newspapers published a false story claiming there was to be a massive new draft call—an announcement sure to stir violent anti-draft riots. The president allowed the editors to be arrested and their papers occupied by the military until it was learned the newspapers got the story from a forged Associated Press dispatch that they had every reason to believe was authentic. As it turned out, the story was fabricated by an unscrupulous journalist who hoped to reap large profits in the stock market during the panic he expected the story to produce.

After the end of the Civil War, the Fourteenth Amendment was approved, requiring the states to safeguard the basic civil liberties of all of their residents. The relevant part of the Fourteenth Amendment reads as follows:

No state shall make or enforce any law which shall abridge the privileges or immunities of citizens of the United States; nor shall any State deprive any person of life, liberty or property, without due process of law; nor

deny to any person within its jurisdiction the equal protection of the laws.

Like the First Amendment, this amendment had far-reaching consequences that were not fully understood when it was adopted. Its immediate impetus came from the desire to protect the former slaves from oppressive legislation in southern states. But during the twentieth century the "liberty" clause of the Fourteenth Amendment was relied upon repeatedly to make the various federal rights guaranteed in the Bill of Rights—including the First Amendment—applicable to the states. Under a modern understanding of constitutional law, no state could enforce a gag law of the sort adopted by many states before the Civil War.

John Stuart Mill's Philosophy

While the United States was preoccupied with the struggle over slavery, John Stuart Mill, an English political philosopher, was refining the theoretical concept of freedom of expression.

Mill's *On Liberty*, first published in 1859, defined the limits of freedom and authority in the modern state. He said that by the mid-1800s the important role of the press as one of "the securities against corrupt or tyrannical government" was well recognized—at least in such countries as England and the United States. He stressed that any attempt to silence expression, even that of a one-person minority, deprives the people of something important. He said that "if the opinion is right, they (the people) are deprived of the opportunity of exchanging error for truth; if wrong, they lose what is almost as great a benefit, the clearer perception and livelier impression of truth, produced by its collision with error."

Mill presented four basic propositions in defense of freedom of expression. First, he said an opinion may contain truth, and if one silences the opinion, the truth maybe lost. Second, there may be a particle of truth within a wrong opinion; if the wrong opinion is suppressed, that particle of truth may be lost. Third, even if an accepted opinion is the truth, the public tends to hold it not on rational grounds but as a prejudice unless forced to defend it. And fourth, a commonly held opinion loses its vitality and its effect on conduct and character if it is not contested from time to time.

In these terms, Mill expanded upon Milton's "marketplace of ideas" concept. The impact of these ideas on the evolution of freedom of expression became evident in the twentieth century.

SEDITION IN THE TWENTIETH CENTURY

Wars and the threat of wars tend to make lawmakers worry more about national security and less about such ideals as freedom of speech. The Alien and Sedition Acts of 1798 were passed at a time when war with France seemed imminent, and the Civil War created pressures for censorship of those who opposed that war effort.

Early in the twentieth century, this nation became involved in what many Americans thought would be the war to end all wars: World War I. In preparing the country for this all-out war, Congress again decided that domestic freedom would have to be curtailed. The result was the Espionage Act in 1917, which was expanded by the Sedition Act in 1918.

In passing these laws, Congress was not merely expressing its own collective desire to suppress unpopular views. In fact, there was a growing worldwide movement for fundamental social change, a movement many Americans found threatening. Already, Marxist revolutionaries were on the move in Russia, and socialists, anarchists and Marxists were also highly visible in this country. Moreover, we were about to undertake a war against Germany, and yet there were millions of persons of German descent living in America. In addition, labor unions such as the Industrial Workers of the World (the "Wobblies") were gaining wide support and calling for basic changes in the capitalist system.

The Espionage Act was passed shortly after the United States entered World War I. It prohibited seditious expression that might hurt the war effort. This federal law was particularly aimed at those who might hamper armed forces recruiting, and it was written so broadly that it was once used to prosecute a grandmother who wrote a letter urging her grandson not to join the army.

Unlike the 1798 Sedition Act, which resulted in only a handful of prosecutions, the 1918 Sedition Act was vigorously enforced. About 2,000 persons were arrested for violating the Espionage and Sedition acts and nearly 1,000 were convicted.

Several of the convictions were appealed to the U.S. Supreme Court, which upheld every conviction it reviewed.

Early Free Expression Decisions

The first Espionage Act or Sedition Act case to reach the Supreme Court was *Schenck v. U.S.* (249 U.S. 47) in 1919. Charles T. Schenck, general secretary of the Socialist Party, and another socialist were convicted under the Espionage Act and state anarchy and sedition laws for circulating about 15,000 leaflets to military recruits and draftees. The tracts denounced the draft as an unconstitutional form of involuntary servitude, banned by the Thirteenth Amendment. They urged the draftees not to serve and called the war a cold-blooded venture for the profit of big business.

When their conviction was reviewed by the Supreme Court, the socialists argued that their speech and leaflets were protected by the First Amendment. The court was thus compelled to rule on the scope and meaning of the First Amendment. In a famous opinion written by Justice Oliver Wendell Holmes Jr., the court rejected the socialists' argument:

> We admit that in many places and in ordinary times the defendants in saying all that was said in the circular would have been within their constitutional rights. But the character of every act depends upon the circumstances in which it is done. The question in every case is whether the words used are used in such circumstances and are of such a nature as to create *a clear and present danger* that they will bring about the substantive evils that Congress has a right to prevent (emphasis added).

In short, the Supreme Court said the First Amendment is not absolute. Congress may abridge freedom of speech whenever that speech presents a "clear and present danger" to some other national interest that is more important than freedom of speech at the moment.

In reaching this conclusion, Holmes made his famous analogy: "free speech would not protect a man in falsely shouting fire in a theatre and causing a panic." Thus, he wrote, free speech can never be considered absolute. Instead, each abridgment of freedom must be weighed against its purpose to decide if it is an appropriate or inappropriate one.

Although the *clear and present danger* test has proved to be vague and difficult to administer, it replaced a common law test for allegedly dangerous speech that was even more difficult to administer without unduly inhibiting freedom. The old common law test, known as the *reasonable tendency* or *bad tendency test*, was established in England in the 1700s and adopted as American common law along with the rest of the English common law. This test could be used to forbid any speech that might tend to create a low opinion of public officials, institutions or laws. It gave prosecutors wide latitude to prosecute anyone charged with the crime of seditious libel.

Whatever its limitations, the clear and present danger test was more precise and offered more protection for unpopular speech than the old reasonable tendency test.

Following the *Schenck* decision, the Supreme Court quickly upheld the convictions of two other persons charged with violating the Espionage Act: Jacob Frohwerk, a German language newspaper editor, and Eugene V. Debs, the famous leader of the American Socialist Party who later received nearly a million votes for president of the United States while in jail.

Eight months after the *Schenck*, *Frohwerk v. U.S.* (249 U.S. 204) and *Debs v. U.S.* (249 U.S. 211) decisions, the Supreme Court ruled on another Espionage Act case, *Abrams v. U.S.* (250 U.S. 616). The convictions of Jacob Abrams and four others who had published antiwar leaflets were upheld, but this time the court had a new dissenter: Justice Holmes had rethought his position and wrote an eloquent defense of freedom of expression that was joined by Justice Louis Brandeis.

In the majority opinion that affirmed the convictions, Justice John Clarke said the primary goal of Abrams and his co-defendants was to aid the enemy. That constituted a clear and present danger to national interests. But on the other hand, Holmes and Brandeis replied:

It is only the present danger of immediate evil or an intent to bring it about that warrants

Congress in setting a limit to the expression of opinion where private rights are not concerned. Congress certainly cannot forbid all effort to change the mind of the country. Now nobody can suppose that the surreptitious publishing of a silly leaflet by an unknown man, without more, would present any immediate danger that its opinions would hinder the success of the government aims or have any appreciable tendency to do so.

Elsewhere in the dissenting opinion, Justice Holmes echoed the views of John Milton and John Stuart Mill in writing this appeal for a free exchange of ideas:

… When men have realized that time has upset many fighting faiths, they may come to believe even more than they believe the very foundations of their own conduct that the ultimate good desired is better reached by free trade in ideas—that the best test of truth is the power of the thought to get itself accepted in the competition of the market, and that truth is the only ground upon which their wishes safely can be carried out.

This opinion was very influential in later years, but at the time it was a minority view. Neither the country nor the Supreme Court was in a mood to be tolerant toward political radicals.

In the last Espionage Act case it reviewed, the Supreme Court affirmed a lower court ruling that denied second-class mailing privileges to the *Milwaukee Leader*, the best known Socialist paper in the country. The high court found that articles in the *Leader* "sought to convince readers … that soldiers could not be legally sent outside the country," and thus the sanctions were appropriate (*U.S. ex rel. Milwaukee Social Democratic Publishing Co. v. Burleson*, 255 U.S. 407, 1921).

By today's standards, these Supreme Court decisions seem repressive. The expression of views that would have been considered well within the protection of the First Amendment in more recent times led to criminal prosecutions during World War I. Obviously, First Amendment law was in its infancy at that point. The courts felt little obligation to observe the niceties of constitutional law at a time when left-ists seemed threatening to many Americans.

THE FIRST AMENDMENT AND THE STATES

During the first part of the twentieth century, at least 20 states enacted their own laws against various kinds of political radicalism. The common element in these laws was a fear of groups that sought to change the American political and social system and advocated force as a means of accomplishing their goals. The constitutionality of these laws was soon challenged by those convicted under them, and it wasn't long before some of these cases reached the U.S. Supreme Court.

Probably the most important of these state sedition cases was *Gitlow v. New York* (268 U.S. 652), which reached the Supreme Court in 1925. Benjamin Gitlow, a New York socialist, and three others were convicted of violating a state criminal anarchy law by writing a document called the "Left Wing Manifesto." They were also convicted of distributing a paper called *The Revolutionary Age.*

Gitlow argued that the New York law violated his freedom of expression, as guaranteed under the First Amendment. In so doing, he was asking the high court to reverse an 1833 decision that said the Bill of Rights only applied to the federal government (*Barron v. Baltimore*, 7 Peters 243). Gitlow contended that the Fourteenth Amendment's requirement that the states safeguard the "liberty" of their residents meant the civil liberties guaranteed in the Bill of Rights could no longer be violated by the states.

Enacted after the Civil War and intended to safeguard the civil rights of the former slaves, the Fourteenth Amendment applies specifically to the states. Among other things, it has a provision known as the *due process clause*, which says, "… nor shall any state deprive any person of life, liberty or property, without due process of law. …" Gitlow argued that "liberty," as the term is used in the Fourteenth Amendment, includes all of the freedoms guaranteed in the First Amendment.

By making this argument, Gitlow won a tremendous long-term victory for freedom of expression, but he lost his own appeal. In an amazingly brief passage, the Supreme Court completely rewrote the

rules on constitutional law, acknowledging that the Fourteenth Amendment had indeed made the First Amendment applicable to the states (known as the *incorporation doctrine*). But then the court said the First Amendment did not protect Gitlow's activities, thus upholding the New York conviction.

The court said, "A state in the exercise of its police power may punish those who abuse this freedom by utterances inimical to the public welfare, tending to corrupt public morals, incite to crime, or disturb the public peace."

Although Gitlow's conviction was affirmed, the Supreme Court had almost offhandedly rewritten the basic rules governing free expression rights at the state and local level. By requiring the states (and their political subdivisions such as city and county governments) to respect freedom of speech, press and religion, the Supreme Court had vastly expanded the rights of Americans.

Two years after the *Gitlow* decision, the Supreme Court affirmed another state conviction in a case that produced a famous opinion defending freedom of expression. In that case (*Whitney v. California*, 274 U.S. 357), Charlotte Anita Whitney was prosecuted for violating a California criminal syndicalism law, a law that made it a felony to belong to a group that advocated forcible change. Whitney was a member of the Communist Labor Party, but she had argued against its militant policies at a meeting just before her prosecution.

Despite these mitigating circumstances, the Supreme Court affirmed her conviction. For technical reasons, Justice Brandeis concurred in the court's decision rather than dissenting, but his concurring opinion (which Justice Holmes joined) was a powerful appeal for freedom:

> Those who won our independence by revolution were not cowards. They did not fear political change. They did not exalt order at the cost of liberty. To courageous self-reliant men, with confidence in the power of free and fearless reasoning applied through the processes of popular government, no danger flowing from speech can be deemed clear and present, unless the incidence of the evil apprehended is so imminent that it may befall

before there is opportunity for full discussion. If there be time to expose through discussion the falsehood and fallacies, to avert the evil by the processes of education, the remedy to be applied is more speech, not enforced silence.

Brandeis said he believed that free speech should be suppressed only in times of emergency and that it was always "open to Americans to challenge a law abridging free speech and assembly by showing that there was no emergency justifying it."

The Supreme Court finally reversed a conviction for expressing radical ideas for the first time in another 1927 case, *Fiske v. Kansas* (274 U.S. 380). In that case, a defendant was prosecuted merely for belonging to the Industrial Workers of the World, and the primary evidence against him was the preamble to the "Wobblies'" constitution. There was no evidence that he had advocated or engaged in any violent or otherwise unlawful acts. The court said the preamble simply didn't present sufficient evidence of unlawful goals to justify the conviction.

POSTWAR SEDITION AND DISSENT

The 1918 Sedition Act, like its 1798 predecessor, was only in force a short time: most of its provisions were repealed in 1921. Major portions of the 1917 Espionage Act were not repealed, but that law was specifically written so that it only applied in wartime. Thus, for nearly two decades after 1921, there was no federal law prohibiting seditious speech. But as World War II approached, those who felt the need to curtail freedom in the interest of national security again gained support in Congress. Finally, a sedition law was attached to the Alien Registration Act of 1940, popularly known as the Smith Act because one of its sponsors was Congressman Howard Smith of Virginia.

Not only were the new sedition provisions attached to an essentially unrelated bill, but the whole thing happened so quietly that many free speech advocates didn't realize what had happened until months later.

Among other things, the new sedition law made it a crime to advocate the violent overthrow of the government or even to belong to a group that advocated

overthrowing the government by force. In addition, there were provisions making it a crime to proselytize for groups having such goals. The law did not require proof that the group might actually carry out any of those goals before its members could be prosecuted; mere advocacy was sufficient. Nor did this law apply only during wartime.

The 1940 law was rarely used at first. In fact, compared to other wars, World War II elicited little domestic opposition, perhaps because of the manner in which the United States became involved in that war as well as the widely publicized atrocities of the Nazis. However, during the tense "cold war" era that followed World War II, the Smith Act was used to prosecute numerous members of the American Communist Party.

The Smith Act's constitutionality was first tested before the U.S. Supreme Court in a 1951 case involving 12 alleged Communists, *Dennis v. U.S.* (341 U.S. 494). Eugene Dennis and the others were tried on charges of willfully and knowingly conspiring to overthrow the U.S. government by force. After a controversial nine-month trial, they were convicted and the Supreme Court eventually upheld the convictions.

Chief Justice Fred Vinson's opinion, in which three other justices joined, didn't specifically apply the clear and present danger test to the activities of the defendants. Instead, the court adopted a test that had been formulated by Learned Hand, a famous appellate court judge who heard the case before it reached the Supreme Court. Hand's test is this:

> In each case (courts) must ask whether the gravity of the "evil," discounted by its improbability, justifies such invasion of free speech as is necessary to avoid the danger.

By using Judge Hand's *modified version of the clear and present danger test*, it was possible for the Supreme Court to sustain the convictions without any evidence that there was a real danger that the Communists could achieve their stated goals. Justice Vinson ruled that the American Communist movement, tiny though it was, constituted a sufficient "evil" to justify the limitations on freedom of speech inherent in the Smith Act. For the moment, it would be unlawful even to belong to an organization that advocated the violent overthrow of the government. Chief Justice Vinson wrote:

> Certainly an attempt to overthrow the Government by force, even though doomed from the outset because of inadequate numbers or power of the revolutionists, is sufficient evil for Congress to prevent.

Chief Justice Vinson continued:

> Overthrow of the Government by force and violence is certainly a substantial enough interest for the Government to limit speech. Indeed, this is the ultimate value of any society. …

After winning the *Dennis* case, the U.S. Justice Department began a new series of prosecutions under the Smith Act. During the early 1950s at least 121 persons were prosecuted under the act's conspiracy provisions, and many others were prosecuted under the provisions outlawing mere membership in organizations advocating the violent overthrow of the government.

This may seem to be an alarming violation of the American tradition of free speech, but it was in keeping with the mood of the times. The early 1950s were the heyday of McCarthyism, a time when prominent Americans were accused of pro-Communist sympathies, often with little or no proof. For example, a number of well-known writers and motion picture celebrities were blacklisted in the entertainment industry after undocumented charges were made against them. In Congress, the House Committee on Un-American Activities conducted investigations that its critics felt were little more than witch-hunts designed to harass those with unpopular ideas.

However, the times were changing, and so was the makeup of the U.S. Supreme Court. Senator Joseph McCarthy of Wisconsin, the man whose name is synonymous with the red scare, was censured by his Congressional colleagues, and public disapproval of his tactics increased notably by the time of his death in 1957. Meanwhile, the Supreme Court had gained several new members, most notably Chief Justice Earl Warren, who led the court into an unprecedented period of judicial liberalism. Warren was appointed in 1953 after the death of Chief Justice Vinson.

In 1957 the Supreme Court responded to these changes by modifying the *Dennis* rule in another case involving the prosecution of alleged Communists under the Smith Act, *Yates v. U.S.* (354 U.S. 298). In this case, the Supreme Court reversed convictions or ordered new trials for a total of 14 persons charged with Communist activities. In so ruling, the high court focused on the distinction between teaching the desirability of violently overthrowing the government as an abstract theory and actually advocating violent action. The court said the convictions had to be invalidated because the jury instructions did not require a finding that there was any tendency of the advocacy to produce forcible action.

The court said the Smith Act could only be used against "the advocacy and teaching of concrete action for the forcible overthrow of the Government, and not of principles divorced from action." The Supreme Court did not return to the clear and present danger test as such, and the court insisted it was not abandoning the *Dennis* rule. But the new requirement of proof that the defendant was calling for action rather than teaching an abstract doctrine made it very difficult to convict anyone under the Smith Act. As a result, this controversial law was almost never used against political dissidents after that time.

Changing Times: The 1960s

Perhaps it was fortuitous timing that the Smith Act was rarely used against radicals after 1957, because in the 1960s there was a period of political dissent unprecedented in twentieth-century America. Thousands—and eventually millions—of Americans came to disagree with their government's handling of the Vietnam War, and countless numbers of them vociferously demanded changes in the political system that led to this unpopular war. Had that happened at a time when the government was prepared to vigorously enforce the Smith Act (and when the courts were willing to brush aside the First Amendment and let it happen) far more people than were jailed under the World War I Sedition Act might have been imprisoned for opposing the government during the Vietnam War.

The First Amendment protection for those accused of seditious speech was again expanded in a controversial 1969 Supreme Court decision involving a Ku Klux Klansman. In that case, *Brandenburg v. Ohio* (395 U.S. 444), a man convicted of violating an Ohio criminal syndicalism law contended that his conduct was protected under the First Amendment. Brandenburg spoke at a Klan rally that was filmed. Part of the film was later televised nationally. Much of what was said was incomprehensible, but the meaning of other remarks was quite clear. Brandenburg urged sending "niggers" back to Africa and Jews to Israel, and also talked of the need for "revengeance."

Was this a call for action that could be prosecuted under the *Yates* rule, or was it merely the teaching of abstract doctrine? In resolving that question, the Supreme Court went beyond the constitutional protection it had afforded speech in the *Yates* decision. In *Brandenburg*, the court said the First Amendment even protects speech that is a call for action, as long as the speech is not likely to produce *imminent lawless action*. Thus, the point at which the First Amendment ceases to protect seditious speech is not when there is a call for action, but when that call for action is persuasive and effective enough that it is likely to produce imminent results. The court said:

> ... (T)he constitutional guarantees of free speech do not permit (state regulation) ... except where the speech is directed to inciting or producing imminent lawless action, and is likely to incite or produce such action.

Brandenburg's criminal conviction was reversed, and the Supreme Court invalidated the Ohio criminal syndicalism law itself. In so doing, the Supreme Court reversed the 1927 *Whitney v. California* decision, in which a state law virtually identical to Ohio's had been upheld. This provides an interesting illustration of the way a dissenting or concurring opinion of one generation can inspire a majority opinion in another. Justice Brandeis' concurring opinion in *Whitney* argued for an imminent danger requirement: Brandeis said the First Amendment should not permit sanctions for political speech unless it threatens to provoke imminent lawless action. More than 40 years later, the Supreme Court adopted that view in the Brandenburg decision, repudiating the majority opinion in *Whitney*.

Even now—many years after the *Brandenburg* decision—millions of Americans feel passionately that the Supreme Court was wrong: the Ku Klux Klan and other racist organizations do not deserve First Amendment protection, they believe. During the 1980s and 1990s, there was a major national controversy about "hate speech." Many states passed laws forbidding that kind of speech, and the Supreme Court ultimately stepped into the debate by ruling on the issue twice, in 1992 and 1993 (see Chapter Three).

INTERPRETING THE CONSTITUTION

In tracing the development of First Amendment freedoms, we have noted several philosophies and "tests" that have been proposed to aid in interpreting what the First Amendment means. Because interpreting the First Amendment (and the rest of the Constitution) is so central to the study of mass media law, we will summarize some basic principles of constitutional interpretation.

Almost every dispute about constitutional rights involves some kind of a *balancing* test. The courts must weigh conflicting rights and decide which is the most important. That means sometimes one constitutional principle must give way to another: there are few absolutes in constitutional law.

That fact, of course, is unfortunate for the mass media. Were the First Amendment an absolute, many of the legal problems the media face would not exist. Given an absolute First Amendment, there would be no such thing as sedition or prior restraint, and it is doubtful the media could even be held accountable for libel and slander, invasions of privacy, or copyright infringements. Certainly there would be no obscenity law and no limits on media coverage of the criminal justice system. But if that were the case, many of society's other interests would be forced to yield to freedom of speech and freedom of the press.

Fortunately or unfortunately, depending on your point of view, the *absolutist theory* of the First Amendment has never been the majority view on the U.S. Supreme Court. Some of the founding fathers, such as James Madison, may have considered the First Amendment something of an absolute safeguard for free speech, and two well-known Supreme Court justices who served during the 1950s and 1960s (Hugo Black and William O. Douglas) took an almost absolutist position. However, the majority view has always been that the First Amendment must be weighed in the balances against other rights and social needs. Thus, the task for the courts over the years has been to develop appropriate guidelines to assist in this balancing process.

One of the best-known of these guidelines for balancing the First Amendment against other interests has been the clear and present danger test. As already noted, it was first cited by Justice Oliver Wendell Holmes in the 1919 *Schenck* decision. In the years since, it has sometimes been applied to political speech cases, although in recent years the Supreme Court has not mentioned it in the leading decisions on free speech. As Chapter Eight explains, the Supreme Court has also applied the clear and present danger test in resolving conflicts between the media and the courts. In many of those cases, the Supreme Court has been forced to weigh the First Amendment guarantee of a free press against judges' rights to exercise their contempt of court powers; the concept of clear and present danger has been used in this balancing process.

Some constitutional scholars argue for a *preferred position test* as an alternative to balancing the First Amendment against other rights and social interests. In their view, the First Amendment should occupy a preeminent place in constitutional law and should rarely give way to other interests. Some believe that during the era when Earl Warren was chief justice, the Supreme Court leaned toward that view of the First Amendment. Indeed, many of the decisions most favorable to the media were handed down by the Warren Court.

In a more general way, the Supreme Court always uses a kind of preferred position test in weighing constitutionally protected interests against other values. In *U.S. v. C.I.O.* (335 U.S. 106), a 1948 case, Justice Wiley Rutledge articulated this view. He noted that the normal rule of judicial interpretation requires the courts to adopt a presumption in favor of the validity of legislative acts. However, he said, when a legislative act restricts First Amendment rights, the presumption must be reversed so that there is a presumption against the validity of the law rather than in favor of its validity. Thus, he advocated a "reverse presumption of constitutionality" when a statutory law is challenged on constitutional grounds.

The concept that the rights protected by the Bill of Rights occupy a preferred position compared to other interests has been mentioned in a number of other Supreme Court decisions. However, on a practical level that bias in favor of constitutional rights does not necessarily translate into tangible results. What the court still does is balance the competing interests—albeit with the scales tipped slightly toward constitutional rights.

The Supreme Court has also developed a series of more specific guidelines to use in evaluating claims that a statutory law or government action violates a constitutional right.

When a statute (or a state's application of the common law) is challenged, the court normally looks for nothing more than a *rational relationship* between the law and a legitimate government goal. When a state law is challenged, for instance, the state may attempt to defend it by showing that the law bears a rational relationship to its police power or its duty to promote the health and welfare of its citizens.

However, when the claim is that the statute violates a fundamental right protected by the Constitution, the state must show a *compelling state interest* to justify the statute. The state must, in effect, convince the court that its objective in enacting this statute is of such overriding importance that a fundamental right (such as freedom of expression) must give way. A good example of this is described in Unit 11, where the Supreme Court's landmark decisions on the First Amendment and *commercial speech* are discussed. Although advertising generally enjoys less First Amendment protection than most other forms of speech, in some cases the Supreme Court has forced a state to show a compelling state interest to justify restrictions even on some types of advertising (see, for instance, *Bigelow v. Virginia*, 421 U.S. 809, 1975). More often, though, governments must show only a *substantial government interest* rather than a compelling one to justify restrictions on advertising (see *Central Hudson Gas and Electric v. Public Service Commission of New York*, 447 U.S. 557).

These tests are admittedly subjective, and not even all Supreme Court justices agree about when each should apply. Justice Clarence Thomas, for example, has often taken the position that advertising should have no less First Amendment protection than other forms of speech.

Another way the courts, and particularly the U.S. Supreme Court, evaluate challenged state and federal statutes is to decide whether they are *vague* or *overly broad*. If a law that limits constitutionally protected rights is so broad that it inhibits freedom more than is necessary to achieve a legitimate government purpose, or if it is so vague that it is difficult to know exactly what speech or conduct is prohibited, it may be invalidated for overbreadth or vagueness.

If a court is going to invalidate a statutory law, it has two options: (1) to find that the law is unconstitutional and thus void under all circumstances; or (2) to find that it is unconstitutional only as it has been applied to the person challenging the law. Moreover, given an ambiguous law, the courts have an obligation to resolve the ambiguity in such a way as to avoid a constitutional conflict if possible. The U.S. Supreme Court has the final say in construing the language in federal statutes, but the state courts have the final say in interpreting state laws. The U.S. Supreme Court can only decide whether a state law is unconstitutional as interpreted by the state courts; it cannot reinterpret a state statute.

This means the U.S. Supreme Court sometimes has to send a case back to a state court to find out what a state law means. Once the state court spells out the meaning, the nation's highest court can then decide whether the law—as interpreted by the state court—actually violates the U.S. Constitution. If it does, it is invalid, of course. But if the state court can interpret the law in such a way as to avoid a conflict with the U.S. Constitution, the law is valid.

Obviously, determining whether a given statute or government action violates the Constitution is a difficult and subjective job. The Supreme Court has a variety of guidelines that it may choose to follow (or choose to ignore) in any given situation. Critics of the process suspect that whatever test is or isn't applied in a particular case, the ultimate outcome of the case depends more on the values and priorities of the nine justices than on how the facts measure up against one or another set of guidelines. In short, whatever other test may be applied, cases are decided on the basis of a rather subjective balancing process in which various competing values, interests and social objectives are weighed.

In his autobiography, former Justice William O. Douglas described a very revealing conversation he had with then–Chief Justice Charles Evans Hughes soon after being appointed to the Supreme Court:

> Hughes made a statement to me which at the time was shattering but which over the years turned out to be true: "Justice Douglas, you must remember one thing. At the Constitutional level where we work, 90 percent of any decision is emotional. The rational part of us supplies the reasons for supporting our predilections."

In the end, most Supreme Court–watchers would probably agree. Bruce Sanford, longtime First Amendment lawyer for the Society of Professional Journalists, most likely would. After seeing the Supreme Court staunchly uphold *unpopular* First Amendment principles in three different 1989 decisions—and then *limit* First Amendment freedoms in two other cases where most of the public probably didn't care either way, Sanford said the First Amendment remains "the most unpredictable area of Supreme Court jurisprudence." He also said, "There is no clear consensus on First Amendment theory and the manner in which it is applied to cases."

So much for theories that purport to rationalize and reconcile the court's seemingly inconsistent rulings on the meaning of the First Amendment …

THE FUTURE OF FREEDOM IN A TERRORIST ERA

In this unit, we have traced nearly 400 years of struggles for freedom of expression. Of the total history of humanity, that is but a tiny portion. Where, then, is freedom going in the next 400 years? Perhaps more to the point, what will be the future of freedom in the near future—an era that may be dominated by the threat of terrorism in many parts of the world?

Obviously, no one can answer these questions. The status of freedom in America may depend on who runs the country—and the world. It also depends on who is appointed to the U.S. Supreme Court, the federal appellate courts and the appellate courts of the 50 states. And it depends on who is elected to national, state and local offices. It is those people who will shape the law.

In a larger sense, the future of freedom is always decided by the changing mood of the times. As several later chapters explain, there is a growing sentiment in America today in favor of more restrictions on free expression. Polls often show that large numbers of people think the First Amendment should not protect the work of artists, musicians and others whose choice of language or subject matter may be offensive. Many people think the broadcast media, including cable and satellite television, should be subject to tougher government restrictions to curb the use of language and images that may be offensive. Some also believe the Internet should be more regulated to limit the kind of words and images that are allowed. How could such restrictions on free expression be reconciled with the First Amendment, civil libertarians often ask.

In much of the world the Internet has revolutionized the idea of free expression. Even in China, which by some estimates has at least 30,000 government workers policing the Internet for unacceptable content in a program that critics have called the "great firewall," the net has brought new freedom. By 2008, an estimated 250 million Chinese were online, making the regulation of content a difficult challenge. Some American companies have drawn criticism for cooperating with the Chinese government by filtering out content of which the government disapproves. When Microsoft launched a new portal in China called MSN Spaces, some objected to the company's insertion of filters that cause a yellow warning to appear on the screen when someone uses words like "democracy," "capitalism," "liberty" or "human rights." Even "June 4th," a widely understood reference to the 1989 Tiananmen Square killings in Beijing, is filtered out. Microsoft's supporters point out that software companies have to comply with local laws in many countries. Other U.S. companies including Google.com and Yahoo.com have also modified their content to satisfy the Chinese government.

In fact, American software companies have often had legal problems abroad with content that is clearly protected by the First Amendment in the United States. In one widely publicized incident, CompuServe was forced to deny even its American

subscribers access to about 30 sexually oriented sites on the Internet to avoid violating German laws. A French court fined Yahoo.com for allowing the sale of Nazi collectibles on its U.S.-based website. Although Yahoo later banned Nazi items, it faced more than $15 million in French fines at one point.

Within the United States, however, the overriding factor in determining the status of freedom in the near future is likely to be the progress of the war against terrorism. Already, legal controversies have raged over issues such as the propriety of trying some of those accused of terrorist acts in military as opposed to civilian courts, as President George W. Bush decreed by executive order. Military courts lack some of the safeguards guaranteed by the U.S. Constitution in civilian courts.

Whenever a society feels threatened by subversive forces within or powerful enemies abroad, freedom suffers. Over the past 200 years, constitutional freedoms have been curtailed repeatedly in wartime. Former Chief Justice William Rehnquist wrote a book in 1998, several years before 9/11, summarizing some of that history. In *All the Laws but One: Civil Liberties in Wartime*, Rehnquist discussed Supreme Court decisions concerning the constitutionality of military trials for those accused of subversive activities. The history he traced may be even more relevant today than it was during his lifetime. His conclusion was that the Supreme Court has often interpreted the law differently in wartime than in peacetime, but with each successive war, Americans became more protective of civil liberties and less willing to abandon constitutional rights in the name of national security.

Is that still true in this era of terrorism? The events of Sept. 11, 2001 prompted several government actions that affected civil liberties. The USA PATRIOT Act substantially expanded government surveillance powers, leading to unprecedented surveillance of U.S. citizens in an effort to catch terrorists before they can strike.

Although the limits on First Amendment freedoms within the United States since 9/11 have been minimal compared to those imposed during World War I, for example, there have been growing concerns both in the U.S. and abroad about America's respect for human rights overseas. The United States was once something of a beacon to the world in advocating broader human rights. When the United Nations General Assembly approved the Universal Declaration of Human Rights in 1948, the United States was its most prominent advocate. Former first lady Eleanor Roosevelt was the first chairwoman of the U.N.'s Commission on Human Rights. The U.S. was a leading advocate of the 1975 Helsinki Accords, in which 35 mostly European countries pledged to respect basic human rights. The U.S. has also been a leading advocate of human rights within the Inter-American Commission on Human Rights, among other international bodies.

But in the 2000s, many human rights advocates in America and abroad expressed concerns about the way the U.S. government was pursuing the war on terrorism. Perhaps the most controversial practice was "extraterritorial rendition" in which U.S. agents kidnapped suspected terrorists and their supporters in foreign countries and took them to still other countries for questioning that involved torture, using methods that are not legal within the U.S. Many Americans and others asked whether these acts were necessary and appropriate ways to fight terrorism.

Looking beyond the effect of terrorist threats on civil liberties, there are other issues that should not be ignored. The behavior of the mass media themselves may help determine how much freedom we have. Journalistic sensationalism, inaccuracy and arrogance—as well as monopolistic media business practices—invite punitive responses by governments. If the media are to preserve their freedom, they must stand firm against abuses by governments at all levels, but they must also be responsible in exercising their freedom.

UNIT 7

The State or the Public?
The Public Interest Standard in
Telecom Regulation

Faced with competing applicants for usage of the airwaves (which as you will learn in the next unit is considered to be a scarce resource) and with no standard to choose among them, Congress created the Federal Communications Commission (as you've learned in Unit 5). In order to provide it with a tool to compare among those trying to win a license to broadcast, Congress introduced into the Radio Act of 1927 and then into the Communications Act of 1934 the "public interest standard." Giving practical meaning to this abstract standard has been a challenge for the FCC ever since. Legal experts Erwin Krasnow and Jack Goodman summarize in this reading the history of the standard's interpretation by the FCC and by the Courts up until the Telecommunications Act of 1996. Unfortunately, the FCC had not completed its work on updating the public interest obligations of broadcasters in the digital age. Those cases it has, in particular children's broadcasting, will be discussed in the lecture.

The "Public Interest" Standard

The Search for the Holy Grail

Erwin G. Krasnow and Jack N. Goodman

I. INTRODUCTION

An observer of the federal administrative/regulatory system once stated that government agencies can be divided into two categories: "Deliver the Mail" and "Holy Grail."[1] "Deliver the Mail" agencies perform neutral, mechanical, logistical functions; they send out Social Security checks, procure supplies, or deliver the mail.[2] "Holy Grail" agencies, on the other hand, pursue an often more controversial and difficult mandate to realize some grand, moral, civilizing goal.

The earliest regulator of electronic communications in the United States, the Federal Radio Commission (FRC), came into being primarily to "deliver the mail,"—that is to act as a traffic cop of the airwaves. However, both the FRC and its successor agency, the Federal Communications Commission (FCC or Commission), had a vague but oft-repeated Holy Grail clause written into their charters: the requirement that they uphold the "public interest, convenience and necessity."[3]

Perhaps no single area of communications policy has generated as much scholarly discourse, judicial analysis, and political debate over the course of the last seventy years as has that simple directive to regulate in the "public interest." Critics of this public interest standard have often charged that the phrase "is vague to the point of vacuousness, providing neither guidance nor constraint on the [regulatory] agency's action."[4] Moreover, as former FCC Commissioner Ervin Duggan recently observed, "successive regimes at the FCC have oscillated wildly between enthusiasm for the public interest standard and distaste for it."[5] If the history of this elusive regulatory standard makes anything clear, it is the fact that just what constitutes service in the "public interest" has encompassed different things at different times.

This Article identifies the current contours of the public interest standard as they have emerged from statute, regulatory activity, and judicial scrutiny over the last eight decades.[6] First, the Article reviews the historical context of Congress's early efforts at broadcast regulation. Second, it traces the development of the substantive characteristics and elements of the standard through a survey of the pivotal interpretive rulings of the FRC and, later, the FCC concerning the standard. Third, it examines the impact that the United States Supreme Court has had in shaping the standard in a series of important decisions. Finally, the Article offers some general observations about the nature of the public interest standard as a device that: (1) eludes satisfactory definition; (2) remains to a great extent dependent on a consensus that must be repeatedly fashioned anew from among the competing values and interests (economic, social, political, and constitutional) at stake in the decision-making process; and (3) one that, notwithstanding its shortcomings, still enjoys significant support.

II. ORIGINS OF THE PUBLIC INTEREST STANDARD

At a fundamental level, the public interest standard is rooted in statute. Under sections 307 and 309 of the Communications Act, the FCC may grant the use of a frequency for a limited term to an applicant that demonstrates that the proposed service would serve "the public interest, convenience, and necessity."[7] License renewal applicants are to be evaluated under the same standard.[8] Although the standard has become a keystone of contemporary communications regulatory policy, it has not always enjoyed such status. On the contrary, as discussed below, the present contours of the standard, and the concomitant regulatory authority it vests in the FCC, have evolved over the course of time and experience and reflect the changing tapestry of American culture over several generations.

A. The Radio Act of 1912 and the Annual Radio Conferences

The Wireless Ship Act of 1910 applied to the use of radio by ships,[9] but the Radio Act of 1912, enacted in the wake of the Titanic disaster, was the first domestic law for general control of radio.[10] It empowered the Secretary of Commerce and Labor to issue licenses for radio stations to United States citizens upon request and to specify the frequencies to be used by the stations. However, the 1912 Act gave the Secretary no authority to reject applications. Congress had not anticipated the rejection of applications because it presumed that there was sufficient spectrum for all who needed to operate radio stations.

The unregulated growth of radio stations in the early 1920s created intolerable interference. In response, then-Secretary of Commerce Herbert Hoover convened a series of four annual national radio conferences in which representatives of the radio industry and government met to adopt a system of self-regulation. Secretary Hoover first expressed the concept of a public interest in radio communications

in a speech before the Fourth Annual Radio Conference in 1925. He stated:

> The ether is a public medium, and its use must be for public benefit. The use of a radio channel is justified only if there is public benefit. The dominant element for consideration in the radio field is, and always will be, the great body of the listening public, millions in number, countrywide in distribution. There is no proper line of conflict between the broadcaster and the listener, nor would I attempt to array one against the other. Their interests are mutual, for without the one the other could not exist.[11]

The Conference generally endorsed the public interest concept and recommended legislation incorporating it. But the delegates ultimately "gridlocked" on the idea, apparently because no one could come up with an acceptable definition.[12]

Congressman Wallace H. White, Jr., one of the co-authors of the Radio Act of 1927, stated that despite the inability of the delegates to the Radio Conference to agree on a definition, the "public interest" was a central concern in writing the 1927 Act:

> [The radio conference] recognized that in the present state of scientific development there must be a limitation upon the number of broadcasting stations and it recommended that licenses should be issued only to those stations whose operation would render a benefit to the public, are necessary in the public interest, or would contribute to the development of the art. ... If enacted into law, the broadcasting privilege will not be a right of selfishness. It will rest upon an assurance of public interest to be served.[13]

Former FCC Chairman Newton Minow has commented that, starting with the Radio Act of 1927, the phrase "public interest, convenience and necessity" has provided the battleground for broadcasting's regulatory debate.[14] Congress's reason for including such a phrase was clear: the courts, interpreting the Radio Act of 1912 as a narrow statute, had said that the Secretary of Commerce could not create additional rules or regulations beyond that Act's terms.[15] This left Hoover unable to control the rapidly changing technologies. In the words of Senator Clarence Dill, one of the co-authors of the 1927 Radio Act, Hoover "issued everybody a license who has made application, and that has brought the present chaos."[16]

The public interest notion in the 1927 and 1934 Acts was intended to enable the regulatory agency to create new rules, regulations, and standards as required to meet new conditions. Congress clearly hoped to create an act more durable than the Radio Act of 1912.

B. The Radio Act of 1927

In contrast to the 1912 Radio Act's narrow limits on the power of the Department of Commerce to "traffic control," Congress intended in the Radio Act of 1927 to delegate broad regulatory powers to the FRC, limiting that agency's discretion mainly by the requirement that its actions serve the public interest.[17] The 1927 Act employed a utility regulation model under which broadcasters were deemed "public trustees" who were "privileged" to use a scarce public resource. The FRC explained this public trust model as follows:

> [Despite the fact that] [t]he conscience and judgment of a station's management are necessarily personal ... the station itself must be operated as if owned by the public. ... It is as if people of a community should own a station and turn it over to the best man in sight with this injunction: 'Manage this station in our interest ...' The standing of every station is determined by that conception.[18]

Nevertheless, the origin of the phrase "public interest, convenience, and necessity" is not evident from the legislative history of the Radio Act of 1927. Former FCC Chairman Minow recounted a conversation with then Senator Clarence C. Dill, which shed some light on the question. According to Senator Dill, the drafters had reached an impasse in their attempts to define a standard for the regulation of radio stations. A young lawyer who had been loaned to the Senate by the Interstate Commerce Commission said, "[w]ell, how about 'public interest, convenience and necessity'? That's what we [need] there." Dill replied, "[t]hat sounded pretty good, so

we decided we would use it, too."[19] However, while the fortuitous emergence of the public interest standard satisfied the immediate need of the drafters, the difficult work of giving the standard meaning in the context of radio regulation was left unfinished.

III. IMPLEMENTATION BY THE FEDERAL RADIO COMMISSION

A. The 1928 Statement

Following enactment of the 1927 Act, the FRC, in 1928, issued its first comprehensive interpretation of the public interest standard.[20] The Commission indicated that it would apply the standard to programming content as well as technical matters. Broadcasters, the FRC said, should not use their stations for their own private interests, and the interests of the audience should take precedence over those of licensees. The FRC concluded its policy statement with the following observations on the public interest standard:

> In conclusion, the commission desires to point out that the test—"public interest convenience or necessity"—becomes a matter of comparative and not an absolute standard when applied to broadcasting stations. Since the number of channels is limited and the number of persons desiring to broadcast is far greater than can be accommodated, the commission must determine from among the applicants before it which of them will, if licensed, best serve the public. In a measure, perhaps, all of them give more or less service. Those who give the least, however, must be sacrificed for those who give the most. The emphasis must be first and foremost on the interest, the convenience, and the necessity of the listening public, and not on the interest, convenience, or necessity of the individual broadcaster or the advertiser.[21]

Only a year after the release of the policy statement, the FRC expanded upon its new regulatory mandate, providing further guidance on the meaning of the "public interest" in *Great Lakes Broadcasting Co. v. Federal Radio Commission*.[22]

B. The Great Lakes Decision

Great Lakes Broadcasting[23] involved a conflict among three Chicago area stations requesting modification of their technical facilities. In assessing their competing claims, the Commission advanced the following guidelines as a gauge for assessing a licensee's performance under the public interest standard:

> (1) a station should meet the "tastes, needs, and desires of all substantial groups among the listening public ... in some fair proportion, by a well-rounded program, in which entertainment, consisting of music of both classical and lighter grades, religion, education and instruction, important public events, discussions of public questions, weather, market reports, and news, and matters of interest to all members of the family find a place;"[24]

> (2) programming would be considered at renewal time in determining whether a station has met public interest requirements;[25]

> (3) where two stations apply for the same frequencies, the station with the longest record of continuous service has the advantage; where there is a substantial difference between the programming service of the two, the station with superior programming will have the advantage;[26] and

> (4) there is no room for operation of "propaganda stations," as opposed to "general public-service stations."[27]

The *Great Lakes Broadcasting* decision has been considered to be the FRC's most important decision because it "contain[ed] the seeds of concepts that would later germinate into significant regulatory policies. ..."[28] The decision firmly established programming content as a criterion of the public interest, and included notions which later formed the basis for the FCC's requirements governing ascertainment of community needs and the Fairness Doctrine.[29]

C. Denial of Licenses Based on Program Content

The FRC used its powers under the public interest standard to revoke the licenses of two stations based solely on its review of the licensee's programming practices. These actions, described below, were taken despite the no-censorship provision of section 29 of the 1927 Act, which provided in relevant part:

> Nothing in this Act shall be understood or construed to give the licensing authority the power of censorship over the radio communications or signals transmitted by any radio station, and no regulation or condition shall be promulgated or fixed by the licensing authority which shall interfere with the right of free speech by means of radio communications.[30]

1. The Brinkley Case

In 1930, the FRC denied renewal of the license of KFKB, Milford, Kansas, on the ground that the station was being controlled and used by Dr. John Brinkley, the "goat-gland doctor," to further his personal interest.[31] The "Medical Question Box," a program aired in three half-hour segments daily, featured Dr. Brinkley answering questions from listeners on health and medicine. In response to listener questions, Dr. Brinkley usually recommended several of his own prescriptions from his own pharmaceutical supply house. The FRC held that Brinkley's practice of diagnosing patients who he had not seen contravened the public health and safety and therefore, the public interest.[32] It also found that he operated KFKB solely for his own private interests.[33]

In affirming the denial of KFKB's renewal, the Court of Appeals rejected Brinkley's argument that the FRC violated the no-censorship prohibition of section 29 of the Radio Act, stating:

> This contention is without merit. There has been no attempt on the part of the commission to subject any part of appellant's broadcasting matter to scrutiny prior to its release. In considering the question whether the public interest, convenience, or necessity will be served by a renewal of appellant's license, the commission has merely exercised its undoubted right to take note of appellant's past conduct, which is not censorship.[34]

The court agreed with the FRC that broadcasting "is impressed with a public interest" and observed that because "the number of available broadcasting frequencies is limited," the FRC has the authority to "consider the character and quality of the service to be rendered."[35]

2. The Shuler Case

The FRC also denied the application for renewal of license of KDEF, Los Angeles. That station was used primarily to broadcast sermons by Trinity Methodist Church's pastor, Reverend Bob ("Fighting Bob") Shuler, who attacked Jews, the Roman Catholic Church, law enforcement officials in Los Angeles, and many others. Shuler based his appeal on constitutional grounds, namely, that the FRC decision violated his First Amendment right to free speech and his Fifth Amendment right to due process of law.

One of the issues before the Court of Appeals was whether the FRC's refusal to renew Shuler's license was a prior restraint under the then recently decided case of *Near v. Minnesota*,[36] or just a post-publication punishment. The court concluded that while a citizen has in the first instance the right to utter or publish his sentiments, it is "upon condition that he is responsible for any abuse of that right."[37] The refusal of the FRC to renew a license "to one who has abused it to broadcast defamatory and untrue matter," the court found, "is not a denial of the freedom of speech, but merely the application of the regulatory power of Congress in a field within the scope of its legislative authority."[38] The court held that Reverend Shuler's broadcasts did not contribute to the "public interest," the test the FRC was "required to apply" in considering renewal applications.[39]

IV. IMPLEMENTATION BY THE FEDERAL COMMUNICATIONS COMMISSION

Although the decisions in *Brinkley* and *Shuler* vindicated the FRC's powers to review programming to determine whether or not it was in the "public interest, convenience, and necessity," the FCC used its programming regulatory powers cautiously during the 1930s and early 1940s, with the exception of forcing most of the remaining propaganda stations off the air.[40] However, in the mid-1940s,

primarily because of the changing economies of network radio, the FCC decided it was time for another general policy statement and directed its staff to consider the public interest implications of radio programming trends.[41]

A. The Blue Book

In 1946, the FCC released the staff report entitled *Public Service Responsibility of Licensees*, which became more popularly known as the "*Blue Book*" because of its blue cover.[42] The *Blue Book* attempted to clarify the Commission's position on the public interest standard by setting forth programming guidelines for consideration of a licensee's performance at renewal time. The *Blue Book* treated the public interest as encompassing four requirements: (1) "sustaining" (unsponsored) programs; (2) local live programs; (3) programming devoted to the discussion of local public issues; and (4) the elimination of advertising excesses.[43] While license renewal forms were revised to make them compatible with the *Blue Book*, the FCC neither adopted the *Blue Book* nor repudiated it. One commentator observed:

> Its theme of balanced programming as a necessary component of broadcast service in the public interest coupled with its emphasis on a reasonable ratio of unsponsored ("sustaining") programs posed too serious a threat to the profitability of commercial radio for either the industry, Congress, or the FCC to want to match regulatory promise with performance.[44]

B. 1960 Program Policy Statement

Based on a series of hearings which it conducted in the late 1950s, the FCC concluded that additional clarification of the public interest standard was necessary. In 1960, the FCC adopted a *Report and Statement of Policy* (*1960 Programming Policy Statement*) which listed the "major elements usually necessary to meet the public interest:"[45]

1. Opportunity for Local Self-Expression
2. Development and Use of Local Talent
3. Programs for Children
4. Religious Programs

5. Educational Programs

6. Public Affairs Programs

7. Editorialization by Licensees

8. Political Broadcasts

9. Agricultural Programs

10. News Programs

11. Weather and Market Reports

12. Sports Programs

13. Service to Minority Groups

14. Entertainment Programming[46]

These types of programs, in some reasonable mix, were considered to be evidence that broadcasters were serving the public interest. The *1960 Programming Policy Statement* also concluded that broadcasters should determine the tastes, needs and desires of the community and design programming to meet those needs. This led to the FCC's adoption of formal ascertainment requirements, which compelled applicants for broadcast licenses to detail the results of interviews conducted by the applicant with community "leaders" in nineteen FCC specified categories ranging from agriculture to religion.[47]

C. The Marketplace Approach to Interpreting the Public Interest Standard

Against this background of detailed regulation, beginning in the late 1970s, the FCC reinterpreted the public interest standard in the light of the "marketplace." Under this approach, regulation is viewed as necessary only when the marketplace clearly fails to protect the public interest, but not when there is only a potential for failure.[48] Early in his administration, FCC Chairman Mark Fowler, made clear that he intended to take a "marketplace approach" to broadcast regulation:

> Put simply, I believe that we are at the end of regulating broadcasting under the trusteeship model. Whether you call it "paternalism" or "nannyism," it is "Big Brother," and it must cease.
>
> I believe in a marketplace approach to broadcast regulation. ... Under the coming marketplace approach, the Commission

should, so far as possible, defer to a broadcaster's judgment about how best to compete for viewers and listeners because this serves the public interest.[49]

1. Radio and TV Deregulation

In its *Deregulation of Radio*[50] decision in 1981, the FCC eliminated rules and policies governing program logs, commercial time limitations, ascertainment of community problems, and non-entertainment programming requirements. The Commission stated that it recognized that its actions "remove the illusory comfort of a specific, quantitative guideline,"[51] but that Congress deliberately placed the public interest standard in the Communications Act to provide the Commission with maximum flexibility in dealing with the ever-changing conditions in the field of broadcasting:

> The Commission was not created solely to provide certainty. Rather, Congress established a mandate for the Commission to act in the public interest. We conceive of that interest to require us to regulate where necessary, to deregulate where warranted, and above all, to assure the maximum service to the public at the lowest cost and with the least amount of regulation and paperwork.[52]

In 1984, the Commission adopted decisions generally granting to commercial television, and to non-commercial broadcasters, the degree of deregulation afforded commercial radio stations in 1981.[53]

2. "Underbrush" Policies

In repealing a number of policies affecting programming and various commercial practices, the FCC indicated its concern for the First Amendment rights of broadcasters in interpreting the public interest standard:

> [P]olicies cautioning broadcasters not to engage in certain programming practices or establishing rigid guidelines relating to such programming raise fundamental questions concerning the constitutional rights of broadcast licensees, and therefore cannot be retained in the absence of a clear and

compelling showing that the public interest demands their retention.[54]

The United States Court of Appeals for the District of Columbia Circuit affirmed the FCC's elimination of "underbrush" policies in *Telecommunications Research and Action Center v. FCC*,[55] thereby approving the agency's reliance on marketplace forces. The Court held that the public interest standard is best left to the discretion of the FCC, which "may rely upon marketplace forces to control broadcast abuse if the Commission reasonably finds that a market approach offers the best means of controlling the abuse."[56]

3. Postcard Renewal Form
The FCC's decision to issue a shortened renewal form (the so-called "postcard renewal") was challenged by Black Citizens for a Fair Media on the ground that the abbreviated renewal form violated the FCC's mandate to determine that the public interest, convenience, and necessity would be served by granting a license.[57] The Court of Appeals affirmed the simplified renewal process, holding that the Communications Act did not require the FCC to ask program-related questions and that the Commission could make public interest determinations using the simplified procedure.[58]

4. Fairness Doctrine Repeal
In *Syracuse Peace Council*,[59] the FCC abolished the Fairness Doctrine which imposed a two-fold duty on broadcast licensees to provide coverage of "controversial issues of public importance" and to afford "a reasonable opportunity" for the airing of contrasting points of view.[60] The Commission repudiated the spectrum scarcity rationale for those requirements. Although the FCC disavowed any interest in calling into question the validity of the public interest standard or eliminating its public trusteeship model for broadcast regulation by contending that it "may still impose certain conditions on licensees in furtherance of [the] public interest,"[61] one scholar commented that "it is clear that without spectrum scarcity, there can be little left of the notion that a broadcaster must abide by a preordained federal conception of what constitutes broadcasting in the public interest."[62]

V. THE SUPREME COURT AND THE PUBLIC INTEREST STANDARD
The agency actions described in the foregoing sections, while unquestionably important to our present understanding of the reach and flexibility of the public interest standard, do not exist in a vacuum. Equally important to the analysis is the contribution of the judiciary in its review of those agency actions. Several decisions of the United States Supreme Court are particularly noteworthy.

A. *Nelson Brothers v. Federal Radio Commission*
In 1933, the Supreme Court issued its first opinion involving the public interest standard.[63] The FRC had granted full-time operating authority to WJKS, Gary, Indiana, at 560 kilohertz, and revoked the licenses of WIBO and WPCC, stations that shared time on that frequency (the formats of NBC affiliate WIBO, and WPCC, a religious station, were duplicated by other stations serving the Gary market). The Court, in affirming the FRC's decision, held that the Commission was entitled to evaluate and consider programming provided by various stations:

> In granting licenses the commission is required to act "as public convenience, interest, or necessity requires." …
>
> In the instant case the commission was entitled to consider the advantages enjoyed by the people of Illinois under the assignments to that state, the services rendered by the respective stations, the reasonable demands of the people of Indiana, and the special requirements of radio service at Gary.[64]

B. *FCC v. Pottsville Broadcasting*
The Supreme Court upheld the public interest standard which it described as the "touchstone" of authority for the FCC.[65] It said that "[t]he Commission's responsibility at all times is to measure applications by the standard of 'public convenience, interest, or necessity.'"[66] The public interest standard, the Court said, is "as concrete as the complicated factors for judgment in such a field of delegated authority permit" and the approach is "a supple instrument for the exercise of discretion."[67]

C. FCC v. Sanders Brothers Radio

The Supreme Court in the Sanders Brothers case held that the public interest standard did not require the FCC to consider economic injury to existing stations when considering an application for a new broadcast station.[68] The Court offered a narrower interpretation of the public interest standard which suggested that the FCC had no supervisory control over programs, business matters, or station policies:

> [T]he Act does not essay to regulate the business of the licensee. The Commission is given no supervisory control of the programs, of business management or of policy. In short, the broadcasting field is open to anyone, provided there be an available frequency over which he can broadcast without interference to others, if he shows his competency, the adequacy of his equipment, and financial ability to make good use of the assigned channel.[69]

D. NBC v. United States

In the NBC case, the Supreme Court upheld the FCC's "chain broadcasting" network rules which were designed to allow network affiliates to select programming free of network constraints.[70] The NBC case represents the most sweeping statement ever made by the Supreme Court in support of the FCC's authority to regulate the electronic media because it:

(1) affirmed the right of the FCC to exercise broad powers over the broadcasting industry;

(2) affirmed that the public interest standard is the touchstone of FCC authority to exercise broad regulatory powers;

(3) held that the public interest standard is not unconstitutionally vague;

(4) offered a scarcity rationale—the notion that regulation is necessary because the airwaves are limited—as justification for the public interest standard and for content regulation; and,

(5) ruled that regulations that may result in license revocation or nonrenewal do not violate broadcasters' First Amendment rights.[71]

The following quote from the Supreme Court's majority opinion in NBC is the most frequently cited authority for the expansive view of the FCC's regulatory mission:

> The Act itself establishes that the Commission's powers are not limited to the engineering and technical aspects of regulation of radio communication. Yet we are asked to regard the Commission as a kind of traffic officer, policing the wave lengths to prevent stations from interfering with each other. But the Act does not restrict the Commission merely to supervision of the traffic. It puts upon the Commission the burden of determining the composition of that traffic.[72]

E. Red Lion Broadcasting Co. v. FCC

In 1969, the Supreme Court upheld the FCC's Fairness Doctrine as well as its related personal attack and political editorializing rules in its landmark *Red Lion* decision.[73] In unanimously affirming the FCC, the Court emphasized three key principles:

(1) *On the uniqueness of broadcasting:* "Where there are substantially more individuals who want to broadcast than there are frequencies to allocate, it is idle to posit an unabridgeable First Amendment right to broadcast comparable to the right of every individual to speak, write, or publish."[74]

(2) *On the fiduciary principle:* "There is nothing in the First Amendment which prevents the Government from requiring a licensee to share his frequency with others and to conduct himself as a proxy or fiduciary ... "[75]

(3) *On the public interest:* "It is the right of the viewers and listeners, not the right of the broadcasters, which is paramount."[76]

The Court added one significant caveat: if experience with broadcast technology post-1969 proved that "the net effect of [administration of the Fairness Doctrine was to reduce] rather than [increase] the volume and quality of coverage, there [would] be time enough to reconsider the constitutional implications."[77]

F. CBS Inc. v. Democractic National Committee

The Supreme Court has observed in *CBS v. Democratic National Committee* that the FCC must "walk a 'tightrope' to preserve the First Amendment values written into the Radio Act and its successor, the Communications Act."[78] After referring to its *Red Lion* decision, the Court noted that "[t]he problems of regulation are rendered more difficult because the broadcast industry is dynamic in terms of technological change; solutions adequate a decade ago are not necessarily so now, and those acceptable today may well be outmoded 10 years hence."[79]

G. FCC v. Pacifica Foundation

By a five to four vote, the Supreme Court affirmed the decision of the FCC that George Carlin's "filthy words" monologue was "indecent."[80] Justice John Paul Stevens, in the prevailing opinion, explained that Carlin's words might be appropriate on other media, but not over the radio: "[w]e have long recognized that each medium of expression presents special First Amendment problems. And of all forms of communication, it is broadcasting that has received the most limited First Amendment protection."[81] The opinion pointed out that "the broadcast media have established a uniquely pervasive presence in the lives of all Americans"—since listeners are "constantly tuning in and tuning out," prior warnings would not be effective in protecting the unwilling listeners.[82]

H. FCC v. WNCN Listeners Guild

In *WNCN Listeners Guild*, the Supreme Court upheld the FCC's decision not to get involved in the regulation of radio station formats in a case involving the decision of the proposed buyer of WNCN to change the format from classical music to rock.[83] The Court found that marketplace regulation was a constitutionally protected means of implementing the public interest standard of the Communications Act.[84]

I. FCC v. League of Women Voters

In *FCC v. League of Women Voters*,[85] the Supreme Court for the first time found a broadcast regulation unconstitutional, namely, section 309 of the Public Broadcasting Act which forbade editorializing by any noncommercial station receiving funds from the Corporation for Public Broadcasting.

> The prevailing rationale for broadcast regulation based on spectrum scarcity has come under increasing criticism in recent years. Critics, including the incumbent Chairman of the FCC [Mark Fowler], charge that with the advent of cable and satellite television technology, communities now have access to such a wide variety of stations that the scarcity doctrine is obsolete. We are not prepared, however, to reconsider our longstanding approach without some signal from Congress or the FCC that technological developments have advanced so far that some revision of broadcast regulation may be required.[86]

J. Turner Broadcasting System, Inc. v. FCC

In its initial decision involving the FCC's rules requiring cable systems to carry the signals of local television stations, the Supreme Court, in *Turner Broadcasting System, Inc. v. FCC*,[87] gave only lukewarm support for *Red Lion*[88] and other decisions, noting that "the rationale for applying a less rigorous standard of First Amendment scrutiny to broadcast regulation, *whatever its validity in the cases elaborating it*, does not apply in the context of cable regulation."[89]

VI. THE EPHEMERAL YET MALLEABLE PUBLIC INTEREST STANDARD

A precise meaning for the phrase "public interest" is extremely elusive.[90] Avery Leiserson offers a pragmatic but somewhat limited definition, suggesting that "a satisfactory criterion of the public interest is the preponderant acceptance of administrative action by politically influential groups."[91] Such acceptance is expressed, in Leiserson's opinion, through groups that, when affected by administrative requirements, regulations, and decisions, comply without seeking legislative revision, amendment, or repeal.[92] Thus, in order for a policy to be accepted by politically influential groups, it must be relevant to, and must not conflict unacceptably with, their expectations and desires. Defining the interest of the entire general public proves to be considerably more difficult, especially if the general public interest is viewed as more than just the sum of special interests.[93]

Besides providing flexibility to adapt to changing conditions, the concept of the public interest contributes significantly to the regulation of broadcasting in another sense. Even a generalized public belief in an undefined public interest increases the likelihood that policies will be accepted as authoritative. The acceptance of a concept of the public interest may thus engender important support for the regulation of broadcasting and for the making of authoritative rules and policies toward this end.[94] For this reason the courts traditionally have given the FCC wide latitude in determining what constitutes the public interest. As the Supreme Court noted in 1981:

> Our opinions have repeatedly emphasized that the Commission's judgment regarding how the public interest is best served is entitled to substantial judicial deference. … The Commission's implementation of the public-interest standard, when based on a rational weighing of competing policies, is not to be set aside … for "the weighing of policies under the 'public interest' standard is a task that Congress has delegated to the Commission in the first instance."[95]

Judge E. Barrett Prettyman expanded upon the reasons for such deference:

> [I]t is also true that the Commission's view of what is best in the public interest may change from time to time. Commissions themselves change, underlying philosophies differ, and experience often dictates changes. Two diametrically opposite schools of thought in respect to the public welfare may both be rational; e.g., both free trade and protective tariff are rational positions. All such matters are for the Congress and the executive and their agencies. They are political, in the high sense of that abused term.[96]

Despite the usefulness of the public interest concept in keeping up with changing means of communication and the general tendency of the courts to defer to the FCC's decisions, conflicts over the meaning of the public interest have been recurrent in broadcast history. On occasion, the vague statutory mandate to look out for the public interest has hampered the development of coherent public policy because Congress (or influential members of Congress) can always declare, "that is not what we meant by the public interest."

Few independent regulatory commissions have had to operate under such a broad grant of power with so few substantive guidelines. Rather than encouraging greater freedom of action, vagueness in delegated power may serve to limit an agency's independence and freedom to act as it sees fit. As Pendleton Herring put it, "[a]dministrators cannot be given the responsibilities of statesmen without incurring likewise the tribulations of politicians."[97]

Judge Henry Friendly, in his classic work *The Federal Administrative Agencies*, offered the following comment on how the origin of the "public interest, convenience and necessity" standard serves to confuse, not enlighten:

> The only guideline supplied by Congress in the Communications Act of 1934 was "public convenience, interest, or necessity." The standard of public convenience and necessity, introduced into the federal statute book by [the] Transportation Act, 1920, conveyed a fair degree of meaning when the issue was whether new or duplicating railroad construction should be authorized or an existing line abandoned. It was to convey less when, as under the Motor Carrier Act of 1935, or the Civil Aeronautics Act of 1938, there would be the added issue of selecting the applicant to render a service found to be needed; but under those statutes there would usually be some demonstrable factors, such as, in air route cases, ability to render superior one-plane or one-carrier service because of junction of the new route with existing ones, lower costs due to other operations, or historical connection with the traffic, that ought to have enabled the agency to develop intelligible criteria for selection. The standard was almost drained of meaning under section 307 of the Communications Act, where the issue was almost never the need for broadcasting service but rather who should render it.[98]

Since Congress has found it inadvisable or impossible to define specifically for future situations exactly what constitutes the public interest, the political problem of achieving consensus as to the case-by-case application of this standard has been passed on to the FCC. The flexibility inherent in this elusive public interest concept can be enormously significant to the FCC not only as a means of modifying policies to meet changed conditions and to obtain special support but also as a source of continuing and sometimes hard-to-resolve controversy.

Disputes concerning legal prescriptions imposed by the Communications Act often have centered on recurring value conflicts—assumptions about what ought or ought not to be done. One such question is the extent to which broadcasting should pursue social as well as economic and technical goals. The emphasis on the social responsibilities of licensees rests on the view that "the air belongs to the public, not to the industry" since Congress provided in section 301 of the Communications Act that "no ... license shall be construed to create any right, beyond the terms, conditions, and periods of the license."[99] For example, the FCC has adopted rules and policies designed to make broadcasters meet social responsibilities by requiring them to implement equal employment opportunity programs for women and minorities and to provide programming responsive to community needs and interests.

Some of these rules and policies require broadcasters to present, or refrain from presenting, content contrary to what they would choose to do on their own. How far the FCC may go in the direct, or indirect, regulation of content without violating either the Communications Act's own prohibition in section 326 against censorship, or the First Amendment to the U.S. Constitution, remains unsettled.[100]

However, in the Communications Act Congress also directs the Commission to regulate "in the public interest, convenience and necessity."[101] Using that standard, the Commission has promulgated many rules and policies governing broadcast programming that could be regarded by the courts as unlawful censorship of the print media. As noted earlier, court cases involving Dr. Brinkley and Reverend Shuler held that the FRC did not have to ignore content, that it could consider it without necessarily engaging in censorship; later court cases have perpetuated the view that government supervision of broadcast content is somehow more acceptable than review of print. Clearly broadcasting continues to be plagued by divergent views of how to balance freedom with achieving socially desired and responsible service, while still not engaging in censorship.

Complicating this controversy is the conflict between First Amendment provisions guaranteeing the right of broadcasters, like other media owners and operators, to be free of government control over the content of programming, and First Amendment theories developed exclusively for broadcasting holding that the rights of listeners and viewers to receive information to be "paramount" over the rights of broadcasters. The theory is that in the "scarce" medium of broadcasting, some affirmative government intervention concerning content may be needed to ensure that the public hears diverse ideas and viewpoints.[102] J. Skelly Wright, a judge of the United States Court of Appeals for the District of Columbia, has commented:

> [I]n some areas of the law it is easy to tell the good guys from the bad guys. ... In the current debate over the broadcast media and the First Amendment ... each debator claims to be the real protector of the First Amendment, and the analytical problems are much more difficult than in ordinary constitutional adjudication ... the answers are not easy.[103]

These colliding statutory ground rules governing the freedom and obligations of broadcasters have been melded into one of the law's most elastic conceptions—the notion of a "public trustee."[104] The FCC views a broadcast license as a "trust," with the public as "beneficiary" and the broadcaster as "public trustee."[105] The public trustee concept naturally flows from the conflicting statutory goals of private use and regulated allocation of spectrum space. Congress gave the FCC the right to choose among various candidates for commercial broadcast licenses and left it up to the Commission to find a justification for providing a fortunate few with the use of a valuable scarce resource at no cost. Legal scholar Benno Schmidt, Jr., thinks the public trustee concept was designed to dull the horns of the FCC's dilemma: to give away valuable spectrum space, with no strings attached, would pose stubborn problems of justification.[106]

However, as noted above, some of the strings attached—especially those, like the FCC's Fairness Doctrine, that are content-related—have been determined to violate the First Amendment. One option exercised by the FCC to reduce controversy over its activities has been to substitute its "content-neutral" or "structural" policies for policies that involve direct review of content. Many FCC rules and policies—for example, the regulation of station ownership patterns—have been of this type. They do not, on their surface, look normative but are in fact examples of content-neutral means of achieving social objectives.

For some years, however, there was hesitation over the substitution of content-neutral, "structural" regulations for content regulation. Broadcasting was thought to be a scarce medium in which structural regulation could not accomplish enough. Beginning in the mid-1970s, however, arguments began to be made more forcefully that FCC review of content should be reduced and structural regulation preferred. Broadcasters tended to argue that, at least in some instances, even structural regulation was unjustified due to what they believed was reliance on an invalid premise: scarcity. Behind many of these criticisms and controversies were changes in electronic communications technology.

Although many correctly argue that the 1970s, the 1980s and the 1990s have been (and will be) particularly active decades in the development and expansion of communications technology, the fact is that there have long been two complementary and determinative features of American broadcasting: spectrum space scarcity and technological innovation. Scarcity, of course, has always been the underlying *raison d'etre* for broadcast regulation. Because one person's transmission is another's interference, Congress concluded that the federal government has the duty both to select who may and who may not broadcast and to regulate the use of the electromagnetic spectrum to serve the public.

Broadcasters argue that there is little justification for rigid government regulation of ten or twenty or more competing radio stations in a market while monopoly newspapers operate freely. As scarcity

decreases, they have argued, so should regulation. Former FCC Chairman Mark Fowler has noted that "[s]carcity, to my mind, is a condition affecting all industries. Land, capital, labor, and oil, are all scarce. In our society, we allow the marketplace to allocate such goods. In this process, consumers' interests and society's interests are well served."[107] From this analysis of the "myth" of scarcity, plus a review of traditional First Amendment theory, Chairman Fowler concluded that in broadcasting, "[e]conomic freedom and freedom of speech go hand in hand," and advocated reliance on minimally regulated marketplace forces rather than content regulation.[108]

The foregoing discussion highlights some of the issues which have attended attempts to apply the public interest standard in particular regulatory circumstances. As is evident from the recitation of the origins and development of the phrase "public interest, convenience, and necessity," the task of formulating a standard for the digital television is a formidable one. Despite the many criticisms of the standard, there is much support for its retention in any legislation governing the regulation of broadcasters. Former FCC Chairman Newton Minow has written that the words "public interest" are "at the heart of what Congress did in 1934, and they remain at the heart of our tomorrows."[109]

> The heart of the Communications Act is its clear emphasis on the public interest. Whatever the temptations to abandon this notion—and they are many—the stakes are too high. Without commitment to the public interest, all government action vis-à-vis communications would be without meaning.[110]

VII. THE PUBLIC INTEREST STANDARD IN THE DIGITAL AGE

As television broadcasters begin the transition from analog to much more flexible digital technology, there have been calls for reexamination of the public interest standard. The FCC told digital broadcasters that it would consider changes to its public interest requirements,[111] and President Clinton appointed a Presidential Advisory Committee to determine whether digital broadcasters should be given new public interest responsibilities.[112]

An examination of the history of the public interest standard and its application by the FCC and the courts, however, reveals no need for an abrupt change in the evolving meaning of the public interest standard. The genius of the public interest standard is its breadth and flexibility. The public interest standard has steadily changed as the electronic media have grown from a few AM radio stations to the vast panoply of broadcasting stations, multichannel video programming providers, satellite services, and Internet services that Americans enjoy today. Digital television readily fits into this framework.

Justice Stewart once remarked that "[t]here is never a paucity of arguments in favor of limiting the freedom of the press."[113] In deciding how to regulate broadcasting, however, Congress rejected a vision of government control. "Long before the impact and potential of the [broadcast] medium was realized, Congress opted for a system of private broadcasters licensed and regulated by Government."[114] Congress made clear in section 326 of the Communications Act that the FCC possesses no power to control the content of broadcast speech. While the Act explicitly reserves "ownership" of the broadcast spectrum to the Government, this property interest has not been viewed as a significant alteration in the Act's basic premise of licensing privately owned and controlled broadcasters.[115]

The tension between the Government's role in licensing broadcasters and the First Amendment principles that Congress clearly sought to protect in the Communications Act resulted in the "tightrope" that the Court described in *CBS v. Democratic National Committee*. While the path has neither always been clear, nor followed one direction, the history of the FCC's interpretation of the public interest standard exhibits a definite pattern of decreasing regulation in the face of an increasing number of information sources.

In the early years of broadcast regulation, relatively few stations existed. Most markets had only one or two stations, and there had not yet been time for a culture to develop within the broadcasting industry. The regulators opted for specific and intrusive regulation of this new service. The Radio Commission rejected Dr. Brinkley's application because he used a station to advance only his own private interests without regard to the needs of the public. The FCC later expanded this information, taking the view that each station must serve a whole spectrum of interests. Even as late as 1960, the Commission's *Program Policy Statement*[116] strongly encouraged stations in large urban areas to include agricultural programs among the subjects in their program mix.

During these years, the broadcasting industry matured and the number of broadcast outlets steadily multiplied. FM service began slowly, but ultimately eclipsed AM as the dominant radio service. The number of radio stations grew from the few hundred when the FCC began regulation to more than 12,000 today.[117] Television service began and spread across the country.

During the 1960s, the FCC undertook a campaign to encourage the development of competitors to established broadcasters from both within the broadcast industry and from without. In the industry, the Commission worked to increase the number of radio and television stations by, among other things, removing barriers to UHF television service and dramatically increasing the number of FM radio stations. It also adopted rules to prevent the national networks from dominating the television programming market, and rules that helped to develop independent television stations. Outside of broadcast service, the Commission worked to develop competitors to broadcasting such as cable television and satellite broadcasting. These efforts have borne more fruit than their proponents could have even imagined.

The deregulation that began in the 1970s and resulted in the removal of much of the FCC's detailed broadcasting rules in the 1980s appropriately reflected these developments. With a multiplicity of broadcast stations and other communications providers available to the public, the need for each station to serve the interests of all listeners and viewers seemed less crucial. Instead, the FCC reasoned that as stations competed with each other, particular stations would look to meet the needs of segments of the audience that other stations overlooked, thereby increasing the value of broadcasting to the entire community.

Further, the public service role of broadcasting had become part of the industry's culture, as well as expected by the audience. Broadcast stations were and remain the dominant source of news, and broadcasters have been the "glue" holding communities together in times of crisis or natural disaster. The FCC found that the tradition of broadcasting and the demands of the audience would ensure that broadcasters continued to serve the public without the spur of detailed content regulations. Despite the absence of FCC mandates, the time and resources devoted by local stations to news programming has steadily increased.[118]

The FCC also recognized that the marketplace could more efficiently determine the audience's needs and interests than could the government. On that basis, the FCC rejected calls that it regulate radio stations' program formats—a decision that was upheld by the Supreme Court in *WNCN Listeners Guild*.[119] While critics at the time believed such regulation necessary to preserve and protect format diversity, their fears have proven unjustified and the range of radio formats has never been greater.

As the number of broadcast stations increased, and competing electronic media emerged, the FCC shifted the focus of its public interest analysis from detailed prescription of broadcasting content to a reliance on marketplace forces to ensure high quality broadcasting. Only in the case of a perceived market failure—such as children's television—have Congress and the FCC felt the need to return to particularized content regulation.[120]

Moreover, the constitutional foundation for renewed extensive content regulation of broadcasting has become increasingly uncertain. At a time when broadcast outlets were few, one station's refusal to include a particular point of view in its coverage might have prevented advocates of that view from communicating to the public.[121] However, even as the Supreme Court was articulating this "scarcity doctrine" in *Red Lion*, the emergence of more stations and competing media began to sow the seeds of the doctrine's demise. The FCC itself recognized by 1987 when it repealed the Fairness Doctrine that scarcity could no longer justify content regulation.[122] While the Supreme Court has yet to overrule *Red Lion*, it has repeatedly noted the widespread criticism of that decision and announced itself ready to reconsider it in an appropriate case.[123]

Even where content regulation has been permitted, the Court has retreated from treating broadcasting differently than competing media. The "intrusiveness" rationale announced in *Pacifica*[124] was long thought to be limited to broadcasting. Two years ago, however, the Supreme Court extended it to cable in *Denver Area Educational Telecommunications Consortium v. FCC* with virtually no discussion.[125]

In the absence of scarcity, justifying renewed regulation of broadcast content becomes problematical. Professor Sunstein argues in favor of a "Madisonian" approach to the First Amendment, suggesting that the government may intervene in broadcasting to promote certain democratic values.[126] Others, however, contend that such an approach gives the government far too much power, and far too little guidance, to determine which speech is acceptable and which not.[127]

The Supreme Court's recent First Amendment cases provide little support for an interventionist view of the First Amendment. Even without formally rejecting *Red Lion*, strong majorities of the Court have embraced a Holmesian view where ideas compete in the marketplace free of government. In the first *Turner* case, the Court noted that its "cases have recognized that Government regulation over the content of broadcast programming must be narrow. ..."[128] It emphasized that "the FCC's oversight responsibilities do not grant it the power to ordain any particular type of programming that must be offered by broadcast stations."[129] In *Hurley*, relying on its opinion in Turner, the Court went further: "While the law is free to promote all sorts of conduct in place of harmful behavior, it is not free to interfere with speech for no better reason than promoting an approved message or discouraging a disfavored one, however enlightened either purpose may strike the government."[130] Thus, the courts are moving away from any approval of government control over the content of broadcast speech.

In light of these judicial trends, the advent of digital television should not be an occasion for increasing the FCC's public interest mandates on broadcasters. It may be that digital television will not in the end be substantially different from television today and that most broadcasters will provide viewers with programming on one high quality digital signal. In that event, there would be no cause for a change in the FCC's interpretation of the public interest standard. The broadcast audience, however, may instead demand that digital television be used, at least in part, for multiple programs or for data transmission. Rather than justifying new and intrusive public interest requirements, an increase in broadcasters' capabilities would support a decrease in FCC regulations.

If digital broadcasters offer multiple channels or data services in addition to traditional broadcasts, the number of program services available in a community will increase, carrying the potential to serve an even greater range of diverse and unique interests. More channels and available services should give the FCC confidence that a wide variety of needs and points of view would be served. The agency would then have less reason to require each station to provide particular types of service because competition among stations would likely ensure that a need not met by one station or service would be addressed by another seeking to gain a position in the market.

Even if broadcasters benefit from the possibilities offered by digital television, the Communications Act's public interest requirement has not been viewed so much as a *quid pro quo* for broadcasters obtaining spectrum than as a means of ensuring that the system of private broadcasting will respond to public needs. The FCC has also historically viewed licensees' efforts to develop more efficient technologies as a public interest benefit, rather than as a justification for imposing increased responsibilities. The advent of digital technology in other services, such as cellular telephones, has not resulted in any change in those licensees' relationship with the FCC.

This is not to say that the public interest mandate of the FCC should disappear. Broadcast licensees should be responsible for establishing that they have served the public, and have done so with all services they provide. The spectrum flexibility provisions of the 1996 Telecommunications Act so provide.[131] Under the public interest standard of the Act, the FCC and broadcasters have worked together to provide the most diverse system of broadcasting in the world. But the FCC has recognized that as the number of competing electronic "voices" has gone up, there is less need for the government to ensure that individual broadcast stations serve particular functions. The possibilities created by digital television technology comfortably fit within this history and justify, if anything, even greater reliance on broadcasters and

the market to ensure service to the public. As in the past, broadcasters should be afforded the latitude to develop and offer programming best calculated to meet the needs of the communities they serve.

Notes

1. Taylor Branch, *The Culture of Bureaucracy: We're All Working for the Penn Central*, Wash. Monthly, Nov. 1970, at 8, 20.

2. *Id.*

3. Glen O. Robinson, *Title I, The Federal Communications Act: An Essay on Origins and Regulatory Purpose*, in A Legislative History Of The Communications Act Of 1934 3, 14 (Max D. Paglin ed., 1989) [hereinafter Legislative History].

4. *Id.*

5. Ervin S. Duggan, *Congressman Tauzin's Interesting Idea*, Brdcst. & Cable, Oct. 20, 1997, at S18.

6. This Article draws heavily on Erwin G. Krasnow et al., The Politics of Broadcast Regulation (1982); F. Leslie Smith et al., Electronic Media and Government, The Regulation of Wireless and Wired Mass Communication in the United States (1995); and Jonathan W. Emord, Freedom, Technology, and the First Amendment (1991).

7. Communications Act of 1934, ch. 652, §§ 307, 309, 48 Stat. 1064 (codified as amended at 47 U.S.C.A. §§ 307,309 (West 1991 & Supp. 1997)).

8. Congress did not uniformly use the phrase "public interest" in the Communications Act. For example, the standard of "public interest" is specified in sections 201(b), 215(a), 319(c), and 315(a); "public convenience and necessity" in section 214(a) and (c); "interest of public convenience and necessity" in section 214(d); "public interest, convenience and necessity" in sections 307(c), 309(a), and 319(d); "public convenience, interest or necessity" in section 307(a); and "public interest, convenience *or* necessity" in sections 311(b) and 311(c)(3) (emphases added). On September 17, 1986, the FCC recommended that Congress drop all broadcast-related mentions of "convenience" or

"necessity." It called the words "superfluous … To the extent the issues embodied in these terms are relevant to radio regulation, they are subsumed under Commission review of the 'public interest.'" FCC Legislative Proposal, Track 1, 25 (Sept. 17, 1981). Congress did not amend the Act as the FCC had proposed.

9. Wireless Ship Act of 1910, Pub. L. No. 61-262, 36 Stat. 629 (1910).

10. Radio Act of 1912, Pub. L. No. 62-264, 37 Stat. 302 (1912).

11. Proceedings of the Fourth National Radio Conference and Recommendations for Regulation of Radio 7 (Nov. 9–11, 1925) (Government Printing Office 1926).

12. *Broadcasters' Public Interest Obligations and the Fairness in Broadcasting Act of 1991: Hearing on S. 217 Before the Subcomm. on Communications of the Senate Comm. on Commerce, Science, and Transportation,* 102d Cong. 2-3 (1991) (statement of Alfred C. Sikes, Chairman, FCC).

13. 67 CONG. REC. 5479 (1926).

14. NEWTON N. MINOW, EQUAL TIME, THE PRIVATE BROADCASTER AND THE PUBLIC INTEREST 8 (1964).

15. See Hoover v. Intercity Radio Co., 283 F. 1003 (D.C. Cir. 1923), *writ of error dismissed as moot,* 266 U.S.C. 636 (1924), where the Court of Appeals for the District of Columbia Circuit held that Secretary Hoover had the discretion under the Radio Act to select a frequency and set the hours of use, but lacked discretion to deny any application for a license not otherwise specifically barred by the Radio Act of 1912. Two years later, in *United States v. Zenith Radio Corp.,* 12 F.2d 614 (N.D. 111. 1926), the U.S. District Court for the Northern District of Illinois determined that the Radio Act of 1912 did not authorize the Secretary of Commerce to deny the issuance of licenses or to require operation on a precise wavelength or under certain time constraints not specifically provided for in the Act.

16. 16. 68 CONG. REC. 3031 (1927).

17. J. Roger Wollenberg, *Title III, The FCC as Arbiter of "The Public Interest, Convenience, and Necessity',* in LEGISLATIVE HISTORY, supra note 3, at 61, 65.

18. *The Federal Radio Commission and the Public Service Responsibility of Broadcast Licensees,* 11 FED. COMM. BJ. 5, 14 (1950) (quoting *Schaeffer Radio Co.,* an unpublished 1930 FRC decision).

19. NEWTON N. MINOW & CRAIG L. LAMAY, ABANDONED IN THE WASTELAND: CHILDREN, TELEVISION, AND THE FIRST AMENDMENT 4 (1995). The phrase came from an 1887 Illinois railroad statute which was adapted into the Federal Transportation Act of 1920. In *Munn v. Illinois,* 94 U.S. 113, 126 (1876), the Supreme Court held that states may regulate the use of private property when the use was "affected with a public interest." In the Transportation Act of 1920, which amended the Interstate Commerce Act, the device of a certificate of convenience and necessity was first applied to the regulation of interstate commerce.

20. 2 FRC Ann. Rep. 166 (1928).

21. *Id.* at 169-70.

22. Great Lakes Brdcst. Co., 3 FRC ANN. REP. 32 (1929), *aff'd in part and rev'd in part,* 37 F.2d 993 (D.C. Cir.), *cert, dismissed,* 281 U.S. 706 (1930).

23. *Id.*

24. *Id.* at 34.

25. *Id.* at 32–35.

26. *Id.* at 32.

27. *Id.* at 35. In *Great Lakes Broadcasting,* 37 F.2d 993 (D.C. Cir. 1930), the Court of Appeals upheld the FRC's decision to consider programming as a primary criterion of the public interest standard.

28. F. LESLIE SMITH ET AL., *supra* note 6, at 240.

29. *Id.*

30. 47 U.S.C. § 29 (1927). The no-censorship provision was reenacted as section 326 of the Communications Act of 1934. *See* 47 U.S.C. 326 (1994).

31. KFKB Brdcst. Ass'n v. FRC, 47 F.2d 670,672 (D.C. Cir. 1931).

32. *Id.*

33. *Id.*

34. *Id.*

35. *Id.* at 672.

36. *Near*, 283 U.S. 697 (1931).

37. Trinity Methodist Church S. v. FRC, 62 F.2d 850, 851 (D.C. Cir.), *cert, denied*, 284 U.S. 685 (1932).

38. *Id.* The Court also held that the refusal to renew a license is not a taking within the Fifth Amendment, stating that "[t]here is a marked difference between the destruction of physical property and the denial of a permit to use the limited channels of the air." *Id.* at 853 (citation omitted),

39. *Id.* at 852.

40. Donald M. Gillmer et al., Mass Communications Law, Cases and Comment 739 (1990).

41. *Id.*

42. FCC, Public Service Responsibility of Broadcast Licensees (1946), *reprinted in* Documents of American Broadcasting 133–231 (Frank J. Kahn ed., 3d ed. 1978).

43. *Id.*

44. Documents of American Broadcasting, *supra note* 42, at 133.

45. Network Programming Inquiry, *Report and Statement of Policy*, 25 Fed. Reg. 7291, 7295 (1960).

46. *Id.*

47. Primer on Ascertainment of Community Problems by Brdcst. Applicants, *Report and Order*, 27 F.C.C.2d 650, 21 Rad. Reg. 2d (P & F) 1507 (1971).

48. The rationale for marketplace regulation was presented in a law review article by Chairman Fowler and Daniel Brenner, his legal assistant. See Mark S. Fowler & Daniel L. Brenner, *A Marketplace Approach to Broadcast Regulation*, 60 Tex. L. Rev. 207 (1982). Critical of the "trusteeship model" and the use of the "vague" public interest standard to impose programming restrictions, they concluded that in light of advances in electronic radio technology, the scarcity rationale was no longer viable and that the marketplace, the listeners and viewers should define the public interest. In their view, the public interest standard abridged broadcasters' First Amendment rights.

49. Mark S. Fowler, The Public's Interest, Address at a Meeting of the International Radio and Television Society (Sept. 23, 1981), *in* Comm. & L., Winter 1982, at 51, 52.

50. Deregulation of Radio, *Report and Order*, 84 F.C.C.2d 968, 49 Rad. Reg. 2d (P & F) 1 (1981), *aff'd in part and remanded in part sub. nom.* Office of Comm. of the United Church of Christ v. FCC, 707 F.2d 1413 (1983).

51. *Id.* para. 10.

52. *Id.*

53. Revision of Programming and Commercialization Policies Ascertainment Requirements, and Program by Requirements for Commercial TV Stations, *Report and Order*, 98 F.C.C.2d 1075, 56 Rad. Reg. 2d (P & F) 1005 (1984); Revision of Program Policies and Reporting Requirements Related to Public Brdcst. Licensees, *Report and Order*, 98 F.C.C.2d 746, 56 Rad. Reg. 2d (P & F) 1157 (1984). In *Action for Children's Television v. FCC*, 821 F.2d 741 (D.C. Cir. 1987), the Court of Appeals upheld the elimination of program lists mandated by the FCC's TV Deregulation decision, but ruled that the Commission had failed to explain adequately the elimination of commercial guidelines for children's programming.

54. Elimination of Unnecessary Brdcst. Reg. and Inquiry into Subscription Agreements, 54 Rad. Reg. 2d (P & F) 1043 (1983). The FCC eliminated prohibitions against ratings distortion conflicts, of interest of station personnel, promotions of non-broadcasts interests, misleading concert promotions, failure to adhere to sales contracts, and the broadcast of false, misleading, and deceptive commercials.

55. *TRAC*, 800 F.2d 1181 (D.C. Cir. 1986), *cert, denied*, 482 U.S. 919 (1987).

56. Id. at 1185.

57. Black Citizens for a Fair Media v. FCC, 719 F.2d 407, 409 (1983), *cert, denied*, 467 U.S. 1255 (1984).

58. *Id.*

59. Complaint of Syracuse Peace Council against TV Station WTVH, *Memorandum Opinion and Order*, 2 FCC Rcd. 5043, 63 Rad. Reg. 2d (P & F) 541 (1987) [hereinafter *Syracuse Peace Council Opinion and Order*], *reconsideration denied by*

Memorandum Opinion and Order, 3 FCC Rcd. 2035, 64 Rad. Reg. 2d (P & F) 1073 (1988). Finding that the Fairness Doctrine inhibited broadcasters from covering controversial issues, the Commission held "that under the constitutional standard established by Red Lion and its progeny, the fairness doctrine contravenes the First Amendment and its enforcement is no longer in the public interest." *Id.* para. 61. In *Syracuse Peace Council v. FCC*, 867 F.2d 654 (D.C. 1989), *cert denied*, 493 U.S. 1019 (1990), the Court of Appeals for the D.C. Circuit upheld the Commission's public interest finding but declined to address the constitutional issues. Judge Starr, in a concurring opinion, stated that he would uphold the FCC's finding that the Fairness Doctrine was unconstitutional.

60. *See, e.g.*, Committee for the Fair Brdcst. of Controversial Issues, *Report and Order*, 25 F.C.C.2d 283, para. 25, 19 Rad. Reg. (P & F) 541 (1973) (stating "strict adherence to the fairness doctrine" was the "single most important requirement of operation in the public interest—the '*sine qua non*' for grant of a renewal of license.").

61. *Syracuse Peace Council Opinion and Order*, 2 FCC Rcd. 5043, para. 81, 63 Rad. Reg.2d(P&F)541.

62. Emord, *supra* note 6, at 236. Former FCC General Counsel Henry Geller agreed: "[t]he fairness doctrine flows directly from the public trustee notion, and to eliminate the fairness doctrine one must also eliminate the notion that broadcasters should act as public trustees." Henry Geller, *Broadcasting and the Public Trustee Notion: A Failed Promise*, 10 Harv. J.L. & Pub. Pol'y 8, 87 (1987).

63. Nelson Bros. Bond & Mortgage Co. v. FRC, 289 U.S. 266 (1933).

64. *Id.* at 285.

65. FCC v. Pottsville Brdcst. Co., 309 U.S. 134, 138 (1940).

66. *Id.* at 145.

67. *Id.* at 138.

68. FCC v. Sanders Bros. Radio Station, 309 U.S. 470 (1940).

69. *Id.* at 475.

70. NBC v. United States, 319 U.S. 190 (1943).

71. F. Leslie Smith et al., *supra* note 6, at 250.

72. *NBC*, 319 U.S. at 215-16. One commentator characterized the quote as:
[P]erhaps the most misinterpreted words in the judicial history of broadcasting regulation. ... Many readers of this part of the decision have taken this to mean that the Court was approving FCC dictation of program content. In context, however, these two sentences simply say that the Commission has the authority to select licensees as well as to "supervise" them. "Traffic" in the Court's analogy refers to licensees, not to programs.
Documents of American Broadcasting, *supra* note 42, at 100.

73. *Red Lion*, 395 U.S. 367 (1969).

74. *Id.* at 388.

75. *Id.* at 389.

76. *Id.* at 390.

77. *Id.* at 393.

78. CBS v. Democratic Nat'l Comm., 412 U.S. 94, 117 (1973).

79. *Id.* at 102.

80. FCC v. Pacifica Found., 438 U.S. 726 (1978).

81. *Id.* at 748 (citation omitted).

82. *Id.*

83. FCC v. WNCN Listeners Guild, 450 U.S. 582 (1981).

84. *Id.* at 604.

85. *League of Women Voters*, 468 U.S. 364 (1984).

86. *Id.* at 376 n. 11 (citation omitted).

87. *Turner*, 512 U.S. 622 (1994).

88. Red Lion Brdcst. Co. v. FCC, 366 U.S. 367 (1969).

89. *Turner*, 512 U.S. at 637 (emphasis added).

90. "'Public interest, convenience or necessity' means about as little as any phrase that the drafters of the [Radio] Act could have used and still comply with the constitutional requirement that there be some standard to guide the administrative wisdom of the licensing authority." Louis G. Caldwell, *The Standard of Public Interest, Convenience or Necessity as Used in the Radio Act of 1927*, 1 Air L. Rev. 295, 296 (1930).

91. Avery Leiserson, Administrative Regulation: A Study in Representation of Interests 16 (1942).

92. *Id.*

93. Ayn Rand has characterized the "public interest" as the "intellectual knife of collectivism's sacrificial guillotine." "Since there is no such thing as the 'public interest' (other than the sum of the individual interests of individual citizens), since that collectivist catchphrase has never been and can never be defined, it amounted to a blank check on totalitarian power over the broadcasting industry, granted to whatever bureaucrats happened to be appointed to the Commission." AYN RAND, CAPITALISM: THE UNKNOWN IDEAL 126 (1967).

94. *See* VIRGINIA HELD, THE PUBLIC INTEREST AND INDIVIDUAL INTERESTS 163-202 (1970).

95. FCC v. WNCN Listeners Guild, 450 U.S. 582, 596 (1981) (quoting FCC v. Nat'l Citizens Comm. for Brdcst, 436 U.S. 775, 810 (1978)).

96. Pinellas Brdcst. Co. v. FCC, 230 F.2d 204, 206 (D.C. Cir.), *cert, denied*, 350 U.S. 1007 (1956).

97. PENDLETON HERRING, PUBLIC ADMINISTRATION AND THE PUBLIC INTEREST 138 (Russell & Russell 1967) (1936). Vagueness, however, may also serve to protect the agency when its decisions are challenged in the courts, since the judiciary may be loath to overturn actions protected by a broad statutory mandate.

98. HENRY FRIENDLY, THE FEDERAL ADMINISTRATIVE AGENCIES 54–55 (1962) (footnotes omitted).

99. Communications Act of 1934, ch. 652, § 301, 48 Stat. 1064 (codified at 47 U.S.C. § 301 (1994)).

100. Equally troubling is the risk of self-censorship by broadcasters as a consequence of indirect content regulations. Judge David Bazelon noted that while the main threat to broadcasters remains that the government can put a licensee out of business, "the more pervasive threat lies in the *sub rosa* bureaucratic hassling which the Commission can impose on the licensee, i.e., responding to FCC inquiries, forcing expensive consultation with counsel, immense record-keeping and the various attendant inconveniences." Illinois Citizens Comm. for Brdcst. v. FCC, 515 F.2d 397, 407 (D.C. Cir. 1975). He further observed that "licensee political or artistic expression is particularly vulnerable to the 'raised eyebrow' of the FCC; faced with the threat of economic injury, the licensee will choose in many cases to avoid controversial speech in order to forestall that injury." *Id.* For examples of raised-eyebrow regulation, *see* ERWIN G. KRASNOW ET AL., FCC REGULATION AND OTHER OXYMORONS: SEVEN AXIOMS TO GRIND, 5 COMM/ENT L.J. 759, 770–72 (1983).

101. *See generally supra* note 8.

102. *See* Red Lion Brdcst. Co. v. FCC, 395 U.S. 367,390 (1969). For further discussion, see *supra* Part V.E.

103. Judge J. Skelly Wright, Speech Before the National Law Center, George Washington University (June 3, 1973), *reprinted in* FRED W. FRIENDLY, THE GOOD GUYS, THE BAD GUYS AND THE FIRST AMENDMENT: FREE SPEECH VS. FAIRNESS IN BROADCASTING ix(1975).

104. This discussion is based on a theme developed by Benno C. Schmidt, Jr. BENNO C. SCHMIDT, JR., FREEDOM OF THE PRESS VS. PUBLIC ACCESS 157–58 (1976). The phrase "public trustee," however, does not appear in the Communications Act.

105. *Id.*

106. *Id.*

107. Fowler, *supra* note 49, at 53.

108. *Id.* at 6.

109. NEWTON N. MINOW, *Commemorative Message*, in LEGISLATIVE HISTORY, *supra note* 3, at xvi.

110. *Id.*

111. Advanced TV Sys., and Their Impact Upon the Existing TV Brdcst. Serv., *Fifth Report and Order*, 12 FCC Red. 12, 809, para. 50, 7 Comm. Reg. (P & F) 863 (1997).

112. Exec. Order No. 13,038, 62 Fed. Reg. 12,065 (March 11, 1997).

113. CBS v. Democratic Nat'l Comm., 412 U.S. 94, 144 (1973) (Stewart, L, concurring).

114. *Id.* at 116.

115. *See* Time Warner Entertainment Co. v. FCC, 105 F.3d 723, 727 (D.C. Cir. 1997) (Williams, J., dissenting from denial of rehearing en banc) ('There is, perhaps, good reason for the [Supreme] Court to have hesitated to give great

weight to the government's property interest in the spectrum.").

116. *See supra* Part IV.B.

117. FCC News Release, *Broadcast Station Totals as of Dec. 31, 1997* (Jan. 23, 1998) <http://www.fcc.gov/bureaus/Mass_Media/News_Releases/1998/nrmm8002.txt>.

118. See generally Thomas W. Hazlett & David W. Sosa, *Was the Fairness Doctrine a "Chilling Effect"? Evidence from the Postderegulation Radio Market*, 26 J. LEGAL STUD. 279 (1997) (observing an increase in informational radio programming after the repeal of the Fairness Doctrine).

119. *WNCN Listeners Guild*, 450 U.S. 582 (1981).

120. *See* Children's Television Act of 1990, Pub. L. No. 101-437, 104 Stat. 996 (1990) (codified in scattered sections of 47 U.S.C. (1994)).

121. Red Lion Brdcst. Co. v. FCC, 395 U.S. 367 (1969).

122. *Syracuse Peace Council Opinion and Order*, 2 FCC Rcd. 5043, 63 Rad. Reg. 2d (P & F) 541 (1987), *reconsideration denied by Memorandum Opinion and Order*, 3 FCC Rcd. 2035, 64 Rad. Reg. 2d (P & F) 1073 (1988), *aff'd sub nom.* Syracuse Peace Council v. FCC, 867 F.2d 654 (D.C. Cir. 1989), *cer., denied*, 493 U.S. 1019 (1990).

123. FCC v. League of Women Voters, 468 U.S. 364, 376 n.11 (1984); *see also* Turner Brdcst. Sys. v. FCC, 512 U.S. 622, 638 (1994) (recognizing that "courts and commentators have criticized the scarcity rationale since its inception"). Last year, five judges of the D.C. Circuit opined that the time had long come for a reexamination of Red Lion. Time Warner Entertainment Co. v. FCC, 105 F.3d 723 (D.C. Cir. 1997) (Williams, J., dissenting from denial of rehearing en banc); *see also* Arkansas AFL-CIO v. FCC, 11 F.3d 1430, 1443 (8th Cir. 1993) (en banc) ("[D]evelopments subsequent to Red Lion appear at least to raise a significant possibility that the First Amendment balance struck in *Red Lion* would look different today.").

124. *Pacifica*, 438 U.S. 726 (1978).

125. *Denver Area*, 116 S. Ct. 2374, 2386 (1996).

126. *See* CASS R. SUNSTEIN, DEMOCRACY AND THE PROBLEM OF FREE SPEECH 95 (1993).

127. *See* Burt Neuborne, *Blues for the Left Hand: A Critique of Cass Sunstein's Democracy and the Problem of Free Speech*, 62 U. CHI. L. REV. 423 (1995).

128. Turner Brdcst. Sys. v. FCC, 512 U.S. 622, 651 (1994).

129. *Id.*

130. Hurley v. Irish Am. Gay, Lesbian, and Bisexual Group, 515 U.S. 557, 579 (1995).

131. Telecommunications Act of 1996, Pub. L. No. 104–104, 110 Stat. 56 (1996) (codified in scattered sections of 47 U.S.C.A. (West 1991 & Supp. 1997)).

UNIT 8

Sell, Lend, or Lease?
Spectrum Management Issues

Regulating telecommunications is unique not only for the communications and network aspects of the industry, but also for the technologies over which services are delivered. Most distinctive among those is the electromagnetic spectrum. A scarce resource within the public domain, managing the spectrum requires planning and coordination. The public interest standard discussed in the previous unit was chosen as the standard for comparing competing applications for spectrum usage when the Radio Act of 1927 was first passed, but the introduction and popularization of mobile technologies requires new ideas. Legal scholars Stuart Benjamin, Douglas Lichtman and Howard Shelanski describe the principles guiding spectrum allocation and how they have developed over the years.

An Introduction to the Electromagnetic Spectrum[1]

Stuart Minor Benjamin, Douglas Gary Lichtman,
and Howard A. Shelanski

A. THE BASICS: ENCODING, TRANSMITTING, RECEIVING

In nearly every setting, people value the ability to communicate rapidly over long distances. Imagine two mountains separated by a valley ten miles wide. People situated on these mountains would surely like to be able to communicate, for example warning one another about any approaching storm clouds. The same is true for, say, airline passengers and their business colleagues back on the ground, and so on.

Centuries ago, such communication might have occurred by smoke signals.[2] Today, it might take place as a cellular telephone communication. And, although the cellular system seems infinitely more advanced than the smoke signal, these two communications systems have much in common: each transmits encoded information, at the speed of light, to a receiver that decodes the information. In this way, each very quickly sends a large amount of information a long way.

In short, telecommunications technology differs in detail, but not in essential concept or function, from smoke signal technology. Employing telecommunications technologies rather than smoke signals means only that people can pack more information into a second's worth of transmission and can transmit that information over a longer distance. One might understand telecommunications, then, as the latest in an evolving technology for extending the speed and reach of data (or information) transmission.

To progress from smoke signals to wireless radio transmissions required that people learn to convert information to electromagnetic radiation. This is what Marconi taught us. The radio waves he pioneered—waves that today carry sound, pictures, numbers, and other data through the air—are basically sine waves, *encoded* with information, that are generated by a power source and then *transmitted* by that power source to a device (the receiver, radio, or TV set) that searches out the sine wave and strips off the encoded information.[3] Today, a perception exists that there are almost countless telecommunications products, markets, and technologies available. Yet virtually all of them are defined simply by the encoding and transmitting process they employ. That is, telecommunications technologies, and thus telecommunications markets, are usually defined by the manner in which information is encoded and the means by which that information is later decoded.

Encoding

Information—such as pictures on a television screen or voices in a telephone conversation—can be encoded onto sine waves in either of two ways: (1) by

450 B.C. WIRELESS DATA

* Cartoon provided by Phillips Business Information's Wireless Data News

one send the information that differs from one frame to the next. In digital transmissions, the information is encoded as a pattern of "0"s and "1"s. Among other benefits, this approach is particularly resistant to "noise" (misinterpreted information) because a receiver only has to distinguish between two digital possibilities as opposed to many possible analog signal levels. Most telecommunications media initially employed analog coding and transmission but more recently have begun to adopt the newer digital approach.

To retrieve information that has been encoded, of course, one needs a receiver that can decode the signal. This can create substantial problems, particularly where different firms or individuals own the encoder and decoder. For example, the benefits of owning an FM radio transmitter are slight if no one owns an FM radio receiver. In the same manner, digitally encoded television signals cannot be received by most television sets now in use.

varying the waves' amplitude (amplitude modulation, or AM) or (2) by varying their frequency (frequency modulation, or FM).

"Analog" and "digital" are terms frequently employed to describe two ways of transmitting continuous information, such as a moving picture. To transmit a moving picture by analog signal requires encoding the complete picture in each frame transmitted. Digital transmission of a moving picture requires only that

Transmitting

For telecommunication, the medium of transmission can be a wire (*e.g.*, telegraph, wireline telephone, cable television) or the airwaves (*e.g.*, broadcast television, cellular telephone, satellite links) or both.[4] Today, telecommunication by wire usually employs one of two technologies. "Coaxial cable" is a braided metallic cylinder surrounding a wire. The wire carries the radio waves while the cylinder prevents signals from

FIGURE 1.1   Radio Waves

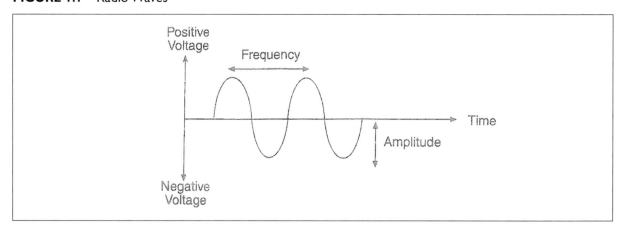

Radio waves typically are transmitted as sine waves, which is to say that they typically follow a pattern in which their energy level varies from high voltage to low voltage and back again, with the transitions accomplished in the gradual manner shown in the figure. Two significant attributes of a sine wave are its *frequency* (which measures how many times per second the wave hits its peak) and its *amplitude* (which measures the magnitude of that peak).

FIGURE 1.2 Amplitude and Frequency Modulation

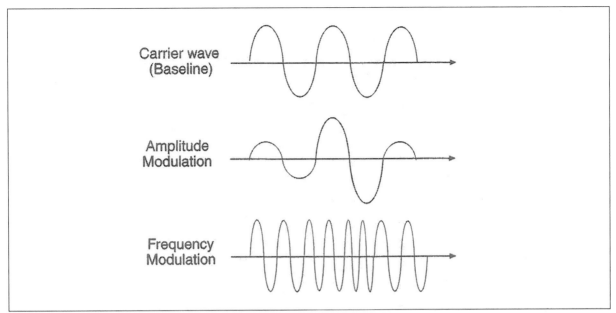

Carrier wave
(Baseline)

Amplitude
Modulation

Frequency
Modulation

Information can be encoded on sine waves by means of amplitude modulation (AM) and also by means of frequency modulation (FM). Compare the AM signal pictured here to the unmodified baseline ("carrier") signal shown above it. Can you see how the amplitude of the AM signal differs from the baseline, thereby possibly communicating information to the recipient? Similarly, can you see how the frequency of the FM signal differs from the carrier, again possibly communicating information to a recipient familiar with this method of encoding?

other wires (or from outside radiation) from interfering with the signals on the wire. The genius of coaxial cable is that the outside cylinder offers superior noise suppression while the braiding allows the cable to remain flexible. "Fiberoptic cable," a technology that entered widespread use in the 1980s, uses light traveling through a very thin glass fiber to transmit data. Fiberoptic cable forms the bulk of the long distance telephone network and the Internet backbone. It is particularly well suited for data transmitted at the highest frequencies, for transmission over very long distances, and for carrying many signals within one cable.

When information is transmitted by wire, the system may be designed so that many streams of data are in the wire and the recipient chooses one stream (*e.g.*, cable television) or so that the wire leading directly to the recipient carries less information (*e.g.*, wireline telephone). In the latter case, decisions as to what goes to the recipient are made, in part, further up the wire by specialized computers called switches and routers.

When information is transmitted through the air, the radio waves can be radiated in all directions or to only a single point. Conventional AM and FM radio stations, like lawn sprinklers, radiate in all directions; a series of microwave transmitters linked together into a 2000-mile hook-up, by contrast, each "radiate" only to a single spot. The direction and characteristic of the radiated signal is determined by the size, shape, and direction of the transmitting antenna. Transmitting through the airwaves also allows the transmitter or the receiver or both to be mobile during the dissemination or exchange of data. The cellular telephone system, for instance, employs transmission and reception through the airwaves to enable people to connect to the telephone system from moving vehicles. The same concept allows dispatchers and taxi drivers to converse via radio waves.

Whether transmission occurs through wire or air, the encoded electrical energy can be sent or radiated at varying degrees of power (compare the "transmitter" that is the portable in-home telephone handset connected to a base station in the house to the broadcast transmitter for a major metropolitan TV station).

The amount of transmission power affects both the distance over which the signal can be transmitted and the signal's clarity at its reception point.

A telecommunications system can be designed so that recipients are also transmitters. Where this two-way communication occurs, the system is usually termed "interactive" or "duplex." Ordinary telephone systems are interactive because one can both receive and transmit voice data through the telephone. Conventional television broadcast systems are not interactive, but the addition of a microwave transmitter from the TV set to the broadcast station could alter that. Cable television systems typically contain a narrow "upstream" channel from the subscriber to the transmitting head-end that can be used for interactive applications.

Of course, it simplifies matters somewhat to describe telecommunication simply as encoding and electronically transmitting information, but most telecommunications technologies and markets are defined principally by these two characteristics. Thus, the difference between AM and FM radio is that one uses amplitude modulation and the other uses frequency modulation to encode the sine waves. Television is simply a mixture of both modulation schemes. The visual data (pictures) are amplitude modulated while the audio data are frequency modulated.[5] Conventional telephone communication is like AM radio in that it requires little spectrum because it transmits only voice data, but is unlike radio in that it transmits locally by wire and so it is somewhat easier to exclude people from listening in on the communication and there is less of a problem with congestion. Communications satellites are very tall transmitting and receiving antennas, and CB radios are portable AM radio stations transmitting at very low power.

Similarly, altering the technology employed in a telecommunications system can change the effects it produces. For example, the extent to which a radio signal creates potential interference with other signals is reduced if the broadcast is not radiated in all directions, but is transmitted only from one point to another, or is radiated at less power. The amount of information that can be transmitted through a cable of a certain size can be increased by switching from coaxial to fiber optic cable. The amount of spectrum necessary to transmit a television signal can be reduced if a digital, rather than an analog, signal is employed. By increasing the power at which a satellite transmits television signals, one can reduce the size of the antenna necessary to receive those signals (and vice versa).

In almost every case, moreover, more than one telecommunications technology can accomplish a given end. Transoceanic cables can substitute for geostationary orbiting satellites. Telephone calls and television signals can be transmitted by wire or over the air. A weak broadcast signal can be strengthened by boosting the power at which it is radiated or by using a relay station to capture and retransmit the signal. In much the same way, coaxial or fiberoptic wires periodically have repeaters that strengthen the signal over long distances. Multi-channel packages of television signals can be sent to the home by cable, microwave, or satellite.

Choosing a telecommunications technology is therefore like choosing virtually any other good. One compares price and quality. There are many ways to transfer data from one place to another. For a specific task, some are cheaper, some are faster, some are more reliable. The distinct advantage of spectrum, for instance, is mobility. A particular telecommunications technology will be chosen for a specific data transmission task based on its price and quality as compared to other ways of getting the job done. Should one write, phone, e-mail or instant message? Presumably, the choice is made by comparing the costs and benefits of each. Further, as new desires arise, new configurations of telecommunications technology will be developed to create cost-effective ways of satisfying these desires. Cable television wedded telephone and radio technology to serve the desires of viewers for more signals of greater clarity. Cellular telephone combined the same technologies to increase accessibility at some cost in clarity and in the ability to exclude unwanted listeners.

B. ALLOCATING SPECTRUM

One major difference between markets for telecommunications goods and markets for other goods is that governmental regulation plays a very large role in determining what kinds and quality of telecommunications services may be offered at what costs. The central issue in telecommunications law and policy today is why telecommunications goods and markets are not treated like most other goods and markets. For most goods (books, desks, shoelaces) government subjects the relevant industry to laws of general applicability—such as antitrust, labor, and securities regulation—but does not control entry, prices, quantity or quality, and does not appoint a regulatory agency to oversee the industry's performance or enact legislation specific to that industry. The question on which all else turns, then, is this: what, if anything, justifies the different treatment accorded telecommunications service providers?

The regulation that most heavily affects the market for telecommunications services is government control over the use of the electromagnetic spectrum, an "input" into the "product" of communicating data electronically via the airwaves. In the United States, no one may broadcast through the airwaves without a license from the federal government.[6] Further, in many cases, that license will specifically limit the types of information the licensee can transmit and the technology that may be employed in transmitting it. This control over who may broadcast and what kinds of broadcasts may be offered substantially constrains the ability of the telecommunications market to adapt to consumer demand. If a faster, cheaper, or more reliable method of quickly getting data to places far away requires over-the-air transmission, one cannot offer that service without first getting the government to grant a license that permits such transmission.

Just to be concrete: no matter how highly consumers in New York City would value the ability to receive telecasts on channel eight, no one can broadcast through the airwaves on channel eight from a transmitter located in New York City because the FCC does not allow it. One cannot simply purchase on the market the right to broadcast on channel eight in New York City; the FCC will not permit such a market to exist.[7]

Once the government decides to issue a broadcast license, it in principle has several ways to decide who will obtain the license. In the case of broadcasting, the government has usually given the license away but imposed public interest requirements on licensees. We will consider the merits of this process in Chapters Three, Four, and Five; but note here that the process likely produces serious inefficiencies.

One example: suppose that someone has the choice between transmitting over a wire and transmitting through the air. In some cases, sending data through the air might be more attractive not because the real cost to society is any less, but because the government does not give away wire in the way it for many years gave away broadcast licenses.

What is this "spectrum" that the government controls so tightly but, in the beginning at least, relinquished without charge? "Spectrum is the entire available range of sinusoidal signal frequencies."[8] Recall that telecommunication through the air involves the transmission of encoded sine waves. These waves can be made to vary in length, which is conventionally measured in meters. The wavelength determines the frequency of the signal. Very long waves have very low frequencies because they repeat infrequently. Short waves are high frequency because they recur more often.

The unit of measurement of frequency is called a "hertz." One hertz is a very low frequency; a one hertz wave would cycle through its sinusoid once every second. AM radio broadcasts in the United States occupy frequencies between 535 kHz (for "kilohertz," one thousand hertz, one thousand sinusoidal cycles per second) and 1605 kHz. FM radio broadcasts occur at the frequencies between 88 MHz (for "megahertz," one million hertz, one million cycles per second) and 108 MHz.

Thus, the spectrum is that range of lengths of radio waves which, to date, people have learned to encode, transmit electronically near the speed of light, and decode. It follows, of course, that the spectrum—like chemistry's periodic table—has expanded substantially during the past 100 years. For example, when the FCC was established in 1934, spectrum capacity was under 300 MHz. By the end of World War II, usable spectrum had increased to 40 GHz (for "gigahertz," one billion hertz).

Different frequencies (*i.e.*, various wavelengths) of radio waves have somewhat different characteristics. Broadcasts at the very lowest frequencies require very large antennas because exceedingly long waves must be propagated. Radio waves in the medium frequency, which include AM radio broadcasts, are reflected back to earth by the ionosphere, particularly at night, thus considerably extending the reach of many of these signals.[9] Transmissions in the very high frequency (VHF) and ultra high frequency (UHF) ranges are not reflected back to earth and so can usually be captured clearly only by a receiver that is within the transmitting antenna's line of sight. Above UHF, which includes the super high and extremely high frequencies, the wavelengths are so small that they can be packed into narrow focused beams of energy, such as are employed in microwave and radar. In general, the higher the frequency (all other things held constant) the more data can be transmitted per unit of time.

The different characteristics of the various frequencies are interesting to note, but they are seldom crucial in determining where in the spectrum the signal carrying particular types of data should be located. This is particularly true for mass communications media. Television signals, for example, not only can be transmitted in both the VHF and UHF bands, but also are clearly and effectively transmitted at much higher frequencies by microwave and through satellites. Radio broadcasting, as noted, takes place all the way from 535 kHz to 108 MHz.

To generate a good quality signal, then, the particular location of that signal in the electromagnetic spectrum is not often crucial. At the very least, a rather wide range of choices will be available. An important qualification, however, is that the presence of other communications media near a particular slice of spectrum may make that slice unsuitable for a particular use. For example, given current technology, a mobile paging service within one slice of the spectrum can create spillover effects that would render a neighboring slice unsuitable for television (say, causing static) but satisfactory for some less complex or less delicate transmission.

Separate from its location in the spectrum (wavelength), the extent of the spectrum that a signal occupies (bandwidth) is also often very important. The preferred amount of bandwidth for a particular use depends on the amount and types of information that must be impressed on the radio waves. For example, much more bandwidth is required to carry a color television signal than to carry the human voice. (Indeed, since television signals contain an audio component, the point is axiomatic.) The preferred amount of bandwidth also depends on the

technology being employed. The same information subjected to traditional analog encoding will require more bandwidth than if encoded digitally and compressed.

By now, it should be apparent that "the spectrum" is just a concept, somewhat like "the multiplication tables." More specifically, the spectrum is a list of wavelengths (frequencies) at which people have learned effectively to transmit data via electrical impulses sent through the airwaves.

C. THE SPECTRUM AS A RESOURCE

The government treats spectrum as if it were a natural resource, one to be allocated both to specific uses and to specific users. This is actually a helpful way to look at spectrum in that it reminds us that spectrum shares many basic properties with other natural resources. For example:

Spectrum can help to create both wealth and value. People are often willing to pay substantial sums for the ability to send or receive large quantities of data quickly and from far away.

Spectrum can be used in varying amounts for the same purpose. To get a television signal from a New York stage to a Los Angeles nightclub one could use no spectrum (send it via wire, door-to-door), some spectrum (wire from New York to Los Angeles, but broadcast to the nightclub), or nothing but spectrum (transmit directly from stage to satellite which transmits, in turn, directly to the nightclub).

Spectrum use is costly in that any spectrum committed to one use can no longer be employed toward a different valuable end. If one person is broadcasting a television signal on channel two in New York, that means someone else cannot use those frequencies for mobile telephony, FM stereo, or dispatching ambulances.

Lastly, while the absolute amount of available spectrum is finite, the amount of usable spectrum can be increased with appropriate investments in technology. Not only do improvements in technology add to the range of usable spectrum, but also within any existing range of usable frequencies, spectrum capacity can be increased by advances in technology. To pick one notable example, digital compression allows a broadcaster to send much more information over the

FIGURE 1.3 Spectrum Management

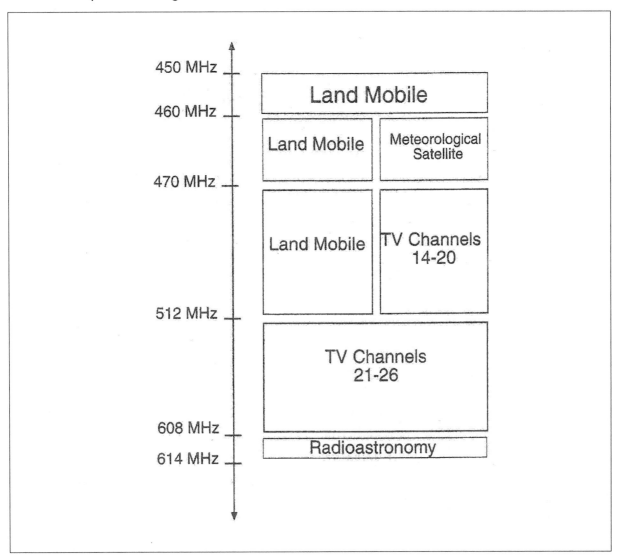

This chart shows the current allocation of spectrum in the range of frequencies between 450 MHz and 614 MHz. Note that some frequencies—for example, the range between 470 MHz and 512 MHz—can be used for any of several uses, in this case both land mobile telecommunication and broadcast television. The National Telecommunications and Information Administration's Office of Spectrum Management produces a full spectrum chart, which is available from that office or at http://www.ntia.doc.gov/osmhome/allochrt.pdf.

same amount of spectrum that would otherwise be occupied by an uncompressed analog signal. In short: "With airwaves, as with other media, the more you spend, the more you can send: it all comes down to engineering and smart management."[10]

D. ALLOCATING SPECTRUM USE

Because spectrum is a costly and productive resource that can be used in different ways and for different purposes, some mechanism had to be devised to "allocate" the spectrum—that is, to decide how much of what parts of it would go to what people for what uses. In a free market capitalist economy, the usual mechanism employed for such purposes is a pricing system. In such a system, potential users of the resource bid for it. These bids establish the value of the resource and, if it goes to the highest bidder, the resource is employed in its highest valued use. This means that the resource is as productive as it can be given present technology, at least within the limits of the market mechanism as an evaluator of value.

At an early stage in the developing science of telecommunication, however, a very different approach was taken toward the problem of allocating spectrum. The government declared that broadcasting without a license was illegal and that only the government could convey a license. Further, licenses were handed out without charge and, although most of them could subsequently be bought and sold, these licenses were valid for only a brief period of time.

How does the process work today? For starters, radio waves do not respect geopolitical boundaries, so it is necessary for spectrum allocation in the United States to conform to rules established by the International Telecommunications Union (ITU), an organization established by treaty. Particularly for terrestrial transmission of radio waves, ITU regulations are not typically very confining. Usually, within any range of the spectrum, international standards permit a wide variety of uses. Further, international law does not restrict any spectrum usage within a country so long as that use does not radiate into other countries.

Within the broad parameters set by the ITU, spectrum allocation inside the United States is, initially, a joint effort of the FCC and the National Telecommunications and Information Administration (NTIA), located within the Commerce Department. NTIA manages those portions of the spectrum that are reserved for federal government use. The FCC manages the rest. The FCC and NTIA jointly decide which frequencies will be reserved for government use.

For those wavelengths not set aside for NTIA's management, the FCC determines permissible uses. Typically, this is accomplished through rulemaking proceedings, in which the agency announces tentatively what portions of the spectrum it will assign to what uses and then reassesses that conclusion in light of comments submitted in response to the announcement. Some tangible results of the spectrum allocation procedure discussed above are illustrated in Figure 1.3.

NOTES

1. Thomas Krattenmaker & Lucas A. Powe, Jr., *Regulating Broadcasting Programming* 6 (1994)

2. The smoke signal analogy is suggested by Don L. Cannon & Gerald Luecke, Understanding Communications Systems 1 (2d ed. 1984).

3. To "invent" broadcast radio, then, one had to discover how to encode the human voice onto energy waves and then to decode that information at a receiver. Similarly, television requires the ability to break a picture down into bits of data (millions of points of light).

4. Many complicated telecommunications employ both wire and air. For example, a domestic long distance telephone call might start out over local telephone lines, move across states through over-the-air microwave transmitters, and then travel through different local telephone lines to reach its destination.

5. Of course, a television signal must convey more data than an FM radio signal, so a television broadcast requires more bandwidth in the spectrum than does an FM radio broadcast.

6. 47 U.S.C. §301.

7. Since, as observed above, a substitute is always available, one could build, or arrange to be carried on, a cable television system in New York City. Whether, however, that substitute is as cost effective in meeting consumer demand is another question.

8. Don L. Cannon & Gerald Luecke, *Understanding Communications Systems 1* (2d ed. 1984)

9. This also means that, for signals at these frequencies, the problem of interference is greater at night than during the day.

10. Peter Huber, Law and Disorder in Cyberspace 75 (1995).

CHAPTER 2

REGULATING THE CONTENT INDUSTRIES

As we have seen so far in this course, telecommunications regulation emerged in order to combat a number of challenges: the need to create a competitive industry and the unique attributes of communications processes, networks and the technologies. As a result of the constraints dictated by the First Amendment and the importance we attribute in the American system to free expression on the one hand, but also as a result of the dictate to serve through broadcasting the public interest and the scarcity of spectrum resources, a body of regulation has developed that dictates the extent and types of speech that should and may be transmitted over the airwaves. These rules are at the center of this chapter in the course, as well as the rules that guide the regulation of non-broadcast content provision: cable and satellite.

UNIT 9

Enough or Too Many?
Media Ownership

The debate over the extent of concentration of media is central to our democracy as much as it is to understanding the regulation of telecommunications. It can also be seen as directly correlated to the regulation of speech over the airwaves, as ownership rules dictate how many media outlets there will be and who will be allowed to own them. Telecommunications scholars Todd Chambers and Herbert Howard discuss in this reading the regulatory and economic aspects of media ownership regulation as well as its history.

The Economics
of Media Consolidation

Todd Chambers and Herbert H. Howard

A hallmark of the American political system is the promise of the First Amendment that the government shall not abridge the freedom of the press. The free press has evolved from printed news pamphlets and the penny press to the wired and wireless forms of electronic mass media. In general, the modern media have been recognized as participants in a theoretical marketplace of ideas where information commodities are offered for public consumption and debate. Democracy demands a free and wide exchange of information from a diverse and antagonistic pool of information sources (*Associated Press v. United States*, 1945). When there is a threat to the number of diverse and antagonistic information sources, such as in the case of consolidation, some policymakers, scholars, and others call for government regulation or deregulation to satisfy the public interest in the marketplace of ideas. There is no doubt that the information in the marketplace of ideas has social, political, and economic value. It is in the economic framework that this chapter seeks to answer questions related to the economics of media consolidation. This chapter seeks to provide an examination of the economics of media consolidation by exploring some of the key issues related to changes in media market structures. Specifically, we define media consolidation, highlight historical trends in the regulation of media

ownership, analyze past research dealing with media ownership and the effects of structural changes in media markets, and make recommendations regarding the future of research in the economics of media consolidation.

DEFINING MEDIA CONSOLIDATION

The merger between America Online (AOL) and Time Warner in 2000 represented the new age of synergy consolidation in the media world. One of new media's largest companies in the Internet world merged with one of old media's largest companies in the movie, cable, magazine, and television world to realize all of the efficiencies that the merger promised to offer—for the business and for the consumers. The Federal Communications Commission (FCC) approved the merger and argued that consumers would receive better service and technology in terms of broadband content and distribution (Federal Communications Commission [FCC], 2001a). After the announcement of the merger in 2000, the new company realized some notable setbacks including billions of dollars in revenue losses. By 2003, the company had decided to drop "AOL" from its company name (Creamer, 2003). This merger as well as dozens of others by companies such as News Corp., Clear Channel Communications, and Viacom has fueled debate and criticism about mergers at the local, regional, national and global level.

The debate about media consolidation has spilled over from the traditional communities of academics and policymakers into the neighborhoods of average citizens. During the 20-month period (Oct. 2001 to May 2003) that the FCC reviewed the broadcast ownership rules, the Commission sifted through more than 520,000 public comments about the issue (FCC, 2003). A Pew Research Center poll found that 48% of respondents to a telephone survey in July 2003 knew about the decision by the FCC to relax the cross-media ownership rule—up from only 26% in February 2003 (Johnson, 2003). In addition, the same poll found that half of the respondents felt that the decision to relax the cross-media ownership rules would be bad for America (Johnson, 2003). The changes in the broadcast rules combined with the growing public interest in the issues of media ownership have highlighted the need to review the specifics of media consolidation and its perceived and actual effects on the welfare of the public.

Overall, media consolidation is a difficult concept to define, much less study. In economic terms, consolidation is a form of merger activity used by firms to combine properties in "a type of merger in which both companies cease to exist after the transaction and an entirely new corporation is formed which retains the assets and liabilities of both companies" (Ozanich & Wirth, 1993, p. 117). From a media perspective, Compaine (1982) concluded there are three general types of mergers in the media industry: horizontal, vertical, and conglomerate. The type of merger is determined by the product markets of the companies involved. If a company merges with another company with similar products in the same market, then the merger is typically characterized as a horizontal merger. A vertical merger can best be described as a company that produces a product buying another company that distributes the product. Finally, a conglomerate merger involves companies with multiple products in different product markets. Since the mid-1990s, there has been a spotlight on media merger activity with companies such as AT&T, TCI, AOL, Time Warner, News Corp., and DirecTV. Overall, these merger activities have created a new media environment with new questions about the consequences of consolidation.

CURRENT TRENDS IN MEDIA CONSOLIDATION

Advances in new technologies such as the Internet, digital broadcast and cable television, and other communication technologies have created new outlets for information. According to the National Cable Television Association, there were 255 national cable television networks in January 2004 (National Cable Television Association, 2004). The FCC reported that there has been a 5% increase in the number of commercial radio stations since the passage of the 1996 Telecommunications Act ("FCC's Adelstein Urges Caution," 2003). Between 1990 and 2000, the number of broadcast television stations experienced a double-digit increase of 12.3% (Levy, Ford-Livene, & Levine, 2002). At the same time, the number of owners for media outlets has decreased in the radio (Williams & Roberts, 2002), television (Howard, 2003) and cable industries (FCC, 2002). According to Howard (2003), almost 86% of all television stations in the United States are owned by multiple-station or group ownership. Likewise, 87% of all cable systems are controlled by the top 10 multiple system operators (MSOs) (FCC, 2002). For radio, one company, Clear Channel Communications, controls more than 1,200 radio stations. Table 17.1 describe the number and value of radio and television transactions since 1994. Based on the transaction information, the spike for radio occurred in 2000 and 2001, whereas there was a jump for television between 2001 and 2002. Since mergers decrease the number of companies in a particular market and may have negative effects on the degree of competition in a market, policymakers evaluate and administer policies related to consolidation activity.

MEDIA CONSOLIDATION FROM A REGULATION PERSPECTIVE

The ideals of the Sherman Antitrust Act of 1890 embody the core concepts when dealing with merger activity in the media industry. Section 2 of the Sherman Act prohibits the monopolization of free

TABLE 17.1   Radio and Television Station Transactions, 1994–2002

Year	Radio	Radio Value	TV	TV Value
1994	494	970,400,000	89	2,200,000
1995	525	792,440,000	112	4,740,000
1996	671	2,840,820,000	99	10,488,000,000
1997	630	2,461,570,000	108	6,400,000,000
1998	589	1,596,210,000	90	7,120,000,000
1999	382	1,718,000,000	86	4,720,000,000
2000	1,794	24,900,000,000	154	8,800,000,000
2001	1,000	3,800,000,000	108	4,900,000,000
2002	836	5,594,141,000	249	2,529,039,000

trade in the United States. Historically, government agencies devoted to regulating the broadcasting industry have used the same ideals to prevent one company from monopolizing the content within the marketplace of ideas.

The U.S. Department of Justice and other agencies such as the U.S. Federal Trade Commission administer the policies of the Sherman Act and attempt to preserve competition within industries. The agency bases its regulatory decisions about mergers using a set of evaluative criteria known as the *Horizontal Merger Guidelines* (Federal Trade Commission [FTC], 1997). These guidelines help regulators evaluate the potential harm to competition and negative consequences on the consumer welfare from the merger of two companies. Specifically, the guidelines outline issues of market concentration, entry barriers, efficiency gains, and economic failure (FTC, 1997). These measures have been used to help shape and formulate policy related to the industries of mass media.

To help prevent the monopolization of ideas, various agencies and branches of the government have used laws and regulations to sustain a diverse marketplace of ideas. The First Amendment guarantees a "freedom of the press" that has been used by all types of organizations claiming "press" status. The general theme behind policies related to ownership is that the more independent owners there are, the better it is for society.

Newspapers

Outside of economic factors, the freedom of the press clause guarantees that anyone can become a newspaper publisher. Unlike the broadcasting industry where a station owner must obtain a license to broadcast and even the cable industry where an individual or company must apply for a local franchise to operate a system, individuals wanting to publish a newspaper do not go through any type of application process. Despite this freedom, the government has argued that it has an interest in protecting the public interest when newspapers attempt to use anticompetitive practices to prevent other papers from operating. In one of the most widely discussed and cited cases, the U.S. Supreme Court upheld the right of competitive newspapers in its *Associated Press v. United States* (1945). According to the Court, the First Amendment "rests on the assumption that the widest dissemination of information from diverse and antagonistic sources is essential to the welfare of the public" (*Associated Press v. United States*, 326 U.S. 1, 1945). Part of the reasoning was to prevent the Associated Press from keeping its services from members' competitors. Although the Court wanted to maintain competition in the daily newspaper industry, it could not account for the economic conditions throughout the 20th century that decimated the number of markets with competitive newspapers.

As a result, Congress passed the *Newspaper Preservation Act* of 1970 that allowed newspaper competitors to form joint operating agreements (JOAs). A JOA permitted a newspaper in a market to take over the business operations of a failing newspaper in order to preserve the publication of both newspapers. According to Lacy (1988), Albuquerque's *Journal* and *Tribune* formed the first JOA in 1933. Throughout the Act's history, there were joint operating agreements in 25 different cities; in 2003, there were 12 JOAs operating in markets such as Cincinnati, Ohio, and Las Vegas, Nevada (Newspaper Association of America, 2003).

Broadcasting

Regulation of broadcasting in the United States was based on several principles including a limited broadcast spectrum that belongs to the public and is legally available through licensing by the government. Consequently, the Federal Radio Commission (FRC) (later the FCC) was granted the power to develop criteria for awarding licenses to applicants for broadcast stations. Under powers granted by the Radio Act of 1927, the FRC determined that broadcast licenses could be issued to business enterprises for commercial purposes, as well as to noncommercial organizations. Both types of licensees are expected to operate stations entrusted to them in the public interest, convenience, and necessity. No policy making action was taken regarding the multiple ownership of stations until much later.

Multiple station ownership has a long history, extending back to the licensee (Westinghouse Electric) of the first commercial radio station, KDKA, Pittsburgh, Pennsylvania. From 1920 to 1940, the regulatory commissions granted numerous licenses for group-owned radio stations. Ownership of radio stations and radio networks became a heated political issue in the late 1930s when the Mutual Broadcasting System sought governmental intervention to reduce the control that NBC and CBS had over numerous stations they operated for other owners. It was Mutual's contention that it was at an unfair advantage in gaining affiliate stations as outlets for its programming. Mutual also asked the government to break up the dual network operation of the National Broadcasting Company.

With the release of the FCC's ownership study, the *Report on Chain Broadcasting* (1941), the Commission expanded its powers to regulate the broadcast industry by exercising a rule that a company should not operate more than one national radio network. Although the FCC had no direct control over the "networks," the Commission used network affiliation to justify regulations in the public interest. Subsequently, after the U.S. Supreme Court upheld the Commission's new network broadcasting rules in *NBC v. United States* (1943), the FCC forced NBC to break up its dual Red and Blue networks. In complying with the Commission's order, NBC sold its Blue Network in 1943 and retained its more popular NBC Red Network. In addition, the FCC forced NBC and CBS to stop operating stations licensed to other entities. Further, in 1943, the Commission adopted an antiduopoly rule, which required that no licensee own two stations of the same broadcast service in the same market area. This rule solidified the FCC's doctrine of localism, which had been developing since the 1920s.

With the network case prominent in its activity, in 1940 the FCC adopted rules to limit multiple station ownership in the two new broadcast services, FM radio and television. In this action, owners were limited to six FM stations and three TV stations per licensee. Although no limits were imposed on AM radio stations at that time, the Commission applied the duopoly principle to the new FM and television services. In 1944, the FCC, responding to a filing by NBC, increased the maximum to five TV stations per licensee.

Critics of multiple station ownership argued that unrestrained group ownership of stations could result in undue control of the communications media that could result in monopoly control of the flow of information received by the public, as well as undue economic control of the media by a few owners. For example, it was said that the latter could result in artificially high advertising rates and other types of trade restraint activity within the radio industry.

The debate concerning multiple station ownership resumed during the post–World War II years and, in 1952–53, the Commission adopted comprehensive rules that limited each owner to seven AM, seven FM, and seven television stations. The arbitrary number of seven stations thus became the FCC's operational limit for acceptable concentration of control of the broadcast media. Unfortunately, the 1952–53 rules did not take into account such relevant matters as station power or the size of markets served by stations. As a result, owners frequently sold stations in order to buy other stations in larger and more economically promising markets while staying within the limit of seven stations. These rules remained in effect until 1986, when the Commission relaxed the ownership limits to 12 stations of each type (AM, FM, and TV). This action also restricted television group owners to coverage of a maximum of 25% of the households in the United States. The relaxation of limits was justified by the fact that the number of stations in each broadcast service had increased by manifold numbers. Group ownership of both radio and television stations expanded greatly following the rules change of 1986.

Whenever more than one applicant sought a broadcast channel, the FCC customarily held comparative hearings to determine which applicant should be awarded the facility. Prominent among the Commission's criteria was its preference for local ownership of stations, which the agency favored as a means of promoting a more diverse body of station owners. As a result, the Commission usually favored local owners over owners of groups of stations. A second preference of the Commission in its comparative hearings was its desire to promote ownership diversity within a market. This preference became manifest in two ways in the agency's comparative hearings, particularly those for new television stations during the 1950s. First, the FCC usually preferred applicants who were not connected with dominant media outlets in a market. The agency, therefore, looked closely at each applicant's other broadcast holdings in a market when granting a new facility. Thus, a TV applicant who had a dominant radio station in the market was less likely to be favored than the owner of a smaller radio station, provided both had a good record of public service. Second, the FCC usually favored applicants who did not have an ownership interest in a local daily newspaper over those who were involved in local publishing.

Concerns were expressed quite strongly about cross-media ownership of newspapers and broadcast stations during the 1930s. The critics believed that a combination of a local broadcast station and a local newspaper could powerfully influence the public on matters of civic importance. No restrictions on local cross-media ownership of a broadcast station and a newspaper were adopted during the 1930s. However, after television became an established medium, controversy arose again concerning local newspaper–broadcast cross-media ownership in the 1960s. The debate climaxed in 1974 when the FCC issued cross-media ownership rules that forbade the formation of new combinations of local broadcast stations and daily newspapers. Established combinations, with a few exceptions, were allowed to remain unaffected by the rule. However, from 1974 forward, the number of newspaper–broadcast combinations declined sharply as many owners decided to sell off one of their properties, usually the broadcasting stations. Most owners who sold either a newspaper or a broadcasting station in the same community received favorable tax inducements to bring about compliance with the Commission's 1974 ruling.

Cable

Prior to 1992, cable system operators had no upper cap on the number or percentage of subscribers they could serve. However, the 1992 Cable Act directed the FCC to establish limits on the number of subscribers a multiple system cable operator (MSO) may serve. The FCC implemented such rules in 1993, allowing operators to serve up to a 30% share of nationwide cable and direct broadcast satellite (DBS) subscribers. Although the U.S. Supreme Court upheld the constitutionality of the Cable Act, the U.S. Court of Appeals for the District of Columbia in 2001 remanded the FCC's limits for cable ownership the following year for further review. The lower court said the Commission "failed to explain why the specific restrictions were justified given the infringement on cable companies' free speech rights" (McConnell, 2001, p. 8). After the court's remanding order, the FCC, in September 2001, launched a proceeding to review its horizontal and vertical limits for cable companies ("FCC Begins Reviewing Cable Ownership Limits," 2001). Early in 2003, FCC Chairman Michael Powell told reporters that the agency would soon review recommendations from the Mass Media Bureau on revising cable-ownership limits. As of August 2004, no further Commission action had occurred on cable ownership limits. In effect, the District Court's order in 2001 abolished the 30% cap on the number of households a cable company could reach.

Deregulation

Since the 1970s, Congress and the FCC have been deregulating the rules and regulations related to the broadcasting and cable industries. The FCC began to allow time brokerage agreements for radio broadcasters in 1971 (Hagin, 1994). A time brokerage or local marketing agreement (LMA) "allows the licensee of another broadcast facility to operate a station in return for a share of the profits" (Creech, 1993, p. 84). Another area of deregulation slowly relaxed restrictions on duopoly arrangements for radio and television. The duopoly rules for radio stations existed until 1992, when the Commission allowed radio duopolies in all markets. According to the duopoly rules, in markets with more than 14 stations an operator could control two AM and two FM stations (FCC, 1992). In smaller markets, the duopoly rules allowed an owner to operate three stations—two of the same service—as long as the duopoly does not attract more than 50% of the audience share of the market (Hagin, 1994). The Commission first relaxed the television duopoly rules for large markets in the fall of 1999 and expanded into other types of markets in June 2003.

In the Telecommunications Act of 1996, Congress changed the national market structure for both television and radio by lifting the limit on the number of properties one company can own on a national basis. For radio, this allowed the development of major radio groups such as Clear Channel Communications and Cumulus Broadcasting. For television, however, the rules retained a national audience reach cap. Under the former rules, a single television group owner could not reach more than 35% of the total potential national audience with no limit on the number of stations. By law, the FCC is required to review ownership rules every 2 years with the provision that any unnecessary rules should be eliminated. In 2003, the Commission voted to raise the cap to 45%. However, Congress and the Bush Administration revised the percentage to 39% in early 2004. In addition, the Act allowed cross-ownership between the cable and telephone industries.

Other decisions by the FCC have stirred public debate among industry, political, and academic communities about the effects of deregulation on media consolidation. After 20 months of review, the FCC adopted broadcast ownership rules in June 2003 that replaced the *Cross Media Ownership Rules* of 1975. In markets with at least nine television stations, the cross-ownership ban between the local newspaper and a local radio and/or a local television station was eliminated, and the local television duopoly rules were further relaxed. At the time of writing, a U.S. Appeals court was scheduled to review the cross-media and duopoly provisions of the FCC's rules changes of 2003.

MEDIA CONSOLIDATION FROM AN ECONOMIC PERSPECTIVE

Media economists applied industrial organization theory as an acceptable framework to analyze media markets (Busterna, 1988a; Wirth & Bloch, 1995). According to the theory, the structure of a market determines the conduct of firms and subsequent performance of a particular market (Scherer, 1980; Sheperd, 1985; Stern & Grabner, 1970). In practical terms, this theory explains that the number and characteristics of organizations will determine the competitive behavior of these firms in the marketplace.

The Market

One of the most important applications of the industrial organization model of economics is the ability to link market structure with market power. If a market contains a firm with market power, then the market might experience certain types of conduct from the dominant firm, resulting in an overall decrease in the market's performance (Ferguson & Ferguson, 1988). In particular, the dominant firm may use various pricing strategies to exclude current or potential competitors; or, a firm may use its power to differentiate its products or services to prevent other firms from entering the market. Through horizontal mergers and/or vertical integration, media companies can benefit from economic efficiencies and leverage market power in either or both of the market for audiences and the market for advertisers.

Economists classify a market as a group of buyers and sellers exchanging substitutable goods and services (Picard, 1989; Sheperd, 1985). Unlike other industries, local media not only exist in geographic markets, but also operate in a product market that is commonly referred to as the dual product market—the market for audience and the market for advertisers (Picard, 1989). Daily newspapers, local television stations and local radio stations compete for audience time at both the intraindustry and an intermedium level. Within a media industry, each medium competes with similar medium types for audience and advertising revenue. For example, a radio station will produce a differentiated product, or format, to attract a listener. Each station will compete against other radio stations for listeners and advertisers. At the intermedium level, each medium type will compete with different medium types for audiences and advertisers. At this level, a radio station might compete with a newspaper in terms of time spent listening rather than time spent reading the newspaper. Likewise, the radio station will compete with a daily newspaper for a share of the local advertising revenue.

Ownership in the Market

Consolidation manifests itself in several different forms within the mass media. In the global or national marketplace, media companies typically combine for mergers, acquisitions, and joint ventures. For local markets, consolidation occurs when companies form joint operating agreements, local marketing agreements, shared service agreements, and duopoly. Although the media may operate like other types of industries in terms of geographic markets, the dual product nature of the media creates unique economic consequences for market conduct and performance.

Studies of media consolidation have typically explored the nature of ownership in descriptive studies or analyzed specific economic effects of ownership in analytical studies. In general, the descriptive studies have focused on identifying the national or local market structure from an intra- or intermedium industry perspective (Compaine, 1982; Compaine & Gomery, 2000; Nixon & Ward, 1961; Sterling,

1975; Waterman, 1991). These studies have used both simple and sophisticated tools to identify market structure. From counts of the number and types of owner in a market to calculations of the Hirschman–Herfindahl index (HHI) or the four- or eight-firm concentration ratios (CR4, CR8), there are a variety of methods available to analyze market structure in media markets (Albarran, 2003). These measures allow analysts to identify the concentration of ownership and evaluate the degree of competition in a market. Market concentration "shows the extent to which production of a particular good or service is confined to a few large firms" (Ferguson & Ferguson, 1988, p. 39). If a market has a dominant firm, that firm will lead to entry barriers and prevent competitors from offering consumers an alternative product or service.

The analytical tools for measuring market structure require clear and precise definitions of the geographic and product markets that will be studied. While all media companies exist in some type of geographic market, not all media companies will compete in the same product market(s). Bates (1993b) emphasized the importance of precision in defining geographic markets and measuring the product market for audiences separately from the product market for advertisers. For example, newspapers such as *The New York Times*, *The Wall Street Journal*, *USA Today*, and *The Los Angeles Times* are typically considered as newspapers with a nationwide market. These papers have a nationwide distribution where they are read and compete for reading time among subscribers in hundreds of other daily newspapers existing in local markets. Table 17.2 provides information about selected studies and how the authors measured market structure.

In addition, a key to exploring the issues of market structure, conduct, and performance is defining the nature of the media firm. In the dual product market, there is a distinction between the market for audiences and the market for advertisers at the firm level. Specifically, all media firms technically act as outlets for information in the audience and advertiser product markets. From this perspective, research in the area of source diversity has considered daily newspapers, local television stations, and local radio stations as participants in a marketplace of ideas (Lacy & Riffe, 1994; Levin, 1954). Whereas

TABLE 17.2 Selected Geographic and Product Market Definitions

Author	Topic	Geographic Markets(s)	Product Market(s)	Market Structure
Bates (1993b)	Televison	Local TV markets	Viewers and advertisers	HHI
Larson	Televions	National TV markets	Viewers and advertisers	CR4, CR8, CR20
Lacy & Davenport (1994)	Newspaper	Local daily newspaper markets	Subscribers	HHI, CR1, CR2, CR3
Drushel (1998)	Radio	Top 50 local radio markets	Listeners	HHI
Berry & Waldfogel	Radio	Local radio markets	Listeners	HHI

all media firms in a market technically act as outlets of information, not all firms exist as independent voices. Economists highlight the need to identify the source of programming or control of access to information (Owen, 1978). Sterling (1975) and Nixon and Ward (1961) defined a media voice as a separate, antagonistic owner of a media property within a local market. It is in this distinction between voices and outlets that the classic debate concerning media consolidation generates the most discussion.

Some scholars have attempted to link diversity of opinion with the number of different media outlets within a local market (Loevinger, 1979). A media outlet differs from a media voice because an owner controls the value of the license through management decisions. Former FCC Commissioner Loevinger (1979) argued that the increasing number of different media outlets ensures diversity within the marketplace of ideas. From this perspective, it would appear that the more outlets available to a market, the greater the diversity of information choices in the market. Another perspective spotlights the need to consider the ownership of these outlets to determine true diversity within the marketplace of ideas.

The primary issue in research related to media ownership is the effect of ownership on the performance of a media market. If a company controls the majority of the media outlets, then that company can monopolize the dual product of media—the audience

and the advertiser. Scholars such as Bagdikian (1997) warned of the consolidation and conglomeration of the mass media. Beginning in 1983, Bagdikian (1983, 1990, 1997) argued that there have been a decreasing number of large conglomerates controlling the media content available to consumers. In most of Bagdikian's work, the findings are based on trend data from several different types of media industries to argue the majority of information and entertainment media are controlled by a handful of companies.

Bagdikian (1997) feared that monopoly control of information outlets would prevent the free expression of ideas in the American democracy. For critics of media concentration, the public interest is not served by monopoly control of local information outlets in all types of media industries. Essentially, this debate focuses on the development of ownership patterns in media markets.

When considering the mass media from an interindustry context, several scholars have addressed the general development and ownership of mass media industries (Compaine, 1982; Compaine & Gomery, 2000; Nixon & Ward, 1961; Sterling, 1975; Waterman, 1991). Most of these studies have focused on general information related to the number of outlets and owners as well as attempting to differentiate as many technical and organizational differences. In general, these studies focused on a national geographic market and included daily newspapers, broadcast television, radio, cable television multiple system operators and cable television networks, motion pictures, magazines and more recently, the top Internet companies. Other studies such as Albarran and Dimmick (1996) and Waterman (1991) added comparative analyses of the degree of ownership concentration across multiple media industries by using HHI and CR4 and CR8 ratios to compare the media industries. Overall, these studies cataloged valuable information related to the type of media owner and level of competition within the industries.

From an intraindustry perspective, studies have dealt with the issues of ownership in the newspaper (Lacy & Davenport, 1994), broadcast television (Howard, 2003; Larson, 1980), radio (Drushel, 1998; Riffe & Shaw, 1990; Rogers & Woodbury, 1996) and cable television industries (Chan-Olmsted & Litman, 1988; Waterman & Weiss, 1997). These studies addressed issues ranging from the concentration of ownership to the effects of market structure on a variety of dependent measures related to consumer welfare. Other researchers addressed the issues of media ownership by exploring mergers and acquisitions (Ozanich & Wirth, 1993). In most cases, the studies focused on the link between the type of media ownership structure and its effect on the diversity of information provided from the outlets controlled by those organizations.

Market Structure

The structure of a market can be defined in terms of the size and distribution of owners, the amount of product differentiation, and the number of entry barriers within a market (Albarran, 2003; Picard, 1989). According to theory, the greater number of similar firms leads to a more competitive market (Picard, 1989). Markets are described using the theoretical framework known as the *theory of the firm*. This framework explains that markets operate in perfect competition, monopolistic competition, oligopoly, or monopoly.

In general, media economists have used the theory of the firm to classify the daily newspaper industry as monopoly (Albarran, 2003; Picard, 1989), the broadcast television industry as an oligopoly (Larson, 1980), and radio as moving from monopolistic competition to oligopoly (Drushel, 1998). In most markets, the newspaper industry has developed into a natural

monopoly where one firm becomes so efficient in producing and delivering its product that it becomes difficult for a competitor to exist in the same market. Researchers have examined the status of newspaper market structure (Busterna, 1988a; Lacy & Davenport, 1994; Picard, 1994; Udell, 1990). Overall, the general trend within the newspaper industry indicated that the number of chain newspapers has doubled since 1960 (Busterna, 1988a). In addition, Lacy and Davenport (1994) concluded that the daily newspaper market was highly concentrated. Litman (1988) attributed the monopolization of the daily newspaper market to economies of scale and joint operating agreements. These results support the notion that the newspaper industry exists within a monopoly market.

The broadcast industries have wavered between oligopoly and monopolistic competition. The majority of research describing the structure of the broadcast industry focused on television (Bates, 1993b; Howard, 2003, 1998; Larson, 1980; Powers, 2001). On a national level, Howard (2003) found that more than 80% of all commercial television stations are under group ownership. At the local level, Bates (1993b) analyzed local television market structure in terms of the audience and advertiser markets, concluding that concentration levels were lower in the audience market than in the advertising market. For cable television, research indicated increases in ownership concentration for the overall industry (Chan-Olmsted, 1996).

Because of the changes in radio ownership rules, there has been a renewed interest in the structure of the radio industry (Berry & Waldfogel, 2001; Chan-Olmsted, 1995; Drushel, 1998; Rogers & Woodbury, 1996; Williams, 1998). Drushel (1998) reported movement toward oligopoly in the Top 50 radio markets. Chan-Olmsted (1995) found support for the notion that the relaxation of duopoly rules was leading to an expansion of ownership within local markets. Overall, the results of broadcast ownership studies suggested higher levels of consolidation at the national and local level. Overall, it appears that each of the traditional, local media industries—daily newspapers, local radio, local television stations, and cable systems—have maintained or moved toward moderate or high levels of ownership concentration. In other words, fewer owners of local media are controlling larger numbers of local media outlets. In addition, it seems the research indicates that the type of media owner is changing as well. Past research indicated that local markets were dominated by chain ownership of newspapers (Lacy & Davenport, 1994), group ownership of television stations (Howard, 2003), and absentee ownership in radio (Chambers, 2003). These policy changes related to television ownership and cross-media ownership will create more opportunities for research into the effects of market structure on the conduct of individual firms in an industry.

Market Conduct

According to the theory of the firm, market structure is characterized by the activities, or conduct, of both the sellers and buyers in the market. In general, market structure predicts specific types of firm conduct such as pricing, product strategy and advertising, research and innovation, plant investment, and legal tactics (Albarran, 2003). From a monopoly market where a single product seller dominates the market and is able to set the price to maximize profits, to a perfect competition market where several sellers of similar products react as price takers in the competitive environment (Albarran, 2003), media exist in various market structures. Monopolistic competition shares some similarities with oligopoly. Under monopolistic competition, a market must have a large number of producers, a degree of product differentiation, no entry barriers, no firm interdependence, and no market share above 10% (Sheperd, 1985). In addition, firms in this environment will have control over the pricing of its products and services; however, these prices will be related to competitors' prices (Organisation for Economic Co-operation and Development, 1993a). Under an oligopoly market structure, the market will have small number of leading firms, some fringe competitors, and a degree of interdependence among firms (Picard, 1989; Sheperd, 1985). Since participants in an oligopoly have control over price, cooperative behavior can lead to joint maximization of prices (Organisation for Economic Co-operation and Development, 1993b). Although all elements are important elements when evaluating media markets, the majority of studies have focused on the pricing and price strategies of firms.

After the passage of the Telecommunications Act of 1996, one of the first responses from the U.S. Department of Justice was to investigate radio mergers in Boston, Philadelphia, Rochester, and Cincinnati to evaluate how radio consolidation affected the market for advertising (Department of Justice, 1996a, 1996b, 1996c). In particular, the Department of Justice wanted to prevent anticompetitive behavior in the pricing of advertising that may or may not have resulted from the radio mergers. Initial industry evidence suggested that consolidation defined as radio duopolies had not raised the price of radio advertising (Price, 1997). Examinations of advertising pricing in media markets have been a popular method of research in media economics.

Scholarly research in the area of advertising pricing and market structures has been mixed. Masson, Mudambi, and Reynolds (1990) studied radio and television advertising prices in terms of viewers and listeners. Overall, the results indicated that prices rise with increased competition. In a study about the Canadian radio industry, McFadyen, Hoskins, and Gillen (1980) found a strong positive relationship between market concentration and the cost of radio pricing. As the number of owners declines in a market, there is an increase in the cost for the price of a commercial. In other words, the dominant firms develop market power and increase the price of advertising.

There have been a variety of approaches to exploring pricing issues in the newspaper industry. Shaver (1995) examined theoretical perspectives of pricing theory by considering the rapidly changing competitive environment for newspapers. Empirical studies of the industry have found mixed results related to market structure and pricing differences between different types of newspaper structures. Picard (1988) reviewed research related to the pricing behavior of newspapers and reported that newspaper monopolies and newspapers in common ownership arrangements such as a joint operating agreement or part of a chain charge higher prices for advertising. A recent study about the economic effects of newspaper joint operating agreements found that newspapers in joint operating agreements actually have advertising rates that are similar to those of newspapers in competitive markets (Romeo, Pittman, & Familant, 2003). These findings highlight the difficulty in measuring issues of conduct related to an evolving media marketplace.

Although advertising pricing is an important component of market conduct, the audience can also enjoy or suffer consequences from changes in pricing behavior. After Congress initially deregulated cable television rates in 1984, consumers called on Congress to reregulate the industry as a result of increasing subscription rates. Jaffe and Kanter (1990) found that after deregulation in the 1980s there was a relationship between markets with more and less competition; in particular, it appeared that in smaller markets the price for cable was higher during deregulation than during regulation. Furthermore, Yan (2002) reported that firm size in the cable industry had negative consequences for consumers in terms of must-carry rules. Specifically, the author found "larger MSOs dropped a larger number of over-the-air television stations to add more cable networks to their lineups" (p. 188). As a natural monopoly, these types of results seem to confirm the exercise of market power by firms in this type of market structure.

Another popular area for research related to market conduct has been in the area of product strategy decisions in terms of newspapers, television, and radio. Several scholars have investigated issues of newspaper product strategy in terms of editorial aspects (Hale, 1988), wire services (Lacy, 1990, 1989), reporting aspects (Picard, 1989), and news content (Wanta & Johnson, 1994). For broadcast television, the research focused on content of television news (Besen & Johnson, 1985) and public interest programming (Busterna, 1988b; Prisuta, 1977; Wirth & Wollert, 1979). For radio, research topics in product strategy have focused on the effect of group ownership on news programming (Lacy & Riffe, 1994; McKean & Stone, 1992; Riffe & Shaw, 1990) and radio formats (Berry & Waldfogel, 2001; Greve, 1996; Rogers & Woodbury, 1996; Romeo & Dick, 2003). A U.S. Department of Justice study about the effect of market structure on radio programming found that major format changes occurred more frequently among radio stations with below-average market shares (Romeo & Dick, 2003). One reason for this trend is that the majority of the stations are large, group-owned radio stations. These studies provided mixed results related to the effect of ownership structure on variables related to market conduct.

Market Performance

Market performance revolves around the concept of efficiency for the firm and for the public. Albarran (2003) outlines the components of market performance as technical and allocative efficiency, equity, and progress. In general, studies in this area have used a variety of measures for performance from both the firm and the market perspective. From a newspaper framework, studies of have measured performance at the firm level by looking at profits (Blankenburg & Ozanich, 1993; Demers, 1998, 1996, 1991) and the market level by examining the effects of a recession on the newspaper economy (Picard & Rimmer, 1998) and the long-term effects of consolidations in The Netherlands newspaper market (van Kraneburg, 2001). Many of these studies focused on public versus private companies and the differences each organizational type has on the various measures of performance. Demers (1998) found that although corporate newspapers are more profitable, they actually place *less* emphasis on profits than do independent newspapers.

At the firm and market levels for the broadcasting and cable industries, the studies focused on the rate of return for Canadian radio (McFadyen, Hoskins, & Gillen, 1980), station trafficking in television and radio (Bates, 1993a, 1993b), and consumer welfare in cable television (Crawford, 2000). McFadyen et al. (1980) found the overall rate of return for Canadian radio companies in 1975 was 18%. Bates (1993a) valued the use of multiples as an indicator of station financial performance. For radio, Bates (1993a) reported multiples averaged about 6–8 for AM, 8.5–10 for FM, and 7–10 for AM/FM combinations (p. 108). In related research about radio station trafficking, Bates (1993a) suggested that the FM radio industry was providing higher than average prices.

Throughout most of the research dealing with market performance issues has been the question: Is monopoly or competition better for consumer choice?

THE STEINER MODEL

The seminal study concerning the effect of monopoly control of a media outlet and its effect on the performance of the market for media content was Steiner's (1952) work in the area of radio program choice. Based on Steiner's 1949 dissertation, the study focused on the degree of competition in the radio industry. Steiner hypothesized that a market operating with a discriminating monopolist would provide a better service to the public than a market operating with a set of competitors. According to the hypothesis, a discriminating monopolist, working with the assumption of audience maximization, has more incentive than participants in a competitive market to provide differentiated products to the entire market. The competitors, working with the assumption of audience maximization, will duplicate their programming according to the most popular program choice available; in other words, in a competitive market, economic theory suggests that competitors will duplicate the most popular program choice because the incentive lies in dividing the audience of the most popular station. Steiner argued that the public welfare was better served under the monopoly model for program choice.

Since Steiner, there have been several attempts to study the effects of broadcast competition and radio program choice (Berry & Waldfogel, 2001; Glasser, 1984; Greve, 1996; Haring, 1975; Owen, 1977; Rogers & Woodbury, 1996). The majority of research in the area of broadcast competition and program choice has focused primarily on television with specific analyses in the structural aspects of advertiser-supported and pay television (Noll, 1978; Noll, Peck, & McGowan, 1973; Owen, 1975; Owen, Beebe, & Manning, 1974; Owen & Wildman, 1992; Spence, 1976; Spence & Owen, 1975, 1977), the number of channels available on cable television (De Jong & Bates, 1991), content aspects related to the conduct of various media such as television and cable television (Grant, 1994), and the home video and theatrical marketplace (Hellman & Soramaki, 1994). Overall, explicit tests of the Steiner model have provided mixed results in studies dealing with program choices.

For the most part, studies dealing with television have rejected the Steiner theory on the basis of audience preferences and the mechanics of the television broadcast industry. Economists such as Noll (1978), Spence and Owen (1975), and Owen and Wildman (1992) have refuted the Steiner examples by analyzing the advertiser-based and pay television-based systems of delivery in terms of audience preferences. Recent studies in radio have suggested confirmation of the initial Steiner hypothesis. Berry and Waldfogel (2001) reported results that showed consolidation increasing the number of radio format choices in local radio markets. Likewise, Rogers and Woodbury (1996) demonstrated that it would take an unrealistic number of new competitors in a radio market to retrieve more diversity in the number of radio program choices. From a theoretical perspective, Gal-Or and Dukes (2003) explored the relationships between product differentiation and the level of advertising in commercial media markets. Because of the nature of an industry that competes for both advertising and audiences, the authors concluded that commercial media outlets involved in a competitive market situation have an interest in a minimum level of product differentiation because it allows stations to sell advertising at a higher rate. Gal-Or and Dukes argued the media have incentives to minimize product differentiation to allow producers to choose a lower level of advertising, consequently paying a higher price for the advertising space.

Overall, the program choice literature indicates the importance of the dual product nature of broadcast programming. Audiences and more important, advertisers, play an integral part in the media diversity equation. In addition, initial tests of the Steiner theory suggested that a monopolist would provide more diversity than a competitor because of the nature of program duplication. Finally, the results showed that although an increase to the number of stations in a market provides some increase in the level of program diversity, it requires a large number of stations in the market. The program choice literature expanded the theoretical basis for analyzing media consolidation.

THE SCP PARADIGM

Overall, the structure-conduct-performance paradigm provides a useful framework for analyzing economic markets. Despite the successful application of industrial organization theory to studies of the media industry, contemporary research suggests the need to reexamine the basic premise of the paradigm because of rapid changes in media market structures (Young, 2000). In particular, convergence and concentration have created new types of multichannel media markets (Chan-Olmsted, 1997). In the cable industry, companies such as Cox Communications represent this type of converged media environment with a portfolio that includes newspapers, radio, television, cable systems, cable networks, Internet network distribution, and production capabilities. The mixed findings related to the consequences of ownership on conduct and performance variables make it difficult to anchor arguments solidly against or in favor of consolidation. In fact, recent studies in radio programming suggest that, contrary to the popular belief that consolidation would be bad for diversity of program choice, there have been increases in overall choice for radio formats. But, as others have pointed out, consolidation does seem to increase the cost of advertising and subscription prices to consumers.

Future studies should consider advancing the theoretical relationships between structure, conduct and performance. After finding that traditional models related to efficiency and market power did not fit data related to vertical integration in the cable industry, Ahn and Litman (1997) argued that consumer welfare was an important consideration when considering cable rate regulation. Few studies have attempted to examine the interplay between market structure, price competition, and the effect of advertising on media consumers within a media market. Hackner and Nyberg (2000) developed a model for analyzing price competition in different market structures while accounting for the nature of the product, advertising externalities, and product differentiation. In theory, the model suggested that exploring the link between the demands of media's dual audiences, the advertiser and the consumer, may reveal policy concerns about excessive media concentration in the public good media marketplace.

Based on a strict interpretation of the industrial organization theory, there are no mechanisms to deal with the product markets of multiple media industries. Outside of HHI and CR calculations using market share, very little research has focused on the effects of the audience on market structure. When the FCC released its Diversity Index with the new ownership rules in 2003, it hoped the index could be used to evaluate the amount of viewpoint diversity in local markets. The index included all of the major variables needed when considering the effects of consolidation—type of media, number of owners, and market share of medium. Despite the fact that it acknowledged the Internet, the Diversity Index assigned weights to media types that may be based on dated information about media use.

A RESEARCH AGENDA

Convergence and policy changes are creating new types of media organizations that, by definition, will behave differently than the media organizations of old. The relaxation of broadcast ownership rules changed the structure of the local media market. Television duopolies, cross-media ownership, radio market clusters, and other new ownership types have restructured the media marketplace. These new ownership structures blur the lines between product markets for media and will require new methods for defining and analyzing market structure, conduct, and performance. Conceptually, these new structures require theoretical development at the firm level.

New technologies such as the Internet are changing the nature of traditional media. There is no doubt that the individual industries of radio, television, newspaper, and cable are becoming more concentrated—but how do you measure the degree of competition among all of these industries in a single market? Part of the problem might be solved by new methods of examining competition, such as the amount of time spent with various media types. Studies by McDonald and Dimmick (2003) and Shaver and Shaver (2003) have considered time as a crucial variable when thinking of issues of competition among the new media and the consequences of market concentration. By examining a variable such as time, researchers might be able to address issues related to global media concentration and intercultural communication patterns as well. These types of studies, combined with works by Napoli dealing with the role of the audience in economics (Napoli, 2001, 2002), could provide new frameworks for exploring market structures with new types of consequences on both industries and audiences.

The research agenda in the area of media ownership and consolidation must move past cataloguing trends and patterns of ownership and address issues related not only to shifts in the structures of media and media industries but also to the fundamental changes in the nature of media consumers in global, national, regional, and local media markets. In general, media economists might deal with these transitions from a variety of disciplines and contexts including strategic and organizational management, audience measurement, and policy assessment.

Future research in the area of media consolidation will continue expanding into the areas of organizational behavior and strategic management to deal with the new combinations of media organizations. In terms of organizational behavior and competitive strategy, researchers can address localism in a variety of contexts ranging from firm strategy to market performance. Young (2000) concluded that future research in industrial organization must get past the interpretation of the relationship between market structure and performance and observe the strategic interactions between competitive firms. Wirth and Bloch (1995) argued: "Strategic behavior undermines the direct links between market structure and conduct, such as those associated with static equilibrium models of perfect competition, monopoly and oligopoly" (p. 24). During the 1970s, research in cross-media ownership (Wirth & Allen, 1979) sought to understand the market structure of organizations with multiple-media platforms. As more markets experience new types of cross-media ownership, future research will apply new understanding about strategic behavior to these models of media organizations.

Already, studies attempting to move in this direction have explored strategic management theory about strategic group interaction between different organizational types of media types (Chan-Olmsted, 1998) as well as cable television (Chan-Olmsted & Li, 2002; Barrett, 1996). Napoli (1997) applied agency theory in an effort to explain the reasons media firms behave the way they do. These types of studies are necessary to deal with the new management models in the media industries.

Although the literature provided some general themes about the effects of consolidation on the conduct and performance of media markets, emerging media technologies raise new questions about an important issue—measurement. From simple geographical definitions of a market to complex definitions of the product market, researchers in the area of media consolidation will need to address new methods for measuring the effects of concentration. At the global level, more research is needed to identify ownership patterns of global media organizations. At the same time, technologies such as the Internet continue to blur the lines of clear product market distinctions and raise issues of being able to clearly identify the audience. Therefore, refinements in the area of audience measurement will need to account for audience mobility and time spent with media, as well as basic reliability and validity concerns.

Finally, the future of media consolidation research will include new methods for assessing the impact of communication policies. International concerns about intellectual property, cross-border information flows, and cultural imperialism will drive more research into the area of media ownership concentration. At the domestic level, policy organizations such as the FCC will continue to ask for assessments to gauge the success or failure related to changes in broadcasting, cable, and other telecommunications. There are numerous opportunities for longitudinal studies using various time series analysis techniques of single or multiple media industries.

In conclusion, the forecasts continue to show increases in the amount of time spent with media. As governments change policies related to market structure and as media industries adapt to technological developments, audiences will both enjoy and suffer from the mechanics of the economic markets. More important, however, is that the same market mechanics that determine the price of the monthly cable bill also determine the number of voices found within the market for ideas. Therefore, it is important for media economists and others to continue asking the questions related to different ownership structures brought about by consolidation and examine the consequences for the audience.

REFERENCES

Ahn, H., & Litman, B. (1997). Vertical integration and consumer welfare in the cable industry. *Journal of Broadcasting & Electronic Media, 41*(4), 453–477.

Albarran, A. (2003). *Media economics: Understanding markets, industries and concepts* (2 ed.). Ames: Iowa State University Press.

Albarran, A., & Dimmick, J. (1996). Concentration and economies of multiformity in the communication industries. *Journal of Media Economics, 9*(4), 41–50.

Associated Press v. United States, 326 U.S. 1 (1945).

Bagdikian, B. (1983). *The media monopoly* (1st ed.). Boston: Beacon Press.

Bagdikian, B. (1990). *The media monopoly* (3rd ed.). Boston: Beacon Press.

Bagdikian, B. (1997). *The media monopoly* (5th ed.). Boston: Beacon Press.

Barrett, M. (1996). Strategic behavior and competition in cable television: Evidence from two overbuilt markets. *Journal of Media Economics, 9*(2), 43–62.

Bates, B. (1993a). Station trafficking in radio: The impact of deregulation. *Journal of Broadcasting & Electronic Media, 37*(1), 21–30.

Bates, B. (1993b). Concentration in local television markets. *Journal of Media Economics, 6*(3), 3–21.

Berry, S., & Waldfogel, J. (2001). Do mergers increase product variety? Evidence from radio broadcasting. *The Quarterly Journal of Economics*, 1009–1024.

Besen, S., & Johnson, L. (1985). Regulation of broadcast station ownership: Evidence and theory. In E. M. Noam (Ed.), *Video media competition* (pp. 364–389). New York: Columbia University Press.

Blankenburg, W., & Ozanich, G. (1993). The effects of public ownership on the financial performance of newspaper corporations. *Journalism Quarterly, 70*(1), 68–75.

Broadcasting & cable yearbook (2003). Newton, MA: Reed Publishing.

Busterna, J. C. (1988a). Concentration and the industrial organization model. In R. G. Picard, J. P. Winter, M. E. McCombs, & S. Lacy (Eds.), *Press concentration and monopoly: New perspectives on newspaper ownership and operation* (pp. 35–53). Norwood, NJ: Ablex.

Busterna, J. (1988b). Television station ownership effects on programming and idea diversity: Baseline data. *Journal of Media Economics, 1*(2), 63–74.

Chambers, T. (2001). Losing owners: Deregulation and small radio markets. *Journal of Radio Studies, 8*(2), 292–315.

Chambers, T. (2003). Structural changes in small media markets. *Journal of Media Economics, 16*(1), 41–59.

Chan-Olmsted, S. (1995). A chance for survival or status quo? The economic implications of the radio duopoly ownership rules. *Journal of Radio Studies, 3*, 59–75.

Chan-Olmsted, S. (1996). Market competition for cable television: Re-examining its horizontal mergers and industry concentration. *Journal of Media Economics, 9*(2), 25–41.

Chan-Olmsted, S. M. (1997). Theorizing multichannel media economics: An exploration of a group-industry strategic competition model. *Journal of Media Economics, 10*(1), 39–49.

Chan-Olmsted, S. (1998). Mergers, acquisitions, and convergence: The strategic alliances of broadcasting, cable television and telephone services. *Journal of Media Economics, 11*(3), 33–46.

Chan-Olmsted, S., & Li, J. (2002). Strategic competition in the multi-channel video programming market: An intra-industry strategic group analysis. *Journal of Media Economics, 15*(3), 153–174.

Chan-Olmsted, S., & Litman, B. (1988). Antitrust and horizontal mergers in the cable industry. *Journal of Media Economics, 1*(1), 63–74.

Compaine, B. (1982). *Who owns the media?* (2nd ed.). New York: Harmony Press.

Compaine, B., & Gomery, D. (2000). *Who owns the media? Competition and concentration in the mass media industry.* Mahwah, NJ: Lawrence Erlbaum Associates.

Crawford, G. (2000). The impact of the 1992 Cable Act on consumer demand and welfare: A discrete-choice, differentiated products approach. *RAND Journal of Economics, 31*(3), 422–449.

Creamer, M. (2003, October 6). AOL Time Warner stresses name change practicality. *PR Week*,

Online Edition. Retrieved January 4, 2004, from Lexis-Nexis Academic Universe.

Creech, K. (1993). *Electronic media law and regulation.* Boston: Focal Press.

De Jong, A., & Bates, B. (1991). Channel diversity in cable television. *Journal of Broadcasting & Electronic Media, 35,* 159–166.

Demers, D. (1991). Corporate structures and emphasis on profits and product quality at U.S. daily newspapers. *Journalism Quarterly, 68,* 15–26.

Demers, D. (1996). Corporate newspaper structure, profits, and organizational goals. *Journal of Media Economics, 9*(2), 1–23.

Demers, D. (1998). Revisiting corporate newspaper structure and profit making. *Journal of Media Economics, 11*(2), 19–45.

Department of Justice. (1996a, August 5). *Justice Department requires Jacor to sell Cincinnati radio station* [News release]. Washington, DC: U.S. Department of Justice.

Department of Justice. (1996b, October 24). *Justice Department requires Boston-based American Radio Systems Corp. to divest three Rochester, New York radio stations* [News release]. Washington, DC: U.S. Department of Justice.

Department of Justice. (1996c, November 12). *Justice Department requires Westinghouse and Infinity to divest radio stations in Boston and Philadelphia in order to go ahead with largest radio industry merger in history* [News release]. Washington, DC: U.S. Department of Justice.

Drushel, B. (1998). The *Telecommunications Act of 1996* and radio market structure. *Journal of Media Economics, 11*(3), 3–20.

FCC's Adelstein urges caution on media ownership rules. (2003, January 13). *Television Digest.* Retrieved November 24, 2003, from Lexis-Nexis Academic Universe.

Federal Communications Commission. (1992). *Radio multiple ownership rule reconsidered.* 7 F.C.C. Rcd. 6387 (1992).

Federal Communications Commission. (1997). Report on chain broadcasting. FCC Pocket No. 5060. Washington, DC.: FCC.

Federal Communications Commission. (2001a). *Fact sheet: FCC's conditioned approval of AOL Time Warner merger.* Retrieved June 24, 2002, from http://www.fcc.gov/Bureaus/Cable/Public-Notices/ 2001/fcc01011 fact.doc

Federal Communications Commission (2001b, September 13). *FCC begins reviewing cable ownership limits* [News release]. Retrieved June 24, 2002, from www.fcc.gov/Bureaus/Cable/NewsReleases/2001

Federal Communications Commission. (2002, January 14). *8th annual video competition report.* Retrieved June 24, 2002, from http://hraunfoss.fcc.gov/edocs_public/attachmatch/FCC-01-389A1.pdf

Federal Communications Commission. (2003, June 2). *FCC sets limits on media concentration* [News release]. Retrieved January 7, 2004, from http://hraunfoss.fcc.gov/edocs_public/attachmatch/DOC-235047A1.pdf

Federal Trade Commission. (1997). *1992 horizontal merger guidelines.* Retrieved December 15, 2003, from http://www.ftc.gov/bc/docs/horizmer.htm

Ferguson, P., & Ferguson, G. (1988). *Industrial economics. Issues and perspectives.* (2nd ed.). London: Macmillan.

Gal-Or, E., & Dukes, A. (2003). Minimum differentiation in commercial media markets. *Journal of Economics & Management Strategy, 12*(3), 291–325.

Glasser, T. (1984). Competition and diversity among radio formats: Legal and structural issues. *Journal of Broadcasting, 28*(2), 127–145.

Grant, A. (1994). The promise fulfilled? An empirical analysis of program diversity on television. *Journal of Media Economics, 7*(1), 51–64.

Greve, H. (1996). Patterns of competition: The diffusion of a market position in radio broadcasting. *Administrative Science Quarterly, 41,* 29–60.

Hackner, J., & Nyberg, S. (2000). *Price competition, advertising and media market concentration.* Stockholm, Sweden: Stockholm University, Department of Economics.

Hagin, L. (1994). *U.S. radio consolidation: An investigation of the structures and strategies of selected radio duopolies.* Unpublished doctoral dissertation, University of Tennessee, Knoxville.

Hale, F. D. (1988). Editorial diversity and concentration. In R. Picard, J. Winter, M. E. McCombs, & S. Lacy (Eds.), *Press concentration* and monopoly: New perspectives on newspaper ownership and operation (pp. 161–176). Norwood, NJ: Ablex.

Haring, J. (1975). Competition, regulation and performance in the commercial radio broadcasting industry. Unpublished doctoral dissertation. New Haven, CT: Yale University.

Hellman, H., & Soramaki, M. (1994). Competition and content in the U.S. video market. Journal of Media Economics, 7(1), 29–49.

Hickey, N. (2002, May–June). Behind the mergers. Columbia Journalism Review. Retrieved December 5, 2003, from www.archives.cjr.org/year/02/3/hickey.asp

Howard, H. (1998). The Telecommunications Act and TV station ownership: One year later. Journal of Media Economics, 11(3), 21–32.

Howard, H. (2003). Television station ownership in the U.S.: A comprehensive study (1950–2002) (Final Report). National Association of Broadcasters.

Jaffe, A., & Kanter, D. (1990). Market power of local cable television franchises: Evidence from the effects of deregulation. RAND Journal of Economics, 21(2), 226–234.

Johnson, P. (2003, July 16). Public unsettled by media consolidation, poll shows. USA Today, p. 3D. Retrieved January 7, 2004, from Lexis-Nexis Academic Database.

Lacy, S. (1988). Content of joint operation newspapers. In R. G. Picard, J. P. Winter, M. E. McCombs, & S. Lacy (Eds.), Press concentration and monopoly: New perspectives on newspaper ownership and operation (pp. 147–160). Norwood, NJ: Ablex.

Lacy, S. (1989). A model demand for news: Impact of competition on newspaper competition. Journalism Quarterly, 68(1), 40–48, 128.

Lacy, S. (1990). Newspaper competition and number of news services carried: A replication. Journalism Quarterly, 69(1), 79–82.

Lacy, S., & Davenport, L. (1994). Daily newspaper market structure, concentration, and competition. Journal of Media Economics, 7(3), 33–46.

Lacy, S., & Riffe, D. (1994). The impact of competition and group ownership on radio news. Journalism Quarterly, 71(3), 583–593.

Larson, T. (1980). The U.S. television industry: Concentration and the question of network divestiture of owned and operated television stations. Communication Research, 7(1), 23–44.

Levin, H. (1954). Competition among the mass media and the public interest. Public Opinion Quarterly, 18(1), 62–79.

Levy, J., Ford-Livene, M., & Levine, A. (2002). Broadcast television: A survivor in a sea of competition (Working Paper Series 37, Office of Plans and Policy). Washington, DC: Federal Communications Commission.

Litman, B. R. (1988). Microeconomic foundations. In R. G. Picard, J. P. Winter, M. E. McCombs, & S. Lacy (eds.), Press concentration and monopoly: New perspectives on newspaper ownership and operation (pp. 3–34). Norwood, NJ: Ablex.

Loevinger, L. (1979). Media concentration: Myth and reality. The Antitrust Bulletin, 24(3), 479–498.

Masson, R., Mudambi, R., & Reynolds, R. (1990). Oligopoly in advertiser-supported media. Quarterly Review of Economics and Business, 30(2), 3–16.

McConnell, B. (2001, March 5). Court scraps cap. Broadcasting & Cable. Retrieved January 7, 2004, from Lexis-Nexis Academic Database.

McDonald, D., & Dimmick, J. (2003). Time as a niche dimension: Competition between the Internet and television. In A. Albarran & A. Arrese (Eds.), Time and media markets (pp. 29–47). Mahwah, NJ: Lawrence Erlbaum Associates.

McFadyen, S., Hoskins, C., & Gillen, D. (1980). Canadian broadcasting: Market structure and economic performance. Montreal: The Institute for Research on Public Policy.

McKean, M. L. & Stone, V. A. (1992). Deregulation and competition: Explaining the absence of local broadcast news operations. Journalism Quarterly, 69(3), 713–723.

Napoli, P. (1997). Rethinking program diversity assessment: An audience-centered approach. Journal of Media Economics, 10(4), 59–74.

Napoli, P. (2001). The audience product and the new media environment: Implications for the economics of media industries. International Journal on Media Management, 3(2), 66–73.

Napoli, P. (2002). Audience valuation and minority media: An analysis of the determinants of the value of radio audiences. *Journal of Broadcasting & Electronic Media, 46*(2), 169–184.

National Broadcasting Company v. United States 319 U.S. 190 (1943).

National Cable Television Association (2004). Industry overview, cable program networks. Retrieved January 9, 2004, from http://www.ncta.com/industry overview/programList.cfm

Newspaper Association of America. (2003). Facts about newspapers. Retrieved December 19, 2003, from http://www.naa.org/info/facts03/17facts2003.html

Nixon, R., & Ward, J. (1961). Trends in newspaper ownership and inter-media competition. *Journalism Quarterly, 38*, 3–14.

Noll, R. (1978). Television and competition. In Federal Trade Commission (Ed.), *Proceedings of the Symposium on Media Concentration* (pp. 243–259). Washington, DC: Federal Trade Commission.

Noll, R., Peck, M., & McGowan, J. (1973). *Economic aspects of television regulation.* (Brookings Institution). Washington, DC: U.S. Government Printing Office.

Organisation for Economic Co-operation and Development. (1993a). *Glossary of industrial organisation economics and competition law.* Paris: Author.

Organisation for Economic Co-operation and Development. (1993b). *Competition policy and a changing broadcast industry.* Paris: Author.

Owen, B. (1975). *Economics and freedom of expression: Media structure and the First Amendment.* Cambridge, MA: Ballinger.

Owen, B. (1977). Regulating diversity: The case of radio formats. *Journal of Broadcasting, 21*(3), 305–319.

Owen, B. (1978). The economic view of programming. *Journal of Communication, 28*(2), 43–47.

Owen, B., Beebe, J., & Manning, W. (1974). *Television economics.* Lexington, MA: Lexington Books.

Owen, B., & Wildman, S. (1992). *Video economics.* Cambridge, MA: Harvard University Press.

Ozanich, G., & Wirth, M. (1993). Media mergers and acquisitions: An overview. In A. Alexander, J. Owers, and R. Carveth (Eds.), *Media economics: Theory and practice* (1st ed., pp. 116–133). Hillsdale, NJ: Lawrence Erlbaum Associates.

Picard, R. (1988). Pricing behavior of newspapers. In R. G. Picard, J. P. Winter, M. E. McCombs, & S. Lacy (Eds.), *Press concentration and monopoly: New perspectives on newspaper ownership and operation* (pp. 147–160). Norwood, NJ: Ablex.

Picard, R. (1989). *Media economics.* Newbury Park, CA: Sage.

Picard, R. (1994). Institutional ownership of publicly traded U.S. newspaper companies. *Journal of Media Economics, 7*(4), 49–64.

Picard, R., & Rimmer, T. (1998). Weathering a recession: Effects of size and diversification on newspaper companies. *Journal of Media Economics, 12*(1), 1–18.

Powers, A. (2001). Toward monopolistic competition in U.S. local television news. *Journal of Media Economics, 14*(2), 77–86.

Price, C. (1997, March). Status quo: Consolidation has little effect on cost per point. *Gavin GM. Radio's Business Edge, 2*(3), 23–24.

Prisuta, R. (1977). The impact of media concentration and economic factors on broadcast public interest programming. *Journal of Broadcasting, 21*(3), 321–337.

Riffe, D., & Shaw, E. (1990). Ownership, operating, staffing and content characteristics of 'news radio' stations. *Journalism Quarterly, 67*(4), 684–691.

Rogers, R. P., & Woodbury, J. R. (1996). Market structure, program diversity and radio audience size. *Contemporary Economic Policy, 14*, 81–91.

Romeo, C., & Dick, A. (2003). The effect of format changes and ownership consolidation on radio station outcomes. Unpublished manuscript.

Romeo, C., Pittman, R., & Familant, N. (2003). Do newspaper JOAs charge monopoly advertising rates? *Review of Industrial Organization, 22*(2), 121–138.

Scherer, F. (1980). *Industrial market structure and economic performance* (2nd ed.). Chicago: Rand McNally.

Shaver, M. (1995). Application of pricing theory in studies of pricing behavior and rate strategy in the newspaper industry. *Journal of Media Economics, 8*(2), 49–59.

Shaver, D., & Shaver, M. (2003). The impact of concentration and convergence on managerial efficiencies of time and cost. In A. Albarran & A.

Arrese (eds.), *Time and media markets*, (pp. 29–47). Mawah, NJ: Lawrence Erlbaum Associates.

Sheperd, W. (1985). *The economics of industrial organization*. Englewood Cliffs, NJ: Prentice-Hall.

Spence, M. (1976). Product selection, fixed costs and monopolistic competition. *Review of Economic Studies, 43*(2), 217–235.

Spence, M., & Owen, B. (1975). Television programming, monopolistic competition and welfare. In B. Owen (Ed.), *Economics and freedom of expression: Media structure and the First Amendment* (pp. 143–165). Cambridge, MA: Ballinger.

Spence, M., & Owen, B. (1977). Television programming, monopolistic competition, and welfare. *Quarterly Journal of Economics, 51*(1), 103–125.

Steiner, P. (1952). Program patterns and preferences, and the workability of competition in radio broadcasting. *Quarterly Journal of Economics, 66*(2), 194–223.

Sterling, C. (1975). Trends in daily newspaper and broadcast ownership, 1922–1970. *Journalism Quarterly, 52*(2), 247–256, 320.

Stern, L., & Grabner, J. (1970). *Competition in the marketplace*. Glenview, IL: Scott Foresman.

Udell, J. G. (1990). Recent and future economic status of U.S. newspapers. *Journalism Quarterly, 67*(2), 331–339.

van Kraneburg, H. (2001). Economic effects of consolidations of publishers and newspapers in The Netherlands. *Journal of Media Economics, 14*(2), 61–76.

Wanta, W., & Johnson, T. (1994). Content changes in the St. Louis *Post-Dispatch* during different market situations. *Journal of Media Economics, 7*(1), 13–28.

Waterman, D. (1991). A new look at media chains and groups: 1977–1989. *Journal of Broadcasting & Electronic Media, 35*(2), 167–178.

Waterman, D., & Weiss, A. (1997). *Vertical integration in cable television*. Cambridge, MA: MIT Press.

Williams, W. (1998). The impact of ownership rules and the Telecommunications Act of 1996 on a small radio market. *Journal of Radio Studies, 5*(2), 8–18.

Williams, G., & Roberts, S. (2002). *Radio industry review 2002: Trends in ownership format and finance* (Media Bureau Staff Working Paper, Federal Communications Commission). Retrieved November 15, 2002, from http://www.fcc.gov/ownership/studies.html.

Wirth, M., & Allen, B. (1979). Another look at cross-media ownership. *The Antitrust Bulletin, 24*(1), 87–103.

Wirth, M., & Bloch, H. (1995). Industrial organization theory and media industry analysis. *Journal of Media Economics, 8*(2), 15–26.

Wirth, M., & Wollert, J. (1979). Public interest programming: Taxation by regulation. *Journal of Broadcasting, 23*(3), 319–330.

Yan, M. (2002). Market structure and local signal carriage decisions in the cable television industry: Results from count analysis. *Journal of Media Economics, 15*(3), 175–191.

Young, D. (2000). Modeling media markets: How important is market structure? *Journal of Media Economics, 13*(1), 27–44.

UNIT 10

Reactive or Proactive?
Regulating Content

This unit consists of a series of lectures and topics, however, they have all been condensed under one heading. There are two ways government can regulate the content of speech: by enhancing forms of desired speech or by restricting forms of undesired speech. The former requires both allocation of resources and a value-laden decision, while the latter, as we have seen in our discussion of the First Amendment, is not easy to do. By introducing all of the proactive policies one following the other, government's view of what is missing from our broadcasting arena is made clear. Because the American media system has emerged as a market-based system, these proactive measures, those enhancing certain forms of speech, represent the government's definition of the market failures inherent in this system.

The four areas in which proactive measures have been taken are:

1. Public broadcasting

2. Political speech

3. Programming for children

4. Minority representation

The one area in which government enforcement of limits on freedom of expression has been most blatant is the regulation of indecent content.

The readings that accompany this series of lectures discuss in detail these regulations. Media scholar Robert McChesney discusses the market failure that led to the evolution of public broadcasting in the United States, while Amit Schejter presents a comparative overview of public broadcasting models elsewhere around the world, as the United States' system seems to be the exception rather than the norm. Legal scholar Adrian Cronauer describes the history of the fairness doctrine, a 40-year policy that has been deserted but continues to loom large over media policy debates. Media scholar Roger Sadler discusses with much detail the special rules that still exist in order to ensure fairness in electoral campaigns. Media law academics Wayne Overbeck and Genelle Belmas briefly describe the rules pertaining to broadcasting for children. Legal scholar LaNelle Owens demonstrates how even though the Supreme Court has found the rules created to enhance minority ownership and representation on the airwaves as constitutional, the FCC has turned its back to them in the name of "economic efficiency." With regards to indecency regulation, the history and principles of this much-debated subject are presented clearly in a chapter written by media law scholars Kent Middleton and William Lee.

Public Broadcasting in the U.S.

Robert W. McChesney

PUBLIC BROADCASTING, YESTERDAY AND TODAY

The United States has never had a "free market" media system in which entrepreneurs competing for profits determined the system's nature. Throughout U.S. history extensive government subsidies have created and altered media systems in ways that the market never could have. By the end of the nineteenth century, however, the rich tradition of public debates over how to deploy large public subsidies to best enhance the breadth and diversity of the press in a democratic society gradually faded into oblivion as powerful commercial media industries began to emerge. Thereafter public subsidies remained—indeed, they were much larger than ever—but they were doled out quietly to the victors of contests between strong commercial media lobbies. The public had no role in this process, virtually no press coverage could draw people into the policy debates, and to the world at large the dominant media firms proclaimed that the United States had a "free market" media system that was the pure embodiment of a free press, as drawn up by Madison and Jefferson.

A radical new development in publicly subsidized media came with the invention of public service broadcasting in the early twentieth century. Unlike previous subsidies, this plan called for the use of public money explicitly to generate media content directly, not simply encourage commercial entities to do so. It stemmed from two other media evolutions. First, radio broadcasting presented an unprecedented problem for every nation: how to best utilize the scarce spectrum that could be devoted to this revolutionary communication technology. Second, the emerging commercial media system, even at its very best, had inherent flaws—*externalities*—that could be damaging to a self-governing or humane society. In combination, these factors prompted the belief that it was not just a right but also a duty of citizens in a democratic society to subsidize and promote a viable nonprofit and noncommercial broadcasting media sector. The result, public service broadcasting, has become a major institution in much of the world, though much less so in the United States. Still, this public service tradition has much to offer democratic media policy making in general.

Public service broadcasting refers to a nonprofit, noncommercial broadcasting service directed at the entire population and providing a full range of programming. At its best, it is accountable to the citizenry, has some distance from the dominant forces holding political power, and does not rely upon the market to determine its programming. Such a setup presents a difficult problem, although not an insurmountable one, for a free society, because it allows the state possibly to control media content far more than classical liberal theory would countenance. In authoritarian political systems, public broadcasting quickly becomes little more than state propaganda. Managing a viable public broadcasting service can be difficult in a democracy, but the international experience shows that it can be done, if there is a political commitment to make it happen. A democratic state can be enhanced by public broadcasting just as an authoritarian state can corrupt such broadcasting. To assume the latter is always the case is to give up the possibility of the former. To some extent, without intending to be overly dramatic, it is to abandon the idea that people can govern themselves.

Several other important variants of nonprofit and noncommercial broadcasting have arisen in the United States, and most stem from specific government policies. Religious institutions, schools, and universities conduct broadcasting as well. Cable TV systems are required to turn over channels (and subsidies) for "public access" broadcasting if communities demand them when local monopoly cable contracts are negotiated. These public access channels are legally content- and viewpoint-neutral—they have no editorial position, and, ideally, they teem with a vibrant range of political opinion. Public access channels tend to be most attractive to those who feel boxed out of the commercial system.[1] Similarly, community radio broadcasting—nonprofit and noncommercial stations dependent largely upon listener donations—exists in scores of U.S. cities. The model was pioneered by the innovative Pacifica system, which has "listener-sponsored" stations in five cities.[2] C-SPAN has provided an invaluable nonprofit and noncommercial service on cable television, though it is not the result of public policy so much as a PR gesture by the cable industry to fend off regulation in the public interest. In other words, the public pays a high price for C-SPAN—to the extent it succeeds as a PR maneuver to permit cable companies to jack up their rates—and the public has no control over its operations.[3]

By far the largest government expenditure to create nonprofit and noncommercial broadcasting has been for the Voice of America and various clandestine services like Radio Free Europe. But these programs are designed for overseas audiences—for diplomatic or propagandistic purposes, depending upon one's perspective—and are not meant to be consumed by the people who pay for them. Most Americans barely know they exist.

But it is public service broadcasting that has the broadest and richest tradition. In most democratic nations of the world, a significant section of the spectrum is devoted to nonprofit (and usually noncommercial) radio and television. The most notable example in the English-speaking world is the British Broadcasting Corporation (BBC). Maintaining public service broadcasting has been a difficult task in the United States for any number of reasons, but in particular because the dominant commercial interests have little interest in coexisting with a strong nonprofit sector that would peel away "their" audience. Today U.S. public service broadcasting is in crisis. Never lavishly funded or supported, the system struggles to survive in a fairly small niche of the media market. Its most vociferous critics charge that public broadcasting is a dubious institution in principle and now has become a bureaucratically ossified relic of a bygone era made irrelevant by the plethora of new cable channels and Internet websites. These critics argue that the market, combined with new technologies, can do a superior job of serving the public interest—and with no public broadcasting subsidy to boot. Because public broadcasting retains an element of political support, especially from the influential upper middle class, its existence is accepted by most of its critics, but only if it remains marginal and poorly subsidized.

To provide some sense of public broadcasting's dilemma, consider this: in 2003 public broadcasting received a federal subsidy of around $365 million, about what Disney's ESPN receives in subscriber fees from cable TV systems every two months.[4] If the United States subsidized a public broadcasting service at rates comparable to Britain's per capita rate for public broadcasting, for example, it would have an annual subsidy in the $15 billion range.[5] This would make it one of the three or four largest media operations in our country and provide an enormous spur to audiovisual production—conceivably large enough to change the industry's direction. In Europe, a huge and impressive variety of programming that would never pass commercial muster has been produced as a result of these subsidies.[6]

Why has public service broadcasting been a marginal phenomenon in the United States in comparison to elsewhere? The main reason is that proponents in other nations were able to get their systems established before commercial broadcasters had achieved dominance over the airwaves. The defeat of the broadcast reform movement in 1934 quashed the hope for this caliber of public broadcasting in the United States. At the time, commercial broadcasters argued that few would listen to their stations if people had access to advertising-free stations with quality entertainment—which they conceded that people wanted—so it was unfair to allow public broadcasting to exist and thereby undermine commercial broadcasting. The U.S. government did establish extremely well-funded noncommercial broadcasting services in the 1940s and beyond—but they were directed at those outside the United States. Indeed, the deal made with the commercial broadcasting industry was that those services—Voice of America, Armed Forces radio and television, Radio Free Europe—would not be accessible in the United States. The explanation was that explicit government propaganda should be restricted to foreigners, but a clear concern for the commercial broadcasters was that the American public not be exposed to well-funded noncommercial fare.

In the 1960s, the commercial broadcasting lobby finally relented, and a national public radio and television service started, but it was not a BBC type of operation, providing a full range of noncommercial programming to the entire population. The plan for what became the Public Broadcasting Service (PBS) and National Public Radio (NPR) did not call for such a system—the commercial dominance of the airwaves was a given—but rather for a broadcasting service that concentrated exclusively upon providing the public service programming that commercial stations were constantly lambasted for avoiding. The commercial broadcasters laid first claim to popular programming, and public broadcasters were left with programming that had less immediate audience appeal.

At its best, as envisioned in the Carnegie Commission reports that helped birth the system, U.S. public broadcasting was seen as producing cutting-edge political and creative programming that commercial broadcasting found unprofitable, and serving poor and marginalized audiences of little interest to commercial networks.[7] As Senator Hugh Scott of Pennsylvania said during the congressional debates on the matter in 1967, "I want to see things on public television that I hate—things that make me think!"[8] In the minds of the original Carnegie Commission, this was to be a well-funded service based on an excise tax on the sale of television sets that would eventually reach 5 percent; this money would be placed in a trust fund over which politicians would have no direct control.[9] When the Public Broadcasting Act of 1967 was passed, this key element of the Carnegie plan was dropped. Had it been fully implemented, public broadcasting would enjoy an annual subsidy in the $3 billion range in 2003 dollars.[10]

The Carnegie vision was doomed from the start because the independent funding mechanism had been sabotaged. When PBS broadcast muckraking programs such as 1970's *Banks and the Poor*, it sent some politicians into a tizzy. President Nixon vetoed the public broadcasting budget authorization in 1972 to express his displeasure.[11] The Democratic platform that year, arguably the most left-wing one since the New Deal, stated, "We should support long-range financing for public broadcasting, insulated from political pressures. We deplore the Nixon Administration's crude efforts to starve and muzzle public broadcasting, which has become a vital supplement to commercial television."[12] PBS eventually did get its funding, but with it public broadcasters got a clear message: be careful in the coverage of political and social issues and expect resistance if you proceed outside the political boundaries that exist in commercial broadcast journalism.

This pattern recurs. Conservatives use what little money Congress provides as leverage continually to badger public broadcasters to stay within the same ideological range found on commercial networks.[13] Conservatives are obsessed with public broadcasting because in it the traditional sources of control in commercial media—owners and advertisers—are absent, so a greater possibility exists that the public system will produce critical work. Milton Friedman has called for subjecting public broadcasting to "market discipline."[14] Soon after the Republican takeover of Congress in the 1994 elections, Speaker Newt Gingrich announced his plan to "zero out" public broadcasting due to its alleged liberal bias. He abandoned the plan when Republicans were flooded with public opposition, much of it from well-to-do people who vote and make campaign contributions.[15]

Accordingly, NPR and PBS at a national level tend to provide a bland variant of mainstream and conventional journalism, comparable to what's on the commercial networks, especially on highly sensitive matters such as the economy and the U.S. role in the world. Public broadcasting is so obsessed with conservative criticism, even more than commercial news media journalists are, that it bends over backwards to appease the Right and appear "balanced." When the conservative pundit Bill O'Reilly stormed off Terry Gross's NPR radio interview program in 2003 because he was upset with the tenor of her questions—by all accounts much milder than how O'Reilly routinely badgers his guests—the response by the NPR ombudsman sent a chilling message to all public broadcasters. "Listeners were not well served by this interview," he said. "Unfortunately, the interview only served to confirm the belief, held by some, in NPR's liberal bias."[16] The message is loud and clear: hands off the Right.

A traditional concern surrounding public broadcasting was that it would become a propaganda agency for the reigning political party and therefore would be insufficiently independent as a democratic force. In nations with poorly designed systems or too much corruption, such as France, this anxiety has had legitimacy. By 2003 irony abounded when U.S. commercial television companies stridently supported the war in Iraq, while some of the most unflattering and critical journalism of pro-war allies Britain and Australia came from their public broadcasters. If sufficiently insulated, public broadcasting can indeed be a critical force. In the United States, thanks to structural constraints, its capacity for being an independent and critical force is greatly compromised.

Entertainment and cultural fare has had a slightly different experience. U.S. public broadcasters were consigned to do programming for which there was little audience, so members of Congress concluded that an underutilized service (with little popular support) did not need a lavish budget. Public broadcasters rarely dared to schedule prime-time entertainment

programs with mass appeal. Such shows would have helped develop the broad audiences and public support that European public broadcasters enjoyed, but U.S. public broadcasters understood that such an approach was political suicide; the muscular commercial broadcasting lobby would have complained to Congress that the government was subsidizing unfair competition, and thus interfering with the free market. Public broadcasters quickly realized they could count on the federal government for only a fraction of their budgets if they were to produce anything at all. They turned almost entirely away from their original commitment to experimental programming and to marginalized and poor audiences, and instead began cultivating an upper middle class sliver with business and high-culture programming. This tactic provided a solid base for periodic "pledge drives" as well as a political constituency that commanded respect in Washington. It also made public broadcasting increasingly attractive to advertisers—or "underwriters," as they were euphemistically termed.

The prospect of government subsidy continues to decline because as public broadcasting grows more and more commercial within the limits allowed to it, its justification for a subsidy decreases. Similarly, management of public stations increasingly adopts the mores and obsession with ratings and target demographics of commercial broadcasting, because the stations must rely on delivering a wealthy audience to stay afloat.[17] In this context public broadcasters have come to brag about their affluent audience, rather than bemoan their lack of a working-class following.[18] Public broadcasting becomes increasingly dependent upon corporate money, and that requires it to compete with commercial media for those funds, with all that that suggests.[19] By 2003 PBS formally authorized the airing of 30-second advertising spots.[20] As all of this happens, the government sees less and less justification for public subsidy. Between the government and the market, U.S. public broadcasting experiences the worst of both worlds.

This, too, has become the dilemma faced by more established public broadcasters outside the United States. As their media systems become increasingly regarded as commercial undertakings rather than public service institutions, these public broadcasters face difficulty in winning their subsidies and considerable pressure to turn to commercial revenues, thereby undermining their case for receiving public subsidies. What was once the U.S. exception is becoming the global rule. As the director-general of the BBC put it, "The accusation is that the BBC is too successful, too powerful and too competitive. This is one of the few jobs where you get crap for losing and crap for doing well."[21]

In fairness to U.S public broadcasters, many are principled and dedicated public servants who have done wonders with often inadequate resources. Local PBS and, especially, NPR stations have often been jewels in their local media environments. The children's programming on PBS, at least until commercialism intruded, offered a welcome respite to commercial fare.[22] But the overriding pressures have been too great; libraries and bookstores are filled with tomes by former public broadcasters and scholars chronicling the failure of the institution.[23] Although public broadcasting still has life in it because of its public and corporate support and because it has built its own "brand name," its long-term trajectory is toward oblivion. In the short term, the challenge simply to maintain the status quo is daunting.[24] Public radio has fared better than public television, if only because the costs of production are dramatically lower, and commercial radio has gone into a hyper-commercial free fall since 1996, making NPR's programming more attractive. A private bequest to NPR of $200 million in 2003 will help put NPR on a solid footing for the foreseeable future, but there is little reason to think it will move beyond being a relatively marginal medium in the lives of most Americans, or that it move toward aggressive, independent journalism.[25]

INVIGORATING PUBLIC MEDIA

So where does this leave U.S. public broadcasting? What needs to be done to turn it into a powerful force in our society? We first must recognize that we need a strong nonprofit and noncommercial media sector. Such a sector is necessary for high-quality children's programming, experimental entertainment, and high-quality material frowned upon by the market. Most important, a nonprofit media sector is mandatory for providing some, perhaps much, of the journalism and public affairs material

befitting a democracy. If such a sector is well funded and well managed, it can have repercussions across the entire media system, across the entire social culture, and across the entire political culture. As economists would put it, public broadcasting can have a "multiplier" effect. Recent developments in our media culture do not undermine the need for public broadcasting; they make it a more necessary institution than ever before.

Although the United States desperately needs a strong nonprofit and noncommercial media sector, today's public broadcasting is nowhere near satisfactory. Because it is severely limited by the manner in which it has developed, it is at best a marginal and semi-commercial enterprise. The United States could easily generate a public broadcasting network that would dwarf what currently exists, but it will require an entirely new strategic approach and a much more sweeping vision of its mission. A crucial problem for U.S. public broadcasting, and for the nonprofit media sector in general, is that it has been relegated to the margins. The commercial system "gives the people what they want," while the nonprofit sector gives them what they need and they accept it only grudgingly. Public broadcasting needs to reject its marginal status and the structural constraints under which it has been forced to live; until then, it will be impossible to mobilize the popular support necessary to generate the resources the system needs to be truly effective.

This means rethinking the organizational structure of public broadcasting. It means abolishing commercialism. It means infusing public broadcasting with a localism that is largely absent in commercial broadcasting. And, more than anything, it means critiquing the limitations of the corporate media system—not merely its worst transgressions but also its inner logic. Advocates need to make a strong case that public broadcasting, rather than being a paternalistic enterprise that ignores popular wishes, is actually capable of generating a democratic relationship with the audience that is not mediated by advertisers or determined by the need for profit maximization. We need to develop concrete proposals for a revamped public system. Professor William Hoynes has drafted a new model for public broadcasting that directly addresses the matter of funding.[26] The point is not to tout Hoynes's proposal as the final word, but simply to make it clear that there are alternatives to the status quo. If there is a political will, there is a way that addresses all of these issues.

The movement for a supercharged public broadcasting may well have to come from without, because those within it may be too structurally bound to the *ancien régime*. Moreover, if people inside public broadcasting are too critical of the commercial media system, it would only enrage their enemies on Capitol Hill, making the budget fights in Washington that much more difficult. Hence, those within public broadcasting are prodded toward the easy road—to see the dreadful state of journalism and mainstream media as acceptable because it makes such a clear and overwhelming case for the need for PBS or NPR as an alternative. This is the public broadcasting of fools. It makes a virtue of a (let us hope short-term) necessity. The historical record and the international experience are clear: viable public broadcasting cannot survive if it is to remain an island of virtue in a sea of vulgarity and commercialism. Public broadcasting has been at its best in an environment where there is a healthy commercial sector that produces quality content. Conversely, commercial media are forced to better serve the public when there is a viable public system.

This new vision for public broadcasting will have to draw new communication technologies into its core. How ironic that opponents of public broadcasting use the emergence of new communication technologies as the basis for their argument against its necessity. There is nothing inherently commercial about digital communication. It can be deployed to further public service media just as much as commercial media. Why cannot the emergence of new digital channels lead to a plethora of diverse noncommercial media, rather than, or in addition to, an expansion in commercial channels? It all comes down to policy, to politics.

Indeed, in view of the new technologies, the very term public service *broadcasting* may be misleading; it is truly public service *media*. We need to conceive of public media as including a variety of institutions—for example, community and low-power radio and television stations, public access channels, and Independent Media Centers, along with a strengthened public broadcasting sector. When NPR sided with the commercial broadcasters in 2000 and worked against the creation of one thousand new noncommercial low-power FM radio stations, it was one of the darkest moments for democracy in recent U.S. media history. Let us hope it is never repeated. Public broadcasting must see itself in a cooperative, not a competitive, relationship with other nonprofit and noncommercial media. We need a broad and diverse nonprofit, noncommercial media sector. Some participants could receive direct state support, and some might receive none, but effective means of generating effective subsidies must become a central component of democratic media policy making.

What this all points to is that the traditional inside-the-Beltway lobbying for public broadcasting is a dead-end street or, at best, a dimly lit cul-de-sac. Polls show widespread support for public broadcasting, but this support must be nurtured and invigorated. To do so, the campaign for public broadcasting has to strike out boldly in a new direction at the grassroots level. It needs to generate a whole new tier of support from sectors of the population that have felt no connection to public broadcasting. A grassroots campaign for public broadcasting must see itself as an integral part of a broader movement for democratic media and media policy making. Indeed, only as part of a broader media reform movement does the campaign for renewed and recharged public broadcasting stand much chance of success. As Saul Alinsky famously noted, to defeat organized money, one needs organized people—and in the realm of media, corporate money is highly organized.

This point applies to all the various media policy issues that currently galvanize popular interest: media ownership limits, copyright, open Internet access, hyper-commercialism, low-power radio, vulgar media content, spectrum giveaways, global trade agreements weakening public interests, inadequate journalism, and the commercialization of education, to mention but a few. Only when those citizens and organizations come together to find common ground to work on each other's battles, and to reach out to untapped sectors of the citizenry, will they have much hope for success. The question to be answered is whether or not this will happen.

NOTES

1. See Laura R. Linder, *Public Access Television: America's Electronic Soapbox* (Westport, Conn.: Praeger, 1999).

2. Matthew Lasar, *Pacifica Radio: The Rise of an Alternative Network* (Philadelphia: Temple University Press, 1999).

3. Stephen Frantzich and John Sullivan, *The C-SPAN Revolution* (Norman, Okla.: University of Oklahoma Press, 1996).

4. Aaron Barnhart, "In Public TV We Trust," *Electronic Media,* 22 July 2002, p. 10.

5. See Jean Seaton, "Public Broadcasting: Imperfect but Essential," openDemocracy.net, 2001, p. 3.

6. See Kristin Hohenadel, "Where Television Sponsors the Film Industry," *New York Times,* 11 June 2000.

7. See Carnegie Commission on Public Television, *Public Television: A Program for Action* (New York: Harper & Row, 1967).

8. Roger Smith, "Public Broadcasting as State Television," www.tompaine.com, 11 March 2003.

9. Carnegie Commission, *Public Television,* p. 8.

10. Barnhart, "In Public TV We Trust," p. 10.

11. Linder, *Public Access Television,* p. 2.

12. "Democratic Platform 1968" in Donald Bruce Johnson., compiler, *National Party Platforms, Volume 2 1960–1976* (Chicago: University of Illinois Press), pp. 718–743.

13. Jerry Landay, "Failing the Perception Test," *Current,* June 2001; David Hatch, "PBS Decision Irks Tauzin," *Electronic Media,* 15 May 2000, p. 4.

14. Quotes from Lawrence Jarvik, *PBS: Behind the Screen* (Rocklin, Calif.: Forum, 1997), back cover.

15. Tom McCourt, *Conflicting Communication Interests in America: The Case of National Public Radio* (Westport, Conn.: Praeger, 1999), pp. 2–3.

16. John Nichols, "Here's One Cut NPR Can Afford to Make," *Capital Times* (Madison, Wis.), 23 October 2003.

17. The press teems with stories on this matter. See, for example, Sean Mitchell, "Public Radio, Under the Influence," *Los Angeles Times,* 27 May 2001; Sally Beatty, "Critics Claim PBS Has Gotten Too Close to Its Underwriters," *Wall Street Journal Online,* 11 July 2002; Pamela McClintock, "Blurbs Blur Line between PBS, Nets," *Variety,* 15–21 July 2002, p. 18; Paula Bernstein, "Not Your Parents' PBS," *Variety,* 16–22 April 2001, p. 13; Samuel G. Freedman, "Public Radio's Private Guru," *New York Times,* 11 November 2001; "Minnesota Grabs the Marketplace," *Brill's Content,* July/August 2002, pp. 106–107.

18. "Myths and Realities," advertising sales pamphlet of the Public Broadcasting Cooperative of Illinois, 2002. Available online at www.pbcionline.org/myths.htm.

19. Elizabeth Jensen, "Corporate Funding Squeezing Public Television," *Los Angeles Times,* 5 February 2003; available online at www.theledger.com.

20. Elizabeth Jensen, "PBS Votes to Accept 30-Second Ad Spots," *Los Angeles Times.* 4 February 2003.

21. Steve Clarke, "Ball Bawls Out Fat Cat BBC," *Variety,* 1–7 September 2003, p. 22.

22. Jennifer Gilbert, "CTW Hunts Eyes, Ads with Sesame Street," *Advertising Age,* 3 January 2000, p. 24; Kimberley Pohlman, "The Commercialization of Children's Television: PBS's Ads Sell Toys, Drugs, and Junk Food to your Kids," *Extra!,* May/June 2000, pp. 13–14.

23. For a few recent titles, and this is just a small sample, see William Hoynes, *Public Television for Sale: Media, the Market, and the Public Sphere* (Boulder, Colo.: Westview Press, 1994); Roger P. Smith, *The Other Face of Public TV: Censoring the American Dream* (New York: Algora, 2002); Tom McCourt, *Conflicting Communication Interests in America* (Westport, Conn.: Praeger, 1999); B. J. Bullert, *Public Television: Politics and the Battle Over Documentary Film* (New Brunswick, N.J.: Rutgers University Press, 1997); James Day, *The Vanishing Vision: The Inside Story of Public Television* (Berkeley: University of California Press, 1995).

24. Joseph Weber, "Public TV's Identity Crisis," *Business Week,* 30 September 2003, pp. 65–66;

John Motavalli, "PBS Facing Crisis," *Television Week,* 20 October 2003, pp. 1, 24.

25. Tom Lowry, Joseph Weber, and Catherine Yang, "Can NPR Bear the Burden of Wealth?" *Business Week,* 15 December 2003, p. 77.

26. William Hoynes, "Independent Public Broadcasting for the 21st Century," unpublished paper, November 1998. A summary of the Hoynes proposal is at: www.cipbonline.org/trustmain.htm.

Public Broadcasting, the Information Society, and the Internet

A Paradigm Shift?

Amit M. Schejter

The information society is dawning upon all industrialized nations. It carries with it great promise, as well as an unknown social challenge. It could make known social institutions obsolete, while maintaining old social orders. In economic terms, it signifies a move away from an industrial economy to a services-oriented economy (Bell 1973) where information has become a key commodity. In technological terms it is usually associated with the convergence of traditional technologies and the introduction of new ones such as the Internet and digital broadcasting. This chapter takes a new look at public broadcasting and describes what its practitioners have done so far on the Internet. Public broadcasters' appearances on the Internet are then measured against their operational roles, as defined and understood with respect to the preinformation society technologies, radio and television.

The role that public broadcasting has assumed in the early stages of the information society is linked to the importance of information in the new economy and new social structure that the information society represents. For many, the information society is not much more than a parade of new technologies (Schement and Curtis 1995, 103), while for many others it expresses the idea of a novel phase in the development of advanced societies (Lyon 1988, 142). The concept of public broadcasting, an institution

owned by the public, for which information is the main product, seems to require a bit of redefinition in this time of social change.

This chapter describes the four major traditional models of public broadcasting and their theoretical roots. The guidelines that surrounded the creation of public broadcasting, as this chapter demonstrates, were designed by policy-makers in all four models, mostly in the form of what Tatalovich and Daynes have dubbed "social regulatory policies" (1988, 1998). These are policies designed for the preservation of social values, usually the ones shared by ruling elites. The information society is, for some, a phenomenon that carries the potential for democratization; still, some of the policies that would be required to implement this form of democracy are top-down in nature (Brants, Huizenga, and van Meerten 1996). The attempt to conflate the information society's technological wonders with the notion of a new concept of democracy has already been criticized as an effort by an existing elite to secure its own means of democratic communication (Calabrese and Borchert 1996).

PUBLIC BROADCASTING: THE HISTORY OF AN INTERVENTIONIST POLICY

Public broadcasting has developed differently in different parts of the world. Still, today, more than ever before, public media institutions find themselves facing similar challenges. For some, this is due to the emergence of advanced forms of information economies and information technologies; for others, it is due to the potential for such development. In order to identify the crisis of public broadcasting in the context of the information society, the origins and design of existing policy need to be briefly identified. Again, four different models were chosen for this study: the United States, in which public broadcasting emerged as an alternative to a commercially dominated market, thus offering a niche service; Western Europe, where public service monopolies and duopolies existed prior to the introduction of commercial television, and whose fare was based on a broad mandate; the developing world, in which public broadcasting served national needs and goals dictated by government, rather than broad public goals; and the post-Communist arena, in which the party-oriented broadcaster underwent adjustments to a market-based public interest regime. Though the origins and designs of these systems are different, Williams (1974, 1992, 77) notes that the similarities in program fare between public television stations in different countries are larger than those between commercial and public broadcasters in any given country. It is not surprising, then, that the crises experienced by broadcasters of all four types have similarities. It is even less surprising that most of these broadcasters have done little to change, even when new media have provided them with an opportunity to do so.

The tensions and challenges public broadcasters face are similar because even though national systems have emerged differently, they have all emerged within the context of social regulatory policies. They have all reached the same crossroads, and their decisions are based on the same dilemmas: Should public broadcasting aspire to be an alternative to commercial broadcasting or a generalist voice on its own? Should public broadcasting stress its public service side or its role in participatory democracy? And most important, is there room for a public broadcaster in the world of hundreds of available channels?

United States: Public Broadcasting As Niche

Three elements have characterized American public broadcasting from the start: it was to provide some undefined measure of "quality," to serve as a provider of content that the market cannot provide, and to be differentiated from "instructional" media (Carnegie Commission 1967). A later attempt to redefine public broadcasting identified the "functional characteristics and goals of American public broadcasting" as noncommercial, independent, public, and consistently excellent (Carnegie Commission 1979, 25). Oulette (1999) argues that the Public Broadcasting Service (PBS) has put forward a model of "enlightened democracy" in its public affairs coverage that complements commercial television's hegemonic orientation with a different, "governmental" logic. Engelman (1996) and Hoynes (1994) lament American public broadcasting's overcorporatization, at least in terms of funding. The U.S. Supreme Court in *Arkansas Educational Television Commission v. Forbes* (523 U.S. 666, 1997) found that political debates on public television are not to be considered a "public forum." This decision reflects the marginal role public broadcasting plays in American political discourse.

Western Europe: Public Service Broadcasting

Whether a unified Western European model of public broadcasting exists is debatable (Humphreys 1996, 116), though Blumler (1992) has created a generalized model based on the different national experiences of Western European nations. His model includes six elements: a comprehensive coverage remit; a generalized, "broadly worded" mandate; pluralism; a cultural mission; a central place in politics, both in terms of highly politicized broadcasting organizations and as reporters of the political process; and noncommercialism. According to Barendt, the principal features of public service broadcasting in Europe are general geographic availability; concern for national identity and culture; independence from both state and commercial interests; impartiality; range and variety; and substantial financing by a charge on users (1995, 52).

The European Broadcasting Union (EBU), an organization whose membership is limited to public service broadcasters, requires members to fulfill four conditions: they are under obligation to cover the entire national population, they are under obligation to provide varied and balanced programming, they must actually produce a substantial proportion of the programs they broadcast, and they cannot be linked to a sports rights agency that is in competition with the EBU (EBU 1998). The model that arises in Europe, therefore, is significantly different than the American model, most notably in its broad mandate for programming, its focus on national character, and its general scheme of funding.

The Developing Model: Public Television as National Television

The developing nations can be described as those that remained mostly under colonial control until World War II. Many of their borders were drawn along colonial agreement lines rather than along ethnic, cultural, or geographic lines. The concept of self-rule and "Western-style" democracy was introduced (or enforced) by the colonial powers on the eve of their withdrawal, while technology, especially fully functional broadcasting technology, appeared late relative to the West.

Three common goals, or premises, were behind the introduction of broadcasting in the developing countries (or "third world") according to Katz and Wedell (1977): a contribution to national integration, relative to the new formation of nation-states (171); a role in the modernization and socioeconomic development of the state (181); and a balance between cultural continuity and change (191). The first and third goals are definitely at odds with each other. Further, the process for creating broadcasting systems was based on a foreign model. The adoption of foreign systems resulted from political decisions, although Katz and Wedell attribute this process mainly to technological development (67). Technology, or form, was followed by programming, or content.[1]

Frequently, developing nations ended up with media that served the needs of the rulers rather than the principles of free speech and democracy—that is, to the extent that we can identify a universal desire on behalf of governments to control access to, and the content of, state television's news and current affairs programs (French and Richards 1996, 53).

Post-Communist Public Broadcasting: A Model in Process

Broadcasting in the post-Communist world cannot remain unaccounted for in any comparative international study, especially because of its newly found prominence in the "cyber" world. First of all, the Eastern bloc was not part of the "developing world" as conceptualized in the West. Eastern bloc media were dubbed "Soviet-Communist" and described as totalitarian in the seminal book titled *Four Theories of the Press* (Siebert, Peterson, and Schramm 1956), but that description has long been seen as flawed due to its ideological bias (Nordenstreng 1998). Whatever this model stood for in the past, it bears no resemblance to the media models that emerged following the collapse of Communist rule in much of the Eastern bloc and the rise of a local version of democracy and capitalism.

These changes resulted in media infrastructures that are diverse. Most observers agree that public broadcasting systems in the Eastern bloc countries have remained closely tied to their respective political structures, as adjustments to "democratic" reform have been difficult (Sparks 1997). Developing and post-Communist broadcasters thus resemble each other in their lengthy unichannel phase, their strong organizational ties to government, and their ties to the national—some would say "nationalist"—goals of government-related programming.

DISCUSSION

Three stages characterize the development of broadcasting in the United States (Noam 1996), and these stages can be identified in Western Europe, the post-Communist countries, and many developing nations as well: the limited channel stage, the multichannel stage, and the "cyber" stage. The transition from the first to the second stage was characterized by the fact that each broadcasting system tried to survive its crisis of change by offering more of the services it always had while centering its efforts in the meantime on the procurement of more funding.

The critique of public broadcasting in the United States has been that public broadcasters have not yet offered a true alternative to the fare that Americans have come to expect from commercial networks.

The role of "alternative programmer" was eventually taken by new commercial services that audiences have learned to use since the adoption of the Public Broadcasting Act (Shooshan and Arnheim 1988, 10). Some of these commercial ventures have started providing types of programming previously associated with public television. In other words, the "niche" mentality of public broadcasting has found a competitor in other services that believe these niches have commercial potential as well. On the other hand, some of the specialized programs for which public broadcasting seemed the right place raised public opposition, since they seemed to undermine conservative concepts of the ideal American society. Public broadcasting's answer has been to seek new sources of income, independent of precarious government funds, as a means of continuing to supply the same kind of service it has always provided for the American people. According to Hoynes (1994), the resulting increase in support from businesses and listeners has, in effect, "privatized" public broadcasting. In the process, the essential character of noncommercial broadcasting in America—including its niche-marketing mentality—remained unchanged.

European broadcasters, on the other hand, have made efforts to stay general in their missions and to receive protection for both their financial bases and programming philosophies. Thus, political efforts have been made to secure the existence of public broadcasters. These efforts have led to some success, both on the national and pan-European levels, the high point being a protocol to the 1977 European Union Treaty that considers the system of public broadcasting in member states to be "directly related to the democratic, social and cultural needs of each society and to the need to preserve media pluralism." As a result, the Council of the European Union decided in January 1999 that "public service broadcasting must be able to continue to provide a wide range of programming ... [and to] seek to reach wide audiences" (*Official Journal* 1999/C 30/01, 1). Following the collapse of the Iron Curtain in the late 1980s, public broadcasters in the former Eastern bloc joined hands with their Western bloc counterparts and dissolved their union into the European Broadcasting Union.

It is not hard to understand why some public broadcasters had a hard time changing their ways, so long as their efforts centered on traditional radio and TV transmissions. As Ang (1991) has noted, the decision-making processes in public service organizations are slow, and the capability to change is limited.

NOTES

1. For Katz and Wedell, the content of broadcasting was merely a natural follow-up to the introduction of technology, but for other scholars, this content relationship has become the central matter of the developmental theory. Schiller (1969) calls it media imperialism and sees in its part of the process of American cultural imperialism over the third world. This process, he contends, is based on the economic inequality between the first and third worlds and the unidirectional flow of television content from the former to the latter. Lee (1979) describes two competing schools of thought on media imperialism: the Marxist approach, which sees it as a direct and unfavorable consequence of global economic patterns of imperialism; and the non-Marxist approach, which analyzes the flow of communication in terms of diffusion and sees it as part of a more natural acceptance of media products by open societies.

REFERENCES

1. Ang, I. 1991. *Desperately Seeking the Audience.* London: Routledge.

2. *Arkansas Educational Television Commission v. Forbes,* 523 U.S. 666 (1997).

3. Barendt, E. 1995. *Broadcasting Law: A Comparative Analysis.* Oxford: Clarendon Press.

4. Bell, D. 1973. *The Coming of the Post-industrial Society.* New York: Basic Books.

5. Blumler, J., and T. Nossiter. 1991. "*Broadcasting Finance in Transition: A Comparative Handbook,* ed. J. Blumler and T. Nossiter. New York: Oxford University Press, 405–426.

6. Brants, K., M. Huizenga, and R. van Meerten. 1996. "New Canals of Amsterdamn: An Exercise in Local Electronic Democracy." *Media, Culture and Society* 18, no. 2: 233–248.

7. Calabrese, A., and M. Borchert. 1996. "Prospects for Electronic Democracy in the United States: Rethinking Communication and Social Policy." *Media, Culture and Society* 18, no. 2: 249–268.

8. Carnegie Commission of Educational Television. 1967. *Public Television: A Program for Action.* New York: Harper and Row.

9. Carnegie Commission on the Future of Public Broadcasting. 1979. *A Public Trust.* New York: Bantam Books.

10. Engelman, R. 1996. *Public Radio and Television in America: A Political History.* Thousand Oaks, CA: Sage.

11. European Broadcasting Union. 1998. *Statutes.* Geneva: European Broadcasting Union.

12. French, D., and M. Richards, eds. 1996. *Contemporary Television: Eastern Perspectives.* London: Sage.

13. Hoynes, W. 1994. *Public Television for Sale: Media, the Market and the Public Sphere.* Boulder, CO: Westview Press.

14. Humphreys, P. 1996. *Mass Media and Media Policy in Western Europe.* Manchester, UK: Manchester University Press.

15. Katz, E., and G. Wedell. 1977. *Broadcasting in the Third World: Promise and Performance.* London: Macmillan Press.

16. Lee, C. 1979. *Media Imperialism Reconsidered: The Homogenizing of Television Culture.* Beverly Hills: Sage.

17. Lyon, D. 1998. The Information Society. Oxford: Polity Press

18. Noam, E. 1996. "Media Concentration in the United States: Industry Trends and Regulatory Responsese." http://www.vii.org/papers/medconc.htm.

19. Nordenstreng, K. 1998. "Beyond the Four Theories of the Press." In *Media and Politics in Transition,* ed. J. Servaes and R. Lie. Leuvan, Belgium: Acco, 97–109.

20. *Official Journal of the European Communities.* 1999. Resolution of the Council and of the Representatives of the Governments of the Member States, Meeting Within the Council of 25 January 1999 concerning public service broadcasting (1999/C 30/01). *Official Journal* Web site http://europea.eu.int/eur-lex/pri/en/oj/dat/1999/c_030/c_03019990205en00010001.pdf (August 15, 2002).

21. Ouellete, L. 1999. "TV Viewing as Good Citizenship? Political Rationality, Enlightened Democracy and PBS." *Cultural Studies* 13, no. 1: 62–90.

22. Schement, J., and T. Curtis. 1995. Tendencies and Tensions of the Information Age: Production and Distribution of Information in the United States. New Brunswick, NJ: Transaction.

23. Schiller, H. 1969. *Mass Communication and American Empire.* New York: Augustus M. Kelly.

24. Shooshan, H., and L. Arnheim. 1988. *Public Broadcasting.* Washington, DC: Benton Foundation.

25. Siebert, F., T. Peterson, and W. Schramm. 1956. *Four Theories of the Press.* Urbana: University of Illinois Press.

26. Sparks, C. 1997. "Post-Communist Media in Transition." In *International Media Research: A Critical Survey,* ed. J. Corner, P. Schlesinger, and R. Silverstone. London: Routledge, 96–122.

27. Tatalovic, R., and B. Daynes. 1988. "Introduction: What is Social Regulatory Policy?" In *Social Regulatory Policy: Moral Controversies in American Politics,* ed. R. Tatalovich and B. Daynes. Boulder, CO: Westview Press 1–4.

28. ———. 1998. *Moral Controversies in American Politics.* Armonk, NY: M.E. Sharpe.

29. Williams, R. 1974, 1992. *Television: Technology and Cultural Form.* Hanover, NH: University Press of New England.

The Fairness Doctrine

A Solution in Search of a Problem

Adrian Cronauer

I. A HISTORICAL PERSPECTIVE OF THE FAIRNESS DOCTRINE

The development of the Fairness Doctrine is intertwined with the history of American broadcasting. Early commercial uses of radio centered on maritime uses, "mainly for ship-to-shore and ship-to-ship communication."[1] An obstacle quickly developed when transmissions from one source interfered with another. Trying to outshout each other, early broadcasters responded to problems of interference by increasing the power of their transmitters which, of course, accomplished little except to increase the electronic cacophony. The first attempt by the federal government to deal with the confused clamor of competing voices on the airwaves was the Radio Act of 1912, which put the task of bringing order out of the electronic chaos in the hands of the Secretary of Commerce.[2] Secretary of Commerce Herbert Hoover tried to place conditions on licenses, but "his power to regulate radio stations in this way was destroyed by court decisions interpreting the 1912 Act."[3]

The tug of war between the government and the broadcasters for control of the airwaves continued in 1925, when the Senate responded to the general concern of whether broadcasters might exert some sort of squatters' rights over the frequencies. The Senate passed a resolution declaring the electromagnetic spectrum to be "the inalienable possession of the people of the United States."[4] A year later, Congress passed a joint resolution which required licensees to waive any right to the wavelength they used.[5] Even so, the system quickly developed so as to provide licensees with what amounted to de facto property rights. "Even before Congress passed the 1927 Act, most observers recognized that stations were being transferred from one owner to another at prices which implied the right to a license was being sold."[6]

Although few stations were on the air before 1920, by November 1922, 564 broadcasting stations were operating in the United States.[7] By 1927, the confusion of the airwaves had increased to the point where most parties involved agreed on the need for an impartial arbiter to assign frequencies, limit signal strengths, and set out geographical coverage areas.[8]

The chaos that developed as more and more enthusiastic pioneers entered the field of radio was indescribable. Amateurs crossed signals with professional broadcasters. Many of the professionals broadcast on the same wave length and either came to a gentleman's agreement to divide the hours of broadcasting or blithely set about cutting one another's throats by broadcasting simultaneously. Listeners thus experienced the annoyance of trying to hear one program against the raucous background of another. Ship-to-shore communication in Morse code added its pulsing dots and dashes to the silly symphony of sound.

...

... Private enterprise, over seven long years, failed to set its own house in order. Cutthroat competition at once retarded radio's orderly development and subjected listeners to intolerable strain and inconvenience.[9]

But the Radio Act of 1927 went far beyond needed traffic-cop functions.[10] It supplanted the regulatory functions of the Secretary of Commerce with its new creation, the Federal Radio Commission—forerunner of the FCC. Although in one breath the statute explicitly forbade program censorship,[11] it also gave the new Commission authority to regulate the programming of the stations it licensed.[12] The 1927 Act included a requirement that if a legally qualified candidate for public office was allowed to use a licensee's facilities, all other candidates must be allowed equal access.[13]

The federal government thereafter controlled the airwaves' content, and it was not long before the Commission exercised its newly-found power by denying a license renewal to an Iowa station owner.[14] The owner used his station to launch attacks on persons and institutions he disliked.[15] The FCC commented enigmatically, "Though we may not censor, it is our duty to see that broadcast licenses do not afford mere personal organs, and also to see that a standard of refinement fitting our day and generation is maintained."[16]

In 1940, Mayflower Broadcasting unsuccessfully attempted to apply for the license of a Boston station, WAAB.[17] While denying Mayflower the license and renewing the license in favor of the incumbent, the Commission criticized the incumbent licensee for editorializing about controversial public subjects and favoring certain political candidates.[18] The station's license was renewed only after it showed it was complying with a policy to stop editorializing.[19] The result was all too predictable: through the 1930s and early 1940s, broadcasters totally abandoned the practice of editorializing and dropped much programming that might have been thought controversial.[20]

Another important decision in the development of the Fairness Doctrine was *NBC v. United States*.[21] Writing for the Supreme Court, Justice Frankfurter spoke of the situation prior to 1927 as "confusion and chaos" which

was attributable to certain basic facts about radio as a means of communications—its facilities are limited; they are not available to all who may wish to *use* them; the radio spectrum simply is not large enough to accommodate everybody. There is a fixed natural limitation upon the *number of stations* that can operate without interfering with one another.[22]

Two FCC reports were important in early clarification of the Fairness Doctrine because they indicated the government's intent to strictly control content. In 1946, the Commission published the *Public Service Responsibility of Broadcast Licensees*, which warned that the Commission would thereafter pay closer attention to broadcasters' programming.[23] Moreover, in 1948, the Commission reexamined the *Mayflower* decision and issued another report, this time encouraging editorials, but requiring "overall fairness."[24]

In 1959, Congress amended Section 315 of the Communications Act of 1934 and included the phrase: "Nothing in the foregoing sentence shall be construed as relieving broadcasters ... from the obligation imposed upon them under this Act to operate in the public interest and to afford reasonable opportunity for the discussion of conflicting views on issues of public importance."[25] The Commission chose to construe the added phrase as codification of the Fairness Doctrine by Congress,[26] although the Court of Appeals for the District of Columbia later rejected that decision.[27]

In 1967, the FCC created more specific rules insuring a right of reply to both *ad hominem* attacks on an identified person or group and to any position taken by a station for or against legally qualified candidates for any political office.[28]

In 1969, the Supreme Court upheld the constitutionality of the Fairness Doctrine in the *Red Lion* decision.[29] The Court justified this result by noting that more individuals would like to broadcast their views than there are available frequencies, reaffirming the Court's reasoning in *NBC v. United States*.[30]

In response to this "scarcity" argument, broadcasters stressed that the requirements of the Fairness Doctrine had a subtle but powerful "chilling effect,"[31] leading many of them to abandon their coverage of controversial issues in favor of "safe" issues.[32] *Red Lion* noted the broadcasters' arguments, but the Court found the possibility of a chilling effect to be remote.[33] Nevertheless, the door was left open for further consideration: "[I]f experience with the administration of those doctrines, indicates that they have the net effect of reducing rather than enhancing the volume and quality of coverage, there will be time enough to reconsider the constitutional implications."[34]

II. THE DOWNFALL OF THE FAIRNESS DOCTRINE

In 1984, the Supreme Court invited an action which would give it a chance to reverse *Red Lion*. In *FCC v. League of Women Voters of California*, the Court said if the Commission were to show the "fairness doctrine [has] 'the net effect of reducing rather than enhancing' speech," the Court would be forced to reconsider the doctrine's constitutional basis.[35] However, no test case appeared.

In August 1985, the FCC took the bait. The Commission issued a report concluding the doctrine no longer serves the public interest and, instead, chills First Amendment speech.[36] The Commission predicted that without the chilling effect of the Fairness Doctrine, it was reasonable to expect an increase in the coverage of controversial issues of public importance.[37] In 1987, the FCC formally renounced the Fairness Doctrine.[38] Events since then have confirmed the FCC's prediction of more, rather than less, coverage of controversial issues.[39] The amount of opinion-oriented programming "exploded" over the ensuing six years and the number of radio talk shows jumped from 400 to more than 900.[40] Many observers ascribe this growth directly to the absence of the inhibiting effect of the Fairness Doctrine.

Nonetheless, powerful congressional forces have dedicated themselves to reinstating the Fairness Doctrine and have tried to enact it into law.[41] Opposition by both Presidents Reagan and Bush kept it from happening during their terms.[42] With the election of President Clinton, though, such Capitol heavyweights as Ed Markey, Chairman of the House Telecommunications Subcommittee,[43] and John Dingell, Chairman of the House Energy and Commerce Committee,[44] viewed the new Democratic administration as unlikely to veto their attempts to bring the doctrine back.[45]

At first, little resistance was seen to a bill restoring the Fairness Doctrine. Some support for such a bill grew over the summer of 1993.[46] By the winter of 1993, however, talk show hosts, like Rush Limbaugh had generated nationwide publicity producing a large number of letters from listeners, opposing the doctrine at a two-to-one margin.[47] As a result, efforts to write it into law were abandoned.[48] Limbaugh and other talk show hosts assert that legislation to reinstate the Fairness Doctrine is an effort by liberal lawmakers to silence their conservative critics.

Still, considering the long history of the Fairness Doctrine and the determined attempts by some congressmen to resurrect it, it is reasonable to assume we have not seen the last of it.[49] Some speculate congressional pressure may prompt the FCC to reinstate the doctrine as a regulatory policy, while others suggest the current initiatives to rebuild our communications infrastructure may provide an opportunity for Fairness Doctrine backers to do surreptitiously what they have so far been unable to do openly.[50]

Notes

1. R.H. Coase, *The Federal Communications Commission*, 2 J.L. & ECON. 1, 7 (1959).
2. Act of Aug. 13, 1912, ch. 287, 37 Stat. 302, *repealed by* Radio Act of 1927, ch. 169, 44 Stat. 1162; *see also* R.H. Coase, *The Federal Communications Commission*, 2 J.L. & ECON. 1, 7 (1959)., at 2, 4.
3. R.H. Coase, *The Federal Communications Commission*, 2 J.L. & ECON. 1, 7 (1959)., at 4.
4. *Id.* at 6.
5. *Id.* at 5, 31–32.
6. *Id.* at 23.
7. *Id.* at 4.

8. Nicholas Johnson, *Towers of Babel: The Chaos in Radio Spectrum Utilization and Allocation*, 34 LAW & CONTEMP. PROBS. 505, 505 (1969).

9. CHARLES A. SIEPMANN, RADIO, TELEVISION AND SOCIETY 5–6 (1950).

10. Radio Act of 1927, ch. 169, 44 Stat. 1162, *repealed by* Communications Act of 1934, ch. 652, § 602(a), 48 Stat. 1064.

11. Part of the 1927 Act read:

> Nothing in this Act shall be understood or construed to give the licensing authority the power of censorship over the radio communications or signals transmitted by any radio station, and no regulation or condition shall be promulgated or fixed by the licensing authority which shall interfere with the right of free speech by means of radio communications.

Id. at 1172-73; *see also* Mark S. Fowler & Daniel L. Brenner, *A Marketplace Approach to Broadcast Regulation*, 60 TEX. L. REV. 207, 217 (1982) ("The first amendment to the Constitution and section 326 of the Communications Act both forbid censorship of broadcasters.").

12. Radio Act of 1927, ch. 169, 44 Stat. 1162 (repealed 1934). In 1921, long before there had been any consensus about the government's right to control broadcasting or the manner in which they could do it, Herbert Hoover, without any statutory authority, began to issue station licenses. What is little known is that Hoover allotted only a single frequency to all commercial broadcasters: 833 kilocycles. All stations were forced to occupy the same channel. There was bedlam as stations tried to drown each other out. While everyone looked to the government to impartially control the chaos, the government exacerbated the problem and then pointed to the result as justification for further governmental control of broadcasting. By either omitting or burying this critical piece of information, many broadcast historians—including the respected but anti-corporate Erik Barnouw—lead the unwary reader to assume there were as many frequencies to choose from then as there are today. The natural but incorrect inference is that chaos would result even now without benign governmental intervention to assign spectrum space. L.A. POWE, AMERICAN BROADCASTING AND THE FIRST AMENDMENT 58 (1987).

13. Radio Act of 1927, ch. 169, 44 Stat. 1162, 1170 (repealed 1934).

14. R.H. Coase, *The Federal Communications Commission*, 2 J.L. & ECON. 1, 7 (1959)., at 9.

15. *Id.*

16. *Id.* (quoting Edward C. Caldwell, *Censorship of Radio Programs*, 1 J. RADIO L. 441,473(1931)).

17. *In re* Mayflower Brdcst. Corp., *Decision and Order*, 8 F.C.C. 333 (1940).

18. *Id.* at 339–41.

19. *Id.*

20. William F. Baxter, *Regulation & Diversity in Communications Media*, 64 AM. ECON. REV. 392, 394 (1974).

21. NBC v. United States, 319 U.S. 190 (1943).

22. *Id.* at 213 (emphasis added) (footnote omitted).

23. FCC, PUBLIC SERVICE RESPONSIBILITY OF BROADCAST LICENSEES 55 (1946). The report became known as the "Blue Book" for the color of its binding. The Blue Book combined governmental concerns over service to local communities with a curious hostility to the profit motive. It cautioned that, thereafter, the Commission was going to look more closely at stations' programs and would view more favorably those stations that avoided "advertising excesses" and carried sustaining programs, local live programs, and discussions of public issues. The FCC suggested sustaining programs be used for:

> (a) maintaining an overall program balance, (b) providing time for programs inappropriate for sponsorship, (c) providing time for programs serving particular minority tastes and interests, (d) providing time for non-profit organizations—religions, civic, agricultural, labor, educational, etc., and (e) providing time for experiment and for unfettered artistic self-expression.

Id.; *see also* R.H. Coase, *The Federal Communications Commission*, 2 J.L. & ECON. 1, 7 (1959)., at 1; Fowler & Brenner, Mark S. Fowler & Daniel L. Brenner, A Marketplace Approach to Broadcast

Regulation, 60 TEX. L. REV. 207, 217 (1982), at 215. These proposals were never actively enforced.

24. *In re* Editorializing by Brdcst. Licensees, *Report of the Commission*, 13 F.C.C. 1246, para. 7 (1949); *see also* William F. Baxter, *Regulation & Diversity in Communications Media*, 64 AM. ECON. REV. 392, 394 (1974), at 393–94; R.H. Coase, *The Federal Communications Commission*, 2 J.L. & ECON. 1, 7 (1959)., at 10.

25. 47 U.S.C. § 315(a) (1988).

26. *In re* The Handling of Pub. Issues Under the Fairness Doctrine and the Pub. Interest Stds. of the Comm. Act, *Fairness Report*, 48 F.C.C.2d 1, para. 28 (1974) [hereinafter *1974 Fairness Report*].

27. Telecommunications Research and Action Ctr. v. FCC, 801 F.2d 501, 517–18 (D.C. Cir.), *reh'g en banc denied*, 806 F.2d 1115 (D.C. Cir. 1986), *cert. denied*, 482 U.S. 919 (1987).

28. 47 C.F.R. § 73.123 (1968).

29. Red Lion Brdcst, Co. v. FCC, 395 U.S. 367, 401 (1969); *see* Les Brown, *THE NEW YORK TIMES ENCYCLOPEDIA OF TELEVISION* 139 (1977), at 359; FRED W. FRIENDLY, THE GOOD GUYS, THE BAD GUYS, AND THE FIRST AMENDMENT 61–77 (1976).

30. *Red Lion*, 395 U.S. at 388–90. The Supreme Court in *NBC* and *Red Lion* introduced a new principle into our First Amendment jurisprudence: When only a few interests control a major avenue of communication, those able to speak can be forced by government to share their access to that avenue.

31. James Quello, veteran FCC Commissioner and former acting chairman, has consistently opposed the idea of the Fairness Doctrine. "It doesn't belong in a nation that is dedicated to freedom of speech and of press." His opposition to the Fairness Doctrine comes, at least in part, from his early experience as a broadcast executive where he encountered concrete examples of the doctrine's chilling effect. Interview with James Quello, FCC Commissioner, in Washington, D.C. (May 5, 1994).

32. *Freedom of the Press: Hearings Before the Subcomm. on Const. Rts. of the Comm. on the Judiciary,* 92d Cong., 2d Sess. 561 (1972), at 560–61.

33. *Red Lion*, 395 U.S. at 393.

34. *Id.*

35. *League of Women Voters,* 468 U.S. 364, 378–79 n.12 (1984) (quoting *Red Lion*, 395 U.S. at 393).

36. *In re* Inquiry into Section 73.1910 of the Commission's Rules and Regs. Concerning the Gen. Fairness Doctrine Obligations of Brdcst. Licensees, *Report, 102 F.C.C.2d 143, para. 74 (1985)*, paras. 74–76.

37. *Id.* para. 130. The Commission determined that the net effect of the Fairness Doctrine was to reduce coverage of controversial issues of public importance. *Id.* para. 29.

38. *In re* Compliant of Syracuse Peace Council against TV Station WTVH Syracuse, N.Y., *Memorandum Opinion and Order,* 2 FCC Rcd. 5043, para. 82 (1987), para. 2.

39. Four years after the Commission ceased enforcing the Fairness Doctrine, the FCC made evidence public indicating that the marketplace was providing expanded choices of news and information and even more sources for such programming. *Broadcasters' Public Interest Obligations and S. 217, The Fairness in Broadcasting Act of 1991: Hearing Before the Subcomm. on Communications of the Senate Comm. on Commerce, Science, and Transportation,* 102d Cong., 1st Sess. 9–14 (1991) (statement of Alfred C. Sikes, Chairman, FCC).

40. Jim Cooper, *Talkers Brace for Fairness' Assault*, BROADCASTING & CABLE, Sept. 6, 1993, at 44, 44.

41. Some see overwhelming sentiment in Congress to bring back the Fairness Doctrine. As one communications lobbyist, Gigi B. Sohn, deputy director of the Media Access Project, put it, "What there isn't is the courage to do it. Basically they've been inundated by followers of conservative talk-show hosts who've been calling them up and telling them not to. And that's been enough." Rod Dreher, *Congress Cowers To Conservatives On Fairness Doctrine,* WASH. TIMES, July 3, 1994, at A4.

42. Congress attempted to indisputably codify the doctrine with the Fairness in Broadcasting Act of 1987. H.R. 1937, 100th Cong, 1st Sess. (1987);

S. 742, 100th Cong., 1st Sess. (1987). President Reagan vetoed it. 133 CONG. REC. S8438 (daily ed. June 23, 1987). President Bush's threat of a veto caused a similar attempt to codify the Fairness Doctrine to fail in 1989.

43. Chairman Markey told reporters that he is committed to "putting fairness back on the books." He added that although Congress is currently preoccupied with the issue of cable rates, it will eventually focus on the issue of restoring the Fairness Doctrine. Kim McAvoy, *Who's to Blame for Cable Rereg Mess?*, BROADCASTING & CABLE, Oct. 4, 1993, at 60, 60.

44. "Both Telecommunications Subcommittee Chairman Ed Markey (D-Mass.) and Energy and Commerce Committee Chairman John Dingell (D-Mich.) are making the fairness bill a priority." Kim McAvoy, *Fairness Doctrine On a Roll*, BROADCASTING & CABLE, Aug. 2, 1993, at 39, 39. "And with Bill Clinton in the White House, they're no longer concerned about a presidential veto." *Id.* at 40.

45. "The presumption has been since 1987 that the next time we get a Democratic president, there is going to be a Fairness Doctrine," stated Thomas W. Hazlett, an economist at the University of California at Davis. Rod Dreher, *Congress Cowers To Conservatives On Fairness Doctrine*, WASH. TIMES, July 3, 1994, at A4. The question at hand is, will President Clinton follow in the footsteps of President Reagan and President Bush? David Bartlett, president of Radio-Television News Directors Association, was pessimistically watchful of the new administration. "While Mr. Clinton may not have content regulation at the top of his personal agenda, don't count on him to pick fights with the powerful Democratic congressional leaders who see it as their mission in life to control what goes out over radio and television." David Bartlett, *Monday Memo*, Broadcasting, Jan. 25, 1993, at 18, 18.

46. *Washington Watch*, BROADCASTING & CABLE, Sept. 20, 1993, at 44, 44.

47. *Id.* Limbaugh is, perhaps, the most recognizable of the talk show hosts who rail on the Fairness Doctrine. As evidence of Limbaugh's reputation for opposing the doctrine, attempts by Congress to codify the doctrine have been referred to in the popular media as "Hush Rush" legislation. Gigi B. Sohn & Andrew Schwartzman, Fairness Not Silence WASH. POST, Jan. 31, 1994, at A21. In point of face, though, large number of other talk show hosts also helped to generate mail against the Fairness Doctrine. Former Watergate conspirator G. Gordon Liddy, now one of the country's top radio personalities said of attempts to reinstate the Fairness Doctrine, "If they did try to, Rush and I and [Pat] Buchanan would be all over them like a blanket." Rod Dreher, *Congress Cowers To Conservatives On Fairness Doctrine*, WASH. TIMES, July 3, 1994.

48.

"I take my hat off to Rush Limbaugh and the other conservative talk-show hosts," said Gigi B. Sohn, deputy director of the Media Access Project. "I think they're absolutely wrong on the Fairness Doctrine, and I think they know it, but they've done a spectacular job of cowing Congress into not taking action."

Dreher, *supra* note 65, at A4.

Although most of the media attention seemed to center on talk radio, it should be noted that religious broadcasters also lobbied aggressively against such legislation. Harry Jessell, *Congress Urges FCC to Deal with Fairness Doctrine*, BROADCASTING & CABLE, Mar. 14, 1994, at 14, 14.

49. "Clinton advisor George Stephanopoulos assails radio's 'tear-it-down attitude' and calls for 'more of a balance.' The doctrine is 'not on the front burner right now,' he says. 'But there's always a chance that it's something people might want to look at.'" Amy Bernstein, *The Hush-Rush Law*, U.S. NEWS & WORLD REP., June 27, 1994, at 12, 12.

50. It has been suggested by some that the Fairness Doctrine will pave its way back into the legislative arena masked behind politically correct movements concerned with "indecent programming" and "responsible journalism." David Bartlett, Monday Memo, BROADCASTING, Jan. 25, 1993, at 18.

A few see a sinister government seeking more and more control of mass-communications.

Actor Michael Moriarty states that he quit NBC's *Law and Order* because he was being written out of the series due to his stand against the Clinton administration's efforts to halt TV violence. Moriarty claimed "[Attorney General] Reno wants to control mass communications using the oldest ploy—the children." Joe Flint, *Moriarty Quits, Blames Violence Backlash,* Broadcasting & Cable, Feb. 7, 1994, at 22, 22.

Moriarty may be prescient, or he may simply be a good legal scholar. The Children's Television Act of 1990 forced the FCC to reinstate restrictions on advertising during programming aimed at children and imposed an obligation on broadcasters to provide programming that affirmatively addresses the "educational and information" needs of young viewers. Pub. L. No. 101–437, 104 Stat. 996 (codified at 47 U.S.C. §§ 303a–303b, 393a, 394 (Supp. IV 1992)).

The 1992 Petition for Reconsideration of the Commission's abandonment of the Fairness Doctrine—filed by the Arkansas AFL-CIO and the Committee Against Amendment 2—points out the Children's Television Act "regulates broadcast content in a way that arguably requires much greater discretion than the fairness doctrine." They imply that, for this reason it would be fitting and proper to restore the doctrine. Some of the recent filings of August 1994, (In re Enforcement of the Fairness Doctrine, Petition for Emergency Declaratory Ruling of the Coalition for Healthy Cal. In Re Arkansas AFL-CIO v. KARK-TV, Little Rock, Ark., Contingent Petition for Reconsideration of the Coalition for a Healthy Cal.), incorporate this argument.

Political Broadcasting Rules

Roger L. Sadler

Because of such concepts as the scarcity ratio-nale and the "public airwaves," the courts have ruled that various broadcast content regulations are constitutional. For example, the courts have upheld the FCC's right to regulate "in-decent" or sexually explicit material on the airwaves. Children have easy access to broadcasting, and the courts say that restricting indecent broadcast pro-gramming is a way to protect children from what are considered unwholesome messages and images. The courts have ruled this all of part of serving the broader "public interest."

The courts have also upheld other content regu-lations for broadcasters. When it comes to political broadcast content, there are rules to ensure that broadcasters do not use the power of the airwaves to favor one candidate over another.

The "Equal Time" or "Equal Opportunity" Rule

This rule originated in the Radio Act of 1927 and was made part of the Communications Act of 1934. It is known as Section 315 because the rule is included in that section of the Communications Act (for exact wording, see box). The rule applies to radio and TV stations, both broadcast and satellite, as well as com-munity cable systems that originate their own pro-gramming. In simple terms: "If a station gives or sells air time to a legally qualified political candidate, that station must also give or sell a comparable amount of time to every other legally qualified candidate run-ning for that office."

One congressman, at the time the Communications Act was being written, said Section 315 was necessary or else "American politics will be largely at the mercy of those who operate these stations." Politicians know the power of broadcasting. Hundreds of millions of dollars are now spent every 4 years on the U.S. presi-dential race alone, and most dollars from candidates' advertising budgets go to broadcast advertising.

Section 315: The "Equal Time" Rule

(a) If any licensee shall permit any person who is a legally qualified candidate for any public office to use a broadcasting station, he shall afford *equal op-portunities* to all other such candidates for that office in the use of such broadcasting station:

Provided. That such licensee shall have no power of censorship over the material broadcast under the provisions of this section. No obligation is hereby imposed under this subsection upon any licensee to allow the use of its station by any such candidate. Appearance by a legally qualified candidate on any:

1. bona fide newscast,

2. bona fide news interview,

3. bona fide news documentary (if the appearance of the candidate is incidental to the presentation of the subject or subjects covered by the news documentary), or

4. on-the-spot coverage of bona fide news events (including but not limited to political conventions and activities incidental thereto), shall not be deemed to be a use of a broadcasting station within the meaning of this subsection. Nothing in the foregoing sentence shall be construed as relieving broadcasters in connection with the presentation of newscasts, news interviews, news documentaries, and on-the-spot coverage of news events, from the obligation imposed upon them under this chapter to operate in the public interest and to afford reasonable opportunity for the discussion of conflicting views on issues of public importance.

(b) The charges made for the *use* of any broadcasting station by any person who is a legally qualified candidate for any public office in connection with his campaign for nomination for election, or election, to such office shall not exceed—

1. during the 45 days preceding the date of a primary or primary runoff election and during the 60 days preceding the date of general or special election in which such person is a candidate, the lowest unit charge of the station for the same class and amount of time for the same period; and

2. at any other time, the charges made for comparable use of such station by other users thereof.

(c) For purposes of this section—

1. the term "broadcasting station" includes a community antenna television system [CATV, or cable]; and

2. the terms "licensee" and "station licensee" when used with respect to a community antenna television system mean the operator of such system.

[In 1993, the FCC ruled that direct broadcast satellite services—satellite TV providers—must also abide by Section 315 and Section 312 (a) (7). In 1997, the FCC said satellite radio providers also have to abide by these rules.]

(d) The Commission shall prescribe appropriate rules and regulations to carry out the provisions of this section.

SECTION 315 ANALYZED
"Equal Time" Really Means "Equal Opportunities"

Even though Section 315 is frequently called the "Equal Time" rule, it is actually more practical to think of it as the "Equal Opportunities" rule. In Section 315, the FCC explains what it means by *equal opportunities:* If a broadcast station or local cable operator accepts advertising or programming from a legally qualified candidate, it must all allow "equal opportunities" for opposing candidates. This means that a station or cable system operator must give all candidates an equal opportunity to reach the same *potential* audience. For example, it would be unfair for a radio station to offer one candidate ads during the afternoon, when there are many listeners, and offer another candidate ads only late at night, when there are fewer listeners.

This rule applies to all candidates at all levels—federal, state, and local. In all of its practices, the station must not give the appearance that it is favoring one candidate over another.

Deadlines

—**FAQ:** Must a candidate make an "equal time" request within a certain time frame?

A candidate has *7 days* to request equal opportunity from a station or cable system. The candidate must make the request directly to the station within 7 days after an opponent's ad or program has aired. After the 7th day, that candidate no longer can demand equal time for those spots already aired by an opponent.

This rule was put in place so candidates could not come to a station to demand equal time for ads or programs that aired weeks or months earlier. A broadcast station is under no obligation to notify candidates about the airing of an opponent's material. The candidate is ultimately responsible.

Legally Qualified Candidates

The FCC says a person is a legally qualified candidate if he or she publicly announces candidacy for nomination or election to a local, state, or federal office; meets the legal qualifications for that particular office (age, residency requirements, U.S. citizenship, etc.); qualifies to be placed on the ballot or is eligible for legal votes by another method, such as write-in or sticker; *and* has made a substantial showing as a bona fide candidate—*or* has been officially nominated by an established or well-known political party.

A station is not responsible for verifying whether a person is a legally qualified candidate. The burden of proof falls on the candidate.

—**FAQ:** *What qualifies as a "use"?*

Section 315 is supposed to apply only to broadcast ads or other material that constitute a legitimate "use" by a candidate. The FCC says a "use" occurs when a recognizable voice or picture of the candidate appears in an ad or other broadcast campaign appearance.

Ads Without a Candidate's Voice or Picture

—**FAQ:** *What about ads that don't use the candidate's voice or picture?*

In such instances, something called the Zapple Doctrine or Zapple Rule applies. This rule came about in 1972 to address the issue of candidates using spokespersons in their ads to avoid "uses" and subsequent Section 315 obligations.

The Zapple Rule says if a *spokesperson* for a candidate appears in an ad, the station must provide equal access to an *opposing candidate's spokesperson*. The Zapple Rule applies only during campaign periods and only to spokespersons of major political party candidates.

—**FAQ:** *Can a candidate demand "equal time" to respond to an opposing candidate's spokesperson?*

No. The Zapple Rule only allows spokespersons to respond to other spokespersons. The station would *not* be required to offer airtime to the actual opposing candidate in such a situation.

Other "Uses"

To try to alleviate confusion, the FCC in 1978 issued a report to detail instances it considers broadcast "uses" by candidates: (a) any time a candidate secures air time, even when not discussing his or her candidacy; (b) an incumbent politician's "weekly reports" broadcast on radio or TV; (c) a candidate's appearance on a variety program, no matter how brief; (d) any on-air appearances by actors or broadcast station employees who are also running for public office.

Celebrity Candidates

—**FAQ:** *So any "celebrity" who's running for public office puts Section 315 into effect?*

Yes. Much to the dismay of many who work in broadcasting, Section 315 does apply to such people as a radio disc jockey, TV weather announcer, or actor who is running for public office. That was not always the case, though.

The 1960 case *Brigham v. FCC*[1] concerned radio and TV weatherman Jack Woods, who had decided to run for the Texas legislature. Woods' opponent William Brigham said Woods' radio and TV weather reports were a use under Section 315, and Brigham demanded equal time on the air. A federal appeals court upheld an FCC ruling that Woods' broadcasts were part of his regular job and not "something arising out of the election campaign." Thus, Section 315 did not apply to Woods' weather report.

However, the FCC and the courts changed their minds on this matter more than 10 years later, saying that such "uses" result in a kind of free advertising for a candidate.

Paulsen v. FCC

In January 1972, Pat Paulsen was a legally qualified candidate for the Republican presidential nomination. Paulsen was also a professional entertainer who would soon be appearing on television in Disney's *The Mouse Factory*. The producer of the show contacted the FCC to see if Paulsen's appearance would count as a use under Section 315. The FCC said stations airing *The Mouse Factory* would be obligated to provide Paulsen's Republican opponents with equal time if those candidates requested it.

In *Paulsen v. FCC*,[2] a federal appeals court upheld the FCC ruling. Even nonpolitical uses of airtime constitute use of a broadcast station because they are free public relations for a candidate, the court said. "A candidate who becomes well-known to the public as a personable and popular individual through 'nonpolitical' appearances certainly holds an advantage when he or she does formally discuss political issues to the same public over the same media." Section 315 needs to apply here because a station could subtly endorse one candidate by inviting him or her to appear on numerous "entertainment" shows and not inviting other candidates.

Also in 1972, NBC broadcast an old Doris Day movie in which Paulsen was seen for 30 seconds. This also qualified as a use, and two of Paulsen's Republican opponents were given 30 seconds of equal time on NBC in that same time slot.

—**FAQ:** Did Section 315 apply in 2003 when movie actor Arnold Schwarzenegger was running for governor of California?

Yes. In fact, the National Association of Broadcasters (NAB) alerted its member stations in California and neighboring states about potential Section 315 problems. The NAB warned broadcast stations that airing old Schwarzenegger movies such as *Total Recall* or *Conan the Barbarian* would have triggered Section 315. It was, potentially, a huge problem because this was a special recall election, with more than 100 legally qualified candidates, all of whom could have demanded equal time. Also, Section 315 applied to stations in adjacent states that broadcast to large numbers of California voters.

—**FAQ:** What about cable channels airing Schwarzenegger movies? Did they have to abide by Section 315?

No. Remember, Section 315 applies only to broadcasters and *local* cable system operators. Therefore, *national* cable channels could have aired these movies without worrying about equal time requests. By the way, there were other celebrities running for governor of California in 2003, including Gary Coleman, who starred in the 1980s sitcom *Different Strokes,* and Don Novello, who played Father Guido Sarducci on *Saturday Night Live.* Local stations were advised to avoid airing reruns of these shows, but national cable channels continued to air them.

Section 315 also applies to local TV celebrities, such as newscasters.

Branch v. FCC

William Branch was an on-air news reporter for KOVR-TV in Sacramento, CA. He would appear in newscasts roughly 3 minutes each day. In 1984, Branch decided to run for the town council in nearby Loomis. Under Section 315 (a), Branch knew that his on-air reports were a "use of the station by a legally qualified candidate." As a result, his

station determined it would have to give Branch's opponents 33 hours of response time, even though Branch would not be using his reports for political purposes. Branch's news reports would still count as a use.

KOVR told Branch to take an unpaid leave of absence during the campaign, with no guarantee his reporting job would still be available if he lost the election. Branch decided to keep his TV job and drop out of the race. He still took his case to the FCC, feeling it was unfair that his TV job kept him from running for political office. He also argued that he was part of a "bona fide newscast," and he should be exempt from Section 315. In *Branch v. FCC,*[3] a federal appeals court ruled that Section 315 does apply to on-air personalities and performers and that newscasters get no special exemption. The court said that newscasters must *not* be exempt from Section 315 and that this ruling would help prevent "unfair and unequal use of the broadcast media." The court's response to Branch's argument that he had to choose between his TV job and political office was, "Nobody has ever thought that a candidate has a right to run for office and at the same time to avoid all personal sacrifice."

—**FAQ:** So, for example, if a local radio disc jockey decides to run for city council, that disc jockey's time on the air would count as a use?

Yes. If a broadcaster who is running for office chooses to keep a broadcasting job during a campaign, it can create headaches for the broadcast station. The station will have to keep track of how many minutes that broadcaster is on the air each day, including his or her voice work on any commercials and promotions, and then offer comparable time *for free* to all opponents for that political office. It would be free because the candidate-broadcaster is not paying the station to be on the air during these times, and therefore opposing candidates cannot be required to pay either.

—**FAQ:** Does this apply to the primaries as well as to the general election?

Yes, but there are some important differences to keep in mind regarding how Section 315 works during primaries and during general elections.

Section 315 and Primaries

Primaries. Let's say Bob Smith is a Republican running for city council, and there are three other Republicans running against him in the primary. There are three Democrats vying for that party's nomination as well. If Smith buys ads on a station, only his Republican opponents would be allowed to request equal time under Section 315 in response to Smith's ads. The Democrats are not his opponents at that time, so they would not be allowed to request equal time based on Smith's ad. The Democrats *would* be allowed to request equal time if a Democratic primary opponent was given air time.

General Elections. By this time, the parties have chosen their candidates. Now the party lines are gone, and Section 315 applies to all candidates from all parties for a particular office.

No Censorship of Political Ads

Stations are not allowed to censor a use by any political candidate for any reason. Even if the ad is poorly produced, is extremely negative, or is from a radical political party, the station must run the ad as is.

—**FAQ:** What if the ad contains libel? Can't the station get in trouble for running a political ad that is libelous?

Libel in Political Ads

Libel involves untrue statements made about a person that damage that person's reputation or harm that person in other ways. Stations are not legally responsible for any libel in political ads that are considered uses. In *Farmers Educational and Cooperative Union of America v. WDAY*,[4] the Supreme Court ruled in 1959 that a broadcast station did not have a right to remove libelous or defamatory material from a political ad that is a use. The court said it did not want broadcast stations to "set themselves up as the sole arbiter of what is true and what is false." Again, those stations cannot be sued if the ad does indeed contain libelous material. However, candidates can be held liable for any defamatory statements made in political ads or programs.

—**FAQ:** Can a station be held responsible for libelous statements in non-use ads?

Yes. That is why stations are allowed to censor an ad by *spokespersons* for a candidate because this type of ad is not considered a use.

—**FAQ:** Isn't such an ad considered a use when equal time is invoked?

No. Equal time is given because of the Zapple Rule, but that does not make it a use.

Stations are expected to edit any potentially libelous material from such non-use ads. This is important—*stations can be held responsible for airing libelous ads from supporters of candidates.*

—**FAQ:** Are stations allowed to edit ads that may be distasteful or indecent?

No. The following case is a good example.

Aborted Fetuses in Political Ads

In the early 1990s, numerous politicians across the United States used pictures of aborted fetuses in their TV ads. The visuals were graphic, including pictures of fetuses with severed limbs or fetuses with skin that had been blackened by a process called "saline abortion." The politicians running the ads said they were showing the pictures to make people aware of what abortion does to a fetus. These politicians were also aware of the "no censorship" clause in Section 315. They knew stations would have to run the ads uncensored.

One such ad by congressional candidate Daniel Becker ran on WAGA-TV in Atlanta early one evening. The station received complaints from viewers, who said the ads were too graphic for broadcast, especially at that time of day. Becker dismissed the complaints and asked the TV station to give him 30 minutes of airtime for a video called *Abortion in America: The Real Story*, which contained more graphic images of aborted fetuses. Becker wanted the video to air late on a Sunday afternoon after an NFL broadcast. The station said the material was too graphic for that time of day and said it would only air the video after midnight, when there would be fewer children in the audience. Becker argued that the station simply did not like his message and was trying to censor his speech.

The FCC agreed that the ad was disturbing and would be harmful to children. Therefore, the FCC gave WAGA the right to air the ad only during late-night hours, from 10:00 p.m. to 6:00 a.m. A district court later upheld the FCC ruling.[5]

However, in 1996, a federal appeals court overturned that ruling in *Becker v. FCC*.[6] The court pointed out that the images in the ads were not indecent. The FCC's definition of indecency includes only material that has graphic depictions of "sexual or excretory activities and organs." This was not sexual material, the court said.

Channeling Becker's ads to late at night deprived him of reaching "particular categories of adult viewers whom he may be especially anxious to reach." Thus, Becker was deprived of the equal opportunities allowed him in Section 315. The FCC was allowing the station to channel the ads "based entirely on a subjective judgment that a particular ad *might* prove harmful to children." If stations are allowed to channel graphic ads for abortion, the court said, the FCC would have to allow stations to channel graphic political ads about the death penalty, gun control, and animal rights. The court feared this would lead to "content-based channeling." Allowing channeling of such ads might make candidates avoid certain controversial issues. The court concluded that channeling the ads violated Becker's "reasonable access" to the airwaves.

This ruling upheld the principle that government attempts to censor "unpopular" messages run head-on into the First Amendment.

Lowest Unit Rate

This is also known as the *lowest unit charge*. You will also hear broadcasters referring to this as LUR or LUC. All candidates—federal, state, and local—are eligible for the LUR. Lowest unit rates for broadcast uses apply only during certain time periods: 45 days before a primary and 60 days before a general election.

—FAQ: What exactly does lowest unit rate mean?

LUR requires that stations give candidates the cheapest available ad rates. Therefore, a station is not allowed to inflate ad prices for "uses" by political candidates. Stations must charge candidates the lowest unit (per second, per 15-second block, or however that station charges) rate that the station would charge to its most favored advertisers for the same type or class of advertisement, for the same length of commercial, and for the same time of day. Stations need to provide candidates with as much information as they can about classes of ads, rates, terms, conditions, and discounts that are offered to favored advertisers.

Stations should draw up *political rate cards* for politicians so that it is very clear what the station is charging for political ads and for a particular class of advertisement.

—FAQ: What is meant by "class of advertisement"?

Broadcast stations sell different types of ads at different rates. For example, sponsoring a newscast (a "fixed position" ad) will cost an advertiser more money than just running an ad at random times of the day ("run-of-schedule"). Politicians must be made aware of these various classes and the rates that are charged. Politicians will wind up paying different prices for different types of ads during different times of the day, but they must always be given the best possible rate.

—FAQ: I work at a radio station. We sometimes have "fire sales" on ads, where we give advertisers some great bargain ad rates, near the end of the month. Do we have to include these rates in the LUR calculations?

The FCC says such "fire sale" ad rates and other "specials" must be included in LUR. In 1992, the FCC tried to alleviate confusion about LUR by issuing these guidelines:

- The commission recognizes four classes of advertising time: nonpreemptible, preemptible with notice, immediately preemptible, and run-of-schedule.

- Stations may create subclasses for each of these four areas as long as the subclasses are clearly defined.

- All classes must be fully disclosed and made available to candidates.

- Stations may not have a separate "premium period" class of time made available only to candidates.

- Stations may increase ad rates during an election season only if they have good reason, such as an increase in ratings or seasonal program changes.

- LUR may be calculated as often as every week.

- Prices for "bonus spots" given to commercial advertisers must be made available to candidates as well.

—**FAQ:** Our station also does a lot of baiters, or trade-outs, with businesses. Do we have to calculate the values of these arrangements when calculating LUR?

No, as long as the barter or trade-out did not involve any cash payments from the advertiser. If any cash does exchange hands, then the station must calculate the value of such transactions and include it in the LUC.

—**FAQ:** A candidate purchases ads at a certain rate in July. In August, our station offers an ad rate to another client that is lower than the rate given to the candidate. Must our station give this new rate to the candidate?

Yes. First, the station must apply this rate to future ads by the candidate. Second, for ads that have already aired, the station must calculate the cost of those ads at the new rate and refund the candidate the difference (a "rebate"). That candidate also has the option to use the difference as "credit" and apply it to future ads. It is the responsibility of the station to alert candidates to any new rates, and it must be done in a timely fashion.

—**FAQ:** Does the Zapple Rule apply to LUR? Can a candidate's supporters get the LUR for their ads?

No. LUR applies only for "uses" (ads containing the candidate's voice or image). Ads from supporters of a candidate do not qualify for LUR.

—**FAQ:** What if a candidate can't afford to buy ads? In the spirit of fairness, shouldn't the station give that candidate some free time?

Political broadcasting rules do not require stations to give free airtime to any candidate. However, as mentioned, if a station gives one candidate free time for some reason, the station must then grant equal free time to opposing candidates.

Stations may also protect themselves from politicians who try to buy advertising time on "credit" and then never pay their bills. A broadcast station can demand that a *federal* candidate pay for airtime up to 7 days before an ad airs. For state and local candidates, those politicians must follow each station's rule regarding credit or payments in advance. These policies must be reasonable, however, and not unfairly keep a candidate from taking advantage of his or her rights under Section 315.

—**FAQ:** For local races, does a station have to honor Section 315 obligations for candidates who are from districts outside of the station's main listening area?

No. Candidates who represent districts outside of a station's "principle service area" may not demand equal opportunities under Section 315.

SECTION 315 AND NEWS EXEMPTIONS

When a candidate appears in a "bona fide" news story or any other type of broadcast news event, the station is not required to give opposing candidates equal time in present or future news stories and programs. In other words, a news reporter is under no *legal* obligation to grant equal or comparable time to candidates in legitimate news stories.

Debates and the Aspen Rule

—**FAQ:** In 2004, presidential debates on TV only had George Bush and John Kerry. Shouldn't Green Party candidate Ralph Nader and others have been included in these debates under Section 315?

There has been heated debate about whether debates should qualify as "bona fide news events" and thus be exempt from Section 315.

This issue first came up in 1960, with the first televised presidential debate between John F. Kennedy and Richard Nixon. Producers of the debate felt the public was much more interested in hearing from Nixon and Kennedy than from any of the other presidential candidates, who were largely unknown, and Congress agreed. Congress suspended Section 315 for the debates and said the TV and radio networks did not have to include candidates from "smaller" parties. The debates could be treated as "news events" and be exempted from Section 315. There were no presidential broadcast debates in 1964, 1968, and 1972. Then in 1975, the FCC echoed the 1960 congressional ruling in the Aspen Rule: Broadcast debates are bona fide news events and are exempt from Section 315.[7]

However, at the time, the FCC said the debates had to be sponsored by a non-broadcast entity such as the League of Women Voters. In 1983, though, the FCC dropped that requirement and said that broadcasters could directly sponsor and organize the debates and still be exempt from Section 315.

—FAQ: Isn't the Aspen Rule unfair to candidates from smaller parties?

Those candidates certainly think so. In 1976, one small-party presidential candidate named Shirley Chisholm took the FCC to court over the Aspen Rule, but a federal appeals court in *Chisholm v. FCC*[8] ruled that the FCC was justified in exempting broadcast debates from Section 315.

Broadcasters tend to like the Aspen Rule for logistical reasons. For example, there are usually about 25 legally qualified candidates who run for president every 4 years. Broadcasters argue that it would be extremely difficult to have a meaningful debate between 25 people and that such an event would attract fewer viewers than a debate featuring the main candidates. In the next case, the court said the Aspen Rule also helps to avoid a "chilling effect" on broadcasters.

—FAQ: What about state and local races? Does the Aspen Rule apply?

Yes. The Supreme Court addressed such concerns in 1998 in *Arkansas Educational Television Commission v. Forbes*.[9] A public TV station aired a debate between the Republican and Democrat running for Congress in Arkansas' Third District. An independent candidate, Ralph Forbes, argued that he should have been included in the debate, and an appeals court ruled for Forbes. That appeals court caused a public station in Nebraska to cancel a candidate debate in 1996. The station said it would prefer to have no debate at all rather than be forced to invite all candidates to participate.

But in 1998, the U.S. Supreme Court said the Aspen Rule applied in this situation as well. It said TV stations, even public stations supported by tax dollars, do not have to include certain candidates. The court reasoned that (a) a broadcast debate is a "nonpublic forum." It is not a public forum like a park, and candidates do not have an automatic right of access, (b) Broadcasters may exclude candidates based on

judgments of newsworthiness (i.e., the candidate is trailing badly in the polls). However, candidates may not be exempt because of their beliefs or stands on issues, (c) Placing such rules on broadcasters creates a "chilling effect." The court specifically mentioned the Nebraska station canceling a debate after the appeals court's ruling in favor of Forbes. Justice Anthony Kennedy said such a ruling "does not promote speech but represses it."

—FAQ: What about press conferences? If an incumbent politician holds a press conference, is this a bona fide news event? Wouldn't this give the incumbent an unfair advantage to use the news media for free publicity?

Incumbent politicians will often hold numerous press conferences in the months before an election. If the news media cover the press conferences, it can be like free advertising for the incumbent candidate. Many nonincumbent politicians say such press conferences create an unfair advantage for incumbents.

A federal appeals court addressed this issue in 1980 in *Kennedy for President Committee v. FCC*.[10] Earlier in 1980, Senator Edward Kennedy of Massachusetts had challenged President Jimmy Carter for the Democratic presidential nomination. Just before the important New Hampshire primary, President Carter appeared on national TV for a presidential news conference, and he used part of the time to attack the views of Kennedy on several issues. Kennedy said such press conferences were inherently unfair because the president can use "the power of incumbency" to get more media attention.

Kennedy's campaign committee demanded equal time under Section 315 because "millions of viewers were misinformed about Senator Kennedy's views on national and international issues critical to voters in the campaign for the presidential nomination." The Kennedy campaign pointed to a 1964 FCC ruling[11] that said news conferences were a use under Section 315. However, in the 1975 *Aspen* ruling, the FCC had reversed course and decided press conferences were not a use.

Thus, in this case, the FCC ruled that the Carter press conference was a "bona fide on-the-spot coverage of bona fide news events" and would not be considered a use. An appeals court agreed and denied

Kennedy's request for equal time under Section 315. Broadcasting the press conference was not an endorsement, the court said. There was not "even so much as a whisper of network bias in favor of the president." The networks were simply covering a bona fide news event and "had exercised good faith journalistic judgment in concluding the event was newsworthy." Kennedy could not use Section 312(a)(7) to demand "reasonable access" for free; he should have held his own press conference to respond to Carter.

The court said also that a ruling in favor of Kennedy would create a chilling effect: "Broadcasters could never be sure that coverage of any given event would not later result in equal-opportunity obligations to all other candidates: resultantly, broadcaster discretion to carry or not to carry would be seriously if not fatally crippled."

Section 315 and Talk Shows

—FAQ: What about candidates who are guests on radio and TV talk shows? More politicians are using such programs as part of their campaigns these days. Do these appearances count as "bona fide news interviews?"

This issue was first addressed in 1959. Congress said the FCC should give exemptions to more types of programs and not only to "standard" news programs. Congress said this would provide the public with more outlets for political discourse.

Eventually, the FCC developed three criteria to determine if a program should be exempt from Section 315:

- Whether the program is regularly scheduled

- Whether the program is controlled by the broadcaster or an independent producer (programs controlled by the broadcaster are often more likely to be exempt)

- Whether producers of the show choose the format, content, and participants based on newsworthiness and not to help or harm any candidate

By the 1990s, presidential candidates had begun to circumvent the national news media by doing interviews on talk shows such as the *Oprah Winfrey Show* and *Larry King Live*. In many instances, these types of interviews qualify as "news interviews," and Section 315 does not apply. However, it depends on the content and character of the show. If the host of a show is endorsing or "cheerleading" for a candidate, the FCC may rule that Section 315 applies. The FCC has been more lenient in giving exemptions to nontraditional news programs since 1988 and since an appeals court ruling in *King Broadcasting Co. v. FCC*.[12]

King Broadcasting wanted to air two pretaped programs highlighting George Bush and Michael Dukakis, the major party presidential candidates that year. The first program was an hour and gave each candidate 30 minutes to "state his case" to the public. One program was to air at the start of the campaign season and another would air just before the election. King also wanted to air an interview show with both candidates being asked questions by a journalist, and the candidates were allowed rebuttal time.

The FCC ruled the programs did not qualify as legitimate news events because King showed bias by not inviting presidential candidates from smaller parties and because the programs were not regularly scheduled. The FCC also said the format of the programs was more like advertising because it allowed the candidate to make "stump speeches."

The appeals court overturned the FCC ruling and said the King programs should be exempt as bona fide news interview programs. The court pointed out that the FCC had not applied the "newsworthiness test" to King. (The court remanded the case to the FCC, and the commission then determined that the King programs were indeed newsworthy.) The court felt that the King programs were not "ads" or "stump speeches," as the FCC claimed, and that the FCC must consider exemptions for "hybrid formats" such as the King format. (The programs were called *hybrid* because they were not just straight news interviews or news stories. The programs contained a combination of candidate speeches, news interviews, and rebuttals.) The court added that the decision in *Aspen* allowed King to treat its programs like debates and invite only the major party candidates.

In 2003, the FCC ruled that even "shock radio" programs, such as the *Howard Stern Show*, were hybrids and qualified as bona fide news interview shows. Using similar criteria, the FCC has determined that the following programs can qualify as "news" interviews and be exempt from Section 315 obligations:

- "Entertainment talk" shows, such as the *Phil Donahue Show*, the *Oprah Winfrey Show*, the *Rosie O'Donnell Show*
- "Entertainment news" shows, such as *Entertainment Tonight*, *Access Hollywood*
- Cable documentary programs, such as A&E's *Biography*
- News magazine candidate profiles, such as a *Nightline* special "Who is Ross Perot?"
- TV political talk shows that include host commentary, such as *Politically Incorrect*
- Network and cable news interview shows, such as *Meet the Press*, *Face the Nation*, the *Larry King Show*
- Radio talk shows that include listener calls and candidate interviews, such as Rush Limbaugh and Howard Stern's

Sponsorship Identification

The following are the basic rules for *local and state races*.

All political ads and programs must be clearly labeled as such with "disclaimers." For radio ads, there must be a verbal statement indicating that the spot is a political ad. For TV, there must be a visual or audio statement, and it may be placed anywhere in the ad. The ads should contain a phrase such as "sponsored by," "paid for by," or "furnished by." These statements are usually pretty basic: "The preceding [following] ad was paid for by the Jane Jones for Mayor Committee." Make sure all local and state political ads at your station contain these sponsorship identifications and that the complete name of the sponsoring candidate or organization is accurate.

The rules for federal races are a little more complicated.

BCRA (FECA)

Federal Candidate Ads and BCRA

Many members of Congress argued that the FCC's sponsorship rules were too vague, especially for TV ads. One problem concerned special interest groups that ran "attack ads" against candidates. These "third-party" ads would often contain only a visual

disclaimer at the end of the ad, a disclaimer that was often flashed on the screen very quickly or written in very small print. As a result, many voters did not see the disclaimers and assumed the ads were paid for by opposing candidates or parties, creating confusion about who was delivering these messages.

The Bipartisan Campaign Reform Act of 2002 (BCRA) was a response to such third-party ads, as well as other concerns. The act also is known as the Federal Election Campaign Act (FECA), and it was the outgrowth of legislation sponsored by senators John McCain and Russ Feingold. The act was challenged in court as a violation of the First Amendment, but the U.S. Supreme Court upheld most of the act's provisions in 2003 in *McConnell v. FEC*.[13]

The BCRA provides specific guidelines for disclaimers that must be included in political broadcast spots for federal candidates. The act covers all "public communications" paid for by federal candidates or by any person or group advocating the election or defeat of a federal candidate. It also includes all public communications that solicit funding for political purposes. Public communications include spots or programs on radio, TV, cable, and satellite, as well as articles and advertisements in newspapers, magazines, outdoor advertising, mass mailings, telephone banks, and public political advertising. The Federal Elections Commission (FEC) enforces BCRA.

"Stand by Your Ad" Disclaimer

For federal candidates, BCRA mandates that certain disclaimers be included in all radio and TV ads that are authorized or paid for by the candidate. The FEC provides two examples:

- "I am *[name]*, a candidate for *[title of federal office]*, and I approved this advertisement."
- "My name is *[name]*. I am running for *[title of federal office]*, and I approved this message."

For radio, either of the above statements (or statements with reasonable variations of this wording) must be delivered clearly *in the candidate's own voice*.

For TV, the candidate has two options. The candidate may appear in a clear, full-screen shot while personally delivering one of the above disclaimers, *or* the candidate may use a recognizable picture or video of him- or herself that fills at least 80% of the screen and is accompanied by a voiceover of the candidate delivering the disclaimer.

Also, TV ads (whether broadcast, cable, or satellite) must have the candidate's name and approval statement *in writing at the end of the ad*. The writing must take up at least 4% of the vertical picture height and be on screen for at least 4 seconds. The wording should also be easy to read with a "reasonable degree of color contrast" between the lettering and the background.

—FAQ: Does the BCRA require disclaimers for political Web pages or e-mails?

No. The Internet is exempt from these disclaimer rules.

BCRA and Lowest Unit Rate

Federal candidate ads *that have direct references to an opponent* must contain certain disclaimers to qualify for LUR. TV ads must mention the office being sought and contain an identifiable candidate image at the end of the ad. The image must last at least 4 seconds and must display in writing an approval statement from the candidate. The wording must also tell what authorized committee paid for the ad. Radio ads must also tell the office being sought, along with an audio identification of the candidate. The audio must also contain a statement of approval from the candidate.

If a candidate runs ads that directly refer to an opponent, the candidate's ads will not qualify for LUR if the ads lack disclaimers.

—FAQ: What are the rules for political ads that are not authorized or paid for directly by the candidate?

Such third-party ads are often produced by "527 groups," so named because of rules established in Section 527 of the Internal Revenue Code. These 527 groups can accept unlimited donations from unions, corporations, and individuals but cannot coordinate ads with presidential campaigns.

Third-party ads must have disclaimers. For radio, an announcer must clearly say a disclaimer such as "_____ is responsible for this advertising." The blank should be filled with the name of the person or political group paying for the ad. The ad must also clearly

state that the message has not been authorized by the candidate or the candidate's election committee.

For TV, the disclaimer may be read as a voiceover by a representative of the ad's sponsor. The representative is not required to appear on screen. The other option is that the disclaimer be delivered through "an unobscured full-screen view of a representative of the political committee or other person making the statement." Such TV ads must also place the disclaimer in writing at the end of the ad, with the lettering filling at least 4% of the vertical picture height and being visible for at least 4 seconds, with good color contrast.

Within 24 hours of the broadcast, a 527 group must provide the FEC with donor names, amount spent, and the names of the broadcast stations or networks that aired the ads.

Third-Party Restrictions Under BCRA

Third parties are prohibited from running radio or TV ads 30 days before a primary and 60 days before a general election, if the ad names a federal candidate, if the ad is aimed at the candidate's district or voters, and if the ad is paid for with unlimited union or corporate contributions.

—FAQ: What about third-party ads that are funded by unlimited individual contributions?

These ads do not have the 30-day or 60-day restrictions. A 527 group that is funded entirely by unlimited individual contributions may run ads opposing or supporting a candidate up through election day, which happened in the 2004 election campaign. Two 527 groups that gained national attention were the Swift Boat Veterans for Truth, who ran ads critical of Democratic candidate John Kerry, and MoveOn. org, which advertised against President George W. Bush.

—FAQ: Are nonprofit groups bound by these restrictions as well?

No. In 2002, the FEC ruled that these restrictions do not apply to tax-exempt religious, educational, and charitable organizations. Groups such as the Sierra Club had fought for the exemption, saying they should be allowed to run ads prior to an election to inform voters about important issues. The ads can still name a federal candidate but are not permitted to endorse election or defeat of the candidate. However, supporters of the law argued that misleading issue ads by some tax-exempt groups were part of the reason for passing BCRA in the first place. The FEC argued, though, that tax laws already prohibited such groups from directly endorsing or attacking candidates, and the groups risk losing their tax-exempt status if they do so.

—**FAQ:** Are there exemptions for newscasts?

Yes. News reports, editorials, and commentaries are all exempt.

—**FAQ:** What about movies or TV shows that mention political candidates?

In 2002, the FEC ruled that late-night comedy monologues and talk shows that discuss or feature federal candidates would be exempt from BCRA guidelines, although the FEC said it would judge such matters on a case-by-case basis. The FEC added that public service announcements featuring candidates would also be exempt.

Controversy erupted over BCRA in June 2004 when filmmaker Michael Moore released his movie *Fahrenheit 9/11*. The film was extremely critical of George W. Bush's presidency and his handling of the war on terrorism. A Republican group, Citizens United, filed a complaint with the FEC, arguing that ads for the film constituted "electioneering communications" that were designed to alter the outcome of the election. In August 2004, FEC voted unanimously to dismiss the complaint, ruling that the movie ads did not violate BCRA.

Political File

Stations must keep track of ALL requests made for political ads or programs and place them in a "political file." This file should be kept with other papers included in the general "public file" and must be composed of information about how requests were handled, including rates charged to each politician, including discounts or package deals given to candidates or organizations; the date and time the ads or programs aired; classes of time bought; number of spots purchased by each candidate or organization; and amount of free time (if any) given to candidates.

The FCC says all of this information should be placed in the political file "as soon as possible." What does that mean? The FCC elaborates: "As soon as possible means *immediately* absent unusual circumstances." In other words, as soon as you have the paperwork completed on political ads, place it immediately in the political file.

The station must keep this file for 2 years.

SECTION 315 VIOLATIONS

Failure to follow the FCC political broadcasting rules can result in fines as high as $25,000 per day for each day violations occur. Stations that are unsure about certain aspects of political broadcasting rules should consult an attorney. It just might be worth the money.

In 1998, for example, the FCC fined WFXD-FM in Marquette, MI, for failing to maintain an accurate political file and for questionable sales practices regarding political ads.[14] The FCC said that the station did not provide adequate details about how it determined the LUR for the 1994 and 1995 primaries and general election. The FCC said the station's "political rate card did not appear to contain even the most rudimentary elements of [its] sales practices." The station tried to argue that the problems were because of "employee error," but the FCC said the licensee is ultimately responsible for the actions of its employees. Someone should have double-checked to make sure the station was compliant with FCC rules.

The station's political file was also lacking necessary information, such as the dates of advertising purchased by candidates or the rates charged to some candidates. The FCC fined WFXD $6000 for three distinct violations ($2000 each): failure to inform candidates about ad rates and classes, inaccurate calculations of lowest unit rate, and failure to maintain a proper political file.

This is just one example. The FCC frequently hands out fines to stations for violations of political broadcasting rules. Politicians know the rules, and they are often very eager to file a complaint with the FCC about a station that does not follow these rules.

SECTION 315 AND BALLOT ISSUES

—FAQ: Are ballot issues covered under Section 315 or Section 312(a)(7)?

No. Stations do not have to accept advertising for ballot issues if they do not want to. The lowest unit rate does not apply to ads supporting or opposing ballot issues. Stations may charge their standard rates for such ads. The "no censorship" clause also does *not* apply. A station may edit or reject issue ads if the station fears the ads are libelous or indecent (a station can be sued for airing issue ads that are false or defamatory). In fact, a station can reject an issue ad for any reason, just as it is free to reject commercial ads. However, ballot issue ads must have clear sponsorship identification, just like other political ads.

SECTION 315 AND NEWSPAPERS

In 1913, the State of Florida passed a law that was basically a Section 315 for newspapers. It mandated that if a political candidate was attacked in a newspaper editorial or story, the newspaper was required to give that candidate a chance to respond. That law remained unchallenged until 1972.

The challenge concerned Pat Tornillo, a candidate for the state legislature. The *Miami Herald* had printed two editorials in September 1972 criticizing Tornillo, including accusations that he had orchestrated an illegal teachers' strike several years earlier. Under the 1913 Florida law, Tornillo demanded space in the *Herald* to reply to the attacks, but the newspaper refused. Tornillo took the newspaper to court, saying many large cities had only one major newspaper, and it was unfair that a major information source such as a newspaper did not provide opportunities for response. Eventually, the Florida Supreme Court ruled for Tornillo, saying the state law enhanced free speech.

However, in 1974, the U.S. Supreme Court ruled that the Florida law was unconstitutional. In *Miami Herald v. Tornillo*,[15] the court said that press responsibility or fairness "is not mandated by the Constitution." The law made newspapers avoid controversy, said the court: "Government-enforced right of access inescapably dampens the vigor and limits the variety of public debate." Newspaper editors, not the government, must be the ones to decide what opinions and news appear on their pages.

The Florida law imposed *fines* for papers that did not follow the rules. The Supreme Court said this was a "penalty on the basis of the content of a newspaper." Such content restrictions and penalties are unconstitutional. Broadcasters use the public airwaves and are subject to content regulations. Newspapers are "private," and government may not regulate their content.

REASONABLE ACCESS: SECTION 312(A)(7)

—FAQ: Section 315 says "if a station offers time." So, can a station choose to air no political ads? If a station doesn't provide time for any political ads, then it won't have to worry about providing "responses" from opposing candidates.

In 1971, any confusion about this wording in Section 315 was clarified for federal candidates. Congress amended the Communications Act with Section 312(a)(7), which is also called the "reasonable access" rule (see box).

Section 312(a)(7): The "Reasonable Access" Rule

(a) The Commission may revoke any station license or construction permit—… (7) for willful or repeated failure to allow *reasonable access* to or to permit purchase of *reasonable amounts of time* for the use of a broadcasting station by a legally qualified candidate for *Federal* elective office on behalf of his candidacy. (Italics added)

—FAQ: What is considered "reasonable access" or "reasonable amounts of time?"

Rules like this tend to frustrate broadcasters because words like "reasonable" are vague. The Supreme Court attempted to define "reasonable" in a landmark ruling on Section 312(a)(7) in the case of *CBS Inc. v. FCC*.[16]

In 1979, President Jimmy Carter and Vice President Walter Mondale announced they were running for reelection. The Carter-Mondale campaign committee, on October 11, 1979, made what it thought was a "reasonable" request of the three major TV networks. The committee wanted to run a

30-minute political ad between 8:00 p.m. and 10:30 p.m. on any day from December 4 through 7, 1979, and it was giving the networks 2 months advance notice to get ready.

The networks were not eager to accommodate the request. NBC said no, arguing that December was too early to air political ads. ABC said it would not start taking sales for political ads until January 1980. CBS said 30 minutes was too much, but it did offer the Carter campaign two 5-minute segments—one at 10:55 p.m. on December 8 and one in the daytime.

In general, the networks said the request for a 30-minute ad was not reasonable because (a) a 30-minute political ad during "prime time" would greatly disrupt their programming schedules; (b) network news shows were already doing a good job of covering the presidential candidates and keeping the public informed on the major issues; (c) there were numerous candidates for president, and the networks were worried about having to provide "response time" under Section 315; (d) it was 11 months before the 1980 election, which, the networks said, was "too early in the political season" for ads. Should the networks have to follow Section 312(a)(7) before the campaign had even started?

The Carter campaign said the presidential campaign was indeed underway, and the networks were not granting reasonable access as mandated by Section 312(a)(7). The Supreme Court later ruled in *CBS Inc. v. FCC* that the broadcast networks should have given the requested time to the Carter campaign. The Carter campaign gave the networks 2 months advance notice. The campaign was being reasonable in this regard. The rights of viewers and listeners are more important than the rights of broadcasters, the court said. Section 312(a)(7) "makes a significant contribution to freedom of expression by enhancing the ability of candidates to present, and the public to receive, information necessary for the effective operation of the democratic process."

The reasonable access rule does not take effect until the start of the "campaign season," but the court said that the presidential campaign was "in full swing" by December 1979. How is this determined? The court provided guidelines:

Signs That a Campaign Season Has Begun Include: (a) *Announcements of candidacy.* Twelve candidates had already formally announced intentions to run for the Republican and Democratic nominations. (b) *Dates of major political events.* The very important Iowa caucuses were in January, so of course candidates would be campaigning in December. (c) *State delegate selections.* Many states had already begun selecting delegates to the national party conventions. (d) *Fundraising activities.* Most candidates were already actively raising campaign funds. (e) *Media coverage.* Newspapers across the country had been covering the campaign for roughly 2 months. (f) *Campaign organizations.* At the time, many of the candidates had already formed active organizations. (g) *Endorsements.* Candidates were already beginning to get endorsements from various groups and other politicians.

However, many broadcasters were angered by the ruling, saying the Carter campaign's request for 30 minutes of prime time television was disruptive to TV scheduling and was therefore not "reasonable." For example, stations could make more money from advertising during a scheduled program than they would make from the Carter ad. In a dissent, Justice Byron White agreed with broadcasters' arguments, saying, "There is no basis in the statute for this very broad and unworkable scheme of access."

Section 312(a)(7) does not give candidates an *automatic* right of access to the airwaves, but it appears to be a pretty strong right. The Supreme Court said that broadcasters must show compelling reasons for rejecting a candidate's request for time, such as a large amount of time already sold to the candidate, a major impact on broadcast scheduling or programming, or the likelihood of a large amount of equal time requests from other candidates.

Important note: Section 312(a)(7) applies only to *federal candidates*—any person running for the U.S. House of Representatives, the U.S. Senate, or the presidency. *State and local candidates are not covered by this rule.*

—FAQ: So stations must accept advertising from federal candidates, but they can choose not to accept any ads from local and state candidates?

That is correct. Section 312(a)(7) applies only to federal candidates, and stations are not required to provide reasonable access—or *any* access, for that matter—to local and state candidates. However, once a station *has* accepted advertising from a candidate for local or state office, Section 315 kicks in. The station must then give equal opportunities for airtime to other legally qualified candidates running for that same office.

Important Rules Regarding Reasonable Access

These rules apply only to candidates for federal office.

- A station may not limit the length of a political program or ad.

- Candidates are allowed to choose whatever format they want. The station may not demand that a candidate use a specific format.

- A candidate is allowed to choose any time of day for ads.

- However, a station does not have to honor *extremely specific* requests for time (for example, if a candidate asks for an ad to be run at 5 minutes and 35 minutes past the hour and your standard advertising times are at 20 and 50 minutes past the hour, the candidate will have to settle for those times).

- Stations are allowed to restrict political ads during newscasts so as not to give the appearance of favoring a candidate during an "objective" newscast.

- Because of Section 312(a)(7), a station may not place any unreasonable limits on ads for federal candidates. For example, you cannot tell a federal

candidate that he or she is limited to six ads per day. There must be reasonable access.

—FAQ: Section 312(a)(7) talks about advertising. How does this rule apply to noncommercial stations?

In 2000, Congress voted to amend the Communications Act to exempt public broadcast stations from Section 312(a)(7). Therefore, public stations have no obligation to provide airtime to federal candidates. However, public stations must still abide by Section 315.

Also, public stations are prohibited from endorsing or opposing any candidate or public office.

NOTES

1. 276 F.2d 828 (5th Cir. 1960)
2. 491 F.2d 887 (9th Cir. 1974)
3. 824 F.2d 37 (D.C. Cir. 1987)
4. 360 U.S. 525 (1959)
5. *Gillett Communications of Atlanta, Inc. v. Becker*, 807 F. Supp. 757 (D.C. Cir. 1992)
6. 95 F.3d 75 (D.C.Cir.l996)
7. See *In re Aspen Institute and CBS*, 55 F.C.C.2d 697 (1975)
8. 538 F.2d 349 (D.C. Cir. 1976)
9. 523 U.S. 666 (1998)
10. 636 F.2d 417, 432 (D.C. Cir. 1980)
11. See *CBS, Inc.*, 40 FCC 395 (1964)
12. 860 F.2d 465 (D.C. Cir. 1988)
13. 124 S.Ct. 619 (2003)
14. DA #98-447, released March 6, 1998
15. 418 U.S. 241 (1974)
16. 453 U.S. 367 (1981)

Regulating Children's Programming

Wayne Overbeck and Genelle Belmas

In addition to its rules on political broadcasting and indecency, the FCC has at various times enforced a number of other broadcast content regulations.

Programming and advertising aimed at children have been a prime example. After a controversy over children's television programming that lasted for more than 20 years, in 1996 the FCC adopted rules requiring all commercial television stations to offer at least three hours a week of regularly scheduled programming to meet the *educational and informational* needs of children. When a digital TV station airs multiple program streams, each stream must include three hours of children's programming per week.

Under the children's programming rules, each station must provide this special programming in segments at least 30 minutes in length between the hours of 7 a.m. and 10 p.m. The children's programming is not supposed to be preempted, even for news or sports events, more often than 10 percent of the time. This poses a problem for stations on the west coast, because major sports events in the east often begin before the traditional Saturday morning children's program block ends in the Pacific time zone.

The children's educational programming must be clearly identified as such on the air. Also, stations are required to notify program guides, indicating the appropriate age range for each program. In addition, each station must have a staff member who acts as a children's educational programming liaison, and each station must file quarterly reports with the FCC to explain how the children's programming requirements are being met.

The adoption of these rules followed an extended controversy in which advocacy groups argued that all television stations have a duty to provide educational programming for children. The networks and major station groups responded by pointing to the various programming and community services they were already providing that had educational value for children. Some pointed out that despite its widely praised quality, PBS educational programming has had low ratings. Given a choice, most viewers have voted with their remote control units for other kinds of programming.

The trade press and other First Amendment advocates expressed concerns about the implications of the mandatory children's programming requirements for other reasons. Here, they noted, is a government agency dictating program content, telling commercial broadcasters to provide the kind of children's programming that *the government thinks children should be watching*—and then to promote it to persuade viewers to watch what's good for them instead of the programming they might prefer to watch.

By the 2000s, the networks' concerns about mandatory children's programming were greater than ever. With several cable networks offering children's programming full time, major over-the-air networks saw ratings for their children's programming drop even lower.

The 1996 rules were by no means the first FCC initiative in this area. As early as 1974, the FCC issued a policy statement calling on broadcasters to discontinue certain practices, such as allowing children's show hosts to advertise products. The commission also urged broadcasters to voluntarily upgrade their children's programming.

Congress passed a law to regulate children's programming in 1990, the Children's Television Act. It limits advertising on children's shows to 12 minutes per hour on weekdays and 10.5 minutes per hour on weekends. This provision applies only to shows intended for children age 12 and younger. The law also requires broadcasters to prove at license renewal time that they have met the "educational and informational needs" of children age 16 and younger by airing programs *specifically designed for that purpose.* The limits on commercials also apply to cable television, including both cable network shows and locally produced programming.

The advertising limits have been enforced aggressively. The FCC has conducted a number of audits of station compliance, and stations carrying excessive advertising have often been fined. In one 1999 action, the FCC fined two jointly owned Illinois stations, WRSP-TV in Springfield and WCCU(TV) in Urbana, $110,000 for 304 violations of the limits between 1994 and 1996. Another station, WDBD (TV) in Jackson, Mississippi, was also fined $110,000 for 158 violations of the limits between 1993 and 1998. In 2004, the FCC hit two cable networks with large fines for carrying too many commercials during children's television programs. The FCC fined Nickelodeon $1 million and ABC Family $500,000. These fines seemed small in comparison to a record $24 million fine that Univision Communications agreed to pay in 2007. Univision, the United States' largest Spanish-language broadcaster, incurred the FCC's wrath by airing telenovelas to fulfill its obligation to carry three hours of children's educational programs a week. It apparently agreed to pay the fine to win FCC approval of the network's sale to an investor group in Los Angeles.

The Children's Television Act also established a National Endowment for Children's Television to support educational programs. In addition, Congress directed the FCC to address the problem of toy-based shows and determine if they were improper *program-length commercials* because they so clearly promoted toys based on the shows' characters—a concern that was being voiced again a decade later.

Acting in 1991, the FCC adopted new rules concerning toy-based shows in response to the Congressional mandate. The rules forbid commercials within a show (or within one minute on either side of the show) for toys based on characters in that show. And the rules forbid hosts of children's shows from doing commercials on the premise that young children cannot distinguish commercials from the non-commercial segments of the show. The commercials must be separated from non-commercial segments of children's shows. But the FCC declined to ban toy-based shows altogether, a decision that was widely criticized by groups advocating quality children's programming.

The FCC responded by issuing a new notice of proposed rulemaking concerning educational programming for children in 1995. That proposal led to the three-hour mandatory children's educational programming requirement the commission adopted a year later.

Inequities on the Air

The FCC Media Ownership Rules—Encouraging Economic
Efficiency and Disregarding the Needs of Minorites

W. LaNelle Owens*

The portrait of the Negro has seldom been drawn but by the pencil of his oppressor and the Negro has sat for it in the distorted attitude of slavery,

—Carter G. Woodson[1]

INTRODUCTION

Shortly after the Telecommunications Act of 1996 was signed into law,[2] the Federal Communications Commission (FCC) released an order relaxing many of its ownership restrictions, in an effort to increase competition in the radio, telephone, cable, and newspaper industries.[3] The relaxation of ownership restrictions opened the doors for media giants to dominate markets and gain increased bargaining power.[4] There are currently a small number of media corporations that control the majority of the news and entertainment Americans receive on the airwaves.[5] Media concentration has led to placing "in a few hands the power to inform the American people and shape public opinion."[6] Some fear that this problematic trend poses a risk to the marketplace of ideas available to the American public.[7]

As the media landscape perseveres, resulting in large media conglomerates merging and acquiring other media companies, the ability of minority-owned[8] television, radio, and cable outlets to compete may become insurmountable,[9] largely because they may lack the necessary capital to competitively advertise or, even worse, become victims of advertising marginalization where advertisers refuse to purchase advertising time on minority stations.[10] Despite these concerns, the FCC reexamined its media ownership rules, altering its most contested rule by deciding to increase the national ownership cap from 35% to 45%.[11] Shortly after the new rules were released, the rules were challenged. Petitions for review were filed in the Second, Third, Ninth, and District of Columbia Circuit Courts of Appeals, seeking to review the media ownership rules.[12] The Judicial Panel on Multidistrict Litigation consolidated the cases, and following a lottery, ordered that the review be consolidated and transferred to the Third Circuit.[13] On September 3, 2003, the Third Circuit stayed the implementation of the local ownership rules pending resolution of the consolidated proceedings.[14] On January 24, 2004, the House and Senate, through an omnibus bill, reset the national television ownership cap to 39%, instead of the 45% cap instituted by the FCC.[15]

Although the debate about the media ownership rules has centered primarily on democratic principles and preserving the objectivity of the news,[16] the crux of it revolves around money, competition and preserving market share.[17] This Comment suggests that the interests of minorities, specifically how relaxing the ownership rules may affect the minority viewing audience, has largely been ignored in this legal debate. Minority-owned media companies fear that if mega-capitalized corporations are free to own as many media outlets as possible, there will be a detrimental impact on the ability of minorities to enter or remain in the industry.[18] The FCC has stated that its new 2003 ownership rules are "carefully balanced to protect diversity, localism, and competition in the American media system."[19] Unfortunately, minority interests are often ignored because there is either no representation on air or there is a limited focus on minority issues in the media.

Even though Congress decreased the national ownership cap, the ownership rules still provide the necessary mechanism for larger conglomerates to merge, further limiting the number of minority-owned broadcast owners. The National Telecommunications and Information Administration (NTIA) has issued reports surveying the state of minority media ownership, revealing that consolidation has had a detrimental impact on minority owners.[20] Traditional antitrust law is based on preserving competition and is enforced as an economic interest.[21] Unfortunately, the current FCC leadership is focused on economic efficiency without taking into consideration the non-economic factors that are harmful to the minority viewing audiences, such as mergers that limit the minority viewing audience's access to programming devoted to their interests. This economic approach allows the FCC to ignore its public interest standard to protect the interests of the public in the airwaves. The aforementioned minority interests and the consideration of non-economic factors that impact the minority viewing audience should be included in the FCC public interest analysis of merging media corporations.

Part I of this Comment reviews the historical role and function of the FCC in the broadcast industry. Part II addresses the measures taken by the FCC and the Congress to promote diversity by enacting various minority employment and tax certificate incentives. Part III examines the evolution of the media ownership rules. Part IV briefly examines the history of minority broadcast ownership, the impact relaxing the ownership rules may have on minority media owners and audiences, and the FCC's response to the needs

of minorities. In conclusion, Part V suggests that the FCC should supplant its merger review with an analytical framework that focuses on non-economic factors to promote diversity of viewpoint.

I. ESTABLISHMENT OF THE FEDERAL COMMUNICATIONS COMMISSION AND ITS PURPOSE

A. Background

The government's aim in regulating the airwaves dates back to the early 1900s.[22] At the beginning of the twentieth century, a considerable increase in commercial broadcasting and illegal behavior required government intervention[23] because shortly after the invention of the radio, a number of corporations created a "consortium for the purpose of monopolizing the manufacturing of equipment and the dissemination of programming."[24] To curb the ensuing monopolization of the airwaves, Congress adopted a federal licensing scheme under the Radio Act of 1927.[25] The Act created and established the Federal Radio Commission (FRC) as a government agency with licensing and regulatory power over "all forms of interstate and foreign radio transmissions and communications within the United States."[26] Initially, the FRC was to exist for one year and then its duties were to be transferred to the Commerce Department.[27] For seven years, the FRC revoked, reviewed and issued licenses to the airwaves.[28] The Radio Act of 1927 only granted the FRC the authority to grant a license "as public convenience, interest, or necessity require[d]."[29] This has become known as the "public interest standard."

B. Creation of the FCC

Unfortunately, the limited authority of the FRC could not keep pace with the rapid increase of radio stations, interference and shrinking availability of radio frequencies.[30] In response to the continuing growth in the radio industry and the perceived inadequacies of the FRC, Congress enacted the Communications Act of 1934,[31] creating the FCC, with increased power.[32] As a permanent federal agency, the FCC now had the authority to administer permits and licenses governing commercial broadcasting,"[33] and in exchange for an exclusive use of assigned frequencies, "the broadcasters [were] supposed to serve the 'public interest.'"[34] Although the Communications Act of 1934 does not provide a concrete definition of "public interest, convenience and necessity," the FCC "fosters the belief that public interest not only entails content-neutral regulations, but also that the public has the right to a 'diversity of views and information over the airwaves.'"[35]

II. FCC EFFORTS TO ENSURE DIVERSITY OF VIEWPOINT FOR MINORITIES

A. Absence of African Americans in the Media Spawns a Number of FCC Initiatives to Increase Diversity On and Off the Screen

The FCC has applied diversity of viewpoint as the cornerstone of many of its orders and rules in support of its "public interest standard."[36] In 1969, the Supreme Court ruled that FCC rules and regulations designed to increase viewpoint diversity were not in conflict with the First Amendment,[37] and that "the people as a whole retain their interest in free speech ... and their collective right to have the medium function consistently with the ends and purposes of the First Amendment."[38] One commentator states that the FCC holds the position that "diverse programming is a constitutionally guaranteed right of the public."[39] Unfortunately, minorities have not always enjoyed diverse programming representing their viewpoint. For many years, issues related to the minority community were absent from the airwaves.[40] Any interest in changing the status quo did not arise until the release of a report by the National Advisory Commission on Civil Disorders, known as the Kerner Commission, in the late 1960s.[41] The Kerner Commission reported that the media did not communicate "'to the majority of their audience—which is [W]hite—a sense of the degradation, misery, and hopelessness of living in the ghetto,'"[42] and "unless the media became more sensitive to its portrayal of minorities, and Blacks in particular, these stereotypical images would persist."[43] In response, the FCC initiated race-neutral regulatory policies to increase and encourage broadcasters to employ Blacks as a means to ensure the inclusion of the minority viewpoint.[44] The FCC also adopted rules forbidding employment discrimination.[45] Unfortunately, the minority employment incentives did not result in any real increase in minority representation in the broadcasting industry.[46] As late as 1971, minorities owned only 10 of the 7500 radio station licenses in the United States.[47]

In an effort to fulfill its mission to increase the public's access to the minority voice, the FCC established the Minority Ownership Task Force (MOTF) to research ways in which minorities could be included in the broadcasting industry.[48] The FCC supported the idea that "[a]dequate representation of minority viewpoints in programming serves not only the needs and interests of the minority community but also enriches and educates the non-minority audience."[49] In 1978, MOTF issued a report concluding that minorities needed to become participants in the broadcasting business as owners.[50] The Task Force surmised that "[u]nless minorities are encouraged to enter the mainstream of the commercial broadcasting business, a substantial proportion of our citizenry will remain underserved, and the larger non-minority audience will be deprived of the views of minorities."[51] After the report, it was clear that the absence of the minority viewpoint was "detrimental not only to minority audiences but to all of the viewing and listening public."[52]

Initially, the FCC did not embrace increasing minority ownership as a means to diversify content, taking the position that the Communication Act was colorblind.[53] The presumption that a nexus existed between minority ownership and diversity of viewpoint, originated in *TV 9, Inc. v. FCC*.[54] In *TV 9*, the FCC refused to award a comparative minority merit to a corporate applicant with African American investors living in the relevant community, claiming that "Black ownership [could not] and should not be an independent comparative factor."[55] This argument was rejected by the D.C. Circuit Court, which held that the Constitution permitted "a view of our developing national life which accords merits to Black participation"[56] and that "when minority ownership is likely to increase diversity of content, especially of opinion and viewpoint, merit should be awarded."[57] Two years later, the court further acknowledged that "[B]lack ownership and participation together are themselves likely to bring about programming that is responsive to the needs of the [B]lack citizenry and those reasonable expectations without advance demonstration [of a public interest benefit from increased minority ownership] gives them relevance."[58] Since the primary objective of comparative hearings is to determine which applicant would provide the best "service" when media companies have competing broadcast license applications,[59] after *TV 9*, the FCC "began considering ownership and participation in station management by members of minority groups"[60] when reviewing license applications of minority broadcast owners.

In 1978, the FCC adopted two additional policies to help alleviate the absence of minorities in the airwaves.[61] The two minority initiatives were a tax certificate program and a distress sale policy.[62] The tax certificate program offered tax deferrals, as an incentive, on any gains from transactions with minority purchasers and an owner of an existing broadcast facility.[63] The distress sale policy was designed to allow a broadcast licensee with a pending revocation hearing to sell the station to a minority-controlled entity at a lower fair market value of seventy-five percent or less.[64] The FCC argued that these policies were of paramount importance: "[Because of the] present lack of minority representation in the ownership of broadcast properties[,] ... [w]e believe that diversification in the areas of programming and ownership—legitimate public interest objectives of this Commission—can be more fully developed through our encouragement of minority ownership of broadcast properties."[65] Comparative hearings were eventually eliminated and replaced with competitive bidding procedures.[66] The distress sale policy still exists but is rarely utilized.[67] Unfortunately, Congress repealed the tax incentive program on the grounds that the FCC policy was not a legitimate means of increasing minority ownership and that the tax certificate program did not have any internal checks by the Internal Revenue Service (IRS).[68] Optimistically, members of Congress and the FCC have shown a renewed interest in reviving the tax certificate program.[69]

B. The Judicial Branch Questions the FCC "Diversity of Viewpoint" Policies and Minority Preference Programs

Prior to the FCC minority preference programs of the 1970s, the Supreme Court ruled, in *Associated Press v. United States*, that diverse programming is a First Amendment right that "rest[s] on the assumption that the widest possible dissemination of information from diverse and antagonistic sources is essential to the welfare of the public. ..."[70] As time progressed, the courts began to question the use of minority preference programs supported by the government. Despite Congress and the Supreme Court previously upholding the nexus argument,[71] when affirmative action came under attack, many of the FCC policies that promoted diversity were challenged based on the ownership and diversity nexus rationale. In 1985, the D.C. Circuit Court of Appeals turned away from its acceptance of the nexus argument in *TV 9* to support minority preference programs.[72] The court reasoned that:

> The minority preference rests on the assumption that first, membership in an ethnic minority causes members of that minority to have distinct tastes and perspectives and, second that these differences will consciously or unconsciously be reflected in distinctive editorial and entertainment programming. The validity of the first of these assumptions is not obvious on its face. ... Indeed, to make such an assumption concerning an individual's taste and viewpoint would seem to us as mere indulgence in the most simplistic kind of ethnic stereotyping. ... With respect to the second assumption[,] ... [t]o suggest that these dubious, ethnically determined tastes will outweigh the economic imperative of what the audience wants to hear ... strikes us as more than a little implausible.[73]

The court questioned whether there was any public benefit in increasing the number of minorities in the broadcast industry.[74] Additionally, several Supreme Court decisions implicated the FCC's minority preference programs. In *Metro Broadcasting, Inc. v. FCC*,[75] the FCC's minority preferential policies were challenged. The first policy promoted minority ownership in review proceedings for new broadcasting licenses.[76] The second policy restricted the sale of minority-owned radio and television broadcast stations to other minority-owned firms.[77] The FCC defended the two policies by arguing that a legitimate nexus existed between race and expression, and that the licensing scheme was consistent with "its long-standing view that ownership is a prime determinant of the range of programming available" to the public and in line with the First Amendment.[78]

The Supreme Court, utilizing an intermediate scrutiny test, narrowly upheld both FCC policies that encouraged minority ownership of broadcast licenses.[79] The Court analyzed a number of empirical studies that supported the idea that a link between minority ownership and content existed.[80] The most compelling research came from a report prepared by the Congressional Research Service entitled, *Minority Broadcast Station Ownership and Broadcast Programming: Is There a Nexus?*[81] The report concluded that "to the degree that increasing minority programming across audience markets is considered adding to programming diversity, then, based on the FCC survey data, an argument can be made that the FCC preference policies contributed, in turn, to programming diversity."[82] The Court reasoned that the policies advanced important First Amendment interests and were an acceptable measure in remedying past discrimination and diversifying programs.[83] Justice Brennan stated: "[T]he interest in enhancing broadcast diversity is, at the very least, an important governmental objective. ... [T]he diversity of views and information on the airwaves serves important First Amendment values. ... [T]he benefits redound to all members of the viewing and listening audience."[84] However, *Adarand* overruled *Metro Broadcasting* by holding that congressional programs that differentiate among groups based on race shall be subject to strict scrutiny.[85] The *Adarand* standard required that any preferential programs must have empirical statistical evidence to prove past discrimination and that any program implemented is narrowly tailored to rectify that past discrimination.[86] As a result, in order for the FCC to establish any program that gives preferential treatment to any class of people based on race, it must be narrowly tailored to eradicate prior discrimination.[87] As affirmative action programs required stringent justifications,[88] the FCC abandoned many of its efforts to increase minority ownership and instead supported relaxing ownership restrictions as a means to promote diversity of viewpoint and competition.[89]

III. THE HISTORY OF MEDIA OWNERSHIP

The principal means of regulating broadcasting is through the control of station ownership. The FCC regulates media ownership "to guard against the feared formation of a monopoly and to expand the number of voices with access to the airwaves."[90] This section discusses the evolution of the media ownership rules.

A. Media Ownership Policy Prior to the Telecommunications Act of 1996

The FCC did not institute a national television ownership restriction prohibiting one company from reaching a particular percentage of American households until the 1940s, when it limited nationwide ownership of broadcast stations to three stations.[91] The number was increased to five stations in 1953, and in 1954, the FCC eventually raised the cap to seven stations.[92]

The seven-station rule remained intact for nearly thirty years before the FCC considered a major transformation of its media ownership rules.[93] In 1984, the agency raised the ownership limit to twelve television stations.[94] This change was not considered to impair the promotion of viewpoint diversity or the prevention of media concentration because the seven-station limit was no longer needed due to technological changes and the growing number of media outlets.[95] This rule was rejected by Congress and after reconsidering its findings, the FCC established an audience reach cap of 25% to measure nationwide ownership.[96]

The 25% cap restricted a single entity from owning television stations that reached more than 25% of American households.[97] The FCC reasoned that a national audience cap would "temper dramatic changes in ownership structure by the largest group owners in the largest markets."[98] The local television ownership rules were not created until the mid-1960s, when the FCC instituted a policy that prohibited an entity from owning two television stations in the same local market.[99] This rule did not undergo any significant changes until the enactment of the Telecommunications Act of 1996.[100]

B. The Telecommunications Act of 1996

Since the passage of the Act, a number of mergers and acquisitions of television networks, radio stations and cable companies have occurred, owing in large part to the FCC's media ownership policies.[101] The Act eliminated the long-standing restriction on the number of television stations a person or corporation could "directly or indirectly own, operate, or control, or have a cognizable interest in nationwide."[102] The Act also required the FCC to review its ownership rules and to "repeal or modify any regulation it determines to be no longer in the public interest."[103] The FCC modified the national television ownership rule and increased the audience reach cap from 25% to 35% of American households,[104] due to the increased number of broadcasting stations, radio stations, cable television systems, and satellite carriers.[105] For example, in contrast to the three broadcasting networks in 1975, there are currently seven national commercial broadcast network stations on the air.[106]

The Act delegated to the FCC the authority to review the local television market.[107] The local television ownership rule, adopted in 1999, allowed common ownership of two television stations in the same local market as long as one of the stations was not among the four highest ranked stations in the market and at least eight independently owned operational television stations remained in that market after any merger.[108] This rule is referred to as the "top four ranked/eight voices test."[109] The FCC set the number of independently owned television stations at eight to maximize the available viewpoints given in a local market.[110] When the FCC reexamined its media ownership rules during its 1998 Biennial Review and concluded that the rules did not warrant a repeal or modification,[111] media corporations challenged the validity of the decision and lobbied for an increase in the ownership cap rules.

C. D.C. Circuit Court Questions the Validity of the 1998 FCC Ownership Decision

The D.C. Circuit Court of Appeals reviewed the national ownership rule and local ownership rules in two cases: *Fox Television Stations, Inc. v. FCC*[112] and *Sinclair Broadcasting Group, Inc. v. FCC*.[113] In *Fox*, television broadcasters challenged the FCC's decision not to repeal or modify its national ownership rules.[114] The broadcasters argued that the FCC failed to show how competition would be hindered by the current ownership rules.[115] The FCC countered

and explained that retaining the national television ownership rules would allow smaller affiliates to bargain with larger networks so that they could better serve their local communities, and that repealing the national ownership rule would reduce competition and diversity.[116] The court remanded the national television ownership rules to the FCC for further consideration, holding that it acted arbitrarily and capriciously by retaining the rule.[117]

The court in *Sinclair Broadcasting Group, Inc. v. FCC*[118] remanded the local television ownership rule for further consideration because the court did not accept the FCC's justification for establishing the top four ranked/eight voices test. The FCC believed that because the media marketplace had changed considerably, a relaxed local ownership rule was in the public's best interest.[119] The court ruled that the local ownership rules demanded that the FCC utilize empirical evidence to support its rule making proceedings with respect to ownership restrictions.[120]

D. The FCC Relaxes Its Media Ownership Rules

Applying *Fox* and *Sinclair*, the FCC set out to review its media ownership rules once more in its 2002 Biennial Review. The FCC set forth four objectives in its review:

(1) To more accurately define its policy goals of diversity, competition, and localism, (2) to determine the best way to promote these goals in the media industry consistent with the 1996 Act, (3) to establish the best measure for these goals, and (4) to establish a balancing test to prioritize the goals if tension exists between them.[121]

Under the direction of Chairman Michael Powell, the FCC seriously considered weakening its restraints on media ownership. The FCC initiated an extensive review of its media ownership rules in an effort to collect as much empirical evidence as possible.[122] Chairman Powell stated that:

This effort is the most comprehensive look at media ownership regulation ever undertaken by the FCC. As the courts have made clear, it is critical that the FCC has a solid factual base to support its media ownership rules. Collectively, these studies represent an unprecedented data gathering effort to better understand market and consumer issues so that we may develop sound public policy.[123]

In October 2002, the Media Bureau of the FCC released twelve empirical studies that examined the current state of the media industry, including the impact media ownership may have on diversity, local markets and competition.[124] One study found that the number of media outlets (radio stations, television stations, newspapers, and cable systems) available to consumers has increased considerably by an average of 195% since 1960.[125]

The FCC eventually decided to relax and eliminate several key media ownership restrictions, reasoning that competition from various media, and the changing media marketplace, lent themselves to less stringent ownership rules.[126] The FCC increased the national television ownership cap, allowing broadcast entities to own a group of stations reaching 45% of the national audience,[127] until the cap was reduced to 39% by Congress in January 2004.[128] The local ownership rules were also challenged. The Prometheus Radio Project (PRP) brought an action to stay the implementation of the rules until judicial review, arguing that the FCC's rules were arbitrary, and that the agency failed to recognize the public interest harm that would result if the rules were made effective.[129] PRP also charged that the FCC ignored its public interest mandate and instead focused only on economic factors, such as competition in advertising sales.[130] The Third Circuit decided to stay the implementation of the media ownership rules until further review.[131] Until a decision has been made by the Third Circuit, local ownership rules and its impact on diversity viewpoint is speculative, at best.[132]

IV. HISTORY OF MINORITY BROADCAST OWNERSHIP

There is a theory that deregulation of the media industry serves the public interest by providing more inter-industry competition, leveling the playing field for those who provide "free, over-the-air commercial television."[133] Unfortunately, the playing field has never been level for minorities, partly due to past economic barriers of entry and legislatively approved racial discrimination. African Americans were virtually shut out of ownership of the broadcasting industry until 1978 when the FCC adopted its policies to promote minority ownership of broadcast stations.[134] It is likely that the current media ownership rules may eliminate much of the progress of that 1978 initiative.

A. Obstacles to Minority Station Acquisitions

The FCC issued many broadcast stations during the formative years of the regulated broadcasting industry when minorities were not able to take advantage of these opportunities. As such, "the effects of past inequities stemming from racial and ethnic discrimination have resulted in a severe under-representation of minorities in the media of mass communications, as it has adversely affected their participation in other sectors of the economy as well."[135] As a result of racial discrimination, when African Americans were eventually able to obtain licenses, the number of minority owned stations was very small.[136] While reliable statistics are not available, it has been reported that there was not a single African American–owned television station until the early 1970s.[137] The first minority-owned television station Detroit's WGPR-TV received its permit in 1973,[138] when the regulatory paradigm recognized the merits of minority ownership and its contribution to viewpoint diversity.[139]

The less restrictive ownership rules have also contributed to the disproportionate participation of minorities in media ownership, partly because minority media owners are primarily single station operators.[140] According to the 2001 report by NTIA, the "relaxation of the ownership rules and consolidation have contributed to higher broadcast station prices. The skyrocketing prices, in some instances up to [twenty] times or more the amount of a station's actual cash flow, have exacerbated minority broadcasters' historic difficulty accessing sufficient capital for entry or expansion."[141] According to the Diversity and Competition Supporters, the success of the tax certificate policies promoting minority ownership helped alleviate some of the financial constraints associated with media ownership, but this effort has been limited by the FCC and the numerous lawsuits challenging affirmative action.[142]

B. The Ownership-Viewpoint Diversity Debate from the Minority Perspective

In *Metro Broadcasting, Inc. v. FCC*, the Supreme Court recognized that the FCC's ownership-viewpoint diversity nexus was consistent with the Communications Act and that "diversification of ownership [would] broaden the range of programming available to the broadcast audience."[143] This principle of a "broadened" programming range does not necessarily transfer to the diversity of viewpoint needs of the minority viewing audience. The FCC measures viewpoint diversity through news and public affairs because "it relates most directly to [its] core policy objective of facilitating robust democratic discourse in the media."[144] Despite this commitment, the National Association of Hispanic Journalists (NAHJ), recently released a report that documented how minorities are continually depicted in the media in a negative light.[145] The report, entitled *Network Brownout Report*, stated that despite the increase of the Latino population in the United States, "Latinos were the subject of less than 1% of stories that aired on network television in 2002."[146] The NAHJ believes that the informational needs of the Latino community are ill-served due to the lack of Latinos working in newsrooms and broadcast management.[147] As indicated in *Metro Broadcasting*, "[d]iversity of ownership ... promote[s] diversity of views. Minority ... broadcasters serve a need that is not as well served as others. They address issues that others do not."[148] Examples like this illustrate that the D.C. Circuit Court's opinion in the 1970s that "[minority] ownership and participation together are themselves likely to bring about programming that is responsive to the needs of the [minority] citizenry ...,"[149] has not been achieved, and perhaps the nexus between viewpoint and ownership among minorities has some validity and should be supported by the FCC's public interest mandate.

Justice O'Connor's dissent in *Metro Broadcasting* argued that there is no justification to benefit a group based entirely on race if it is premised on a "rigid assumption about how minority owners will behave in every case,"[150] and further stated that

> a racial criterion embodies the related notions that a particular and distinct viewpoint inheres in certain racial groups, and that a particular

[minority broadcast owner], by virtue of race or ethnicity alone, is more valued than other [broadcast owners] because they are "likely to provide [that] distinct [minority] perspective."[151]

As the NAHJ Report illustrates that minorities are being depicted in a stereotypical fashion, the causal connection between minority ownership and programming viewpoint is relevant, despite criticism that "race-based means of achieving the FCC's diversity goal tends only to reinforce racial stereotyping."[152]

C. Media Ownership Limits and Its Impact On Stereotypes in the Media

The FCC is "entitled to reconsider and revise its views as to the public interest and the means needed to protect that interest."[153] Therefore, the agency should utilize its broad public interest directive to provide the necessary resources for people of color to have access to the broadcasting industry; perhaps this will assist in countering the use of negative images presently found in the media.[154] Messages and imagery in the media have helped to create and mold the image of minorities to the world partly because there is no other medium that engages in the creation and distribution of content, other than the media, at such a high level of consumption.[155] Some suggest that a solution to improving the negative imagery of minorities on screen is to increase the number of minorities that have a controlling interest in a media corporation.[156]

Despite the fact that Black Entertainment Television (BET) was started and predominantly run by African Americans, and the network's claim that it is a place African Americans can go to find news and content geared towards their interests, one critic laments that BET "has taken on a new meaning for many African Americans: Black Embarrassing Television,"[157] due to the sexually charged and one-dimensional characters of color presented on the network.[158] Some critics blame the lack of quality programming on Viacom's acquisition of BET;[159] however, prior to the sale, BET displayed the same stereotypical programs.[160] Although "[t]here were no [B]lack dramas or other intellectually stimulating programs being shown,"[161] BET's ability to provide news and public affairs specifically addressing the concerns of African American people is unprecedented. "BET Nightly News" is one of the only nightly news shows to report the day's national and international headlines with a uniquely Black perspective on cable.[162] Despite the firing of a prominent news anchor, BET's news show provides in-depth interviews with prominent and local African Americans regarding important issues facing the community.[163]

Minority-owned media corporations have the ability to provide public affairs programming addressing news stories unreported, or considered minor stories by other mainstream media outlets. In testimony before the Senate Committee on Commerce, Science and Transportation, Robert Short, Jr., President of Short Broadcasting Co., Inc. and former owner of WRDS radio station in Syracuse, testified about the negative effects deregulation has had, and will continue to have, on minority news content. "WRDS provided local news and public affairs programming without regard to oversight from any distant corporate parent. WRDS carried news stories that other media ignored."[164] Furthermore, Native Americans, the least represented minorities among media owners, "usually rely on non-commercial station ownerships to serve their communities,"[165] which eludes that community the opportunity of utilizing the "power of the mass media to improve community building, self-determination, and preservation and protection of [their] cultural identity."[166] There is a compelling interest to restrict media concentration because, although African Americans and Latinos make up a significant portion of the population, until a critical mass of individuals of color gain access and have a controlling interest in the broadcast industry, diversity of viewpoint from a minority perspective will be *de minimis.*[167]

D. Minority Media Owners Question the Validity of Relaxing the Ownership Rules

Many minority organizations filed comments with the FCC expressing concern that the rules have allowed larger companies to consume many minority-owned stations, resulting in minorities losing access to the broadcasting industry.[168]

"Ownership in the radio industry is becoming concentrated in the hands of fewer owners and

there has been a decline in ownership by Black entrepreneurs. ... The Telecommunications Act of 1996 served to accelerate the trend towards market consolidation by removing limits on the national ownership of radio and greatly relaxing ownership limits in the local markets."[169]

Hence, minority viewpoints are increasingly less likely to find ready access on the airwaves.

In a recent op-ed piece, Chairman Powell and Senator John McCain noted that minorities are an under-represented group with respect to media ownership.[170] They cite to a 2001 report released by the National Telecommunications and Information Administration (NTIA) that "minorities owned 449 of the 11,865 full-power commercial radio and television stations in the United States, or 3.8%. Such figures stand in sharp contrast to the population figures as a whole for 2001, in which minorities represented nearly a third of the total U.S. population."[171] More importantly, the FCC has acknowledged that,

"minority broadcast station owners, when compared to non-minority owners, *provide more public affairs programming on events or issues concerning ethnic or racial minority audiences,* are more likely to broadcast in languages other than English, are more likely to staff their station with minority employees and *are more likely to participate in minority-related events in their communities.*"[172]

To increase minority ownership, Chairman Powell and Senator McCain believe that Congress should adopt the Telecommunications Ownership Diversification Act, which "would remedy this problem by allowing large businesses to defer certain taxable gains when communications assets are sold to qualifying small businesses."[173] According to the NTIA, "between 1978 and March 1996, the [FCC] issued 359 tax certificates to promote minority ownership in broadcasting."[174] The termination of the tax certificate program, coupled with the *Adarand* decision, has greatly curtailed the FCC's efforts to promote minority ownership.

The FCC has also established a Federal Advisory Committee on Diversity for Communications in the Digital Age.[175] Similar to the Minority Task

Force that helped to create the tax certificate and distress sales policies in the late 1970s, the Diversity Committee will "develop a set of recommendations including potential regulatory actions and education initiatives to promote and enhance opportunities for minorities and women."[176] Although there seems to be a commitment to improving the opportunities for minorities in the communications industry, with the implementation of the Diversity Committee and a renewed interest in implementing the tax certificate program, the promise of these initiatives is unclear. The Minority Media and Telecommunications Council (MMTC), in its brief filed in the pending *Prometheus Radio Project v. FCC* action, states that it is not convinced that the FCC will consider any new minority ownership policies with much fervor.[177] Within the past couple of years, the organization has submitted ingenious methodologies to improve the condition of minority ownership in the broadcasting industry of which the FCC has not actively pursued.[178]

Most notably, the organization suggested a Staged Implementation of Deregulation Plan for the media ownership rules.[179] This Plan offered a two-year guideline that would allow the FCC to measure minority ownership, competition, localism and diversity more effectively.[180] This Plan allows the FCC to make incremental adjustments to its ownership rules to "avoid causing irreversible damage if a deregulatory step proves to be a mistake."[181] The Plan was modeled after the *Brown v. Board of Education*[182] cases aimed at desegregating public schools in an incremental fashion. MMTC reasons that as the implementation plans gave school districts the flexibility to adapt to the changing hue of the classroom, a similarly careful and exact implementation of the media ownership rules affords the economy to adapt to changes in the market.[183] It is paramount that the FCC alters its course and genuinely re-commits itself to improving the status of minority ownership.

V. BROADER NON-ECONOMIC MEDIA REVIEW NEEDED TO CURB MEDIA MERGERS

A. Traditional Antitrust Review vs. The FCC Public Interest Standard: Two Conflicting Principles

Today, United States antitrust enforcement is based primarily on economic factors to preserve and protect competition.[184] The media plays an essential role in disseminating ideas and promoting democracy. As a consequence, merging media corporations impact more than economic concerns protected by antitrust laws; the combination of media corporations can directly impact the marketplace of ideas for the viewing audience. The FCC is in a critical position to protect the potential harm to the minority media owners and the minority viewing audience because as recognized in *Metro Broadcasting*, "it is upon ownership that public policy places primary reliance with respect to diversification of content. ...."[185]

Although mergers and acquisitions are governed by the Sherman Act,[186] proposed mergers are generally reviewed under Section 18 of the Clayton Act.[187] The Act stipulates that "no person ... shall acquire ... any part of the assets of another person ... where in any line of commerce ... in any section of the country, the effect of such acquisition may be substantially to lessen competition, or tend to create a monopoly."[188] The Clayton Act focuses on the "reasonable probability" of anticompetitive or monopolistic behavior.[189] Current merger analysis rests mainly on the potential economic effects of a proposed merger with respect to market power.[190]

Mergers and acquisitions are normally under the review of the Department of Justice (DOJ) or Federal Trade Commission (FTC),[191] but the FCC shares concurrent jurisdiction with the other regulatory agencies over mergers or acquisitions involving radio license transfers or telecommunications common carriers which may have the effect of substantially lessening competition or tending to create a monopoly with respect to the FCC public interest mandate.[192] As the primary focus of merger review under the DOJ and FTC is a quantifiable economic measure, the FCC is the appropriate agency to protect viewpoint diversity because it can take into account other factors not afforded within the confines of "reasonable probability." This Comment does not propose that the FCC terminate its regulatory function in analyzing media mergers, but recognizes that due to the delicate nature of the marketplace of ideas, media mergers require a more aggressive review and necessitates a regulatory paradigm that seeks to protect diversity viewpoint.[193]

The Supreme Court, in *Associated Press*, emphasized the FCC's duty to promote source and viewpoint diversity as a First Amendment right that "rest[s] on the assumption that the widest possible dissemination of information from diverse and antagonistic sources is essential to the welfare of the public …"[194] Because the FCC operates under an independent public interest standard "with the aim of promoting source diversity, outlet diversity, and viewpoint diversity,"[195] it should heed this directive and in its assessment of likely competitive benefits or harms, not limit its merger review to an economic analysis.

In an effort to base its media ownership rules on empirical evidence as directed from *Sinclair Broadcasting*, the FCC utilized a Diversity Index, an economic qualitative tool, similar to the Herfindahl-Hirschmann Index (HHI) used in traditional antitrust law.[196] The Diversity Index measures and analyzes available media outlets that contribute to viewpoint diversity in local media markets with respect to cross ownership.[197] One commentator asserts that "the FCC devoted much discussion to … evidence that cross-ownership creates efficiencies and synergies that enhance the quality and viability of media outlets, thus enhancing the flow of news and information to the public."[198]

The aim of antitrust law is to not only protect consumers from unfair price increases, but also, and perhaps most importantly, protect consumer choice, but in economic terms. Twenty years ago, Robert Pitofsky, the former chairman of the FTC, proposed that non-economic factors should be considered in antitrust analysis.[199] He believed that "It is bad history, bad policy, and bad law to exclude certain political values in interpreting the antitrust laws."[200] This was also supported in *Metro Broadcasting* in that the FCC "has never relied on the market alone to ensure that the needs of the audience are met."[201]

The FCC should employ a merger review model under this "consumer choice" ideology that encompasses non-economic factors that go beyond market power and economic efficiency[202] because "antitrust

is more than economics."[203] Unfortunately, the FCC has not taken advantage of its broad discretionary power to protect "public convenience, interest, or necessity [as] require[d]"[204] by easing its media ownership restrictions. Focusing heavily on market power and economic efficiency in the communications industry ignores a fundamental principle of antitrust law–consumer choice. Unless the FCC takes note and broadens its public interest mandate to protect viewpoint diversity, the media ownership restrictions will create an environment that may limit consumer choice, making it easier for larger corporations to dominate certain sectors of the media spectrum and stifle the minority viewpoint.

B. Minority Viewing Audiences as a Submarket

The new media ownership rules accept the assumption that with the advent of cable, satellite, and digital systems, source, outlet and viewpoint diversities are not compromised because information access is to some extent limitless.[205] Even though minority audiences have access to a number of alternative media sources, they may have different interests that are not being displayed in the media and this separate market of interests is usually not considered under the FCC's merger review process.[206]

Although minorities have access to many media outlets, recognizing their interests is important. According to the Nielsen Media Research, African Americans out of all other populations, are the largest television viewing audience in the United States,[207] and interestingly, minority viewing patterns differ from the rest of the American population, particularly for Spanish speaking homes, because "language usage in [Latino] homes has an important impact on TV viewing choices."[208] African Americans and Latinos are the two largest ethnic television viewing audiences sampled by the Nielsen Media Research and the information compiled is utilized by the media industry "to buy and sell television time as well as to increase the effectiveness of television advertising and programming."[209] If the media industry relies on the viewing choices of minorities, it begs the question why the FCC has chosen not to recognize the minority audience as a separate market with respect to its merger review process?

The FCC has the authority to protect the interests of the minority viewing audience by adhering to its public interest mandate, but has opted to focus heavily on economic factors, such as efficiency and preserving market share. This economic methodology has caused the FCC not to adhere to its previous commitment to "encourage diversity in the ownership of broadcast stations so as to foster a diversity of viewpoints in the material presented over the airwaves."[210]

A non-economic analysis, focused on minority audiences as a submarket within the broader communications market, should be considered when a merger has the potential of impacting minority viewing audiences. Under traditional antitrust law, submarkets are an economic evaluative measure,[211] however, it should be extended and applicable to the public interest standard as a non-economic factor. The concept of a submarket evolved from the Supreme Court's recognition, in *Brown Shoe Co. v. United States*, that a separate market may exist within a primary one.[212]

> The outer boundaries of a product market are determined by the reasonable interchange-ability of use or the cross-elasticity of demand between the product itself and substitutes for it. However, within this broad market, well-defined submarkets may exist which, in themselves, constitute product markets for antitrust purposes. The boundaries of such a submarket may be determined by examining such practical indicia as industry or *public recognition of the submarket as a separate economic entity, … distinct customers, …* Because § 7 of the Clayton Act prohibits any merger which may substantially lessen competition "in any line of commerce," it is necessary to examine the effects of a merger in each such economically significant submarket to determine if there is a reasonable probability that the merger will substantially lessen competition. If such a probability is found to exist, the merger is proscribed.[213]

Submarkets are relevant to minority audiences because they can be "distinct customers" within the larger media landscape when it comes to the type of information minorities seek in the media. As stated earlier, minority-owned media stations are more likely to provide public affairs information relevant to the minority community than non-minority outlets and therefore, should be considered as a submarket. The recent Hispanic Broadcasting Corporation's (HBC) acquisition by Univision Communications, Inc. illustrates why it is important that the FCC consider the needs of minority audiences as a relevant submarket in its merger review analysis.

The FCC and DOJ recently approved the merger of two dominant Latino-oriented media corporations,[214] even though the merger implicated the radio/television cross-ownership rules in San Francisco and San Jose, California.[215] The rule requires "a resulting combination [that] contains stations in more than one … radio market"[216] to satisfy the voice count prong standard. The voice count prong allows a party to own "1 television station and up to 6 radio stations in any market where at least 20 independently owned media voices remain in the market after the proposed transaction."[217] The FCC refused to recognize the Latino viewing audience as a separate market despite receiving complaints that the merger would "diminish the diversity of sources available to Spanish-language speakers."[218] The FCC held the position that diversity of viewpoint was not compromised for viewers that speak primarily or only Spanish and that there was no impact or harm to the Spanish-speaking audience to justify a "Spanish-language submarket due to the availability of other media alternatives for that audience."[219]

This decision does not take into account that economic forces do not account for other intangible factors that may potentially harm or impact minority audiences and business owners. For example, FCC Commissioners Adelstein and Copps, in their dissent, argued that the Latino audience will be disadvantaged by the merger because media concentration does not consider language barriers and cultural affairs specific to that population as a factor.[220] Allowing the market to dictate the composition of a submarket solely based on economics may, as FTC Chairman Pitofsky alluded to in the late 1970s, result in an "economy so dominated by a few corporate giants that it will be impossible for the [government] not to play a more intrusive role in economic affairs."[221]

Although the FCC has had a tradition of not defining product markets based on programming format or language, and has taken the position that format choice should be dictated by market forces,[222] it is difficult to promote viewpoint diversity if the market effectively forces the minority audience and minority broadcast owners to seek alternatives that are owned by a small number of non-minority media conglomerates that may not offer sufficient content alternatives for that audience. Perhaps this offers a basis for the FCC to supplant its merger review to concentrate on the resulting social and political effects of ownership diversity with respect to the minority viewing audience. At a minimum, the FCC should recognize that its public interest standard should be paramount in all of its decisions, instead of promulgating policies cabined in economics.

CONCLUSION

The Telecommunications Act of 1996, under the guise of promoting competition, modified or eliminated many longstanding rules governing market concentration and cross ownership. By removing these concentration and ownership barriers, the Act encouraged media mergers by large media conglomerates, making it more difficult for minority media owners to compete. As a result, the Act has helped big media organizations control competition and diversity in the marketplace of ideas. The FCC should, through its public interest directive, play a more aggressive role in media merger analysis by focusing on social and political factors and protect diversity and competition in the marketplace of ideas. In the past, the FCC, Congress and other government agencies have focused on increasing diversity viewpoint by increasing the number of minority owners. However, the critical question has always been what constitutes a minority viewpoint? Is there one set of individuals that can capture the entire "voice" of one race? The problem is that people are all different; therefore, minorities do not all think alike. The experiences of African Americans in low-income neighborhoods in Chicago may result in a much different perspective than a middle-class African American family residing in Phoenix. Moreover, it is not necessarily accurate to depict all low-income individuals as having the same

experiences. Family values, economics and environment form how individuals view the world.[223] If there is no way to capture a more inclusive view, does a nexus between ownership and diversity really exist?

This Comment surmises that perhaps it does. The quandary is that due to the small number of minority broadcast owners, there is an assumption that a link does not exist. The National Association of Black-Owned Broadcasters, in comments to the FCC, challenged the agency to adopt policies "to enhance viewpoint and source diversity, and stem the tide of consolidation which is destroying viewpoint and source diversity, and ... reducing the number of minority broadcast stations owners."[224]

This Comment contends that perhaps some mergers harm the welfare of the minority viewing audience by diminishing viewpoint diversity available to that audience. Consumers should be free to make choices by any criteria they choose: quality, price, or as in the case of media organizations, by viewpoint diversity. The potential injury to minorities is that as the concentration of ownership drives out more and more small "mom and pop" urban stations, the probability that a monopoly of the marketplace of ideas will foreclose any choice for "minority news" increases from a minority perspective.

Antitrust law can be an effective weapon against massive media corporate consolidation in general, but the FCC's ownership rules and merger review, specifically, should not focus merely on economic factors. The public interest standard is broad enough to encompass more than an economic analysis for media mergers; therefore, the FCC should also take into account the social and political aspects of every proposed merger deal.[225]

There is a nexus between ownership and diversity because our decisions are based on the experiences individuals have and the media especially influences perceptions and behaviors about race.[226] "Because the prevailing view is that a large amount of power to shape society resides in the hands of television executives, directors, and writers, it is imperative that remedies are found to remake the composition of television shows and the executive suites that produce them."[227] Critics argue that the current media marketplace "allows for greater diversity without regulation;"[228] however, even with the expansion of media networks, people of color are primarily absent from television. More importantly, the Internet and other technological advancements are not a suitable or sufficient substitute because minorities rely heavily on radio and television for news and information.[229] Former FCC Commissioner Gloria Tristani eloquently surmised that large media mergers and the resultant economies of scale are not always a good thing.

> How information is presented and what stories are covered and, often more important, *what stories are not covered*, has a significant impact on public perceptions and the discussion of public issues. More channels do not necessarily mean that additional views are being expressed. More channels often just mean that the same voice can express their views over and over again.[230]

The Supreme Court has held that, "It is the right of the public to receive suitable access to social, political, aesthetic, moral, and other ideas and experiences. … That right may not constitutionally be abridged either by Congress or by the FCC."[231] Until the FCC augments its current merger review with a renewed commitment to increase minority ownership, the promise of the Telecommunications Act of 1996 will never reach its goal to expand diversity of viewpoint.

NOTES

* J.D. Candidate, Howard University School of Law, 2004; M.M.C., 2001; B.S., 1996. Executive Notes & Comments Editor, HOWARD LAW JOURNAL, 2003–2004. I must give honor to God for blessing me with this opportunity to engage in legal discourse and to expound upon my legal and graduate studies in Mass Communications. I appreciate the hard work and diligence of my Associate Articles Editors, Alexis Hall and Tameka N. Simmons, and the valuable feedback received from Howard Law Professors Michael deHaven Newsom and Andrew I. Gavil, and Associate Dean Patricia M. Worthy. I also extend extreme gratitude to my friend and Managing Editor, Lindsay N. Kendrick, and my mentor, Clint E. Odom, for all of the support given to me during the writing process.

1. Carter G. Woodson, *The Mis-Education Of The Negro* 180 (Associated Publishers 1977) (1933).

2. Telecommunications Act of 1996, Pub. L, No. 104–104, 110 Stat. 56 (codified at 47 U.S.C §§ 151–641 (1996)).

3. See 47 U.S.C. § 202(c) (1996); Implementation of Sections 202(c)(1) and 202(e) of the Telecommunications Act of 1996 (National Broadcast Television Ownership and Dual Network Operations), 61 Fed. Reg. 10,691 (Mar. 15, 1996) (to be codified at 47 C.F.R. pt. 73); KOFI OFORI ET AL., BLACKOUT? MEDIA OWNERSHIP CONCENTRATION AND THE FUTURE OF BLACK RADIO 3, 13–14 (1997) [hereinafter OFORI, BLACKOUT?].

4. Recently, the cable corporation, Comcast, made an unsolicited bid offer to merge with the Walt Disney Corporation. Frank Ahrens & Christopher Stern, *Comcast Bid Shows Power of Cable TV*, Wash. Post, Feb. 16, 2004, at Al.

5. Young African-Americans Against Media Stereotypes, *The World's 10 Biggest Media Companies and What They Own: 10 Companies Control 90% of the Information and Entertainment You Receive, at* http://www.yaaams.org/topten.shtml (last visited Feb. 7, 2004). Some of the biggest media companies are AOL Time Warner, Walt Disney, Viacom, Inc., News Corporation (headed by Rupert Murdoch), Sony, Vivendi Universal, and NBC (owned by General Electric). *Id.* Each company owns a large number of other media outlets. *Id.* For example, Time Warner owns a publishing house that includes magazines such as *Time, Sports Illustrated,* and *Life,* a music division that includes Interscope and Elektra Records, a studio that owns a part of Warner Brothers Television Network, and the largest owner of cable systems in the U.S. and cable channels, CNN, HBO and Cinemax. *Id.*

6. Miami Herald Publ'g Co. v. Tornillo, 418 U.S. 241, 250 (1974).

7. *See* Jonathan Krim, *Offer Raises Concern About Ownership of TV, Internet Access,* Wash. Post, Feb. 12, 2004, at E1.

8. As used herein, "minority" and "minorities" refers to African Americans, Latino Americans, Asian Americans and Native Americans.

9. *See FCC Oversight: Hearing to Discuss Federal Communications Commission June 2nd Decision on Various Media Ownership Rules Before the Senate Committee on Commerce, Science, and Transportation,* 108th Cong. 6–7 (2003) (statement of Michael J. Copps, Commissioner, Federal Communications Commission), *available at* http://hraunfoss.fcc.gov/edocs_public/attachmatch/DOC-235127A3.pdf.

10. *See* Robert Millar, Comment, *Racism is in the Air: The FCC's Mandate to Protect Minorities from Getting Shortchanged by Advertisers,* 8 COMM. L. CONSPECTUS 311 (2000) (discussing how discrimination plays a role in how advertisers decide where to place their advertising dollars).

11. Broadcast Ownership Rules, Cross-Ownership of Broadcast Stations and Newspapers, Multiple Ownership of Radio Broadcast Stations in Local Markets, and Definition of Radio Markets, 68 Fed. Reg. 46,286 (Aug. 5, 2003) (to be codified at 47 C.F.R. pt. 73) [hereinafter 2003 Broadcast Ownership Rules]. The FCC limits the signal control a single entity may have in a particular region based on a percentage of the national viewing audience. *See id.* at 46,356. For a historical discussion of the ownership rules, see discussion *infra* Part III.

12. *See* FCC's Consolidated Opposition to Motions for Stay Pending Judicial Review (Nos. 03–3388, et al.) at 7, 2003 WL 22052896 (3d Cir. 2003). On August 6, 2003, Media General, Inc., the National Association of Broadcasters, and the Network Affiliated Stations Alliance filed motions in the D.C. Circuit Court of Appeals. *Id.* The Third Circuit received a petition from the Prometheus Radio Project. *Id.* Media Alliance filed a petition in the Ninth Circuit and the National Council for Churches of Christ in the United States filed a similar petition in the Second Circuit. *Id.* Three additional petitions for review were filed in the D.C. Circuit by Fox Entertainment Group, Inc., Viacom, Inc., and the National Broadcasting Company, Inc. *Id.*

13. Consolidation Order of the Judicial Panel on Multidistrict Litigation (J.P.M.L. 2003), *available at* http://www.ca3.uscourts.gov/staymotion/rtc67.pdf. The Panel has the authority to consolidate and transfer cases to one court. *See* 28 U.S.C. § 2112(a) (2000).

14. Prometheus Radio Project v. FCC, 2003 WL 22052896 (3d Cir. 2003). As of the final publication deadline of this article, the Third Circuit has not made a ruling.

15. Consolidated Appropriations Act, Pub. L. No. 108–199, § 629, 118 Stat. 3 (2004).

16. Paul Davidson & David Lieberman, *FCC Eases Rules for Media Mergers,* USA Today, June 3, 2003, at 1.

17. *Id.*

18. Comments of the National Association of Black Owned Broadcasters, Inc. (NABOB) & the Rainbow/Push Coalition, Inc., In the Matter of 2002 Biennial Regulatory Review—Review of the Commission's Broadcast Ownership Rules and Other Rules Adopted Pursuant to Section 202 of the Telecommunications Act of 1996 [hereinafter 2002 Biennial Review], 6–10 (Jan. 2, 2003), (on file with author) [hereinafter NABOB]; Comments of the National Association of Hispanic Journalists (NAHJ) 2002 Biennial Review, 7 (Jan. 2, 2003), *available at* http://www.nahj.org/pdf/NAHJ_FCC.pdf. [hereinafter NAHJ]; "Minority-owned stations at least provide a platform for [minorities] to be heard on broader issues and to reach both ethnic and general audiences that are searching for a diversity of viewpoints." Hugh Price, Address at the FCC Martin Luther King Observance 5 (Jan. 30, 2003) (transcript available in the Comments of the Diversity and Competition Supporters, 2002 Biennial Review (on file with author)).

19. Press release, FCC, FCC Sets Limits on Media Concentration, Unprecedented Public Record Results in Enforceable and Balanced Ownership Rules (June 2, 2003), *available at* http://www.fcc.gov/headlines2003.html. Localism is a regulatory objective of the FCC to maintain viewpoint diversity in local markets. *Id.* Congress and the Supreme Court have historically recognized the importance of the FCC's public interest standard

to require that local media markets serve the needs and interests of their local communities. The Communications Act directs the FCC to "make such distribution of licenses, frequencies, hours of operation, and power among the several States and communities as to provide a fair, efficient, and equitable distribution of radio service to each of the same." 47 U.S.C. § 307(b) (2003). In *NBC v. United States,* the Supreme Court explained that, "Local program service is a vital part of community life. A station should be ready, able, and willing to serve the needs of the local community." 319 U.S. 190, 210–14 (1943); *see also Fox Television Stations, Inc. v. FCC,* 280 F.3d 1027, 1042 (D.C. Cir. 2002) (affirming the FCC's duty to preserve localism, explaining "'the public interest' has historically embraced diversity (as well as localism), and nothing in § 202(h) signals a departure from that historic scope") (internal citation omitted).

20. NTIA, CHANGES, CHALLENGES, AND CHARTING NEW COURSES: MINORITY COMMERCIAL BROADCAST OWNERSHIP IN THE UNITED STATES (2000), *available at* http://www.ntia.doc.gov/reports.html [hereinafter NTIA].

21. See discussion regarding the purpose of antitrust law, *infra* Part V.

22. *See generally* NBC v. United States, 319 U.S. 190, 210–214 (1943) (describing the history of federal regulation of airwaves).

23. *See* CHARLES H. TILLINGHAST, AMERICAN BROADCAST REGULATION AND THE FIRST AMENDMENT 41 (2000); *see also* Judith C. Aarons, *Cross-Ownership's Last Stand?, The Federal Communications Commission's Proposal Concerning the Repeal of the Newspaper/Broadcast Cross-Ownership Rule,* 13 Fordham Intell. Prop. Media & Ent. L.J. 317, 321–27 (2002) [hereinafter Aarons, *Cross-Ownership's Last Stand*],

24. OFORI, BLACKOUT?, *supra* note 3, at 2. General Electric, Westinghouse, AT&T, and Western Electric dominated and controlled the manufacturing of radio transmitter equipment. *Id.* at 3.

25. Radio Act of 1927, Pub. L. No. 69–632, §§ 1–41, 44 Stat. 1162 (1927) (repealed 1934).

26. Radio Act of 1927 §§ 1-3; *see also* Aarons, *Cross-Ownership's Last Stand, supra* note 23, at 324.

27. *See* Tillinghast, *supra* note 23, at 49, Congress extended the life of the Commission on an annual basis until 1934. *Id.*

28. *Id.*

29. Radio Act of 1927 § 4.

30. Aarons, *Cross-Ownership's Last Stand, supra* note 23, at 322–24 (discussing frequency interference problems in the radio broadcast industry).

31. Communications Act of 1934, 48 Stat. 1064 (1934) (current version at 47 U.S.C § 151 (2003)).

32. *See* Patricia M. Worthy, *Diversity and Minority Stereotyping in the Television Media: The Unsettled First Amendment Issue,* 18 HASTINGS COMM. & ENT. LJ. 509, 519 (1996) [hereinafter Worthy, *Diversity and Minority Stereotyping*].

33. *Id.*

34. Amber McGovern, *Neutralizing Media Bias Through the FCC,* 12 DEPAUL-LCA J. ART & ENT. L. & POL'Y 217, 223 (2002).

35. Aarons, *Cross-Ownership's Last Stand, supra* note 23 at 326–28; *see also* FCC v. WNCN Listeners Guild, 450 U.S. 582, 593 (1981) (discussing the Supreme Court's interpretation of the public interest standard and its deference to FCC rules and regulations based on that standard).

36. *See* Aarons, *Cross-Ownership's Last Stand, supra* note 23, at 326–28.

37. Red Lion Broad. Co. v. FCC, 395 U.S. 357 (1969).

38. *Id.* at 390.

39. McGovern, *supra* note 34, at 224.

40. Worthy, *Diversity and Media Stereotyping, supra* note 32, at 511. During the Civil Rights Movement, a Jackson, Miss, radio station failed to air any programs that supported racial integration in the South. United Church of Christ v. FCC, 359 F.2d 994 (D.C. Cir. 1965). The D.C. Circuit vacated the station's license and ordered the FCC to offer the license to other applicants. Office of Communication of the United Church of Christ v. FCC, 425 F.2d 543, 550 (D.C. Cir. 1969).

41. Exec. Order No. 11,365, 32 Fed. Reg. 11,111 (July 29, 1967).

42. Worthy, *Diversity and Media Stereotyping, supra* note 32, at 511 (quoting KERNER COMM'N, REPORT OF THE NAT'L ADVISORY COMM'N ON CIVIL DISORDERS 1 (1968) [hereinafter KERNER REPORT]).

43. *Id.* at 512.

44. *Id.* at 512–15; *see also* Petition for Rulemaking to Require Broadcast Licensees to Show Nondiscrimination in Their Employment Practices, 13 F.CC.2d 766, 774 (1968).

45. Nondiscrimination in the Employment Policies and Practices of Broadcast Licensees, 54 F.C.C2d 354, 358 (1975). In its continuing effort to increase minority ownership, the FCC also adopted rules requiring licensees to file annual employment reports. Statement of Policy on Minority Ownership of Broadcasting Facilities, 68 F.C.C.2d 979, 979 (1978) [hereinafter 1978 Minority Policy Statement].

46. The FCC noted that although it had initiated programs "to assure that minorities and women [were] given equal and full consideration for job opportunities," the numbers were still too low. 1978 Minority Policy Statement, *supra* note 45, at 979–80.

47. NTIA, *supra* note 20, at 18.

48. Worthy, *Diversity and Media Stereotyping, supra* note 32, at 524–25.

49. 1978 Minority Policy Statement, *supra* note 45, at 981.

50. *Id.* The Minority Ownership Task Force reported that:

    It is apparent that there is a dearth of minority ownership in the broadcast industry. Full minority participation in the ownership and management of broadcast facilities results in a more diverse selection of programming. In addition, an increase in ownership by minorities will inevitably enhance the diversity of control of a limited resource, the spectrum. *Id.* at 981 n.10.

51. *Id.* at 981.

52. *Id.* at 980–81.

53. *See* Jeff Dubin & Matthew L. Spitzer, *Testing Minority Preferences in Broadcasting,* 68 S. CAL. L. REV. 841, 844 (1995).

54. 495 F.2d 929 (D.C. Cir. 1973).

55. *Id.* at 935.

56. *Id.* at 936.

57. *Id.* at 938.

58. Garrett v. FCC, 513 F.2d 1056, 1063 (D.C. Cir. 1975). The FCC denied the application of a Black owned radio station to change its Huntsville, Ala. operation from a day-time only broadcast to an unlimited one. *Id.* The court held that not giving weight to the public interest benefit of expanding a minority radio voice to serve the minority population did not reconcile with the principles of *TV 9. Id.*

59. *See* Leonard M. Baynes, *Life After* Adarand: *What Happened to the* Metro Broadcasting *Diversity Rational for Affirmative Action in Telecommunications Ownership,* 33 U. MICH. J.L. REFORM 87, 91 (2000) [hereinafter Baynes, *Life After* Adarand].

60. *Id.* at 92.

61. *Id.* at 982–83.

62. *Id.* at 982-83; *In re Applications of WPIX, Inc., N. Y., N. Y. For Renewal of License,* 68 F.C.C.2d 381, 411–12 (1978).

63. Baynes, *Life After* Adarand, *supra* note 59, at 94.

64. *Id.* at 95–96. The tax certificate program was inapplicable to women because the FCC believed that the needs of minorities were paramount to diversity and that "the historical and contemporary disadvantagement suffered by women" paled to what minorities had suffered. *See id.* at 94 n.34 (quoting Nat'l Telecomms. & Info. Admin., 69 F.C.C.2d 1591, 1593 n.9 (1978)).

65. 1978 Minority Policy Statement, *supra* note 45, at 981.

66. 47 U.S.C. § 309(j) (2000). See Bechtel v. FCC, 10 F.3d 875, 878 (D.C. Cir. 1993) (invalidating credit enhancements based on race in comparative hearings).

67. *See* Bill McConnell, *Rich, Including Some Minorities, Get Richer: NTIA Report Shows Consolidation Generally Pushed Out Small Minority Operators but Rewarded Some of the Bigger Players,* BROAD. & CABLE, Jan. 22, 2001, at 102.

68. Baynes, *Life After* Adarand, *supra* note 59, at 95.

69. Senator John McCain introduced the Telecommunications Diversity Act of 2003 to the Senate. S 267, 108th Cong. (Jan. 30, 2003), On May 9, 2003, the bill was transferred to the House of Representatives. H.R. 2044, 108th Cong. (2003); *see also* Press Release, FCC, Statement of FCC Chairman Michael Powell on Senator McCain's Telecommunications Ownership Diversification Initiative (Jan. 30, 2003), *available at* http://www.fcc.gov/commissioners/powell/mkp_statements_2003.html. After the tax certificate and distress sales programs were terminated and with the implementation of the Telecommunications Act of 1996, the number of minority-owned stations decreased. *See* NTIA, *supra* note 20, at 34. For additional discussion on the FCC's renewed interest in the tax certificate program, see Part IV.D.

70. *Associated Press,* 326 U.S. 1, 20 (1945).

71. Congress noted that the "nexus between diversity of media ownership and diversity of programming sources has been repeatedly recognized by both the Commission and the courts." H.R. Conf. Rep. No. 97–765, at 40 (1982), *reprinted in* 1982 U.S.C.C.A.N. 2261, 2284. The Supreme Court, in *NAACP v. Federal Power Comm'n,* observed that FCC policies "can be justified as necessary to enable the FCC to satisfy its obligation under the Communication Act of 1934 … to ensure that its licensees' programming fairly reflects the tastes and viewpoints of minority groups." 425 U.S. 662, 670 n.7 (1976).

72. Steele v. FCC, 770 F.2d 1192 (D.C. Cir. 1985). In an opinion written by then-Judge Clarence Thomas, the D.C. Circuit also reversed the FCC policy of awarding merit based on gender as a means to support the ownership-viewpoint nexus. *See* Lamprecht v. FCC, 958 F.2d 382 (D.C. Cir. 1992). "But what difference does it make, if a woman owns a station or if women owned all the stations? … Does it make a difference in programming, does it make a difference in content of the points of view[?]" *Id.* at 396 n.5.

73. *Steele,* 770 F.2d at 1198–99. In his dissenting opinion, Judge Wald argued that, "Promotion of diverse sources of information through diversification of ownership is a well established public interest mandate." *Id.* at 1205.

74. *Id.*

75. 497 U.S. 547 (1990).

76. *Id.*

77. *Id.*

78. *Id.* at 549.

79. *Metro Broadcasting* was a 5–4 plurality decision. *Id.* The Court reasoned that: The judgment that there is a link between expanded minority ownership and broadcast diversity does not rest on impermissible stereotyping. Congressional policy does not assume that in every case minority ownership and management will lead to more minority-oriented programming or to the expression of a discrete "minority viewpoint" on the airwaves. Neither does it pretend that all programming that appeals to minority audiences can be labeled "minority programming" or that programming that might be described as "minority" does not appeal to non minorities. Rather, both Congress and the FCC maintain simply that expanded minority ownership of broadcast outlets will, in the aggregate, result in greater broadcast diversity. A broadcasting industry with representative minority participation will produce more variation and diversity than will one whose ownership is drawn from a single racially and ethnically homogeneous group. *Id.* at 579.

80. *Id.* at 582–83.

81. *Id.* at 582 n.31.

82. *Id..*

83. *Id.* at 601.

84. *Id.* at 568.

85. Adarand Constructors, Inc. v. Pena, 515 U.S. 200, 202 (1995) ("Requiring strict scrutiny is the best way to ensure that courts will consistently give racial classifications a detailed examination, as to both ends and means.").

86. *Id.* at 215.

87. *See* Worthy, *Diversity and Minority Stereotyping, supra* note 32, at 529 (explaining that any preferential program for minorities to remedy prior discrimination must be supported by statistical evidence).

88. After the *Adarand* decision, other FCC minority policies were challenged in the courts. In *Lutheran Church-Missouri Synod v. FCC,* the court met an *Adarand*-based challenge concerning the FCC's Equal Employment Opportunity (EEO) guidelines. 141 F.3d 344 (D.C. Cir. 1998). In defending the regulation against the Equal Protection Clause, the FCC argued that the regulations were necessary to achieve its objective of fostering diverse programming content. *Id.* The court ruled in favor of the Lutheran Church, holding that the FCC could not precisely define how the regulations would promote broadcast diversity. *Id.* at 351. The court further reasoned that it was "impossible to conclude that the government's interest, no matter how articulated[,] is a compelling one." *Id.* at 351. The FCC later adopted a report and order revising the EEO guidelines to comply with the holding in *Lutheran Church. See* Review of the Commission's Broadcast and Cable Equal Employment Opportunity Rule and Policies and Termination of the EEO Streamlining Proceeding, 15 F.C.C.R. 2329 (2000).

89. The Supreme Court decision in *Grutter v. Bollinger* was narrowly applied to admissions policies at educational institutions. 539 U.S. 306 (2003). The impact of the decision on federally funded programs is still questionable. Jan Crawford Greenburg, *Supreme Court Narrowly Upholds Affirmative Action; 'Effective participation by members of all racial and ethnic groups in the civic life of our nation is essential if the dream of one nation, indivisible, is to be realized.'—Justice Sandra Day O'Connor, 5–4 Ruling Permits Colleges to Weigh Race,* CHI. TRIB., June 24, 2003, at 1; *see also* Andrea L. Johnson, *Redefining Diversity in Telecommunications: Uniform Regulatory Framework for Mass Communications,* 26 U.C DAVIS L. REV. 87, 97 (1992) (discussing that during the Reagan Administration, the FCC abandoned its support of the minority ownership efforts). A 1980 Commission report claimed that ownership restrictions had produced minimal public benefit and that therefore no causal connection existed between the programs and the goals of competition and diverse viewpoints. *Id.*

90. Wendy M. Rogovin, *The Regulation of Television in the Public Interest,* 42 CATH. U.L. REV. 51, 76 (1992).

91. *See In re* 1998 Biennial Review—Review of the Commission's Broadcast Rules & Other Rules Adopted Pursuant to Section 202 of the Telecommunications Act of 1996, 15 F.C.C.R. 11,058, 11,066 (1998) [hereinafter 1998 Biennial Review].

92. *Id.* at 11,067.

93. *Id..*

94. *Id.*

95. *Id.* at 11,067–68. The nature of broadcasting had experienced a transformation with the advent of cable television. *Id.*

96. *Id.* at 11,068.

97. *Id.* at 11,068–69.

98. *Id.* at 11,069.

99. *Id.* at 11,081.

100. *Id.* at 11,083.

101. The most notable media mergers have included Viacom and CBS, AT&T and Comcast, AOL and Time Warner, and Disney and Capital Cities/ABC. *See generally* Aaron Moore, Who Owns What, COLUM. JOURNALISM REV. *at* http://www.cjr.org/owners (last visited Apr. 15, 2003) (offering a listing of the most recent media mergers); *see also supra* nn. 4–5, 7 and accompanying text.

102. 47 U.S.C. § 202(c)(1)(A) (1996).

103. *Id.* § 202(h).

104. *Id.* § 202(c)(1)(B).

105. *Id.*

106. Aarons, *Cross-Ownership's Last Stand?, supra* note 23, at 330.

107. 47 U.S.C. § 202(c)(2).

108. Review of the Commission's Regulations Governing Television Broadcasting; Television Satellite Stations Review of Policy and Rules, 64 Fed. Reg. 50,651, 50,652 (Sept. 17, 1999) (to be codified at 47 C.F.R. pt. 73) [hereinafter 1999 Local Ownership Rules].

109. *Id.* at 50,654.

110. *Id.*

111. 1998 Biennial Review, *supra* note 91, at 11,072–75.

112. 280 F.3d 1027 (D.C. Cir. 2002).

113. 284 F.3d 148 (D.C. Cir. 2002).

114. *Fox,* 280 F.3d at 1027.

115. *Id.*

116. *Id.*

117. *Id.* at 1033.

118. 284 F.3d at 169.

119. *Id.* at 160.

120. *Id.*

121. 2002 Biennial Regulatory Review—Review of the Commission's Broadcast Ownership Rules and Other Rules Adopted Pursuant to Section 202 of the Telecommunications Act of 1996 Cross—Ownership of Broadcast Stations and Newspapers Rules and Policies Concerning Multiple Ownership of Radio Broadcast Stations in Local Markets Definition of Radio Markets, 67 Fed. Reg. 65,751, 65,753 (Oct. 28, 2002) (to be codified at 47 C.F.R. pt. 73) [hereinafter 2002 Biennial Review].

122. Press Release, FCC Releases Twelve Studies on Current Media Marketplace Research Represents Critical First Step in FCC's Fact Finding Mission, (Oct. 1, 2002), *available at* http:// hraunfoss.fcc.gov/edocs_public/attach-match/DOC-226838A1.pdf (last visited Jan. 12, 2004).

123. *Id.*

124. *Id. See* Scott Roberts et al., Media Bureau, FCC, A Comparison of Media Outlets and Owners for Ten Selected Markets (1960, 1980, 2000) (2002), *available at* http://hraunfoss.fcc.gov/ edocs_public/attachmatch/DOCs2268A2.txt.

125. *Id.*

126. 2003 Broadcast Ownership Rules, *supra* note 11, at 46,286. The new FCC Order relaxed broadcast-newspaper and radio-television cross-ownership. Media companies no longer were held to the prohibition against owning a newspaper and either a television, or radio station in the same city. *Id.*

127. *Id.* at 46,356. Some of today's networks are very close to the 39% cap. *See* Frank Ahrens, *FCC Rule Fight Continues in Congress; Opponents of Ownership Consolidation Also Plan Legal Strategy,* Wash. Post, June 4, 2003, at E01. (discussing that CBS (Viacom) is at 40%, NBC (General Electric) has a 34% audience,

ABC (Walt Disney Corp.) is around 24%, and Fox (News Corp) is at 37%). The FCC still prohibits one of the top four broadcasting networks from buying one of the other four. 2003 Broadcast Ownership Rules, *supra* note 11, at 46,300–01.

128. Consolidated Appropriations Act of 2004, Pub, L. No. 108–199, § 629,118 Stat. 3 (2004). After public outcry, Congress issued a resolution stating its disapproval of the media ownership rules the FCC ordered in June 2003. *See* S.J. Res. 17, 108th Cong. (2003).

129. Motion for Stay Pending Judicial Review of Prometheus Radio Project, Prometheus Radio Project v. FCC, No. 03–3388, 2003 WL 22052896, at *1 (3d Cir. Sept. 3, 2003), *available at* http://www.ca3.uscourts.gov/staymotion/Petition.htm (last visited Feb. 27, 2004).

130. *Id.* at 9.

131. Prometheus Radio Project v. FCC, No. 03–3388, 2003 WL 22052896, at *1 (3d Cir. Sept. 3, 2003) (per curiam).

132. The oral arguments occurred on February 11, 2004. Third Circuit Court of Appeals website, *at* http://www.ca3.uscourts.gov/staymotion/ Petition.htm. The appellate court has not issued an opinion as of this date.

133. Stuart A. Shorenstein & Lorna Veraldi, *Defining the Public Interest in Terms of Regulatory Necessity,* 17 St. John's J. Legal Comment. 45, 49 (2003).

134. *See* 1978 Minority Policy Statement, *supra* note 45.

135. David Honig, Comment, *The FCC and Its Fluctuating Commitment to Minority Ownership of Broadcast Facilities,* 27 How. LJ. 859, 873 (1984). For a discussion on racism in America and its effects on African Americans, see Derrick A. Bell, Jr., Faces at the Bottom of the Well: The Permanence of Racism (1992); Derrick A. Bell, Jr., Race, Racism and American Law (5th ed. Aspen Publishers 2004) (1973).

136. Brief of Amicus Curiae FCC at 7 n.4, Metro Broad., Inc. v. FCC, 497 U.S. 547 (1990), (No. 89–700), *available at* 1990 WL513123 (1990).

137. *Id.* The first minority-owned radio station did not occur until 1949. NTIA, *supra* note 20, at 16.

138. *In re Request by WGPR, Inc., Detroit, Mich., For Waiver of Grant Fee,* 54 F.C.C.2d 297 (June 4, 1975).

139. *See* TV 9, Inc. v. FCC, 495 F.2d 929 (D.C. Cir. 1974).

140. NTIA, *supra* note 20, at 35.

141. *Id.* at 33.

142. *See Initial Comments of Diversity and Competition Supporters,* 2002 Biennial Review, at 22–31 (Jan. 2, 2003) [hereinafter *Initial Comments*]; *see also Reply Comments of Diversity and Competition Supporters* 2002 Biennial Review, at 5, n.4 (Feb. 3, 2003) [hereinafter *Reply Comments*]. Minority television ownership in the local television market has suffered as well. Minority ownership has dropped from thirty-three to twenty stations. *Id.* at 5.

143. *Metro Broad., Inc.,* 497 U.S. at 570.

144. 2003 Broadcast Ownership Rules, *supra* note 11, at 46,288.

145. Press release, NAHJ, Latinos Remain Marginalized by Network News Coverage, NAHJ Study Finds (Dec. 11, 2003), *available at* http://www.nahj.org/release/2003/prl21103.html.

146. *Id.*

147. *Id.*

148. *Metro Broad,, Inc.,* 497 U.S. at 577 n.25.

149. Garrett v. FCC, 513 F.2d 1056, 1063 (D.C. Cir. 1975).

150. *Metro Broad., Inc.,* 497 U.S., at 619 (O'Connor, J., dissenting) (citation omitted).

151. *Id.* at 618.

152. Brief of Amicus Curiae the Washington Legal Foundation, at 9, Metro Broad., Inc. v. FCC, 497 U.S. 547 (1990), (No. 89–700), *available at* 1990 WL 10012794.

153. Black Citizens for a Fair Media v. FCC, 719 F.2d 407, 411 (D.C. Cir. 1983).

154. The use of African Americans in a negative light can be traced back to minstrelsy which was the first and most popular form of mass culture in the nineteenth-century United States. *See* Michael Rogin, Blackface, White Noise: Jewish Immigrants in the Hollywood Melt ing Pot (1996) (providing a historical discussion of the "blackface" form in the United States).

155. *See generally* DONALD BOGLE, TOMS. COONS, MULATTOES, MAMMIES, & BUCKS (Continuum Publ'g 1991) (1973) (providing an interpretive analysis of African Americans in American films from a historical context). African Americans are not the only group faced with the dilemma of marginalization in portrayals. Italian Americans are divided about the portrayal of their heritage in the HBO hit show, "The Sopranos." According to the National Italian American Foundation, the show reinforces the stereotype that all Italian Americans are criminals. *See* Nat'l Italian Am. Found,, Zogby Report, National Survey: American Teenagers and Stereotyping (2001) *available at* http://www.niaf.org/research/report_zogby. asp. The National Council on La Raza recently issued a report documenting the stereotypical media representation of Latinos. *See* Leonard M. Baynes, *Racial Stereotypes, Broadcast Corporations, and the Business Judgment Rule,* 37 U. RICH. L. REV. 819, 845 (2003). Native Americans have often been relegated to roles of ambivalent servants to White "masters." See *also* Baynes, *infra,* discussing Native American stereotypes in Western films. Asian Americans and individuals from the Middle East are often ridiculed with characters exhibiting heavy accents that are also limited to roles that stereotype their race or ethnicity. *See* Keith Aoki, *Is Chan Still Missing? An Essay About the Film Snow Falling on Cedars and Representations of Asian Americans in U.S. Films,* 7 ASIAN PAC. AM. LJ. 30 (2001); Leonard M. Baynes, *Racial Profiling, September 11th and the Media: A Critical Race Theory Analysis,* 2 VA. SPORTS & ENT. L.J. 1 (2002).

156. *See generally* NABOB, *supra* note 18.

157. Andre Brown, *A Message to BET: Black Embarrassing Television,* Young African-Am. Against Media Stereotypes, *at* http://www. yaaams.org/bet.htm (last visited Feb. 4,2003); *see also* Aaron McGruder, A Right to be

Hostile: The Boondocks Treasury 50, 55, 90–91 (2003).

158. *Id.*

159. Christopher Stern, *Viacom Cements Purchase of BET; Johnson to Remain CEO; Network to Stay in D.C.,* Wash. Post, Nov. 4, 2000, at A1.

160. *Brown, supra* note 157, *at* http://www.yaaams. org/bet.htm. BET will have competition from TV One in the year 2004. Cathy Hughes, owner of Radio One, has collaborated with the Comcast Cable system corporation to provide a rival cable network geared toward African Americans. Jeff Clabaugh, *Comcast Takes TV One To The Masses,* Wash. Bus. J., Nov. 20, 2003, *available at* http://washington.bizjour-nals.com/washington/stories/2003/11/17/daily25.html (last visited Feb. 21, 2004). According to BET executives, "[t]he idea of launching another cable channel option targeting African Americans—or somehow competing with BET, for that matter—is not new." Press release, BET, BET Responds to Comcast–Radio One Venture (Jan. 13, 2003), *available at* http://www.bet.com/articles/0,,c3gb-5881,00.html.

161. *Brown, supra* note 157, *available at* http://www.yaams.org/bet.htm.

162. *Id.*

163. Tavis Smiley was fired from BET when he entered into an exclusive interview with Sara Olsen that appeared on ABC instead of CBS, which is a subsidiary of the BET-owned parent company, Viacom. Lisa de Moraes, *BET Terminates Contract of Talk Show Host Tavis Smiley,* Wash. Post, Mar. 24, 2001, at C7, *available at* 2001 WL 17615361.

164. *Media Ownership: Radio Industry: Hearing Before the Comm. on Commerce, Science and Transp.,* 108th Cong. 1 (2003) (statement of Robert Short, Jr., President, Short Broadcasting Co.), *available at* http://commerce.senate.gov/pdf/short013003.pdf.

165. NTIA, *supra* note 20, at 33.

166. *Id.*

167. "In 1997, the United States Department of Commerce reported that while African Americans and Latinos comprised approximately 27% of the U.S. population, members of these groups owned only 2.7% of the nation's 1342 commercial television stations." Gary Williams, *"Don't Try To Adjust Your Television—I'm Black": Ruminations on the Recurrent Controversy Over the Whiteness of TV,* 4 J. Gender Race & Just. 99, 107 (2000). That number increased to 3.8% by the year 2000, despite the fact that minorities are an estimated 29% of the U.S. population. NTIA, *supra* note 20, at 34.

168. *See generally, supra* notes 18, 20.

169. OFORI, BLACKOUT?, *supra* note 3, at xiii.

170. John McCain & Michael K. Powell, *Clear Signal, Static Response,* Wash. Times, Mar, 3, 2004, *available at* http://washingtontimes.com/op-ed/20040302-085047-6972r.htm.

171. *Id.*

172. *Id.* (emphasis added).

173. *Id.*

174. NT1A, *supra* note 20, at 23.

175. Press release, FCC, Chairman Powell Announces Intention to Form a Federal Advisory Committee to Assist FCC on Diversity Issues, (May 19, 2003), *available at* http:// http://www.fcc.gov/DiversityFAC/.

176. *Id.*

177. Brief of Intervenors MMTC, at 7–12, Prometheus Radio Project v. FCC, 2003 WL 22052896 (3d Cir. 2003) (Nos. 03–3388 et al.), *available at* http://www.mmtconline.org/briefs/04/BroadcastOwn%20Brief.pdf. [hereinafter MMTC Brief].

178. *Id.* at 7. "The FCC has exhibited a pattern of ignoring rulemaking proposals aimed at advancing minority ownership." *Id.* at 8.

179. *Reply Comments, supra* note 142, at 29–32.

180. *Id.*

181. MMTC Brief, *supra* note 177, at 29.

182. 347 U.S. 483 (1954) (Brown I); 349 U.S. 294 (1955) (Brown II).

183. *Id.*

184. *See* Walter Adams & James W. Brock, *Antitrust, Ideology, and the Arabesques of Economic Theory,* 66 U. COLO. L. REV. 257, 282 (1995). The Chicago School of Economics has dominated the way antitrust is analyzed, focusing on

economic effects in the market. This approach is based on the premise that "economic power poses no significant social problems so long as liberty of contract and free market—both defined as an absence of government interference—are allowed to function in an untrammeled fashion." *Id.*

185. Metro Broad., Inc. v. FCC, 497 U.S. 547, 570–71 (1990) (quoting TV 9, Inc., 495 F.2d 929, 938) (D.C. Cir. 1973).

186. 15 U.S.C. §§ 1–7 (2000).

187. *Id.* § 18.

188. *Id.*

189. Brown Shoe Co. v. United States, 370 U.S. 294, 323 n.39 (1962); *see also* Conrad M. Shumadine & Michael R. Katchmark, *Antitrust and the Media, in* Communications Law 2003, at 307–08 (PLI Patents, Copyrights, Trademarks, & Literary Prop. Course, Handbook Series No. 770, 2003) (providing expansive discussion regarding the function of antitrust law within the boundaries of the First Amendment and communications law).

190. The Department of Justice (DOJ) and the Federal Trade Commission (FTC) collaborated and created a number of Merger Guidelines which outline its present antitrust enforcement policies. *See* Department of Justice and the Federal Trade Commission Merger Guidelines, *available at* http://www.usdoj.gov (last visited Jan. 11, 2004). As horizontal mergers are motivated by the prospect of financial gains, the primary focus of analysis rests on market power. The Horizontal Merger Guidelines are designed to predict whether a merger will create or enhance market power or facilitate the exercise of dominant market power to the harm of consumers. *Id.* The Guidelines lay out a five-step review process in its merger analysis. *Id.* First, it is assessed whether the proposed merger will "significantly increase concentration and result in a concentrated market" by a defined and measured market *Id.* The second element evaluates whether the merger will result in market concentration that will have the potential to adversely affect competition. *Id.* The third step assesses whether entry barriers

will result that may detect or counteract competitive concerns. *Id.* The fourth and fifth steps analyze the efficiency gains and the probability of a failing firm exiting the market but for the merger. *Id.*

191. The DOJ and the FTC have authority to enforce federal antitrust statutes. *See* 15 U.S.C. § 4 (2000); 28 C.F.R. § .40 (2004). The FTC is also given authority from the FTC Act, 15 U.S.C. §§ 45, 46 (2000), 16 C.F.R. § 0.16 (2004).

192. Clayton Act, 15 U.S.C § 21(a) (2000); Communications Act, 47 U.S.C. § 214(a) (2000).

193. *See* Harold Feld, *The Need for FCC Merger Review,* 18 Comm. Law. 20 (2000) (discussing the importance of the FCC to remain an integral function of the merger review process in the communications industry); *see also* Maurice E. Stucke & Allen P. Grunes, *Antitrust and the Marketplace of Ideas,* 69 Antitrust L.J. 249 (2001) (discussing the Telecommunications Act of 1996 and its relation to antitrust law). Within the Telecommunications Act of 1996, Congress added an antitrust savings clause that the Act itself does not "modify, impair, or supersede the applicability of any antitrust laws." 47 U.S.C. § 601(b)(l) (2000), *reprinted in* 47 U.S.C. § 152, Historical and Statutory Notes.

194. Associated Press v. United States, 326 U.S. 1, 20 (1945); *see* Turner Broad. System, Inc. v. FCC, 512 U.S. 662, 663 (1994).

195. Christine DeFrancia, *Ownership Controls in the New Entertainment Economy: A Search for Direction,* 7 Va. J.L. & Tech. 1, 11 (2002).

196. 2003 Broadcast Ownership Rules, *supra* note 11, at 46,316.

197. *Id.*

198. Richard E. Wiley et al., *Changes and Challenges, in* Communications Law 2003, at 376 (PLI Patent, Copyrights, Trademarks, & Literary Prop. Course, Handbook Series No. 773, 2003).

199. Robert Pitofsky, *The Political Content of Antitrust,* 127 U. Pa. L. Rev. 1051 (1979).

200. *Id.*

201. *Metro Broad., Inc.,* 497 U.S. at 571.

202. Donald R. Simon, *Big Media: Its Effect on the Marketplace of Ideas and How to Slow the Urge to Merge,* 20 J. Marshall J. Computer & Info. L. 247, 286 (2002).

203. Alec Klein, *A Hard Look at Media Mergers; FTC Chief Likely to be Key Force In AOL Decision,* Wash. Post, Nov. 29, 2000, at E1, *available at* 2000 WL 29918451 (quoting Robert Pitofsky, FTC Chairman).

204. 47 U.S.C. § 303 (2000).

205. *See* 2003 Broadcast Ownership Rules, *supra* note 11, at 46,291 (describing the present media marketplace).

206. As a policy, the FCC does not consider station formats to serve its public interest man- date. *See* Development of Policy Re: Changes in the Entertainment Formats of Broadcast Stations, 57 F.C.C.2d 580 (1976); FCC v. WNCN Listeners Guild, 450 U.S. 582 (1981) (upholding FCC policy that the public interest is best served by promoting program diversity through market forces, and not by considering station formats in ruling on applications for license renewal or transfer); *but cf.* Johnson, *supra* note 89, at 97 (discussing the shift of the FCC's objective to support minority ownership).

207. Nielsen Media Research, *Measuring the Ethnic Television Audience, available at* http:// www. nielsenmedia.com/ethnicmeasure/index.html (last visited Apr. 16, 2004).

208. Nielsen Media Research, *Hispanic-American Television Audience, available at* http:// www. nielsenmedia.com/ethnicmeasure/hispanic-american/indexHisp.html (last visited Apr. 16, 2004).

209. Nielsen Media Research, *supra* note 207.

210. 1999 Local Ownership Rules, *supra* note 108, at 12,903.

211. Andrew I. Gavil et al., Antitrust Law in Perspective: Cases, Concepts & Problems in Competition Policy 473 (2003).

212. *See* Jonathan B. Baker, *Stepping Out in an Old Brown Shoe: In Qualified Praise of Submarkets,* 68 Antitrust L.J. 203 (2000) (discussing how courts have used, and in some cases abused, antitrust submarkets analysis).

213. Brown Shoe Co. v. United States, 370 U.S. 294,325 (1962) (citations omitted) (emphasis added).

214. Frank Ahrens, *FCC Clears Univision-Hispanic Broadcasting Deal; Republicans in Favor, Democrats Opposed, Merger to Create Spanish-Language Media Giant,* Wash. Post, Sept. 23, 2003, at A5.

215. In the Matter of Shareholders of HBC and Univision for Transfer of Control of HBC, (Docket No. MB 02-235, FCC File Nos. BTC-20020723ABL et al.), Memorandum Opinion & Order 4 (Sept. 22, 2003), *available at* http://hraunfoss.fcc.gov/edocs_public/ attachmatch/FCC-03-218Al.pdf [hereinafter FCC HBC Univision Merger Order].

216. *Id.* at 4 n.13.

217. *Id.* at 5.

218. *Id.* at 23.

219. *Id.*

220. *Id.* at 32.

221. Pitofsky, *supra* note 199, at 1051.

222. *See supra* note 207 and accompanying text.

223. *See generally* bell hooks, Rock My Soul: Black People and Self-Esteem (2002).

224. NABOB, *supra* note 18, at 9.

225. The Supreme Court, on several occasions, has stated that antitrust law should not be solely focused on economics. *See Simon, supra* note 202, at 286; *see also* Fed. Trade Comrm'n v. Indiana Fed'n of Dentists, 476 U.S. 447, 459 (1986) (stating that "an agreement limiting consumer choice ... cannot be sustained"); United States v. Cont'l Can Co., 378 U.S. 441, 455 (1964) (observing that consumer decisions are not solely based on price); Times-Picayune Publ'g Co. v. United States, 345 U.S. 594, 611–12 (1953) (recognizing that the "'market' ... cannot be measured by metes and bounds; obviously no magic inheres in numbers.").

226. Rogovin, *supra* note 90. "In the United States of America, broadcast television substantially shapes society, society's perception of itself, and society's definitions of culture. Television is so much a part of life in this country that, like breathing, its impact is rarely recognized." *Id.* at 52; *see also,* Camille O. Cosby, Television's

Imageable Influences: The Self-Perceptions of Young African-Americans 133 (1994) (discussing the negative images of African Americans on television and the impact it has on perceptions of other races).

227. Williams, *supra* note 167, at 107.

228. Aarons, *Cross-Ownership's Last Stand?, supra* note 23, at 339.

229. *See generally* NTIA, supra note 20.

230. Simon, *supra* note 202, at 286. (emphasis added).

231. Red Lion Broad. Co. v. FCC, 395 U.S. 367, 390 (1969).

Indecency

Kent R. Middleton and William E. Lee

INDECENCY

Obscene content has no First Amendment protection. If material appeals to the prurient interest, is patently offensive, and has no serious social value, the government may ban the material, criminally punish its creators and distributors, or take a variety of other actions.

Indecent material is sexually oriented but does not meet the *Miller* definition of obscenity. Indecency, much like obscenity, depicts or describes sexual or excretory activities or organs in a patently offensive manner. Indecency, in contrast to obscenity, need not arouse a prurient interest in sex. In addition, an indecent broadcast program, unlike one that is obscene, can have serious value and still violate the law. The FCC has said that the "serious merit" of a program will be considered as a factor, but not necessarily the deciding factor, in determining whether a broadcast is indecent.

Unlike obscenity, indecency receives some First Amendment protection, which varies from medium to medium. Courts analyze indecency regulations according to the technological attributes of a medium and the level of effort required of the reader or viewer to receive messages. For example, the Supreme Court regards the Internet as similar to the highly protected print media because both require affirmative effort by the recipient to receive a message. In contrast, broadcast indecency is restricted because broadcasting is "uniquely accessible to children," even those who are too young to read.

Broadcasting

As was noted in Chapter 3, in 1969, the Supreme Court held in *Red Lion Broadcasting Co. v. FCC* that spectrum scarcity justified regulations designed to promote the presentation of a range of views.[1] If only select licensees may use the public airwaves, those station owners must accept certain public interest obligations not demanded of print media owners.

The regulation of broadcast indecency, however, is not justified on spectrum scarcity grounds. Instead, the Supreme Court's decision in *FCC v. Pacifica Foundation*, upholding the FCC's power to punish a broadcaster for airing indecent content, justifies broadcasting's reduced First Amendment protection in this context because broadcasting is intrusive and accessible to children.[2] Writing for the Court, Justice Stevens said that broadcasting "is a uniquely pervasive presence in the lives of all Americans." Broadcasting "confronts" citizens in public but also "in the privacy of the home, where the individual's right to be left alone plainly outweighs the First Amendment rights of an intruder." Even though listeners could change channels or turn off the receiver after encountering offensive depictions of sexuality, this was "like saying that the remedy for an assault is to run away after the first blow." Justice Stevens also said that society's interest in protecting children, coupled with the ease with which even young children could gain access to broadcasting, justified broadcasting's special treatment. In a dissenting opinion, Justice Brennan questioned whether listening to broadcasts, even in the home, implicated "fundamental" privacy interests.

Although a federal statute outlaws the broadcasting of obscene, indecent, or profane material,[3] the FCC's enforcement has focused on indecency. Broadcasters almost never air hard-core sexual depictions that meet the *Miller* test for obscenity. Also, the statutory reference to profane material has rarely been enforced. In the 1930s, blasphemous statements such as *By God* were regarded as profane.[4] Since the 1960s, however, statements such as *God damn it* have been treated as protected expression.[5] In a 2004 decision treating the word *fuck* as both indecent and profane, the FCC announced a new approach that classifies "vulgar and coarse" language as profane.[6] The FCC left the status of words other than *fuck* unsettled; broadcasters were warned that the agency would analyze other potentially profane words or phrases on a case-by-case basis. Subsequently, in two 2005 decisions discussed below, the FCC ruled that words such as *dick* are not sufficiently graphic to be profane and that blasphemous statements, such as *God damn it,* are not actionable as profanity. In 2006, though, the FCC ruled that *shit* was sufficiently vulgar to be both indecent and profane.

The FCC's new interest in profanity, like its attention to indecency, reflects the ebb and flow of political pressure. In 2001, for example, the FCC received just 346 indecency complaints and the agency levied $91,000 in fines. As shown in Table 9.1, since 2003, indecency and profanity in broadcast programming have been issues of intense political interest. The FCC's enforcement bureau ruled in October 2003 that an isolated utterance of *fuck* in a live entertainment broadcast was not indecent; this ruling prompted 237,215 letters of protest. Amid intense political pressure, the FCC in March 2004 overturned its enforcement bureau and held that even a single utterance of *fuck* in live entertainment programming is indecent and profane. The FCC also received more than 542,000 complaints about Janet

Jackson's "wardrobe malfunction" exposing her breast at the 2004 Super Bowl halftime show; in September 2004, the FCC fined CBS-owned television stations $550,000 for the Super Bowl broadcast.[7] The agency also negotiated consent decrees with the Viacom, Emmis, and Clear Channel broadcast groups in 2004.[8] In exchange for dismissal of pending indecency cases, these broadcasters agreed to collectively pay $5.5 million in "voluntary contributions" to the U.S. Treasury. Each broadcaster also agreed to implement indecency compliance plans including training of on-air talent and producers, use of time delay equipment on live programming, and suspension or termination of employees involved in future indecency violations. Howard Stern decried the FCC's actions as a "witch hunt" and moved his program in 2006 to Sirius, an unregulated subscription satellite service.

Until recently, FCC fines for indecent broadcasts have been rare and only a small amount.[9] As discussed below, a new law enacted in 2006 increases the amount of fines tenfold. Faced with a difficult regulatory environment and the loss of audience to cable and satellite services that can legally carry graphic programs, like *The Sopranos*, the major television networks in 2006 filed suit against the FCC, claiming it is time to revisit the indecency rules. As discussed below, the Supreme Court in 2009 narrowly ruled the FCC's new policy toward "isolated expletives" was not arbitrary under the Administrative Procedure Act. The Court did not discuss constitutional questions but directed an appellate court to consider First Amendment issues.

Limiting Indecent Broadcasts

The First Amendment protects indecency because the Supreme Court has said only those sexually oriented materials meeting the *Miller v. California* test for obscenity fall outside constitutional protection. However, in 1978, in *FCC v. Pacifica Foundation*, the Supreme Court ruled that the FCC could regulate the times of indecent broadcasts without violating the First Amendment.[10]

The dispute in *Pacifica* began with an afternoon broadcast of a George Carlin monologue, "Filthy Words," on New York City radio station WBAI (FM). A New York father complained to the FCC after hearing the Carlin satire on the use of language

TABLE 9.1 Indecency Complaints and Fines 2000–June 2006

	Number of Complaints	FCC Proposed Fines*
2006 (Jan–Jun)	327,198	$3,962,500
2005	233,531	0
2004	1,405,419	2,428,080
2003	166,683	440,000
2002	13,922	99,400
2001	346	91,000
2000	111	48,000

*In some instances, the fine may be reduced or rescinded. Also, the fine may relate to a complaint from a prior year.

Source: FCC Enforcement Bureau

while driving with his son.[11] Carlin begins his twelve-minute monologue by saying he will talk about "the words you couldn't say on the public, ah, airwaves, um, the ones you definitely wouldn't say, ever." Then he frequently repeats in a variety of contexts seven "dirty" words: *shit, piss, fuck, cunt, cocksucker, motherfucker,* and *tits.*

The FCC said Carlin's "dirty" words were indecent because they depicted sexual and excretory activities and organs in a patently offensive manner. The commission said the words were "obnoxious, gutter language" that were indecent because they "debased" and "brutalized" human beings "by reducing them to their bodily functions." The commission said Carlin repeated the offensive words "over and over" during the early afternoon when children were "undoubtedly" in the audience.

Although the FCC did not penalize the Pacifica Foundation, the WBAI licensee, for the Carlin broadcast, the commission said additional complaints about indecent programming from listeners could lead to sanctions. Broadcasters airing indecency not only risk fines and the loss of their licenses under the 1934 Communications Act,[12] but they also can be fined and jailed for up to two years under the federal criminal code.[13]

The FCC's decision to warn Pacifica for the broadcast of the Carlin monologue was reversed by the U.S. Court of Appeals for the District of Columbia but reinstated by a divided U.S. Supreme Court. Justice John Paul Stevens, in an opinion supported in part by four other justices, said the FCC's warning to WBAI did not violate the 1934 Communications Act or the First Amendment.

Stevens said the FCC did not censor WBAI's broadcast of the Carlin monologue, as Pacifica contended. As was discussed in Chapter 3, the prohibition on censorship in the 1934 Communications Act has never forbidden the FCC to evaluate broadcasts after they were aired. The commission had not edited the "Filthy Words" monologue in advance. Rather, the FCC had reviewed the program after the broadcast as part of the commission's responsibility to regulate licensees in the public interest. Stevens said review of program content after a broadcast is not censorship.

Stevens also rejected Pacifica's argument that Carlin's monologue could not be regulated because it was not obscene. Pacifica had argued that *obscenity* and *indecency* mean the same thing under federal law. Pacifica contended that indecent language, like obscene language, must appeal to the prurient interest before it can be punished. However, Stevens said the words *obscene* and *indecent* have different meanings when applied to broadcasting. The term *indecent* refers "to nonconformance with accepted standards of morality," the justice said. Hence, the Court accepted the FCC's conclusion that Carlin's monologue was indecent but not obscene.

Justice Stevens said, in a part of the opinion supported by only three other justices, that the First Amendment might have protected the Carlin monologue if it had been offensive political or social commentary. However, Carlin's use of the "seven dirty words" did not deserve absolute First Amendment protection because they were not essential to the "exposition of ideas" and were of such little use in the search for truth that any benefit "is clearly outweighed by the social interest in order and morality." Because the words Carlin used were patently offensive and ordinarily lacked literary, political, or scientific value, they could be regulated in some contexts, Stevens said.

In a part of the opinion in which he again spoke for the Court's majority, Stevens said important considerations in indecency cases include the time of day of the broadcast; the nature of the program containing the offensive language; the composition of the audience; and perhaps the differences among radio, television, and closed-circuit transmissions. The Court said the Carlin monologue could be regulated because of the repetitive use of the offensive words at a time when children could reasonably be expected to be a part of the audience.

Justice Lewis Powell, Jr., joined by Justice Harry Blackmun, concurred with most of the Stevens opinion, including the need to protect children from offensive speech on the broadcast media. However, Powell disagreed with Stevens's attempt to regulate speech on the basis of social value. He said the justices should not be deciding which speech is protected by the First Amendment by assessing the social and political value of its content. The social value of speech "is a judgment for each person to make," said Powell, "not one for the judges to impose on him."

Justice William Brennan, Jr., in a dissenting opinion, said the FCC's regulation of the Carlin speech was unconstitutional. In an opinion joined by Justice Thurgood Marshall, Brennan said the Court's majority was for the first time prohibiting minors from hearing speech that was not obscene and therefore is protected by the First Amendment. Brennan said that "surely" preserving speech entitled to First Amendment protection is important enough that listeners could be required to suffer the "minimal discomfort" of briefly hearing offensive speech before they turned off the radio. Brennan chastised Justice Powell and the majority for "censoring" speech like the Carlin monologue solely because the justices found the words offensive. Brennan accused the Court of attempting "to impose its notions of propriety on the whole of the American people."

All four dissenting justices, in an opinion written by Justice Potter Stewart, said the FCC could not constitutionally regulate the "seven dirty words" because, as the Court determined, the Carlin monologue was not obscene. Stewart said that when Congress passed the law banning "any obscene, indecent, or profane language" from the airwaves, no legislator said that the word *indecent* meant anything different from the word *obscene*.

Defining Broadcast Indecency

After the *Pacifica* decision, the FCC at first emphasized the limits of its supervision of indecent programming. For more than a decade, the FCC limited its definition of indecency to the frequent repetition of sexual or excretory expletives such as *fuck* and *shit* and did not punish a broadcaster for airing indecent programming.

However, in April 1987, the FCC warned broadcasters that the term *indecent* meant much more than the repetition of George Carlin's "seven dirty words." The commission said, unlike the recent past, any broadcast would be indecent if it included a description or depiction of sexual or excretory activities or organs in a manner patently offensive by contemporary community standards for the broadcast medium. The commission said the context of a broadcast would be an important factor in determining whether the words or depictions are "vulgar" or "shocking" and therefore indecent. Context, the commission said, includes the manner in which the words or depictions are portrayed, whether the portrayal is isolated or fleeting, "the merit" of a program, and whether children might be listening or viewing.[14] The FCC said it would take action against indecent programming when "there is a reasonable risk that children are in the audience." The FCC emphasized broadcasters must precede indecent material with a warning even if children could not reasonably be expected to be in the audience.[15]

The Court of Appeals for the District of Columbia Circuit upheld the FCC's new enforcement policy for indecency. In *Action for Children's Television v. FCC*, the court agreed the FCC's previous policy of limiting indecency actions to programs containing the seven dirty words was an "unduly narrow" interpretation.[16] The court affirmed the FCC's assessment that it made "no legal or policy sense" to regulate Carlin's monologue but not other offensive descriptions or depictions of sexual or excretory activity that avoided the specific words that led to the Supreme Court's *Pacifica* decision. The D.C. Circuit said the commission had rationally decided that a broader definition of indecency was needed.

Under the new indecency policy, the FCC fined dozens of radio broadcasters in the early 1990s for programs featuring bawdy humor and double entendres concerning sexual organs or activities. Infinity Broadcasting paid $1.7 million after the FCC found several broadcasts by Howard Stern were indecent.[17] Stern, the self-proclaimed "King of all Media," frequently talks crudely about sexual activity, discusses his own sexual fantasies, and describes women disrobing in his studio.[18]

FIGURE 9.1 Recent FCC Rulings on Indecency

CONSISTENT OR INCONSISTENT?	
Indecent	*Not Indecent*
Fuck Uttered by U-2's Bono on an awards show. The FCC regarded the remark as "gratuitous."	Vs. **Fuck** Uttered repeatedly by actors during *Saving Private Ryan*. The FCC concluded the language was "integral" to the film.
Shit Uttered by Nicole Richie on an awards show. The FCC regarded the remark as "gratuitous."	Vs. **Bullshitter** Uttered by a *Survivor* contestant during a news interview. The FCC said the news context weighs against indecency findings.
Janet Jackson's Breast Briefly exposed during the Super Bowl Halftime Show. The FCC regarded the segment as overtly sexual.	Vs. **Nicollette Sheridan's Naked Back** Shown during an introduction to *Monday Night Football*. Despite the sexually suggestive nature of the segment, there was no graphic depiction of sexual organs.
Howard Stern's discussions of sex Stern discusses various sexual activities such as oral sex. The FCC concluded Stern was pandering to the audience interest in sexuality.	Vs. **Oprah Winfrey's discussions of sex** Winfrey discusses various sexual activities such as oral sex and terms used by teenagers. The FCC claimed the segment was designed to help parents.
A teen-age girl wearing a bra and panties Briefly shown straddling a teen-age boy during an episode of *Without A Trace*. The FCC found the scene to be "highly sexually charged."	Vs. **A couple in bed passionately kissing, caressing, and rubbing** Briefly shown during an episode of *Alias*. The FCC said there was no display of sexual organs.

The FCC and Evergreen Media Corporation agreed to settle lawsuits filed against each other over the commission's punishment of indecent programming.[19] The FCC agreed to drop several indecency actions against Evergreen and publish a document interpreting its indecency enforcement policies. In return, Evergreen agreed to drop its countersuit and to pay the FCC $10,000. Evergreen also agreed to issue an internal policy memorandum advising employees the company may discipline them if they violate indecency rules.

Eight years later, in 2001, the FCC issued the guidelines Evergreen sought in its agreement with the commission.[20] The guidelines say a radio or television broadcast will be found indecent if, first, it describes sexual or excretory organs or activities and, second, it is patently offensive to an average viewer or listener. The commission said it uses a national standard for determining whether a program is patently offensive, not a local community or statewide test. The FCC also said it considers the "full context" of the program. For example, a newscast employing explicit language might not be indecent, but a disk jockey repeatedly using language implying sexual activity might be indecent programming.

The guidelines reveal that the FCC has no bright-line test to define indecency. Instead, the agency makes case-by-case determinations, balancing several factors to decide whether a program is indecent. Critics, who believe the FCC's indecency decisions are arbitrary and inconsistent, claim that indecency determinations reflect "little more than the personal tastes" of the commissioners.[21] Figure 9.1 contrasts recent FCC indecency rulings.

One factor examined by the FCC is the program's explicit or graphic nature. The more explicit the language or pictures, the more likely the program will be found indecent. Thus, the FCC cited Howard Stern's references to testicles, penis size, masturbation, and sodomy and Bubba the Love Sponge's description of oral sex techniques as examples of explicit content. However, the commission also said sexual innuendo, although not explicit or graphic, may be indecent. For example, the FCC sanctioned a radio station for playing a song containing the following lyrics using candy bar names to symbolize sexual activities and organs:

I whipped out my Whopper and whispered, Hey, Sweettart, how'd you like to Crunch my Big Hunk for a Million Dollar Bar? Well, she immediately went down on my Tootsie Roll and you know, it was pure Almond Joy. I couldn't help but grab her delicious Mounds, this little Twix had the Red Hots.

To the FCC, the pandering nature of the song made the thought of candy bars "peripheral at best."[22]

In decisions issued in 2004 and 2006, the FCC found that nudity need not be depicted for a television program to be found indecent. A *Married by America* episode featuring topless strippers was found to be indecent even though breasts were digitally obscured. Although the nudity was obscured, "even a child would have known the strippers were topless," the FCC stated.[23] Similarly, an episode of *Without A Trace* briefly depicting partially clothed teenagers at a party was found to be indecent. A teenage girl was shown wearing bra and panties, straddled on top of one male character in a "highly sexually charged" scene.[24]

In contrast, in a 2005 decision, the FCC found that the introduction to a *Monday Night Football* game was not indecent because the nudity shown was not graphic. During the introduction, Nicollette Sheridan, appearing as her *Desperate Housewives* character and wearing only a towel, attempts to seduce Terrell Owens in the Eagle's locker room. After he rebuffs her advances, she drops her towel, prompting Owens to say, "Aw, hell, the team's going to have to win without me," and she leaps into his arms. Sheridan is briefly shown from the back, nude from the waist up. The FCC concluded that although the scene was sexually suggestive, there was no graphic depiction of sexual organs or activities.[25] Also in 2006, the FCC found an episode of *Alias* featuring a couple in bed, "kissing, caressing and rubbing against each other" not to be indecent because there was no display of sexual organs.[26]

A second factor is the persistent repetition of sexual or excretory words such as in George Carlin's recording in the *Pacifica* case. In his "Filthy Words" monologue, Carlin repeats various words such as shit:

At work you can say it like crazy. Mostly figuratively, Get that shit out of here, will ya? I don't want to see that shit anymore. I can't *cut* that shit, buddy. I've had that shit up to here. I think you're full of shit myself. He don't know shit from Shinola.

The FCC regards repeated sexual or excretory references, such as those in Carlin's monologue, to be indecent. Until 2004, the FCC generally treated isolated expletives, such as a news announcer's on-air blunder, "Oops, fucked that one up," as not indecent. In 2004, however, the FCC announced a new policy, discussed below, that regards even a single utterance of *fuck* to be both indecent and profane. In 2006, the FCC found a single utterance of *shit* was found to be both indecent and profane. For less offensive sexual or excretory language, the FCC requires repetition if the expression is to be deemed indecent.[27]

Brief visual images of nudity can also be indecent, depending on the context. For example, the FCC found the 2004 Super Bowl halftime show to be indecent, even though Janet Jackson's breast was shown for only 19/32 of a second. The segment featured song lyrics and choreography that discussed or simulated sexual activities. After singing "gonna have you naked by the end of this song," Justin Timberlake pulled off part of Ms. Jackson's costume to briefly reveal her breast to the television audience, which included millions of children. Although Jackson and Timberlake claimed the breast exposure was accidental, the FCC concluded that CBS was aware of the "overall sexual nature" of the segment and promoted it as "shocking" to attract viewers.[28]

A third factor is a program's intentional pandering to the audience or intending to shock listeners. The context, or the way in which material is presented, is important in defining indecency. The FCC guidelines contrast Bubba the Love Sponge's monologues with discussions of sex on the *Oprah Winfrey Show.* For example, an *Oprah* program was ruled not to be indecent when a psychologist advised a woman about masturbation:

> You need to at least know how to make your body get satisfied by yourself. Because if you don't know how to do it, how is he going to figure it out? He doesn't have your body parts, he doesn't know.

The FCC concluded that the *Oprah* discussion was not presented in a pandering or titillating manner, unlike the technique of radio "shock jocks." In a 2006 case again involving *Oprah,* the FCC also found a graphic discussion of sexual slang terms used by teenagers not to be indecent. To the FCC, the program was designed to help parents, rather than to titillate. "To the extent that the material is shocking, it is due to the existence of such practices among teenagers rather than the vulgarity or explicitness of the sexual depictions or descriptions."[29]

The FCC also said a news report airing a recording of organized crime figure John Gotti was not indecent, even though Gotti used *fuck* or *fucking* ten times in seven sentences. The FCC believed the explicit language was an integral part of a bona fide news story about organized crime.[30] The commission said it was reluctant to second-guess the editorial judgments of broadcasters "on how best to present serious public affairs programming to their listeners." As will be shown below, in 2006 the FCC again expressed its reluctance to find news programs to be indecent.

Although the FCC is unlikely to challenge expletives in news programs, the commission announced in 2004 that it considers even a single utterance of what it called "the F-word" both indecent and profane in live entertainment programs.[31] In its 2004 ruling, the FCC overturned its own enforcement bureau, which had ruled that U-2's Bono had not expressed indecency when he exclaimed, "This is really, really, fucking brilliant," upon winning the 2003 Golden Globe Award for best original song. The enforcement bureau found that in this context, as in the Gotti broadcast, the word *fucking* did not describe sexual activities. Moreover, drawing upon the 2001 guidelines, the bureau concluded that fleeting and isolated remarks did not warrant FCC sanctions.[32]

In overturning the enforcement bureau's decision, the FCC announced that its precedents allowing isolated or fleeting use of the "F-word" in similar contexts were no longer good law. Any use of the "F-word" inherently has a sexual connotation, the commission said. Furthermore, use of the "F-word" was patently offensive because it "is one of the most vulgar, graphic and explicit depictions of sexual activity in the English language." The FCC described Bono's use of the "F-word" as gratuitous, and indicated that political, scientific, or other uses of the "F-word" might mitigate its offensiveness. The FCC noted that a factor in its decision to target isolated use of the "F-word" was the ease with which broadcasters can delay live broadcasts and bleep offending material. In response to this ruling, many broadcasters began using delays on live broadcasts.

Due to uncertainty about the FCC's standards in the wake of the Bono ruling, sixty-six ABC television network affiliates preempted the November 2004 Veteran's Day broadcast of the film *Saving Private Ryan,* which has numerous uses of the F-word. In early 2005, the FCC dismissed complaints filed against some of the ABC affiliates airing the film, holding the film's coarse battlefield language, unlike that of Bono, was neither gratuitous nor intended to shock. "Indeed, it is integral to the film's objective of conveying the horrors of war through the eyes of these soldiers, ordinary Americans placed in extraordinary situations," the agency stated. ABC provided parents with ample warnings about the film's content; thus, the FCC concluded the presentation was not intended as family entertainment. Also, the FCC ruled that uses of the words *God damn* and similar blasphemous phrases were not profane.[33]

In another decision issued in 2005, the FCC held that the words *dick, penis, testicles, bastard, bitch, hell, damn, orgasm, breast, nipples, pissed,* and *crap* were not profane when used in a fleeting manner in entertainment programs such as *Friends, Will and Grace,* and *Scrubs.* The FCC claimed these words, in context, were not sufficiently graphic to be patently offensive.[34]

In 2006, the FCC ruled that *shit,* "one of the most offensive words in the English language," was both indecent and profane.[35] Nicole Richie, a presenter at the *2003 Billboard Music Awards* program, asked, "Have you ever tried to get cow shit out of a Prada purse?" Even when used in an isolated manner in entertainment programming, the FCC found the S-word was likely to "disturb the peace and quiet of the home." The FCC cautioned broadcasters that only in rare circumstances would the S-word, like the F-word, be regarded as essential to an artistic, educational, or political message. To emphasize its view that the S-word was almost always indecent, the FCC found a documentary about blues musicians airing on a public television station to be indecent. The licensee failed to

demonstrate to the FCC's satisfaction that phrases such as "that shit is crazy" were essential to informing the public about a matter of public importance. In setting aside the artistic judgment of acclaimed filmmaker Martin Scorcese, the FCC said the documentary's educational purpose could have been fulfilled "without the repeated broadcast of expletives."

In an important clarification of its policy on isolated expletives, the commission announced in November 2006 that live news programs provide a context that weighs against an indecency finding. At issue was a live interview on *The Early Show,* a two-hour morning program airing on the CBS television network. During the interview, a contestant in the CBS program *Survivor: Vanuatu,* described another contestant as a "bullshitter." The FCC initially found the broadcast to be indecent, but subsequently concluded its earlier decision did not give "appropriate weight" to the news context of the program. Citing the Gotti case discussed earlier, the FCC explained that news programs were at the core of the First Amendment's protection. The FCC cautioned broadcasters that "there is no outright news exemption from our indecency rules. Nevertheless, in light of the important First Amendment interests at stake as well as the crucial role context plays in our indecency determinations, it is imperative that we proceed with the utmost restraint when it comes to news programming."[36] Commissioner Jonathan Adelstein, in a dissenting opinion, claimed the FCC's reversal of its earlier decision illustrated the "arbitrary, subjective and inconsistent nature" of the FCC's indecency decision making. Further, he questioned the treatment of "infotainment" as news; the segment was merely a promotion of the network's primetime entertainment programming. "The only news here is how far this Commission is willing to stretch the definition of 'news,'" Adelstein stated.

The FCC's new policy on "isolated expletives" was sustained in 2009 by the Supreme Court in a 5–4 ruling based on administrative rather than constitutional law.[37] The majority concluded the FCC did not act arbitrarily in violation of the Administrative Procedure Act when it began punishing single utterances of fuck and shit. "The Commission could reasonably conclude," Justice Scalia wrote for the majority, "that the pervasiveness of foul language, and the coarsening of public entertainment in other media such as cable, justify more stringent regulation of broadcast programs so as to give conscientious parents a relatively safe haven for their children." It was rational for the FCC to believe that a permissive policy toward fleeting expletives would lead to increased use of expletives, Justice Scalia wrote.

Justice Breyer's dissenting opinion, joined by Justices Stevens, Souter and Ginsburg, argued the agency provided inadequate explanation for its new policy. Breyer noted that there was no evidence of an increase in the airing of expletives during the twenty-five years the FCC did not punish isolated utterances. The FCC's lack of an adequate explanation for its policy change suggested that the FCC's answer to the question, "Why change?" is, "We like the new policy better," an action Breyer found to be arbitrary.

Even though the Court ruled the FCC's policy did not violate the APA, the Court remanded the case to a lower court to determine whether the policy violated the First Amendment. Several justices indicated they might be receptive to a First Amendment challenge. Justice Thomas, who joined the majority, questioned the viability of *Red Lion* and *Pacifica*, opinions he described as "unconvincing." Justice Stevens, the author of *Pacifica*, claimed that the *Pacifica* ruling treated indecency narrowly by focusing on repetition of language with sexual or excretory meaning. The FCC's new policy ignored the fact that a word such as fuck can be used to express an emotion "miles apart" from any sexual meaning. "As any golfer who has watched his partner shank a short approach knows, it would absurd to accept the suggestion that the resultant four-letter word uttered on the golf course describes sex or excrement and is therefore indecent," Stevens wrote.

Fining Indecency

On June 15, 2006, President Bush signed the Broadcast Decency Enforcement Act, which increased the maximum penalty the FCC can impose per indecency violation from $32,500 to $325,000.[38] This tenfold increase was necessary, President Bush stated, because the prior amount was not a deterrent to many broadcasters, and in recent years "broadcast programming has too often pushed the bounds of decency."

Although Congress sets the maximum amount that can be assessed for an indecency violation, the FCC can impose a lesser amount if it concludes the violation is not egregious. The agency also has substantial discretion in determining whether any fine is assessed. For example, in 2006 the FCC resolved complaints about programs, such as the *2003 Billboard Music Awards* show, involving isolated use of expletives such as *fuck* and *shit*. These programs aired prior to the FCC's decision in the Bono case; the agency found the broadcasts to be indecent but imposed no fines because FCC policy at the time of the broadcasts tolerated isolated use of expletives.[39]

The FCC's discretion also affects its assessment of who is liable for fines. As part of its recent crackdown on indecency, the agency began multiplying the fine by the number of stations carrying a program, but currently the FCC fines only licensees who are the subject of viewer complaints to the FCC. In 2004 the FCC proposed fining all Fox Network affiliates that broadcast an episode of *Married by America* featuring whipped cream, spanking, and strippers, but in 2008 the agency held liable only those 13 Fox affiliates subject to viewer complaints.[40] In another 2008 action, the FCC imposed a $1.2 million fine against 45 ABC Television Network affiliates subject to viewer complaints about a February 25, 2003 episode of NYPD Blue airing at 9 p.m. in the Central and Mountain time zones. In the program, a woman's naked buttocks were shown in several close-range shots, including one the FCC described as "lingering." The maximum fine applicable at the time of the broadcast, $27,500 per station, was levied due to the titillating nature of the scene and because the stations could have declined to air the prerecorded program, the FCC said.[41]

Channeling Indecency

Although the FCC has said broadcasters can air indecency only during the hours when children are not expected to be listening and watching, it has had difficulty finding a safe harbor for indecency that is acceptable to both Congress and the courts. All three branches of government have struggled to find a time for broadcast indecency that shields children from offensive programming but allows adults access to constitutionally protected speech.

In 1995, the U.S. Court of Appeals for the D.C. Circuit held constitutional a restriction of broadcast indecency to the hours of 10 P.M. to 6 A.M. At the same time, the court ruled unconstitutional an attempt by Congress to limit the hours of indecency for most but not all broadcast stations from midnight to 6 A.M.[42] In the Public Telecommunications Act of 1992, Congress had prohibited indecent programming between 6 A.M. and midnight for all broadcast stations except public radio or television stations that left the air at or before midnight. Only the public television stations with shortened hours could begin broadcasting indecency at 10 P.M.

The D.C. Circuit, sitting en banc, voted 7–4 that although a ban of indecency from 6 A.M. to midnight met most constitutional requirements, Congress had not properly justified treating commercial and public broadcasting stations differently. The court said Congress had not explained how the disparate treatment of broadcasters met the compelling governmental interest of protecting children from indecent broadcast programming.

However, the D.C. Circuit's majority said it had to set aside the midnight standard in favor of the 10 P.M. standard—the hour that some public broadcasters could begin airing indecent programming—so all broadcasters would be treated the same. Congress, the court said, did not provide evidence that minors are less likely to be corrupted by sexually explicit material broadcast by a public station than by a commercial station. The court said allowing public broadcasters to air indecency before midnight undermined the argument for prohibiting indecent speech before midnight on other stations.

In separate dissents, Chief Judge Harry Edwards and Judge Patricia Wald argued the statute channeling indecency was unconstitutional; Congress and the FCC had assumed, rather than provided evidence, that indecency harmed children, Edwards and Wald said. Both Edwards and Wald suggested that instead of prohibiting indecency during much of the broadcast day, the government consider equipping television sets with computer technology that would allow parents to block indecent programs from their homes. As discussed later in this chapter, Congress enacted such a requirement, known as the V-Chip, in 1996.

Telephone

For years, there was little concern about content communicated over the telephone. However, when dial-a-porn services proliferated in the 1980s, parents complained the services were readily available to children, who may try to imitate the sexual activities described and who sometimes incurred charges of thousands of dollars listening to dial-a-porn. In 1988, Congress banned obscene and indecent messages delivered via commercial telephone services.

The U.S. Supreme Court held that Congress could constitutionally ban obscene sexual messages provided by commercial telephone services. At the same time, however, the Court said a ban on indecent dial-a-porn services violated the First Amendment.

In *Sable Communications v. FCC*, the Supreme Court ruled that sexually explicit phone messages that are indecent but not obscene cannot be banned but can be regulated. The Court said that since indecency, unlike obscenity, is constitutionally protected, Congress invalidly banned indecent dial-a-porn instead of only restricting access by children. Justice White said the 1988 statute was "another case of burning the house to roast the pig."[43]

The Court acknowledged Congress has a legitimate interest in preventing children from being exposed to dial-a-porn. However, the Court said that since indecent speech is constitutionally protected, as the Court first held in *FCC v. Pacifica Foundation*, the regulation of indecent dial-a-porn must be limited so that access by children is restricted without barring access by adults. In *Sable*, the Court distinguished telephone services from broadcasting:

> The context of dial-in services, where a caller seeks and is willing to pay for communication, is manifestly different from a situation in which a listener does not want the received message. Placing a telephone call is not the same as turning on a radio and being taken by surprise by an indecent message. Unlike an unexpected outburst on a radio broadcast, the message received by one who places a call to a dial-a-porn service is not so invasive or surprising that it prevents an unwilling listener from avoiding exposure to it.

Also, telephone service providers were able to use methods such as access codes to make their messages available to adults but not to children.

Shortly after the Supreme Court ruled in *Sable* that a blanket ban on indecent dial-a-porn is unconstitutional, Congress enacted more limited legislation. Congress adopted a statute prohibiting dial-a-porn services from providing indecent messages to persons younger than eighteen years old and to nonconsenting adults.[44] The law also requires telephone companies that bill for adult messages to block indecent dial-a-porn from the phones of customers who have not subscribed to the service in writing. The statute also allows dial-a-porn services to insulate themselves from prosecution by adhering to FCC procedures limiting children's access to explicit sexual messages.

The FCC, under the authority of the law, adopted rules requiring dial-a-porn providers to restrict access to their services by requiring callers to use credit cards or access codes or by scrambling their calls so that they can be heard only through a descrambling device.[45] Two circuits of the U.S. Courts of Appeals, the Second and the Ninth, have upheld the law and the FCC's interpretation of it. Both courts said the rules were narrowly tailored to meet the compelling government interest in protecting the "physical and psychological well-being of minors."[46]

Cable Television

When determining the constitutionality of cable regulations, as when regulating other media, the Supreme Court grapples to protect the First Amendment rights of system operators to control their content, to protect the rights of adults to access constitutionally protected content, and to protect children from indecency. At the same time, Congress and the courts want to encourage the development of new technologies.

In some ways, cable is like print, suggesting that cable operators can be accorded maximum First Amendment freedoms without exposing children to great amounts of indecency. Cable systems, like print, offer diverse voices through scores of channels, enough channels to distinguish cable from broadcasting, which is licensed and regulated because of the narrow broadcast band. Cable is also like print

because householders control entry of the medium into the home. Cable subscribers, like newspaper and magazine readers, order cable and pay for it regularly. Unlike broadcasting, cable is not as pervasive a "free" medium that enters the home, sometimes intrusively. Cable is also unique because system operators can block channels at the command of individual subscribers, permitting subscribers to protect children from unwanted content.

Although cable can be analogized to print, the medium also embodies qualities of the more ubiquitous and intrusive broadcasting medium, suggesting that cable might be more regulated than print to protect children. The scores of channels offered by the typical cable system can appear every bit as pervasive and intrusive as over-the-air broadcast channels, even though the cable service is invited into the home.

Recently the graphic content on cable program services has drawn fire from politicians. Kevin Martin, chair of the FCC, has argued for extending the indecency rules to the programming included in the expanded basic packages offered by cable and DBS providers. Alternatively, Martin has advocated a change in the way cable systems package their programming so parents can "get Nickelodeon and Discovery without having to buy other adult-oriented fare."[47] In response to Martin's suggestion, Comcast and Time Warner began offering family-friendly packages. The National Cable and Telecommunications Association (NCTA), cable's primary trade association, is opposed to government-mandated programming packages; the NCTA says that parental use of measures such as channel blocking or the V-chip are more appropriate ways to control children's access to indecent programming.

Generally, the courts have ruled that cable operators enjoy nearly the same First Amendment rights as publishers or Internet operators. The Court has noted that cable companies originate programming and exercise editorial discretion.[48] In another case, the Court referred to cable as "part of the press" because cable operators deliver news, information, and entertainment to their subscribers.[49] In yet another case, the court said cable operators are entitled to largely the same First Amendment protection as publishers.[50]

Of course, cable operators, like operators of other media, have no right to disseminate obscenity. But cable operators may transmit indecency. In a case emphasizing the similarity between cable operators and publishers, the Supreme Court upheld lower court rulings that indecency cannot be banned on cable. In *Wilkinson v. Jones*, the Court upheld lower court rulings striking down a Utah statute barring indecency on cable.[51] The federal district court said that cable could not be regulated like broadcasting because cable offered so many more channels. The court also said that cable, unlike broadcasting, is invited into the home. Indeed, cable viewers pay extra for HBO, Showtime, and other premium channels that sometimes carry sexually oriented programming, the court noted. Furthermore, cable subscribers can control children's access to indecency by installing "lockboxes" provided by cable companies, the court said.

In *United States v. Playboy Entertainment Group, Inc.*, the Court reaffirmed the rights of cable operators by striking down part of a statute designed to protect children from inadvertently being exposed to sexual video and audio.[52] The Court struck down a section of the Telecommunications Act of 1996 that attempted to halt the "bleed" of sexual pictures and dialogue from adult cable channels to channels children might be watching in the basic cable service. The statute required cable operators carrying Playboy channels, AdulTVision, Spice, and other channels "primarily dedicated to sexually oriented programming" either to completely scramble the signals, to block them entirely, or to cablecast them between the hours of 10 P.M. and 6 A.M., to lessen the possibility that children might glimpse a breast or hear suggestive dialogue bleeding from an imperfectly scrambled transmission. Another alternative allowed cable operators to block delivery of the sexually oriented channels only to cable subscribers who requested the block. However, only a tiny fraction of cable subscribers requested the house-by-house block. Most cable systems therefore chose the time-shifting alternative—telecasting indecency after 10 P.M.—because establishing a bleed-proof scrambling technique was too expensive, a complete block ended the transmission of constitutionally protected sexual expression, and few households requested individual blocks.

Playboy and other adult programmers challenged the statute, arguing that even the required time-shifting was unconstitutional because it restricted cable operators, programmers, and adult viewers who desired nonobscene sexual programming before 10 P.M., when 30–50 percent of adult programming is normally viewed. In a 5–4 ruling in which the Supreme Court applied strict scrutiny to the regulations, the Court held that the required scrambling, total blocks, and time-shifting were unconstitutional content restraints because a less restrictive method was available to protect children from a signal bleed, a problem that the Court was not convinced was very serious in the first place. The Court ruled that cable operators' and programmers' First Amendment rights could be served and children protected if cable operators followed the less restrictive alternative of notifying subscribers that the cable companies would block indecent programming to individual homes if subscribers asked. Requiring notification allows subscribers to take advantage of cable's unique technology, the Court said, the ability of cable operators to block individual channels to individual homes. Through notification and blocking, programmers could provide sexual content via cable twenty-four hours a day to adult viewers with a right to view it. At the same time, children would be protected, the Court concluded.

Although cable operators have broad First Amendment rights to control the types of programs they will carry, cable systems are monopolies in most localities and are required to provide channels for voices that the cable operator does not choose. To diversify voices in often-monopolistic cable systems, the federal government requires larger cable systems to lease up to 15 percent of their channels to anyone who will pay to rent a channel.[53] Through local franchises, cities and counties require cable systems to set aside "PEG" channels for public, educational, and government programming.[54] The Supreme Court has ruled that cable operators can ban indecency on leased access channels but not on public, educational, and government channels.

Leased Access

Under a 1984 cable act, Congress requires larger cable systems to designate 10–15 percent of their channels for use by others on a commercial or "leased" basis. Smaller cable systems are not required to lease channels.

A section of a 1992 law permits cable operators to ban indecency on leased channels if the cable system provides written policies that explain the law and the cable company's procedures.[55] The law also allowed cable operators to permit sexually oriented programming over leased channels, but only if the cable operators "segregated" indecent programming on a single channel that would be available within thirty days if subscribers requested it in writing. In a decision affirming the First Amendment rights of cable operators, the Supreme Court ruled that cable operators can permit or forbid indecency on leased access channels but cannot be required to segregate the sexually oriented programming onto a single channel that would be blocked to all subscribers or opened only to those who requested it. In *Denver Area Educational Telecommunications Consortium, Inc. v. FCC* the Court struck down the segregation requirement because it unconstitutionally restricted sexual content of the cable system operators, programmers, and adult viewers.[56]

In a plurality opinion that most justices concurred in, the Court ruled that the law allowing cable operators to ban or allow indecency on cable channels was constitutional. But the portion of the statute requiring the segregation and written request was unconstitutional, the Court said, because it restricted protected programming entirely during the thirty-day period while subscribers were waiting for cable installation. The Court also said the written-request requirement was unconstitutional because it inhibited subscribers whose reputations might be damaged if a cable operator revealed they requested a restricted channel. Furthermore, the Court feared cable operators might forgo disseminating protected sexual expression to avoid the costly and time-consuming government regulations. As for the children, they would be adequately protected, the Court said, through the content decisions of cable operators on leased channels and by technological remedies, including lockboxes.

Peg Channels

Local governments may require cable systems to provide public, educational, and government (PEG) channels as a repayment to the community for being allowed to lay cables under city streets and to use city rights-of-way. PEG channels are used for the telecast of city council and school board meetings, educational panels, and public announcements. In *Denver Consortium*, the Supreme Court ruled the First Amendment permits the government to bar cable operators from restricting indecency in PEG channels. The Court concluded that a cable operator's "veto" over indecency was much less necessary to protect children on public access channels than on leased access channels. Unlike leased access channels, which are controlled by a third party who rents a channel, public access channels typically are operated cooperatively by local community and governmental organizations, often including an access channel manager appointed by the municipality. Elaborate screening and certification processes protect children from indecency on public access channels, the Court concluded, precluding the need for content controls by cable operators.

Internet

In 1996, Congress attempted to prohibit indecency on the Internet, but the U.S. Supreme Court found the law unconstitutional. The Court said the Internet should have the same level of First Amendment protection as the print media have. Because indecency is not prohibited in the print media, it may not be proscribed on the Internet.

The Communications Decency Act (CDA), which was part of the Telecommunications Act of 1996, prohibited deliberately using the Internet to send indecent, patently offensive, or obscene material to people under eighteen years old. The CDA also made it illegal for any person or company—such as America Online—to allow dissemination of obscene or indecent material to minors over Internet facilities it controlled. Violators could be fined or imprisoned for up to two years. Internet providers could defend themselves if they acted "in good faith" to take "reasonable, effective, and appropriate actions" to prevent minors from receiving indecent material through the Internet.[57]

In *Reno v. ACLU*, the Supreme Court found the CDA unconstitutional, saying that the Internet should receive expansive First Amendment protection.[58]

The government argued that the Internet should be subject to extensive regulatory control, as is broadcasting. The Court disagreed, stating that the Internet is not as "invasive" as broadcasting. Gaining access to content on the Internet requires a user to take deliberate actions, from turning on a computer to connecting to an Internet Service Provider such as AOL to accessing a specific website. The Court said because certain steps must be taken, it is unlikely that an Internet user would accidentally encounter indecent material.

The Court also distinguished the Internet from broadcasting because there was no spectrum scarcity justifying government regulation. The Internet did not have physical limitations similar to those of broadcasting. At any given time, tens of thousands of people are discussing a range of subjects on the Internet, where content is "as diverse as human thought." And the Internet provides a low-cost means for "publishers" to reach a global audience. The Court recognized that the Internet is used as a worldwide soapbox.

Applying strict scrutiny in the *Reno* decision, the Court agreed the government had a compelling interest in protecting children from obscene and indecent material. But the Court said the CDA was unconstitutional because it was not narrowly drawn to restrict speech as little as possible.

Justice Stevens, writing for the 7–2 Court majority, said important words in the CDA were unconstitutionally vague. The Court said that criminal laws and laws limiting speech—and the CDA was both—must define terms carefully. The CDA was imprecise, the Court said, not allowing Internet users to know what speech was illegal. Communities were left to define *patently offensive* and *indecent* because Congress did not clearly define them, the Court said. The word *indecent* is not defined in the law at all. The term *patently offensive* is defined as material involving "sexual or excretory activities or organs" as taken "in context" and "measured by contemporary community standards." The Court said these phrases, meant to give context to "patently offensive," are themselves not defined.

Without clear definitions, the Court said, the words "will provoke uncertainty among speakers about ... just what they mean." Users might have censored themselves, the Court said, suppressing their speech rather than communicating protected material that they incorrectly feared the CDA might have prohibited. The Court said the statute's undefined terms would cause self-censorship. Some speakers would silence themselves, fearing they would violate the law, even though their "messages would be entitled to constitutional protection," the Court said. Therefore, the Court said, the community using the narrowest, most confining definitions would set the standard for the entire country. Justice Stevens said an e-mail message about birth control a parent sent to a child at college might violate the law if people in the college town considered birth control to be indecent or patently offensive.

The Court also found the CDA was overbroad, prohibiting communications that are constitutionally protected, as well as content that lawfully can be prohibited. The Court noted the CDA constitutionally prohibited obscenity on the Internet but unconstitutionally banned indecent and patently offensive material. The First Amendment does not protect obscene material in any mass medium, including the Internet. But the CDA also banned offensive or indecent material that has literary, artistic, political, or scientific value, the Court said, although that material would be protected for adults if published in other media. Although the Court's obscenity test shelters sexual speech with social value, the CDA did not. Justice Stevens said the CDA might have penalized otherwise protected messages about homosexuality, prison rape, or the First Amendment.

The Court also said the CDA was broader than a New York law protecting children from print indecency that the Court found acceptable. In *Ginsberg v. New York*, discussed earlier in this chapter, the Court upheld a statute making it illegal to sell minors sexually oriented material that would not be obscene if sold to adults.[59] The Court said the New York law was not overbroad but the CDA was too broad because it prohibited not only the sale of indecent material to minors but also the gift of constitutionally protected indecency, even by a parent. Further, the constitutional New York statute barred indecency to anyone under seventeen years old, but the broader CDA barred indecency to anyone under eighteen.

The Court also said the CDA was broader than a statute using zoning laws to restrict where adult movie theaters may be located. In *City of Renton v. Playtime Theatres*, discussed later in this chapter, the Court said it was constitutional for Renton, Washington, to limit adult theaters to certain areas of the city.[60] But the Court said it was not constitutional for the CDA to bar indecency entirely. The zoning law was not an attempt to prohibit content but to channel it to certain places. The CDA was a ban on content, the Court said.

The Court did follow its reasoning in *Sable Communications v. FCC*, discussed earlier in this chapter, in which it upheld a congressional ban on obscene messages transmitted by telephone.[61] But in *Sable* and in the CDA decision, the Court said the First Amendment protects indecent messages transmitted from adults to adults when users must take affirmative steps to receive indecent material, as both "dial-a-porn" customers and Internet users do.

The Court suggested parental control or blocking software would be constitutionally acceptable ways to prevent children's access to indecent material. The Court majority said a more precisely and narrowly drawn statute preventing children's access to indecent material on the Internet might be constitutional.

After the Court ruled the CDA unconstitutional, Congress attempted to protect children on the Internet with a narrower law. In 1998, Congress enacted the Child Online Protection Act (COPA) prohibiting commercial material "harmful to minors" on the World Wide Web. The overbroad CDA had prohibited noncommercial as well as commercial materials on the whole Internet.

To overcome vagueness and overbreadth, Congress drew on the Supreme Court's ruling in *Miller v. California* to define "harmful to minors" in the Child Online Protection Act. A commercial work is harmful to minors under COPA if jurors applying "Contemporary community standards" would find the work as a whole appeals to the prurient interest of minors, is patently offensive and lacks serious value. COPA provides a defense to website operators who use age verification techniques to prevent minors from gaining access to prohibited materials.

An appeals court found COPA to be unconstitutionally overbroad because material disseminated nationally on the World Wide Web might be ruled harmful to minors according to the community standards of a jury in one of the "most puritan of communities." But the U.S. Supreme Court ruled that COPA could not be declared unconstitutional only because different juries would interpret "contemporary community standards" differently. In *Ashcroft v. American Civil Liberties Union*, the Supreme Court ruled that "community standards need not be defined by reference to a precise geographic area."[62]

The Supreme Court sent COPA back to the appeals court to determine whether the statute was sufficiently narrow when all three prongs of the *Miller* test—patent offensiveness, appeal to the prurient interest, and lack of social value—were applied. The Court noted that the overbroad CDA, unlike COPA, allowed punishment of expression that was patently offensive but did not necessarily appeal to the prurient interest or lack social value. "When the scope of an obscenity statute's coverage is sufficiently narrowed by a 'serious value' prong and a 'prurient interest' prong, we have held that requiring a speaker disseminating material to a national audience to observe varying community standards does not violate the First Amendment," the Court said in an opinion written by Justice Thomas.

Eight justices concurred for various reasons that COPA should be remanded to the lower court. Justice Stevens, dissenting, argued that COPA, like CDA, is overbroad. Stevens said that much expression that is lawful for adults will be prohibited if the "contemporary community standards" of conservative communities determines what is patently offensive to minors and appeals to minors' prurient interests. Stevens also argued that juries might bar constitutionally protected expression for adults by easily determining that the work lacks serious value for children.

On remand, the appellate court found COPA to be unconstitutional because the law was not narrowly tailored, nor did it employ the least restrictive means available, such as blocking or filtering technology.[63] The Supreme Court affirmed by a 5–4 vote, holding that the government failed to prove that age verification techniques were more effective than software filters installed by parents. Justice Kennedy, writing for the majority in *Ashcroft v. American Civil Liberties Union II*, noted that COPA was suspect because a blue-ribbon commission created by Congress concluded that filters were more effective than age verification techniques.[64] Kennedy concluded that if Congress promoted the use of filters, parents could control what their children see "without subjecting protected speech to severe penalties."

Justice Breyer argued in a dissenting opinion that COPA's burden on protected speech is modest; it only requires providers of sexual material to restrict minors' access. Moreover, he regarded filters to be faulty, costly, and dependent upon parental willingness to supervise children's use of the web.

The Court remanded the case so the trial court could consider the effectiveness of various technical methods of controlling children's access to harmful material. After a trial, a federal district court in March 2007 held COPA violated the First Amendment because software filters were a more effective, but less restrictive means of blocking access to sexual materials than the age verification schemes authorized by COPA.[65] Additionally, the court ruled that COPA was unconstitutionally vague because it did not define how terms like "as a whole" would apply to the World Wide Web. "There is no question that a printed book or magazine is finite, and, as a result, it is very easy to discern what needs to be examined in order to make an 'as a whole' evaluation," the district court wrote. The same is not true for a webpage or websites since pages and sites are hyperlinked to other pages and sites. A publisher of a website could only guess at what undefined portion of the "vast expanse" of the web would be considered to be the whole work by a court, and this imprecision was unconstitutional, the district court wrote. The Third Circuit affirmed this ruling in 2008; when the Supreme Court denied certiorari in 2009, the ten-year battle over COPA ended.

Public libraries that accept federal funds may be required to limit access to sexually explicit Internet material, the Supreme Court ruled in 2003. By a 6–3 vote, the Court upheld a federal statute requiring that public libraries use filtering software or risk losing federal subsidies for Internet access.

By 2000, 95 percent of public libraries in the United States provided public Internet access. Patrons of all ages regularly searched for online pornography, often exposing other patrons unwillingly to pornographic images. In 2001, Congress required libraries receiving federal funds to install software filters to block adults from accessing obscenity or child pornography and children from accessing material harmful to minors. But software filters are imprecise, often "overblocking" materials adults and children have a First Amendment right to see. Thus, Congress, in the Children's Internet Protection Act (CIPA), also permitted libraries to disable filters for patrons engaged in "bona fide research or other lawful purposes."[66]

In *United States v. American Library Association*, the Supreme Court upheld CIPA, ruling that libraries may restrict patrons' access to Internet material of "requisite and appropriate quality," just as librarians have traditionally decided which books to purchase.[67] Writing for the Court, Chief Justice Rehnquist noted that most libraries already exclude pornography from their print collections because they deem it inappropriate. "It would make little sense to treat libraries' judgments to block online pornography differently, when these judgments are made for just the same reason," Rehnquist said.

The majority of the Court concluded that CIPA does not seriously burden library patrons' access to constitutionally protected Internet content. The Court was unsympathetic to the claim that some patrons would be too embarrassed to ask librarians to unblock sites or disable filters. "The Constitution does not guarantee the right to acquire information at a public library without any risk of embarrassment," the Court said.

Justice Souter, in a dissenting opinion joined by Justice Ginsburg, viewed CIPA as unconstitutional censorship. Souter feared that library patrons would be denied access to protected expression by librarians who can refuse under CIPA to unblock sites or disable filters. Justice Souter also disputed Chief Justice Rehnquist's argument that blocking access to Internet sites is analogous to choosing books for library shelves. Souter argued that blocking sites is analogous to cutting pages from an encyclopedia or removing books already purchased. Justice Stevens also dissented, claiming that libraries can allow adults unfettered access to lawful Internet content while protecting other patrons from unwanted exposure to sexual materials by installing privacy screens on terminals or buying recessed monitors.

Summary

Obscenity is prohibited in any medium of expression. The regulation of nonobscene sexual depictions varies from medium to medium. Broadcasters may be punished for airing depictions or descriptions of sexual or excretory activities or organs in a manner that is patently offensive to community standards for the broadcast medium. In *FCC v. Pacifica Foundation*, the Supreme Court ruled that broadcasters can be constitutionally restricted to airing indecency only at those times of day when children are not likely to be in the audience. The current "safe harbor" for broadcasting indecent material is between the hours of 10 P.M. and 6 A.M.

Dial-a-porn services can transmit indecent material at any time of day. However, these services must employ techniques, such as access codes, to limit their audiences to adults. Cable systems may transmit indecent material at any time of day on channels controlled by the cable operator. Cable companies may prohibit indecent material on leased access channels; municipal officials overseeing PEG channels may also prevent these channels from being used for indecent programs. Finally, the Supreme Court has ruled that communicators using the Internet, like print publishers, have a First Amendment right to disseminate indecency.

VIOLENT PORNOGRAPHY

Violence in the media is a recurrent concern among the public and politicians. Congress periodically holds hearings to determine if violence in the media contributes to violence in society. As will be shown later in this chapter, industry organizations have adopted various systems of labeling comic books, movies, recordings, video games, and Internet sites in response to political pressure. In 1996, Congress passed legislation requiring violent television programming to be labeled and parents to be afforded the technology to block it from home TV screens. In 2005, Congress authorized the use of software to render "imperceptible" portions of films displayed in homes.

American courts have never found that violence alone lacks First Amendment protection. Violence is not included in the definition of obscenity. If violence is combined with sexual content and the material is found to be obscene, it is the sexual matter, not the violence, that is the basis for the finding.

Effects of Violent Pornography

Social science research is not conclusive about the effects of violent pornography. Nonetheless, in 1986 the Attorney General's Commission on Pornography (the Meese Commission) asserted that exposure to violent pornography depicting the degradation, domination, or coercion of women increases aggressive behavior toward women, including sexual violence. The Meese Commission lacked solid scientific proof for this claim and acknowledged that its conclusions were based in part on its members "own insights and experience" with violent pornography.[68] Two commissioners objected to the commission's efforts to "tease the current data into proof of a causal link."[69]

Social scientists questioned the Meese Commission's conclusions, arguing that a causal relationship between exposure to sexually violent images and aggression toward women is found in laboratory studies measuring short-term effects, but that these studies do not support conclusions about long-term effects. Further, it is unclear whether the adverse effects of violent pornography are caused by the combination of violence and sexual imagery, or are due to depictions of violence against women. Social scientific evidence suggests that exposure to violent pornography may increase one's tolerance for sexual crimes, but evidence linking violent crime to pornography is not clear. According to its critics, the Meese Commission used social science studies "selectively to confirm certain moral/political beliefs."[70]

Women and Violence

The Meese Commission advocated stricter enforcement of obscenity law, but feminists claimed that violent and degrading portrayals of women should be illegal even when not obscene. In the 1980s, a number of feminists argued that violent pornography violated women's civil rights; objectionable portrayals of women contributed to discrimination against women in settings such as employment and education.[71] In response, Indianapolis declared the "graphic sexually explicit subordination of women" to be illegal. The ordinance outlawed the verbal or pictorial representation of women in "subordinate" ways, including as sexual objects enjoying pain, humiliation, or rape or in "scenarios of degradation."

The U.S. Court of Appeals for the Seventh Circuit declared the ordinance unconstitutional because it did not assess a work as a whole, nor did it include the elements of patent offensiveness, prurient appeal, and lack of social value as required by *Miller*.[72] Speech treating women in an approved way—premised on equality—was lawful under the ordinance no matter how sexually explicit. "Speech treating women in the disapproved way—as submissive in matters sexual or as enjoying humiliation—is unlawful no matter how significant the literary, artistic, or political qualities of the work taken as a whole," the appellate court wrote. The First Amendment "forbids the state to declare one perspective right and silence opponents."

The Seventh Circuit observed that violent pornography, like racist or anti-Semitic speech, is protected expression even though political majorities find it to be insidious. Otherwise, the government would become "the great censor and director of the thoughts which are good for us."

Video Games

In recent years, the depiction of violence and sexuality in top-selling video games such as *Grand Theft Auto* has become a matter of great concern to social scientists and legislatures.[73] In response to the belief that these games harm children, a number of cities and states have enacted laws limiting or prohibiting children's access to violent and sexually explicit games; each law has been found to be unconstitutional.

In *American Amusement Machine Association v. Kendrick*, the Court of Appeals for the Seventh Circuit found unconstitutional an Indianapolis ordinance limiting the access of minors to video arcade games containing "graphic violence."[74] Although the law also restricted access to games with "strong sexual content," the plaintiffs only challenged the aspects of the law relating to violence.

Because Indianapolis was fearful that violent video games engender aggressive attitudes and behavior, the court of appeals required that the city prove violent video games caused players to commit violent acts. Without strong empirical support, governmental claims about the effects of violent depictions would be a pretext for censorship.

Writing for the court of appeals, Judge Richard Posner found that the social science studies relied on by Indianapolis showed only that violent video games increase aggressive feelings but do not cause anyone to commit a violent act. The city's claim of harm to its children from these games was "wildly speculative."

Posner described video games as a form of constitutionally protected storytelling; the themes presented in games such as *The House of the Dead* are also described in ancient and modern literature. The law was unlikely to reduce children's exposure to media violence, Posner said, because the city was not restricting children's access to violence in other media, such as books and movies.

Children have First Amendment rights, Posner noted, and it was important that children receive "uncensored speech" before they turn eighteen so that their minds are not blank when they first vote. "People are unlikely to become well-functioning, independent-minded adults and responsible citizens if they are raised in an intellectual bubble," he wrote.

Following *Kendrick*, courts in several states have invalidated laws restricting children's access to video games.[75] For example, in late 2005, an Illinois law prohibiting the sale or rental of violent or sexually explicit video games to minors was ruled unconstitutional.[76] The federal district court carefully reviewed a series of social science studies and concluded that a solid causal link between violent video game exposure and violence had not been established. Applying the *Brandenburg* incitement test discussed in Chapter 2, the court held there was no evidence that violent video game content was "directed to inciting or producing imminent lawless action."

The Illinois law was also flawed because it did not restrict children's access to other media, such as DVDs and CDs, which may portray violence. And because the law banned any sexual imagery in games—even a brief scene—it departed from the traditional requirement that sexual depictions be considered as part of a whole work. "Such a sweeping regulation on speech—even sexually explicit speech—is unconstitutional even if aimed at protecting minors," the district court wrote.

The V-Chip

The FCC has been reluctant to restrict violence in broadcast programming.[77] However, in 1996, Congress adopted legislation requiring ratings of "violent" and "sexual" programming and the installation of computer chips in television sets that would allow parents to block the rated programming.

The so-called V-chip law was enacted as part of the Telecommunications Act of 1996. The law mandates that television receivers with thirteen-inch or larger screens sold in the United States contain a computer chip allowing television set owners to block programs containing violence, sexual content, "or other indecent material about which parents should be informed before it is displayed to children."[78] The law does not define *violence*, *sexual content*, or *indecency*, although indecency has been defined by the FCC. The V-chip could be coded by parents to automatically block programming that they find objectionable. In 1998, the FCC said V-chips must be installed in half the television receivers made for sale in the United States by July 1, 1999, and in all sets by January 1, 2000.[79]

For the V-chip to block programs, violent or sexually oriented programming must be accompanied by program ratings sent through the television signal. Congress told video program distributors that they had one year to "voluntarily" implement a program rating system that was acceptable to the FCC. Otherwise, the FCC was empowered to create its own advisory committee to develop a ratings system. In March 1998, the FCC gave final approval to the television program rating system developed by the National Association of Broadcasters, the National Cable Television Association, and the Motion Picture Association of America.[80] The ratings, assigned to all television programs except news, sports, and unedited MPAA-rated movies on premium cable channels, alert parents to program material they might not want their children to watch.

The ratings are as follows:

Programs designed for children:

TV–Y   Appropriate for all children

TV–Y7   Programs directed to children seven years old and above

TV–Y7–FV   Fantasy violence may not be appropriate for children under seven years old

Programs designed for general audiences:

TV–G   For general audiences

TV–PG   Parental guidance suggested; the program may contain material unsuitable for younger children. The program also may contain: (V) moderate violence; (S) some sexual scenes; (L) occasional coarse language; or (D) some suggestive dialogue.

TV–14   Parents strongly cautioned; the program may contain material unsuitable for children under fourteen years of age. The program also may contain: (V) intense violence; (S) intense sexual scenes; (L) strong coarse language; or (D) intensely suggestive dialogue.

TV–MA   Mature audiences only; the program may contain material unsuitable for children under seventeen years of age. The program also may contain: (V) graphic violence; (S) explicit sexual scenes; (L) strong coarse language.

Ratings are applied to programs by broadcast and cable networks. Syndicated programs, such as talk shows, are rated by the program distributor. To ensure that program ratings are applied accurately and consistently, the television industry established the Oversight Monitoring Board. The board includes members from broadcast television, cable television, program production, and the public. The board has no enforcement power except public pressure.

Despite being available for nearly a decade, use of the V-Chip is very low. A 2005 study by the Kaiser Family Foundation found that among seventh through twelfth graders, only 6 percent reported parental use of the V-Chip.[81] Low parental use of the V-Chip was recently cited by FCC as a reason for continuing regulation of broadcast indecency.[82]

In an attempt to fend off increased indecency fines on broadcasters and an extension of indecency rules to cable and satellite services, in 2006 a cross-section of media companies and trade associations announced a $300 million national public service advertising campaign to increase parental awareness of the V-Chip. The advertisements encourage parents to visit a website, TheTVBoss.org, which provides information on managing children's television usage.

The limited effectiveness of the V-Chip and the ratings system, however, was cited by the FCC in an April 2007 report on television violence.[83] The FCC found that of the 280 million television sets in U.S. households, only 119 million sets are equipped with the V-chip. Additionally, the FCC found few parents used the V-Chip and many parents lack understanding of the ratings system. Further, the FCC reported programs are often inaccurately rated.

Although the FCC did not initiate any new rules relating to television violence, it outlined several policy options for Congress to consider. One policy recommended by the FCC was a time-of-day channeling of violent programming, similar to the time channeling of indecency. Such a scheme would require that Congress define violence, an especially nettlesome problem that must include factors such as context, presence of weapons, and realism. Congress had asked the FCC for a definition of violence, a task the agency avoided. This prompted Commissioner Jonathan Adelstein to note that the FCC "has not been able to formulate and recommend a definition of violence that would cover the majority of violent content that is inappropriate for children, provide fair guidance to programmers, and stand a decent chance of withstanding constitutional scrutiny, in light of judicial precedent."

NOTES

1. 395 U.S. 367 (1969).
2. 438 U.S. 726, 748–49 (1978).
3. 18 U.S.C. § 1464.
4. *See, e.g.,* Duncan v. United States, 48 F.2d 128 (9th Cir. 1931).
5. Gagliardo v. United States, 366 F.2d 720 (9th Cir. 1966); Raycom, Inc., 18 F.C.C.R. 4186 (2003).
6. Complaints Against Various Broadcast Licensees Regarding Their Airing of the "Golden Globe Awards," Memorandum Opinion and Order, 18 F.C.C.R. 4975 (2004).
7. Complaints Against Various Television Licensees Concerning Their February 1, 2004 Broadcast of the Super Bowl XXXVII Halftime Show, Notice of Apparent Liability for Forfeiture, 19 F.C.C.R. 19230 (2004). This case was excluded from the scope of the Viacom consent decree.
8. Viacom, Inc., Order (FCC 04-268) (Nov. 23, 2004); Emmis Communications Corp., Order (FCC 04-199) (Aug. 12, 2004); Clear Channel Communications, Inc., Order (FCC 04-128) (June 9, 2004).
9. *See, e.g.,* Frank Aherns, "Delays, Low Fines Weaken FCC Attack on Indecency," *Wash. Post,* Nov. 10, 2005, at A1.
10. 438 U.S. 726 (1978).
11. Pacifica Foundation Station WBAI (FM), 56 F.C.C.2d 94 (1975).
12. 47 U.S.C. § 312(a)(6).
13. 18 U.S.C. § 1464.
14. *In re* Infinity Broadcasting Corp. 2 F.C.C.R. 2705 (1987).
15. In *re* Pacifica Foundation, Inc., 2 F.C.C.R. 2698 (1987).
16. 852 F.2d 1332 (D.C. Cir. 1988).
17. Sagittarius Broadcasting Group. 10 F.C.C.R. 12 (1995).
18. Mel Karmazin, 8 F.C.C.R. 2688 (1992).
19. United States v. Evergreen Media Corp., Civ. No. 92-C 5600 (N.D. Ill. Feb. 22, 1994) (agreement for settlement and dismissal with prejudice).
20. Industry Guidance on Broadcast Indecency, 16 F.C.C.R. 7999 (2001).
21. Stephen Weiswasser and Robert Sherman, "*Oprah* and Spielberg vs. *Without a Trace* and Scorsese: Indecent Inconsistency at the FCC," 24 *Comm. Lawyer* (2006).
22. W1OD, Inc., 6 F.C.C.R. 3704 (1989).
23. Complaints Against Various Licensees Regarding Their Broadcast of the Fox Television Network Program "Married By America" on April 7, 2003, Notice of Apparent Liability for Forfeiture, 19 F.C.C.R. 20191 (2004).
24. Complaints Against Various Television Licensees Concerning Their December 31, 2004, Broadcast of the Program "Without A Trace," Notice of Apparent Liability for Forfeiture. (FCC 06-18) (Mar. 15, 2006).

25. Complaints Against Various Television Station Licensees Regarding the ABC Television Network's November 15, 2004, Broadcast of "Monday Night Football," Memorandum Opinion and Order (FCC 05-53) (Mar. 14, 2005).

26. Notices of Apparent Liability and Memorandum Opinion and Order (FCC 06-17) (Mar. 15, 2006).

27. *See, e.g.,* Infinity Broadcast Operations, Inc., Notice of Apparent Liability for Forfeiture (FCC 04-49) (Mar. 18, 2004).

28. Complaints Against Various Television Licensees Concerning Their February 1, 2004, Broadcast of the Super Bowl XXXVII Halftime Show, Notice of Apparent Liability for Forfeiture, 19 F.C.C.R. 19230 (2004). *See also* Young Broadcasting of San Francisco, Inc., Notice of Apparent Liability for Forfeiture, 19 F.C.C.R. 1751 (2004) (brief exposure of penis found to be indecent).

29. Complaints Regarding Various Television Broadcasts Between February 2, 2002 and March 8, 2005, Notices of Apparent Liability and Memorandum Opinion and Order, (FCC-06-17) (Mar. 15, 2006).

30. Peter Branton, 6 F.C.C.R. 610 (1991).

31. Complaints Against Various Broadcast Licensees Regarding Their Airing of the "Golden Globe Awards," Memorandum Opinion and Order, 19 F.C.C.R. 4975 (2004).

32. Complaints Against Various Broadcast Licensees Regarding Their Airing of the "Golden Globe" Awards, Memorandum Opinion and Order, 18 F.C.C.R. 19859 (Enf. Bur. 2003). *See generally* Anne Marie Squeo, "A Job for Solomon: Was Bono's Blurt a Verb or Modifier?" *Wall Street Journal,* Mar. 11, 2004, at A1.

33. Complaints Against Various Television Licensees Regarding Their Broadcast on November 11, 2004, of the ABC Television Network's Presentation of the Film "Saving Private Ryan," Memorandum Opinion and Order, 20 F.C.C.R. 4507 (2005).

34. Complaints by Parents Television Council Against Various Broadcast Licensees Regarding Their Airing of Allegedly Indecent Material, Memorandum Opinion and Order, 20 F.C.C.R. 1931 (2005).

35. Complaints Regarding Various Television Broadcasts Between February 2, 2002 and March 8, 2005, Notices of Apparent Liability and Memorandum Opinion and Order (FCC 06-17) (Mar. 15, 2006).

36. Complaints Regarding Various Television Broadcasts Between February 2, 2002 and March 8, 2005, Order, (FCC 06-166) (Nov. 6, 2006).

37. FCC v. Fox Television Stations, Inc., 2009 U.S. Lexis 3297 (Apr. 28, 2009).

38. Pub. L. No. 109-235, 120 Stat. 491 (2006).

39. Complaints Regarding Various Television Broadcasts Between February 2, 2002 and March 8, 2005, Notices of Apparent Liability and Memorandum Opinion and Order at ¶¶ 101–45 (FCC 06-17) (Mar. 15, 2006).

40. Complaints Against Various Licensees Regarding Their Broadcast of the Fox Television Network Program "Married by America" on April 7, 2003, Forfeiture Order, (FCC 08-63) (Feb. 22, 2008).

41. Complaints Against Various Licensees Concerning Their February 25, 2003 Broadcast of the Program "NYPD Blue" Forfeiture Order (FCC 08-55) (Feb. 19, 2008).

42. Action for Children's Television v. FCC (Act III), 58 F.3d 654 (D.C. Cir. 1995), *cert. denied,* 516 U.S. 1043 (1996).

43. 492 U.S. 115 (1989).

44. 47 U.S.C. §223.

45. Regulations Concerning Indecent Communications by Telephone, 5 F.C.C.R. 4926 (1990).

46. Dial Information Servs.Corp. v. Thornburgh, 938 F.2d 1535 (2d Cir. 1991), *cert. denied,* 502 U.S. 1072 (1992); Information Providers' Coalition for Defense of the First Amendment v. FCC, 928 F.2d 866 (9th Cir. 1991).

47. Testimony of Kevin Martin before the U.S. Senate Committee on Commerce, Science and Transportation (Nov. 29, 2005).

48. Los Angeles v. Preferred Communications, Inc. 476 U.S. 488 (1986).

49. Leathers v. Medlock, 499 U.S. 439 (1991).

50. Turner Broadcasting Sys., Inc. v. FCC, 512 U.S. 622 (1994).

51. 800 F.2d 989 (10th Cir. 1986), *aff'd without opinion,* 480 U.S. 926 (1987).

52. 529 U.S. 803 (2000).

53. 47 U.S.C. § 532.

54. 47 U.S.C. § 531.

55. 47 U.S.C. § 532(b).

56. 518 U.S. 727 (1996).

57. Pub. L. No. 104-104, § 502, 110 Stat. 56 (1996).

58. 521 U.S. 844 (1997).

59. 390 U.S. 629 (1968).

60. 475 U.S. 41 (1986).

61. 492 U.S. 115 (1989).

62. 535 U.S. 564 (2002).

63. ACLU v. Ashcroft, 322 F.3d 240 (3rd Cir. 2003).

64. 542 U.S. 566 (2004).

65. ACLU v. Gonzales, 478 F. Supp. 2d 775 (E.D. Pa. 2007), *aff'd,* 534 F.3d 181 (3rd Cir 2008), *cert. denied,* 2009 U.S. LEXIS 598 (Jan. 21, 2009).

66. 20 U.S.C. § 9134(f)(3).

67. 539 U.S. 194 (2003).

68. Attorney General's Commission on Pornography, Final Report (1986).

69. *Id.* (separate statement of Commissioners Judith Becker & Ellen Levine).

70. Daniel Linz, Neil Malamuth, & Katherine Beckett, "Civil Liberties and Research on the Effects of Pornography," in *Psychology and Social Policy* 149 (P. Suedfeld and P. E. Tetlock, eds., 1992).

71. *See, e.g.,* Catherine MacKinnon, *Only Words* (1993).

72. American Booksellers Ass'n, Inc. v. Hudnut, 771 F.2d 323 (7th Or. 1985), *aff'd without opinion,* 475 U.S. 1001 (1986).

73. *See, e.g.,* Craig Anderson et al., "Violent Video Games: Specific Effects of Violent Content on Aggressive Thoughts and Behavior," 36 *Advances Experimental Soc. Psychol.* 199 (2004).

74. 244 R 3d 572 (7th Cir. 2001).

75. *See, e.g.,* Interactive Digital Software Ass'n v. St. Louis County, 329 F.3d 954 (8th Cir. 2003); Video Software Dealers Ass'n v. Schwarzenegger, 401 F. Supp. 2d 1034 (N.D. Cal. 2005); Entertainment Software Ass'n v. Granholm, 404 F. Supp. 2d 978 (E.D. Mich. 2005); Video Software Dealers Ass'n v. Maleng, 325 F. Supp. 2d 1180 (W.D. Wash. 2004).

76. Entertainment Software Ass'n v. Blagojevich, 404 F. Supp. 2d 1051 (N.D. Ill. 2005).

77. Report on the Broadcast of Violent, Indecent, and Obscene Material, 51 F.C.C.2d 418 (1975).

78. Pub. L. No. 104-104, § 551, 110 Stat. 56 (1996). *See also* 47 U.S.C. § 303 (x).

79. Blocking of Video Programming Based on Program Ratings, 13 F.C.C.R. 11248 (1998).

80. Video Program Ratings, 13 F.C.C.R. 8232 (1998).

81. Kaiser Family Foundation, *Generation M: Media in the Lives of 8–18 Year-olds* 20 (2005).

82. Complaints Regarding Various Television Broadcasts Between February 2, 2002 and March 8, 2005, Order at ¶ 51, (FCC 06-166) (Nov. 6, 2006).

UNIT 11

Speech or Transaction?
Regulation of Commercial Speech

The commercial character of American broadcasting contradicts somewhat the fact that American jurisprudence has traditionally downplayed the social importance of commercial messages. In this reading Michael Parkinson and Marie Parkinson review the limitations on commercial speech in a historical context. Indeed, straightforward advertisements are easy to identify, however in recent years we have seen the proliferation of surreptitious forms of advertising in broadcasting in the form of product placements, undisclosed video news releases, unabashed self-promotion ("plugola") and straightforward corrupt promotion of media products for bribe ("payola"). These forms of stealth and ethically questionable forms of advertising will be discussed in the accompanying lecture.

Commercial Communications

Rights and Regulations

Michael G. Parkinson and L. Marie Parkinson

[T]he suppression of advertising reduces the information available for consumer decisions and thereby defeats the purpose of the First Amendment.[1]

OVERVIEW

Commercial messages are granted fewer rights and are subjected to more regulation than other forms of communication. In fact, until fairly recently most courts ruled that the First Amendment did not even cover messages proposing commercial transactions. The limited First Amendment protection of commercial messages results from the federal government's obligation to simultaneously protect both commerce and freedom of communication. Understanding how these obligations are balanced and the resulting treatment of business-related communication is particularly important to people practicing in commercial advertising. The concepts are also important to journalists covering business and to public relations practitioners working in the areas of investor relations or commercial product promotions.

In this chapter, we first define *commercial communication*. We then describe the limited rights of free speech that are afforded commercial messages. We also detail the extensive regulations on commercial communication that are imposed by the Federal Trade Commission (FTC) and explore actions in civil court for fraudulent messages. We also describe limitations on advertising to children, advertising about tobacco products, and advertising attorneys' services. We conclude with practice notes that describe media, client, and agency liabilities for false or dangerous advertising, and the restrictions on political advertising and lobbying. We realize that political advertising and lobbying are not commercial communication but feel this information is helpful to communications practitioners whose practice in commercial communication may overlap with political communication.

WHAT IS COMMERCIAL COMMUNICATION?

To facilitate understanding how the law balances obligations to commerce and to free speech, we begin by explaining the difference between commercial communication (sometimes called commercial speech) and advertising. Because not all advertising is commercial communication, FTC regulations do not apply to all advertising. However those regulations

Michael G. Parkinson and L. Marie Parkinson, "Commercial Communications: Rights and Regulations," from *Law for Advertising, Broadcasting, Journalism, and Public Relations: A Comprehensive Text for Students and Practitioners*, pp. 367–380. Copyright © 2006 by Lawrence Erlbaum Associates. Permission to reprint granted by Taylor & Francis.

do apply to some forms of mass communication that are not usually thought of as advertising.

We must be able to recognize "commercial advertising" before we can know which of our messages do not enjoy full First Amendment rights and which ones are subject to governmental regulations. **Commercial communication**, as legally defined, does include most advertising but it does not include all advertising. Furthermore, commercial communication, as legally defined, includes a great many messages that are not traditional advertisements. It may be helpful for mass communications students and practitioners to note that the courts and regulatory agencies usually use the term *commercial advertising* to label the advertising that is subject to regulations.

Communication Definition of Advertising

Those of us in mass communications were probably taught that we can define advertising based on how the medium of the communication was financed. We consider a message to be advertising and the practitioner who places it an advertiser if he or she purchased the newspaper space, Internet page, or broadcast time for the message. This definition of advertising has advantages. It allows us to easily differentiate between what we label advertising, public relations, or journalism. However, in order to understand the legal limitations on the rights of commercial communication and the governmental regulation of commercial communication it is essential for us to understand that the law uses a different and more complicated system of identification. The law not only considers whether the time or space for a message was purchased, the law also considers the intent of the message itself.

Because of the legal definition of commercial communication, rights of free speech can be restricted for advertisers, public relations practitioners, and even journalists. Free speech rights can be restricted for any communications practitioner if his or her communication activities have a commercial purpose. The FTC regulations that many people believe can only control those in the advertising profession can be applied with equal force to those in other mass communications professions when they produce commercial communication. Furthermore, not all advertising is subject to the

regulation of the FTC. Some pure advertising escapes FTC regulation and enjoys the full protection of the First Amendment.

Legal Definition of Commercial Communication

In 1964, in its decision in *New York Times v. Sullivan*, the U.S. Supreme Court had to determine if an advertisement placed in *The New York Times* was a commercial communication. In that decision the Court said: "That the Times was paid for publishing the advertisement is as immaterial in this connection as is the fact that newspapers and books are sold."[2] Almost 20 years later, the Court affirmed this position in *Bolger v. Young's Drug Products Corp.* In that case, the Court was trying to determine whether a postal regulation was constitutional. The regulation prohibited delivery of unsolicited pamphlets offering contraceptives for sale. There the Court ruled the federal regulation of speech would be constitutional only if the pamphlets were commercial communication. After determining the pamphlets were advertisements, the Court said, "The mere fact that these pamphlets are conceded to be advertisements does not compel the conclusion that they are commercial speech."[3] Very specifically, the U.S. Supreme Court has ruled that not all advertising is regulated as commercial communication. In the *Bolger* decision the Court did say that messages that do "no more than propose a commercial transaction" are at "the core" of commercial communication[4] but even messages that only proposed a commercial transaction have been ruled not to be commercial communication if the transaction is related to an activity that is traditionally protected by the First Amendment. Specifically, in both *Murdock v. Pennsylvania*[5] and *Jamison v. Texas*,[6] the Supreme Court ruled that advertisements offering religious books for sale were not commercial communication and enjoyed full First Amendment protection.

Similarly, the FTC's regulations do not apply to all advertising. Limitations of the FTC's authority to regulate commercial communication is seen in the 1931 case of *Federal Trade Commission v. Raladam*[7] and the 1938 amendment to the FTC's enabling statutes. Raladam advertised and sold an obesity cure and the FTC enjoined Raladam from advertising the product without adding a disclaimer to the advertisements. The U.S. Supreme Court unanimously ruled that the FTC's statutory authority was limited to protecting business competitors from unfair business practices and did not give the FTC authority to control false advertising to protect consumers. Responding to this decision, in 1938 the U.S. Congress amended 15 USC § 45 (a) (1). This section formerly gave the FTC authority to control "unfair practices." After the amendment it gave the FTC authority to control "unfair or **deceptive** practices in commerce" (emphasis added). The current FTC authority to regulate false advertising arises entirely from this clause and is limited to the regulation of "commercial" advertising.

It is obvious that not all advertisements are commercial communication. It is equally obvious that some messages not included in advertisements are commercial communication. One example of commercial communication that is not typically labeled advertising is in-person solicitation.[8] Other examples include letters, news releases, and editorials. News releases, editorials, and letters were the focus of the conflict between Marc Kasky and Nike, Inc. This case, perhaps more than any other, emphasizes the fact that some commercial communication falls outside the definition of advertising used by communications practitioners.

Nike, Inc. v. Kasky

"Beginning in 1996, Nike was besieged with a series of allegations that it was mistreating and underpaying workers at foreign facilities. Nike responded to these charges in numerous ways, such as by sending out press releases, writing letters to the editors of various newspapers around the country, and mailing letters to university presidents and athletic directors."[9] Clearly, press releases, letters to the editor, and letters to university officials do not use the paid media typically associated with advertising. Nike itself has characterized its actions as a public relations campaign. As part of its public relations campaign,

In 1997, Nike commissioned a report by former Ambassador to the United Nations Andrew Young on the labor conditions at Nike production facilities. After visiting 12 factories, Young issued a report that commented favorably on working conditions in the factories and found no evidence of widespread abuse or mistreatment of workers.[10]

Nike publicized Young's report in news releases and letters.

In 1998, Marc Kasky sued Nike saying the company had violated California laws against unfair or deceptive business practices and false advertising. Nike responded to Kasky's suit with a legal response called a demurrer. In effect, Nike asked that the suit be dismissed and said that Kasky could not sue because the challenged messages were not commercial communication and were therefore not subject to laws governing false advertising or deceptive business practices. The trial court granted Nike's request to dismiss the case and the California Court of Appeals upheld that decision saying, "Our analysis of the press releases and letters as forming part of a public dialogue on a matter of public concern within the core area of expression protected by the First Amendment compels the conclusion that the trial court properly sustained the defendants' demurrer without leave to amend."[11] In more simple terms, the trial court and the appeals court both said the messages were not commercial communication and were therefore not subject to laws governing false advertising.

The California Supreme Court reversed and ruled that the news releases, editorials, and letters about labor practices and working conditions in factories where Nike products are made were "commercial speech."[12] In its decision, the Court said, "such representations, when aimed at potential buyers for the purpose of maintaining sales and profits, may be regulated to eliminate false and misleading statements because they are readily verifiable by the speaker and because regulation is unlikely to deter truthful and nonmisleading speech." The Court concluded, "contrary to the Court of Appeals, that Nike's speech at issue here is commercial speech."[13]

The California Supreme Court used the same rules articulated by the U.S. Supreme Court in its 1983 decision in *Bolger*. The California Supreme Court looked at three factors—advertising format, product references, and commercial motivation—that in combination supported a characterization of commercial communication in that case.[14]

The U.S. Supreme Court initially granted certiorari, agreeing to hear an appeal of the California Supreme Court's decision. Later, the Supreme Court reversed itself and ruled that the grant of certiorari had been "improvident." The Court gave several reasons for deciding not to hear the case. The first two of their reasons were based on arguments dealing with the Court's jurisdiction and are beyond the scope of this book. However, while explaining the third reason for its decision, the Court made several points that support the conclusion that news releases, editorials, or letters to university officials may be treated exactly like commercial advertising. In this explanation, the Court said, "This case presents novel First Amendment questions because the speech at issue represents a blending of commercial communication, noncommercial communication, and debate on an issue of public importance."[15] Apparently, the Court found that news releases, editorials, and letters could contain commercial communication because they involved "direct communications with customers and potential customers that were intended to generate sales—and possibly to maintain or enhance the market value of Nike's stock."[16]

The U.S. Supreme Court remanded the matter back to the California courts. Before the California courts could review the facts and determine whether Nike's communications were commercial or noncommercial, Nike settled with Kasky. For the time being, all we know for sure is that the kinds of media used by Nike in its campaign might be commercial communication if a court found they met the criteria described in *Bolger v. Youngs Drug Products.*[17]

The Bolger Test

The California Supreme Court, in *Kasky*, relied on the *Bolger* test to determine if Nike's communications were commercial. Since the Supreme Court's decision in *Bolger v. Youngs Drug Products* in 1983, the definition of commercial communication or commercial advertising has depended on the admittedly vague and imprecise test, which is summarized in Exhibit 12.1. In a preliminary step, the test says that communication that does "no more than propose a commercial transaction" is commercial

communication.[18] However, if the communication mixes both commercial and noncommercial components or includes more than a proposal to sell a product then three factors are examined. The three factors are (a) advertising format, (b) product references, and (c) commercial motivation. What makes the test ambiguous is that the Court has not only rejected the notion that any of these factors is sufficient by itself, but it has also declined to hold that all of these factors in combination, or any one of them individually, is necessary to support a commercial communication characterization.[19]

A review of how courts have applied the *Bolger* test produces some limited clarification. It appears that communications that are in the format of advertisements must be reviewed but the fact that a message is in a purchased medium and in the format of an advertisement does not, by itself, mean that the message is commercial communication. Similarly, a reference to a specific product does not, by itself, make a message commercial and the fact that the speaker has an economic motivation for delivering the message is insufficient to turn a message into commercial communication. The combination of all three factors provides strong support that the message can be characterized as commercial communication.[20]

For those in advertising, public relations, journalism, or broadcasting this means that they must be careful about any message that meets any one of these criteria. Messages that look like advertisements or that mention specific products or in which practitioners or their clients have a financial interest may not enjoy full First Amendment protection and may be subject to some government regulations. Of course, this does not mean practitioners cannot deliver messages that fit one, or all, of the above criteria. Journalists obviously cover stories about the stock prices of their newspapers, public relations practitioners deliver news releases about their client's products, and advertising professionals place their advertisements while complying with all legal restrictions and regulations. Even commercial communication enjoys some First Amendment protection.

Step 1	A. Can the communication be construed to propose a commercial transaction? If no, *stop here.* It is NOT commercial communication.
	B. Does the communication propose a commercial transaction and do nothing else? If so, *stop here.* It is commercial communication.
	If the communication does not fit either A or B, then proceed to Steps 2–3.
Step 2	Answer the following questions:
	A. Is the communication in the "format" of an advertisement?
	B. Does the communication include a reference to a specific product or service?
	C. Does the person or company creating the communication have a financial motivation for creating and delivering the message?
Step 3	Do the answers to the three questions in Step 2 lead a reasonable person to believe the communication is commercial? If yes, it is commercial. If no, it is not.
	(Remember you do not have to answer all three questions "yes" to find that the combination of answers makes the message commercial communication, nor is a message commercial speech just because one or two of the questions was answered yes. It is a subjective and somewhat vague test.)

RIGHTS AFFORDED COMMERCIAL COMMUNICATION

Current legal doctrine holds that any message fitting the definition of commercial communication is afforded less First Amendment protection than is given noncommercial communication. However, the First Amendment protects even purely commercial messages as long as the message is not false, misleading, potentially misleading, or coercive, and does not encourage an illegal act. The doctrine granting some limited First Amendment protection to commercial communication is fairly recent. Historically, commercial communication was totally subject to government regulations and enjoyed no First Amendment protection.

Historical Perspective

At one point, speech intended to generate marketplace transactions was governed by the principle of *caveat emptor* or "let the buyer beware." Under this principle, it was the buyer's responsibility to identify any deception in commercial communication. This doctrine encouraged self-serving deception by advertisers whose messages were often perceived as socially worthless. There was no social movement or governmental motivation to protect that kind of advertising. Not only was there no impetus to protect commercial communication, there was an opposite drive to protect consumers from fraud and deception. Commercial communication was, therefore, susceptible to virtually unlimited governmental regulation.

In 1942, the U.S. Supreme Court specifically said commercial communication was not protected by the First Amendment. This decision came in a conflict between Valentine, the police commissioner of New York, and Christensen, a Florida resident who sought to advertise tours of a submarine he had moored in New York Harbor. Initially, Christensen printed handbills announcing the tours. He was told the handbills violated a New York sanitary ordinance prohibiting handbills. The ordinance only permitted handbills about public protest. Christensen, being a dedicated entrepreneur, had the handbills reprinted. The new version of Christensen's handbills omitted the price of the tour and, on the reverse side, included a protest against the City of New York. Christensen argued that these new handbills either were not commercial advertising or that they so intermingled commercial and noncommercial messages that their distribution was protected by the First Amendment. Valentine said he would permit distribution of the handbill protesting the city's actions, but would not permit distribution of the handbill if even one side of it contained information about the submarine tours. Lower courts issued an injunction ordering the police commissioner to permit Valentine to distribute his handbills, complete with tour information. The U.S. Supreme Court reversed saying, in part:

> This court has unequivocally held that the streets are proper places for the exercise of the freedom of communicating information and disseminating opinion and that, though the states and municipalities may appropriately regulate the privilege in the public interest, they may not unduly burden or proscribe its employment in these public thoroughfares. We are equally clear that the Constitution imposes no such restraint on government as respects purely commercial advertising.[21]

The Court also noted it thought Christensen was trying to evade the anti-advertising ordinance by adding the protest. The Court said, "If that evasion were successful, every merchant who desires to broadcast advertising leaflets in the streets need only append a civic appeal, or a moral platitude, to achieve immunity from the law's command."[22]

Without citing any prior authority at all, the Court simply said that purely commercial advertising had absolutely no First Amendment rights. Furthermore, the Court found that even mixed commercial and noncommercial messages had no protection where some part of the message was intended to advance a commercial purpose. The police commissioner was allowed to prevent Christensen from distributing his handbill advertisements.

Beginning of Commercial Communication Protection

The U.S. Supreme Court first began to recognize some rights for commercial speech in its decision in *Bigelow v. Virginia*.[23] The Bigelow case dealt with advertisements placed in Virginia newspapers announcing that abortion services were available and legal in New York. A Virginia statute prohibited circulation of any message encouraging abortion. In its opinion, the U.S. Supreme Court ruled the Virginia statute unconstitutional because it suppressed speech that was protected by the First Amendment. The Court effectively reversed its earlier decision in *Valentine v. Christensen* saying that in their *Christensen* decision,

> The ordinance was upheld as a reasonable regulation of the manner in which commercial advertising could be distributed. The fact that it had the effect of banning a particular handbill does not mean that *Christensen* is authority for the proposition that all statutes regulating commercial advertising are immune from constitutional challenge.[24]

It might be noted the Court seemed unwilling to admit it was reversing itself. The decision in *Valentine v. Christensen* dealt with a challenge to an ordinance that only applied to commercial advertising and specifically exempted protest messages. A careful reading shows it was not the "time, place, and manner" restriction the Court claimed it had been. It seems obvious the Court, in *Bigelow*, was trying to find a way to grant First Amendment rights to some commercial advertising.

Within a year after the Supreme Court issued its decision in *Bigelow*, it found the courage to acknowledge First Amendment protection for commercial speech. In 1976, the Court reviewed a challenge to a Virginia law that prohibited advertising the price of prescription drugs. After finding the challenged messages were the purest form of commercial communications that did no more than propose a lawful commercial transaction, the Court said, "It is a matter of public interest that those economic decisions, in the aggregate, be intelligent and well informed. To this end, the free flow of commercial information is indispensable."[25] This decision effectively gave commercial advertising some First Amendment protection. It recognized that information about products and prices is essential for decisions by consumers and that such information also is valuable in a free enterprise system where government and concerned citizens can use the information to regulate or challenge commercial practices.

This decision was followed quickly by other decisions affirming the First Amendment rights of commercial communication. However, these decisions also made it obvious that commercial communication did not enjoy full First Amendment protection. The first of these cases was *Lindmark Associates, Inc. v. Township of Willingboro.*[26] The Township of Willingboro created an ordinance that prohibited real estate "for sale" signs. They prohibited the signs because they feared the signs in interracial neighborhoods would create "white flight." In its analysis, the Court said that the township's interest in protecting real estate values and residential integration could be met in other ways that did not require such a significant infringement on the First Amendment rights of those who wanted to sell their property.

The second of these cases is *Carey v. Population Services International.*[27] *Carey* addressed several issues related to the sale and advertising of birth control products. Part of that decision declared unconstitutional a New York statute prohibiting the advertisement of condoms. The Court did recognize a First Amendment right to distribute truthful information about condoms through advertising, but also said, "even a burdensome regulation may be validated by a sufficiently compelling state interest."[28] Later, the Court said that such regulation "may be justified only by compelling state interests, and must be narrowly drawn to express only those interests."[29] In effect, the Court held that, although commercial communication enjoys First Amendment protection, protection is not absolute. The Court said New York could regulate or limit a constitutional right if (a) it could demonstrate an adequate governmental interest, and (b) the restriction on constitutional rights was only as great as was necessary to meet the governmental interest.

After describing this logic, the Court applied it to the New York statute prohibiting advertising of condoms. It ruled that the complete suppression of truthful information about a lawful product was too broad to be constitutional even if New York had a legitimate interest in protecting its citizens from potentially offensive advertising."[30]

When *Virginia Pharmacy*, *Lindmark*, and *Carey* are all read together they do show that the Supreme Court had recognized some First Amendment rights for commercial speech, even commercial advertising. However, they also make it obvious that the Court was not giving commercial communication the same First Amendment protection that is enjoyed by noncommercial communication. This balance of protection and limitation was made a bit clearer by the Court's decision in what is commonly called the *Central Hudson* decision.

The *Central Hudson* Test

Three years after the decisions in *Virginia Pharmacy*, *Lindmark*, and *Carey* the Supreme Court decided a case brought by Central Hudson Gas and Electric against the New York Public Service Commission.[31] The case arose because a New York utility commission ordered Central Hudson to stop all advertising that promoted the use of electricity. The utility commission's decision was based on their belief that the New York electrical system did not have sufficient fuel stocks or electrical generation capacity to meet consumer demands. The ban on advertising was originally imposed because the commission anticipated particularly high demand for power during the winter of 1973–1974. However, the commission did not lift the ban after that winter because it thought advertising would encourage consumption contrary to its policy to conserve energy. Central Hudson challenged the order through the New York court system and lost at every level. The company then appealed to the U.S. Supreme Court saying that the public service commission's order violated the First and Fourteenth Amendments to the U.S. Constitution. The Supreme Court reversed the New York courts and held that the ban on energy advertising was unconstitutional. In this decision, the Court finally detailed specific rules that could guide future decisions about what First Amendment rights are given to commercial communication. First, the Court explained that commercial communication is not afforded the same First Amendment protection as is given to noncommercial communication. Justice Powell, writing for the Court, explained that,

> [t]wo features of commercial speech permit regulation of its content. First, commercial speakers have extensive knowledge of both the market and their products. Thus, they are well situated to evaluate the accuracy of their messages and the lawfulness of the underlying activity. In addition, commercial speech, the offspring of economic self-interest, is a hardy breed of expression that is not "particularly

susceptible to being crushed by overbroad regulation."[32]

In other words, because those who produce commercial communication are unlikely to accidentally misstate facts and because they are so well motivated financially that they will not be easily deterred by regulations, the Court would permit greater regulation of commercial communication than noncommercial communication.

In addition to explaining why commercial communication could be more aggressively regulated than other forms of communication, the Court also explained when commercial messages would be afforded First Amendment protection. This four-part standard for balancing the First Amendment rights of commercial communication with other government interests that could justify restriction of First Amendment rights has come to be called the **Central Hudson Test**.

The first step of the test is to determine whether the communication has any First Amendment protection at all. In order to even be considered for First Amendment protection, commercial communications must not promote an illegal product, service, or activity and it must not be false or misleading. Messages that promote illegal products or activities, or that are false or misleading simply are not given any First Amendment protection and for such messages it is not necessary to consider the next steps of the *Central Hudson* Test.

The second step of the *Central Hudson* Test is to determine if the governmental body that seeks to regulate the speech has asserted a substantial interest. This means that the state or other government entity that wants to restrict the free expression of the commercial speaker or advertiser must show it has some duty to protect that is important enough to justify a restriction on free expression. For example, the government entity may say that it has a duty to protect its citizens from being exposed to offensive images.

The third step in the *Central Hudson* Test is to assess whether the restriction on free expression actually will advance the asserted governmental interest. Here the Court asks, for example, if citizens will actually be protected from offensive images by the restriction of free expression.

The fourth step requires the Court to determine if the restriction on free expression is no greater than necessary to meet the governmental interest. Continuing the example of a government trying to protect its citizens from offensive images, the Court would ask if there is another way to protect the citizens that does not require as much restriction of free expression.

The *Central Hudson* Test has the advantage of giving some rules that may guide a state or regulatory agency trying to decide whether it may limit commercial communication. However, the test still has major weaknesses. Each of the four steps requires very subjective judgments and even justices of the U.S. Supreme Court have noted the test cannot be consistently applied and its results cannot be predicted. The difficulty of applying the test can be seen in the Court's decision in *Metromedia, Inc. v. San Diego*,[33] which was decided just 1 year after the *Central Hudson* decision. In *Metromedia*, the justices wrote five separate opinions, each attempting to apply the logic of the *Central Hudson* Test to an ordinance that banned most outdoor advertising. Ultimately, they concluded that the ordinance was unconstitutional. However, in his dissent, Justice Rehnquist called the decision a "tower of Babel." The confusion over how to apply the *Central Hudson* Test was further exacerbated a few years later when in its decision in *City Council v. Taxpayers for Vincent*,[34] the Supreme Court ruled that an ordinance banning political signs on public land was constitutional. In 3 years, applying the same test, the Court found commercial signs could not be restricted by city ordinance but that political signs could be restricted. These holdings are particularly confusing because the rulings seem inconsistent with the governmental interests advanced and the type of communication involved. In *Metromedia* the city of San Diego asserted its ban on off-site billboards advanced a governmental interest in "eliminating hazards to pedestrians and motorists brought about by distracting sign displays, and to preserve and improve the appearance of the city." In *Vincent*, the city of Los Angeles asserted an interest in "esthetics and in preventing visual clutter." Application of the second stage of the *Central Hudson* Test would seem to favor the city of San Diego yet the ordinance was declared unconstitutional, while the Los Angeles ordinance challenged in *Vincent* was upheld. The decisions are even more puzzling when one considers that the ordinance in Vincent addressed political signs and political messages have traditionally received the highest First Amendment protections.

Application of the *Central Hudson* Test was made more difficult in 1986 when the Court decided *Posadas de Puerto Rico Associates v. Tourism Company of Puerto Rico.*[35] The legislature of Puerto Rico passed a law prohibiting advertising of casino gambling that was directed to the local residents. That same legislature passed laws making casino gambling legal and making it legal to advertise for the casinos as long as the advertisements targeted only tourists or prospective tourists. In its decision, the Court ruled that the government of Puerto Rico had a substantial interest in limiting corruption and crime that would attend increases in gambling by locals. Furthermore, the Court ruled there was a connection between advertising and demand by local residents for gambling, but the Court did not consider whether any alternative that imposed lesser restrictions on free expression could advance the governmental interest. The Court simply did not require any support for the third or fourth steps of the *Central Hudson* Test. Complicating the decision even further was the Court's observation that the Puerto Rican legislature had the power to completely ban casino gambling and that the power to ban an activity included the lesser power to ban advertising of the activity.[36] This last assertion has led many to believe the *Central Hudson* Test need not be applied to commercial messages about any activity that could be prohibited by government.

More confusion followed in 1999 when in *Greater New Orleans Broadcasting Association v. United States*[37] the Court ruled that advertisements for legal casinos in Louisiana and Mississippi could not be banned. The Court ruled the state failed to meet the third step of the *Central Hudson* Test because its asserted interest in the control of social costs like crime, corruption, and financial burdens on the poor was not supported by a ban on advertising. Not only is the *Central Hudson* Test itself vague and subjective, there are even serious questions about whether it will always be applied.

Clarification of *Central Hudson* Test—Maybe?

There have been some attempts to clarify or even operationalize some of the *Central Hudson* Test steps. These are summarized in Exhibit 12.2. In 1989, in *Board of Trustees of the State University of New York v. Fox,*[38] the Court offered some explanation of what it meant by the phrase "no greater than necessary to meet the governmental interest" as that phrase is used in the fourth step of the *Central Hudson* Test. The case arose in a challenge to a State University of New York (SUNY) regulation banning most commercial enterprises from its campuses. Enforcing this regulation, the SUNY police broke up a Tupperware party in a university dorm. Fox and other students at SUNY sought a court order challenging the regulation.

The courts reviewed several issues, one of which was whether a total ban on commercial activity was "greater than necessary to meet the governmental interest." The governmental interests asserted by SUNY were (a) promoting an educational rather than a commercial atmosphere on the university's campuses, (b) promoting safety and security, (c) preventing commercial exploitation of students, and (d) preserving residential tranquility.[39] One question presented to the Court was whether some narrower restriction like controlling the hours during which parties could be held might still meet these interests. Justice Scalia, writing for the Court, simply redefined the word "necessary" and said what is required to meet the fourth step of the *Central Hudson* Test is not the least abridgment of free expression "necessary" but only a "fit" between the regulation abridging free expression and the asserted governmental interest. He explained further that what is required to meet the fourth step is,

> not necessarily the least restrictive means but … a means narrowly tailored to achieve the desired objective. Within those bounds we leave it to governmental decisionmakers to judge what manner of regulation may best be employed.[40]

The decision in *Board of Trustees of the State University of New York* does not completely vitiate the fourth step of the *Central Hudson* Test. In 1993, the U.S. Supreme Court in *City of Cincinnati v. Discovery Network, Inc.,*[41] ruled that the "fit" between the restriction on free expression and the governmental interest must be substantial. In *City of Cincinnati*, the Court reviewed a decision by Cincinnati authorities to revoke the Discovery Network's right to place newsracks on the city's property. The city's decision was based on an ordinance prohibiting commercial handbills. The Court found that the city did permit other newsracks and that the number of newsracks used for commercial handbills was small in comparison to the total number of newsracks. The Court ruled that the city's interest in safety and esthetics could be adequately met by regulating the number of racks or their size and location. A total ban on newsracks for commercial handbills was ruled unconstitutional. As recently as 2003, in *Atlanta Journal and Constitution v. City of Atlanta Department of Aviation*,[42] the court of appeals supported such a conclusion by declaring the city's power to cancel a publisher's airport newsrack license unconstitutional.

It appears that even though the fourth step of the *Central Hudson* Test was modified, it must still be met before a governmental agency can restrict the free expression of commercial communication.

Social Conformist Applications

The Supreme Court has never specifically said it uses a **social conformist** approach when deciding what is and what is not commercial communication. Nor has it offered such a philosophical explanation for its decisions regarding the propriety of government regulation of commercial communication. However, neither the *Bolger* Test nor the *Central Hudson* Test can be applied with the kind of precision that an absolutist or literalist approach makes possible. A review of how the *Central Hudson* Test has been applied suggests an unspoken rule. The Court does appear to use the social function component of the social conformist approach to constitutional interpretation. Speech that advances goals the Court sees as socially important is given greater First Amendment protection than is communication that does not have a socially important function.

EXHIBIT 12.2   The *Central Hudson* Test Used to Determine Whether Commercial Speech May Be Subjected to Government Regulation

Step 1	A. Does the communication promote an illegal product, service, or activity? If yes, stop here; it has no First Amendment protection and is subject to government regulation.
	B. Is the communication false or misleading? If yes, stop here; it has no First Amendment protection and is subject to government regulation.
	If the answer to Questions A and B are both no, the communication may have some First Amendment protection; go to Steps 2–4.
Step 2	Does the government body attempting to regulate the commercial communication assert a substantial and legitimate government interest? If no, stop here; the regulation probably does violate the First Amendment. If yes, go to Step 3.
Step 3	Is the government interest described in Step 2 advanced or helped by the proposed regulation of the commercial communication? If no, stop here; the regulation probably does violate the First Amendment. If yes; go to Step 4.
Step 4	Is there a substantial "fit" between the regulation and the government interest described in Step 2? (This does not mean that the regulation is absolutely "necessary" to meet the government interest but it cannot be a much broader or more invasive regulation than is needed to meet the government interest.) If no, stop here; the regulation probably does violate the First Amendment. If yes, the regulation probably does not violate the First Amendment

Decisions regarding government impositions on commercial communication follow a rough pattern from the middle 1970s to the late 1990s. Beginning with the Supreme Court's decision in *Roe v. Wade*,[43] the Court apparently found protecting personal decisions about health, particularly reproductive health, an important social goal. Many of the cases that imposed limits on governmental control of commercial communication after that date all seem to advance the goal of protecting personal decisions about health. The first case to restrict governmental impositions on commercial communication was *Bigelow v. Virginia*, a case dealing with information about abortion availability. The other major cases granting greater constitutional protection to commercial communication in the 1970s addressed similar health issues. For example, in 1976 the Court protected drug price advertising and in 1977 it protected messages about contraceptives. The other major area where constitutional protection was expanded was real estate advertising and in those cases racial integration, another important social function, was being protected.

Restrictions on the protection of commercial communication can also be seen to follow a social function approach. After granting extensive protection to commercial communication in the 1970s, the Court began to limit those protections in a series of cases that addressed other important social functions like the government's ability to control gambling, and liquor consumption. In 1977, the Court reasoned that prohibitions against attorney advertising should be overturned to meet the social goal of encouraging access to the legal system.[44]

NOTES

1. *New York Times Co. v. Sullivan*, 376 U.S. 254, 265 (1964).
2. *Bolger et. al. v. Youngs Drug Products Corp.*, 463 U.S. 60, 65 (1983).
3. *Id.* at 66.
4. *Murdoch v. Pennsylvania*, 319 U.S. 105 (1943).
5. *Jamison v. Texas*, 318 U.S. 413 (1943).
6. *Federal Trade Commission v. Raladam*, 283 U.S. 643 (1931).
7. *Ohralik v. Ohio State Bar*, 436 U.S. 447 (1978).
8. *Nike, Inc. v. Kasky*, 539 U.S. 654 (2003).
9. *Id.* at 656.
10. *Marc Kasky v. Nike, Inc.*, 79 Cal. App. 4th 165, 178 (2000).
11. *Id.* at 968.
12. *Id.* at 970.
13. *Id.* at 957.
14. *Nike, Inc. v. Kasky*, 539 U.S. 654, 663 (2003).
15. *Id.* at 664.
16. *Bolger v. Youngs Drug Products*, 463 U.S. 60 (1983).
17. *Id.* at 66.
18. *Marc Kasky v. Nike, Inc.*, 27 Cal. 4th 939, 957, 45 P. 3d 243 (2002).
19. *Bolger*, 463 U.S. at 66–67.
20. *Valentine v. Christensen*, 316 U.S. 52, 54 (1942).
21. *Id.* at 55.
22. *Bigelow v. Virginia*, 421 U.S. 809 (1975).
23. *Id.* at 819–820.
24. *Virginia State Bd. of Pharmacy v. Virginia Citizens Consumer Council Inc.*, 425 U S 748 765 (1976).
25. *Lindmark Associates, Inc. v. Township of Willingboro*, 431 U.S. 85 (1977).
26. *Carey v. Population Services International*, 431 U.S. 678 (1977).
27. *Id.* at 686.
28. *Id.*
29. *Id.* at 700.
30. *Central Hudson Gas & Elect. Corp. v. Public Service Comm'n*, 447 U.S 557 (1980)
31. *Id.* at 564 n.6.
32. *Metromedia, Inc. v. San Diego*, 453 U.S. 490 (1981).
33. *City Council v. Taxpayers for Vincent*, 466 U.S. 789 (1984).
34. *Posadas de Puerto Rico Associates v. Tourism Company of Puerto Rico*, 478 U.S. 328 (1986).
35. *Id.* at 346.
36. *Greater New Orleans Broadcasting Association v. United States*, 527 U.S. 173 (1999).
37. *Board of Trustees of the State University of New York v. Fox*, 492 U S 469 (1989).
38. *Id.*
39. *Id.* at 480.
40. *City of Cincinnati v. Discovery Network, Inc.*, 507 U.S. 410 (1993).

41. *Atlanta Journal and Constitution v. City of Atlanta Department of Aviation* 322 F3d 1298 (11th Cir.2003).

42. *Roe v. Wade,* 410 U.S. 113 (1973).

43. *Bates v. State Bar of Arizona,* 433 U.S. 350 (1977).

44. The original FTC act was passed on September 26, 1914, as Chapter 311 § 5. It is codified at 15 U.S.C. § 45 (2004).

UNIT 12

Must or Must Not Carry?
Regulation of Multiplatform
Video Delivery Systems

While so much regulatory attention has been drawn to broadcasting, 85% of Americans receive their video intake over cable and satellite networks. These networks are not, for the most part, subject to the same content regulations as broadcasters, as their regulatory environment is not limited by the scarcity dictated by the technological attributes of the spectrum. At the same time cable and satellite distribution systems raise many challenges to regulators, as they dominate the delivery to consumers, compete directly and indirectly with broadcasters, and create within their own industry a whole new market of operators and content providers. The readings in this unit cover most of the rules that pertain to these systems, while the lectures focus more on staging them within the context of relations with consumers, broadcasters, and other players exclusively in the MPVD market.

A chapter from Roger Sadler's book on the regulation of electronic media provides the details of multi platform video distribution regulation. The accompanying lecture will provide further insight to the differences between cable and satellite regulation.

Cable and
Satellite Regulation

Roger L. Sadler

Regulation of emerging video technologies requires a delicate balancing act of competing interests.

—*Quincy Cable TV, Inc., v. FCC*[1]

Because of its nature, cable television presents a unique regulatory problem. Cable TV, also known as CATV or Community Antenna Television, got its start in the United States in the late 1940s. As the name indicates, CATV involves a community or business erecting a large antenna to receive television station signals more clearly. These clearer TV signals are then sent to individual homes via cable. At first, most CATV systems were located in smaller, more remote communities where it was difficult to pick up TV stations with just an antenna on a TV set or a roof. People could pick up TV signals with an antenna very easily in larger cities, so cable TV did not grow as quickly in metro areas. At that time, cable systems mostly retransmitted the signals of broadcast stations.

The Communications Act of 1934 gave the FCC the power to regulate "all interstate communication by wire or radio." The government soon had to determine how it would regulate this emerging technology, but cable TV presented interesting regulatory issues:

- *Is it "interstate"?* Most cable systems' wires do not cross state lines, so they technically are not "interstate communication." However, cable systems do retransmit TV signals from other states, so they are interstate in that regard.

- *Is it broadcasting?* CATV is technically not a broadcast medium because the signals are carried over wires. At the same time, though, cable operators do retransmit broadcast station programming.

- *Is it a common carrier?* CATV is transmitted over wires, so it is similar to a common carrier such as a telephone company. However, CATV does not fit into that category because cable companies choose what material goes over their wires, and common carriers do not.

These were just some of the issues considered as the government tried to determine how cable needed to be regulated. Cable TV does not use the public airwaves, and the courts do not consider it "pervasive," like broadcasting. Broadcast airwaves come into a home uninvited, but consumers must choose to invite cable into the home. As a result, the FCC does not have the same kinds of regulations for cable systems as it does for broadcast stations.

EARLY CABLE REGULATION

In 1959, there were only 550 cable systems nationwide, and the FCC said it had no plans to regulate cable TV. In 1960, a bill to give the FCC authority over the cable industry died in a congressional committee. Still, the FCC would soon make some rules to try to regulate the cable industry. One of the main concerns was the economic effect that cable systems could have on local broadcasters, and this highlighted the FCC's concept of *localism*. Localism is directly related to the "public interest" standard and says that broadcast stations must air programming to serve the needs and interests of their communities. Therefore, the FCC will take steps to ensure that other media do not hinder broadcast stations' ability to serve the public interest or hinder the public's access to broadcast station programming.

This concept of localism was tested in 1962. The FCC ruled that cable systems could use microwave relay systems to bring in broadcast signals from distant cities, but the cable companies had to prove that this signal importation would not economically damage broadcasters and hinder localism. Still, broadcasters complained. These distant stations from larger cities often carried more movies and better overall programming than smaller local stations did, and cable companies soon found that the big city stations were popular with cable subscribers. As a result, local broadcasters feared they would go out of business as a result of lost viewers and reduced advertising revenue. Most of the population (especially in rural areas) did not have access to cable at this time. Therefore, if these small broadcasters went off the air, localism would be severely damaged because many citizens would have no access to a local broadcast station.

These were the kinds of concerns that arose later that year in Wyoming. The FCC had given permission to the Carter Mountain Transmission Corporation to use microwave links to provide distant TV station signals to cable companies in the towns of Riverton and Thermopolis. KWRB-TV in Riverton fought the FCC decision and, after a hearing, the FCC reversed itself and ruled in favor of KWRB. The commission decided that the microwave relays did indeed pose a genuine economic threat to KWRB and could result in the loss of TV service to a large rural population that did not have access to cable TV. The FCC said it would reconsider the ruling if Carter could guarantee the cable companies would carry KWRB and would not carry distant stations that duplicated KWRB's programming. Carter decided not to appeal to the commission and instead took the FCC to court. A federal appeals court upheld the FCC's decision in 1963 in *Carter Mountain Transmission Corporation v. FCC*.[2] The court reaffirmed the FCC's doctrine of *localism* by ruling that the commission's decision in this matter was a "legitimate measure of protection for the local station and the public interest."

By 1965, the number of cable systems had grown to 1847, more than tripling in just 6 years, and the FCC was seeing a greater need to regulate the rapidly growing industry. The commission was also becoming more concerned about cable's effects on local broadcast stations. In its *First Report and Order*[3] on CATV in 1965, the FCC used the *Carter Mountain* ruling as a justification for giving itself more power to regulate cable TV, and it did so with two rules:

- "Must-carry": The FCC said cable systems must carry the signals of local broadcast stations if the cable system is within the "A" contour of the station. (The A contour is the area in which a broadcast station's signal provides quality reception the majority of the time.)

- "Nonduplication": Cable systems could not carry distant stations that duplicated programming on a local station. Cable systems were allowed to carry duplicated programming on distant stations as long as it did not air within 15 days of the local station airing that same programming. (This would later be called the *network nonduplication rule*.)

With these rules, the FCC further demonstrated its commitment to localism by protecting the interests of local broadcast stations. It was becoming clear that the FCC was viewing cable systems as supplements to local stations and not as substitutes.

In the *Second Report and Order*[4] in 1966, the FCC said its regulations would now apply to all cable systems. It also decided to give more protection to fledgling UHF stations by prohibiting cable systems in the top 100 markets from importing distant signals. The commission also wanted to have more control over telephone companies entering the cable business. In 1968, the commission required that telephone companies obtain a Certificate of Public Convenience before building a cable system. Two years later in 1970, the FCC further greatly restricted telephone companies' entrance into the cable industry by prohibiting phone companies from owning a cable system within their telephone service areas.

Leapfrogging

Many cable systems up until 1968 had been carrying distant stations on their systems without the permission of those stations. The FCC instituted an "antileapfrogging" rule in the top 100 markets that required cable systems to get permission from distant stations before placing those stations on their systems. This rule was eliminated in 1976.

The FCC Is Allowed to Regulate Cable

Some cable operators were becoming increasingly uncomfortable with the FCC's cable rules, but broadcasters appreciated the FCC's protection of their economic interests. One broadcasting company, Midwest Television, used these rules to its advantage. The company complained to the FCC, saying that Southwestern Cable Company in San Diego was carrying TV stations from Los Angeles and that this was having a negative impact on Midwest's station in San Diego, KFMB-TV.

In 1968 in *U.S. v. Southwestern Cable*,[5] the U.S. Supreme Court upheld the FCC's concept of localism and said the San Diego cable system's actions were "disrupting Commission-licensed broadcasting in the San Diego market." The court upheld the FCCs cable regulations and indicated that the FCC had authority to regulate cable TV. The Telecommunications Act of 1934 granted the FCC the right to regulate "all interstate communication by wire or radio," the court said; the FCC's "regulatory authority over CATV is imperative if it is to perform with appropriate effectiveness certain of its other responsibilities."

As for the extent of the FCC's power to regulate cable, the court said that question would be answered in the future: "There is no need here to determine in detail the limits of the Commission's authority to regulate CATV."

—**FAQ**: What impact did the Southwestern Cable case really have on cable regulation?

Even though the Supreme Court did not provide explicit detail about the extent of the FCC's power to regulate cable, the justices had upheld the FCC's basic right to regulate cable. The court had also reiterated the doctrine of "localism," ruling that local broadcast stations needed to be protected to serve the public interest. That protection, if necessary, could come in the form of certain restrictions on cable providers.

CABLE AND "PUBLIC INTEREST"

As cable became more popular in the late 1960s, the FCC decided that cable systems had to serve the public interest in some way. In 1969, the commission required cable systems with more than 3500 subscribers to provide locally originated programming, as well as facilities for production. Many cable operators did not like the government mandating that certain types of programs be provided on cable systems, and in *U.S. v. Midwest Video*,[6] a cable company took the FCC to court over these local programming rules. In a 5–4 ruling, the Supreme Court in 1972 upheld the FCC's right to regulate cable. The court said that FCC could require cable companies to serve the public interest in some ways as long as the rules are "not inconsistent with law, and as the public interest, convenience, or necessity requires." Local programming rules were not a great burden, the justices said: These larger cable systems were capable of producing local programs "without impairing their financial stability, raising rates, or reducing the quality of service." The court said that providing facilities for original local programming was usually simple, requiring only a camera and a videotape recorder.

The Supreme Court agreed with the FCC's argument that the "unregulated explosive growth of CATV," as well as cable practices such as leapfrogging, threatened to "deprive the public of the various benefits" of local broadcasting stations. Therefore, cable regulation was necessary in this regard. Cable is part of the "broadcasting system," the court said. "CATV is dependent totally on broadcast signals and is a significant link in the system as a whole and therefore must be seen as within the jurisdiction of the [Communications Act of 1934]."

—FAQ: Didn't this ruling give the FCC a lot more power to regulate cable?

The four dissenting justices believed so. Justice Douglas argued that these FCC cable regulations gave the commission too much power and were a violation of cable operators' First Amendment rights. Douglas said cable operators, not the government, should be the ones to decide what programs are placed on their systems.

The dissenters brought up arguments that continue to be made today by opponents of cable regulation. Douglas wrote that the majority ruling allowed for "no limits short of complete domination of the field of communications by the Commission." Regarding cable regulations in general, Douglas wrote that "Congress is the agency to make the decision," not the FCC. CATV should not be regulated like broadcasting because "CATV systems do not in fact broadcast or rebroadcast. Broadcasters select the programs to be viewed; CATV systems simply carry, without editing, whatever programs they receive." As for the majority argument about CATV being "dependent totally on broadcast signals," Douglas argued that the court could apply the same reasoning and regulations to manufacturers of TV sets.

That same year, the FCC, under the leadership of Dean Burch, put even more emphasis on local cable programming and mandated other rules for the cable industry.

The 1972 Cable Television Report and Order[7]

As the number of cable systems exploded, the FCC realized it could not "license" cable companies, but the commission needed some means of record keeping. In its 1972 Report and Order,[6,7] the commission required all cable companies to get a *certificate of compliance* from the FCC to operate a cable system or to add a TV broadcast signal.

The FCC also mandated that all cable systems be built with the capacity to handle at least 20 channels. The FCC then imposed some "broadcasting rules" on many cable systems. Any cable operator who originated local programming had to abide by such rules as sponsorship identification, the Fairness Doctrine, and Section 315. The FCC required that cable operators file annual reports with the commission and maintain employment and financial records.

The 1972 *Report and Order* also instituted a wide range of rules that included cross-ownership, technical standards, access channels, franchise rules, and syndicated program exclusivity. Many of these rules would be modified or eliminated in the years to come, as will be discussed shortly.

Antisiphoning Rule Struck Down

In 1975, the FCC was concerned that popular movies were being "siphoned" away from broadcasters by cable television. It was simple economics. Filmmakers could usually make more money by placing their movies on pay cable channels than on advertiser-supported broadcast television. Fearing that the cable industry was again threatening local broadcast stations, the FCC established rules that prohibited cable companies from offering pay movie channels with feature films less than 3 years old. The rules also prohibited cable channels from offering paid access to certain major sporting events (such as the World Series) if these events had been shown on broadcast TV within the previous 5 years. The FCC said the siphoning of such programs away from broadcast stations would limit the public's ability to access such programs on "free TV." Also, the FCC said that pay programming involving sports programs and feature films could not make up more than 90% of total cable pay operations.

—FAQ: Didn't the cable industry find the antisiphoning rules unfair?

Yes, and HBO took the commission to court over the rules and won. The DC Circuit Court of Appeals invalidated the antisiphoning rules in 1978 in *Home Box Office (HBO) v. FCC*.[8] The court ruled that the FCC exceeded its authority and provided "no evidence to support the need for regulation of pay cable television." The court said the commission did not prove that broadcasters were actually being harmed by "siphoning." The court basically said that the FCC was trying to solve a problem that did not exist.

—FAQ: Didn't the HBO ruling signal a change in how the courts viewed FCC regulation of cable?

Yes. The *HBO* case was important because the court demanded that the FCC provide concrete rationale for its cable regulations. The FCC was forced to recognize that cable operators had the right to make independent programming choices free of FCC interference. Subsequently, the ruling also opened the doors for other cable pay channels, which would soon result in a rapid growth of the cable industry.

The Cable Communications Policy Act of 1984 (The 1984 Cable Act)

This act is credited with spurring the rapid growth of cable in the late 1980s. It was designed to "encourage the growth and development of cable systems," and in it, Congress amended the Communications Act of 1934 to give the FCC official authority to regulate cable television. Cable regulations established in the 1960s became law under this act, and this gave the FCC more freedom in passing regulations affecting cable television. At the same time, the 1984 Cable Act would lead to a substantial deregulation of cable at the federal level and shift more power to local authorities.

Before 1984, many local governments and cable operators were confused about how much power they had in the cable regulation arena. Congress helped to clarify some of their concerns in the 1984 Cable Act, which was negotiated between cable industry and broadcasting groups. Congress ruled as follows.

- Cable operators must *obtain franchises* granted by local governments, which act as *local franchising authorities* (LFAs).

- Franchise fees could not exceed 5% of the cable system's gross revenues.

- Local governments may establish technical requirements for the cable system.

- The franchise renewal process must be orderly and not unfairly deny renewals to existing cable operators. LFAs may deny renewal to a cable operator for reasons such as violations of a franchise agreement, providing inferior service to the community and being technically unqualified.

- The local government is not allowed to dictate cable system programming.

- The local government may request that cable systems set aside channels for educational, governmental, or public access use.

- Cable operators must run wires in the entire franchise area. (Some companies had a practice of not stringing wires in "less profitable" neighborhoods.)

- The FCC is allowed to establish certain technical standards for cable system equipment and facilities.

- In general, neither the local government nor the FCC may regulate rates. However, the act allowed the FCC to regulate basic cable rates for systems in places where there was no effective competition in the market. Later, the FCC would define *competition* very broadly so that most cable systems wound up being exempt from FCC rate regulation of basic cable service.

- Cable systems were not allowed to own a TV station within the same market. (This rule was later dropped. See chapter 5.)

- Local governments may award more than one cable franchise in the community

—FAQ: Don't most communities, though, have only one cable franchise?

Yes, and it was the case back then as well. The majority of local governments often granted "exclusive franchises" in which only one cable company was permitted to operate in the community. There were various reasons for this. Most small communities did not have enough customers to support two cable companies. Also, smaller cable companies would not even make a bid for a franchise in many communities because they could not afford to compete with the established bigger cable companies. In any case, the result was a cable company with a monopoly on cable service in a community. That situation has changed today because cable companies now have more competition, mostly from satellite TV providers. However, in 1986, when cable was the "only game in town," the issue of exclusive local cable franchises made its way to the Supreme Court.

Franchises

Companies must use public utility poles to string cables across communities. Local and state governments have authority over these public structures, and governments are therefore allowed to exercise some control over the cable companies that use these poles. The local government thus acts as an LFA and has the power to give a cable system the right to operate in the community. (In some states, state public utility commissions oversee cable TV regulation.)

The major Supreme Court ruling concerning franchising is *City of Los Angeles v. Preferred.*[9] Cable operator Preferred Communications wanted to lease space on Los Angeles utility poles and underground conduits to run its TV cables. However, the city's Department of Water and Power said it could not lease any space unless Preferred had a franchise from the city. The city refused a franchise request because Preferred had not taken part in the city's franchise auction process. Preferred sued the city, saying it had a First Amendment right to operate a cable system in Los Angeles. Preferred argued there was "sufficient excess physical capacity" on poles and underground conduits and enough customer demand in the area to support a second cable company. Preferred also said the city's auction process was unfair, allowing only one cable company to operate based on which company the city considered "best." The city argued that there was limited economic demand for cable services in the community and that there was limited space on public utility structures. The city also expressed concerns that the installation process would create traffic problems and the extra cables on poles might be unattractive.

An appeals court agreed with Preferred and said the cable company had a First Amendment right to use these public rights of way. The U.S. Supreme Court generally agreed with the appeals court that cable operators have basic First Amendment rights, but the court also said that a city has the right to award a franchise to only one company. The Supreme Court remanded the case to a district court, where the judge ruled for Preferred because the city utility structures could handle more than one cable company and the city's rule about granting only one cable franchise was a violation of the First Amendment rights of cable operators.

—FAQ: Did this ruling prohibit all exclusive cable franchises?

It certainly set the wheels in motion. In 1992, Congress gave some teeth to the judge's ruling when it banned communities from awarding exclusive franchises.

ACCESS CHANNEL RULES

The 1972 *Report and Order*[6, 7] said that access channels would help increase citizen involvement in community affairs and give "third parties" access to the cable system. The FCC established four basic types of access channels to meet these needs and mandated that cable systems in the top 100 markets carry them. Cable systems were also required to provide facilities for access channel program production. If there was no public demand for all four types of channels, cable companies would be allowed to carry fewer than four.

In 1976, the FCC expanded the access channel rule to include cable systems with more than 3500 subscribers, but these cable systems were still required to provide facilities for production of local access programs. In addition, the FCC required cable systems of this size to have a 20-channel capacity by 1986.

—FAQ: Weren't these access channel rules another violation of cable operators' rights to make independent programming decisions?

Many cable operators thought so, and they argued that these rules were similar in nature to the antisiphoning rules, which the courts had struck down. Midwest Video Corporation challenged the access channel rules on First Amendment grounds, arguing that the FCC was trying to treat cable companies like broadcasting. In 1979, in *FCC v. Midwest Video* (also called *Midwest Video II*),[10] the Supreme Court ruled that the FCC had gone beyond the authority granted to it in the Communications Act of 1934. The FCC could not make cable systems carry public access channels or abide by channel capacity requirements. The court ruled that making cable systems carry original local programs turned CATV into a "common carrier" like a telephone system. The court said the FCC needed the permission of Congress to treat cable as a common carrier and to enforce such rules. In fact, Congress got involved in the matter 5 years later with the Cable Act of 1984.

PEG Channels No Longer Mandatory

Section 611 of the Cable Act says that a local franchising authority *may* require cable companies to set aside channels for public, educational, or governmental (PEG) use. Again, the Supreme Court, in *Midwest Video II*, said the FCC could not force cable companies to carry access channels. In 1984, however, Congress said that franchising authorities could require cable companies to do so. In this way, the decisions about access channels were placed in the hands of local governments instead of the FCC. Usually, the LFA and cable company negotiate over the types of access channels to be offered, or they may choose not to carry any PEG channels. The 1984 Cable Act allowed LFAs to determine their own policies for use of these channels.

—**FAQ:** Does the 1984 Cable Act lay out any basic rules regarding PEG channels?

Yes. Some of the major rules from the 1984 act include the following:

- Franchising authorities may require cable companies to provide facilities, services, or equipment for use of PEG channels.

- A cable company can require certain production standards for PEG programs.

- A cable company can require users to undergo training (how to operate cameras, how to do proper lighting, etc.).

- A cable company is not allowed to refuse a request for time on an access channel based simply on the content of the material.

- Access channels are designated for nonprofit activities, and therefore commercial programs of any sort are not allowed, except on leased access channels.

- Cable companies may grant time on these channels on a first-come-first-served basis.

- Cable companies are allowed to enforce age restrictions, such as requiring persons younger than 18 to have an adult cosign on requests for time.

—**FAQ:** What are the differences between the four types of access channels?

Public Access. These channels are supposed to be open for free use by the general public, and the cable company may not censor content. Franchising authorities may designate a third party to oversee these channels. Public access channels were designed to allow free "first-come nondiscriminatory access," but cable operators may charge users for any costs involved in producing programs. The FCC originally said that public access channels should not allow any advertising, lottery information, obscenity, or indecent material. However, the rules against indecent material were overturned, which will be discussed in more detail in chapter 11.

Educational Access. These channels are set aside for educational institutions and are to be used solely for educational purposes. The franchising authority or cable operator works in conjunction with local schools and universities to allocate time on these channels. The FCC says that "educational authorities" are to control the content on these channels. Therefore, an educational access channel is not a "public" channel, and the general public does not have an automatic right to air programs on this channel. The same holds true for the next type of channel.

Governmental Access. In most cases, the franchising authority controls access to these channels to show local government programming, such as city council meetings. In 1972, the FCC said that local governments were allowed to control the content on these channels.

Leased Access. These are also called *commercial access* channels. They may be rented or "leased" by third parties who wish to air programming and, as the name indicates, the channels may be used for commercial purposes. The channels often air programming such as infomercials, local sports events, foreign language shows, real estate programs, and political shows.

Cable operators may not control content on these channels, but, at the same time, cable systems are not legally liable for access channel content. It is the program producers who are liable for such things as false advertising, obscenity, and libel. When these access channels are not being used by third parties, a cable system may use the channels for whatever purposes it wishes.

—FAQ: May cable companies or LFAs regulate content on PEG channels?

No. The 1984 Cable Act says that cable companies are not allowed to censor any material on PEG channels. A 1989 case reaffirmed this concept in a public access channel controversy involving the Ku Klux Klan.

The KKK and Public Access

Congress intended for cable access channels to be open to all citizens, no matter what their viewpoints. Controversy arose in the late 1980s in Kansas City when a cable company allowed members of the Ku Klux Klan to use the public access channel. The KKK appearance on the channel created community outrage, and the cable company argued it had no choice—public access channels were designed to be open to anyone.

Soon after the KKK appearance, the LFA in Kansas City decided it would simply get rid of its public access channel to help avoid such controversies. The city argued that the *Midwest Video II* ruling made it clear that a cable system could not be forced to carry access channels. However, the KKK said the LFA was pulling the access channel to deny the Klan a future venue for its speech, so the KKK took the matter to court.

In 1989, in *Missouri Knights of the Ku Klux Klan v. Kansas City*,[11] a federal district court judge called access channels a "public forum." The judge said that an LFA did indeed have the right not to offer access channels. However, in this case, the judge said that the Kansas City LFA had pulled the channel because it did not like the Klan's message. An access channel is a "public forum," the judge said, and the city should not manipulate its use or nonuse to silence certain viewpoints.

The judge said the KKK had a legitimate argument here, and he refused to dismiss the complaint. To avoid more legal hassles, the Kansas City LFA and the cable company agreed to reinstate the public access channel and to pay the KKK's legal fees. This case did not establish any true legal precedent because the parties involved settled their differences out

of court. Still, the ruling reinforced the 1984 Cable Act's prohibition on censorship on access channels.

—FAQ: These rulings involved PEG channels. Are there any FCC rules regarding leased access channels?

Although the 1984 Cable Act made PEG channels an *option* for LFAs, leased access channels were made a *requirement* for many cable systems.

Mandatory Leased Access

Congress felt that independent programmers should have some means of access to cable systems. To meet that need, the 1984 Cable Act mandated that cable systems with 36 to 54 activated channels had to set aside 10% of channel space for leased access. Systems with 55 or more activated channels must set aside 15%. (*Activated* means channels that are regularly available to customers, including PEG channels.) Cable systems with fewer than 36 channels do not have to provide leased access channels. Cable operators must charge "reasonable" rates for the use of leased access channels.

"MUST-CARRY" RULES

In 1965, the FCC established its first broad-based "must-carry" rules. Must-carry meant that cable systems were required to carry every "local or significantly viewed" broadcast station in the area. In 1966, the rule was amended so that it applied only to cable systems that carried at least one local station. (In other words, if a cable system carried one local broadcast station, it had to carry all other local broadcast stations.) These rules were designed to prevent cable companies from "shutting out" local broadcasters and to help ensure "the financial viability of free, community-oriented television."

By 1984, the must-carry rules were modified and required cable systems to carry the signals of all television stations within a 35-mile radius of the community served by the cable company, as well as stations "significantly viewed in the community." Carriage of local stations was mandatory for most cable systems.

—FAQ: Weren't the must-carry rules yet another attempt by the FCC to force programming rules on cable operators?

A cable company in Quincy, WA, certainly thought so and challenged the rules in *Quincy Cable TV, Inc. v. FCC*.[12] The cable company had refused to carry two television stations from nearby Spokane, choosing instead to carry selected cable channels. The FCC fined the cable company $5000 for violating the must-carry rules.

In 1985, a federal appeals court struck down the must-carry rules and said they were a violation of the First Amendment. The "scarcity rationale" cannot be applied to cable TV as a justification for content regulation, the court said. The rules are intrusive and force cable companies to carry certain stations they may not want to carry. Also, the rules "favor one group of speakers over another" because "local broadcasters are guaranteed the right to convey their messages over the cable system while cable programmers must vie for a proportionately diminished number of channels." (The Quincy cable system back then had a capacity of only 12 channels.)

The court said that the government's interest in protecting broadcast stations "is insufficient to justify the subordination of First Amendment freedoms" of cable operators. It pointed out that the FCC had provided no real proof that the lack of must-carry rules would significantly harm local broadcast stations. The court felt that the must-carry rules were "overinclusive," forcing some cable systems to carry 20 local stations. The rules also required carriage of local stations even if those stations provided no local programming.

The FCC tried to reinstate must-carry rules in 1987, but a federal appeals court struck down the law that same year in *Century Communications v. FCC*.[13] However, must-carry rules in a new form would emerge 5 years later in the Cable Act of 1992.

THE CABLE TELEVISION CONSUMER PROTECTION AND COMPETITION ACT OF 1992

If the 1984 Cable Act helped to deregulate cable, then the 1992 act was a major reregulation of the cable industry. There were several significant changes implemented by the 1992 Cable Act, and Congress showed that it was beginning to look at cable more as a multichannel service provider instead of as a direct threat to broadcasters. Still, Congress recognized a need to provide some protection to broadcasters.

As cable expanded rapidly in the 1980s, broadcasters continued to see their market share erode. In 1970, the major broadcasters drew 90% of viewers at any given time. By the early 1990s, that audience share had dropped to less than 60%. (In November 2003, ratings information from "sweeps" showed that the cable audience share exceeded the broadcast audience share for the first time in history.) The once dominant broadcasters were steadily losing audiences to cable. The 1992 Cable Act recognized this situation and introduced modified must-carry rules.

"Must-Carry" and "May-Carry"

For decades, cable companies carried local broadcast stations on their cable systems without paying those stations any fees. Many broadcasters said that the cable companies should pay the stations for the rights to carry their signals. Cable companies argued that the broadcasters should not complain because carriage on the cable system provided the broadcast station with a larger audience, and those audiences would usually get clearer reception than they would through an antenna.

The 1992 Cable Act addressed this issue by giving broadcast stations two options regarding carriage on a local cable system:

- *Must-Carry*: If a station chooses must-carry, then the cable system in its service area is required to carry that station. However, the cable system is not required to pay the station for the mandatory use of its signal.

- *May-Carry (or "Retransmission Consent")*: If the station chooses may-carry, or retransmission consent, then the cable system has to get permission from the station before carrying the station's signal and must usually pay the station in some way. A cable system is not permitted to carry a broadcast station's signal if a retransmission consent deal has not been reached. These deals are considered private and do not have to be divulged to the public.

The rules did provide relief for smaller cable companies. The smallest cable systems (with 12 or fewer channels) did not have to carry more than 3 commercial stations and one noncommercial station. Cable operators with more than 12 channels had to set aside up to one third of their channels for must-carry. The FCC provided an example: If a cable system has 60 channels, it must set aside up to 20 channels for must-carry. If there are 25 stations in the market that choose must-carry, the cable system may choose not to carry 5 of those stations. Of course, the company may carry all 25 if it wishes, but it is not a requirement. However, if there are only 15 stations electing must-carry, the cable system must carry all 15 stations in that market. (The FCC says a *market* for a television station is that station's designated market area [DMA] as determined by Nielsen Media Research.)

—**FAQ:** The courts had recently struck down similar must-carry rules. Wouldn't these new rules suffer the same fate?

To the surprise of many, the Supreme Court upheld the new rules in *Turner Broadcasting v. FCC*.[13, 14] There were actually two *Turner* rulings, one in 1994 and one in 1997. In *Turner I*,[13] the court ruled 5–4 that cable companies are still monopolies in most communities, and the FCC is justified in enforcing the must-carry rules.

In *Turner II*,[14] the Supreme Court looked at the must-carry rules again and, once again, ruled 5–4 in favor of the FCC's rules.

—**FAQ:** Why did the court say that must-carry rules were now OK?

Remember, the previous must-carry rulings were in lower courts, and the Supreme Court simply chose to ignore those rulings. The court argued that there was substantial evidence to show that many local broadcast stations would go out of business without must-carry rules (thus upholding the FCCs concept of localism). Keeping local broadcast stations around is important in serving local communities and providing diverse viewpoints, the court said. Also, cable systems now have more channel capacity, so a requirement to carry local stations is not a great burden and does not shut out cable channels.

The bargaining for retransmission consent, or may-carry, has led to some situations in which cable companies "black out" local stations because agreements for payment have not been reached; however, these blackouts are usually brief. Probably the most famous of these blackouts occurred in May 2000, during ratings sweeps. Time Warner Cable and ABC could not reach a retransmission consent deal for the carriage of ABC affiliates in several large cities, so Time Warner began to black out those ABC signals. The FCC said the blackout was unjustified, and Time Warner and ABC eventually reached a retransmission consent deal. The blackout lasted for 36 hours.

Television stations and cable channels must renegotiate these contracts every 3 years. The contract renewal dates were established in the Telecomm Act of 1996. The next, contract deadline is October 1, 2005, with the contracts becoming effective January 1, 2006.

Rate Regulation ... for a Time

Congress discovered that the deregulation of the 1980s had led not only to rapid growth of the cable industry but also to rapidly increasing cable rates, often at two or three times the rate of inflation. Consumers began to complain. LFAs had been allowed to regulate rates for basic cable service but, prior to 1992, the FCC did not regulate cable rates. The 1992 Cable Act instituted rate regulations that would last for several years.

Cable Equipment and Basic Cable Tier

"Basic cable" is the cheapest type of service available to cable customers. It usually includes local broadcast channels, access channels, and public television. In areas where there was no "effective competition" for the cable operator, the 1992 Cable Act said, local and state governments were allowed to regulate rates for cable equipment and basic cable.

—**FAQ:** What is "effective competition"?

Effective competition means that there is at least one other cable system in the area or some other multichannel distribution system, such as satellite TV. At least half of the households in the area must have access to both systems, and the smallest system has to have a market share of at least 15%. Also, cable system subscribers must constitute fewer than 30% of households in the franchise area.

—**FAQ:** Isn't the concept of effective competition now obsolete because of the widespread availability of satellite TV?

For the most part, yes. The 1996 Telecomm Act revisited the 1992 rate regulations and set most of them to expire in 1999. Any rate regulations that did remain applied only if there was "no effective competition." However, by 1999, most Americans had access to satellite TV services, which provided the effective competition. As a result, cable rate regulation is basically nonexistent now.

The 1992 Cable Act also regulated cable rates in other areas:

Cable Programming Service Tier

The 1992 Cable Act had allowed local governments to regulate rates on the cable service tier (which includes all cable channels and video programming not available on basic cable). However, the Telecommunications Act of 1996 mandated that local governments would no longer be allowed to regulate rates on the cable service tier as of March 31, 1999.

Per-Channel or Per-Program Tier

This includes "premium" cable channels, such as Showtime and pay-per-view channels, for which customers pay extra fees to receive the programming. Neither the FCC nor an LFA have the right to regulate rates for these channels.

Also, the FCC was no longer allowed to act on consumer complaints regarding rates on the cable service tier. In 1999, FCC chairman William Kennard defended the rate regulations. He announced that cable rate regulations in effect from 1993 to 1999 saved customers $3 billion to $5 billion. During that time, the FCC had also ordered cable companies to pay approximately $100 million in refunds to 40 million cable subscribers who had been overcharged.[15]

Rate Rollbacks

The Cable Act mandated that cable rates be reduced by about 17% over a 2-year period. Cable companies challenged these mandatory rate reductions, but in 1995 a federal appeals court ruled in *Time Warner Entertainment v. FCC*[16] that the FCC had a right to enforce the rate rollbacks.

Proportional Rates

Cable systems were required to charge rates that were directly proportional to their costs for the various kinds of programming offered. They were also told to distribute the costs of the system among the various basic and premium channels appropriately.

Satellite TV

The Satellite Home Viewer Improvement Act of 1999

Because of something called the 1988 Satellite Home Viewer Act, the cable industry had a huge competitive advantage over satellite TV providers. The satellite companies were not allowed to provide subscribers with signals from local TV stations. As a result, many potential satellite TV customers stayed with cable so they could receive their favorite local stations.

The situation changed, though, with the Satellite Home Viewer Improvement Act of 1999. Congress voted to allow satellite companies to provide "local-into-local service." This meant satellite TV subscribers could now get local TV stations through their satellite dishes as long as those subscribers lived in the local TV station's DMA as defined by Nielsen Media Research.

It is important to note that the Satellite Home Viewer Improvement Act does not require that satellite TV providers offer local stations. It is simply an option. A satellite TV service still has to negotiate with local TV stations for the rights to carry their signals.

There are two basic types of satellite services. There is C-band, which uses a large dish. There is also direct broadcast satellite (DBS), which uses smaller dishes to receive the satellite TV signals.

Satellite TV Regulations

As noted in chapter 3, satellite TV providers must abide by political broadcasting rules, such as Section 315 and Section 312(a)(7).

The "Carry One, Carry All" Rule

As of January 1, 2002, if a satellite TV service has chosen to offer local-into-local service, it must also provide its subscribers with signals from all local TV stations in that particular DMA that have requested carriage on the satellite service. This includes all noncommercial educational stations as well.

The following rules apply to "carry one, carry all:" Just as with cable, local TV stations may choose mandatory carriage on the satellite system or may negotiate for retransmission consent. The satellite service may offer the local stations to subscribers as a package deal or "a la carte." The satellite provider may require subscribers to purchase additional equipment (such as an extra dish) to receive all of the local signals in a market. However, a satellite provider may NOT require the purchase of additional equipment for the reception of only *some* local stations. The satellite service is allowed to charge subscribers for carriage of local stations.

—FAQ: What if my satellite service chooses not to provide local TV signals? Can I still get network programs?

Yes. There's always a roof-top antenna. However, if that type of antenna does not provide quality signals, you may qualify as an "unserved household." That means your household is unserved by local TV stations. Unserved households are allowed to receive up to two "distant" network station signals for each network. Satellite services are allowed to provide unserved households with up to two distant affiliates from each of the major networks (ABC, CBS, NBC, Fox). A "distant" signal comes from a station outside of a subscriber's DMA. People who have dishes permanently attached to commercial trucks or motor homes can also qualify as "unserved households."

To clarify, if you can receive local signals for CBS, NBC, and Fox through a rooftop antenna, you count as a "served" household for those local affiliates. If, however, you cannot receive a local ABC station via antenna, you are "unserved" for ABC. The satellite provider is required to offer you only the local CBS, NBC, and Fox affiliates but is permitted to offer you a "distant" ABC affiliate.

In 2000, the FCC voted that satellite TV must follow three rules that also apply to cable systems,

with some modifications. These rules apply to both C-band (large dish) and DBS (small dish) systems.

The Network Nonduplication Rule

An example of this rule is a local CBS affiliate that requires a satellite service to black out CBS programs being carried on a nationally broadcast superstation. This rule applies even if the satellite service does not carry the local CBS affiliate.

The Syndicated Exclusivity Rule ("Syndex")

An example of this rule is a local TV station that has exclusive rights to air a syndicated show in the market. The station may require a satellite service to black out that same syndicated show when it airs on a national super-station. This rule applies even if the local station is not carried by the satellite service.

In regard to these two rules, the FCC says six broadcasters qualify as "national superstations": KTLA-TV (Los Angeles), KWGN-TV (Denver), WGN-TV (Chicago), WPIX-TV (New York), WSBK-TV (Boston), and WWOR-TV (New York).

The Sports Blackout Rule

This rule applies to satellite services and concerns sporting events carried on network stations and nationally distributed superstations. The rule gives protection to a sports team or league's exclusive distribution rights to a local sporting event or sports team. Therefore, the rule applies only if a local TV broadcast station is not carrying a local game. Then all other broadcasters' signals showing the game may not be shown in the protected local blackout zone.

These three rules do not apply to satellite services with fewer than 1000 subscribers in "zones of protection."

Notes

1. *Quincy Cable TV, Inc, v. FCC,* 768 F.2d 1434 (D.C. Cir. 1985)
2. 321 F.2d 359 (D.C. Cir. 1963)
3. FCC First Report and Order, 38 F.C.C. 683 (1965)
4. FCC Second Report and Order, 2 F.C.C.2d 725 (1966)
5. 392 U.S. 157 (1968)
6. 406 U.S. 649 (1972)

7. 36 F.C.C.2d 143 (1972)
8. 567 F.2d9 (D.C. Cir.1978)
9. 476 U.S. 488 (1986)
10. 440 U.S. 689 (1979)
11. 723 F. Supp. 1347 (WD Mo. 1989)
12. 768 F.2d 1434 (D.C. Cir. 1985)
13. 835 F.2d 292 (D.C. Cir. 1987)

CHAPTER 3

REGULATING THE TELECOMMUNICATIONS INFRASTRUCTURE

UNIT 13

Monopoly or Competition? History of Common Carrier Regulation and the Telecommunications Act of 1996

In order to fully understand telecommunications policy in the United States, one needs to be acquainted with its historical roots and in particular with the major role the term "common carrier" has played in this history along with AT&T, the corporation that dominated the industry for nearly a century, a domination whose ramifications still loom largely. An introductory reading by Sterling, Bernt and Weiss describes the technological attributes of the telephone industry, and a reading derived from legal experts Henk Brands and Evan Leo's book *The Law and Regulation of Telecommunications Carriers* provides a historical perspective of the development of the regulation of telephony. A reading from Sharon Black's (an international telecommunications attorney) book on telecommunications law provides a historical context for the overhaul of American law in 1996.

The Telecommunications Act of 1996 marks the final stage in the introduction of competition in American telecommunications. While the historical review provides context of the major crossroads in which competition was developed, the dramatic change in 1996 was the evolution of local competition. This required regulatory treatment of three pillars of reform: interconnection, universal service and removal of barriers to entry (unbundling). A historical discussion of interconnection is derived from the work of Columbia University economist Eli Noam; the concept of universal service and its origins in the United States are described by Syracuse University professor Milton Mueller; and the pitfalls of the unbundling regime in the United States as they test the boundaries between antitrust and telecommunications law are illustrated through the analysis of the *Verizon v. Trinko* case as discussed by Dennis W. Carlton and Hal Sider. In order to be able to assess the uniqueness of the American system, a comparative context is provided through a reading on universal service in Europe by British media scholar Nicholas Garnham, a reading on unbundled access to the local loop by German scholar Anne Gabelmann, and a comparative analysis of both regimes written by Amit Schejter.

Introducing
Telecommunications

Christopher H. Sterling, Phyllis W. Bernt
and Martin B.H. Weiss

More than other sectors of a nation's economy, telecommunications operates through a unique melding of technology, economics, and policy. At the most basic level, telephone, wireless or radio communication, and Internet connectivity all rely on technology. All forms of telecommunication involve a message, a sender, and a receiver that utilize telecommunications transmission. There are many variations in this transmission process—telephone networks and data networks may move, or switch, a message differently; and messages may be sent over narrow copper wires or over larger capacity fiber optic cables or through the air. Each mode operates under fundamental principles, and a basic knowledge of these is needed to understand how a telephone call takes place, or a byte of data moves through a network, or an Internet connection is made.

An understanding of telecommunications also requires knowledge of economic and policy factors. U.S. telecommunications has developed from a long history of monopoly and regulation. While until recently telecommunication systems in virtually every other country in the world were government owned, in the United States telecommunications has operated as a commercial enterprise almost from its mid-19th-century inception. Government involvement in deployment and development of telecommunications took place here more through regulation than ownership. For decades the U.S. telephone system was largely controlled by the Bell System and a host of small local telephone companies dependent on Bell.

The potential for substantial economic gain can, of course, lead to abuses when an essential service (like local telephony) is provided by a monopolist free from competitive pressures when making pricing and production decisions. Regulation at both the federal and state levels emerged early in the 20th century as the best way to control these possible abuses of monopoly power. In regulating telecommunications, the Federal Communications Commission (FCC), the 50 state public utility commissions (PUCs), and the D.C. commission do more than just control the price of service. Through regulatory decisions they have also structured the industry, determined how services would be provided and by whom, and set service quality standards. Understanding the sometimes convoluted development of telecommunication thus requires some knowledge of these regulators' modes of operation, sources of authority, and motivating principles.

This reading introduces the fundamentals of telecommunications technology, economics, and policy, including basic principles that will be helpful in understanding the history, issues, and concepts discussed in the readings that follow.

TECHNOLOGY—THE MEANS

As the historical core of telecommunications for more than 130 years, *telephony* is the process of transmitting sound—usually the human voice—through electrical signals. For this transmission to occur, sound waves must be converted to electrical signals at the originating point of a call and then the electrical signals must be reconverted to sound waves at the terminating point of the call. A microphone, or *transducer,* converts the human voice to electrical signals and then a speaker converts the electrical signals back to sound waves. In a modern telephone, the microphone and speaker are combined into one telephone handset, so that the telephone set can both generate and receive calls. A *transmission medium,* such as a copper wire, a fiber optic cable, or the air waves, carries the electrical signals between telephone handsets.

Basics

Human speech occupies a variable range of frequencies that depend on the speaker and the moment (as when people raise and lower the pitch of their voices to convey meaning). Generally human speech—and hearing—can range from a low of about 300 Hz (Hertz) to a high of about 10,000 Hz (or 10 kHz). Experiments have found that language can be understood and speakers readily identified using a narrower frequency range of 300 to 3400 Hz. The International Telecommunication Union (ITU) recommends that telephone systems be designed to carry at least this range, referred to as a signal's *bandwidth.*

While telephone systems have long been designed to transmit human speech, increasingly systems are used for other purposes as well, such as connecting computers (via modems) and transmitting documents (via fax). The traditional telephone network was largely analog; in other words, the electrical signals transmitted were analogous to, or replicated, the sound waves formed by human speech. Data emanating from computers, on the other hand, consisted, not of electrical waves, but rather of bits and bytes of data, or combinations of zeros and ones. Modems (modulator/demodulators) were needed to convert the digital data stream of bits and bytes into an analog speech-like signal (unintelligible to most

people) that the largely analog telephone network could carry.

The transmission medium traditionally consisted of copper wires which were connected to the transducer via a circuit called a *hybrid.* The function of the hybrid was (and is) to separate signals being sent from those being received so that the received signal can be directed to the speaker, as illustrated in Fig. 1.1.

By the early 20th century, the most widely used transmission medium was a *twisted pair* of copper wires. Earlier transmission most commonly utilized a single strand of iron wire, which had also been the standard for telegraph systems. Such "open wire" systems were relatively cheap but were more prone to interference, especially from the electric power systems that were proliferating in the late 19th and early 20th centuries. Today, *fiber optic* cable is beginning to replace twisted pair copper.

All transmission media can be evaluated according to their attenuation and their susceptibility to noise. *Attenuation* is the reduction of signal strength, and this increases with both distance covered and the frequency used. A weaker signal is, of course, more difficult to hear. The *bandwidth* of a transmission medium really is the range of frequencies that a transmission medium can carry with acceptable attenuation for a specified distance. The history of transmission media can be seen as a quest for increases in acceptable bandwidth. Twisted pair copper was able to transmit a wider range of frequencies over longer distances than iron wire; today, fiber optic cable is able to transmit much higher bandwidth than twisted pair copper. As is discussed in later chapters, local telephone companies (providers of traditional telephone network service based on twisted pair copper) are under increasing pressure to replace copper with more fiber optic cable, also called broadband facilities. The questions of how the local telephone companies will pay for these broadband facilities, and how they will recover the cost of the twisted pair copper already in use, are major issues of concern to telecommunications policymakers.

Noise refers to unwanted signal energy (sometimes called *interference)* from any source. In other words, the intended signal is the electrical energy that has been converted from the sound waves; noise is any other electrical energy that manages to invade the

FIGURE 1.1 Basic Telecommunications Link

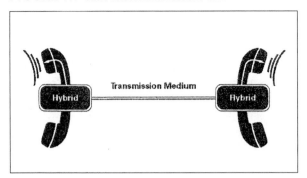

transmission path of the intended signal. Although intended signals suffer attenuation, noise normally does not because it can enter the transmission medium at any point, not just at the beginning point of the signal. Thus the effect of attenuation is not just that the signal (the desired information) becomes weaker, but also that the signal becomes more difficult to distinguish from noise. Engineers capture this notion in the *signal-to-noise ratio,* in which the signal power is divided by the noise power. If this ratio is small, then the signal will be more difficult to discern than when the ratio is large. It is the combination of the bandwidth of a transmission medium and the signal-to-noise ratio that governs the capacity of a channel to carry information.

Telephone Systems

Telephone systems involve key components that must fit and work together to enable telephone service. To place a telephone call, a subscriber must have equipment, usually a telephone, through which he or she is able to connect with the telephone network in order to send a message to a desired telephone number. The subscriber establishes a connection to the network by going "off hook," or lifting the telephone receiver. By doing so, the subscriber establishes a connection with a switch. The subscriber then "tells" the switch the number he or she wishes to reach by dialing that number. The switch recognizes the number and routes the call—or rather establishes a channel through other switches and transmission media—between the calling subscriber and the called number.

For policy reasons that will be discussed farther (*see sections 6.4, 7.1, and 7.2*), telephone network service is provided by two different types of companies: local telephone companies or local exchange carriers (LECs) and long distance companies or interexchange carriers (IXCs). LECs provide local service and own the facilities closest to the subscriber; IXCs provide long distance service and use the LECs' facilities, along with their own facilities, in order to provide long distance calls. This relationship is illustrated in Fig. 1.2.

A LEC's network is structured as shown in Fig. 1.3, with the LEC owning the local connection to the subscriber (the loop); as well as Central Office (CO), or local, switches; tandem switches through which LECs accumulate traffic from several central office switches; and transmission systems connecting switches. IXC networks do not include the local connection to the subscriber or local switches. Instead IXC networks consist of large capacity long distance switches and transmission systems that haul telephone calls from city to city and state to state. (As is discussed in section 9.2, this neat distinction is changing because of Congress's passage of the Telecommunication Act of 1996. As a result of that act, such LECs as Verizon are now offering long

FIGURE 1.2 Industry Structure

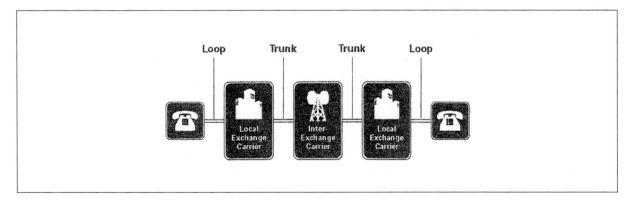

FIGURE 1.3 Local Exchange Network

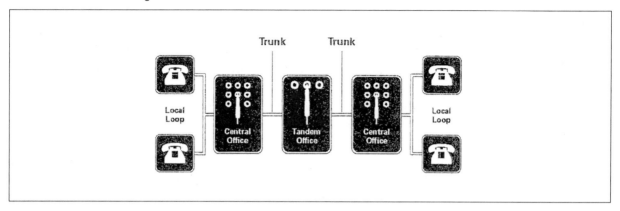

distance service once restricted to IXCs, and some IXCs, such as AT&T, are offering local service once reserved for LECs.)

The components of a telephone network consist of customer premise equipment (CPE), such as telephones, modems, and fax machines; the local loop; switches (CO and tandem); and transmission systems. Since the late 1970s, subscribers have been able to purchase the CPE of their choice (as long as it meets specific FCC technical standards); earlier CPE could only be leased from the local telephone company.

The contracts that long governed the interconnection of the LEC and IXC networks were termed the "separations and settlements" procedures discussed later, since replaced by "access charge" arrangements. IXCs pay LECs access charges for the use of the LEC network. As a result of Congress's desire to see the development of competition in all parts of the telephone system, competitive local exchange carriers (CLECs) developed in parallel to the LECs. IXCs negotiate arrangements with the CLECs to use their facilities, just as they have used the LECs' facilities. For reasons explored later, however, few CLECS have survived into the 21st century.

Local Loop

The *local loop* refers to the set of technologies used to connect end user locations with the LEC's CO. From the late 19th century well into the 20th, this was done via a direct connection between these users over twisted pair wire. This type of wire is inexpensive and easy to manage, though its transmission characteristics are far from ideal. The local loop has been one of the costliest components of a network, in large part

because a separate connection is required for virtually every customer. Shared telephone infrastructure used by multiple consumers did not appear until development of the CO switch.

In the last 40 years, local loop technology has undergone significant changes. The consequence of these changes has been to move the point at which the infrastructure is shared gradually closer to the customer, so that the local loop could become less costly. Today's local loop consists of a combination of loop carrier systems and remote switching partitions/concentrators.

Loop carrier systems are designed to connect clusters of customers with the CO over transmission facilities shared by many end users. That is, individual customers no longer have dedicated connections to the CO. Under most circumstances, this is transparent to customers because most people use their telephone for only a small percentage of the time. Unlike loop carrier systems, *host-remote switches* consist of a portion of the CO switch that has been placed among a cluster of customers. Host-remote switches handle some of the switching functions, which can further reduce the capacity needed to connect the remote to the main CO switch. In effect, the switch is partially *distributed* throughout the service area using such an architecture.

Local loop facilities will appear in this book as a point of controversy. While local telephone companies have sought ways to reduce loop costs through carrier systems and host-remote switching configurations, existing loop investment remains a major portion of LEC costs. The issue of how this cost should be recovered, whether through local rates or through long distance charges, has been a major point of contention since the 1930s and continues to be controversial today.

Digital Transmission Systems

Transmission systems are facilities intended to connect switches with other switches. Since the 1920s, they have often been high capacity systems. As twisted pair cables offer relatively poor performance over longer distances, engineers developed such other media as coaxial cable, waveguides, microwave, satellite, and, most recently, optical fiber, all of which are superior to twisted pair in capacity and noise performance.

To overcome the attenuation effects associated with distance, engineers developed electronic (vacuum tube-based) amplifiers early in the 20th century. These systems boosted the power of the incoming signal (as well as the incoming noise, unfortunately), which meant that the signal-to-noise ratio deteriorated over distance despite the amplifiers, limiting the information-carrying capacity of telephone channels. The only solution to this problem was to discover ways of regenerating only the desired signal and not the noise—the solution being the development of *digital* transmission beginning in the 1950s.

Unlike traditional analog transmission techniques, in which every incremental signal level had meaning, digital systems depended only on two signal levels. Analog amplifiers had no choice but to amplify noise because there was no way to distinguish signal from noise. Digital systems, however, would detect only high or low voltage levels, so any additive noise was not meaningful and could be discarded. Thus digital repeaters could be engineered to regenerate signals that were nearly indistinguishable from the original signal, thus avoiding the deterioration of the desired signal-to-noise ratio over distance. With digital transmission systems, however, the end-to-end signal can still deteriorate if the signal-to-noise ratio at the input of any repeater is too low for it to correctly distinguish a high or a low voltage; this inability would result in bit errors, which, though correctable, introduce noise on an end-to-end basis.

Since voice or music signals originate at a microphone in analog format, it is necessary to convert them to a digital format if the full advantage of digital transmission systems is to be gained. The location of this conversion has evolved over time, starting at the transmission system terminal, then moving to the local loop side of the CO switch. There has been a slow attempt to finally shift this process to the telephone itself, though this has not happened yet on a widespread basis. A *codec* device converts an analog signal into the digital pulse code modulation (PCM) format. To accomplish this, the codec samples the analog telephone signal 8000 times per second, and then converts each sample into digitized samples of zeros and ones which are converted back to analog format at the other end without loss of fidelity.

High-Capacity Channels

Since the bandwidth of a voice signal remains constant, higher capacity media like optic cable would be of little value without some additional equipment to

FIGURE 1.4 Frequency Division Multiplexing

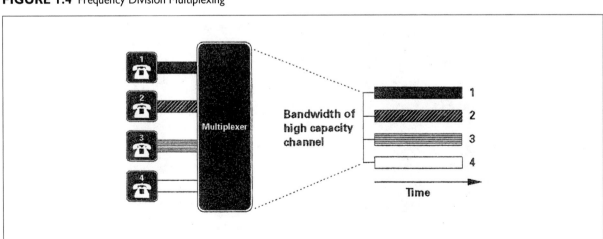

take advantage of this higher capacity by finding ways to transmit multiple voice channels across a single medium. In other words, instead of handling one voice channel, these media would handle hundreds of voice channels at once. The collection of technologies that achieve this are referred to as multiplexers, and are of two types: frequency division multiplexing (FDM) and time division multiplexing (TDM).

FDM is the technique used initially and consisted of subdividing the high bandwidth media into many subchannels, each of which matched the bandwidth of a telephone channel. This is completely analogous to the broadcast spectrum, in which AM and FM bands are separated into many different channels, each of which is occupied by a single broadcaster per location. Figure 1.4 illustrates the operation of FDM.

In order to flexibly provide resources to the network as needed, and because different media had different capabilities, *multiplex hierarchies* were developed. These allowed managers to use a building block approach to provisioning capacity and allowed for manufacturing efficiencies. The basic level of multiplexing in the FDM hierarchy was a *group* of just 12 telephone channels. The next level was a *supergroup* (five groups, or 60 telephone channels), or a *master-group* (10 supergroups, or 600 telephone channels), which could be multiplexed onto a transmission system. Higher capacity systems were also available, up to a *jumbogroup*, which consisted of 10,800 telephone channels over a single transmission system.

Carrier systems based on this multiplex hierarchy were the mainstay of the telephone network until the 1960s, when they were gradually supplanted by digital transmission systems that used the time division multiplex hierarchy. Just as FDM was well suited to analog transmission, so too is TDM suited to digital transmission. Unlike FDM, in which the bandwidth of the transmission system is subdivided into subbands, TDM allocates the entire bandwidth to a single channel for a short period in regular intervals. This is illustrated in Fig. 1.5.

With TDM, each time the bandwidth of the transmission system is devoted to a particular telephone channel, the entire digitized sample (i.e., 8 bits) must be transmitted. Since the telephone channel is sampled 8000 times per second, the transmission system must devote a slot to each voice channel every 125 microseconds (μsec) (=1/8000). As more channels are carried, the amount of time in which the 8 bits must be transmitted decreases, so that the bit rate of the transmission system must increase. It can be demonstrated relatively easily that an increase in bit rate is directly proportional to an increase in the bandwidth required by the system. Thus, using a different technique, TDM systems perform essentially the same functions with the similar trade-offs as do FDM systems.

As with FDM systems, TDM employs a multiplex hierarchy. The original digital transmission system was the T1 carrier system and represented the first level of multiplexing in the TDM hierarchy. The

FIGURE 1.5 Time Division Multiplexing

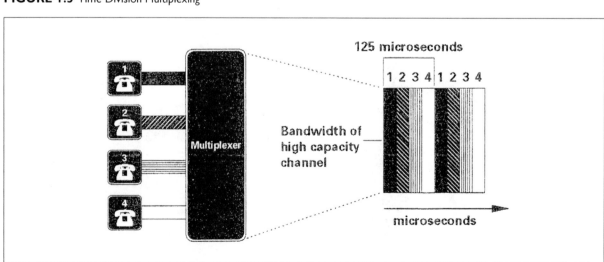

T2 system consists of 24 telephone PCM telephone channels (and is sometimes called a *digroup* because it is equivalent to two FDM groups). The next level of TDM that is in common use is the T3 carrier system, which consists of 28 T1 channels or 672 telephone channels. As was the case with FDM, the TDM hierarchy defined by the ITU is not consistent with this one. In the 1980s, an international standard-setting effort sought development of a very high speed multiplex hierarchy called SONET (for Synchronous Optical NETwork) or SDH (Synchronous Digital Hierarchy). SONET is now the standard for most heavy-duty (carrier grade) networks, although T1 and T3 services are still used as well.

Development of multiplexing changed the relationship between the telephone companies and their users, especially larger customers. As the telephone industry developed an ability to handle 24 calls over one digital T1 line, large customers demanded T1 service at a discount, rather than paying for 24 single voice channels. In effect, the large customers wanted to profit from the cost savings that multiplexing provided, rather than letting the telephone companies reap all of the benefits. To retain their customers, telephone carriers (still heavily regulated at the time) asked state utility commissions and the FCC for the authority to provide T1, T3, and higher capacity services at discounted rates.

Data Networks

Telephone networks operate using a technique called *circuit switching*. This process dedicates bandwidth exclusively to a specific call. In other words, a transmission path is created through the network for the call and that path is maintained until the call is ended. Circuit switching made a lot of sense historically and is generally well suited to voice communications which involves a continuous stream of communication.

As digital computers emerged in the 1950s and 1960s, users soon sought to interconnect them. The ubiquitous (though analog) telephone network was the obvious medium for such interconnection. To allow the network to carry such digital signals, engineers had to develop *modems* that would convert the data stream from computers to tones that could be transmitted over the telephone network. As users gained experience with data transmission, it soon became clear that using circuit switching for data networks was not efficient because computers tend to send bursts of data followed by pauses. A sporadic rather than a dedicated transmission path would be more efficient.

A better technique for data is to collect the transmitted data from many computers, carry them over a common network, and then distribute them to their respective destinations. To accomplish this, it was necessary to encapsulate the data in *packets*, which would provide instructions on where to send the enclosed data and how to treat it. This technique, called *packet switching*, makes more efficient use of the network because it is highly likely that each computer will send its burst of data at different times than other computers.

Since devices made in different nations need to interconnect, data communications was an area ripe for standardization. Initially, standardization was provided within a given manufacturer's set of products. As the need for more and faster data communications capabilities grew and demand for public data networks emerged, manufacturer standards were no longer sufficient. To address these emerging needs, the Swiss-based International Standards Organization (ISO) and International Telecommunication Union (ITU) began to develop standards for data communications. While they coordinated their efforts, each had different objectives. The ITU sought standards for public data networks, while ISO was developing architectures and protocols for general computer interconnection.

The eventual product of the ITU's work was recommendation X.25, which specified the interconnection between a public data network and a user. By contrast, ISO produced its Open Systems Interconnection Reference Model (OSI-RM) and eventually many of the protocols within the reference model. The OSI-RM is a standard way to organize the required functionality of data communications systems. It is organized around seven layers, each of which can be implemented by one or more distinct network protocols. Another similar, though unrelated, set of protocols were also developed under the auspices of the ARPANET project of the U.S. Department of Defense. These TCP/IP and associated protocols became the *de facto* worldwide standards, despite the work of ISO and ITU. These are routinely used to interconnect computers worldwide and are the underlying protocol for the Internet.

While traditional telephone networks form the industry's underlying infrastructure, the dynamic growth of today's data networks (and especially the Internet) strongly suggests that data networks will replace traditional voice links. Until recently, voice and data networks were separate, with voice traffic traversing circuit switched networks and data being carried across packet networks. As technology developed, it became increasingly possible to "packetize," combine, and transmit all video, audio, data, and voice signals across one network. For large businesses, this presented the opportunity to save money by combining voice and data services. Telephone company owners of the traditional voice network have also recognized, as they continue to install digital transmission media and digital switches, that there are efficiencies inherent in moving from a network based on circuit switching to a packetized network.

Even more significant perhaps, newer telephone company competitors recognize huge business opportunities inherent in offering *Voice over Internet Protocol* (VoIP). By packetizing voice and sending it over the Internet, competitors including cable television and Internet Service Providers (ISPs) can offer customers an alternative to the public circuit switched telephone network, often at substantial savings. Because the Internet is not regulated, these VoIP providers do not face the regulatory costs and restrictions borne by the telephone companies. As the quality of VoIP improves, and as CPE capable of handling VoIP is developed, VoIP is fast emerging as a viable competitor to the traditional voice network—and, as we shall see, raises new policy concerns.

Competition and Divestiture

Henk Brands and Evan T. Leo

Starting in the 1950s, competitors began nibbling at the edges of the Bell System's end-to-end telecommunications monopoly. In the ensuing decades, the FCC, spurred by the courts, slowly but surely eliminated *de jure* barriers to entry. The coexistence of the Bell System and its rivals generated an enduring and increasing tension, with competitors demanding ever more "equal" access to the Bell System's networks, and the Bell System seeking to defend its monopolies, or at least compete unshackled by regulation.

Ultimately, the Bell System's response to increasing competition unleashed a drastic governmental response. Frustrated by what it saw as the Bell System's resistance to competition and the FCC's failure to address this adequately, the Department of Justice in 1974 brought an antitrust action against AT&T that, after a 1982 settlement, led to what may have been the most far-reaching industry restructuring in the history of the U.S. economy: the Bell System's divestiture, in which AT&T was required to shed its local-exchange operations.

In this chapter, we review in turn the history of increasing competition with the Bell System, the background and substance of the government's claims, and the eventual resolution of the government's action.

COMPETITION IN THE PREDIVESTITURE ERA

After the heady days of local-exchange competition ended in the 1920s, the telephone industry settled into a long period of end-to-end monopoly. AT&T's Long Lines Department commanded a close to 100% market share in long-distance service, the Bell System's local telephone companies controlled more than 80% of all local access lines (the balance being controlled by noncompeting independents), and Western Electric dominated customer premises equipment (CPE) (because Bell System subscribers were required to buy or lease telephone handsets, key systems, and PBXs from Western Electric) and network equipment such as telephone switches (because of self-dealing within the Bell System). Far from finding this state of affairs objectionable, federal and state regulators thought it unavoidable, in that they saw "the telecommunications market" as a monolithic natural monopoly. In addition, many thought this state of affairs desirable, in that it eliminated the inconvenience of network fragmentation and facilitated the pursuit of universal-service policies.

However, in time, competition would not be stopped, particularly in CPE and long-distance markets. As for CPE, economic conditions had always permitted competition: Clearly, the manufacture and sale

Henk Brands and Evan T. Leo, "Competition and Divestiture," from *The Law and Regulation of Telecommunications Carriers*, pp. 247–253, 262–266, 272–276. Copyright © 1999 by Artech House. Permission to reprint granted by the publisher.

of CPE is no more a natural monopoly than the manufacture and sale of pogo sticks. Why then should Bell be allowed to prohibit attachment of non-Bell CPE? In the abstract, one might be satisfied with the answer that non-Bell CPE might jeopardize the integrity of the network, or that the prohibition was necessary so as to provide Bell with a source of subsidies toward low basic rate. But the more specific the factual context, the less tenable such answers. As for long-distance service, once microwave technology made competition economically viable, why should high-volume telecommunications users not be permitted to "make" rather than "buy" long-distance service—that is, why should they not be permitted to erect and operate their own microwave facilities? Also, if that were allowed, why shouldn't upstart companies like MCI be permitted to offer private-line service to these customers in competition with AT&T? Further, if MCI were permitted to offer private-line long-distance service, why not switched service?

As more fully explained later, the events that unfolded in CPE and long-distance markets are remarkably similar. The FCC first permitted inroads that seemed innocuous in that they were more of a complement than a substitute to the Bell System's products and services, but the FCCs orders were vague and failed to meet fundamental issues head-on, permitting competitors to widen the breach in Bell's defenses over time. What followed was a period of confusion and paralysis at the FCC, which was uncertain how to adjust to the changing environment. With some small nudges from the D.C. Circuit, the FCC ultimately adopted a policy that virtually without qualification favored competition. In one sense, however, the FCC's conversion came too late: frustrated with the FCC's stewardship of the industry (and egged on by AT&T's new competitors), the Department of Justice wrested control over the industry from the FCC, only to place it, as it would later find to its discomfort, in the hands of a single federal judge.

Competition in CPE Markets

For decades, the Bell System relied on its monopoly power in local-exchange service to monopolize the adjacent markets for the manufacture and marketing of CPE. It did so by including provisions in its tariffs filed with regulators that prohibited end users from connecting non-Bell-supplied CPE to the public network.[1] The ostensible justification for this prohibition was the preservation of the integrity of the public network: Bell claimed that, unless it were allowed to control the attachment of equipment to the network, improperly designed equipment might cause injury to the network, AT&T employees, and the public. Moreover, the Bell System had a policy of leasing (not selling) residential CPE, so that subscribers over time often paid a multiple of their CPE's value in monthly subscription fees. State and federal regulators were long complicit in AT&T's conduct: They counted on inflated CPE charges (particularly for business equipment like PBXs) as contributing to low rates for basic residential service.[2]

The FCC first broke with its unconditional acceptance of Bell's prohibition on "foreign attachments" (Bell's term for non-Bell CPE) in 1947. In *Use of Recording Devices in Connection with Telephone Services,* Report, 11 FCC 1033 (1947), the FCC found that a device supplied by a third party that recorded telephone conversations could be used "without causing any perceptible effect on the functioning of the telephone apparatus or the quality of the telephone service," *id.* at 1036, and ruled that the devices would be permitted to be sold and used. Seven years later, however, the FCC reversed course. In 1954, the FCC let stand Bell tariffs that prohibited the attachment of a predecessor of today's answering machine, the Jordaphone. *See Jordaphone Corp.*, Decision, 18 FCC 644 (1954). The FCC distinguished the recording devices it permitted to interconnect in 1947 on the ground that the Jordaphone opened and closed circuits on the telephone network; the FCC accepted as true Bell's assertion that this could harm the network.

The FCC's solicitude to accommodate AT&T in this regard crested in 1955, when the FCC agreed with AT&T that end users should not be permitted to attach to their receiver a cup designed to muffle the sound of a telephone conversation.

Competition in Long-Distance Markets

FCC-erected *de jure* entry barriers to long-distance competition fell by the wayside in similar incremental steps. Technological advances during World War II made it possible to use microwave technology to transmit long-distance telephone signals. With this new technology, economies of scale were much less pronounced than they had been when coaxial cable was still the long-distance carrier medium of choice. Thus, it became economically easier for large users to erect their own microwave facilities, and the FCC authorized the first petition to this effect in 1959. *See Allocation of Frequencies in the Bands Above 890 MHz*, Report & Order, 27 FCC 359 (1959), *recon. denied*, 29 FCC 825 (1960). Once this hurdle had been cleared, it was no great leap to argue that licensees ought to be permitted to offer microwave-carried long-distance service to third parties, and, in 1963, Microwave Communications, Inc., filed a petition requesting a license to provide such service between Chicago and St. Louis. Six years later, the FCC finally approved MCI's application in a split decision, rejecting AT&T's arguments that (among other things) MCI merely sought to engage in "cream skimming," that MCI proposed to make inefficient use of scarce spectrum, and that MCI's service would be unreliable. The contentiousness of the FCC's internal debate on the matter is well reflected in the following opinion.

THE LAWSUIT AGAINST AT&T

Ever since the 1956 consent decree terminated the government's antitrust action against Western Electric, there had been a considerable and growing appetite within the Justice Department's Antitrust Division to take on the Bell System again. Division lawyers took offense at the way AT&T reacted to growing competition in markets for CPE and long-distance service, and felt that antitrust enforcement action was necessary to save fragile competition. While the Nixon administration was in office, however, there was scant political will to mount a bruising antitrust battle with the biggest company in the world. Thus, preparations for a lawsuit languished.

In 1974, however, all planets aligned favorably. *See generally* P. Temin, *The Fall of the Bell System* 99–112 (1987). In the wake of the Watergate scandal, the Ford administration left the Justice Department considerable political leeway, and deButts's 1973 NARUC speech was seen as signaling a hardening of AT&T's attitudes in response to the growing competitive threat. At the same time, the confusion in the wake of the *Specialized Common Carrier* decision appeared to underscore the FCC's inability to check the Bell System's anticompetitive conduct. On November 20, 1974, the government filed its action in federal district court in Washington D.C, charging AT&T with monopolization in violation of Section 2 of the Sherman Act.

Oversimplifying a little bit, Section 2 requires an antitrust plaintiff (whether a private party or the government) to prove two things. *First*, the plaintiff must prove that the defendant possesses monopoly power: the ability profitably to charge prices above the level that would prevail in a competitive market. Monopoly power is often proved through indirect evidence: for example, by showing that the defendant has a dominant market share of, say, more than 50%. The idea is that, where a defendant's rivals' combined market share is small, rivals probably will be unable quickly to expand output in response to a price increase by the defendant because they will lack capacity. That inability gives the monopolist a certain amount of power over price.

Second, the plaintiff must prove that the defendant has either acquired or maintained its monopoly power through anticompetitive conduct—conduct whose likely anticompetitive effect decidedly outweighs whatever redeeming procompetitive or efficiency-enhancing merit it may have. Unlike Section 1 of the Sherman Act, Section 2 has not given rise to case law holding certain practices to be *per se* unlawful; nevertheless, various doctrines have developed that identify certain kinds of conduct that are more likely to be unlawful than others. An example is "predatory pricing," that is, pricing below cost. We will revisit predatory pricing principles later.

Although the government's claims were wide-ranging and changed considerably while the lawsuit dragged on, the thrust of the government's 1974 action was that AT&T had monopolized two markets: one for long-distance service (including both private-line and switched service) and one for equipment (including both CPE and network equipment). According to the government, the Bell System (including Western Electric) had monopoly power in each of these markets and had maintained this power through anticompetitive conduct. The most damaging of the government's wide-ranging allegations of "bad" conduct fell into two categories.

First, the government alleged that AT&T had unreasonably denied its new long-distance and equipment rivals access to the Bell System's local-exchange facilities (as compared with the access AT&T provided to itself). With respect to long-distance, the claim was that AT&T had refused to provide MCI and others with technically adequate and appropriately priced connections to AT&T's local networks. With respect to CPE, the government pointed to AT&T's tariffs, which first forbade all foreign attachments and later required PCAs. With respect to network equipment, the government's argument was based on the Bell System's long-standing procurement practices, under which the local Bell Operating Companies purchased equipment only from Western Electric. In each instance, the government alleged, the Bell System had denied its rivals access to the local exchange so as to afford a competitive advantage to its own long-distance, CPE, and network-equipment businesses.

In antitrust law, an access-discrimination claim of this nature is analyzed under the "essential facilities" (or "bottleneck monopoly") doctrine, which holds that the possessor of a facility that is essential to competitive survival must provide its rivals with reasonable access to this facility.[3] As a general matter, antitrust courts and commentators are somewhat skeptical of essential-facilities claims, believing that forced sharing among competitors can have deplorable effects on desirable incentives to invest and innovate.[4] But it is fairly well accepted that incentives-related concerns are at a low point where the defendant's control over an essential facility is the result of a natural monopoly. In such a case, the defendant became the owner of a unique facility not because of its ingenuity or business acumen, but simply because economic conditions cannot sustain competition. Thus, an important part of the government's case was its allegation that the local exchange was a natural monopoly.

Second, the government argued to a lesser extent that the Bell System had engaged in predatory pricing through cross-subsidization. The claim was that, whenever competitors entered a market, AT&T would lower its prices in that market to below-cost levels, drawing on profits from other, noncompetitive, markets to subsidize the strategy. This practice would either scare off competitors altogether or, to the extent competitors attempted to match or beat AT&T's below-cost prices, force them into bankruptcy. There was little evidence that AT&T had cross-subsidized in equipment markets; thus, the government's cross-subsidization theory was largely limited to its long-distance claims. In particular, the government argued that AT&T used switched long-distance service (with respect to which there was no competition until MCI launched its Execunet service) to subsidize private-line service (with respect to which there had been some competition ever since the 1959 *Above 890* decision). *See United States v. AT&T*, 524 F. Supp. 1336, 1365 (D.D.C 1981).

In antitrust law, predatory-pricing claims are surrounded by perhaps an even more noxious odor than essential-facilities claims; again, the concern is that sustaining such claims may deter desirable conduct. As a general matter, antitrust law encourages price cutting because lower prices in a very direct and tangible way benefit consumers; thus, courts are properly hesitant to do anything that might inhibit firms (even monopolists) from engaging in this salutary conduct. It is therefore fairly well established that low prices cannot sustain liability unless a defendant has sold its products below some relevant measure of its costs.[5] The point of this limitation is that a defendant selling its products below cost probably has in mind something other than competition on the merits: No rational firm would want to sell its products at a price that results in a loss on each unit sold (at least in the long run).

The government never succeeded in proving that AT&T had priced its products below a relevant measure of cost. The problem was that AT&T's business was so riddled with joint and common costs that it was just about impossible to untangle the cost question. Indeed, in discovery, it quickly became apparent that AT&T itself did not possess accurate cost data, and that it did not rely on such data to determine its rates. Undeterred, the government proposed a novel antitrust theory: The government claimed that the very fact that AT&T did not know what its costs were should give rise to antitrust liability. The idea was that a monopolist's pricing "without regard to cost" should be just as unlawful as pricing below cost.

An additional reason why predatory-pricing claims are unpopular with antitrust courts is that predatory pricing is rarely a profitable strategy in the long run and thus unlikely to occur. By definition, predatory pricing is a money-losing proposition in the short run. The monopolist loses money with each unit sold. Thus, a monopolist will engage in predatory pricing only if it has some reasonable hope of recouping money lost in the short run by raising prices in the long run. Higher prices of course attract competition, so the long-term price hikes will be impossible unless there are barriers to entry—barriers that apparently did not prevent entry previously (witness the existence of the competitors that were the target of the defendant's predation in the first place).

To address *this* concern, the government, relying on the unique context of rate-of-return regulation, advanced an argument that we have already briefly discussed in Chapter 4. In the case of a vertically integrated monopolist like the Bell System, the government argued, the defendant does not need to wait for post-predation recoupment; it can recoup immediately. The theory is that the defendant has the enduring ability and incentive to misallocate costs related to the "target" market (here private line long-distance service) to an adjacent market where it is under rate-of-return regulation (here switched long-distance service). In this way, the defendant can essentially get for free what its competitors have to buy with real dollars, thus giving rise to a persistent competitive advantage. Because of rate-of-return regulation, any costs misallocated this way will lead to a revenue increase that can immediately offset any predation losses incurred in the target market.

For some years, little happened in the government's action because Judge Waddy, the judge to whom the action had been assigned, fell seriously ill. Eventually, the case was reassigned to newly appointed Judge Harold Greene, who immediately made clear that he would pursue a speedy trial. A bench trial before Judge Greene began on January 15, 1981—more than six years after the government had filed its complaint. The government's presentation of its case would consume four months and involve about 100 witnesses. After the government rested, AT&T filed a motion to dismiss pursuant to former Rule 41(b) of the Federal Rules of Civil Procedure, which empowered district courts to enter judgment for the defendant if "upon the facts and the law the plaintiff has shown no right to relief." Judge Greene denied AT&T's motion in virtually all respects.

NOTES

1. The tariffs provided: "No equipment, apparatus, circuit or device not furnished by the telephone company shall be attached to or connected with the facilities furnished by the telephone company, whether physically, by induction or otherwise. … In case any such unauthorized attachment or connection is made, the telephone company shall have the right to remove or disconnect the same; or to suspend the service during the continuance of said attachment or connection; or to terminate the service." *Use of the Carterfone Device in Message Toll Service,* Decision, 13 FCC2d 420, App. A (1968). Bell first included these provisions in private contracts with subscribers in 1899, and incorporated them into its tariffs in 1913.

2. *See, e.g., North Carolina Utils. Comm'n v. FCC/552* F.2d 1036, 1048 (4th Cir.) *(NCUCII)* ("The state commissions contend that they currently subsidize residence and one-phone consumer service by charging more for business equipment (PBXs and key phones) and for extension phones than the unit costs of such equipment."), *cert. denied,* 434 U.S. 874 (1977).

3. "An often cited example involves an early Supreme Court case in which a consortium of railroads had acquired all bridges and terminals in St. Louis that were necessary for railroads to cross the Mississippi. In that case, the Court held that the consortium was required to allow its railroad rivals reasonable access to the bridges and terminals. *See United States v. Terminal Railroad Assn. of St. Louis,* 224 U.S. 383 (1912).

4. For example, if the consortium in the *Terminal Railroad* case had known that it would be required to share its bridges with competitors (in other words, if it had known that it would not be able to reap supracompetitive profits after investing in these bridges), the consortium might never have made the investment in the first place, and society might have been worse off.

5. Courts and commentators have quarreled as to the precise relevant measure of cost—a disagreement that we will not discuss here.

The Telecommunications
Act of 1996

Sharon K. Black

"... *to promote competition and reduce regulation in order to secure lower prices and higher quality services for American telecommunications consumers and encourage the rapid deployment of new telecommunications technologies.*"

Purpose of the Telecommunications Act of 1996.[1,2]

The Telecommunications Act of 1996, passed by congress on February 1, 1996,[3] and signed into law on February 8, 1996 by President William J. Clinton, was the most extensive change in U.S. communications law in the 62 years since the Communications Act of 1934. It altered the structure and operation of the industry in at least four significant ways. First, it opened the local telephone markets to competition, completely reversing the historical concept of a *natural monopoly* in telephones. As such, it removed previous barriers to entry for multiple market participants.

Second, it removed divisions between technologies. For example, cable television (CATV) companies and electric and gas utilities can now provide telephone service. It also allowed other equipment manufacturers and entertainment companies to provide new services that are redefining what "basic" communications is and how it is delivered to customers. These changes, in turn, are redefining how people communicate.

Third, it affected all sectors of the telecommunications industry. Unlike the Kingsbury Commitment, the 1956 Decree and the 1982 Modified Final Judgment (MFJ),[4] which affected only AT&T and its subsidiaries in the Bell system, the 1996 Act affects all sectors of the telecommunications industry. This includes existing local telephone service providers; independent providers such as GTE, United, and Continental; small, independent telephone companies; long-distance carriers; equipment manufacturers; and new entrants to the market.

Fourth, it removed the restrictions imposed by prior consent decrees, including the 1956 Decree and the 1982 MFJ, that are inconsistent with the 1996 Act.[5] This means that the 1996 Act supersedes most of the provisions of these historical agreements with the new obligations of the 1996 Act.

Considering the breadth and depth of these changes, the 1996 Act will direct how the communications industry will be organized and will function for many years to come. Understanding the Act is critical when evaluating the opportunities available to companies in the new competitive telecommunications environment and the restrictions that define their market strategies. Therefore, the purpose of this chapter is to describe (1) the intent, general structure, and organization of the 1996 Act; (2) the new definitions and provisions it provides; (3) the overall duties and responsibilities it imposes on the various segments of the industry; and (4) challenges to the Act.

To accomplish this, Section 3.1 describes the purpose of the 1996 Act, while Section 3.2 outlines the Act's general structure and organization. Section 3.3 provides several key definitions, and Section 3.4 discusses several key provisions to open competition in the local telecommunications market. Section 3.5 describes the duties and obligations of the various categories of carriers identified in the 1996 Act, while Section 3.6 discusses four constitutional challenges to certain of these duties and obligations.

PURPOSE OF THE TELECOMMUNICATIONS ACT OF 1996

In general, the 1996 Act is part of an ongoing effort to protect the public from the potential negative domination of large, powerful companies and to encourage innovation. In the decade following the breakup of the Bell System in 1984,[6] the U.S. Congress and state legislatures noted that three positive results had occurred from competition in long distance. First, long-distance prices dropped significantly from nearly $3.00 per minute to less than 10¢ per minute. Second, new technology was introduced to consumers more quickly than had occurred previously; and third, these changes resulted in more equipment and service options for consumers. The state and federal legislators hoped to (1) obtain the same three results for consumers with competition in the local market, (2) bring communications law more into line with the technological developments that integrated voice and data services, and (3) thus place the U.S. communications industry in a better position for the Internet Age. To accomplish these goals, the Act introduced competition in the local exchange market.[7]

Federal Action

In detailing its objectives, Congress declared in an early draft of Senate Bill S. 652, printed on June 23, 1995,[8] that

> (1) Competition, not regulation, is the best way to spur innovation and the development of new services. A competitive marketplace is the most efficient way to lower prices and increase value

for consumers. In furthering the principle of open and full competition in all telecommunications markets, however, it must be recognized that some markets are more open than others.

> (2) Local telephone service is predominantly a monopoly service. Although business customers in metropolitan areas may have alternative providers for exchange access service, consumers do not have a choice of local telephone service. Some States have begun to open local telephone markets to competition. A national policy framework is needed to accelerate the process.

> (3) Because of their monopoly status, local telephone companies and the Bell operating companies have been prevented from competing in certain markets. It is time to eliminate these restrictions. Nonetheless, transition rules designed to open monopoly markets to competition must be in place before certain restrictions are lifted.

> (4) Transition rules must be truly transitional, not protectionism for certain industry segments or artificial impediments to increased competition in all markets. Where possible, transition rules should create investment incentives through increased competition. Regulatory safeguards should be adopted only where competitive conditions would not prevent anticompetitive behavior.

> (5) More competitive American telecommunications markets will promote United States technological advances, domestic job and investment opportunities, national competitiveness, sustained economic development, and improved quality of American life more effectively than regulation.

> (6) Congress should establish clear statutory guidelines, standards, and timeframes to facilitate more effective communications competition and, by so doing, will reduce business and customer uncertainty, lessen regulatory processes, court appeals, and litigation, and thus encourage the business community to focus more on

competing in the domestic and international communications marketplace.

(7) Where competitive markets are demonstrably inadequate to safeguard important public policy goals, such as the continued universal availability of telecommunications services at reasonable and affordable prices, particularly in rural America, Congress should establish workable regulatory procedures to advance those goals, provided that in any proceeding undertaken to ensure universal availability, regulators shall seek to choose the most procompetitive and least burdensome alternative.

(8) Competitive communications markets, safeguarded by effective Federal and State antitrust enforcement, and strong economic growth in the United States which such markets will foster are the most effective means of assuring that all segments of the American public command access to advanced telecommunications technologies.

(9) Achieving full and fair competition requires strict parity of marketplace opportunities and responsibilities on the part of incumbent telecommunications service providers as well as new entrants into the telecommunications marketplace, provided that any responsibilities placed on providers should be the minimum required to advance a clearly defined public policy goal.

(10) Congress should not cede its constitutional responsibility regarding interstate and foreign commerce in communications to the Judiciary through the establishment of procedures which will encourage or necessitate judicial interpretation or intervention into the communications marketplace.

(11) Ensuring that all Americans, regardless of where they may work, live, or visit, ultimately have comparable access to the full benefits of competitive communications markets requires Federal and State authorities to work together affirmatively to minimize and remove unnecessary institutional and regulatory barriers to new entry and competition.

(12) Effectively competitive communications markets will ensure customers the widest possible choice of services and equipment, tailored to individual desires and needs, and at prices they are willing to pay.

(13) Investment in and deployment of existing and future advanced, multipurpose technologies will best be fostered by minimizing government limitations on the commercial use of those technologies.

(14) The efficient development of competitive United States communications markets will be furthered by policies which aim at ensuring reciprocal opening of international investment opportunities.

These Congressional "findings" translated into the following explanations of Congress's goal for the 1996 Act:

To provide for a national policy framework designed to accelerate rapidly private sector deployment of advanced telecommunications and information technologies and services to all Americans by opening all telecommunications markets to competition, and for other purposes.

… to establish a national policy framework designed to accelerate rapidly the private sector deployment of advanced telecommunications and information technologies and services to all Americans by opening all telecommunications markets to competition, and to meet the following goals:

(1) To promote and encourage advanced telecommunications networks, capable of enabling users to originate and receive affordable, high-quality voice, data, image, graphic, and video telecommunications services.

(2) To improve international competitiveness markedly.

(3) To spur economic growth, create jobs, and increase productivity.

(4) To deliver a better quality of life through the preservation and advancement of universal

service to allow the more efficient delivery of educational, health care, and other social services.

States' Action

While Congress was outlining the goals and directives of the federal Telecommunications Act of 1996, approximately two-thirds of the states' legislatures changed their state laws in 1995 to open their local markets to competition. Most of these laws allowed one year for the state public utilities commission (PUC), representatives of industry, public interest groups, and legislative committees to write the rules and regulations implementing the law. This meant that most of the states required local telephone competition to be in place and operating in their states before the federal Telecommunications Act of 1996 was enacted. This was difficult because the precise format, details, and dates of the federal implementation were unknown. For the states, this required meeting state-imposed statutory deadlines, while still tracking the federal activity to avoid as much inconsistency with the federal law as possible. It was also a time of cooperation within the states as the representatives of industry, public interest groups, staffs of the PUCs, and legislative committees met to draft the implementing rules in each state. In addition, the states often consulted with the staffs of other states to trade ideas, discuss processes, and determine the best approaches and solutions to common issues and problems. This level of cooperation among the states helped stabilize implementation ideas from one state to another and is the primary reason that some similarity exists among the state laws. This similarity is crucial for telecommunications companies seeking to offer products in multiple states.

STRUCTURE AND ORGANIZATION OF THE 1996 ACT—47 U.S.C. §§ 151 *ET SEQ.*

The Telecommunications Act of 1996 is not a new law that replaces the Communications Act of 1934. Instead, it amends the 1934 Act by modifying certain portions of the older Act, and adding new sections to accommodate technological changes and the new competitive environment. Thus, to find the 1996

Act, one must go to the 1934 Act, found at 47 U.S.C. §§ 151 *et seq.*, and look for the 1996 updates.

When the 1996 updates are printed separately as the Telecommunications Act of 1996 Act, four general trends emerge. First, the sections of the Telecommunications Act are non-sequential, in that the sections start at Sections 1, 2, and 3, then jump to Sections 101 through 104, and then to section 151. The remaining sections move forward in a similar hopscotch manner throughout the Act, identifying only those portions of the 1934 Act that were changed or added as new sections.

Second, both the 1996 Act, when printed alone, and the 1934 Act, printed in its entirety, each have seven titles, or chapters, but they have different names and address different topics. For example, the seven titles in the 1996 Act are as follows:

Title I:	Telecommunication Services
Title II:	Broadcast Services
Title III:	Cable Services
Title IV:	Regulatory Reform
Title V:	Obscenity and Violence
Title VI:	Effect on Other Laws
Title VII:	Miscellaneous Provisions

The seven titles in the 1934 Act are as follows:

Title I:	General Provisions
Title II:	Common Carrier (Wireline)
Title III:	Radio (Wireless)
Title IV:	Procedural and Administrative Provisions
Title V:	Penal Provisions—Forfeitures
Title VI:	Cable Communications
Title VII:	Miscellaneous Provisions

Nonetheless, since the 1934 Act is the fuller law, the industry follows the 1934 titles when referring to Information and Enhanced Service Providers as Title I providers; to common carriers, incumbent local exchange carriers and competitive vocal exchange carriers, as Title II providers; wireless companies as Title III providers, and cable television companies as Title VI providers.

Because of this difference in the titles within the two Acts, a particular citation for information may not be the same in the two Acts. Where the location of an item differs, this book provides both citations so the reader can find the correct citation in either document.

Third, the 1996 Act provides mainly broad, over-arching goals for U.S. communications in the new competitive environment. For example, Congress mandated in the 1996 Act that (1) telecommunications facilities must be interconnected at any "technically feasible point,"[9] (2) rates, terms, and conditions in the new competitive environment shall be "just, reasonable, and nondiscriminatory,"[10] and (3) the Federal Communications Commission (FCC) and each state commission "shall encourage the deployment on a reasonable and timely basis of advanced telecommunications capability to all Americans ... in a manner consistent with the public interest."[11] Congress delegated to the FCC[12] and the states[13] the task of determining (1) where the "technically feasible point" is for each product or system;[14] (2) what "just, reasonable, and nondiscriminatory" mean; and (3) how to best implement these goals. While the state interpretations cannot conflict with the FCC's interpretation, they often vary widely among themselves and are usually more detailed than the federal interpretations. Where different states have different interpretations of what these mean and how to best achieve them, implementation of a nationwide product becomes difficult for companies.

Fourth, the 1996 Act begins with three introductory sections, Sections 1, 2, and 3. Section 1 states that the short title and citation for the 1996 Act is the Telecommunications Act of 1996, and the 1996 Act, "[e]xcept as otherwise expressly provided," amends the Communications Act of 1934. Section 2 then provides the table of contents, listing the seven titles and their subsections, and Section 3 provides new and modified definitions to the 1934 Act, many of which significantly alter the structure and direction of the new competitive environment. These are discussed in greater detail below.

DEFINITIONS—SECTION 3 OF THE TELECOMMUNICATIONS ACT OF 1996

One of the most important aspects of Section 3 of the 1996 Act is the modified and new definitions it provides to the industry.[15] Among the more surprising changes and additions are the definitions of telecommunications, carriers, and equipment. Since each is a common word, one would expect the definitions to be quite straightforward. However, each has a peculiar twist that has a great impact on the new competitive industry. Each term also has subsections, for example, (1) *telecommunications* includes definitions of telecommunications service, telecommunications carriers, and the telecommunications industry; (2) *carrier* includes definitions of local exchange carriers, including both incumbent and competitive local exchange carriers, Bell Operating Companies, and the two exceptions provided for mobile service providers and small, rural telephone companies; and (3) *equipment* includes definitions of telecommunications equipment and customer-provided equipment. The details of each are discussed below.

Three-Pronged Definition of Telecommunications

The 1934 Act did not contain a definition for the word *telecommunications*. Instead, it defined only the word *communications*. The 1996 Act, however, updated this by providing definitions for telecommunications, telecommunications service, and telecommunications carrier, creating what is known as the three-pronged definition of telecommunications.[16] In addition, it provides a definition of the telecommunications industry.[17] The four definitions concerning telecommunications follow.

Telecommunications, § 3(a)(2)(48)

The 1996 Act defines the term *telecommunications* as "the transmission, between or among points specified by the user, of information of the user's choosing, without change in the form or content of the information as sent and received."[18]

The three key elements in this definition, (1) between or among points specified by the user; (2) carrying information of the user's choosing, and (3) without change in the form or content of the information as sent and received, seem quite familiar. We recognize that users specify the points of communications when they dial phone numbers or address e-mails. Similarly, we recognize that the information in the communication is unchanged in form or content when phone conversations include mispronounced words and e-mails include misspelled words. However, during implementation of the 1996 Act, it was noted that modern communications generally convert most communications from analog to digital as they pass through various equipment in the network and that this was a change in the form of the information. It was subsequently decided that since these digitization changes are made only to facilitate the transmission process and are transparent to the users, they are not to be considered changes in the form or content of the information as sent and received. Instead, Congress defined telecommunications as the transmission of messages "passed through" just as the user communicated it, with its content unedited by a third party.

Telecommunications Service, § 3(a)(2)(51)

The term *telecommunications service* is defined in the Telecommunications Act of 1996 as "the offering of telecommunications for a fee directly to the public, or to such classes of users as to be effectively available directly to the public, regardless of the facilities used."[19]

The three key phrases in this definition are the offering of telecommunications (1) for a fee, (2) to the public, and (3) regardless of the facilities used. These highlight three specific characteristics of a telecommunications service not specified previously.

Telecommunications Carrier, § 3(a)(2)(49)

The term *telecommunications carrier*, is defined in the 1996 Act, as "*any* provider of telecommunications services, except ... aggregators of telecommunications services (as defined in Section 226). A telecommunications carrier shall be treated as a common carrier under this Act only to the extent that it is engaged in providing telecommunications services, except that the Commission shall determine whether the provision of fixed and mobile satellite service shall be treated as common carriage."[20]

This definition has three surprising portions. First, it defines a telecommunications carrier as any provider of telecommunications services. Since two of the elements of a telecommunications service are *for a fee* and *to the public*, this definition means that a telecommunications carrier is anyone who offers a telecommunications service for a fee. This is a much larger group than we have previously considered to be telecommunications carriers. It can include such groups as (1) business centers in airports or shopping centers that send or receive faxes and other communications for a fee; (2) colleges that add the price of a phone in the fee for a dorm room; and (3) office-building owners who add fees for telecommunications facilities in the rent. Traditionally, these groups have not considered themselves to be telecommunications carriers and thus have applied for exemptions from the FCC or the state legislators or PUCs. Some exemptions have been granted, others have not. The second surprising portion of this definition is that the only exemption provided in the 1996 Act is for "aggregators," such as hotels, where the price of the phone is included in the room rental cost. The difference between considering dorms and office buildings as "carriers," and hotels as "not carriers" appears to be in the length of time of a tenant's stay. Shorter or temporary stays seem to be excluded, although no clear distinction is provided in the statute or legislative history. The third surprising portion of this definition is that it states that the FCC will make a later determination about whether a satellite communications system is to be considered a common carrier. No explanation concerning this deferral was provided in either the legislation or the Joint Explanatory Statement of the Conference Committee.

Telecommunications Industry, § 714(k)(3)

The term *telecommunications industry*, as defined in the 1996 Act, means "communications businesses using regulated or unregulated facilities or services and includes broadcasting, telecommunications, cable, computer, data transmission, software, programming, advanced messaging, and electronics businesses."[21] This definition indicates Congress's partial acknowledgement of the convergence of technologies and the variety of potential new providers of telecommunications services in the new competitive environment.

Definitions of Carriers

With the extended definition of telecommunications carriers, the 1996 Act further divides the term *carriers* into four specific categories including the following: (1) local exchange carriers, (2) incumbent local exchange carriers, (3) competitive local exchange carriers, and (4) Bell Operating Companies, as well as two important exclusions, (5) wireless companies, and (6) small, rural telephone companies. All six categories are described in more detail below.

Local Exchange Carriers, § 3(a)(2)(44)

The 1996 Act defines the term *local exchange carrier* (LEC) as "any person that is engaged in the provision of telephone exchange service or exchange access. Such term does not include a person insofar as such person is engaged in the provision of a commercial mobile service under Section 332(c), except to the extent that the Commission finds that such service should be included in the definition of such term."[22]

As one would expect, this definition includes anyone who provides local telephone exchange service to the public for a fee. Surprisingly, however, the definition includes two additional elements. First, it includes any company providing exchange access. *Exchange access* is defined in the 1996 Act as "the offering of access to telephone exchange services or facilities for the purpose of the origination or termination of telephone toll services."[23] Hence, a local exchange carrier is not just a local service provider, but *any* service provider that originates or terminates toll traffic. With the introduction of technologies such as satellite, fiber, microwave, cable, and Internet service providers (ISPs), toll service could be originated and terminated without the use of the local telephone company's facilities.

Second, the definition of local exchange carriers specifically excludes *commercial mobile service providers*. These wireless companies provide radio communications service between mobile stations and fixed, land stations, or among mobile stations,[24] and include services such as cellular telephone, personal communications systems, and enhanced specialized mobile radio (ESMR) services. This exclusion means that these wireless companies are not considered local exchange carriers, even if no wire facilities exist in the area and the wireless companies provide the only telephone service available. This exclusion also means that the mobile service providers are not responsible for most of the duties and obligations of local exchange carriers, but they are considered new entrants and thus can receive all of the benefits and privileges provided to new entrants in the 1996 Act.

Exclusion—Mobile Service Providers

Congress exempted the commercial mobile service providers for several reasons. First, wireless service had always been viewed as a supplemental service to basic landline telephone service. For this reason, it had never been regulated as a local telephone company. Second, the advanced wireless systems tend to provide combined voice, data, and video services, each addressed differently by the 1996 Act. Third, Congress wanted competition to start immediately after the 1996 Act was signed. It recognized that the migration from monopoly to competition could take years if duplicate wired systems had to be installed. Instead, a much quicker method to provide a duplicate local infrastructure was through wireless systems. Congress realized that it was the easiest, fastest technology to bring about competition and thus to encourage the expansion of wireless facilities. Congress (1) made certain federal land available for wireless antenna sites, (2) reduced the time required for antenna site approval, (3) created an appeal process if a site request were denied, and (4) placed the research and responsibility for setting radio frequency emission standards with the FCC.[25]

Incumbent Local Exchange Carriers, § 251(h)(1)

The 1996 Act defines an *incumbent local exchange carrier* (ILEC) as, "with respect to an area, the local exchange carrier that

(A) provided telephone exchange service in the area on the date of enactment of the Telecommunications Act of 1996; and

(B) (i) was deemed to be a member of the National Exchange Carrier Association [pursuant to section 69.601 (b) of the Commission's regulations (47 C.F.R. 69.601 (b))] on such date of enactment; or

(B) (ii) is a person or entity that, on or after such date of enactment, became a successor or assign of a member described in clause (i); ...[26]

Beyond recognizing that the telephone companies providing local service on February 8, 1996 are incumbent carriers, this definition adds three future elements to the definition of an incumbent local exchange carrier. It states that the FCC may consider a local exchange carrier to be an incumbent local exchange carrier if

(A) such carrier occupies a position in the telephone exchange service market that is comparable to the position occupied by the existing ILEC;

(B) such carrier has substantially replaced an incumbent local exchange carrier described in paragraph (1); and

(C) such treatment is consistent with the public interest, convenience, and necessity and the purposes of this section.[27]

The qualification that an incumbent local exchange carrier (ILEC) must be deemed to be a member of the National Exchange Carrier Association (NECA),[28] excludes small rural telephone companies that may have been providing the telephone service in an area for many years prior to 1996 and are technically incumbent local exchange carriers, but whom Congress is excluding from the responsibilities of incumbent local exchange carriers because of their small size. Congress did not want to place undue burden or cost on the subscribers of companies who may not experience competition.

Exclusion—Rural Telephone Companies, § 3(a)(2)(47)

A number of the smaller, rural carriers feared that the duties and responsibilities placed on incumbent local exchange carriers by the 1996 Act could bankrupt them. Therefore, to relieve the small carriers' concerns, Congress exempted rural telephone companies in the 1996 Act, defining a *rural telephone company* as a local exchange carrier[29] that

(A) provides common carrier service to any local exchange carrier study area that does not include either—

(i) any incorporated place of 10,000 inhabitants or more, or any part thereof, based on the most recently available population statistics of the Bureau of the Census; or

(ii) any territory, incorporated or unincorporated, included in an urbanized area, as defined by the Bureau of the Census as of August 10, 1993;

(B) provides telephone exchange service, including exchange access, to fewer than 50,000 access lines;

(C) provides telephone exchange service to any local exchange carrier study area with fewer than 100,000 access lines; or

(D) has less than 15 percent of its access lines in communities of more than 50,000 on the date of enactment of the Telecommunications Act of 1996.

While this definition and exclusion are important to the smaller carriers, Congress also stated that if a carrier grew beyond these qualifications, the carrier loses this rural telephone company exclusion and must meet the obligations of the incumbent local exchange carriers.

Congress exempted small, rural telephone companies from the definition of a local exchange carrier, and therefore from the duties and obligations imposed on local exchange carriers (by Sections 251 and 252)[30] because it was anticipated that few competitive companies would likely enter this market. Therefore, preparing for competition would be an unnecessary expense for the customers. However, in case new opportunities, such as demand for high-speed Internet connections, changed the market dynamics, Congress stated that this exemption lasted only until the rural markets received a request from a competitive local exchange carrier to interconnect their systems. At that point, the smaller, rural systems would be required to interconnect in a nondiscriminatory manner. Section 251(f)(2) also states that local exchange carriers with less that 2% of the nation's lines may petition the state for suspension or modifications of any of the requirements of Section 251(c) (local exchange carrier and incumbent local exchange carriers duties).

Both allow the states to provide some flexibility in the application of the Act. The carriers requesting the exemption bear the burden of proof in their request.

Competitive Local Exchange Carriers

Surprisingly, the 1996 Act does not contain a definition of the term *competitive local exchange carrier*. It is, however, the term used by the industry to identify the new entrants providing switched services in local markets. In addition, throughout the 1996 Act, Congress reiterates that various providers are free to enter the opened local exchange markets as new competitive carriers. These include the following: (1) long-distance service providers or interrexchange carriers; (2) cable television companies; (3) wireless carriers; (4) competitive access providers, including microwave and fiber-based carriers; (5) public utilities such as the gas and/or oil and electricity providers; and (6) entrepreneurs.

Bell Operating Companies, § 3(a)(2)(35)

The 1996 Act defines the term *Bell Operating Company* (BOC) as

(A) any of the following companies: Bell Telephone Company of Nevada, Illinois Bell Telephone Company, Indiana Bell Telephone Company, Incorporated, Michigan Bell Telephone Company, New England Telephone and Telegraph Company, New Jersey Bell Telephone Company, New York Telephone Company, US West Communications Company, South Central Bell Telephone Company, Southern Bell Telephone and Telegraph Company, Southwestern Bell Telephone Company, The Bell Telephone Company of Pennsylvania, The Chesapeake and Potomac Telephone Company, The Chesapeake and Potomac Telephone Company of Maryland, The Chesapeake and Potomac Telephone Company of Virginia, The Chesapeake and Potomac Telephone Company of West Virginia, The Diamond State Telephone Company, The Ohio Bell Telephone Company, The Pacific Telephone and Telegraph Company, or Wisconsin Telephone Company; and

(B) includes any successor or assign of any such company that provides wire line telephone exchange service; but

(C) does not include an affiliate of any such company, other than an affiliate described in subparagraph (A) or (B).[31]

The first part of this definition, the list of 20 companies, is important because the 1996 Act placed the heaviest obligations on the Bell Operating Companies. These duties and responsibilities are described in Section 3.5.4, but it is interesting to note that many large, non-Bell companies providing local service, such as GTE, Sprint, and AT&T, were not given the same level of obligations. It is also intriguing that in some cases whole Regional Bell Operating Companies, such as US WEST and Southwestern Bell Co. (SBC), were included in the list, while others, such as Ameritech, BellSouth, Bell Atlantic, and NYNEX were named only as individual companies. No explanation for this was given in the legislative history.

The second part of this definition, the inclusion of any successor, applies directly to the companies, such as (1) US West, bought by Qwest; (2) Ameritech, Pacific Bell, and Southern New England Telephone, merged with SBC; and (3) NYNEX merged with Bell Atlantic. It guaranteed that these companies could not escape the heavy responsibilities of being a BOC by changing ownership, name, or stock allocations.

The third part of this definition, the exclusion of affiliates, links directly back to the issues of *Computer I, II,* and *III* discussed in Chapter 2.

Definitions of Equipment

The 1996 Act further provides two clarifying definitions regarding telecommunications equipment. The first identifies the equipment used by the carriers to provide services, and the second identifies the equipment used by customers, on their premises, to access the services.

Telecommunications Equipment, § 3(a)(2)(50)

The 1996 Act states that "the term *telecommunications equipment* means equipment, other than customer premises equipment, used by a carrier to provide telecommunications services, and includes software integral to such equipment (including upgrades)."[32]

The two key elements in this definition are the distinction between telecommunications equipment and customer premises equipment and the inclusion of software, with upgrades, integral to the equipment. The first element underscores the shift from the vertical structure of the Bell Companies, which provided end-to-end communications. The second element recognizes the importance of computers and software in today's telecommunications industry.

Customer Premises Equipment, § 3(a)(2)(38)

On the other hand, the 1996 Act defines the term *customer premises equipment* as "equipment employed on the premises of a person (other than a carrier) to originate, route, or terminate telecommunications."[33] A major part of the new competitive market opens opportunities in the customer premises equipment market and thus is important to all new service providers, facilities entrants, and customers seeking new applications of telecommunications.

PROVISIONS TO OPEN THE COMPETITIVE MARKET

Since one of the stated purposes of the 1996 Act was to open the local telecommunications market to competition, Section 251 provides three ways for competitive companies to enter the market, a clear process and timetable for implementation of the provisions of the 1996 Act, and the requirements for negotiating and writing interconnection agreements. A discussion of each follows.

Three Ways to Enter the New Competitive Market, 251 (c)(2–4)

The 1996 Act provided three basic ways for companies to enter the new competitive telecommunications market: facilities-based systems, unbundled access, and resale networks. Specifically, the 1996 Act requires an incumbent local exchange carrier (1) to interconnect its facilities with the facilities of a requesting new entrant in the incumbent local exchange carrier's local market in order to facilitate local telephone services over both facilities-based systems;[34] (2) to provide competing telecommunications

carriers with access to individual elements of the incumbent local exchange carrier's own network on an unbundled basis (unbundled access);[35] and (3) to sell to its competing telecommunications carriers, at wholesale rates, any telecommunications service that the incumbent local exchange carrier provides to its customers at retail rates, in order to allow the competing carriers to resell the services (resale).[36] The Eighth Circuit Court of Appeals refers to these three duties as "the local competition provisions."[37]

Facilities-Based Interconnection, § 251(c)(2)

To accomplish facilities-based interconnection, the 1996 Act requires the incumbent local exchange carriers to

provide, for the facilities and equipment of any requesting telecommunications carrier, interconnection with the local exchange carrier's network—

(A) for the transmission and routing of telephone exchange service and exchange access;

(B) at any technically feasible point within the carrier's network;

(C) that is at least equal in quality to that provided by the local exchange carrier to itself or to any subsidiary, affiliate, or any other party to which the carrier provides interconnection; and

(D) on rates, terms, and conditions that are just, reasonable, and nondiscriminatory, in accordance with the terms and conditions of the agreement and the requirements of this section and section 252.[38]

These requirements seek to ensure the interconnection of separate, facilities-based systems for transparent exchange of communications traffic between carriers so that all customers can seamlessly call any other person no matter which company serves each customer.

Unbundled Access, § 251(c)(3)

The 1996 Act defines *unbundled access* as

the duty to provide, to any requesting telecommunications carrier for the provision of a telecommunications service, nondiscriminatory access to network elements on an unbundled basis at any technically feasible point on rates, terms, and conditions that are just, reasonable, and nondiscriminatory in accordance with the terms and conditions of the agreement and the requirements of this Section and Section 252. An incumbent local exchange carrier shall provide such unbundled network elements in a manner that allows requesting carriers to combine such elements in order to provide such telecommunications service.[39]

This option allows companies, such as cable television, wireless providers, and electric/gas utilities, who already have customers, installation and maintenance crews, and billing systems, to lease the network elements they are missing, such as a voice switches, or electronic ordering systems, to complete their local telephone system. The 1996 Act, thus mandates that the traditional vertical hierarchy of the telephone industry be divided into parts, known as *unbundled network elements,* so that competitive new entrants can choose what they need to provide competitive local telecommunications service.

Resale, § 251(c)(4)

The 1996 Act defines the third form of entry, *resale,* as

the duty of ILECs—

(A) to offer for resale at wholesale rates any telecommunications service that the carrier provides at retail to subscribers who are not telecommunications carriers; and

(B) not to prohibit, and not to impose unreasonable or discriminatory conditions or limitations on, the resale of such telecommunications service, except that a State commission may, consistent with regulations prescribed by the Commission under this section prohibit a reseller that obtains at wholesale rates a telecommunications service that is available at retail only to a category of subscribers from offering such service to a different category of subscribers.[40]

Congress realized that when a new carrier entered a local market, it would take time for that new carrier to build its own facilities in order to serve customers and would be a significant investment for those companies. Both factors meant a delay in the start of competition and thus a delay in realizing the benefits of competition for consumers. Instead, Congress wanted competition in the telecommunications industry to start the day the 1996 Act was signed and thus made provisions for new entrants to resell the incumbent local exchange carriers services. By purchasing at wholesale and reselling at retail, the new entrants would be able to make a profit. Telecommunications services are available for resale in accordance with the requirements of 47 U.S.C. §§ 251(b)(1), 251(c)(4), 252(d)(3), and 271(c)(2)(B)(xiv).

Implementation of the 1996 Act, § 251(d)(1)

Congress required in the 1996 Act that "within 6 months after the date of enactment of the Telecommunications Act of 1996, the commission [FCC] shall complete all actions necessary to establish regulations to implement the requirements of this section." This meant that since the Act was signed on February 8, 1996, the FCC was required to complete the implementing rules for the Act by August 8, 1996. It also meant that the states already offering local competition must wait until August, 1996 before the federal government's final directions on the 1996 Act were available.

Notice of Proposed Rulemaking

To complete the rules needed to implement the 1996 Act, the FCC first drafted a set of more than 80 new rules addressing (1) interconnection, (2) unbundling, (3) resale, (4) universal service, (5) access charges, (6) local number portability, (7) interconnection agreements, (8) the procedures by which companies could enter the new markets, and (9) new ownership rules. Second, before a government agency, such as the FCC, can impose new rules on an industry, the federal Administrative Procedures Act requires that the agency publish a draft of the rules and request public comment on them. This process is known as issuing a Notice of Proposed Rulemaking (NPRM) and is meant to ensure due process. Thus, in May 1996 the FCC published its proposed rules and requested comments on them from all interested persons.[41]

In any proposed rulemaking process, two rounds of public comment are provided for. In the first round, parties comment on the rules, and in the second round, parties review the responses of all other parties and comment on which they agree or disagree with and why. Over 450 parties responded to the two rounds in the May 1996 NPRM concerning the 1996 Act, including the governments of all 50 states; the U.S. territories, including Guam, the Virgin Islands, and Puerto Rico; the major telephone carriers, industry associations, and consumer groups including the offices of consumer council of most states; and associations representing retired persons and disabled.

During June and July 1996, both sets of public responses were considered by the FCC and many comments were incorporated into the FCC's final set of rules, issued on August 8, 1996, in the FCC's *First Report and Order, Implementation of the Local Competition Provisions in the Telecommunications Act of 1996*.[42] The FCC's rules are now codified throughout various sections of Title 47, Code of Federal Regulations,[43] and require uniform, nondiscriminatory interconnection, unbundled network elements, reciprocal rates for transport and termination, collocation of equipment, and rates based on forward-looking cost methodologies.

Initial Opposition to the Rules

Despite the broad-based public review of the FCC's proposed implementation rules in the two rounds of the NPRM, parties in nearly every jurisdiction of the United States filed court cases opposing the rules within the first few days and weeks following the FCC's release of its First Report and Order. These motions to stay the First Report and Order, were filed mainly by incumbent LECs and state utility commissions protesting pricing.

Although most of the petitioners requested the court to stay the entire First Report and Order, their specific attacks focused primarily on the FCC's rules regarding pricing.[44] The petitioners opposed the rules regarding both: 1) the prices that the incumbent LECs could charge their new competitors for interconnection, unbundled access, and resale; and

2) the prices for the transport and termination of local telecommunications traffic.[45] "Transport and termination of telecommunications" is the process whereby a call that is initiated by a customer of a telecommunications carrier is routed to a customer of a different telecommunications carrier and completed by that carrier. The telecommunications carrier that "terminates" or completes the call to its customer typically charges the other telecommunications carrier for the cost of terminating the call. The Act imposes a duty on all local exchange carriers, incumbents and new entrants, to establish reciprocal compensation arrangements for such transport and termination of phone calls.[46] The petitioners argued that the FCC exceeded its jurisdiction in establishing prices for what are essentially local intrastate telecommunications and that the pricing rules violate the terms of the Act.[47]

Eighth Circuit Court Review

When multiple cases are filed on an issue in several jurisdictions, multiple courts do not hear the cases because it would be inefficient and could lead to inconsistent decisions. Instead, the cases are consolidated in one court, pursuant to Rule 24 of the *Rules of Procedure of the Judicial Panel on Multidistrict Litigation*.[48] In the case of the complaints against the FCC's *First Report and Order Implementing the 1996 Act*, the motions were consolidated at the U.S. Eighth Circuit Court of Appeals in St. Louis, Missouri, by the September 11, 1996 order of the Judicial Panel on Multidistrict Litigation, Docket No. RTC-31. This was surprising to many people, because it was one of the few times a court outside of Washington, D.C. reviewed a telecommunications law and its implementing rules that would affect all aspects of the industry throughout the United States.

The Eighth Circuit Court spent most of September 1996 reviewing the FCC's findings and rules in the First Report and Order, and found most of the rules to be "good law." On October 3, 1996, in *Iowa Utilities Board v. FCC*,[49] the court stayed, temporarily, only two sections: (1) the operation and effect of the pricing provisions, and (2) the *pick and choose* option.[50] *Pick and choose* is a portion of the 1996 Act that allows a CLEC negotiating an interconnection agreement with an incumbent local exchange carrier to pick and choose provisions from other interconnection agreements previously negotiated by that incumbent local exchange carrier with other competitive local exchange carriers. The intent of the provision is to level the negotiating "playing field" so that all competitive local exchange carriers can obtain similar provisions from the incumbent local exchange carrier. Several applications to vacate these stays by the Eighth Circuit Court were sent to the U.S. Supreme Court, but all were denied.[51] During the remainder of 1996 and early 1997, the Eighth Circuit Court reviewed these two sections more fully and issued its decision on July 18, 1997 in *Iowa Utilities Board v. FCC [II]*.[52] The Eighth Circuit Court's decision was amended upon rehearing on October 14, 1997.

Process for Writing Interconnection Agreements, § 252

Whichever of the three ways a company selects to enter a telecommunications market, facilities based, unbundled, or resale, the primary method of doing business in the new environment is through written contracts between two (or more) telecommunications carriers, called *interconnection agreements*. These contracts are very detailed documents that include all aspects of the business relationship between the two carriers, including the technical interconnections between their equipment and facilities, how they will exchange communications traffic, and how and at what rate the two companies will financially compensate each other for the traffic. In the case of equipment or service failure, the interconnection agreements identify which carrier will respond, how quickly, and in what manner. The contract also describes coverage of obligations such as local number portability and universal service, as well as which jurisdiction and method of resolution will be used if a contract dispute arises. Examples of interconnection agreements can be found on the Internet Web pages of most state PUCs.

Section 252 of the 1996 Act establishes the process, timing, and constraints by which these interconnection agreements are to be developed.[53] First, in each case, the interconnection agreements must be filed in each state in which the two carriers will do business. This is true even if the two negotiating carriers plan to offer the same services in several states.

Second, if the parties cannot independently negotiate an agreement, the 1996 Act provides for mediated or arbitrated agreements.

Third, to begin the process of writing an interconnection agreement, the competing carrier sends a formal, written *Request to Negotiate* to the incumbent carrier. The ILEC must then notify, in writing, the utility commission of each state affected by the request. This is because the 1996 Act sets a very tight, nine-month calendar in which an interconnection agreement must be completed and signed. Congress included this deadline in the 1996 Act to keep the negotiation process from stalling, thwarting, or slowing the introduction of competition in the local market. The start date of the nine-month calendar begins with the incumbent carrier's acknowledgment of the receipt of the competing carrier's CLECs *Request to Negotiate*.

Negotiated Agreements, § 251(c)(1), § 252(a)(1)

During the process of drafting an interconnection agreement, Congress's first preference is for the carriers to negotiate voluntary agreements among themselves. Section 252 of the 1996 Act states that each party, the incumbent local exchange carrier and the competing local exchange carrier, has a duty to negotiate, in good faith, the terms and conditions of an agreement that accomplishes the Act's goals.[54] The carriers may meet and negotiate the details of their agreement and, when completed, submit the agreement to the state utility commission for approval. Again, the state commission then has three months to review such agreements and to approve or deny them.

Mediated Agreements, § 252(a)(2)

However, if at any point during the negotiation process, the negotiations are not going well, either party may request that the state utility commission or its designees, usually its staff or an outside contractor hired by the commission, attend the negotiations and participate in the process as a *mediator*. In a mediated agreement, the mediator simply facilitates the process, while the decision making remains with the parties. When a mediated agreement is signed, it must also be submitted to the state utility commission for approval. The commission has three months in which to approve or deny the agreement.

Arbitrated Agreements, § 252(b)

If the mediation process does not improve the situation, either party may request that the state utility commission arbitrate the interconnection agreement. However, this request may only be made during a window from 135 to 160 days (inclusive) into the negotiations, calculated from the date of the CLEC's *Request to Negotiate*. This window is approximately four and one-half months into the mandated nine-month limit. The main difference between mediation and arbitration is that with arbitration the decision moves from the parties to the arbitrator. Thus, while the mediator serves as a facilitator of the process, the arbitrator becomes the judge. Additionally, pursuant to Section 252, the arbitrator's decision is *binding* on both parties, although Section 252(b) limits the arbitrator's authority to resolving only the *open issues* as specifically stated in the petition requesting arbitration. Once an arbitrated interconnection agreement is completed and presented to the state utility commission for approval, the state commission has only 30 days in which to review and approve or deny the agreement. This is because with arbitration, Congress assumed that the state commission would be intimately familiar with the details of the agreement and may have mandated many of them. Thus Congress felt that the commission needed time only to ensure that its directions were clearly included in the written contract, and a shorter review period was in the best interest of the public.

Post-Approval Issues

Once an interconnection agreement has been approved by the state utility commission, it must be made publicly available within 10 days. Usually, this is done by posting it on the state PUC's Internet Web site and providing an archived paper copy at the state PUC's offices. After that, however, issues such as tariffs and problem resolution may continue to arise. Generally, the 1996 Act does not address these, but the states have provided for them as follows.

Tariffs

A carrier's tariff is more than just a price list. It contains detailed descriptions of each service offered, complete with technical specifications, product guarantees, and quality of service parameters. It also details the respective obligations of the carrier and the customer and the resolution procedures to be used when problems arise. As such, it is a written contract between the telecommunications provider and its customers.

While the 1996 Act explicitly removed rate-of-return regulation, many states still require carriers doing business in their states to file tariffs. Unlike in the previous regulated environment, the states do not hold rate hearings to approve or deny the tariffs, but many require companies to file tariffs in order to have a publicly available, written statement from each carrier outlining its obligations and agreements with its customers. Some states require all companies, both incumbent local exchange carriers and competitive local exchange carriers, to file tariffs, and other states require only the incumbent local exchange carriers to file tariffs.

Problem Resolution

As with other contracts, problems can arise after the interconnection agreements are filed with the state. When this occurs, the parties can, of course, sue one another and seek judicial relief. However, most states realized that this could thwart or restrict competition, and thus they provided for mediation and arbitration to resolve disputes.[55]

DUTIES AND OBLIGATIONS OF CARRIERS

Title 1 of the 1996 Act, "Telecommunications Services,"[56] established two new sections to be added to the 1934 Act, specifically in Title 2, "Common Carriers."[57] The two new sections are "Part II—Development of Competitive Markets" and "Part III—Special Provisions Concerning Bell Operating Companies." The significance of these two new sections is that they delineate the rights and obligations of each participant in the new competitive local market. As such, these new laws establish the parameters in which the market participants must operate, the

TABLE 3.1 Chart of Carriers' Duties: Who Must Do What Under the Act (Part 1)

Duty	Statute	All Carriers	LECs	Incumbent LECs	BOCs
Interconnection	251 (a) (1)	A-1			B-1
Persons with Disabilities	251 (a) (2)	A-2			
Network Coordination	251 (a) (2)	A-3			
Resale	251 (b) (1)	—	L-1	I-4	B-14
Number of Portability	251 (b) (2)	—	L-2		
Dialing Parity	251 (b) (3)	—	L-3		B-12
Poles, Ducts, Conduits, and Rights-of-Way	251 (b) (4)	—	L-4		B-3
Reciprocal Compensation	251 (b) (5)	—	L-5		B-13
Duty to Negotiate	251 (c) (1)	—	—	I-1	
Interconnection Plus	251 (c) (2)	—	—	I-2	B-1
Network Elements	251 (c) (3)	—	—	I-3	B-2
Resale at Wholesale Rates	251 (c) (4)	—	—	I-4	
Notice of Changes	251 (c) (5)	—	—	I-5	
Collocation	251 (c) (6)	—	—	I-6	

Source: Used by permission of Telecommunications Research Associates.
Note: LECs, local exchange carriers; BOCs, Bell Operating Companies.

opportunities open to them, and the requirements that each competitor must meet.

The new Part II starts at Section 251, and includes Sections 251 through 261.[58] The new Part III starts at Section 271 and includes Sections 271 through 276.[59] Section 251 lists the obligations and duties of the new companies competitive local exchange carriers, while Section 271 contains the Competitive Checklist that the Bell Operating Companies must pass before they can provide ancillary services beyond basic local and long-distance telephone service. Sections 272–276, generally known as the special provisions or BOC safeguards, establish the parameters around four new ancillary services, including (1) equipment manufacturing, (2) electronic publishing, (3) alarm monitoring, and (4) payphone services. To clarify the rights and responsibilities of market participation, Sections 251 and 271 of the 1996 Act group the competitive market participants into the following four categories: (1) All telecommunications carriers; (2) all local exchange carriers; (3) all incumbent local exchange carriers, and (4) the Bell Operating Companies. Tables 3.1 and 3.2 summarize the rights and obligations of each group.

All Telecommunications Carriers, § 251(a)

The category of *telecommunications carriers* as defined in the 1996 Act[60] includes all incumbent local exchange carriers, all new entrants, and all long-distance service providers. For specific items, the category also includes equipment providers, wireless carriers, and satellite service providers, but generally these three

TABLE 3.2 Chart of Carriers' Duties: Who Must Do What Under the Act (Part 2)

Duty	Statute	All Carriers	LECs	Incumbent LECs	BOCs
Interconnection	271 (c) (2) (B) (i)	A-1			B-1
Network Elements	271 (c) (2) (B) (ii)	—	—	I-3	B-2
Poles, Ducts, Conduits, Rights-of-Way	271 (c) (2) (B) (iii)	—	L-4		B-3
Access to Local Loop	271 (c) (2) (B) (iv)	—	—	—	B-4
Trunk-Side Local Transport	271 (c) (2) (B) (v)	—	—	—	B-5
Local Switching	271 (c) (2) (B) (vi)	—	—	—	B-6
911/Directory Assistance/Operator	271 (c) (2) (B) (vii)	—	—	—	B-7
White Pages Listings	271 (c) (2) (B) (viii)	—	—	—	B-8
Telephone Numbers	271 (c) (2) (B) (ix)		—	—	B-9
Databases for Call Handling	271 (c) (2) (B) (x)	—	—	_	B-10
Interim Number Portability	271 (c) (2) (B) (xi)	—	—	_	B-11
Info re Local Dialing Parity	271 (c) (2) (B) (xii)	—	L-3		B-12
Reciprocal Compensation	271 (c) (2) (B) (xiii)	—	L-5		B-13
Resale at Wholesale Rates	271 (c) (2) (B) (xiv)	—	—	I-4	B-14

Source: Used by permission of Telecommunications Research Associates.
Note: LECs, local exchange carriers; BOCs, Bell Operating Companies.

groups are exempt from any specific obligations. The 1996 Act identifies only three duties that all telecommunications carriers must meet: interconnection, consistency with U.S. laws regarding persons with disabilities, and coordinated network planning. Each is described further below.

All Carriers' Duty 1: Interconnection, § 251(a)(1)

First, the 1996 Act requires that all telecommunications carriers "interconnect directly or indirectly with the facilities and equipment of other telecommunications carriers."[61] This requirement dramatically changed U.S. communications law by making each carrier's duty to interconnect immediate with no required finding of need. For 62 years, from 1934 to

1996, U.S. communications law supported the concept of a *natural monopoly* in each market and resisted the addition of any other company's equipment to the telephone network, arguing that it might degrade the performance of the network. For this reason, the 1934 Act required a lengthy and complicated process to prove that each interconnection was "in the public necessity, interest, and convenience."[62] Typically the process took several years, was rarely granted, and thus was generally avoided. The 1996 Act reversed that process and made the *duty to interconnect* explicit, immediate and applicable to all telecommunications market participants.[63]

All Carriers' Duty 2: Persons with Disabilities, § 251(a)(2)

Second, the 1996 Act requires that the products and services of all telecommunications carriers be consistent with the Americans With Disabilities Act of 1990.[64] It states that all telecommunications carriers have the duty "not to install network features, functions or capabilities that do not comply with the guidelines and standards established pursuant to Section 255." Section 255 requires that manufacturers of telecommunications equipment, manufacturers of customer premises equipment, and providers of telecommunications services, shall ensure that their equipment or services are "accessible to and usable by individuals with disabilities, if readily achievable."[65]

Beyond placing payphones at wheelchair level, redesigning phone booths, placing larger numbers on telephones, and volume controls on handsets, this requirement helps to bring the benefits of digital communications to persons with disabilities to provide them with fuller access to enhanced communications. For example, it could make it possible for visually impaired persons to have Internet information, books, and other research and written communications be "read" to them through a *codec*. The word *codec*, is a shortened form of coder/decoder, a device that converts analog to digital communications and back again. It can convert digital or computerized information into analog form so the human ear can understand it. At present these systems often sound like very mechanical voices, but technology is improving. Codecs can also convert spoken or oral communications into written communications for hearing-impaired persons. This has exciting potential for the future, but also places significant responsibilities on the manufacturers of telecommunications equipment and providers of telecommunications services. Most surprising of all, the federal agency given the responsibility for developing the guidelines in this area is the U.S. Architecture and Transportation Board, a group previously not prominent in telecommunications equipment and services, but now responsible for the final approval of all new telecommunications equipment and services.

All Carriers' Duty 3: Coordinated Network Planning, § 251(a)(2)

Third, the 1996 Act requires all telecommunications carriers to not "install network features, functions or capabilities that do not comply with the guidelines and standards established pursuant to Section 256." Section 256 requires the FCC to establish procedures for FCC oversight of coordinated network planning for effective and efficient interconnection of public telecommunications networks.[66]

Historically, the individual Bell Operating Companies in the United States coordinated their network and equipment planning with one another to seamlessly transfer calls across the country. While they were separate companies, they were also part of the Bell System, and it increased the value of the phones to their customers to be able to call anyone. The companies also had monopoly control of a geographic area, so even interconnection with independent companies following the 1913 Kingsbury Commitment did not mean market loss for them. The 1996 Act continues this tradition of seamless communications by requiring all local exchange carriers to interconnect with one another even in a competitive environment. Taking this one step further, the 1996 Act requires all telecommunications carriers to coordinate the planning and system design of public networks to allow a free flow of calls from one company to another in a nondiscriminatory manner.[67]

Duties of Local Exchange Carriers, § 251(b)

Within the larger group of *all carriers* is a subset of companies called the *local exchange carriers*. The 1996 Act defines local exchange carriers as any person who provides telephone exchange service or exchange access, including the (1) incumbent local exchange carriers, (2) new competitive local exchange carriers, (3) Bell Operating Companies, and (4) non-Bell Operating Companies or independent telephone companies. It does not include, however, two very important groups within the industry, the commercial mobile service providers (wireless), operating pursuant to 47 U.S.C. 332(c), and small, primarily rural telecom providers,[68] except to the extent that the FCC finds that their services should be included in certain cases.

In addition to the three general duties of *all carriers* described in the section above, the 1996 Act adds five additional duties that the local exchange carriers must meet. In its Joint Explanatory Statement, Congress stated that these five *additional* duties make sense only in the context of a specific request from another telecommunications carrier or any other person who actually seeks to connect with or provide services using the local exchange carrier's network.[69] The five duties are presented below.

Local Exchange Carriers' Duty 1: Resale, § 251(b)(1)

First, the 1996 Act, requires all local exchange carriers "not to prohibit, and not to impose unreasonable or discriminatory conditions or limitations on the resale of its telecommunications services."[70] This requirement is significant for three reasons. First, it protects the resale option of market entry discussed earlier in Section 3.4.1. Second, the requirement does not apply to wireless systems, because they are not considered local exchange carriers. Third, it does not require that the resale occur at a wholesale price, as is the case with resale by the Bell Operating Companies, discussed later in Section 3.5.4.

Initially, companies even as large as AT&T announced that it would use resale contracts to enter at least 30% of the local markets by the end of 1996.[71] However, after the first several such resale agreements, competitive local exchange carriers became frustrated with the level of service provided under the resale agreements and decided instead to purchase local facilities on which they could enter the market. AT&T, for example, purchased companies such as TCG and TCI and began to integrate all of its facilities to provide services in the local market.

Local Exchange Carriers' Duty 2: Number Portability, § 251(b)(2)

Second, the 1996 Act requires all local exchange carriers "to provide, to the extent technically feasible, (local) number portability" in accordance with FCC requirements.[72] The Act defines *number portability* as "the ability of users of telecommunications services to retain, at the same location, existing telecommunications numbers without impairment of quality, reliability, or convenience when switching from one telecommunications carrier to another."[73]

This duty is important because it allows customers to keep their phone number if they change local service providers. It is an enormously active part of the post-1996 competitive environment that eventually will impact every phone call in the United States. Likely also, it will create a third portion of the industry to manage phone number assignments, and ultimately will continue to raise serious cost issues because the database of "ported" telephone numbers must be continually maintained and updated. The process and issues surrounding *local number portability* are discussed in greater detail in Chapter Four. It is also an obligation that applies to the wireless industry. Commercial mobile providers, including cellular, personal communications systems and certain specialized mobile radio carriers, will also participate in the long-term solution so that customers may also keep their wireless telephone numbers when they switch providers. Currently, the date for this to occur is November 24, 2002, but that date may change.

Local Exchange Carriers' Duty 3: Dialing Parity, § 251(b)(3)

Third, the 1996 Act requires all local exchange carriers "to provide dialing parity to competing providers of telephone exchange service and telephone toll service, and to permit all such providers to have nondiscriminatory access to telephone numbers, operator services, directory assistance, and directory listing, with no unreasonable dialing delays."[74] It defines *dialing parity* as enabling a person that is not an affiliate of a local exchange carrier to "provide telecommunications services in such a manner that customers have the ability to route automatically, without the use of any access code, their telecommunications to the telecommunications services provider of the customer's designation from among 2 or more telecommunications services providers (including such local exchange carrier)."[75]

Since the introduction of competition in the long-distance industry in 1984, many customers have grown accustomed to (1) dialing codes to access their long-distance service provider, (2) then dialing the phone number they are calling, and (3) finally entering their personal identification number. This process often requires 25 or more dialed digits. Recognizing this, Congress stated in the 1996 Act that parity must exist in local dialing.[76] Thus, if local calls can be made by dialing seven digits, then the customers of the competitive local exchange carriers must also be able to make local calls by dialing seven digits. Similarly, if the region has adopted a 10-digit local dialing requirement, then the customers of both incumbent local exchange carriers and competitive local exchange carriers must be able to make local calls with 10 digits. Congress did not want competition to be discouraged by the evolution of a situation similar to the "special access code," which required some customers to dial more digits to make a call in the long-distance market. Congress, instead, mandated *parity* in the number of digits dialed by customers of both the competitive local exchange carriers and incumbent local exchange carriers to place local calls.

Additional Services

In addition, section 251(b)(3) of the 1996 Act requires that the incumbent local exchange carrier in each region must also provide to the competitive exchange carriers in that region, nondiscriminatory access to (1) telephone numbers to assign to customers, (2) operator services, (3) directory assistance, and (4) white-page directory listings. In this manner, Congress determined that if five telephone companies provided local telecommunications services in a city, residents would not have to have five different telephone books. Instead, the incumbent local exchange carrier is required to print, and distribute for free, the white pages. The yellow pages can be marketed and printed for profit in whatever manner the incumbent local exchange carrier selects. Similarly, operator services and directory assistance must be provided as separate *network elements* by the incumbent local exchange carriers, so that the competitive local exchange carriers can choose to purchase them from the incumbent local exchange carrier or provide their own service.

Network Elements

The 1996 Act defines a *network element* as "a facility or equipment used in the provision of a telecommunications service. Such term also includes features, functions, and capabilities that are provided by means of such facility or equipment, including subscriber numbers, databases, signaling systems, and information sufficient for billing and collection or used in the transmission, routing, or other provision of a telecommunications service."[77]

The FCC's implementing rules identify the following eight network elements:[78]

(1) Local loop

(2) Local switching

(3) Tandem switching

(4) Interoffice transmission

(5) Databases and signaling systems

(6) Operation support system

(7) Operator service

(8) Directory assistance

The *local loop* is the transmission link between the distribution frame at the central office and the network interface at the customer premises. The incumbent local exchange carrier must include conditioning requested by the customer, although unbundling of subloop elements, between concentrators and local drops, are not required by the 1996 Act or the FCC at this time.

Local switching is the connection between the local loop and trunk. It includes all lineside and trunkside functions, plus all vertical functions including dial tone, 911, and Custom Local Area Signaling Services.

Tandem switching is the connection between trunks, including all related switch functions. *Interoffice transmission* is the link between the central office or wire center of the ILEC and CLEC, with all relevant network functions.

Databases and signaling systems are the functional and Advanced Information Network (AIN) databases that allow access to and work with the Signaling System 7 (SS7). They include the carriers' *Operation Support System* (OSS) or electronic service-ordering systems. At present, OSS is a key reason that many of the incumbent local exchange systems have not passed their section 271 checklist and was an area of tremendous activity from 1997 through 2001.

Operator service and *directory assistance* are two services that may be confusing to customers if widely duplicated. Thus, if a competitive local exchange carrier obtains these services from an incumbent local exchange carrier under a resale agreement, the incumbent local exchange carrier must provide each service as a separate element and rebrand if technically possible, or if not possible, use no brand.

Before 1996, when a customer dialed *O* for the operator, or 411 for directory assistance, the customer heard something like "Thank you for calling US WEST. What city please?" After 1996, to meet the *nondiscriminatory* requirement in operator and directory assistance services, the ILEC operators answering calls for several companies either had to identify each company by name or use no company name or *brand* at all. In early experiments, it became too confusing for the operators to identify each company correctly. When they did not, it was confusing to customers who thought they were dialing the operator of one company, only to have a second company answer the call. For these reasons, most ILECs have chosen to use no brand. Instead, callers now hear something generic such as, "What city please?" with no identification of the carrier providing the operator service.

Local Exchange Carriers' Duty 4: Access to Rights-of-Way, § 251(b)(4)

Fourth, the 1996 Act requires all local exchange carriers "to afford access to the poles, ducts, conduits, and rights-of-way of such carrier to competing providers of telecommunications services on rates, terms, and conditions that are consistent with Section 224."[79]

Section 244 states that, "All utilities must allow new entrant telecom providers to use their rights-of-way." Section 703 extends these duties to all public utilities including gas, electric, and water providers.

This requirement is critical because, as seen in the development of telegraph, telephone, cable television, and fiber optics systems today, rights-of-way are crucial to telecommunications distribution systems. Competition cannot evolve unless competing carriers have affordable access to equal rights-of-way. The four main points of concern with this requirement include the following: (1) the states are to determine the *reasonableness* of the rates on a case-by-case basis; (2) the owner of the right-of-way, pole, or duct may not reserve space for its own future needs; but (3) a CLEC may reserve space based on a long-range growth plan; and (4) other than section 252 of the 1996 Act, no guidance exists about how to resolve contention among companies for the limited space available.

Local Exchange Carriers' Duty 5: Reciprocal Compensation, § 251(b)(5)

Fifth, the 1996 Act requires all local exchange carriers "to establish reciprocal compensation arrangements for the transport and termination of telecommunications."[80] Initially, this requirement that local carriers compensate one another for communications traffic exchanged between them seemed quite reasonable. However, the interpretation and implementation of this requirement has become one of the most litigated issues in the post-1996 telecommunications industry.

Reciprocal compensation mandates that payments to a terminating carrier must be equal regardless of the direction of the flow of traffic or the type of carrier receiving the traffic. It requires that the fees paid be nondiscriminatory, or equal among carriers, and be applied only to traffic that is originated and terminated in a local area. The states are to define what is meant by "local area." This has raised several issues. First, in most cases, the difference between local and long-distance traffic is readily defined, but for commercial mobile radio wireless service carriers, reciprocal compensation applies to all traffic that originates and terminates in a single metropolitan trading area. Metropolitan trading areas are the license area of personal communications service carriers and only 51 MTAs exist in the United States. Therefore what is considered local for wireless carriers covers a much larger area than for wireline communications. A second issue concerns traffic to and from ISPs. Payments to terminate this traffic are disproportionate among companies, raising issues about whether Internet-bound traffic is local or not. The details of the litigation analyzing this are discussed in Chapter 4.

Duties of Incumbent Local Exchange Carriers, § 251(c)

As defined in Section 3.3.2, an incumbent local exchange carrier (ILEC) is any local carrier that (1) provided telephone exchange service on February 8, 1996; (2) is large enough to be a member of the National Exchange Carrier Association (not a small, rural carrier); or (3) acquired sufficient market share to match or absorb the previous incumbent carrier's serving area. Therefore, the term incumbent local exchange carrier includes both the Bell Companies and the non-Bell companies such as GTE and dozens of other larger independent telephone companies that were providing telephone service on February 8, 1996. Since the incumbent local exchange carriers are also part of the *all carriers and local exchange carriers* categories discussed previously, they are responsible for the 8 duties required of those two groups. In addition, the 1996 Act imposes the following six specific obligations on the incumbent carriers making a total of 14 duties required of all incumbent local exchange carriers.

Incumbent Local Exchange Carriers' Duty 1: Negotiate, § 251(c)(1)

First, the 1996 Act requires all ILECs "to negotiate in good faith" interconnection agreements with other competing carriers. The interconnection agreements must include specific acknowledgements of and accommodations for all of the duties of the LECs [local exchange carriers] and ILECs [incumbent local exchange carriers], including the three duties of telecommunications carriers all five additional duties of LECs, and all six duties of ILECs.[81] The requesting telecommunications carrier also has a duty to negotiate the terms and conditions of the agreement in good faith. Section 252 addresses the details of the negotiation process and alternatives,

such as arbitration, if either party delays, obscures, or thwarts the negotiations in some manner.

Incumbent Local Exchange Carriers' Duty 2: Interconnect, § 251(c)(2)

Second, the 1996 Act requires all incumbent local exchange carriers to

interconnect the facilities and equipment of any requesting telecommunications carrier, with the local exchange carrier's network—

(A) for the transmission and routing of local telephone traffic and access to long distance service;

(B) at any technically feasible point within the carrier's network;

(C) with quality that is at least equal to that which the local exchange carrier (LEC) provides to itself, a subsidiary, affiliate, or any other party; and

(D) on rates, terms, and conditions that are just, reasonable, and nondiscriminatory.[82]

This duty is more detailed than "Duty 1: Interconnection" of *all telecommunications carriers* and thus is less arguable.

Incumbent Local Exchange Carriers' Duty 3: Unbundle Access to Network Elements, § 251(c)(3)

Third, the 1996 Act mandates that an incumbent local exchange carrier shall

provide, to any requesting telecommunications carrier for the provision of a telecommunications service, nondiscriminatory access to network elements on an unbundled basis at any technically feasible point on rates, terms, and conditions that are just, reasonable, and nondiscriminatory in accordance with the terms and conditions of the agreement and the requirements of sections [251] and 252. An incumbent local exchange carrier shall provide such unbundled network elements in a manner that allows requesting carriers to combine such elements in order to provide such telecommunications service.[83]

While the concept and purpose of *unbundling* and *network elements* were discussed in Section 3.4.1, this portion of the 1996 Act places specific responsibility on the incumbent local exchange carriers to unbundle the local network into elements and make them available to the new entrants "in a manner that allows requesting carriers to combine the elements in order to provide telecommunications service." Second, the law requires the incumbent local exchange carriers to provide these network elements at the same quality as they provide for their own customers, with no limitations on their use. Third, the incumbent local exchange carriers must provide the network elements upon request, not in a delayed manner. Fourth, the elements must be provided at *any technically feasible point* and at *rates, terms, and conditions that are just and reasonable*. Different states have divided the network into as many as 22 different elements, and the rates charged vary widely.

Incumbent Local Exchange Carriers' Duty 4: Resale, § 251(c)(4)

Fourth, the 1996 Act mandates that an incumbent local exchange carrier must "offer for resale any telecommunications service that the carrier provides at retail to subscribers who are not telecommunications carriers."[84] The Act also requires that this be done at wholesale rates and in a manner that does "not prohibit or impose unreasonable or discriminatory conditions or limitations on the resale of such telecommunications service." However, "a State commission may, consistent with regulations prescribed by the Commission [under the 1996 Act], prohibit a reseller that obtains at wholesale rates a telecommunications service that is available at retail only to a category of subscribers from offering such service to a different category of subscribers."

Congress included this requirement to allow new entrants to enter the local telecommunications market earlier than they could if they had to first build and install their own facilities. The new entrant can obtain full service, or any portion needed, from the incumbent local exchange carriers at wholesale rates and sell it to customers at retail rates. Each state determines the difference between the retail price of the service and the wholesale price to the competitive local exchange carrier.

The only guidance the 1996 Act provides to the states concerning setting the wholesale rate is found in Section 252(d)(3) of the 1996 Act. It states that "The wholesale rates for services to be resold shall be the retail rates minus the costs of marketing, billing, collection, and other costs that will be avoided" by the incumbent local exchange carrier since it no longer serves those customers. The issue that exists for the state commissions is the difference between *avoided* and *avoidable*. Many incumbent carriers argue that very few costs are avoided because even if they lose some customers, they must still have a billing system and run marketing campaigns. Beyond the cost of the stamps and envelopes to those few customers, all other costs remain despite the number of customers the incumbent local exchange carrier has or loses to other carriers. This argument is countered by the competitive local exchange carriers who argue that more costs could be avoided if the incumbent local exchange carriers were more serious about avoiding costs.

Incumbent Local Exchange Carriers' Duty 5: Notice of Changes, § 251(c)(5)

Fifth, the 1996 Act states that incumbent local exchange carriers have a duty "to provide reasonable public notice of changes in the information necessary for the use or interoperability of the ILEC's facilities and networks." The purpose of this duty is to prevent any surprises from the ILEC that would restrict interconnection and interoperability from occurring.

Incumbent Local Exchange Carriers' Duty 6: Collocation, § 251(c)(6)

Sixth, the 1996 Act states that incumbent local exchange carriers have a duty "to provide (for) physical collocation of equipment necessary for interconnection or access to unbundled network elements: (1) on rates, terms, and conditions that are just, reasonable, and nondiscriminatory; (2) at the premises of the local exchange carrier; and (3) the carrier may provide for virtual collocation only if the local exchange carrier demonstrates to the State commission that physical collocation is not practical for technical reasons or because of space limitations."

Webster's Dictionary defines *collocation* as residing side by side. *Physical collocation* means that both the incumbent local exchange carriers' (ILEC's) and competitive local exchange carriers' equipment are located in the ILEC's switch room. *Virtual collocation* means that two companies' equipment are connected through high-capacity trunks, but are actually located often miles apart. The 1996 Act's requirement for physical collocation was a surprise to many of the people working in the industry because most observers were expecting that Congress would require virtual collocation. The advantage to new entrants of physical collocation is that their equipment is in the same environment as the incumbent local exchange carrier's equipment. The disadvantage is that it complicates the ability of the competitive carriers to get to their equipment without an escort from the incumbent carrier. Both generally are items discussed in negotiating interconnection agreements.

Duties of Bell Operating Companies, § 271

Section 271 of the 1996 Act places 14 additional duties on the 20 Bell Operating Companies (BOCs) listed at 47 U.S.C. 153(4).[85] The definition of a Bell Operating Company also includes any successor or assignee of the above companies that provides wireline telephone exchange service. The definition excludes any affiliate of the above companies, other than an affiliate providing local telephone service. The 1996 Act defines an *affiliate* as "a person that (directly or indirectly) owns or controls, is owned or controlled by, or is under common ownership or control with, another person. For purposes of this paragraph, the term 'own' means to own an equity interest (or the equivalent thereof) of more than 10 percent."[86]

Since the Bell Operating Companies are also part of all carriers, local exchange carriers, and incumbent local exchange carrier categories discussed previously, they are responsible for the 14 duties required of those three groups. The additional 14 obligations required in Section 271 therefore make a total of 28 duties required of the Bell Operating Systems. The 14 extra duties for the Bell Operating Companies, are known as the *Fourteen-Point Checklist* to "pass their [section] 271 [requirements]."

Two important points should be noted concerning Section 271. First, its requirements do not affect GTE, Continental, United, or any of the hundreds of other non-Bell incumbent local exchange carriers. Second, Section 271 contains four subsections covering the following: (1) the markets and services that the Bell Operating Companies can provide immediately, (2) the markets and services that the Bell Operating Companies cannot enter until after it passes its Section 271 requirements, (3) the 14 points, and (4) the process to be followed by each company to pass their 271 requirements. Each is described next.

In-Region versus Out-of-Region Services, § 271(a)

Section 271(a) of the 1996 Act divides the new competitive U.S. telecommunications market into two groups: those that the Bell Operating Companies can enter immediately after February 8, 1996, and those in which the Bell Operating Companies must have FCC approval of the companies' Section 271 applications before they can enter.[87] These two markets are defined primarily as *in-region* and *out-of-region* markets, respectively.

In-region markets are the markets in which the Bell Operating Company was the previous monopoly holder[88] and in which it is still considered the dominant provider. In this market, the Bell Operating Company has the "home team advantages" of an installed base of customers, name recognition, and established billing systems to the majority of customers. In contrast, in the out-of-region markets, the Bell Operating Company is simply another competitive local exchange carrier (CLEC) that must attract customers from the established incumbent local exchange carrier (ILEC). First, when providing services out-of-region, the Bell Operating Company is a competitive local exchange carrier CLEC. For this reason, the 1996 Act allows the Bell Operating Companies, or their affiliates, to provide out-of-region services immediately after February 8, 1996[89] so long as the Bell Operating Companies do so through separate subsidiaries and subject to section (j) of the FCC's rules. In-region services are more regulated and cannot be openly provided until after the Bell Operating Company "passes its 271."

Among the regulated services are interLATA long-distance services. The 1996 Act defines the term *interLATA service* as "telecommunications between a point located in a 'local access and transport area' and a point located outside such area."[90] It also defines the term *local access and transport area (LATA)* as

> *a contiguous geographic area: (A) established before the date of enactment of the Telecommunications Act of 1996 by a Bell operating company such that no exchange area includes points within more than 1 metropolitan statistical area, consolidated metropolitan statistical area, or State, except as expressly permitted under the AT&T Consent Decree; or (B) established or modified by a Bell operating company after such date of enactment and approved by the Commission.*[91]

In long-distance services, however, the 1996 Act primarily distinguishes between long-distance services based on their point of origination. For example, the 1996 Act restricts a Bell operating company from providing interLATA long-distance services *originating* in any of its in-region states until it has "passed its 271" and obtained FCC authorization to do so. The only services excepted from this requirement are those services that are previously authorized, as defined in Section 271(f), or are *incidental* to the provision of another service, as defined in Section 271(g).[92] On the other hand, if the long-distance service originates out of region, the BOC may provide it immediately.

Incidental InterLATA Services, § 271(b)(3)
Similarly, the 1996 Act requires no authorization for a

> *Bell operating company (BOC), or any affiliate, to provide incidental InterLATA services*[93] *originating in any State (in-region and out-of-region) after February 8, 1996, including:*
>
> *(A) audio, video, or other programming services—such as cable television.*
>
> *(B) customer interactive services providing the ability to select or respond to the audio, video or other programming services.*
>
> *(C) alarm monitoring services, if the BOC was already providing them before February 8, 1996. The service must be continued, however, through a separate subsidiary.*

> *(D) two-way interactive video services or Internet services over dedicated facilities to or for elementary and secondary schools as defined in Section 1996 Act 254(h)(5);*
>
> *(E) commercial mobile services, including long-distance calls to and from the BOCs' cellular and PCS customers,*
>
> *(F) services that permit a customer, located in one LATA, to retrieve stored information from, or file information in, information storage facilities operated by the BOC but located in another LATA;*
>
> *(G) signaling information used in connection with the provision of telephone exchange services or exchange access by a local exchange carrier; or*
>
> *(H) network control signaling information to, and receipt of such signaling information from, common carriers offering interLATA services at any location within the area in which such Bell operating company provides telephone exchange services or exchange access.*[94]

Special Provisions, §§ 272–276
In addition to the InterLATA opportunities described in Section 271, Sections 272 to 276 of the 1996 Act outline several *special provisions* and additional opportunities open to the BOCs in the new competitive environment once they obtain approval of their separate 271 applications. The sections include:

272: Separate affiliate, safeguards
273: Manufacturing by Bell Operating Companies
274: Electronic publishing by Bell Operating Companies
275: Alarm-monitoring services
276: Provision of payphone service

Fourteen-Point Checklist, § 271(c)(2)(B)
The 1996 Act, Section § 271(c)(2)(B), is titled the "Competitive Checklist," but, as discussed earlier, it is also known as the "271 Fourteen-Point Checklist."[95] Its purpose is to answer the question of When does sufficient competition exist in a market to allow the Bell Operating Company in that market to be able to

enter the restricted lines of businesses of out-of-region long distance, manufacturing of equipment or other services? Is the answer 10%, 40%, or 50%. By how many companies? The passage of § 271 is the benchmark adopted to answer these important questions, and thus it is critical to both the incumbent local exchange carriers and the competitive exchange carriers.

The checklist identifies fourteen items, that the Bell Operating Company must convince the FCC that it has met or accomplished in each state in which it provides local service as the incumbent local exchange carrier. The burden of proof rests on each Bell Operating Company to prove that it has adequately enabled competition in that local market. Table 3.2 on page 77 provides a summary of the 14 points. As can be noted from Table 3.2, the first two of the 14 points repeat two of the duties placed on all incumbent local exchange carriers: (1) proof that the Bell Operating Company has provided nondiscriminatory access for its competitors to its network elements, and (2) proof that it adequately interconnects with all competitors who request interconnection. The next 8 points, points 3 through 11, list the eight network elements identified in the FCC's *First Report and Order*. The Bell Operating Company (BOC) must show that it has made each element available in a nondiscriminatory manner and at a *reasonable price*. The last 3 of the 14 points, numbers 12 through 14, check that the requirements for interconnection, reciprocal compensation, and resale at a wholesale rate have been adequately met. The 14 points are as follows:

Access or interconnection provided or generally offered by a Bell operating company [BOC] to other telecommunications carriers must include each of the following requirements:

1. Interconnection: The BOC must show that it has adequately interconnected with the facilities and equipment and meets the requirements of sections 251(c)(2) and 252(d)(1).

2. Nondiscriminatory access to network elements: The BOC must show that it is offering nondiscriminatory access to unbundled network elements (UNEs) in accordance with the requirements of sections 251(c)(3) and 252(d)(1).

3. Nondiscriminatory access to the poles, ducts, conduits, and rights-of-way owned or controlled by the Bell Operating Company: The BOC must show that it is providing nondiscriminatory access to its poles, ducts, conduits and rights-of-way at just and reasonable rates in accordance with the requirements of section 224.

4. Local loop transmission from the central office to the customer's premises: The BOC must show that it has unbundled local loop transmission from local switching or other services, and is providing it as an unbundled service to its competitors on a nondiscriminatory basis at a fair and reasonable price.

5. Local transport from the trunk side of a wireline local exchange carrier switch: The BOC must show that it has unbundled from switching or other services.

6. Local switching: The BOC must show that it has unbundled local switching from transport, local loop transmission, or other services.

7. Nondiscriminatory access to—The BOC must show that it has unbundled 911 and E911 services; directory assistance services; and operator call completion services.

8. White pages: The BOC must show that it has unbundled directory listings for customers of the other carrier's telephone exchange service.

9. Until the date by which telecommunications numbering administration guidelines, plan, or rules are established, nondiscriminatory access to telephone numbers for assignment to the other carrier's telephone exchange service customers. After that date, compliance with such guidelines, plan, or rules.

10. Nondiscriminatory access to databases and associated signaling necessary for call routing and completion.

11. Until the date by which the Commission issues regulations pursuant to section 251 to require number portability, interim telecommunications number portability through remote call forwarding, direct inward dialing trunks, or other comparable arrangements, with as little impairment of functioning, quality, reliability, and convenience as possible. After that date, full compliance with such regulations.

12. Nondiscriminatory access to such services or information as are necessary to allow the requesting carrier to implement local dialing parity in accordance with the requirements of Subsection 251(b)(3).

13. Reciprocal compensation arrangements in accordance with the requirements of Subsection 252(d)(2).

14. Resale at wholesale rates. Telecommunications services are available for resale in accordance with the requirements of Subsections 251(c)(4) and 252(d)(3).

The "271" Approval Process, § 271(d)

Although the Bell Operating Company must pass its 14-Point Checklist in each state, it is not the state PUC that makes the determination. Instead, the written application is approved by the FCC. However, the FCC does not make a unilateral decision. Instead it "consults" with two groups before it makes its decision: the PUC in the state concerned with the Bell Operating Company's application, and the attorney general at the U.S. Department of Justice. The question asked of the Department of Justice is primarily whether the Bell Operating Company is under investigation for corporate misdeeds, such as tax evasion, fraud, or sexual discrimination, and thus whether it is a good corporate citizen before the Bell Operating Company can be cleared to enter into other markets. The law requires that the Department of Justice respond within 30 days, which is reasonable given that the Department of Justice can simply check its records for past and current proceedings.

The question asked of the state PUC, on the other hand, is whether the Bell Operating Company has adequately met the 14 points in *that* state. Pursuant to state and federal Administrative Procedure Acts (APAs),[96] the PUC cannot unilaterally answer this question. Instead it must hold hearings to consider comments on the issue from the public, affected competitors such as AT&T, MCI, Sprint,

and other competitive local exchange carriers, and any other party with standing. However, a public hearing requires at least 20 days notice before the hearing can begin, and for some reason, the 1996 Act only provided 20 days for the state to respond to the FCC's request for comment. Recognizing this conflict in timing, the telecommunications industry came up with a unique solution. The National Association of Regulatory Utility Commissioners (NARUC) drafted a "best practices letter" to be sent to the corporate executive officer of each affected Bell Operating Company, suggesting that it provide a 90-day *prior notice* to its state PUC *before* the Bell Operating Company made application to the FCC. This would allow the PUC time to hold the hearings and determine a response before the Bell Operating Company applied for "271" clearance from the FCC. All Bell Operating Companies readily agreed to do this since it was in their best interests. Without such correction in the timetable, the Bell Operating Companies would have great difficulty "passing their 271" at the FCC.

Once the FCC has the proper information, it then considers the responses and must make its determination on each Bell Operating Company's application within 90 days. Within 10 days following its approval, the FCC must publish a brief description of the determination in the Federal Register.[97] Once a Bell Operating Company passes its 271 requirements, it can become a full competitor in all markets, just as other companies.

CHALLENGES TO THE CONSTITUTIONALITY OF SECTION 271 REQUIREMENTS

Frustrated by the difficulty of clearing the Section 271 hurdle, the Bell Operating Companies challenged the constitutionality of Section 271. The process involved several steps.[98] As the Fifth Circuit Court of Appeals described it:

> On April 11, 1997, plaintiff SBC Communications, which is of course one of the RBOCs (Regional Bell Operating Companies), applied to the FCC pursuant to § 271 to have the long distance line-of-business restriction lifted for its local service area of Oklahoma. The FCC

determined that the statutory criteria had not been met, and therefore denied the application on June 26, 1997. SBC appealed the ruling to the D.C. Circuit, where it was affirmed on March 20, 1998.[99]

Without waiting for the outcome of that appeal, however, on July 2, 1997, SBC and its subsidiaries filed suit against the United States and the FCC in the Federal District Court for the Northern District of Texas, alleging that all of the Special Provisions were facially unconstitutional under the Bill of Attainder and Equal Protection Clauses [of the U.S. Constitution] and that § 274 violated the Free Speech Clause as well. Several long distance companies, including MCI Telecommunications Corp., Sprint Communications Company, and AT&T, the BOCs' erstwhile parent, intervened on the government's side in the dispute, and two other RBOCs, U.S. West Communications and Bell Atlantic Corp., intervened on SBC's. Bell Atlantic added a slightly more nuanced separation of powers challenge to SBC's other constitutional complaints.[100]

On December 31, 1997, ruling on cross-motions for summary judgment, District Judge Kendall held that the Special Provisions constituted an unconstitutional bill of attainder and that they were severable from the rest of the Act. He therefore granted SBC's motion and declared the challenged sections void."[101]

The United States, the FCC, and the defendant-intervenors appealed to the United States Court of Appeals for the Fifth Circuit. The Fifth Circuit Court of Appeals reviewed the constitutionality of the federal statute *de novo* and, on September 4, 1998, reversed the lower court, holding that the special provisions are constitutional.[102] Since *bill of attainder* is a less familiar term, it warrants additional explanation.

Bill of Attainder
Article I, sec. 9, cl. 3 of the United States Constitution provides that "[n]o Bill of Attainder or ex post facto law shall be passed [by Congress]. Article I, sec. 10, cl. 1 contains a parallel provision applicable to the states."

The term, *bill of attainder*, is not a commonly used or understood phrase, so as

> the Supreme Court has often clarified, [i]n forbidding bills of attainder, the draftsmen of the Constitution sought to prohibit the ancient practice of the Parliament in England of punishing without trial 'specifically designated persons or groups.'[103] Consistent with this characterization, the Court has generally defined a bill of attainder as 'a law that legislatively determines guilt and inflicts punishment upon an identified individual without provision of the protections of a judicial trial.'[104] Where, as here [in the Special Provisions in the 1996 Act], the liability in question clearly attaches by operation of the legislative act alone, the constitutional test may be summarized in the following two-pronged test: First, has the legislature acted with specificity? Second, has it imposed punishment?[105]

Concerning the first prong, *specificity,* the U.S. Fifth Circuit Court of Appeals, stated that

> Notwithstanding beguiling arguments that support the district court's holding, at bottom, we simply cannot find a constitutional violation in this case. Even assuming that the Bill of Attainder Clause applies to [specific] corporations, and even assuming that the Special Provisions are sufficient to meet the specificity prong of the test, there simply cannot be a bill of attainder unless it is also the case that the Special Provisions impose punishment on the BOCs."[106]

Concerning the second prong, *punishment,* the Fifth Circuit discussed the various arguments and held that

> For all of the foregoing reasons, we find that the Special Provisions ultimately are nonpunitive as an historical, functional, and motivational matter. They are therefore not an unconstitutional and odious bill of

attainder as that term has been defined by the Supreme Court. To the extent that the district court concluded otherwise, it was in error, and its decision on that point is accordingly reversed."[107]

As noted above, however, SBC and the other appellees also urge three additional constitutional arguments as alternate bases for affirming the judgment of the district court. Having found the Special Provisions not to constitute a bill of attainder, we must obviously consider these alternate theories. We do so only briefly, however, as they are far less substantial."[108]

Separation of Powers

First, the appellees contend that the Special Provisions violate separation of powers because they address themselves to a particular judicial consent decree—the MFJ—in such a way as to alter the result. They rely on the well accepted rule that it violates separation of powers principles for Congress to reopen any adjudication that represents the "'final word of the judicial department' on a case. Yet under Pennsylvania v. Wheeling and Belmont Bridge Co., 59 U.S. (18 How.) 421, 15 L.Ed. 435 (1855), it has long been clear that Congress may change the law underlying ongoing equitable relief, even if, as in Wheeling itself, the change is specifically targeted at and limited in applicability to a particular injunction, and even if the change results in the necessary lifting of that injunction. … In the light of [numerous precedents], we simply cannot see a separation-of-powers problem based on the Special Provisions' interference with the MFJ in this case."[109]

Therefore, the "Special provisions of Telecommunications Act of 1996 imposing line-of-business restrictions on named Bell operating companies (BOCs) do not violate the constitutional requirement of separation of powers by replacing restrictions imposed by judicial consent decree."[110]

Equal Protection Clause

The appellees next argued that the Special Provisions violate the Equal Protection Clause by discriminating against the BOCs by name. Under City of New Orleans v. Dukes, *427 U.S. 297, 96 S.Ct. 2513, 49 L.Ed.2d 511 (1976), however, specification of named parties in economic regulation is clearly permissible for equal protection purposes so long as the regulation is rationally related to a legitimate governmental interest and does not trammel fundamental personal rights or draw upon inherently suspect distinctions such as race, religion, or alianage. As should be manifest from the entire history of this area of the law, regulation of an LEC's conduct in the local telephone service market neither restricts fundamental individual rights nor lacks rational relation to the government's legitimate interest in ensuring greater competition in all telecommunications markets. Furthermore, the specification of the BOCs in the Special Provisions at issue here was not based on invidious criteria like race, religion, or alienage. As such, the Special provisions are not inconsistent with the Equal Protection Clause.*[111]

Bell Operating Companies' Right to Free Speech

Finally, the appellees urge that, even if the other Special Provisions are allowed to stand, § 274 must go as it impermissibly infringes the Bell Operating Companies' right to free speech. The D.C. Circuit Court recently rejected an identical challenge to § 274 by another regional Bell Operating Company, however, see BellSouth, 144 F.3d at 67–71, and we can find no reason to disagree with the result and analysis. Because § 274 does not in any way differentiate speech on the basis of content, its speech restricting provisions are subject only to (at most) intermediate scrutiny review under *Turner Broadcasting System, Inc. v. FCC*, 512 U.S. 622, 642, 114 S.Ct. 2445, 129 L.Ed.2d 497 (1994) (Turner I). Under that standard, a restriction will be upheld if it advances important governmental interests unrelated to the suppression of free speech and does not burden substantially more speech than necessary to further those interest. Obviously the competition-embracing interests discussed above are manifestly sufficient to meet the first hurdle. Furthermore, because § 274 merely imposes a structural separation requirement on speech activities, not an absolute bar, its restrictions are practically de minimis in this necessarily corporate context, and certainly do not burden substantially more speech than necessary to accomplish its legitimate goals. For these reasons, the contention that § 274 violates the BOCs right to free speech is entirely lacking in merit.[112]

CONCLUSION

The details, duties, and obligations incorporated in the Telecommunications Act of 1996 create the most extensive change in U.S. communications law since 1934. While the Act is constantly being challenged and refined, it is important for participants in the telecommunications industry to understand the Act in order to more fully evaluate the opportunities and restrictions that it presents to them. This understanding also assists participants in analyzing the ongoing issues as discussed in Chapter Four.

NOTES

1. The author sincerely thanks Roger Newell, J.D., a colleague at Telecommunications Research Associates (TRA), for Mr. Newell's and TRA's permission to use in this chapter the materials developed by Mr. Newell summarizing the duties and obligations of telecommunications carriers. Mr. Newell can be reached at *www.rnewell@tra.com.* TRA can be reached at *www.tra.com* or 1-800-872-4736 in St. Marys, Kansas.

2. Telecommunications Act of 1996, Pub. L. No. 104–104, purpose statement, 110 Stat. 56, 56 (1996) [hereinafter Telecommunications Act of 1996].

3. The Telecommunications Act of 1996 was sent to Congress for enactment on January 3, 1996 as S. 652. Its final form was a compromise created by the Conference Committee from versions drafted by the House of Representatives (HR) in HR Report 104–458, 104th Congress, 2d Session, and the Senate in Senate Report S. 652, 104th, 2d Session, passed on July 19, 1995, and printed on June 23, 1995 [hereinafter S.652].

4. The MFJ refers to the order entered August 24, 1982, in the antitrust action *United States v. Western Electric,* Civil Action No. 82-0192, in the United States District Court for the District of Columbia and implemented on January 1, 1984 [hereinafter MFJ]. The term "AT&T Consent Decree" was substituted for "Modification of Final Judgment" in the Joint Explanatory Statement "in order to characterize more accurately the intent of the Senate bill and House-amendment with respect to the supersession issues addressed in title VI. In Section 3(a)(34) of the 1996 Act, the term 'AT&T Consent Decree' includes any judgment or order with respect to such action entered on or after August 24, 1982" [hereinafter AT&T Consent Decree].

5. Telecommunications Act of 1996, *supra* note 2, at § 601(a).

6. MFJ, *supra* note 4.

7. Iowa Utilities Bd. v. FCC, 109 F.3d 418, 421 (8th Cir. 1996) [hereinafter Iowa I].

8. S. 652, *supra* note 3, at § 5.

9. 47U.S.C. §251(c)(2)(B).

10. 47 U.S.C. § 251(c)(2)(D), 252 and 271.

11. Telecommunications Act of 1996, *supra* note 2, at § 706(a).

12. *See, for example,* 47 U.S.C. § 251(d)(1) (1996).

13. *See, for example,* 47 U.S.C. §§ 251(d)(3), 251(f), and 252 (1996).

14. 47 U.S. C. §§ 251(d)(1), 251(d)(3), 251(f), and 252 (1996).

15. The changes are codified at 47 U.S.C. § 153 (1996).

16. Kevin Werbach, Counsel for New Technology Policy, *The Digital Tornado: The Internet and Telecommunications Policy,* FCC, Office of Plans and Policy, Working Paper No. 29, March 1997, at 30.

17. Telecommunications Act of 1996, *supra* note 2, at §714.

18. *Id.* at § 3(a)(2)(48); codified at 47 U.S.C. § 153(43) 1996).

19. *Id.* at § 3(a)(2)(51), codified at 47 U.S.C. § 153(46) (1996).

20. *Id.* at § 3(a)(2X49), codified at 47 U.S.C. § 153(44) (1996).

21. *Id.* at § 714(k)(3).

22. *Id.* at § 3(a)(2)(44), codified at 47 U.S.C. § 153(26) (1996).

23. *Id.* at § 3(a)(2)(40), codified at 47 U.S.C. § 153(16) (1996).

24. *Id.* at § 3(a)(2)(44), codified at 47 U.S.C. §§ 153 (26), (27), and (33) (1996).

25. *Id.* at § 704, codified at 47 U.S.C. § 332(c) (1996).

26. *Id.* at § 251(h)(1) (1996).

27. 47 U.S.C. §251(h)(2) (1996).

28. 47 U.S.C. § 251(h)(1)(B)(i) (1996).

29. Telecommunications Act of 1996, *supra* note 2, at § 3(a)(2)(47), codified at 47 U.S.C. § 153(37) (1996).

30. *Id.* at § 251(9(1), codified at 47 U.S.C. § 251(f) (1) (1996).

31. *Id.* at § 3(a)(2)(35), codified at 47 U.S.C. § 153(4) (1996).

32. *Id.* at § 3(a)(2)(50), codified at 47 U.S.C. § 153(45) (1996).

33. *Id.* at § 3(a)(2)(38), codified at 47 U.S.C. § 153(14) 1996).

34. 47 U.S.C. § 251(c)(2) (1996).

35. 47 U.S.C. § 251(c)(3) (1996).

36. 47 U.S.C. § 251(c)(4). *See also,* Iowa Utilities Board v. FCC, 120 F.3d 753, 753 (1997) [hereinafter Iowa II].

37. *Id.* at note 3.

38. Telecommunications Act of 1996, *supra* note 2, at § 251(c)(2), codified at 47 U.S.C. § 251(c) (2) (1996).

39. 47 U.S.C. § 251(c)(3) (1996).

40. 47 U.S.C. § 251(c)(4) (1996).

41. Notice of Proposed Rulemaking (NPRM) Concerning Implemention of the Local Competition Provisions in the Telecommunications Act of 1996, CC Docket No. 96–98 (May 1996). [hereinafter May 1996 FCC NPRM to implement 1996 Act].

42. First Report and Order, Implementation of the Local Competition Provisions in the Telecommunications Act of 1996, CC Docket No. 96–98 (Aug. 8, 1996) [hereinafter August 8, 1996, FCC Order implementing 1996 Act].

43. Iowa II, *supra* note 36, at note 6.

44. *Id.* at 755–756.

45. *Id.*

46. *Id.* at note 7 citing § 251(b)(5) of the 1996 Act.

47. *Id.* at 754–755.

48. See 28 U.S.C. § 2112(a)(3) (1994).

49. Iowa I, *supra* note 7, motion to vacate stay denied, 117 S. Ct. 429 (1996).

50. 47 U.S.C. § 252(i); 47 C.F.R. § 51.809.

51. Federal Communications Commission and the United States, applicants, v. Iowa Utilities Board, et al., No. A-299, Nov. 12, 1996 [Former decision, 117 S.Ct. 378]; and the Association for Local Telecommunications Services, et al., applicants, v. Iowa Utilities Board, et al., No. A-300, Nov. 12, 1996 (Former decision, 117 S.Ct. 379).

52. Iowa II, *supra* note 36.

53. Telecommunications Act of 1996, *supra* note 2, at § 252, codified at 47 U.S.C. § 252 (1996).

54. *Id.* at §§ 251(c)(1), 252(a)(1), codified at 47 U.S.C. §§ 251(c)(1), 252(a)(1) (1996).

55. 47 U.S.C. § 252 (1996).

56. Telecommunications Act of 1996, *supra* note 2, at Title 1, Subtitles A and B.

57. 47 U.S.C. SS 202–276 entitled Title II— Common Carriers.

58. 47 U.S.C. §§ 251–261.

59. Telecommunications Act of 1996, *supra* note 2, at §§ 271–276, codified at 47 U.S.C. §§ 271–276.

60. 47 U.S.C. § 153(44) (1996).

61. Telecommunications Act of 1996, *supra* note 2, at § 251(a)(1), codified at 47 U.S.C. § 251(a) (1) (1996).

62. Communications Act of 1934, 47 U.S.C. § 201(a).

63. Telecommunications Act of 1996, *supra* note 2, at § 251(a)(1), codified at 47 U.S.C. 251(a)(1) (1996).

64. *Id.* at § 251(a)(2), citing § 255, codified at 47 U.S.C. § 251(a)(2) (1996).

65. *Id.* at § 255, codified at 47 U.S.C. § 255 (1996).

66. *Id.* at § 251(a)(2), citing § 256, codified at 47 U.S.C. § 251(a)(2) (1996).

67. *Id.* at § 256.

68. 47 U.S.C. §251(f) (1996).

69. Joint Explanatory Statement of the Committee of Conference, Conference Agreement on New Section 251—Interconnection (1996).

70. Telecommunications Act of 1996, *supra* note 2, at § 251(b)(1), codified at 47 U.S.C. § 251(b)(1) (1996).

71. *AT&T Competitive Strategy,* Wall St. J., June 12, 1996.

72. Telecommunications Act of 1996, *supra* note 2, at § 251(b)(2); codified at 47 U.S.C. § 251(b)(2) (1996).

73. *Id.* at § 3(46); codified at 47 U.S.C. § 153(30) (1996).

74. *Id.* at § 251(b)(3); codified at 47 U.S.C. § 251(b)(3) (1996).

75. *Id.* at § 3 (39); 47 U.S.C. § 153(15) (1996).

76. 47 U.S.C. §251(b)(3) (1996).

77. Telecommunications Act of 1996, *supra* note 2, at § 3 (45); 47 U.S.C. § 153(29) (1996).

78. *In re* Implementation of the Local Competition Provisions in the Telecommunications Act of 1996, First Report and Order, FCC 96-325, 11 FCC Red 15499, 1996 FCC LEXIS 4312 (1996).

79. Telecommunications Act of 1996, *supra* note 2, at § 251(b)(4); codified at 47 U.S.C. § 251(b)(4) (1996).

80. *Id.* at § 251(b)(5); codified at 47 U.S.C. § 251(b)(5) (1996).

81. *Id.* at § 251(c)(1); codified at 47 U.S.C. § 251(c)(1) (1996).

82. *Id.* at § 251(c)(2); codified at 47 U.S.C. § 251(c)(2) (1996).

83. *Id.* at § 251(c)(3); codified at 47 U.S.C. § 251(c)(3) (1996).

84. *Id.* at § 251(c)(4); codified at 47 U.S.C. § 251(c)(4) (1996).

85. *Id.* at § 3(35); codified at 47 U.S.C. § 135 (4) (1996).

86. *Id.* at § 3(33); codified at 47 U.S.C. § 135 (1) (1996).

87. 47 U.S.C. § 271(d)(3) (1996).

88. 47 U.S.C. §271(i)(1) (1996).

89. 47 U.S.C. § 271(b)(2) (1996).

90. Telecommunications Act of 1996, *supra* note 2, at § 3(42); codified at 47 U.S.C. § 135 (21) (1996).

91. *Id.* at § 3(43); codified at 47 U.S.C. § 135 (25) (1996).

92. Joint Explanatory Statement of the Committee of Conference, Conference Agreement on New Section 271 (1996).

93. 47 U.S.C. §271(g) (1996).

94. 47 U.S.C. § 271(b)(3) (1996).

95. Telecommunications Act of 1996, *supra* note 2, at § 271(c)(2)(B); codified at 47 U.S.C. § 271(c)(2)(B) (1996).

96. Administrative Procedure Act, 60 Stat. 237, (5 U.S.C).

97. 47 U.S.C. §271(d)(5) (1996).

98. Eric M. Swedenburg, *Promoting Competition in the TC Market: Why the FCC Should Adopt a Less Stringent Approach to 271*, Cornell L. Rev., V. 8, at 1418, 1420 (1999).

99. SBC Communications, Inc. v. FCC, 154 F.3d 226, 232–233 (5th Cir. 1998), describing SBC Communications, Inc. v. FCC, 138 F.3d 410 (D.C. Cir. 1998).

100. *Id.* 154 F.3d 226, 233 (5th Cir. 1998).

101. *Id.*

102. United States v. Bailey, 115 F.3d 1222, 1225 (5th Cir. 1997), *de novo* review: as cited in SBC Communications, Inc. v. FCC, *supra* note 99, at 233.

103. Selective Service v. Minnesota Public Interest Research Group, 468 U.S. 841, 847 (1984) (quoting United States v. Brown, 381 U.S. 437, 447 (1965)).

104. *Id.,* quoting Nixon v. Administrator of General Services, 433 U.S. 425, 468 (1977).

105. SBC Communications, Inc. v. FCC, *supra* note 99, at 233.

106. *Id.* at 234, citing Plaut v. Spendthrift Farm, Inc., 514 U.S. 211(1995).

107. *Id.* at 244.

108. *Id.*

109. *Id.*

110. *Id.* at 221.

111. *Id.* at 246.

112. *Id.* at 247.

Interconnecting the Network of Networks

Eli M. Noam

Period of No Agreements in the United States

Interconnection is not a new issue but goes back a full century. Control over interconnection was used to establish the monopoly system, as it was later used to introduce competition.

In 1876 Alexander Graham Bell, a teacher of the deaf in Boston, introduced a workable telephone. One year later Bell's father-in-law and other investors launched the Bell Telephone Company, later renamed AT&T, after its long-distance subsidiary. Various Bell companies were franchised across the country.

Once the basic Bell patents expired in the 1890s, independent competitors entered those areas not serviced by Bell concessioners, especially in underserved rural districts and in central business districts. Between 1894 and 1902, 3,039 commercial companies and 979 mutual associations and farmer cooperatives were formed to enter the U.S. telephone industry.[1] By 1904 independents competed head-to-head against Bell in communities in New York, Texas, Illinois, and California.[2] In several cities multiple systems competed side by side without interconnection.[3]

After a few years the independents were nearly equal in size to Bell and covered a much greater geographical area. Robust competition existed not only in the provision of local service but also in the manufacturing of switching and customer equipment manufacture. However, the independents were far from being on an equal par with the Bell System. The main difference between the Bell System and the independents was interconnection. While the Bell Telephone system was fully interconnected on a national level through its long-distance network of AT&T Long Lines, the independents operated on a fairly limited regional scale.

After 1894 the Bell Company's policy was to refuse interconnection to the independents. By denying interconnection the Bell company was attempting to establish dominance. Its strategy centered on the *control of interconnection*: of equipment into their network, of rival local networks into the Bell local networks, and of rival networks to the Bell long-distance system. Without regulatory intervention to contest its control over interconnection into its networks, AT&T was able to keep the independents at bay. Plans for new long-distance entrants did not succeed, partly because they too were denied interconnection into the Bell local networks. In 1897 independent forms attempted to put together a long-distance network to connect its members. However, nothing came of it.

Period of Contracted Agreements

In 1902 the Bell Company changed its policy and used its power over interconnection to manage a cartel instead of establishing a full monopoly. Bell agreed to allow interconnection to its toll lines and exchanges with three conditions: the independent could not be located in a town with a Bell exchange, the independent had to lease Bell-manufactured instruments, and the independent could not interconnect with the toll lines of Bell competitors. For its part, Bell would not compete with nor provide service to a direct competitor of the independent telco.[4]

The terms of the agreements greatly favored the Bell system in a number of ways. Contracting independent telcos were limited to the territories that did not infringe on Bell's territories,[5] mostly rural areas of no commercial interest to Bell. Bell could set high equipment standards, thus protecting itself against being undercut in price by lower-quality independents. Bell gained access to the independents' customers, thereby enhancing the value of telephone service for its now customers. And Bell preempted the development of rival long-distance carriers and, in part, could head off regulation.

Road to Regulated Interconnection

AT&T preferred to grant interconnection through a contractual agreements because this allowed it to exercise its bargaining power. In contrast, the independents preferred interconnection as a matter of *right* and sought mandatory interconnection supervised by the state. This scenario is classic, and it has reappeared around the world. In 1904 a high federal court ruled that a state could mandate the interconnection of a rival network. By 1910 five states required interconnection, and by 1915 more than thirty states.[6] All still do today.

The politics of interconnection, however, were convoluted. Many of the independents only wanted to obtain interconnection rights into long-distance networks but did not want to give interconnection rights into their own local networks, where they had market power. Thus, in Wisconsin, both Bell *and* the independent companies opposed interconnection requirements in each state legislative session between 1901 and 1909.[7] Market power soon led

to the establishment of a regulatory system of utility commissions on the state level which supervised privately owned utilities, including telephone companies. This arrangement contrasted sharply with the system of national and state-owned telephone administrations emerging in most other countries.

In the absence of any state interconnection requirements, customers often subscribed to two telephone companies. Usually an independent phone would be used for local service, and the Bell system would be used for toll calls. In La Crosse, Wisconsin, 80 percent of all subscribers had a subscription with both Wisconsin Bell and the local independent. Unhappy with this situation, the citizenry petitioned the State Regulatory Commission to order interconnection. The Wisconsin Bell Company opposed the petition, questioning the Commission's right to order interconnection on the grounds that regulated interconnection would deny a company equal protection of the law and trial by jury, and that it would constitute taking of property without due process of law and without due compensation. Bell also argued that mandated interconnection would lead to a technically inferior network, interfere with interstate commerce, and expose confidential business information.[8]

Nevertheless, the Wisconsin Commission mandated interconnection[9] based on a 1911 state law, finding, as the law required that (1) the connection was required by public convenience and necessity, and (2) that it would not result in irreparable injury to the owner or users of the network, or to the service.[10] The statute also required the companies to negotiate appropriate interconnection charges. When the parties predictably failed to reach such an agreement, the Commission set the rate for interconnection at 5 cents per local telephone call, 10 cents for calls between 50 and 100 miles, and 15 cents for calls over longer distances.[11] In other words, the interconnection charges were value based, not cost based. Wisconsin Bell took the case all the way to the U.S. Supreme Court, but lost.[12]

After the Wisconsin statute, interconnection soon moved to the federal level of government. Several independent telephone companies brought antitrust complaints against AT&T, based on its refusal to offer interconnection, and they were joined by the Justice Department in 1913. Under pressure AT&T chose to negotiate an agreement with them, known as the *Kingsbury Commitment*, making the U.S. government a partner in its cartel. Under its terms, AT&T guaranteed existing independent telephone companies interconnection to its long distance network and agreed not to expand geographically by acquiring competitors or entering their territories. AT&T also promised to limit its activities to communications and to leave the telegraphy market, where it had acquired the previously dominant telecommunication company, Western Union. The Kingsbury Commitment's interconnection requirement for the Bell System applied only to long distance toll calls of more than 50 miles, and for these calls customers had to pay a surcharge of 10 cents in addition to normal toll rates.[13]

The Kingsbury Commitment stabilized the industry. AT&T granted the independents interconnection, this time as a matter of right, in return for joining an AT&T led cartel. Under the Kingsbury Commitment, a system of de facto exclusive franchises emerged in which only one telephone company served any particular area. That company was protected from rival entry because no rival had a right to interconnection.

In effect, the policy of Theodore Vail, AT&T's president, allowed interconnection to sublicensees of Bell but linked the independent telcos in the role of cooperating junior partners. In return for its cooperation, Bell protected the local independent's monopoly by denying interconnection to another telco in the same territory. Thus the independents now had an interest in an effective Bell system as an interconnecting agent, technology driver, standard setter, and, ultimately, cartel enforcer. As a result of the interconnection requirement contained in the Kingsbury Commitment, the telephone industry moved from extensive competition to extensive oligopolistic cooperation.

Once the collaborative cartel system was established, price and service competition declined. This historic episode illustrates that the creation of interconnection, by itself, does not necessarily bring about competition, and can in fact lead to close cooperation that turns new carriers into complements rather than competitors.[14] Thus interconnection does not assure competition, but the lack of such interconnection has historically prevented its emergence. Interconnection has been a necessary but not sufficient condition for competitive telecommunications.

Establishment of a Regulatory System

The U.S. government's action in seeking in 1913 the Kingsbury Commitment, which was designed to limit AT&T from total market dominance, was part of a general trend of antitrust policy. Americans had become concerned with the enormous growth of business entities in the decades following the Civil War, and a strong populist current opposed domination by big firms. This distrust was shared by the political left, midwest farmers, small businesses, and westerners. That sentiment also led roughly at that time to the emergence of regulatory commissions.

Soon after regulatory commissions were established in telecommunications, their pro-competition rationale gave way to the desire to stabilize the monopoly system in return for universal service. In 1918 the California state public utility commission supported the position that "there should be one universal service, as this will enable complete interchange of communication … this [is] in addition to the usual advantages of consolidation of utility properties resulting from the elimination of duplicate property and duplicate operating expense."[15]

Similarly the Missouri Public Service Commission concluded in 1919 that while "competition between public service corporations was in vogue for many years as the proper method of securing the best results for the public … The consensus of modern opinion, however, is that competition has failed to bring the results desired … Nearly all of the states in this country have adopted laws providing for the regulation of public service corporations … It is the purpose of such laws to require public service corporations to give adequate service at reasonable rates, rather than to depend upon competition to bring such results."[16]

Thus supported by public policy and a wide political coalition, AT&T's dominance grew. By 1934 AT&T built and owned 80 percent of all telephones and access lines in the United States and operated the only national long-distance network. The remaining

20 percent of the market were serviced by about 2,000 mostly small and rural independents, interconnecting into AT&T and sharing in the periphery of the monopoly. Competing local telcos rarely persisted until in 1945 the last remnant of competitive local loop service in the United States, the Keystone Telephone Company in Philadelphia, shut down.

Equipment Interconnection: The Beginning of Interconnection as a Tool for Competition

For over seventy years AT&T's control over interconnection provided it with the tools to establish a monopoly shared with small independent carriers. This control was sanctioned by federal and state regulatory bodies. However, the power that AT&T had ceded to the government to regulate interconnection had the potential to turn against it. This began to happen in the 1960s, and interconnection now became a tool for destabilizing AT&T. Interconnection policy moved into its second stage, that of opening markets.

As soon as the Federal Communications Commission was created in 1934, one of its members investigated AT&T's vertical integration. The charges, which were presented in the "Walker Report," asserted that AT&T had created a monopoly over equipment manufacturing through its control over the interconnection of such equipment. The business purpose behind such vertical integration went beyond operational advantages, which economists describe as economies of scope. It enabled AT&T to shift earnings to the unregulated-manufacturing activities and away from the profit-regulated network services, and to shift costs in the other direction. In other words, the regulated networks overpaid for their equipment, thereby deflating the profits subject to regulatory ceilings. The Walker Report hence recommended a divestiture of AT&T's manufacturing arm, the Western Electric company. However, the position found only limited support on the full FCC and World War II soon thereafter delayed any follow-up. But after the war, under President Truman, the Justice Department filed an antitrust suit against AT&T, in 1949, seeking to split off equipment manufacturing.

Intervention by the Defense Department, as well as the 1952 Presidential election, stalled the case. In 1956, under a more supportive Republican administration, AT&T achieved a favorable settlement. It was not forced to divest its Western Electric manufacturing arm or to open up to non-AT&T equipment, but its activities were limited to telephony. Western Electric was confined to telephone-related research and manufacturing operations, and was ordered to establish a more liberal policy in the licensing of its patents. Overall, despite the fact that it had to close some of its routes of expansion, AT&T had succeeded in avoiding a potentially disastrous antitrust judgment. Furthermore the government's main concern was the shifting of profits, namely an issue of price regulation, rather than the opening of the equipment market. However, this changed soon.

After 1956 the United States hesitantly began a policy of entry and interconnection. The Communications Act of 1934 authorizes the FCC to mandate interconnection when this is in the public interest. Under pressure from both the electronics industry—whose importance grew with World War II, the Korean conflict, and the consumer prosperity of the 1950s—equipment interconnection ceased to be unthinkable. The two key decisions were *Hush-A-Phone*[17] and *Carterfone*,[18] which allowed non-AT&T equipment to be owned by customers and to be connected to the network. In *Hush-A-Phone*, AT&T had even prohibited the attachment of a plastic cap to the telephone handset, whose function was to shield the conversation from background noise. In *Carterfone*, AT&T had banned a device that permitted the "patching" of radio calls into the network.

In response to *Carterfone*, AT&T required that non-AT&T equipment be attached through elaborate and expensive connection devices supplied only by AT&T. The FCC initially went along, despite howls of protests by the interconnectors. Consequently the market share for competitors' equipment increased only modestly, from 0.03 percent in 1969 to 3.7 percent in 1974.[19]

With equipment competition stalled, the FCC reconsidered and turned to the National Academy of Sciences to investigate direct connection of competitor equipment to the network. Following recommendations, the FCC established in 1975 a registration and certification program as a substitute to AT&T's complex protective devices. Interconnection now would be permitted through standardized plugs, jacks and other standards for terminal equipment that were designed to prevent harm to the network. The installer of equipment had simply to attest to the work and to allow AT&T to inspect the work, if it so desired. The states' public utility commissions, egged on by AT&T, tried to overturn the FCC, arguing jurisdiction, consumer protection, and the loss of cross-subsidies. However, they lost in the courts, in the landmark case of *North Carolina Public Utilities Commission v. FCC*.[20]

The FCC's rules provide technical protection to ensure that the attached terminal equipment did not damage Bell system facilities, injure employees, or impair service to other users, as feared by AT&T. FCC "Part 68" rules set minimum equipment requirements, covering vibration, physical shock, voltage surges, signal leakage, signal power, and the like.

The Part 68 rules helped the interconnection equipment industry to take off. While in 1969 there were only four PBX vendors in the U.S. market, by 1980 more than 30 vendors existed.[21] Prices dropped, and options proliferated.

This liberalization affected primarily customer equipment. In contrast, for *network* equipment, mostly AT&T equipment was used because the AT&T network bought mostly its own equipment. Until 1984 the vast Bell System and all of its customers—comprising 80 percent of the total market equipment—were substantially closed to other suppliers because of the vertical integration with AT&T's manufacturing subsidiary, Western Electric. This changed with the AT&T divestiture in 1984. Many observers expected the RBOCs to cling to AT&T as their equipment supplier out of habit or convenience, but in fact, the RBOCs rapidly embraced non-AT&T equipment. AT&T's national market share for central office switches, in terms of revenues, dropped from 70 percent in 1983 to 53 percent in 1989, while Northern Telecom (Nortel) reached 40 percent.[22] In subsequent years, as the conflicts between AT&T and its RBOC progeny grew acrimonious, AT&T's equipment became disfavored by its customers/rivals. Eventually AT&T spun off its equipment operations as *Lucent Technologies*, which achieved a better market access.

Long-Distance Interconnection and the Demise of the Bell System

The interconnection of *equipment* is closely related to the interconnection of *carriers* because interconnected equipment may be merely the termination point for aggregated traffic by an alternative service provider or carrier. The issue in *Carterfone*, for example, had been the use of terminal equipment as an entry point of non-AT&T radio communications into the network by "patching" it in. Equipment interconnection had tended to be less strictly controlled in most other countries of the world than in the United States, since the vertical integration of manufacturing and networks was rare. However, when it came to the next chapter, the interconnection of long-distance networks, the United States began to move into uncharted waters.

World War II military research, especially in the radar field, had opened the microwave spectrum to communications. The availability of microwave transmission equipment drastically lowered economic and technological entry barriers and raised the demand by large organizations to provide for some of their own communications. In 1959 the FCC's *Above 890* regulatory decision[23] permitted large users to operate in-house microwave long-distance service. These users, typically large entities, felt that they were increasingly subsidizing local service and small customers, and they sought to move at least part of their traffic off the common system. Taking the next step, in 1969 one microwave delivery company, Microwave Communications, Inc. (MCI) won a court ruling against a reluctant FCC and an adamant AT&T to provide private line service for *other* users.[24] This set the stage for a battle over long-distance interconnection.

MCI soon wanted to expand beyond private line services into generally available public switched service. To do so successfully, it wanted to interconnect with AT&T's local networks in order to connect its subscribers to nonsubscribers, and vice versa. The FCC ruled against MCI, but MCI appealed the decision. MCI won its appeal with a ruling known as the *Execunet* decision (1978).[25] *Execunet* held that a common carrier such as AT&T has to provide access to all users, whether they are small residential households or competitors.

The logic of the equipment interconnection also spilled into enhanced services. It is hard to distinguish the interconnection of equipment such as computers from the computer-based enhanced services. As Peter Huber put it, an enhanced service is simply CPE sold retail, by the minute, rather than wholesale, by the pound.[26]

Thus, in 1974, the FCC permitted services by *value-added* networks that leased services from the common carrier and enhanced them with additional features and capabilities. Regular value-added services, in turn, are hard to distinguish from the simple resale of transmission capacity, if only minimal value is added.

Two years later, in 1976, the resale and shared use of interstate private lines were permitted, even where they did not add value. Previously AT&T was left to its own judgment as to whose resale it approved. AT&T had prohibited the resale and shared use by some private companies, but it leased lines to others, such as the telegraph company Western Union.[27] Through the FCC's actions, the reselling of domestic local and long-distance transmission became possible, extensive, and virtually unregulated.

Thus, by 1978, AT&T found itself, after almost a century of long-distance exclusivity, facing both facilities-based and resale competition in telephony.

Interconnected competition had cataclysmic effects on the U.S. telecommunications industry. Eventually it led to the breakup of the world's largest telecommunications company, AT&T. The breakup was brought about by a Justice Department antitrust suit filed in 1974, as well as a private antitrust case by MCI, which asserted that AT&T had used unfair practices to suppress its competitors, especially through discriminatory interconnection practices. The government's case resulted, after a 1982 consent decree, in the most massive corporate reorganization in business history. The divestiture agreement spun off AT&T's local Bell operating companies (the BOCs)—accounting for approximately two-thirds of the company's assets and employees—into seven regional holding companies (RHCs, often called "Baby Bells" or RBOCs). The RBOCs initially provided local exchange telephone and mobile service, but they increasingly sought other opportunities.

The government's main argument for splitting up AT&T was that it was inherently incapable of providing its long-distance competitors with equal interconnection to its local network. To buttress its case, the Justice Department introduced evidence of AT&T's resistance to competition through its unequal interconnection arrangements. Since regulatory requirements did not work in the face of AT&T persistence, it was necessary, the government argued, and the court basically agreed, to split off the company's local operations, which had been the source of its bottleneck power. Thus the resistance to interconnection brought down the world's foremost telecommunications provider.[28]

As a result of the divestiture decree (supervised by district judge Harold Greene and known more formally as the Modified Final Judgment, or MFJ), LECs had to grant equal access to all long-distance carriers and to all telephone users. Customers could indicate their "primary" carrier to which domestic and international long distance calls are automatically routed by a local exchange company offering service in the customer's region, or local access and transport area (LATA). Customers can also access carriers other than the primary carrier by dialing a prefixed number on a call-by-call basis. The LEC and an interexchange carrier (IXC) exchange traffic at the IXC's point of presence (POP).

By 1998 long-distance service, when it is defined as including intra-LATA interexchange service (i.e., short-haul toll calls), AT&T accounted for only 42 percent of the market. Using the narrower definition of long-distance inter-LATA service, AT&T's market share fell from 90 percent in 1984 to 51 percent in 1998.[29] RBOCs provide long distance within their own LATAs, accounting for about 15 percent of the long-distance market in 1998. Even if AT&T's market share remained quite substantial, its prices had to come down for the company to keep its share from eroding still further.[30]

The Modified Final Judgment required the LECs to provide adequate capacity to transport entrants' anticipated requirements and to provide signaling and directory assistance "equal in type and quality to that provided for the interexchange telecommunications services of AT&T and its affiliates."[31] Since dialing parity did not work in the older generation of electro mechanical switches, timetables were established for a transition to digital exchanges. The RBOCs had to offer substantial equal access by 1986, and others were required to grant equal access within three years of an IXC request. By 1989, 95 percent of all RBOC lines accommodated equal access. Correspondingly the share of "inferior" access minutes dropped from 16.7 percent in 1985 to 2.7 percent in 1989.[32]

AT&T's long-distance rates dropped by 40 to 45 percent in real terms in the 1980s. (However, the end-user line charge, which reduced the IXCs' access charges payable to the LECs, partly offset this.) Between 1986 and 1993, AT&T's volume increased at an average annual rate of 6.7 percent, but that of its competitors increased even faster, from a lower base.[33]

Marketing competition between IXCs to gain consumer market share became fierce, often more so than price competition. From gift certificates to free frequent flyer miles, interexchange carriers have tried to attract consumers in many ways. Retail prices stabilized and even increased briefly after 1996. But in 1998, a new wave of long-distance carriers, seeking to serve as Internet backbone providers, such as Qwest, Level 3, ICG, Metromedia, Global Crossing, and Williams, entered in a significant way; and the Bell companies' participation in long-distance service had been given a green legislative light, with Bell Atlantic first to gain regulatory approval in late 1999 in New York. Significantly, the approval for the Bell companies to offer long-distance service hinged on their offering full and nondiscriminatory interconnection to their own networks.

Thus the trend to open markets to rival networks through interconnection proceeded from equipment, resale, private long distance, switched long distance, to short-haul long distance, and, as we will see below, to local switching, and finally to local transmission.

Interconnection Regime after the 1996 Telecommunications Act

The 1996 Telecommunications Act, a comprehensive amendment to the Communications Act of 1934, changed many aspects of competition and regulation. A new section, entitled "Interconnection Requirements,"[34] was included in the law. BOCs were subject to several conditions on local competition before they could provide long-distance service within their regions. RBOCs had to comply with a "competitive checklist" of steps to open up the local market. Among others, they were required to provide interconnection to new entrants, unbundle their network, allow the resale of their services by competitors, and provide for number portability.

The Act directed the FCC to establish within six months the necessary rules and regulations for interconnection. After feverish efforts the FCC issued later that year a voluminous order on the "Implementation of the Local Competition Provisions in the Telecommunications Act of 1996."[35] It addressed three paths available for the entry of competitors into the local telephone market, namely full facilities-based entry, lease of unbundled network elements from incumbent LECs, and the resale of the incumbent's retail service by the new entrant. The fourth path—per-minute access—was addressed in another proceeding. As described in greater detail in chapter 5, the FCC prescribed minimum points of interconnection as well as adopted a list of unbundled network elements (UNEs) that the incumbent LEC must make available for competitors. These were initially: network interface devices, local loops, local and tandem switches, interoffice transmission facilities, signaling and call-related database facilities, operations support systems and information, and operator and directory assistance facilities. Incumbent LECs were required to provide equal and nondiscriminatory access to these elements in a manner that allowed the entrant to combine such elements as they chose and prohibited incumbent LECs from imposing any restrictions on the use of these elements.

The order determined that network elements be priced at a "forward-looking" long-run incremental cost basis, a system called "TELRIC," including a reasonable share of forward-looking joint and common costs (for a discussion of TELRIC, see chapter 4). However, if states were unable to conduct a TELRIC study within nine months, the FCC established default ceilings and ranges which the states could apply on an interim basis. The default range was set at 0.2 to 0.4 cents per minute for local switching UNE and a ceiling of 0.15 cents per minute for tandem switching.

Resale, the third entry strategy provided by the Act, was an important option for new entrants that could not afford the time or expertise to compete in the local exchange market by purchasing unbundled elements or by building their own networks, or who wanted to bundle local service with their own services. The FCC established a default discount range of 17 to 25 percent off retail prices, based, as mandated by the law, on "avoided cost." States were given the discretion to set the specific rate within that range. (For a discussion of wholesale pricing refer to section 4.2.)

In 1997 the FCC took a further step to flat access charges for terminating traffic by the minute rather than by the month.[36] The FCC claimed to adopt a market-based approach, though it is not clear what that term means in a highly regulated context such as access charges. It imposed charges that were to reflect costs, and removed some implicit universal service transfer that was distortive in favor of explicit support mechanisms.

The most direct change of the access charge reform was in the recovery of cost of common line usage. Non-traffic-sensitive costs, would be recovered through flat-rate charges. Since the cost for usage of an ILEC's local loop does not increase with usage it should be recovered through a flat rate. The previous usage sensitive per-minute CCLC was too high for high-volume customers, encouraging uneconomic bypass. Striving to make a gentle transition, the FCC raised the flat charge second residential lines and multi-line business lines to $9.00.[37]

Subscriber line charges were raised, and ILECs were authorized to assess another flat charge, a "pre-subscribed interexchange carrier charge" (PICC) on the IXC chosen by the end user. The PICC was capped for primary residential and single-line business lines at $.53 per month for the first year and increased by $.50 per year until the sum of the SLC and the PICC recovered non-traffic-sensitive cost.

In the interim, the ILECs were permitted to impose a per-minute CCLC on originating minutes. Such a charge, however, was meant to decrease to zero as revenues increased because of the raised PICC for second residential and multi-line business lines. Similarly, after the CCLC was eliminated, the PICC for multi-line business lines and second residential lines would decrease as the SLC and PICC for primary residential and single-line business lines recovered full revenues.

The FCCs financial reform increased the subscriber line charges (SLC) by $1.3 billion (to $9.2 billion).[38] The new pre-subscribed interexchange carrier charge (PICC) amounted to $2.3 billion. These flat-rate increases were offset by reduction in the traditional traffic-sensitive carrier access charges by $3.6 billion. Other reductions were $0.8 billion in subsidies from small LECs, and $1 billion reduction in revenues due to the price cap, whose productivity factor was raised from 5.3 to 6.5 percent.

The FCC reform also included $2.6 billion for the support of universal service for schools, libraries, and rural health care providers. This was funded from a percentage charge on the revenues of IXCs, LECs, and other telecommunication providers. This access charge system was again modified in 2000, when the FCC, in Order 00-193, largely adopted a reform compromise worked out by an inter-industry group, the Coalition for Affordable Local and Long Distance Services (CALLS). The basic principles for the industry were that any change would be revenue-neutral to the ILECs; that the burden on the IXCs would be reduced; that charges would not be distortive of efficiency; and that subsidies would be made more explicit. In consequence, the presubscribed interexchange carrier charge (the PICC) was eliminated, and replaced by a gradual increase in the authorized subscriber line charge (the SLC) to $6.50 per month per residential and business line. Furthermore, the usage-sensitive per-minute carrier access charge paid by IXCs to the LECs was reduced from about 1.5 cents per minute to the target of 0.55 cents per minute for the BOCs and GTE, 0.95 cents for primarily rural LECs, and 0.65 cents for the remaining LECs. To reach these levels, prices would decline by a factor of 6.5% percent per year, minus inflation. Once these prices were reached, the automatic reductions would cease and merely offset inflation; that is, real prices would be frozen. The significance of these numbers was also that they were likely to become proxies for local interconnection charges more generally. The total reduction was calculated at $3.2 billion. In return, the major long-distance companies committed themselves to eliminate any minimum usage charge (though on the implementation of that commitment AT&T and the FCC clashed almost immediately), and to pass through to consumers the reductions in access charges. Lifeline transfers to low-income users were also adjusted upwards to make up for the increase in the SLC, increasing from $60 to $125 million within five years. Rural high cost areas kept their allocation of $650 million of transfers under federal rules, though they were now collected by an assessment on all carriers' interstate revenues, and placed in a universal service fund that was available to CLECs, too, if they served customers in high-cost areas.

Thus, by the year 2001, usage-sensitive access charges had declined considerably and were moving toward elimination (bill-and-keep).

Local Competition and Interconnection

Competition in local infrastructure is the toughest challenge for entrants.[39] It also the key to a "level playing field" for the other telecom services. Since almost every communications flow has a local component, a monopolistic local segment affects all of telecommunications. It is therefore not surprising that policy makers, once they have embarked on a pro-competition strategy, were eager to remove the last bottleneck. Although deregulatory-minded, they have become activist, and interconnection policy was their chief tool.

In the mid-1980s a second wave of rival entry into local communications began. As in long-distance service, local competition started with dedicated, unswitched services such as private lines. However, that market, accounting for only about 6 percent of total LEC revenues at the time, was relatively small. In contrast, 85 percent of total LEC revenues came from switched services: local service, switched access, and local toll calls. This became the next target of competitive entry.

The new types of local service providers became known as "bypassers," "alternative local telephone service companies" (ALTs), "competitive access providers" (CAPs) when they predominantly provided dedicated services, or "competitive local exchange companies" (CLECs) (pronounced "see-lecks"), when they offered switched local services.

One major segment targeted by the early CAPs was the transport of calls from a long-distance carrier's points of presence (POP) to the LEC's end-office (or to large corporate users, or to other IXCs), known as "local transport." Local transport can either be "common transport," where traffic is routed through an LEC access tandem switch together with other traffic, or "dedicated transport," where a dedicated line connects the LEC end-office to a particular IXC's POP. New providers also began to aggregate the traffic of multiple smaller users and transport it to the IXC point of presence.

In New York, dedicated local service alternative to Nynex was approved in 1985 by the Public Service Commission, and subsequently offered by Teleport Communications, MFS and LOCATE, as well as by microwave companies and cable television providers. In Illinois, Chicago Fiber Optic used abandoned coal-delivery tunnels beneath the city to lay fibers that linked up long-distance services and customers. New York was also the first state to permit competitive-switched, local exchange service, and to determine that CAPs were entitled to their own number blocks. Not all states were equally hospitable to this development. But by 1995 most states had begun to approve some type or competitive entry. The evolution of alternative local access accelerated after a major fire in 1988 at the Illinois Bell central office in Hinsdale, local-network failures in New York and elsewhere, and a national failure by AT&T in 1990. These events caused telecommunication-dependent users, such as financial institutions, to diversify risk, and to put their eggs into more than one basket.

The 1996 Telecommunications Act

While these regulatory and court actions were occurring, the U.S. Congress was also tackling the issue of local competition. There were major efforts in 1994 and 1995 to rewrite the 1934 Communications Act. A central provision in the various drafts was the creation of local competition in those states which had resisted such competition. In return the ILECs were promised an easier entry into long-distance service. Other industries were also offered various incentives in the legislation. In consequence the new

Telecommunications Act was passed nearly unanimously by Congress in 1996.[40]

The Act requires each telecommunications carrier to interconnect directly or indirectly with other telecommunications carriers, and to comply with the technical guidelines and standards established for equipment interconnectivity. Interconnection agreements need to be approved by the respective state utility commission.

To qualify for approved for long distance service, an ILEC must pass the following "competitive checklist" (Section 271):

- Interconnection, at any technically feasible point, that is equal in quality to that provided by the local exchange carrier to itself, and at reasonable and nondiscriminatory rates and conditions.

- Nondiscriminatory access to network elements on an unbundled basis, unbundled local loops and local transport, which can be recombined

- Reasonable or nondiscriminatory conditions for the resale of its telecommunications services at wholesale rates.

- Number portability.

- Dialing parity and access to telephone numbers, operator services, directory assistance, and directory listing.

- Access to its poles, ducts, conduits, and rights-of-way.

- Access to databases and associated signaling.

- Reciprocal compensation arrangements for the transport and termination of traffic.

- Physical collocation where practicable.

- Good faith negotiations on all the terms.[41]

These obligations did not apply to rural telephone companies until they received a bona fide request for interconnection, and if the relevant state commission determined that such request was economically and technically feasible, and consistent with universal service requirements.[42]

To implement these statutory provisions, the FCC, under its chairman Reed Hundt, issued its Interconnection Order in August 1996 in a 700-page document which defined and enumerated the number of unbundled network elements (UNEs)

which incumbent LECs must make available to requesting carriers.[43] (This is discussed in Chapter 6.) The rules set the conditions under by which ILECs have to make UNEs available to interconnectors, and specified how states must determine the rates that the ILECs can charge for such access.

These rates are calculated using the total element long-run incremental cost (TELRIC) methodology described in chapter 4.[44]

In general, the 1996 *Telecommunications Act* gave the states three ways to proceed on interconnection agreements. First, where the parties to interconnection reached agreement among themselves, the states had to accept the agreement as long as it was not discriminatory or against the public interest. Over time, most parts of the thousands of agreements became negotiated. Second, where the parties could not reach agreement, states could engage in mandatory arbitration within about four months, subject to varying procedures that varied from informal to highly structured.

The third method was to approve an "opting-in" by which interconnectors could choose to be governed by an agreement entered by the same ILEC with another interconnector. This was to prevent discrimination and speed up the process. However, the FCC, in an activist mood to open local markets, interpreted the law expansively in its rules, by creating the possibility of a "pick-and-choose" opt-in, in which interconnectors could select terms from various interconnection agreements. The incumbents opposed this methodology because it required them to open their networks at a hypothetical rather than historic price. They challenged the order in court. Numerous state utility regulatory commissions joined in the challenge, challenging the FCC's jurisdiction as intruding on the powers of the states. An appellate court agreed with the states that they, and not the FCC, had the power to determine this methodology for calculating interconnection rates because the Telecommunications Act left this question to them. It also invalidated the FCC's pick-and-choose rule.[45] But this was rejected by the Supreme Court, which upheld pick-and-choose. Nevertheless, the FCC recognized that its rules could be counterproductive, and refashioned them to make pick-and-chose less flexible.

However, the court found that the FCC had correctly included among "network elements," the operational support systems (OSS), operator services, directory assistance, and switching features such as caller ID, call forwarding, and call waiting. Similarly the appellate court upheld the FCC's determination that the ILEC requirement to provide network elements that are "technically feasible" for unbundled access does not include consideration of economic, accounting, billing, space, or site concerns. The cost of such considerations, according to the court, will be taken into account in determining just and reasonable rates, terms, and conditions for services.[46]

Of course, everyone appealed, and the case reached the U.S. Supreme Court in *AT&T Corp. v. Iowa Utilities Board.*[47] Justice Antonin Scalia, normally a staunch state rights supporter, restored the FCC's jurisdiction to author rules and policies governing the pricing and unbundling for interconnection agreements subject to state implementation. The question whether TELRIC was a proper pricing rule was remanded to the lower courts, where the 8th Circuit court in August 2000 decided partly against the method. It upheld the concept of forward-looking and incremental pricing but rejected the FCC's use of a hypothetical network, as opposed to actual costs. As it turned out, however, the FCC itself was beginning to get cold feet as it realized the impact of the concept of hypothetical cost. The cost models indicated that often such cost, for rural areas, was actually far higher than the actual cost of fully depreciated networks, which would have led to higher rural prices, a politically sensitive outcome. The case went on to the U.S. Supreme Court.

While this legal wrangling was taking place, the state public utility commissions proceeded. They adopted various variants of long run incremental pricing, usually following the FCC even while denying its authority. Prices varied widely, however, from $1 to $2 per unbundled loop in Chicago, to $25 in some other states.

However, the FCC's primary unbundling rule was held invalid because it did not correctly apply the 1996 law in regard to the pick-and-choose rules, since it gave CLECs requesting interconnection overbroad access to network elements.[48] In deciding which elements must be unbundled, the FCC had to consider, the court held, whether access to proprietary network elements is "necessary" for entry.

The details of the FCC's rules are further discussed in various sections of this book, such as under unbundling, pricing, access charges, and universal service.

In 1998 four of the Bell companies applied for permission to offer interLATA service.[49] All were rejected for not meeting some of the requirements of the checklist. For example, Bell South, the FCC held, only six of the fourteen points of the competitive checklist, and part of a seventh. Bell South failed to demonstrate that it did not discriminate in its transactions with unaffiliated competitors. It also failed to provide equal access to its operation support systems (OSS). Similarly Ameritech failed to offer nondiscriminatory access to its 911 and E911 services.[50] Going back to the drawing board, Bell Atlantic filed another petition with the FCC for interLATA service, after obtaining a green light for compliance by the New York PSC, and its long-sought application was granted a few days before the end of the twentieth century. Texas, Oklahoma, Kansas, and Massachusetts followed.

While these proceedings were slowly progressing an anticipated problem of asymmetric traffic arose, known as the issue of "reciprocal compensation." Reciprocal compensation is a system of carrier-to-carrier payments that compensate one local telephone company for carrying over its own network a local call that originates on another local carrier's network. The amount of the payment between carriers is determined by the duration of the calls between them, and it most logically operates "reciprocally" in both directions. For voice traffic, the exchange of calls between ILECs and CLECs tends to be about even, making the reciprocal compensation payments essentially a wash.

The situation is different for Internet dial-up calls to an ISP where the duration tends to be several times that of a voice call, and in one direction, from the end user to the ISP, whereas the ISP rarely initiates a call.

ILECs ended up with fewer ISP customers than their CLEC counterparts, because the latter offered lower prices or additional services. This created an asymmetry in the number of minutes of calls terminations exchanged between incumbent and competitive LECs in the same area. On average, the ILECs' customers spend a greater number of minutes dialing up the CLECs' ISP customers than the CLECs' customers spend dialing up the ILECs. Because the incumbent was terminating fewer minutes of local calls in their networks relative to their competitors, they had pay to their competitors far more than they received, due to the surplus of inbound minutes to the CLEC. The asymmetry in the exchange of minutes of calls created an imbalance in the flow-of-traffic payments, until the interconnection contracts were renegotiated. This led to major regulatory skirmishes. The roles had been reversed. Whereas in the past it was the incumbents who wanted high transport and termination charges while the newcomers clamored for low rates, they now switched positions when the traffic balance, under the impetus of the Internet and the stronger ability of the CLECs to capitalize on it, swung unexpectedly in favor of the CLECs. The states, called upon to sort out the disputes, generally settled on a cost methodology of long-run incremental cost.

The ILECs also sought to offer broadband residential data service for Internet use and video. The question arose on what conditions they could do so. For example, did they have to offer such service to resellers? The FCC, following Section 706 of the 1996 Act, facilitated the competitors' entry. They were able to install their equipment, so-called digital subscriber line multiplexers (DSLAMs) necessary for high speed packet service, in the physical premises of the incumbents. The ILECs must also offer access to unbundled network elements; ILECs must also remove unused equipment to create space for their competitor's equipment. When space is exhausted at a particular location, ILECs must offer collocation in its adjacent structures. The price for the access to ILEC facilities and network elements was regulated.

In time, the FCC was required by a court to modify its collocation requirements to include only equipment "necessary" for interconnection, excluding equipment that was merely convenient to have in the central office. This, the Washington, DC, circuit court held in *GTE v. FCC*, 205 F3rd 416, 2000, was an excessive interpretation by the FCC of the 1996 *Telecommunications Act*, and in violation of the ILECs' property rights.

ILECs were permitted to offer high-speed services, also on an interstate basis through fully separated subsidiaries. While these legal skirmishes took place, many CLECs faltered in the marketplace as their financing

dried up. Local competition remained rare for residents, though it was increasingly vigorous for business.

NOTES

1. A. Stone, *Public Service Liberalism,* Princeton: Princeton University Press, 1991, p. 132.

2. Ibid, p. 138.

3. J.W. Stehman, *The Financial History of the American Telephone and Telegraph Co.*, Boston: Houghton Mifflin, 1925, p. 52.

4. M. Mueller, Open interconnection and the economics of networks: An analysis and critique of current policy, Columbia Institute for Tele-information Working Paper, 344, 1988.

5. D. Gabel and D.F. Weiman, Historical perspectives on interconnection between competing local exchange companies, Columbia Institute for Tele-information Working Paper 671,1994 (citing AT&T CA, Box 66, Sub-Licensing Policy, 1907–1908. Hall-French, 5/16/1908). See also K. Lipartito, System building on the margin: The problem of choice in the telephone industry, *Journal of Economic History* 49: 30–31 (1989); G. W. Brock, *The Telecommunications Industry: The Dynamics of Market Structure,* Cambridge: Harvard University Press, 1981.

6. Gabel, Weiman, op. cit.

7. F. Winter, With the fight for physical connection of telephone systems, *La Crosse County Historical Sketches,* Series 4:70; National Civic Federation, "compilation and analysis of laws of 43 for the regulation of central commissions of railroad and other public utilities," pp. 318–4\325. See also *Frank Winter v. La Crosse Telephone Company and Wisconsin Telephone Company,* U-317,11 Wisconsin Railroad Commission Reports 748, 1913. See Gabel.

8. *Frank, Winter v. La Crosse Telephone Company and Wisconsin Telephone Company,* U-317, 11 Wisconsin Rail Road Commission Reports 748 (1913).

9. *D. McGowan v. Rock County Telephone Co. and Wisconsin Telephone Co.,* U-500, 14 Wisconsin Railroad Commission Reports 529 (1914).

10. *Frank Winter v. La Crosse Telephone Company and Wisconsin Telephone Company,* U-317,11

Wisconsin Railroad Commission Reports 748, p. 9 (1913).

11. D. Gabel and D. F. Weiman, Historical perspectives on interconnection between competing local exchange companies, Columbia Institute for Tele-Information Working Paper 671, 1994.

12. D. F. Weiman, and R. C. Levin, Preying for monopoly? The case of Southern Bell Telephone Company, 1894-1912, *Journal of Political Economy* 102:103–26 (1994).

13. *Wisconsin Telephone Company v. Railroad Commission of Wisconsin and others,* 162 Wisconsin Reports 383 1916.

14. Mueller, Milton, op. cit.

15. In Re Pacific Telephone & Telegraph Co., 15 Cal. R.C.R. 993 (1918), quoted in Stone, op. cit, p. 126. An identical conclusion was reached by an Indiana regulatory board which concluded that the merging of competing operations "should be encouraged even if it is resisted." *Central U. Teleph. Co.,* PUR 1920B, p. 813; and *Indiana Bell Teleph. Co.,* PUR 1922C, p. 348.

16. Johnson County Home Telephone Co., 9 Mo. P.S.C.R. 637 (1919. Quoted in Stone, op. cit. 9. 127.

17. *Hush-A-Phone Corporation v. U.S. and FCC,* 238 F.2d 266 (1956).

18. *Carter v. AT&T,* 250 F. Supp. 188,192(N.D. Tex. 1966).

19. G. W. Brock, *The Telecommunications Industry, the Dynamics of Market Structure,* Cambridge: Harvard University Press, 1981, p. 244.

20. *North Carolina Public Utilities Commission v. FCC* 537 F.2d 787 (4th Circuit), cert, denied, 429 U.S. 1027 (1976).

21. OECD, Telecommunications, Washington: OECD Publications and Information Services, 1983. p. 76.

22. B. L. Egan and L. Waverman, The state of competition in telecommunications, in B.G. Cole, ed., *After the Breakup: Assessing the New Post-AT&T Divestiture Era,* New York: Columbia University Press, 1991, pp. 285–304.

23. In re Allocation of Frequencies in the Bands above 890 Megacycles, Reports and Order, 27 F.C.C. 359 (1959).

24. In re Microwave Communications, Inc., Initial Decision, 18 F.C.C. 2d 979,1010 (1969).

25. *MCI Telecommunications Corporation v. FCC,* 561 F. 2d 365 (D.C. Or. 1977).

26. P. W. Huber, Competition and Open Access in the Telecommunications Market of California, Unpublished report, p. 69, February 8,1994.

27. R. Wiley, *Telecommunications in the United States: Trends and Policies.* Norwood: Artech House, 1981, pp. 53–54. (Special Report in C.C. Docket 79–164; adopted 12/19/79.)

28. R. W. Crandall, *After the Breakup: U.S. Telecommunications in a More Competitive Era.* Washington: Brookings Institution, 1991; P. W. MacAvoy and K. Robinson, Losing by judicial policy menacing: The first year of the AT&T divestiture, *Yale Journal on Regulation* 2:225–62(1985).

29. P. DeGraba, Bill and Keep at the Central Office as the Efficient Interconnection Regime. OPP Working Paper Series 33, Federal Communications Commission, December 2000.

30. L. D. Taylor, *Telephone Demand: A Survey and Critique,* Cambridge, MA: Ballinger, 1985; L. D. Taylor, Telecommunications Demand, New York: Kluwer Academic, 1993; W. Taylor, *Effects of Competitive Entry in the U.S. Interstate Toll Markets,* National Economic Research Associates, New York, 1993.

31. Modified Final Judgment (AT&T Consent Decree), Appendix B, A.1; U.S. *v. AT&T Co.,* 552 F. Supp. 226 (D.D.C. 1982).

32. Federal Communications Commission, Industry Analysis Division, *Trends in Telephone Service,* Washington, DC, Government Printing Office, February 1991.

33. Telecommunications Act of 1996, 47 U.S.C. § 251 Pub. L. No. 104–104,110 Stat. 56.

34. In the Matter of Implementation of the Local Competition Provisions in the Telecommunications Act of 1996, First Report

and Order, FCC 96–325, CC Docket No. 96–98, Adopted August 1,1996, Released August 8,1996.

35. In the Matter of Access Charge Reform, First Report and Order, FCC 97–158, CC Docket No. 96–262, Adopted May 7, 1997, Released May 16, 1997, Reply Date July 11, 1997. This access reform order was released in conjunction with the even lengthier FCC 97-157, Report and Order In the Matter of Federal-State Joint Board on Universal Service, CC Docket No. 96–45.

36. In the Matter of Access Charge Reform, First Report and Order, FCC 97–158, Par. 38, Released May 7,1997, Adopted May 16, 1997.

37. M. A. Noll, The costs of competition: An analysis of the FCC telecommunication orders of 1997, *Telecommunications Policy,* p. 7, August 14,1997.

38. R. W. Crandall, Regulating communications: Creating monopoly while "protecting" us from it, *Brookings Review* 10: 3 (1992). I. Vogelsang and B. M. Mitchell, *Telecommunications Competition: The Last 10 Miles,* Washington, DC: AEI, 1994. D. Waterman, Local monopsony and free riding, *Information Economics and Policy* 8: 337–55 (1996).

39. Telecommunications Act of 1996, 47 U.S.C. §§ 151 *et seq.,* Pub. L. No. 104–104,110 Stat 56 (1996).

40. 47 U.S.C. § 251(c) (1996).

41. 47 U.S.C. § 251(f)(l)(A) (1996).

42. Specific Unbundling Requirements, 47 CFR § 51.319 (1996)

43. Availability of provisions of agreements to other telecommunications carriers, 47 CFR §51.809 (1996)

44. *Iowa Utilities Board v. FCC,* 120 F.3d 753, 800, 804, 805–806 (8th Cir. 1997).

45. *Iowa Utilities Board v. FCC,* 120 F.3d 753 (8th Cir. 1997).

46. *AT&T Corp. v. Iowa Utilities Board,* 119 S.Ct. 721 (1999).

47. *AT&T Corp. v. Iowa Utilities Board,* 119 S. Ct. 721 (1999).

48. Bell Atlantic filed for petition on January 26,1998 (FCC Docket NO. 98–11); US West filed on February 25,1998 (FCC Docket No. 98–26); and Ameritech filed on March 5,1998 (FCC Docket No. 98–26).

49. FCC Report, *http://www.fcc.gov/Bureaus/common_Carrier/Orders/1998/da980513.txt*

50. The reference made to (47U.S.C.A.271(b)(ii) is found in FCC Report No. CC97-45, Common Carrier Action, August 19,1997.

Universal Service

A Concept in Search of a History

Milton L. Mueller, Jr.

niversal service entered the vocabulary of American telecommunications in 1907. The slogan "one system, one policy, universal service" was coined by Theodore Vail, president of AT&T, and propagated in the company's annual reports from 1907 to 1914. Its appearance came at the peak of a fierce competitive struggle between the Bell System and thousands of independent telephone companies. The idea of universal service served as the linchpin of the Bell System's argument for transforming the telephone industry into a regulated monopoly. The emergence of the concept thus marked an important turning point in the history of American telecommunications.

Most historians and policy makers believe that when Vail invoked "universal service" he meant the same thing we mean by it today: regulatory policies to promote the affordability of telephone service through cross-subsidies.[1] That widely accepted view is incorrect. There is an important difference between Vail's concept of universal service in 1907 and the conception prevailing now. Understanding that difference is what this book is all about. At stake is not simply a question of historical semantics, but a reinterpretation of the history of telecommunications with significant implications for current and future telecommunications policies.

In contemporary discourse, universal service policy is synonymous with government policies to promote the affordability of telephone service and access to the network. More commonly, it refers to attempts to maintain affordable local rates by means of rate averaging and cross-subsidies within the nation's telecommunications system. That might mean, for example, higher charges for long-distance service than for local service, or charging the same rates for all long-distance calls, even when economies of scale make one call far less expensive than another. Whatever the mechanism, pushing telephone penetration toward 100 percent is a policy goal of sufficient importance to justify various forms of public intervention in the industry.

Universal service in that respect is an expression of liberal egalitarianism. More than just a telephone in every home, the phrase implies that a ubiquitous communications infrastructure can contribute to national unity and equality of opportunity. In debates over the emergence of competition in the telephone industry in the last three decades, the concept has become a pillar of the developed world's postal, telephone, and telegraph monopolies.[2] Telephone companies and regulators warned that universal service could not have been achieved without the regulated monopoly structure, and that competitive market forces had to be thwarted or tempered lest those goals be undermined. More recently, advocates of a new "information superhighway" have also drawn upon the concept to promote broadened access to new technologies.[3]

That is the contemporary construction of universal service—one that has prevailed from about 1975. Indeed, that modern idea of universal service comes with a full-blown version of its own historical origins. According to the conventional wisdom, universal telephone service was a public policy mandated by the federal Communications Act of 1934 and consciously brought into being by regulators acting in conjunction with telephone monopolies. "Telecommunications public policy crystallized in America with the Communications Act of 1934. Its goal was clear: the provision of universal service to every citizen in the country … Telephones at the time were viewed as a 'social necessity' that should be provided to all."[4] The crowning achievement of that system, so the story goes, was the fact that 92 percent of American homes had telephones just before the AT&T divestiture.

The authors of that claim offer no supporting evidence. Indeed, they merely repeat ideas that most business people, academics, and regulators involved in the telephone industry take as true. To that group, universal service is the offspring of a near-holy trinity comprising the Communications Act of 1934, regulated monopolies, and rate subsidies.

It is, however, surprisingly easy to cast doubt upon that belief. The words "universal service" do not appear in the Communications Act. Neither do they appear in any of the thousands of pages of the *Congressional Record* during the period that Congress was preparing the legislation. The bill's House sponsor, Speaker Sam Rayburn (D-Texas), explicitly stated that the act did not change existing law.[5] Indeed, no mechanism for subsidizing telephone service was created or authorized in the legislation. The Communications Act of 1934 was, in fact, little more than consolidation. Its stated purpose was to put federal authority over communications into one specialized agency. To do so, the drafters took those parts of the Interstate Commerce Act of 1910 that authorized the Interstate Commerce Commission to regulate interstate telephone service and combined them with the Radio Act of 1927, which regulated broadcasting. The result was a consolidated communications act and a single regulatory agency, the Federal Communications Commission.

Indeed, federal regulation could not have had much impact on the universality of telephone service in the 1930s or 1940s, or even the 1950s. The Communications Act gave the FCC jurisdiction over interstate telecommunications only, and in the years shortly before 1934 less than 2 percent of all telephone traffic crossed state lines.[6] The 1934 act thus affected only a small portion of the overall telephone marketplace.

That brings us back to the point at which this chapter began. If the universal service concept originated not in the Communications Act of 1934 but in the Bell-independent competition of the early 1900s, why did a debate about universality emerge at that time? And if, as I have asserted, Theodore Vail and his contemporaries did not mean by universal service what we mean today, what did they mean? As usual, historical reality is more interesting than myth.

The universality of telephone communications became an issue in the early 1900s because the local telephone exchanges of the Bell System and the independents were not connected to one another. Competition took the form of two separate telephone systems in a city or town vying with each other for subscribers and for connections to other localities. Subscribers who joined one system could not call subscribers of the other—unless, as happened about 13 percent of the time, they subscribed to both systems. Duplicate subscribers (mostly businesses) had two separate telephone instruments, one Bell, one independent. Even when there was only one exchange in a community, that duplicate service divided subscribers. A Bell exchange could not make connections with subscribers of a competing independent exchange in another city, and vice versa. In effect, telephone users confronted the same kind of barriers to communication as IBM-compatible and Macintosh computer users of the 1980s and 1990s. The incompatibility, however, was usually due more to the companies' refusal to deal with each other than to technological incompatibility.[7]

"Dual service" was the contemporary name for competing, noninterconnected telephone exchanges in the same community. Dual service diverges so radically from our current universally interconnected telephone system that it is hard to appreciate just how widespread and long-lived the phenomenon was. It existed in some form for thirty years, from 1894 to 1924. From 1900 to 1915, at least 45 percent of the U.S. cities with populations over 5,000 had competing, noninterconnected telephone exchanges. During the peak of the independent movement's strength, between 1902 and 1910, that percentage was more than 55 percent.

Vail and other Bell spokesmen decried the fragmentation and duplicate subscriptions caused by competing telephone exchanges. Independents defended the fragmentation as a small price to pay for the price restraints, service improvement, and innovation promoted by competition.

"Universal service" was put forward in that environment by the Bell System as a policy alternative to dual service. To Bell, the term meant consolidating competing telephone exchanges into local monopolies so that all telephone users could be interconnected. It did not mean a telephone in every home, affordability, or government policies to subsidize telephone penetration.[8]

After 1907, the Bell-independent business rivalry was transformed into a political and ideological struggle between two opposing principles of industry organization: dual service and universal service. It was true that dual service competition restricted universality by fragmenting subscribers. But, paradoxically, such competition also rewarded the pursuit of universality by the telephone companies themselves in a way that regulation and monopoly have never been able to do. A telephone system with more people on it is, *ceteris paribus*, more valuable than one with fewer subscribers.[9] Competing systems that are not connected to each other gain a competitive advantage over their rivals as they extend service to more users and more locations. That dynamic was the driving force behind the Bell-independent rivalry of the early 1900s. Dual service propelled both systems into a race to wire all parts of the country and attract as many subscribers as rapidly as possible. Penetration and geographic coverage in the United States, particularly in rural areas, made the most rapid gains in that period.

Perhaps most important, recasting that period of telephone history leads to a fundamental reinterpretation of why the telephone system became a monopoly. Odd as it may seem, after three antitrust cases and scores of journal articles, the monopolistic character of telephone service is still a subject of intense historical and theoretical controversy. Traditionally, economists grounded their explanation in the theory of natural monopoly and believed that the structure of the telephone industry was the most efficient form of organization owing to the presumed existence of supply-side economies of scale and scope. Many historians and economists have rejected the natural monopoly explanation, however, and have insisted that the monopoly resulted from abusive and predatory actions of the Bell System. Until now, those two positions have defined the spectrum of opinion on the subject.

We should reject both views. A different explanation, which might be called the universal service theory of monopoly, is more persuasive. That theory portrays the telephone monopoly as a product of a conscious, publicly mediated policy decision to "unify the service"—that is, to eliminate the user fragmentation created by dual service. In chapter 3, I characterize that outcome in terms of economic theory as an attempt to realize what may be termed demand-side economies of scope. That characterization represents a new theoretical position, in that it shifts the explanation for the efficiency of monopoly from the supply side to the demand side, and from economies of scale to economies of scope. It is also a distinct historical position in that it stresses that the elimination of dual service was the product of a political consensus rather than a unilateral product of the Bell System.

Another historiographical issue that merits revisiting is the role of interconnection and its absence in the development of the American telephone infrastructure. That is a neglected and often misinterpreted topic in the historical literature. The most influential account of the competitive period, the *Telephone Investigation* of the Federal Communications Commission in 1939, devotes only a few dismissive sentences to dual service competition.[10] Its incomplete and inaccurate treatment of the subject has misled two generations of historians. Lipartito, Langdale, Fischer, and others with access to primary sources, barely mention dual service competition.[11]

Since dual service has not been taken seriously by historians, data about its nature and extent have not been systematically collected or quantified. When the phenomenon of noninterconnection has not been simply overlooked, it has often been misrepresented. Policy analysts and economists who have written about the early competitive period generally treat the lack of interconnection as an anticompetitive abuse. From their work has arisen the general interpretation that Bell's refusal to interconnect with the independents ultimately defeated them. The truth, as subsequent chapters will show, is very different. Until 1910, the independents were as uninterested as Bell in interconnecting. Further, Bell's refusal to interconnect utterly failed to stop the independents from proliferating throughout the country. Conversely, Bell's decisions from 1901 to 1908 to aggressively interconnect its toll lines to noncompeting independent exchanges was a damaging blow to dual service and the most powerful method of promoting universal service. Furthermore, the Kingsbury Commitment of 1913, which is almost unanimously represented by historians as the "end" of the dual service era and the beginning of universal interconnection, has been completely misinterpreted.

If revisiting the dual service era leads to substantial revisions in the way we understand and categorize telephone history, it also has important implications for current and future telecommunications policies. Indeed, current conceptions about the competitive consequences of interconnection and the need for "equal access" are derived mainly from interpretations of telephone and telegraph history. The important issue is whether decision makers will be guided by history or myth.

This book reframes the debate about universal service. If the standard historical assumptions about regulated monopoly's role in the creation of universal service are true, then nations considering competition and liberalization must control and limit competitive forces to promote universal access. If, on the other hand, dual service competition played a critical role in the development of a ubiquitous telephone infrastructure, and that experience accounts for the tremendous U.S. lead in the extension of telecommunications service, government policies should be very different.

NOTES

1. See, e.g., Herbert S. Dordick, Toward a Universal Definition of Universal Service, in Universal Telephone Service: Ready for the 21st Century? (Annual Review of the Institute for Information Studies 1991) [hereinafter Ready for the 21st Century].

2. Nicholas Garaham, *Universal Service in Western European Telecommunications,* in European Telecommunications Policy Research (IOS 1989).

3. For a skeptical view of that trend, see Robert W. Crandall & J. Gregory Sidak, *Competition and Regulatory Policies for Interactive Broadband Networks,* 68 S. Cal. L. Rev. 1203 (1995).

4. Barbara J. Farrah & Mike Maxwell, *Building the American Infostructure,* Telephony 45 (Apr. 20, 1992).

5. "[T]he bill as a whole does not change existing law, not only with reference to radio but with reference to telegraph, telephone, and cable, except in the transfer of jurisdiction [from the ICC to the new FCC] and such minor amendments as to make that transfer effective." 78 Cong. Rec. 10,313 (1934).

6. Smith *v.* Illinois Bell Tel. Co., 282 U.S. 133 (1930).

7. Technological differences did play a role, however, as independents often used automatic switching during those years whereas the Bell System was still relying on manual switching.

8. That interpretation, which is vehemently disputed by historians whose work has been supported by the Bell System, is documented in chapters 8, 9, and 11.

9. That phenomenon is known as the "network externality" in economics. Chapter 3 contains more formal analysis of its properties and its implications

10. Duplication of exchange service is dismissed as "wasteful from the viewpoint of investment and burdensome to the subscriber." Federal Communications Commission, Investigation of the Telephone Industry 133 (Government Printing Office 1939).

11. Kenneth Lipartito, The Bell System and Regional Business: The Telephone in the South (Johns Hopkins University Press 1989); John V. Langdale, *The Growth of Long Distance Telephony in the Bell System, 1875–1907,* 4 J. Hist. Geo. 145 (1978); Claude Fischer, *Revolution in Rural Telephony, 1900–1920,* 21 J. Soc. Hist. 5 (1987); Claude Fischer, America Calling: A Social History of the Telephone to 1940 (University of California Press 1993).

Regulation, Antitrust, and *Trinko* (2004)

Dennis W. Carlton and Hal Sider[*]

INTRODUCTION

Regulation and antitrust have the common aim of promoting competition and maximizing social welfare but differ widely in how this aim is implemented. Antitrust operates through general rules established by courts under the principles set forth in antitrust laws, primarily the Sherman Act, the Clayton Act, and Section 5 of the FTC Act. Regulation, on the other hand, often requires firms to comply with detailed industry-specific rules. Antitrust law attempts to deter certain conduct that allows a firm to create or preserve market power but does not treat the mere possession of market power as an offense. However, regulation, among its other aims, often has affirmative, legislatively established goals of creating competition and eliminating or constraining the market power of regulated firms.

The Supreme Court directly addressed the overlapping and sometimes conflicting goals of antitrust and regulation in its 2004 decision in *Verizon Communications Inc.* v. *Law Offices of Curtis V. Trinko, LLP*.[1] The case involved claims that Verizon, the incumbent provider of local telephone service in New York, harmed competition and violated the Sherman Act by discriminating against AT&T, a rival telecommunications supplier that provided service by leasing portions of the Verizon network.

The case was brought by the law office of Curtis Trinko (Trinko), a New York firm that purchased local telephone service from AT&T. In a unanimous decision, the Court concluded that the antitrust laws did not obligate Verizon to deal with AT&T and other rivals. The Court concluded that Trinko's claim of discrimination, even if true, was not a sufficient basis to bring an antitrust claim under Section 2 of the Sherman Act. That is, the Court concluded that even if Verizon violated its regulatory obligations by failing to provide adequate assistance to rivals, these actions would not violate the antitrust laws.

Trinko narrowed the circumstances in which antitrust laws create an obligation for a firm to deal with its rivals and more clearly distinguished a firm's regulatory obligation to deal with rivals from any such obligation that might arise under the antitrust laws. The Court relied heavily on economic reasoning in explaining its conclusions. The decision recognized that imposition of a general obligation to deal with rivals can harm social welfare by reducing a firm's incentives to invest, innovate, and compete. It also recognized that judges are typically at a significant informational disadvantage relative to industry regulators in setting the terms of trade that arise from an imposition on a monopolist of a duty to deal with rival firms. In drawing these conclusions, the Court assessed the comparative advantage of regulation relative to that of antitrust in the formation of competition policy.

This chapter reviews the facts and circumstances of *Trinko* and evaluates the Supreme Court's decision from an economic perspective. The next section of this chapter briefly addresses the competing and complementary roles of regulation and antitrust in the formation of competition policy and provides background on the regulatory obligations faced by Verizon that were at issue in the *Trinko* case. In the following section, we review the allegations made by Trinko and the procedural history of the case. We then review the Court's decision from an economic perspective, highlighting key aspects of the decision and evaluating the Court's economic reasoning. Finally, we attempt to compare from an economic perspective the Court's ruling in *Trinko* with the economic logic of related cases, including the Department of Justice's antitrust suit that led to the breakup of AT&T in 1984 and the Court's decision in *Aspen Ski*, in which the Court affirmed a firm's obligation to deal with a rival under certain circumstances.

ANTITRUST AND REGULATION UNDER THE TELECOMMUNICATIONS ACT OF 1996

The Competing and Complementary Roles of Regulation and Antitrust[2]

Regulation and antitrust laws play both competing and complementary roles in the formation of competition policy. Regulators can attempt to protect consumers from situations in which competition may not work well, such as natural monopoly, and may attempt to promote competition in these industries by establishing industry-specific obligations on regulated firms as to how to deal with rivals as well as setting penalties for firms that fail to comply with these requirements.

While regulators in industries such as telecommunications, electric power, and natural gas often require regulated firms to interconnect with rivals, antitrust law has never created a universal obligation for firms to deal with rivals. For example, and as discussed below, the Supreme Court has never recognized claims under the "essential facilities" doctrine, although some lower courts have done so.

The caution used by courts in creating obligations for firms to deal with rivals is consistent with the traditional goals of antitrust law of deterring conduct that creates or preserves market power (as opposed to penalizing firms that possess market power) as well as the recognition that the imposition of a duty to deal with rivals can diminish pro-competitive rivalry among firms. In contrast, regulators can and do obligate regulated firms to deal with rivals and specify the prices and other terms of trade governing these transactions.

A regulated firm's failure to satisfy its regulation-mandated obligation to interconnect with rivals can raise price and restrict output relative to the level expected in the absence of this failure. This is the hallmark of conduct that harms competition, which is the economic prerequisite for creating antitrust liability. However, imposition of a duty to deal creates a tension between the goal of discouraging actions that restrict output and raise price and the goals of preserving interfirm rivalry. In addition, the treble-damage penalties assessed under antitrust law can vastly exceed those typically imposed by regulators and raise basic questions about the specification of economically appropriate penalties for various types of regulatory and antitrust offenses.

The *Trinko* case addressed a variety of fundamental issues that relates to the economically appropriate scope of regulation and antitrust enforcement. The Court found that this scope depends upon the comparative advantages of each institution in identifying anticompetitive conduct and designing appropriate remedies.

Regulators often have specialized industry knowledge and explicitly attempt to set rules that balance the interests of regulated firms with the interests of different groups of consumers. In telecommunications, for example, regulators attempt to set prices that protect consumers and preserve incumbent firms' incentives to invest. Regulators also attempt to balance the interests of different groups of consumers by establishing different prices to different groups of consumers (e.g., specifying different prices for business and residential consumers as well as different prices in urban and rural areas). Of particular relevance to *Trinko*, the Telecommunications Act of 1996, which is enforced by the Federal

Communications Commission (FCC) and state public utility commissions, requires incumbent local exchange carriers (ILECs) to interconnect with rival firms and to lease elements of their networks to rivals and not to discriminate against rivals in providing such interconnections. State regulators require ILECs to develop systems that enable regulators to monitor their performance in providing service to competitive local exchange carriers (CLECs) in a nondiscriminatory manner. These systems provide the basis for regulators' ongoing monitoring activities and regulatory assessments of financial penalties for ILEC failure to comply.

Even with detailed industry expertise, regulators are not always successful in establishing policies that properly balance the interests of consumers and firms. Regulators can err in attempting to implement technical regulatory goals, and there is a well-recognized concern that regulators will cater to special interests such as the regulated firm or specific consumer groups.

For example, attempts by state regulators to implement the FCC-mandated framework for pricing network elements led to wide differences in prices for the same network elements in different states. The data from the National Regulatory Research Institute (2003) indicate that state regulators in Illinois established a monthly lease rate of $2.59 per month for "local loops" (the copper wires used to connect customers to the phone network) in urban areas in 2003. The national average rate at that time was $10.92. In addition, many state regulators have substantially changed their rates for local loops in a relatively short span of time, although the underlying FCC framework being applied did not change. Between 2001 and 2003, for example, Arkansas dropped its monthly rate for local loops in urban areas from $71.05 to $23.34, and Washington, D.C., reduced its monthly rates from $10.81 to $4.29.

Since it is unlikely that these changes over time or differences across urban areas reflect cost differences alone, the data indicate that regulators have substantial latitude in mandating the terms under which firms are obligated to interconnect and suggest that regulated prices may differ substantially from the economically appropriate level. This in turn can have important consequences with respect to incumbent firms' incentives to expand and maintain their infrastructure and to invest in developing new technologies because incumbent firms know that they may be forced to share this infrastructure and investments with rivals.

In contrast to the detailed rules promulgated by regulators (with varying levels of success), antitrust courts operate by attempting to establish general rules. While judicial opinions impose obligations only on the parties involved in a dispute, they often have far-reaching implications by providing guidance for firms in related situations. Administration by federal judges is both a major strength and weakness of antitrust. Compared with regulators, federal judges are further removed from pressures from special interests but, at the same time, typically do not have the industry-specific expertise required to design and implement industry-specific remedies. As discussed below, attempts by courts to administer the Modified Final Judgment (MFJ) that settled the Department of Justice's 1974 antitrust suit against AT&T provide a stark reminder of the difficulties faced by courts in attempting to implement industry-specific remedies to competitive problems.

While courts and regulators each have comparative advantages and disadvantages in implementing competition policy, judges are likely to be poorly suited to define the terms of trade when creating an obligation for a firm to deal with its rivals. The establishment of the terms of trade is particularly complicated in the telecommunications industry, which requires coordination and the establishment of standards among a large number of parties.

Verizon's Obligations under the 1996 Telecom Act

There is a long history of antitrust scrutiny of the telecommunications industry, including the U.S. Justice Department's antitrust suit against AT&T, which was settled in 1984 and is discussed below.[3] In that case, the DOJ claimed that AT&T, then the incumbent provider of local telephone services, harmed competition by discriminating against rival long-distance carriers, including MCI. The case was settled in 1982 with a consent decree that, with some modification by Judge Harold Greene, became the MFJ.[4] The MFJ divided the old AT&T into seven large, regional Bell operating companies (RBOCs) and the "new" AT&T,

which provided long-distance and other less-regulated telecommunications services and also produced telecommunication equipment. Subsequently, two RBOCs—Bell Atlantic and Nynex—merged and, together with GTE, formed Verizon (which later bought MCI). Three other RBOCs—SBC, Pacific Telesis, and Ameritech—also merged in a series of transactions and later acquired the "new" AT&T, retaining the AT&T name. The new AT&T has since merged with BellSouth, another RBOC. The remaining RBOC, US West, merged with Qwest, and the combined company retained the Qwest name.

As discussed in more detail below, the MFJ was overseen by the courts from 1984 until Congress enacted the Telecommunications Act of 1996. The 1996 Act attempted to create competition in the provision of local telephone services by establishing a "carrot and stick" approach that linked entry by RBOCs into the provision of long-distance service to their success in opening their local networks to competition. In order to meet these goals, ILECs were required to meet a number of conditions established by the FCC and state regulators relating to leasing portions of their network and providing interconnection to competitive local exchange carriers. These conditions include factors such as complying with the network-sharing obligation of the 1996 Act, providing rivals with "nondiscriminatory" access to the incumbent's network, and providing regulators and rivals access to operations support systems (OSS). These systems are used by ILECs to, among other things, monitor performance in meeting service requests by affiliated and nonaffiliated entities. Both the FCC and state public utility commissions created financial penalties for firms that failed to meet regulatory requirements for opening their networks to competition. CLECs and ILECs entered into a wide variety of interconnection agreements governing the mechanics of the operational aspects of their dealings.

The 1996 Act also established a general framework for establishing the price at which ILECs were to lease network elements to CLECs, which was to be implemented by state regulators. The establishment of the appropriate price for network elements generated widespread debate among economists and further generated substantial litigation. The FCC's framework for pricing leased network elements

was established "to give aspiring competitors every possible incentive to enter local retail telephone markets."[5] Thus, the 1996 Act required that ILECs such as Verizon deal with rivals and also required that ILECs lease network elements to these rivals at rates well below those that would be established through arms-length negotiation. The data on the regulated prices of one set of network elements—local loops—summarized above show massive price differences across states, suggesting that regulator-established rates created sizable subsidies for entrants in at least some states.

Under these circumstances, an ILEC's failure to comply with the requirements to provide inputs to rivals at these rates would be expected to raise price and reduce output relative to the level that would have existed if the ILEC complied fully with these requirements. However, if rates are not set at economically appropriate levels, an ILEC's failure to comply with regulatory requirements would not necessarily have an adverse effect on consumer welfare relative to that expected based on economically appropriate interconnection prices.

Finally, the 1996 Act also included an explicit antitrust "savings clause" that established that the 1996 Act did not preempt antitrust laws. The Act stated: "[n]othing in this Act or the amendments made by this Act … shall be construed to modify, impair, or supersede the applicability of any of the antitrust laws."[6]

THE *TRINKO* CASE

As noted above, Trinko is a New York City law firm that obtained local telephone services from AT&T, a CLEC providing service using certain network elements leased from Bell Atlantic (later renamed Verizon).[7] In 2000, Trinko filed a class action complaint in the Southern District of New York in which it claimed that Bell Atlantic:

> [f]ulfilled orders of other Local Phone Service providers' customers after fulfilling those for its own Local Phone Service, has failed to fill a substantial number of orders for other Local Phone Service providers' customers substantially identical in circumstances to its own Local Phone Service Customers for whom it

has filled orders, and has systematically failed to inform other Local Phone Service providers of the status of their orders with Bell Atlantic concerning [the Local Phone Service providers'] customers.[8]

Trinko claimed that these discriminatory actions violated both the 1996 Telecommunications Act and Section 2 of the Sherman Act and that these actions harmed competition by slowing the expansion of CLEC-provided services.[9] The Trinko complaint was filed one day after the FCC entered into a consent decree with Bell Atlantic relating to provisioning problems similar to those identified in the Trinko complaint. As part of the consent decree, Bell Atlantic paid a $3 million fine and also agreed to pay $10 million to CLEC customers for claims related to problems in handling their orders.[10]

As noted above, the amended Trinko complaint alleged that members of the proposed class were damaged by Bell Atlantic's provision of a service that was below that accorded Bell Atlantic customers. In response, Bell Atlantic argued that Trinko's claim should be dismissed because, among other reasons, the complaint failed to meet the accepted legal standard for establishing an antitrust claim under Section 2 of the Sherman Act. As the circuit court explained, "[g]enerally, a plaintiff can establish that a defendant violates section 2 of the Sherman Act by proving two elements. '(1) the possession of monopoly power in the relevant market; and (2) the willful acquisition of maintenance of that power, as distinguished from growth or development as a consequence of a superior product, business acumen or historic accident.'"[11] Bell Atlantic argued that Trinko failed to meet the second element of this test.

In a December 2000 opinion, the District Court for the Southern District of New York agreed with Bell Atlantic and dismissed the case. The district court concluded:

> The complaint points to only one act or series of acts taken by Bell Atlantic to maintain its monopoly power: Bell Atlantic's failure to cooperate with local competitors as required by [the 1996 Act]. Even a monopolist, however, has no general duty under the antitrust laws to cooperate with competitors. [...] The affirmative duties imposed by the

Telecommunications Act are not coterminous with the duty of a monopolist to refrain from exclusionary practices.[12]

The U.S. Court of Appeals for the Second Circuit reinstated the antitrust claim in 2002, concluding that the district court adopted an overly narrow interpretation of Trinko's antitrust claims. The Second Circuit concluded:

> The allegations in the amended complaint describe conduct that may support an antitrust claim under a number of theories. [...]

> First, the amended complaint may state a claim under the 'essential facilities' doctrine. The plaintiff alleges that access to the local loop is essential to competing in the local phone service market, and that creating independent facilities would be prohibitively expensive. The defendant allegedly has failed to provide its competitor, AT&T, reasonable access to these facilities. [...]

> Second, the plaintiff may have a monopoly leveraging claim. [...] The amended complaint alleges that the defendant has monopoly power over a wholesale market in which it sells access to the local loop to telecommunications carriers. It also alleges that the defendant used that power to gain a competitive advantage in a retail market in which telecommunications carriers sell local phone service to consumers.[13]

The Second Circuit's opinion was inconsistent with an earlier decision by the Seventh Circuit in *Goldwasser* v. *Ameritech*,[14] in which the plaintiff also argued that discrimination by the incumbent local exchange carrier violated Section 2 of the Sherman Act.[15]

The Supreme Court granted certiorari and heard arguments in the *Trinko* case in October 2003. On January 13, 2004, the Court issued a unanimous opinion concluding that "Verizon's alleged insufficient assistance in the provision of service to rivals is not a recognized antitrust claim ..."[16] The Court added that "we do not believe that traditional antitrust principles justify adding the present case to the few existing exceptions from the proposition that there is no duty to aid competitors."

The Court's opinion relied extensively on economic reasoning. The Court recognized the tension between the antitrust laws' goals of fostering competition and the imposition of obligations on firms to deal with rivals. The Court noted that the desire to charge "monopoly prices" motivates pro-competitive business activity and that imposition on a monopolist of an obligation to deal with its rivals can reduce a firm's incentives to invest, innovate, and compete. The Court concluded:

> The opportunity to charge monopoly prices—at least for a short period—is what attracts 'business acumen' in the first place; it induces risk taking that produces innovation and economic growth.[17]

> Firms may acquire monopoly power by establishing an infrastructure that renders them uniquely suited to serve their customers. Compelling such firms to share the source of their advantage is in some tension with the underlying purpose of the antitrust law, since it may lessen the incentive for the monopoly, the rival, or both to invest in those economically beneficial facilities.[18]

As this suggests, much of the Supreme Court's reasoning, as well as its conclusion that with few exceptions "there is no duty to aid competitors," has implications beyond regulated industries. Nonetheless, the Court also stressed that the regulated nature of Verizon's activity limits the need to impose an antitrust obligation to deal with rivals.

The Court recognized that the 1996 Telecommunication Act's aim of promoting competition goes beyond the traditional goals of antitrust law. The Court highlighted the distinction between legislative and regulatory goals of promoting entry from antitrust goals of preserving competition.

> The mere possession of monopoly power, and the concomitant charging of monopoly prices, is not only not unlawful; it is an important element of the free market system. [...] The 1996 Act is in an important respect much more ambitious than the antitrust laws. It attempts *'to eliminate the monopolies* enjoyed by the inheritors of AT&T's local franchises.' Section 2 of the Sherman Act, by contrast seeks merely to prevent unlawful monopolization. It would be a serious mistake to conflate the two goals.[19]

The Court also stressed the regulatory nature of Bell Atlantic's interconnection requirements in choosing (again) not to recognize an "essential facilities" doctrine as the basis for creating an obligation for a firm to deal with a rival. As noted above, Trinko argued that access to Bell Atlantic's network was "essential"[20] and that Bell Atlantic's failure to meet its regulatory obligation to provide equal access to its network violated the Sherman Act by raising price and reducing output (relative to the levels that would have existed in the absence of the violation). The Supreme Court chose not to review under the "essential facilities" doctrine accepted by some lower courts and concluded instead that Bell Atlantic's regulatory obligations undercut any need for courts to impose "forced access" remedies.

> We have never recognized [an essential facilities] doctrine, and we find no need either to recognize it or to repudiate it here. It suffices for present purposes to note that the indispensable requirement for invoking the doctrine is the unavailability of access to the "essential facilities"; where such access exists, the doctrine serves no purpose [...] Respondent believes that the existence of sharing duties under the 1996 Act supports its case. We think the opposite: The 1996 Act's extensive provision for access makes it unnecessary to impose a judicial doctrine of forced access.[21]

The Supreme Court further acknowledged that regulation is often an adequate substitute for antitrust because "[w]here such a [regulatory] structure exists, the additional benefit to competition provided by antitrust enforcement will tend to be small, and it will be less plausible that the antitrust laws contemplate such additional scrutiny."[22]

Finally, the Supreme Court also stressed that judges are at a comparative disadvantage relative to industry regulators in setting prices and other terms of trade as typically is required when a court imposes a duty to deal with a rival. The Court noted that the "incessant, complex, and constantly changing interaction of [...] would surely be a daunting task for a generalist antitrust court"[23] and that "[a]n antitrust court is unlikely to be an effective day-to-day enforcer of these detailed sharing obligations.[24] More pointedly, the Court concluded:

> Enforced sharing also requires antitrust courts to act as central planners, identifying proper price, quantity and other terms of dealing—a role for which they are ill suited. Moreover, compelling negotiation between competitors may facilitate the supreme evil of antitrust: collusion.[25]

ECONOMIC EVALUATION OF THE COURT'S OPINION

The Supreme Court's opinion in *Trinko* relies extensively on economic logic and arguments, both in its evaluation of the competitive effects of forced sharing rules and its evaluation of the appropriate role of antitrust in regulated industries. This section evaluates the Court's economic reasoning.

Effect of Forced Sharing on Incentives to Invest and Compete

As noted above, there is a basic tension between the antitrust laws' goal of encouraging competition and the goals of facilitating competition by obligating a firm to deal with rivals. As the Court recognized, this type of an obligation can discourage investment and innovation both by the monopolist, which is forced to share the results of its investments with rivals, but also by rivals. That is, if regulators set interconnection fees that do not reflect all relevant economic costs of production, then entrants have an incentive to lease the incumbent monopolists' facilities instead of undertaking to construct their own facilities.

The effect of forced sharing rules on investment incentives has been a long-standing concern of telecommunications policy.[26] Requirements that ILECs offer to lease unbundled network elements in turn require the specification of lease rates in addition to specifying measures of service quality. As discussed above, rates have often been set by regulators in order to subsidize competition. The obligation by ILECs to facilitate entry, and in many cases to subsidize entrants, necessarily reduces their incentive to invest in their networks and to innovate.

While the analysis of investment incentives in *Trinko* is specific to the telecommunications industry, the same general logic and economic concerns arise any time that a court requires a firm to deal with rivals. The court must take on the role of establishing not only the price at which the parties transact but also other terms of trade. In the absence of a court requirement, firms have an incentive to enter into efficient bargains if there are gains from trade. Imposition by a court of a duty to deal with a rival is required only if one party finds the deal that could be achieved through private negotiation is not as good as the court-imposed deal. Price and other contract terms established by a court will typically be at terms less favorable to the incumbent firm than those that would have been achieved without court intervention. The obligation to offer services to rivals at subsidized rates reduces a firm's incentive to undertake the investment required to offer services in the first place.

Rivalry between incumbents and entrants also increases incentives to innovate as firms attempt to retain customers by developing and offering higher-quality products.[27] Indeed, it can be argued that the breakup of AT&T helped spur the major technological changes in the telecommunications industry in recent decades, including the development of wireless telephony, high-speed data networks, and the Internet. Of course, it also can be argued that line-of-business restrictions in the MFJ slowed the adoption of new technologies by limiting the ability of RBOCs to offer these services. While of great interest, this question is beyond the scope of this chapter.

Nonetheless, it is important to recognize that although forced sharing requirements can help subsidize entry and innovation, forced sharing requirements can also discourage investment and innovation by the entrants. CLECs that obtain access to network elements at subsidized rates are likely to defer investments in new equipment in favor of leasing network elements from incumbent carriers. The CLEC competition that results reflects a form of "regulatory arbitrage" resulting from the establishment of economically inappropriate prices for network elements and can displace facilities-based competition. The latter would yield greater opportunities for innovation and real price competition, as opposed to price competition resulting from regulator-imposed transfer prices that subsidize the purchase of key inputs.

Economic Literature on Exclusionary Conduct

In recent years, economic analysis has identified a number of circumstances in which exclusionary conduct can adversely affect competition and consumer welfare.[28] This literature identifies a number of circumstances in which a monopolist's refusal to deal can harm competition and other circumstances in which competition would not be adversely affected. In particular, exclusionary practices by a monopolist may have the effect of preventing rival producers of complementary products from operating at an efficient scale. In addition, a monopolist may have the incentive to use exclusionary practices to slow the development of complementary new technologies that may present a future challenge to the monopolist. The IBM[29] and Microsoft[30] cases each raise these types of issues.

While economic understanding has grown in recent years with respect to how various business strategies, including types of exclusionary conduct, can be used to preserve market power, there is a separate question of how courts should make use of these theories. It is often difficult to distinguish harm to competition from harm to a rival, and this task is complicated by the fact that there can be an efficiency rationale for many types of exclusionary behavior.[31]

Courts and Administration of Forced Sharing Rules

As stressed above, regulators have specialized expertise and fashion detailed rules that attempt to balance the competing interests of various groups of firms and consumers. In contrast, antitrust establishes general rules administered by nonspecialists. The Supreme Court's decision in *Trinko* was based in part on its view that antitrust courts are poorly suited to establish and administer the terms of forced sharing requirements.

Forced sharing obligations generally require the establishment of prices and other terms of trade. As summarized above, the Supreme Court observed that courts typically lack sufficient industry knowledge or experience to do this properly. The problems faced by courts in administering the Modified Final Judgment that settled the government's antitrust case against AT&T provide a stark reminder of problems that arise when courts take on an ongoing oversight function.[32] Judge Harold Greene approved the MFJ that settled the antitrust suit brought by the Department of Justice against AT&T and resulted in the breakup in 1984 of AT&T. Judge Greene's oversight of the industry continued until the Telecommunications Act of 1996, which transferred Judge Greene's remaining oversight responsibilities to the FCC. The MFJ, in effect, left one man responsible for implementation and ongoing supervision of the largest industrial restructuring undertaken in the history of the United States. Following the divestiture, Judge Greene had continuing responsibility for drawing, and redrawing, the lines that defined the types of services that the regional Bell operating companies (RBOCs) were permitted to offer and the conditions under which service could be offered. Between 1982 and 1996, Judge Greene issued thousands of advisory letters, received six thousand briefs, and often took years to resolve unopposed motions.

The adverse impact of inefficient administration of forced sharing rules is likely to be greatest in industries such as telecommunications, which are characterized by rapidly changing technology and innovation. New products and services are major sources of economic growth and increases in consumer welfare,[33] and a variety of recent studies shows that the introduction of new products such as cellular phones and later the Internet has resulted in enormous gains in consumer welfare.[34] Consumer harm from delays in the deployment of new services due to improper court oversight can defeat any desirable goals associated with impositions of duties to deal.

Exceptions to *Trinko*

It is important to emphasize that *Trinko* did not establish a blanket rule that eliminates in all circumstances the obligation under the antitrust laws to deal with competitors. The Court emphasized that "[u]nder certain circumstances, a refusal to cooperate with rivals can constitute anticompetitive conduct and violate Section 2."[35] As noted above, Verizon's regulated status played an important role in the Court's reasoning, and the Court stressed that "antitrust analysis must always be attuned to the particular structure and circumstances of the industry at issue."[36]

Still, the Court stressed that the circumstances that trigger the obligation to deal with one's rival under Section 2 are quite limited and referred to *Aspen Ski*,[37] in which such obligations were imposed as "… at or near the outer boundary of Section 2 liability."[38] The Court distinguished *Trinko* from *Aspen Ski*—*Aspen Ski* involved termination of an ongoing (and thus presumably profitable) joint venture, while, in *Trinko*, Verizon's regulatory obligation to open its network to CLECs was "something brand new."[39] The Court emphasized the importance of this distinction.

From an economic perspective, this is a very thin reed on which to base a distinction. Changes in economic circumstances can convert an "ongoing" business relationship into "something brand new" requiring renegotiation between the parties.[40] The imposition of a duty to deal with a rival in such circumstances may alter the bargaining positions of the parties, but the division of rents from a profitable venture is not a matter of antitrust concern. Court-imposed obligations to deal with rivals in such circumstances can impair economic efficiency by discouraging firms from entering into agreements in the first place and by interfering with ongoing economic relationships.[41]

Although *Trinko* did not overrule *Aspen Ski*, the Court's emphasis on the limited circumstances in which *Aspen Ski* applies makes it clear that an antitrust duty to deal will generally be difficult to establish. Similarly, the bipartisan Antitrust Modernization Commission recently concluded that "[r]efusals to deal … should rarely, if ever, be unlawful under antitrust law, even for a monopolist."[42]

Antitrust Damages and Penalties for Regulatory Violations

Application of antitrust liability when firms fail to meet regulatory obligations to deal with rivals has the further effect of replacing the regulator-established system of penalties with treble damages under the antitrust laws. As discussed above, the 1996 Act established a "carrot and stick" approach that penalized RBOCs that failed to meet their interconnection obligations by preventing them from obtaining permission to provide long-distance service. In addition, state regulations established detailed interconnection requirements and penalties for failure to comply with these requirements.

While both regulation and antitrust laws embody penalties for violations, the circumstances at issue in *Trinko* leave little economic rationale for the imposition of potentially enormous antitrust penalties on top of the specified penalties established by regulators. More specifically, Verizon was subject to a variety of regulatory obligations, including Verizon's interconnection agreement with AT&T (the CLEC from which Trinko wished to obtain service), industry wide guidelines agreed to by Verizon, the CLECs, and the New York Public Service Commission, as well as the "Performance Assurance Plan" that established detailed measures of Verizon's performance in providing service to CLECs and established penalties for Verizon's failure to meet specified standards. Under the plan, the size of the penalty depended on the magnitude of the performance shortfall, Verizon's historical performance in meeting this standard, and the impact on the CLECs business.[43]

The transformation of Verizon's failure to provide sufficient assistance to rivals into an antitrust violation would have added treble damages suffered by plaintiffs as an additional penalty. Where there is no antitrust liability in the absence of regulation, it follows that the public interest goal can be adversely affected by making regulatory violations triggers for additional antitrust penalties. For example, the risk of very large antitrust penalties can lead to "excessive" cooperation by incumbent firms with rivals, which in turn can harm consumer welfare by discouraging investment, innovation, and competition between ILECs and CLECs.

Moreover, the traditional economic rationale for trebling damages under the antitrust laws does not apply in *Trinko*, or likely in a variety of related settings. The trebling of antitrust damages is typically justified by the difficulty of detecting violations—if violations are difficult to detect, then establishment of the appropriate incentives for deterring violations requires that violators once detected face penalties that exceed the harm to the plaintiff, and trebling is one way to accomplish this.[44] However, the extensive monitoring of Verizon's performance by state regulators and by CLECs and the ability to compare Verizon's performance with that of other ILECs implies that violations by Verizon or other ILECs will not go undetected. There is little economic rationale for adding trebled antitrust penalties to those of regulators under these circumstances.

ADDITIONAL ISSUES RAISED IN THE TRINKO OPINION
Verizon v. Trinko and U.S. v. AT&T

Several observers have noted the similarities in the economic issues raised in *Trinko* and those in the Justice Department's antitrust suit against AT&T (which was settled with the MFJ in 1982), as well as the difference in the outcomes.[45] The economic foundation of both cases is the well-recognized principle that a local exchange monopolist facing a regulated retail price (presumably set below the profit-maximizing level) has an incentive to discriminate against rival firms that can purchase network access from the monopolist at a regulated input price (set below the profit-maximizing level) that is so low that it allows the rival to price profitably at or below the regulated retail price. In the Department of Justice case, it was alleged that AT&T—then the incumbent ILEC—denied network access to rivals in order to exclude competition for its long-distance business; in *Trinko*, it was alleged that Bell Atlantic denied access to rivals in order to exclude competition for its local telephone business.

While *U.S. v. AT&T* settled before going to a complete trial and appellate review, the discrimination-based antitrust claims resulted in a massive industrial restructuring and resulted in the creation of separate firms providing local telephone service and long-distance service. In *Trinko,* of course, the Court failed even to recognize that discrimination against rivals by an incumbent monopolist was sufficient to establish an antitrust claim. The outcomes of the two cases reflect divergent views about the comparative advantages of antitrust and regulation in addressing competitive problems.

Both the Department of Justice's allegations in *U.S. v. AT&T* and the MFJ itself reflect a distrust of (1) the ability of regulators to design and implement rules that foster entry into the segments of the telecommunications industry that could sustain competition and (2) the ability of regulators to identify and penalize discrimination by an incumbent monopolist against rivals attempting to obtain network access.[46] If regulators are unable to perform these functions adequately, then discrimination incentives can be eliminated only through structural remedies and prohibitions on ILEC activities such as those embodied in the MFJ.

Time has demonstrated that there are significant costs associated with the MFJ's divestiture remedy. Divestiture and the line-of-business restrictions in the MFJ precluded the RBOCs from offering a variety of services for which they were likely efficient providers and eliminated their ability to realize likely economies of scope. While the divestiture and the MFJ circumvented a number of concerns about the efficacy of regulation, they introduced a number of new ones and put in place an extraordinarily cumbersome mechanism for administering the settlement. The 1996 Telecommunications Act introduced new problems. Regulatory issues relating to the pricing of network elements have been disputed almost continuously both before and since passage of the 1996 Act.

There is little doubt that the Court's decision in *Trinko* was shaped by this well-known history, with the *Trinko* decision highlighting the limitations faced by generalist judges and courts in these circumstances. More generally, the Court in *Trinko* also had a more favorable view of the ability of regulators to detect and remedy discrimination compared with the views held by the Department of Justice at the time of *U.S. v. AT&T*. For example, the Court's opinion in *Trinko* describes at considerable length how "[t]he regulatory framework that exists in this case demonstrates how, in certain circumstances, 'regulation significantly diminishes the likelihood of major antitrust harm.'"[47] More specifically, the Court favorably cites the success of the FCC's process for authorizing RBOC entry into the provision of long-distance service, the

New York Public Utility Commission's Performance Assurance Plan, and concludes that "[t]he regulatory response to the OSS failure complained of in respondent's suit provides a vivid example of how the regulatory regime operates."[48]

Reconciling *Trinko* with the 1996 Act's "Savings" Clause

As noted above, the 1996 Act has an antitrust "savings" clause that states that "nothing in this Act [...] shall be construed to modify, impair, or supersede the applicability of any of the antitrust laws." The complaint in *Trinko* relies on this clause to argue that regulatory violations that raise price and reduce output relative to the level that would have existed in the absence of the violation are anticompetitive and thus are appropriately interpreted as antitrust violations.

The Supreme Court quickly dismissed this approach and concluded that the savings clause in the 1996 Act "does not create new claims that go beyond existing antitrust standards" and evaluated Trinko's claims based on existing antitrust standards regarding a firm's obligation to deal with its rivals. Trinko's argument, if accepted by the Court, would have transformed many regulatory violations into antitrust offenses.

Does the Court's opinion here leave any role for antitrust in regulated industries? Yes, albeit one that is more limited than the simple application of an economic test of assessing antitrust liability based on considerations of price and output alone. Even in regulated industries, many activities remain unregulated, and antitrust violations can arise in a variety of activities outside the scope of a regulated firm's failure to comply with regulatory obligations. For example, although the FAA's regulatory authority regarding airline safety gives it the ability to influence how aircraft are maintained, that would not immunize the airlines from antitrust liability if they engaged in price fixing. In addition, regulators often rely on markets instead of specific rules to govern some aspects of regulated firms' activities, and the Court's decision continues to subject these activities to the antitrust scrutiny that exists in unregulated sectors.

The recommendation adopted by the Antitrust Modernization Commission fits closely to the rules applied by the Supreme Court for defining the scope of antitrust in regulated industries. The commission recommended:

> When the government decides to adopt economic regulation, antitrust law should continue to apply to the maximum extent possible, consistent with that regulatory scheme. In particular, antitrust should apply wherever regulation relies on the presence of competition or the operation of market forces to achieve competitive goals.[49]

CONCLUSION

The Supreme Court's unanimous decision in *Trinko* relies heavily on economic reasoning in drawing a sharp line distinguishing a firm's regulatory obligation to deal with rivals from any such obligation that might arise under the antitrust laws. The Court reasoned that the imposition of a general obligation to deal with rivals can harm social welfare by discouraging a firm's incentives to invest, innovate, and, more generally, compete. The Court also concluded that courts are typically at a significant informational disadvantage relative to regulators in addressing the pricing and other terms of trade that necessarily arise from imposition on a monopolist of a duty to deal with rival firms. The Court explained that only in rare circumstances does there arise a duty to deal with rivals under the antitrust laws. The Court refused to expand those circumstances when a firm is regulated.

NOTES

1. *Verizon v. Trinko*, 540 U.S. 398 (204).
2. Some of the issues discussed in this section are presented in greater length in Carlton and Picker (2006).
3. See also Noll and Owen (1994).
4. *United States v. AT&T,* 552 F. Supp. 313 (1982).
5. *Verizon v. FCC,* 535 U.S. 467, 528 (2002).
6. 47 U.S.C. Section 152, Historical and Statutory Notes.
7. *Trinko* also raised issues regarding whether the plaintiff, who was not a direct purchaser of service from Verizon, had legal standing to bring an antitrust claim in federal court. While this

issue was not addressed in the Court's opinion, a concurring opinion by Justice Stevens, together with Justices Souter and Thomas, concluded that Trinko did not have standing to bring a mandatory dealing claim because "… it remains the case that whatever antitrust injury respondent suffered because of Verizon's conduct was purely derivative of the injury that AT&T suffered. And for that reason, respondent's suit […] runs the risk of duplicative recoveries and the danger of complex apportionment of damages." *Verizon v. Trinko,* 540 U.S. 398, 417. This issue is addressed in Picker (2006).

8. Amended Complaint, *Trinko, v. Bell Atlantic,* No. 00-1910 (SDNY) ¶21.

9. Ibid., ¶55.

10. 540 U.S. 398, 404 (2004).

11. *Trinko v. Bell Atlantic Corp.,* 305 F.3d 89, 107 (2002), citing *Volvo N. Am. Corp. v. Men's Inter. Prof'l Tennis Council,* 857 F.2d 55 (1988).

12. 123 F. Supp. 2d 738, 742 (2000).

13. 305 F.3d 89, 108.

14. *Goldwasser v. Ameritech Corp.,* 222 F.3d. 390 (2000).

15. In that case, the Seventh Circuit concluded that the alleged discrimination "cannot survive as a pure antitrust suit […] freed from the specific regulatory requirements Congress intended. Only if Section 2 somehow incorporates the more particularized statutory duties the 1996 Act has imposed on ILECs would Ameritech's alleged failure to comply with the 1996 Act be, in itself, also an antitrust violation." Ibid, at 396.

16. 540 U.S. 398,410 (2004).

17. Ibid. at 407.

18. Ibid.

19. Ibid.

20. Complaint, *Trinko v. Bell Atlantic Corp.,* No. 00-1910 (SDNY) ¶2.

21. 540 U.S. 398, 411.

22. Ibid. at 412.

23. Ibid. at 414.

24. Ibid. at 415.

25. Ibid. at 407.

26. See, for example, FCC 96–325, First Report and Order in the Matter of Implementation of the Local Competition Provisions in the Telecommunications Act of 1996, August 8, 1996 (¶282), which stated, "[w]e acknowledge that prohibiting incumbents from refusing access to proprietary elements could reduce their incentives to offer innovative services." Similarly, in congressional testimony, FCC Chairman Kevin J. Martin stated that open access regulation in telecommunications "… calls for a delicate balance: we need to make sure that incumbent networks are open to competition, but, at the same time, provide incentives for both incumbents and new entrants to build new facilities." Kevin J. Martin, "Statement on Competition Issues in the Telecommunications Industry," before the Committee on Commerce, Science and Transportation, United States Senate, January 14, 2003.

27. Carlton and Perloff (2005), pp. 560–564.

28. See, e.g., Ordover, Saloner, and Salop (1990), Whinston (1990), Bernheim and Whinston (1998), and Carlton and Waldman (2002). The application of the types of models discussed in these papers to antitrust is discussed in Carlton (2001).

29. *United States* v. *IBM Corp.,* Dkt No. 69-Civ2000 (S.D.N.Y. 1969).

30. *United States* v. *Microsoft Corp.,* 87 F. Supp. 2d 30 (2000). See the discussion by Daniel Rubinfeld in Case 20 in this volume.

31. See Carlton (2003).

32. This history is briefly retold in Thorne (2005), which provides a brief history of the administration of the MFJ, and the examples below are taken from this testimony. This history is told in more detail in Huber et al. (2004, 2005).

33. Robert Solow's (1957) classic study showed that technological innovations accounted for nearly seven-eighths of the growth in output per hour between 1909 and 1949. In his Nobel Lecture, Solow (1988, p. 313) concluded that his prior result "has held up surprisingly well in the thirty years since then during which time 'growth accounting' has been refined quite a lot …"

34. Hausman (2004) estimated that cellular phones generated consumer surplus of between $80 billion and $150 billion in 2002 alone. On a per capita basis, this means that the average surplus

per consumer is between roughly \$600 and \$1110 per year. Goolsbee and Klenow (2006) estimated that the Internet generates annual consumer surplus of \$2500 to \$3800 per consumer.

35. 540 U.S. 398, 408.

36. Ibid. at 411.

37. *Aspen Skiing Co.* v. *Aspen Highlands Skiing Corp., 472* U.S. 585 (1985).

38. Ibid. at 409.

39. Ibid. at 410. In discussing circumstances that trigger an obligation to deal with rivals, the *Trinko* opinion also mentions *Otter Tail Power* v. *United States,* 410 U.S. 366 (1973), and highlights that, in that matter, "the defendant was already in the business of providing a service to certain customers (power transmission over its network), and refused to provide the same service to other customers."

40. Similarly, differences between new and existing customers can make a transaction with a new customer "something brand new."

41. See Carlton (2001) and Areeda (1990) for more extensive evaluations of the Court's decision in *Aspen Ski.*

42. Antitrust Modernization Commission (2007, p. 101). Carlton was a member of this commission.

43. Some aspects of the regulatory oversight and penalties faced by Verizon are summarized in 540 U.S. 398 412-3 (2004). This regulatory framework is described in more detail in Thorne (2005).

44. See Posner (2001), pp. 271–272.

45. See Brennan (2005) and related articles in the Winter 2005 issue of the *Antitrust Bulletin.*

46. See Brennan (2005), pp. 640-643.

47. 540 U.S. 398, 412.

48. Ibid. at 413.

49. Antitrust Modernization Commission (2007), p. 22.

REFERENCES

Antitrust Modernization Commission. *Report and Recommendations.* Washington, D.C.: AMC, 2007.

Areeda, Phillip. "The Essential Facilities Doctrine: An Epithet in Need of Limiting Principle." *Antitrust Law Journal* 58 (1990): 841.

Bernheim, B. Douglas, and Michael Whinston. "Exclusive Dealing." *Journal of Political Economy* 106 (February 1998): 64–103.

Brennan, Timothy. "*Trinko* v. *Baxter:* The Demise of *U.S.* v. *AT&T.*" *Antitrust Bulletin* 50: (Winter 2005): 635–664.

Carlton, Dennis W. "A General Analysis of Exclusionary Conduct and Refusal to Deal—Why *Aspen* and *Kodak* Are Misguided." *Antitrust Law Journal* 68(3) (2001): 659–684.

Carlton, Dennis W. "The Relevance for Antitrust Policy of Theoretical and Empirical Advances in Industrial Organization." *George Mason Law Review* 12 (Fall 2003): 47–64.

Carlton, Dennis W., and Jeffery M. Perloff. *Modern Industrial Organization,* 4th ed. New York: HarperCollins, 2005.

Carlton, Dennis W., and Randal C. Picker. "Antitrust and Regulation." Olin Working Paper No. 312, University of Chicago Law and Economics, Chicago, 2006.

Carlton, Dennis W, and Michael Waldman. "The Strategic Use of Trying to Preserve and Create Market Power in Evolving Industries." *RAND Journal of Economics* 33 (Summer 2002): 194–220.

Goolsbee, Austan, and Peter Klenow. "Valuing Consumer Products by the Time Spent Using Them: An Application to the Internet." *American Economic Review* 96 (May 2006): 108–113.

Hausman, Jerry. "Cellular 3G Broadband and WiFi" In *Frontiers of Broadband, Electronic and Mobile Commerce,* edited by Russell Cooper and Gary Madden, 9–25. Heidelberg: Springer, 2003.

Huber, Peter W., Michael K. Kellogg, and John Thome. *Federal Telecommunications Law,* 2d edn. New York: Aspen Law & Business, 1999 & Supps. 2004, 2005.

National Regulatory Research Institute (NRRI). *UNE Surveys,* July 2003.

Noll, Roger, and Bruce Owen. "The Anticompetitive Uses of Regulation: *United States* v. *AT&T.*" In *The Antitrust Revolution* 2nd edn, edited by John E. Kwoka, Jr., and Lawrence J. White, 328–375. New York: Oxford University Press, 1989.

Ordover, Janusz, Garth Saloner, and Steven Salop. "Equilibrium Vertical Foreclosure." *American Economic Review* 80 (March 1990): 127–142.

Picker, Randal. "Mandatory Access Obligations and Standing." *Journal of Corporation Law* 31 (Winter 2006): 387–400.

Posner, Richard. *Antitrust Law,* 2d edn. Chicago: University of Chicago Press, 2001.

Solow, Robert. "Technical Change and the Aggregate Production Function." *Review of Economics and Statistics* 39 (August 1957): 312–320.

Solow, Robert. "Growth Theory and After." *American Economic Review* 78 (June 1988):307–317.

Thome, John. Testimony before the Antitrust Modernization Commission, 2005.

Whinston, Michael. "Tying, Foreclosure and Exclusion." *American Economic Review* 80 (September 1990): 837–859.

Universal Service

Nicholas Garnham

WHAT IS UNIVERSAL SERVICE?

There is now widespread agreement on a definition of universal service in telecom which in the words of OFTEL in the UK, is the provision of "affordable access to basic voice telephony or its equivalent for all those reasonably requesting it, regardless of where they live." The problem for the regulator is that neither affordability nor reasonableness are terms that can be defined with scientific precision. They remain a matter for subjective judgement by the regulator.

The EC Draft Interconnection Directive defines universal service more narrowly as "the provision of service throughout a specified geographical area, including—where required—geographical averaged prices for the provision of that service," but introduces the additional concept of common tariffs.

Universal service can be widened to include the provision of other services considered, for whatever reason, to be socially desirable, such as public payphones. Within the context of the information society debate, the question is now widely raised as to whether the definition of universal service should be broadened to include the provision of service levels above that of simple narrowband dialtone,

for instance services provided by digital exchanges such as itemised billing, call forwarding, caller line identification, etc.

From a regulatory point of view there are thus two sets of issues raised by universal service provision, depending on whether we are dealing with established services over a mature network, or new services where the network facilities are still in the roll-out phase. In the former case the issue is: What services should licensed public telecom operators be required to deliver that they would not otherwise deliver under competitive market conditions, why and how should these obligations be funded? In the latter case, whether we are dealing with basic telephony in less developed national contexts or with information society type developments of a mature telephone network, there is the issue of whether, through regulatory intervention, to attempt to accelerate network and service roll-out beyond that which market demand pull would produce.

THE HISTORY OF UNIVERSAL SERVICE

Current debates on universal service are largely based on myth and a dangerous misunderstanding of history. It is assumed that pre-liberalisation monopoly PTTs, or in the US, the monopoly regulated private

Nicholas Garnham, "Universal Service," from *Journal of Economic Issues*, pp. 199–204. Copyright © 1998 by the Association for Evolutionary Economics. Permission to reprint granted by Cengage (Gale).

operator AT&T, were obliged to provide and did in fact provide universal service and that this was made possible by a system of cross-subsidy and cost averaging which is unsustainable under competitive conditions as prices are driven closer to costs.

In fact the concept of universal service was dreamt up by Theodore Vail as part of a deal with the state and federal governments to maintain AT&T's monopoly. It was always more rhetoric than reality. In the conditions of the US, AT&T could use cross-subsidies derived from its monopoly control of the continental long distance network to price local access artificially low as a barrier to entry. Thus local telephony was more "affordable" than it would otherwise have been. But AT&T never provided geographical universality of access; the growth of telephone penetration rates followed a normal demand driven curve, not taking off to achieve penetration levels we would now regard as those approaching universal service until the 1960s.

European PTTs have not even resorted to the rhetoric of universal service, and in general the provision of telephony lagged behind demand. Operations were governed by principles not of universal service, but of public service, which derived from the absolute powers of monarchy. The public service mission, although this was never explicitly stated, implied that the State took responsibility for providing universal geographical coverage within its borders and for providing a guarantee of continuity, rather than universality of supply. It gave citizens no right to telephony; to the contrary it protected the operator against legal action for damages for failing to provide service.

The concept of universal service has been placed on the European regulatory agenda by liberalisation. It and the mythic history I have just outlined, have been mobilised as an attempted defence of the telephone monopoly. In fact the scare stories of people being priced off the network in significant numbers as a result of rate rebalancing have not been realised and in liberalised regimes, such as the UK, penetration rates have significantly risen. This does not mean that such rises, and the related fall in the real cost to subscribers of telephone service, can be *attributed* to competition. They can just as easily be attributed to the effects of technology and rising income levels. This however, is not to say that there

do not remain pockets of socially and economically sub-optimal levels of penetration which properly require regulatory attention.

UNIVERSAL SERVICE TODAY

In the context of a regulated competitive telecom market universal service obligations have to be seen as one of a range of regulatory interventions designed to achieve economic or socially desirable outcomes that would not be achieved by market players if left to their own unregulated devices.

All such interventions, however desirable the goal, bring with them two well known dangers. First, the distortion of economic incentives may bring with it losses to overall efficiency which outweigh the gains. For instance in the case of universal telephone penetration cross-subsidies designed to raise the affordability and thus penetration of telephone service may be cancelled out by rising costs such that real prices and thus real barriers to entry remain static. Second, subsidy tied to the consumption of a given service, in this case residential telephony, may override consumers' actual preferences and thus distort consumption patterns. Any form of support for the economically or socially disadvantaged which, in effect, forces them to consume a given pattern of goods and services rather than allowing them to choose requires special justification. There is danger of policymakers attaching more relative importance to telephone service than those potential subscribers whom universal service is meant to benefit. It is this problem that makes the concept of "affordability" less than useful in the definition of universal service. Affordable to whom and in comparison with what?

The Economic Case for Universal Service

Notwithstanding the caveats above, there is special case for universal service in telecom not shared by most other markets for goods and service. These derive from:

- Network externality—the greater the size of the network, the greater the benefit to other users of the network. Therefore, the true economic value of service to customers is greater than the willingness to pay of the individual customer and it is appropriate to provide support to some customers whose costs of service provision exceed the revenues that they generate.

- The special levels of network externality in a two-way network—users may generate significant levels of profitable incoming traffic, while themselves generating, and thus paying for, few, if any, outgoing calls.

- Telecom use as a substitute for other services, such as transport, may generate economy-wide benefits which are not reflected in the price of telecom itself.

- Increasingly, in an information society and economy, telecom may provide vital infrastructural access to other goods and service, especially vital public services, which justify a general subsidy to ensure universal access, as with the analogy of roads.

UNIVERSAL SERVICE AND THE REGULATOR
The Mature Network

The provision of universal service is regarded as a regulatory problem because it is assumed that provision in the past has required cross-subsidy—and will continue to require cross-subsidy in the future. And further, competitive market entry, by forcing prices closer to costs, will make such cross-subsidy unsustainable. This then raises the following questions for the regulator:

- Does the provision of universal service require cross-subsidy?

- If so, is such subsidy justified?

- How much subsidy is required?

- What mechanism is best for providing the subsidy? In particular, should the money be raised from the telecom industry and distributed within the telecom regulatory structure, or by and through the general system of taxation and social security payments?

How Much Subsidy?

It is clear from recent studies that the levels of cross-subsidy claimed by incumbent dominant operators have been grossly exaggerated. Recent detailed studies undertaken in the UK by OFTEL in collaboration with BT, when taking into account the benefits to the operator (incoming traffic generated, costs of connection and reconnection, market presence, brand visibility), as well as the cost of providing universal service, have whittled the annual net costs down from BT's opening claim of £400 million to between £0 and £40 million per annum depending on assumptions. The results of such studies are likely to differ from country to country depending upon such factors as the density or otherwise of population, nature of terrain to be covered, income levels and usage patterns. They are, however, unlikely to differ significantly. And, they are an essential starting point for any regulatory intervention.

If the costs to the dominant operator of its universal service obligations are marginal it may make sense either to ignore them and simply regard them as their costs of doing business, or to provide support to low income customers through general taxation and the social security budgets rather than by elaborate, distorting and potentially expensive interventions in the telecom market itself.

Funding Methods

In the real world there will be persistent pressure from the dominant operator, and from regulatory economists who like tidy models, to "level the playing field" by off-loading some of the costs of provision onto its competitors through a form of access charging. This can be done either by factoring it into interconnection charges or by setting up a Universal Service Fund financed by a levy on the industry based on some estimate of share of use of the access network.

Whichever method is chosen, any attempt to reimburse the costs of universal service obligations through intra-industry transfers will generate pressure for increased accounting separation and transparency, and will suck the industry and regulator into increasingly arcane, costly and ultimately unresolvable disputes over cost allocation.

A universal service levy and fund if combined with a system of either an auctioning of universal service franchises or a subscriber-based universal service voucher, thus allowing any market player to provide the service, avoids this problem. The auctioning of franchises is particularly appropriate as a means of dealing with geographical universality and ensuring service delivery to rural areas.

Barriers to Universal Access

Research increasingly demonstrates that many of the barriers to universal access do not lie, in any simple sense, in the cost to the consumer, but in the way that service and billing and payment options are structured. A major disincentive for low income users are relatively high up-front connection and rental charges and the inability to control usage and thus cost. The availability of digital exchanges makes it increasingly easy for operators to offer a range of services and tariffs to minimise these disincentives at no net cost to themselves. If maximising penetration is the name of the game, regulators are probably more usefully employed ensuring that operators offer such services than in setting up elaborate cross-subsidy mechanisms.

Developing Networks and Services

The above considers universal service as the regulatory problem of maximising access to telephone service penetration in the context of a mature network. The situation is quite different as regards the roll-out phase of the basic telephone network or the provision of more advanced service, such as broadband, in addition to access to telephone dialtone. Insofar as the development of the basic network is concerned, the mythic version of universal service is placing quite unrealistic pressures on telecom operators and regulators who face this situation.

The roll-out of a network requires long-term investment planning, and the installation of capacity ahead of demand. Nonetheless, no network in the world has been rolled out without regard to the flow of revenues from realisable demand. The result has been that high use business subscribers have always taken priority over residential subscribers and the growth of penetration levels has broadly mirrored per capita income growth, both nationally and regionally. The availability of wireless to distribute telecom traffic eases the problem of targeting high revenue producing groups in order to finance a faster expansion than would have been possible with a pure fixed link network. But, in my view, the case has not been made for an acceleration of network development beyond the norm in the name of universal service. Such an acceleration is likely to lead simply to highly inefficient patterns of investment with a large amount of fixed plant earning unacceptably low rates of return. The result of this will either delay long-term network development and traffic growth, by asking existing subscribers to pay more than they otherwise would for this excess capacity, or by diverting tax revenue from where it could be spent more efficiently and with equal or greater social and economic benefit.

This is not of course to say that it is not reasonable for regulators to ensure that those building and operating developing networks maximise coverage and roll-out speed within existing economic constraints and do not divert revenues to other purposes.

Widening the Definition of Universal Service

There is at present much discussion as to whether to widen the definition of universal service beyond the provision of telephone dialtone. This is taking place, in particular, within the context of the so-called Information Superhighway. The same considerations apply here as to developing telephone networks. Is regulatory intervention required or justified with the aim of accelerating the general availability of advanced services beyond that which the industry would supply subject to market forces? If so what services should be covered by a new universal service obligation, over what time scale, and who should pay?

In my view, no convincing general case has been made for such an intervention, or for the massive diversion of investment funds that would be required. The uncertainties of demand and the dangers of wasteful investment are simply too great.

There may be a case for a wider definition of universal service which is based upon the change in the social and economic status of a service once it passes a certain penetration threshold. One can argue that once a service becomes very widely used access to it becomes a definition of social membership and a condition of full economic participation. Thus one could argue that once, say 2 Mbit access to Internet reaches 70 percent penetration, regulatory steps should be taken to ensure universal access. But it needs to be stressed that even if one does accept this argument such a situation lies a long way in the future. And historically the telephone was never regarded in this light. Thus a very strong, and historically unprecedented, case would have to be made.

CONCLUSIONS

1. The provision of universal service is not mandated by history and is thus not threatened by liberalisation.

2. Industry or service specific subsidies need to be viewed with suspicion in terms of their market and consumption effects. They cannot be assumed to be favouring those they are designed to help.

3. The cross-subsidies involved in meeting universal service obligation are likely to be minimal to zero and thus the necessity and desirability of elaborate and costly, industry-specific, mechanisms for income transfers need to be examined with care.

4. The case for accelerated network development in the name of universal service provision or the redefinition of universal service to cover higher levels than simple telephone dialtone are weak to non-existent.

There are steps that can be taken in the design of service and tariff packages, not involving subsidies, to ensure maximum penetration. Regulatory effort should be focused on these.

Regulating European Telecommunications Markets

Unbundled Access to the Local Loop Outside Urban Areas

Anne Gablemann*

ABSTRACT

This paper examines the topic of unbundled access to the local loop in areas which show characteristics of non-contestable natural monopolies outside the large cities. Under the heading 'local loop unbundling' three variants are discussed, full unbundling, line sharing, and bitstream access. An obligation to provide competitors access to local networks on an unbundled basis is a strong intervention into the property rights of the regulated firm. In this light, the following points particularly come into question: Who should be granted the right to access local loops on an unbundled basis? Which form(s) of local loop unbundling should be enforced? © 2001 Elsevier Science Ltd. All rights reserved.

KEYWORDS: Fixed line communications; Network access; Local loop unbundling

INTRODUCTION

As soon as the telecommunications markets in most of the member states of the European Union had been fully liberalized in January 1998, intense competition developed in the field of long distance communications, which led to the construction of alternative long distance networks and an immense decrease in prices for national long distance calls as well as international calls. In contrast, competition has just started to emerge in the area of local networks. In many countries the construction of alternative local infrastructures has so far been limited to the densely populated areas of large cities. Usually, the lion's share of access networks is owned by an incumbent carrier. Since there are economies of scale in combination with sunk costs, access networks outside urban areas constitute monopolistic bottlenecks, which are an insurmountable barrier for would-be competitors. An extensive network duplication is neither compatible with the incentives of a new market player nor efficient from a social point of view. This requires regulatory action.

This paper focuses on access to local networks in peripheral and rural regions. The concept of unbundled access to the local loop is an instrument for disciplining market power, which can serve to foster the development of comprehensive competition in markets which are vertically related to the monopolistic infrastructure. The background for the following considerations is the conviction that regulatory action should be limited to what is absolutely necessary.

The following section presents the concept of local loop unbundling as a special case of network interconnection. The different forms of local loop unbundling—'full unbundling', 'line sharing', and 'bitstream

Anne Gablemann, "Regulating European Telecommunications Markets: Unbundled Access to the Local Loop Outside Urban Areas," from *Telecommunications Policy*, vol. 25, issues 10–11, pp. 729–741. Copyright © 2001 by Pergamon. Permission to reprint granted by Elsevier Science & Technology Journals.

access'—are depicted and briefly discussed. Section 3 presents a normative framework for regulating access to local telecommunications networks. This is the 'disaggregated regulatory approach' in conjunction with the 'essential facilities doctrine'. Section 4 considers the necessity for unbundled access to local loops, differentiating between long distance carriers and suppliers of local services. In Section 5, the qualitative effects of the three forms of unbundling on competition and on the ownership rights of the regulated firm are discussed and a possible design for an unbundling obligation is provided. In Section 6 the closely related aspect of local loop pricing is touched upon. Finally, Section 7 provides a summary of the main findings.

THE CONCEPT OF LOCAL LOOP UNBUNDLING

Unbundled Access to the Local Loop as a Special Case of Network interconnection

Local loops cover the distance between the network termination point at the customer's house and the subscriber main distribution frame (see Fig. 1). On their way to the switch, the local loops of different customers are combined to form one single cable. At the switch the individual loops are separated again and connected to the subscriber main distribution frame.[1]

'Interconnection' comprises the physical as well as the logical connection of telecommunications networks. The precondition for the physical connection is the existence of adequate technical interfaces securing the compatibility of the different infrastructures. There are different locations which can be used as points of interconnection with access networks.

First, access is possible at the trunk side of the local switching facility, which enables the network operator demanding access to make use of all of the functions (conveyance, switching, and network management) of the established carrier's network.

Second, access can take place at the line side of the incumbent's local switch, i.e. at the subscriber main distribution frame,[2] the serving area interface or the network termination point.[3] In these cases the 'package' of transmission and switching services is forced open and the entrant is enabled to get *unbundled*

access solely to the local transmission function of the incumbent carrier's network.

In addition to physical interconnection, telecommunications networks need to be logically interconnected so that the logical resources of one network can provide control and information services accessible to the other network. This is important for technical reasons, e.g. in the course of call routing. Moreover, logical interconnection makes it possible to access databases storing e.g. transmission data or content necessary for offering value added services (see Mitchell & Vogelsang, 1994, pp. 19–21). Logical interconnection is realized by means of software interfaces.

The main difference between unbundled access and 'usual' local network interconnection is that the newcomer demands physical interconnection only. So the logical interconnection is not realized by the incumbent but by the entrant himself. Of course this difference affects the pricing of network access. Instead of a usage dependent interconnection charge the competitor pays a fixed amount of money to the incumbent monthly for using the local loop.

Another difference is in the intensity of intervention by the regulator in the property rights of the established firm. While with usual interconnection the incumbent keeps full control over his local network, this is not true for all forms of local loop unbundling. E.g. in the case that the access line is separated from his network and fitted into the entrant's network the technology which is to be employed on the local loop is typically chosen by the competitor, not by the incumbent.

The Different Versions of Local Loop Unbundling

Full Unbundling

With this version of unbundling[4] the selected local loops are taken over by the market entrant completely.[5] Fig. 2 shows this form of network access for the case that access takes place at the subscriber main distribution frame.[6]

At the switch the local loops of different customers are separated and connected to the subscriber main distribution frame, the interface at which the competitors can access each individual local loop without using the switching facilities of the incumbent. That

FIGURE 1 Access network and points of interconnection

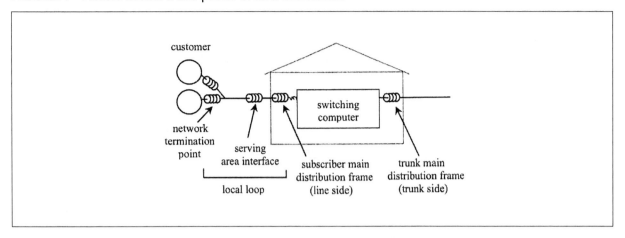

FIGURE 2 Full unbundling of the local loop

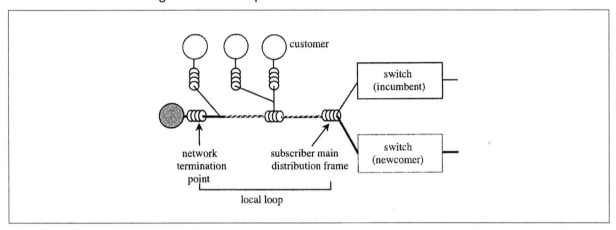

means that the entrant is able to supplement his own local facilities with the transmission capacities of the incumbent in a very flexible way at low risk, being generally free to decide which transmission technology should be employed.[7]

The incumbent is not able to offer his services to his former customers any more, because the full frequency spectrum of the local loops in question is used by the entrant. Further, what was before a local call within the same switching area may have the character (and the price) of a long distance call now (see Engel & Knieps, 1998, p. 28).[8]

Line Sharing

When line sharing is realized, one and the same local loop is used both by the incumbent and the entrant (see Fig. 3).

The incumbent continues offering voice telephony to his customers, whereas the newcomer offers broadband services like fast internet access using his own xDSL-modems.[9]

Voice telephony and data are separated by means of an xDSL-filter (the so-called 'splitter') before reaching the incumbent's switching computer (see European Commission, 2000a, pp. 12–15). Whilst telephone calls are transmitted to the switch of the incumbent, data traffic is branched off and handed over into the newcomer's network directly. In contrast to full unbundling, the local loop remains integrated in the incumbent's network.

High Speed Bitstream Access

With this form of unbundled access, the incumbent carries out the upgrading of his copper loop himself (or maybe the substitution of certain parts of it by fibre) and creates a broadband connection between the end-user and the local exchange (see Fig. 4). The newcomer is granted access to a specified bandwidth

FIGURE 3 Line sharing

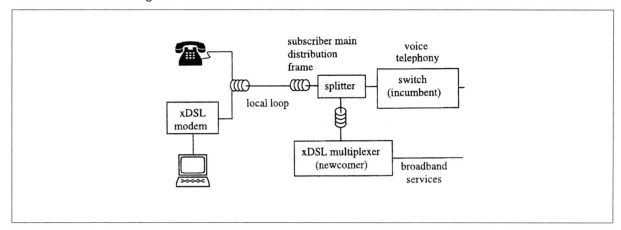

FIGURE 4 High speed bitstream access

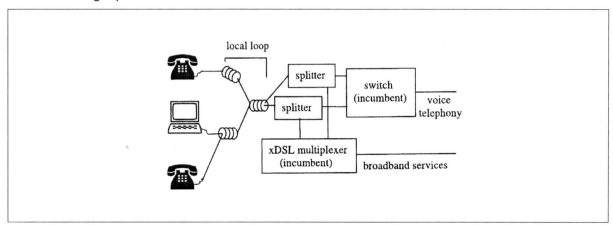

for the provision of broadband services (see European Commission, 2000a, p. 15f).

As with line sharing, voice and data traffic are separated from each other by a splitter. With bitstream access, the entrant has neither physical access to the copper pairs nor influence on the functionality of the access service. As depicted in Fig. 4, with high-speed bitstream access the incumbent is still able to serve his customers with voice telephony.

A NORMATIVE FRAMEWORK FOR REGULATING NETWORK ACCESS

The Essential Facilities Doctrine

The appropriate framework for the assessment whether an incumbent carrier should be forced to grant competitors access to his local infrastucture is the essential facilities doctrine, which has its roots in the tradition of American anti-trust law. It

may be used to enforce access to a facility which is 'essential'.

For a facility to be 'essential', several conditions have to be fulfilled simultaneously (see Glasl, 1994, p. 308).[10] The facility in question must be owned by a monopolist who refuses access to potential downstream competitors although this would be feasible. Further, the facility has to be not reasonably duplicable by potential entrants with the consequence that they cannot enter the downstream market without being granted access to precisely this facility—in short, if there exist neither active nor potential (perfect or imperfect) substitutes.

Areeda stresses that the doctrine should be applied restrictively—not anything "one has that another wants" should be called an essential facility (see Areeda, 1990, p. 844). But at least for the moment with respect to local loops outside the large cities[11] these conditions seem to be fulfilled as a rule.[12] Access to essential facilities should be granted, if this is "likely substantially to improve competition in the marketplace by reducing price or by increasing output or innovation" (Areeda, 1990, p. 852).

The essential facilities doctrine does not only apply in the context of competition law, but can also be integrated into a framework of sector-specific regulation.

The Disaggregated Regulatory Approach

With the aim of avoiding unnecessary interventions and therefore keeping regulation as light as possible, the disaggregated approach offers principles for sector-specific regulation in network industries, based on clear-cut criteria for the assessment of market power (see Knieps, 2000, pp. 95–100). Market power prevails if a natural monopoly exists in conjunction with sunk costs ('monopolistic bottleneck').[13] These explicit economic criteria put the definition of an essential facility in concrete form.

Regulatory measures should be carefully directed only to those parts of the market where a market power problem exists. An extension of the regulatory basis in the sense of a 'global regulation' is rejected, because from a constitutional economic point of view unnecessary interventions into the market mechanism cannot be justified. Besides, the cost of regulation has to be considered.[14]

A related issue is the intensity of interventions. If regulatory action is necessary, it should be measured out in such a dose as to ensure that market power is neutralized without restricting the regulated firm unnecessarily. This implies that the price regulation should be restricted to the price *level* and leave the design of price *structures* as far as possible to the regulated firm, as it is the case with price-cap regulation.[15] Consequently, if a regulation which was necessary in the past has become superfluous in the meantime, it should be abolished as soon as possible.

THE RELEVANCE OF UNBUNDLED ACCESS TO THE LOCAL LOOP FOR COMPETITION IN DOWNSTREAM MARKETS

Unbundled Access for Long Distance Carriers?

The adoption of the regulatory approach presented in the previous section to the problem of local loop unbundling requires a differentiation between long distance carriers and suppliers of local services.

Long distance carriers are dependent on getting access to the incumbent's local network. Otherwise there would be no sense in operating a long distance network, because it would be impossible to reach customers as senders or receivers of messages. Unbundled access to the local loops enables them to transport long distance calls to and from the customers themselves, but in their function as long distance carriers the crucial thing is to get access to the customers *generally* (see Engel & Knieps, 1998, pp. 24, 27). For that, interconnection at the trunk side of the local switch (see Fig. 1) is sufficient.

This makes clear that an unbundling obligation which favours long distance carriers is unnecessary from the perspective of a disaggregated regulatory approach as well as questionable from a legal perspective. Such an obligation might be in conflict with the principle of proportionality,[16] as there exists a weaker instrument for disciplining market power in the form of usual interconnection regulation.

Unbundled Access for Suppliers of Local Services?

The term 'local services' includes narrowband as well as broadband services. Narrowband voice telephony consists of a package of local transmission and switching services.[17] Local broadband services like fast internet access deal with the transmission of large quantities of data towards the customer as well as away from the customer, usually the latter to a minor extent only.

At present new competitors can enter local service markets outside densely populated areas only by two means, either on the basis of unbundled local loops or by reselling the incumbent's services.

With resale the entrant buys local telecommunications services offered by the incumbent at wholesale rates and then sells those services on his own behalf and on his own account, thereby passing on a portion of the wholesale discount to his customers. The reseller's scope for competitive action is confined to the enrichment of existing services by new features and to marketing efforts, e.g. the improvement of the quality of service and the design of new tariff structures. Since the reseller has to make use of loopholes in the established firm's retail price structure (arbitrage), his possibilities to create innovative tariff structures are limited.

The entrant cannot influence the technical features of the retail services. That is why the reseller's possibility of standing in contrast to the incumbent and the range of feasible new services are restricted. Given price regulation upstream, tariff arbitrage will lead to lower prices in the field of existing services like local voice telephony. But there is no scope for competition as to the deployment of innovative transmission technologies which might be the source of many new services.

With unbundled access to the incumbent's local loops, new market players are capable of carrying out the local transmission of messages or data on their own. By renting transmission capacities complementary to their own switching devices they are able to offer an alternative connection to the public telecommunications network also to those customers for whom selective bypass would not be profitable. In the case of full unbundling (see Fig. 2) and line sharing (see Fig. 3) the newcomer gains certain degrees of freedom as to the choice of transmission technology. It is to be expected that the pressure of competition will foster the spread of innovative technologies like xDSL (see European Commission, 2000a, p. 5), which will lead to a larger variety of services being offered to the customer.

It is apparent that resale is no close substitute for local loop unbundling. An obligation on the part of the incumbent carrier to sell his local services to downstream competitors on the wholesale market cannot overcome the monopolistic bottleneck completely. It follows that but for an unbundling obligation some of the competition potential in local markets would remain unused. From this point of view resale regulation and unbundling regulation are complements rather than substitutes.[18]

In the long run 'sustainable' competition, i.e. competition that need not be kept alive by permanent market power regulation, is only possible if efficient network competition is evolving gradually. In this context unbundled access may serve as a first stage for new market players.[19] By means of hired local loops, entrants can gather information on the demand and cost conditions on local markets without having to run the risk of enormous sunk investments initially. Instead, new infrastructure can be set up step by step when the number of customers is going up. Seen from this perspective, the concept of local loop unbundling might support the development of competition based on an efficient variety of local networks.[20]

THE DESIGN OF AN UNBUNDLING OBLIGATION

Effects on Competition and Property Rights
Full Unbundling
This form of unbundling reveals theoretically the largest scope for competition, because the competitors take over the local loops completely and may choose from the whole range of the xDSL family, opening the way for competition in transmission technologies which may yield a multitude of innovative services not yet offered by the incumbent.

But in reality the freedom to choose the transmission technology is restricted by technical boundaries, because not all lines are qualified for all types of xDSL.[21] Additionally, assume that different entrants employ different xDSL-technologies on loops which belong to the same cable. These different technologies are likely to interfere with each other and with existing digital connections of the incumbent carrier, which might at worst cause the breakdown of the whole transmission system.

The main shortcoming of full unbundling is that the incumbent cannot use his property for his own purposes any more, because he is uncoupled from his former customers. The essential facilities doctrine cannot be used to justify such a drastic measure.

Line Sharing
With line sharing both the incumbent and the competitor have access to the customer. The competitor can choose from a range of transmission technologies operating on the higher frequency spectrum of the local loops, e.g. ADSL or *universal DSL* (UDSL), and offers broadband services to his customers. If the customer decides to change the supplier of broadband

services, the incumbent can continue offering voice service using the low frequency spectrum—his property rights are infringed upon only to the extent which is necessary to enable competition in the field of broadband services.

On the other side with this form of unbundling, high-powered technologies like *symmetric DSL* (SDSL), *high speed DSL* (HDSL) and VDSL (*very high bitrate ADSL*) cannot be employed, because this would require the usage of the full frequency spectrum of the local loop (see European Commission, 2000a, annex I). This limits the potential for innovation, but reduces the coordination problem mentioned above. Besides, line sharing poses special difficulties as to the pricing of network access (see Section 6).

Bitstream Access

With bitstream access the incumbent keeps full control of his network. He is obliged to offer access to a specified bandwidth on his local loop, being free to decide which technology is used.[22] Therefore, the coordination problem as to the use of different technologies in one and the same cable (or the substitution of copper by fibre) is internalized in the course of the incumbent's network optimization. Bitstream access is the least burdensome solution for the incumbent.

The other side of the coin is that the competition effects of this form of unbundling are limited. The entrant is enabled to compete in the area of broadband services, but has no influence on the transmission technology. Innovation can therefore only take place at the service level. The incumbent has the power to decide which local loops should be upgraded first and thus which consumers can be served with broadband services, whether by himself or by the newcomer (see European Commission, 2000a, p. 16). For these reasons requiring bitstream access is too weak an instrument for substantially improving competition in local telecommunications markets.

Suggestions for the Design of an Unbundling Obligation

The different forms of unbundled access to the local loop can be seen as complements or as substitutes. If seen as complements, 'the market' can decide which form of access best meets user needs (see European Commission, 2000a, p. 6). In unregulated markets

this argument is indisputable, but it is too vague in the context of a sector-specific regulation which intervenes into the market mechanism.

Local loop unbundling goes along with an intrinsic trade-off—the more comprehensive the scope for competition a form of unbundling reveals, the stronger the property rights of the incumbent carrier are infringed upon.

A 'regulatory menu' which consists of different forms of unbundling from which entrants may choose à la carte goes too far from the perspective of the disaggregated regulatory approach. It overstrains the essential facilities doctrine and is likely to destroy the incumbent's incentives to invest in its local networks. The more comprehensive the duty to share its local loops (at cost-based prices), the less is the incentive of the incumbent firm (and its competitors) to invest in new, risky technologies. The regulated firm has to bear the whole risk of failure, but has to share the fruits of the investment if it turned out to be successful (see Kahn, Tardiff, & Weisman, 1999, p. 346f).

Based on the previous considerations, line sharing seems to be suitable to enable competition in local markets. An obligation to provide shared access could be seen as a minimum requirement the incumbent has to meet. An entrant preferring fully unbundled access might get it, if the incumbent decided to offer this form of access voluntarily. On the other side, bitstream access could be the result of private negotiation, if the entrant voluntarily waives his right to get unbundled access in the form of line sharing.

The regulatory instrument of local loop unbundling does not have to provide competitors with a *perfect* substitute for a local network of their own, but to enable competition in vertically related markets.

It should be only a temporal substitute, because the development of (efficient) network competition in the long run is the precondition for the elimination of market power and the phasing-out of sector-specific regulation. In this context, the pricing of unbundled access to the local loop plays a central role.

THE PRICING OF UNBUNDLED LOCAL LOOPS

The pricing of unbundled local loops is crucial for the entrants' investment decisions. If the regulator sets the price of the local loops 'too low,' investment incentives are destroyed. If the price is set 'too high,' inefficient network competition might occur in the long term.[23] Prices of local loops should reflect their long run incremental costs (LRIC) plus a mark-up to ensure that costs which are common to the line and other services of the incumbent carrier can be recovered.[24]

The problem of common cost allocation gains further importance when a local loop is used by two parties, because there are costs which are incremental to the local loop as a whole and not to its higher frequency or lower frequency portion.[25] These costs need to be split and allocated between the voice and non-voice portion of the local loop. In this context, different approaches are under consideration.

One of them is based on ad hoc rules. Assume that there are one voice service and one data service operating on the local loop in question. Criteria for cost allocation might be the number of services, which would lead to a split of 50:50, or the amount of bandwidth which is used by the services, i.e. roughly a split of 5:95 (see OFTEL, 2000, p. 11). Alternatively, the whole of the common costs could be allocated to the voice telephony portion of the line.[26]

Another approach deals with mark-ups which are proportionate to the incremental cost of the services provided on it. Under the assumption that the broadband service goes along with higher incremental costs than the voice service (e.g. because xDSL-splitters have to be installed), a higher portion of common costs would be ascribed to the supplier of the broadband service.

Finally, the allocation of common costs can be related to the price elasticity of demand for the services run on the local loop. This is the allocative mechanism to be preferred from an economic point of view. The higher the price elasticity, the smaller the mark-up allocated to the service in question. This approach ensures the recovery of common costs while minimizing allocative distortions which are likely to occur in the context of the two above mentioned approaches, but it requires a very flexible price regulation.

Since the efforts and the costs of creating and enforcing an elaborate regulatory scheme which takes explicit account of price elasticities are high, it should be discussed whether to include the prices for unbundled network elements into a price-cap mechanism together with other bottleneck elements.

SUMMARY

In this paper, an approach is adopted which postulates that regulatory measures should be restricted to what is absolutely necessary. Seen against this background the following conclusions can be drawn with regard to local loop unbundling.

A general unbundling obligation of incumbent carriers is questionable. Long distance carriers are not dependent upon unbundled access to the incumbent's local loops. Bundled access in the form of usual interconnection is sufficient to assure their participation in the competition process. The unbundling obligation of the incumbent should focus on alternative suppliers of local broadband services.

What has to be emphasized is that in the light of a restrictive application of the essential facilities doctrine the different forms of unbundling should not be seen as complements.

In order to open up local telecommunications markets for competition comprehensively, unbundled access in the form of line sharing seems to be a suitable instrument. Suppliers of local services like fast internet access can influence the transmission technology employed on the hired local loops to a certain degree, thereby strengthening competition in this area. This is the main advantage of line sharing compared with bitstream access. Further, the property rights of the regulated firm are infringed upon no more than is necessary, because the connection to its customers is maintained. This is the main advantage of line sharing compared with full unbundling.

An obligation of the incumbent carrier to provide line sharing should be embedded in a flexible framework for price regulation which takes account of the price elasticity of demand.

Due to the prospect of network competition in the long run, the need for an unbundling regulation has to be reviewed from time to time.

ACKNOWLEDGEMENTS

Comments by Günter Knieps are gratefully acknowledged. For comments on an earlier version of this paper the author would like to thank Christian Dippon and an anonymous referee.

NOTES

1. For a detailed description of the structure of an access network see Mitchell and Vogelsang (1994, p. 13), and WIK(1998, p. 25ff).

2. In Europe, only about 20% of the copper local loops terminate directly at a switch site. Most customers are connected indirectly with the local switch via a so-called remote concentrator unit (see Lewin & Matthews, 1998, p. 65). In this case the subscriber main distribution frame is located at the remote concentrator unit which is connected with a specific local switch by fibre.

3. If access is granted at the serving area interface or at the network termination point, this is called 'subloopunbundling'.

4. In its recent regulation on unbundled access, the European Parliament and the Council oblige operators with significant market power in the provision of fixed public telephone networks and services to offer fully unbundled as well as shared access to their copper local loops. See European Parliament and Council of the European Union (2000).

5. Although restricted in making use of his property rights, the regulated firm is still the owner of the local loop in a legal sense.

6. Although there are situations imaginable in which access takes place at other interfaces in the local network (see footnote 3), no distinction is made between these different situations, because this is not the central point for the purpose of this paper.

7. The entrant can use the full frequency spectrum on the copper line which enables the usage not only of *asymmetric digital subscriber line* (ADSL) but also of advanced DSL technologies like *very high bitrate ADSL* (VDSL). But it has to be kept in mind that VDSL only operates over short distances. Only with local loops shorter than 300 m the maximum speed of more than 50Mbit/s can be achieved (see Lewin & Matthews, 1998, p. 33). See also Section 5.1.

8. Consider two end-users, A and B, which were both customers of the incumbent carrier initially. Assume that B decides to become a customer of the entrant. When he calls A now, the call does not reach the incumbent's switching computer any more, unless the local networks are interconnected logically at the trunk side of the incumbent's switch.

9. The entrant might offer local voice telephony to his customers, too, by reselling the services of the incumbent or by using the higher frequency spectrum of the hired loop for both broadband and voice services.

10. The leading US essential facilities case in the telecommunications sector is MCI Communications Corp. v. AT&T. In the course of this case the criteria mentioned have been established.

11. In metropolitan areas where network oligopolies have already developed, competitors have obviously managed to enter the market on the basis of their own facilities without dependence upon those of the incumbent. This demonstrates in itself that the local loops of the incumbent are not 'essential' for would-be competitors (see Kahn, 1999, para. 9). A similar argument holds for large business customers, irrespective of whether they are located in large cities or in rural areas, because for them selective by-pass would be viable (e.g. using fibre).

12. The author refers especially to the situation in Germany, where end-users outside the large cities normally do not have the choice between several local carriers. Alternative access technologies using cable TV networks or power distribution networks are not yet ready for widespread use. This is the case in most member states of the European Union. An exception is the United Kingdom where the local infrastructure of alternative carriers (among others cable TV

networks) plays a significant role (see European Commission, 1999, p. 241).

13. The disaggregated regulatory approach is based on the theory of 'contestable markets', in which sunk costs are identified as the reason for non-contestability of a natural monopoly. See Baumol, Panzar and Willig (1982).

14. Besides the direct costs there are indirect costs of regulation. An example for the latter could be the distortion of the market outcome caused by a restrictive price regulation hampering social welfare.

15. Since well-directed regulation of monopolistic bottlenecks gives incentives for leveraging market power into vertically related unregulated markets, access regulation and price-cap regulation have to be accompanied by two further measures. First, the regulated firm must be committed to setting non-discriminatory access charges. Otherwise a local profit constraint could be avoided by setting prohibitively high access charges for third parties and low access charges for one's own downstream departments. Second, the regulated firm must be obliged to keep separate books for the regulated and non-regulated parts of the business to prevent internal shifts of costs or revenues. These points are discussed in Brunekreeft (1997, pp. 6–8).

16. According to this principle an intervention into property rights—which are protected by constitutional law—is only justified if the following three conditions are met: the intervention has to be suitable, the least burdensome solution, and narrowly tailored to the ends (see Stern & Dietlein, 1999, p. 8).

17. This package may be extended by an additional value ('value added service'), e.g. access to a database from which information on local events can be collected.

18. Resale regulation is only sufficient for promoting competition with regard to such services for which innovation at the upstream level plays no central role (e.g. plain voice telephony).

19. FCC (1999), para. 5: "Moreover, in some areas, we believe that the greatest benefits may be achieved through facilities-based competition, and that the availability of requesting carriers to use unbundled network elements, … , is a necessary precondition to the subsequent deployment of self-provisioned network facilities." See also Lewin and Matthews (1998, p. 66).

20. Hard empirical evidence to back up this argument does not exist as far as the author knows. For an overview of the structure of the local access markets within the European Union see European Commission (1999, annex 4.7, 2000b, annexes 1.4 and 3).

21. This is among other things a question of the loop length (see Lewin & Matthews, 1998, p. 33).

22. "'High speed bit stream access' refers to the situation where the incumbent installs a high speed access link to the customers' premises (e.g. by installing its preferred ADSL equipment and configuration in its local access network) …" European Commission (2000a, p. 15). Or, as Lewin and Matthews (1998, p. 68) put it, with bitstream access "… the incumbent would then be free to modify its access network in whatever way it wished, as long as it delivered the required bit stream services." There is no technical regulatory intervention in the sense of the prescription of a special transmission technology.

23. A detailed discussion of the problems related to the pricing of unbundled network elements would be far beyond the scope of this paper.

24. E.g. the costs for the duct used by several lines between the serving area interface and the subscriber main distribution frame (see Fig. 1).

25. E.g. the costs for the copper line and the portion of the duct between the network termination point at the customer's home and the serving area interface at which the lines of several customers are concentrated (see Fig. 1).

26. The latter is favoured by OFTEL in its Consultation Document on shared access to the local loop, not least for pragmatic reasons (see OFTEL, 2000, pp. 11/12). Besides the danger of allocative distortions an additional problem might occur: With line sharing, the subscriber could decide to receive both data and voice services on the higher frequency portion of the local loop. This leads to a dilemma for the incumbent carrier: On the one side he needs to recover the

common costs which were allocated to the low frequency portion of the local loop initially, so he has to charge his remaining subscribers a higher line rental. On the other side this might create incentives for them to cease their voice telephony contract, too. OFTEL proposes as a way out to treat such a line just like a fully unbundled one forwhich the sharing operator offering also voice telepony has to pay the full price (see OFTEL, 2000, p. 12).

REFERENCES

Areeda, P. (1990). Essential facilities: An epithet in need of limiting principles. *Antitrust Law Journal, 58,* 841–853. Baumol, W. L., Panzar, J., & Willig, R. (1982). *Contestable markets and the theory of industry structure.* New York: Hartcourt Brace Jovanovich.

Brunekreeft, G. (1997). *Local versus global price cap: A comparison of foreclosure incentives.* Discussion Paper No. 36. Institute of Transport Economics and Regional Policy, University of Freiburg.

Engel, Ch., & Knieps, G. (1998). *Die Vorschriften des Telekommunikationsgesetzes über den Zugang zu wesentlichen Leistungen. Eine juristisch-ökonomische Untersuchung.* Baden-Baden: Nomos Verlagsgesellschaft.

European Commission. (1999). *Fifth report on the implementation of the telecommunications regulatory package.* Communication from the Commission to the European Parliament, the Council, the Economic and Social Committee and the Committee of the Regions. COM(1999)537. Brussels, November.

European Commission. (2000a). *Unbundled access to the local loop.* Working Document prepared by the Information Society DG, outlining an approach towards a possible Commission Recommendation. Brussels, February.

European Commission. (2000b). *Sixth report on the implementation of the telecommunications regulatory package.* Communication from the Commission to the European Parliament, the Economic and Social Committee and the Committee of the Regions. COM(2000)814. Brussels, December.

European Parliament & Council of the European Union. (2000). *Regulation of the European Parliament and of the Council on unbundled access to the local loop.* 2000/0185 (COD). Brussels, December.

FCC. (1999). *Third report and order and fourth further notice of proposed rulemaking in the matter of implementation of the local competition provisions of the Telecommunications Act of 1996 (FCC 99–238).* Federal Communications Commission, Washington, DC, November.

Glasl, D. (1994). Essential facilities doctrine in EC anti-trust law: A contribution to the current debate. *European Competition Law Review, 6,* 306–314.

Kahn, A. E. (1999). *Declaration before the Federal Communications Commission in response to second further notice of proposed rulemaking in the matter of implementation of the local competition provisions in the Telecommunications Act of 1996.* CC Docket No. 96–98.

Kahn, A. E., Tardiff, T. J., & Weisman, D. L. (1999). The Telecommunications Act at three years: An economic evaluation of its implementation by the Federal Communications Commission. *Information Economics and Policy, 11,* 319–365.

Knieps, G. (2000). Interconnection and network access. *Fordham International Law Journal, 23,* 90–115.

Lewin, D., & Matthews, J. (1998). *Access networks and regulatory measures.* Study prepared by Ovum for DG XIII of the European Commission. Final Report, November.

Mitchell, B., & Vogelsang, I. (1994). *Interconnection of telecommunications networks in the USA.* Discussion Paper No. 138, Wissenschaftliches Institut für Kommunikationsdienste (WIK), Bad Honnef.

OFTEL. (2000). *Access to bandwidth: Shared access to the local loop.* Consultation Document on the implementation of shared access to the local loop in the UK. Office of Telecommunications, London, October.

Stern, K., & Dietlein, J. (1999). Netzzugang im Telekommunikationsrecht (Teil 2)—Zur verfassungsrechtlichen roblematik eines "entbündelten"

Zugangs zu den Teilnehmeranschlussleitungen. *Archiv für Post und Telekommunikation, 1,* 2–15.

WIK. (1998). *Ein analytisches Kostenmodell für das Ortsnetz.* Reference Document commissioned by the Regulierungsbehörde für Post und Telekommunikation (RegTP). Wissenschaftliches Institut für Telekommunikationsdienste, Bad Honnef, March.

'From All My Teachers I Have Grown Wise,[1] and From My Students More than Anyone Else'[2]

What Lessons Can the U.S. Learn from Broadband Policies in Europe?

Amit M. Schejter

ABSTRACT

Rooted in what are already disparate programs of regulatory intervention, the European Union and the United States have identified differently their current challenges in telecommunications policy. This study describes the development of both regulatory frameworks through their philosophical roots and ideological transitions demonstrating how, on the one hand, American influences have affected the European policy language, but, on the other, the European policies have better implemented the same policies and as a result are being seen as contributing to higher levels of broadband penetration. This time around, it seems that attending to the strengths of the European process may help policy-makers in the US reformulate their own home-grown policies.

KEYWORDS: European Union / local loop unbundling / telecommunications policy / United States / universal service

INTRODUCTION

Fearing the eventuality of economic colonization by the United States and Japan, that had demonstrated far greater success in adopting and using information society technologies (Schneider, 2001), the European Commission began taking charge of policy-making in the continent in the 1990s, revolutionizing the European political structure and regulatory landscape (Sandholtz, 1996). While making use of policy terminology coined in the US, the European Union launched its own innovative industrial scheme, which included enforcing local loop unbundling (LLU), a policy that helped it almost catch up (on average), and in some locales, even plunge ahead of the US in broadband penetration levels, after starting out far behind.

While this study describes the evolution of the policies that led to European supremacy in broadband deployment, it compares European policy development to the policy development in the US during the same period. The study concludes that this time around the Europeans may be on the way to taking a more innovative and effective approach to what was once considered a badge of pride of the US telecommunications policy, universal service, by considering the adoption of a universal broadband goal—thus once more adopting an American concept and perfecting it to serve up-to-date policy goals. Highlighting the strengths of the European system—focus, simplicity, relative efficiency and willingness to change the course of policy as needed, an effective balance between centralization and delegation of power, and innovation—the study addresses the question of whether the new European attention to universal service and the apparent disregard of a need for reform by the US might boost the trend of European leadership in broadband deployment. If so, the question that arises is whether the US, in order to stay competitive with the EU, will learn from its past mistakes and adopt an approach that will identify universal service as a policy measure ensuring more rapid diffusion of broadband access, and in an ironic reversal of past trends, will learn from those who once learned from it.

Following a comparison of the development of European and American regulatory frameworks, which takes into account their philosophical roots, this article describes how the American-coined 'unbundling' terminology was adopted in Europe but evolved in different directions in both regimes to different outcomes. This analysis helps explain the emerging differences in the design of universal service in the current regulatory debate, and demonstrates how the US may once again be heading on the wrong course by allowing the distortion and misinterpretation of American homegrown policies while at the same time European policy-makers are refining them to achieve their original social goals. En route to the liberalization of the European telecommunications infrastructure, policy ideas and vocabulary formulated in the US, namely the idea of the open network architecture, helped European regulators arrive at a sound and focused policy to which the success in proliferation of broadband can be attributed. By re-framing the policy debate in the US this time around, using terminology developed in Europe, the US may maintain, or rather regain, its competitive edge.

THE USEFULNESS OF COMPARISONS

Comparing the policies of different regimes in order to learn from them is commonly seen as a justification for conducting comparative research (Livingstone, 2003). National policy-makers, contends Bauer (2003), not only study reforms in other countries, they often end up adopting similar policies. The revolutionary regulatory framework adopted by the EU in the early 2000s has already been the focus of comparative studies with Japan (Fuke, 2003) and with the US (Kubicek et al., 2001; Marcus, 2002).

However, when differences in institutional frameworks are not taken into account, research findings may be more anecdotal than systematic, and their value is questionable. Addressing possible confounding variables, therefore, becomes critical. It is easy to downplay the significance of comparisons and argue that certain things defy comparison. In the case of policies geared toward liberalizing telecommunications markets, however, these comparisons can and should be undertaken, because of the very basic similarities that stem from the common elements that characterize telecommunication networks. Some would argue that the policies of the US and the EU defy comparison. While the former is a national unit, the latter is a loose federation of 27 independent nation-states; while the former has been institutionalized as a uniform political and economic unit for more than 200 years, the latter has been in a constant state of flux, with regards to organizational form and membership; while the former's national policies are guided by an established and court-tested constitution, the latter is unable to form a binding constitution. The EU is a weak confederation, as it has no national sovereignty. Its member states have strong political ties to the incumbent telecommunications operators (the PTTs) they owned during most of the period reviewed in this study, and unlike the Brussels bureaucracy, member state governments and law-makers are held accountable to their constituents. Just like the case in the US, however, there is constant tension in the EU between federal and state rights, although the balancing acts that have eventually evolved in Europe have spawned different approaches to policy formulation. This study takes into account these differences, their effect on policy formulation and outcomes, and it demonstrates that much can be learned from them.

THE STATE OF THINGS

When it comes to broadband penetration, the US has been consistently lagging behind members of the Organization for Economic Cooperation and Development (OECD), the original 15 members of the European Union (the "EU 15") and even countries that traditionally had no prior success in ICT

FIGURE 1   US and EU 15 Broadband Penetration (per 100 inhabitants) Net Increase 2001–7

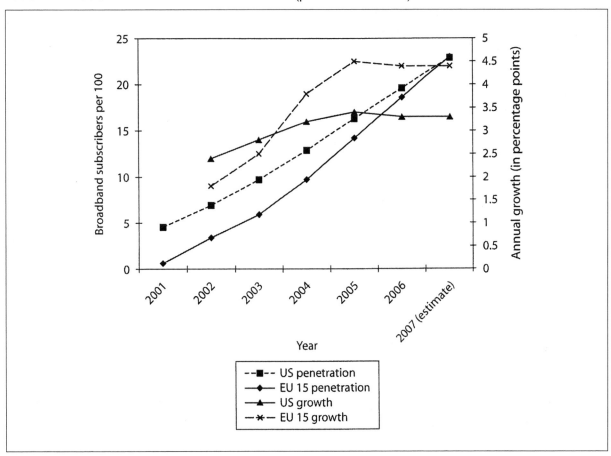

Source: OECD.

development and boast fewer financial resources than the US (Frieden, 2005).

In fact, between 2003 and 2006, the US dropped from 10th to 15th place in broadband deployment among the OECD countries.[3] Between the end of 2005 and the end of 2006, the US stood 20th among the 34 OECD members in the growth rate of broadband adoption. Since 2003, the EU 15 growth rate has passed that of the US, predicting total penetration rate to match that of the US by the end of 2007 (see Figure 1).

The differences between the two unions' performance, however, are not limited to broadband penetration alone. Since the passing of the Telecommunications Act in 1996, there has been no positive change in telephone penetration levels in the US—a slight decline from 93.9 percent in 1996 to 92.9 percent in 2006 can be observed—even though the Federal Communications Commission (FCC) has changed the working definition of 'telephone

penetration' to include wireless access.[4] Most recently, the EU reported that 97 percent of households in the Union had telephone access in 2006.[5] What is clearly similar in both unions is the fact that telephone penetration rates vary along socioeconomic lines. Schement and Mueller (1996) have long identified the correlation between poverty and connectivity in the US, a correlation supported by the FCC's report on telephone subscribership.[6] European statistics demonstrate a similar association between the two (van Zon, 2005).

It would be presumptuous to tie these trends to one specific contributing factor, as several possible configurations of economic circumstances and policy variables can support rapid broadband diffusion (Kim et al., 2003), however, it can be hypothesized that the consistent European growth in connectivity for both low- and high-tech applications and the continued stagnant and declining state of connectivity in the US may be traced to the historical and ideological roots of policy differences between the US and the EU and the way both unions have adjusted them to technological and economic changes of late.

DIFFERING PHILOSOPHIES OF TELECOMMUNICATION REGULATION

Telecommunications policy, or any policy for that matter, reflects the underlying assumptions about social reality that policy-makers share. Policy-making is an attribute of political culture (Homet, 1976; Redford, 1969). Information policy in the US assumes the predominance of civil liberties, economic efficiency and social fairness and equity (Bushkin and Yurow, 1980). This assumption relies on patterns of thought that reflect the western heritage of the Enlightenment (Streeter, 1990: 45). It has also been analyzed as the "outgrowth of the dissension of the European settlers who populated North America—men and women seeking to escape from social rigidities, to exercise a larger measure of economic freedom, to form governments and government structures that they might control than the other way around" (Homet, 1976: 4). Pool (1983), however, argues that historically, American media policy is one of "soft technological determinism," rather than one of market forces. He notes that whenever a new technology emerges on the scene, it is referred to in terms similar to the idea it most resembled that existed at the time. The new policy model offered is, therefore, technologically determined: regulation of the telegraph was adopted from policies that governed the operation of railroads, and cable television was viewed more as a form of television than a form of telephone. Even though a technology can be later better understood, developed and changed, the rules governing it and the institutions built around it remain intact. When technologies have converged, Pool notes, the US government has traditionally chosen to subject the new technology to the regulatory framework that applied to the more restricted of the converging technologies. For that reason, for example, cable television, which is comparable both to television and telephone, is regulated more like the former. Indeed, the US Communications Act, formulated in 1934, has evolved over the years into

a technologically biased law in which different policies are applied to different technologies. The laws pertaining to each technology are listed in separate chapters of the law, a technique that assures that changes in the law regarding one technology need not affect any other technology.

The basic European assumptions around which telecommunications policy has developed are remarkably different. In general, notes Garnham (2001), the provision of telephony was governed by the principles of public service, which derived from the absolute powers of monarchy and gave citizens no particular right. Telecommunications were regarded as both a natural monopoly and a public utility and as such their governance and regulation through state-owned post, telegraph and telephone monopolies (often referred to as PTTs) was considered justified (Sandholtz, 1993). The same can be said of the regulation of mass media, with European governments asserting early on that broadcasting was too important to be left in the hands of the market (Levy, 1999). This commonality in ideological stands allowed for the creation of the EU as a unifying force. The various EU legal apparatuses have developed a dynamic equilibrium between the forces of central authority and member state autonomy, the tension created by this state of affairs being most observable in the regulation of telecommunication markets. But unlike the technologically determined American model, the EU has developed in recent years a unique technologically neutral regulatory framework. Its first manifestation was in the regulatory framework for telecommunications adopted in 2003, subsequently followed up by the adoption of the "Audiovisual Without Frontiers" directive in 2007.

DIVERGENT HISTORIES OF TELECOMMUNICATION DEVELOPMENT

Indeed, the distinct ideological roots of policy have bred separate avenues of policy development on the two sides of the Atlantic. Committed to private enterprise, the US encouraged telecommunication policy to develop through private entrepreneurship. Only when it became clear that power was being abused in this emerging industry, in the late 19th century, was the newly created antitrust regulation applied to the emerging telecommunications monopoly. The initial struggles between the regulators and regulated focused on issues that have been at the heart of telecommunication regulation ever since: interconnection, mergers and acquisitions and universal service. While telecommunications was brought under the auspices of antitrust law in 1914 (the "Clayton Act"), it became regulated as a natural monopoly starting in 1921 (the "Willis–Graham Act"). In fact, as of that time and until the breakup of AT&T in 1984, only one difference existed between European and US telecommunication markets: the monopoly in the US was private, while that in Europe was run by the government. The outcome of this distinction was rather striking: in 1960, the penetration level of telephones in the US was 27.3 per 100 inhabitants, while in France it was 4.8, in Germany 5.8 and in the UK 9.6. This gap was maintained throughout the 1970s and 1980s, and only began narrowing when European PTTs became corporations in the 1980s and telephone penetration reached near saturation levels in the US.

It was the perceived advantage of the US's free enterprise system that led European countries (with the UK at the forefront), starting in the 1980s, to introduce two major policy initiatives: liberalization of the telecommunication markets and privatization of the national PTTs. But it was the publication of the National Information Infrastructure (NII) report in the US in 1993, a report which prompted fears in Europe of American economic colonization, that provided the impetus for a unified European policy (Schneider, 2001). The first cross-European liberalization policy was only introduced in 1988, but by 1990, the EU identified the connection between growth in the information sector and economic competitiveness on a global scale and linked it to liberalization policies. By 1993, it set a 1998 deadline for full liberalization of voice telephony, allowing member states and incumbent PTTs a lengthy period of adjustment (Waverman and Sirel, 1997). During this period, universal service was first introduced as a policy goal in Europe, as part of an 'open network' policy[7] seemingly influenced by policies adopted in the US. The American influence is also visible in the policy language adopted. When the concept of an "information society" was introduced by the Clinton–Gore administration, it was quickly integrated into the European discourse (Servaes and Burgelman, 2000), and its principles, namely the predominance of market forces in designing this new reality, became the focus of the ensuing policy report commissioned by the EU, known as the Bangemann Report (Anttiroiko, 2001; Bangemann, 1994). The Bangemann Report's conclusions were published just as the liberalization of the telecommunications sector was becoming a heated issue in Europe, with the European Commission asserting its position as a supranational governing body (Sandholtz, 1996). The ensuing conflict led to the publication of the "Green Paper on the Liberalization of Telecommunications Infrastructure and Cable Television Networks" in January 1995, which in turn led the council in September of that year to urge the Commission to create a regulatory framework[8] that resulted, among other things, in the first universal service directive, which was enacted in 1997.[9]

This initial European regulatory framework was reconsidered within two years,[10] a review which created a new regulatory framework that became law in 2003.[11] One issue, however, deemed more urgent by the Commission, was resolved by 2000, the adoption of a compulsory local loop unbundling (LLU) regime. Mandatory unbundling of the local loop means that the wires linking a telephone subscriber to the nearest operator facility are deemed an "essential facility," an element of the network without which a newcomer cannot enter the market and over which the incumbent has monopoly power. The regulation on unbundled access to the local loop[12] was enacted in order to "help bring about a substantial reduction in the costs of using the Internet." It mandates unbundled access to the local loops belonging to operators designated as having significant market power in the fixed public telephone network supply market by their national regulatory authorities. So while the entire regulatory framework was to be accepted by member states as of July 2003, the requirement that the PTTs unbundle their networks became law as early as 31 December 2000, and while the focus of liberalization had been voice telephony in 1998, by 2003 the policy was aimed at enhancing Internet access.

Two unique features characterized the 2003 regulatory framework: it was to be "technologically neutral" and it gave preference to competition law over telecommunication law. In practice, the latter meant that specific communication law provisions would apply only to those product markets that would be deemed uncompetitive by competition law standards. Indeed, the local loop was deemed as such.

LLU IN THE EU AND THE US: POLICY, IMPLEMENTATION AND OUTCOME

The adoption of a policy that required incumbent operators to unbundle their local loops was one of the highlights of the transition EU policy-makers made while developing a coherent regulatory framework in the 1990s and early 2000s. At the same time, regulators in the US spent nine years and numerous hours in court only to come up with a formula that, in fact, eliminates the unbundling regime.[13] While the Europeans defined the network element to be unbundled as the local loop and the local loop alone, the American law required mandatory unbundling of all network elements that the FCC would find were necessary and that by refraining from unbundling them a competitor would be significantly impaired. While the Europeans maintained for the regulatory authorities the determination of whether "significant market power" lies with the incumbent while determining a priori the network element regarding which this determination should be made, the American law defined a priori who the incumbents compelled to unbundle are and left the regulators with determining which elements should be unbundled. The result of the EU's approach was its ability to mobilize a far weaker and decentralized union to adopt policies that conflict with incumbent operators' interests for the sake of promoting competition that the central 'government' perceived as serving the public interest, and to do so successfully, contributing to faster penetration of advanced technologies. What is it in the European regulatory mechanism that did the trick?

As noted, the 1999 communication review brought about a rewriting of pan-European policies. But, while the transition to technological neutrality and the predominance given to competition law were introduced in an orderly fashion through the enactment of five directives, LLU was adopted separately, in a relatively short and unambiguous document. The regulation on unbundled access to the local loop[14] is explained in one paragraph of the preamble: local loops are necessary to gain access to consumers; they are controlled by incumbent operators that rolled them over a long period of time while enjoying monopoly status; competitors cannot match the economies of scale and coverage of incumbents. Based on this rationale, only one conclusion is possible, if competitive access to consumers is desired: incumbents should be forced to share the local loop with competitors while the prices they charge for this usage need to be regulated. By adopting this policy, the basic elements of network economics are served, as competitors can overcome the main barrier to entry to the market: the cost of gaining access to the most essential facility of the network without which it is impossible to reach the consumer. In doing so, the EU evoked the "essential facilities" doctrine and made it an integral part of telecommunication regulation. The European Parliament and Council narrowly defined what was to be unbundled, since this was required under the "essential facility" doctrine, and authorized the national regulators to enforce the regulation. It also presented a form of "light touch" or minimal regulatory intervention, due to its focus and simplicity; once technological neutrality was added, the policy took the direction of being even less obtrusive, as the central government could not be seen as dictating technological development, but only overseeing market behavior.

There is, however, considerable controversy regarding the efficacy of LLU. Some maintain it should be adopted as policy only temporarily (Doyle, 2000); that it may deter the development of the economically desired facility-based competition (Bourreau and Dogan, 2004); and that it has failed outright as a policy, as it has been poorly enforced (Spiller and Ulset, 2003). The figures, however, appear to support its advocates, and quite impressively. Bauer et al. (2002) conclude that more aggressive policies in the EU regarding LLU help explain the difference in Internet access among European regions. Marcus (2005) observes that about one in four of the 12 million new Internet subscribers in Europe in the 12 months preceding July 2004 can be explained by regulatory support for competitive access—fully unbundled lines, shared access, bitstream access or simple resale—all made possible as a result of the LLU regime adopted by the Union. Garcia-Murillo (2005) asserts that unbundling has a significant positive impact on the availability of broadband services and that it contributes to a substantial improvement in broadband deployment in middle-income countries, but not in their high-income counterparts. Gideon (2006) asserts that the incentive for investing in cost-reducing innovation did not diminish due to mandatory unbundling, as some operators often claim. The EU itself reports that because of new regulatory measures, in particular those pertaining to pricing, and because of increased investment in infrastructure by new operators, the market for shared lines and unbundled local loops increased in 2003–4 by 110 percent.[15]

Beyond these economic and network benefits, the policy of enforcing LLU on incumbent operators was also handled in a politically savvy manner. While the principle was defined narrowly and precisely, its implementation was left to national regulators. The latter, knowledgeable of local geographic and economic considerations and held accountable by their constituents, control the pricing of the loop and can maneuver between voter dissatisfaction and incumbent protectionism, while the EU's sanction sword hangs above their heads. Indeed, the relative success of broadband deployment attributed to LLU in some member states created additional pressure on national regulators to act and implement the policy. In perhaps the most dramatic of responses, and through extreme implementation of "technological neutrality," the Dutch parliament adopted in October 2006 a law requiring unbundling of cable television networks for the sake of broadband penetration.[16]

By contrast, unbundling in the US evolved in quite a different manner. Although it only became part of the law with the Telecommunications Act of 1996, it has roots in two parallel historic narratives: the interconnection regime that developed when long-distance competition was introduced in the 1970s and the "open network architecture" regime that emerged from the three rounds of "computer inquiries," which tested the boundaries between the regulation of telecommunication and information

services. When MCI started providing long-distance point-to-point service in the 1960s, it needed to connect to AT&T's access network in order to reach consumers.[17] The courts awarded MCI this right of access, which was termed "interconnection." In fact, though, the right awarded was a form of unbundling, as MCI was connecting to the AT&T network, but it was also using AT&T's network to access its consumers. At the time, the court ruled that AT&T's access network was an "essential facility," it cited the appropriate doctrine and applied it to the case. The "computer inquiries" held throughout the 1960s, 1970s and 1980s concluded that the *sine qua non* for the development of competition in data services was the adoption of an "open network architecture," a policy that ensured data providers with access to the consumers of the telephone monopoly (Cannon, 2005). With the development of the Internet, Internet service providers (ISPs) were also deemed as 'information services' (the new terminology for data providers), and thus allowed access to consumers for which the price paid to the access monopoly was determined by cost.

When "unbundling" became law in 1996, it was included in section 251 of the Telecommunications Act, the section dealing with interconnection, even though it is not an interconnection issue, but rather an issue of lowering barriers to entry. Contrary to the narrow European definition made at the legislative level, the Telecommunications Act of 1996 left the FCC with the discretion to decide which network elements need to be unbundled. While the FCC started with as broad as possible a list in its initial Local Competition Order in 1996,[18] the eventual objections by stakeholders on all sides of the debate led to a series of court rulings that one after another voided the FCC's decisions. The FCC could not satisfy the court that its choice of criteria satisfied the law's convoluted definition of what accounts for elements that are "necessary" for the proper functioning of competitors and elements that "impair" their ability to challenge the incumbent local operators. The competitive operators claimed that section 251 of the law "codifies something akin to the essential facilities doctrine,"[19] but the court refused to apply that standard and to accept that "essential facilities" was indeed a doctrine that prevails under US law.[20]

In 2005, after nine years of court proceedings, the FCC eliminated the unbundling requirement altogether,[21] citing the court decision that established cable modem access as an unregulated information service, and putting both technologies on an equal footing. As a result, not only were new telephone service providers essentially blocked from entering the market, ISPs as well lost their unique status. A policy born and bred in the US, which served as a model for the EU, had now become defunct. Ironically, as mentioned before, the Dutch parliament, operating in a country boasting the highest penetration level of broadband Internet access, had also found the need to put cable and landline access on equal regulatory footing, however it chose the exact opposite path, by forcing them both to unbundle their local loops. The fact that cable unbundling is not more widely enforced in Europe can be attributed to the fact that cable penetration levels are not uniform across the continent.

UNIVERSAL SERVICE IN THE EU: A DEVELOPING CONCEPT

Universal service was not a central element of EU policy historically. As Garnham (2001) notes, European policies were designed to guarantee continuity of service and not universality of supply, while protecting the PTTs against legal action for damages incurred for failing to provide service. Universal service, as a pan-European goal, was first mentioned in the 1992 "review of the situation in the telecommunications sector." It was deemed an issue to be "noted," "recognized," "considered" and mentioned as a "major goal" next to the liberalization of all public voice telephony services in a 1993 Council Resolution on the review of the situation in the telecommunication sector and the need for further development in that market.[22] In February 1994, the European Council adopted for the first time a specific resolution on universal service principles in the telecommunications sector,[23] which stipulated that universal service was "mainly a matter of the provision of a basic voice telephony service at an affordable price to all customers reasonably requesting it" and urged the member states to establish the appropriate regulatory framework to ensure its provision. The Bangemann Report issued that same

year, while promoting a market-oriented approach, and widely criticized for its extreme neoliberal premise, identified the main social risk of the evolving information society in "the creation of a two tier society of have and have-nots" (Bangemann, 1994: 5), expressing concern that individual members of society would reject the new information society technologies. The solution recommended was to prepare the European populace through education. The report stated that "fair access to the infrastructure will have to be guaranteed to all, as will provision of universal service, the definition of which must evolve in line with the technology" (Bangemann, 1994: 5–6). With regards to the market mechanisms aimed at ensuring universal service, the Bangemann Report recommended ending the PTT monopolies while ensuring that in the future all licensed operators would take responsibility that the universal service obligation was met.

The 1997 directive[24] accepted that the concept of universal service must evolve in order to keep pace with technological and economic changes and defined it as "a defined minimum set of services of specified quality which is available to all users independent of their geographical location and, in the light of specific national conditions, at an affordable price." Member states and their respective regulatory authorities were held responsible for maintaining and developing a universal service and provided with the authority to rule in cases in which the universal service obligation was an unfair burden on an operator, along with the jurisdiction to establish the appropriate compensatory mechanism. The directive, however, dictated the formula for calculating the burden. This balancing act demonstrates once again the peculiarities of the European model: while the bureaucrats promote a "free market" ideology based within a narrow technocratic vision and dictate mechanisms for calculating universal cost that are purely economic and deny any padding of expenses by the member-state-government-darling-PTT, the member states maintain jurisdiction that reflects both their invested interest in the PTTs and their political responsibilities. The European effort was focused first on creating rate balancing mechanisms, only then on the voluntary member state intervention in assuring affordable rates by creating a universal service fund

(Cherry, 1999). In fact, only two member states (France and Spain) had to establish funding mechanisms for universal service, as the narrow definition of the service allowed fulfilling of the universal service obligation without a need for an additional subsidy (Michalis, 2002).

Indeed, universal service continued to be defined very narrowly, arousing some scholarly criticism. Bauer (1998) lamented the limited nature of the universal service right in Europe, attributing it to the monopolistic history of the industry, the interaction between the EU and its member states and the slow economic growth that characterized Europe in the 1990s. While he believed the policy adopted maximized the "synergies between market forces and information access" (Bauer, 1998: 330), he argued that it "fell short of a more visionary policy." Melody (1999) observed that amid the transition from national PTTs to commercial public telecom operators (PTOs) (as privatization progressed), many PTOs discovered that universal service funding helped quell competition and pad their bottom lines. "Elaborate mechanisms for calculating and sharing extra universal service costs," he noted, "are primarily to blunt the face of serious competition. Those countries that are serious about universal service, e.g. the Nordic countries, have gone about it in the simplest way possible. Denmark and Finland have not even bothered to calculate it" (Melody, 1999: 23). Kiessling and Blondeel (1998), on the other hand, warned that the tendency of some countries, notably Belgium and the Netherlands, to pursue a broader definition of universal service might lead to higher costs on new market players, thus hindering competition. This assertion contradicted Skogerbø and Storsul's (2000) findings that opposition to an expanded universal service definition in small countries (Denmark, the Netherlands and Norway) came at the time from the incumbent PTTs and therefore reduced the possibility of an expanded definition of universal service in Europe.

Indeed, the 1999 public consultation and communication review, conducted for the purpose of jumpstarting a new regulatory framework for the European community, failed to revolutionize the definition of universal service. It concluded that the current scope of universal service should be maintained, while introducing procedures for its review and update.[25] The ensuing regulatory framework, which encompassed five directives, did, however, include, for the second time, a separate directive on universal service. Although the working document published along with the review[26] does not expand the definition of universal service, the 2002 directive on universal service and users' rights[27] does. Although guaranteeing availability, quality and efficient implementation had been left to the member states, universal service was expanded to include the ability to receive and make local, national and international telephone calls, facsimile communications and data communications sufficient to permit "functional Internet access."[28] The latter is to be defined by taking into account the technological choice of the majority of subscribers. At the same time that it added "social obligations" to the universal service obligations—the duty to provide directories, public pay phones, special measures for the disabled and affordability of tariffs—the directive also introduced an important element into the pricing mechanism of the universal service obligations. When calculating the cost of the obligation, regulators are required to subtract any market benefit that arises from providing the service under the obligation. Hence, by 2002, the EU had both expanded the basic obligations of operators and rights of consumers in major legislation, and further weakened the position of the national PTTs, by making consumer demand the determinant of Internet access technology and by taking into account the advantages held by incumbents in the role of local access monopolies. Some national regulators, picking up on the European cues, embarked on their own ambitious re-examination of their internal policies (Simpson, 2004).

The 2006 review of the regulatory framework[29] was already designed to assess the efficacy of the 2003 regulatory framework. As part of this review, the commission noted that a "broadband gap" is emerging in Europe along geographical lines.[30] The Commission staff working document, following the review and previewing the imminent green paper, stops short of establishing broadband as a universal service. It does, however, create the conditions for a debate about a new definition for universal service that distinguishes universal access from universal content, in this way tying the debate on universal service to the debate on "net neutrality." The Commission staff are under the impression that the technologically neutral analysis of significant market power and the powers granted to the national regulatory authorities in this regard provide the NRAs with the authority to guarantee minimum quality levels for transmission levels that will assure that access to certain content services is not blocked.[31] Access to content emerges here as an issue to be framed within a debate on the meaning of universal service. As such, the EU took upon itself to publish a new green paper on universal service, which should have included a road map for a new definition by 2007—yet again setting an expedited timetable to encounter what appear to be problems on the horizon.

Just like unbundling, universal service is a term developed in the US and further expanded. It seems, however, to be heading in the direction of the unbundling regime. Indeed, while many would prefer to believe that universal service has always been a goal of telecommunications policy in the US, as Mueller (1997) reveals, it was in fact a ploy to maintain AT&T's monopoly, and instead of meaning universal access for consumers, it meant a universal network controlled by AT&T. Universal service became law only in the 1996 Act, incorporating the mechanisms created originally for the purpose of subsidizing the local access of consumers through higher prices on long-distance calls. As such, it developed as a subsidy system. Just as it did in the case of unbundling, the law only describes the level of service as 'evolving', leaving it to regulators to determine the specifics, except for the unique provision of subsidizing Internet access to schools, libraries and health care providers (known as the "E-rate").

Indeed, even the most recent attempt to redraft a telecom bill in the US, in 2006, does not address the level of service that needs to be made available to all citizens of the US. The House version simply ignored the issue, while the Senate bill referred only to the funding mechanisms of the existing level of service.

REGULATORY IMPLICATIONS FOR FUTURE POLICY

It is probably axiomatic by now to say that it is a matter of national interest to promote access to broadband, at least as much as it is in the public and individual interest. Observing international broadband adoption trends and rates, one cannot fail to notice that while Europe is plunging ahead, with some countries leaving even Asian powerhouses behind, the US, which was the original leader in both making the first regulatory moves and adopting Internet technology, is slowly falling behind. What is it then that makes Europe different from the US, and what can the US learn from the European experience in order to revive broadband penetration?

On the conceptual level, the differences are pronounced: the Europeans stuck to their goal of crafting an 'information society', did not take their eyes off the ball, and tweaked the policy to meet the goals. A comparison of the unbundling process reveals the following differences regarding the practical implementation level:

1. While in Europe, unbundling was treated as a separate and distinct act, in the US it was buried inside the long and convoluted interconnection section of the law;

2. While in Europe, the law was clear, concise and focused on the particular element to be unbundled, in the US, it left it up to the regulators and the courts to try and decipher which elements needed to be unbundled;

3. While in Europe, the definitions are made at the highest normative level and the analysis for their application is made at the regulator level, in the US only principles are set at the highest normative level, while interpretations that lead to definitions are made on a lower normative level;

4. While the Europeans review and adjust their policies to changing technological and market conditions every two to three years, it has been more than 10 years since the US conducted a major overhaul of its laws;

5. While in Europe, the goal of telecommunications policy is clear and defined in unambiguous terms, namely, to promote competition and avoid inequity between "have and have-nots," in the US, the debate is framed by the stakeholders.

As a result of frequent European reassessment of policies, innovative approaches are tested and policy changes are rapid and efficient, particularly when taking into consideration how diverse and relatively flimsy the union is. Centralized control at the highest level of policy-making, where all union members are represented, makes the eventual enforcement on national regulators relatively painless, or at least less painless than in the US where a federal administrative body, the FCC, is charged with designing the policy, or in the case of universal service, a joint federal–state board, that apparently lacks the ability to interpret the rules in a creative manner. Perhaps the most striking difference, and apparently the most telling, between the two systems is that the Europeans, unlike the Americans, are able to assign the issues their proper level of importance and define them correctly, leaving less room for chaotic legal interpretation.

In "defense" of the chaotic situation in the US, it should be noted that its structure of the telecommunications industry is more complex. The European regulators do not have to deal with the remnants of a system that differentiates between local and long-distance service and "basic" (or "telecommunication") and "enhanced" (or "information") services, applying different rules to them and regulating them separately. The origin of the European system, a national monopoly providing the entire range of telecommunication and information services, makes operating easier. The fact that the European PTTs were state owned at the start provided them with greater leverage in some countries, because of their close ties to government and similar organizational cultures. But the fact that in the US the players are powerful corporations that leverage their wealth to affect the policy process takes its toll on the final outcome.

It is remarkable that the US, where most policy tools developed and whose supremacy in information and communications technology distribution served as the model to be imitated by others, stands to benefit from learning from the Europeans, where 50 years ago the number of telephone lines and penetration rates were only a fraction of those existing in the US. The differences in the policy-making process are so pronounced that it would be a grave mistake not to rethink them as well. This is especially true of the case of universal service, where the US still holds an advantage with regard to access to the Internet by public education and health institutions, as a result of the unique E-rate subsidy policy.

As the author of Psalms wrote nearly 3000 years ago: "from all my teachers I have grown wise," to which later scriptures added "and from my students more than anyone else."[32]

Notes

1. Psalms 119:99.
2. Taanit 7:71.
3. *Source:* OECD Broadband Statistics; at: www.oecd.org/document/7/0,3343, en_2649_34225_38446855_1_1_1_1,00.html (accessed 13 August 2007) (hereinafter: OECD Broadband Statistics).
4. See FCC report on telephone subscribership in the US, November 2006; at:hraunfoss.fcc.gov/ edocs_public/attachmatch/DOC-268003A1. pdf
5. E-Communications Household Survey published by the European Union, July 2006; at: ec.europa.eu/information_society/ policy/ecomm/doc/info_centre/studies_ext_consult/ecomm_household_study/ ebjul06_main_report_en.pdf
6. See note 4.
7. Directive 97/33/EC of the European Parliament and of the Council of 30 June 1997 on Interconnection in Telecommunications with Regard to Ensuring Universal Service and Interoperability through Application of the Principles of Open Network Provision (ONP), *Official Journal* L 199, 26 July 1997, pp. 0032–0052; at: europa.eu.int/ISPO/infosoc/ telecompolicy/en/dir97-33en.htm
8. Council Resolution of 18 September 1995 on the Implementation of the Future RegulatoryFramework for Telecommunications, *Official Journal* C 258, 3 October 1995, pp. 0001–0003;at: eur-lex.europa.eu/LexUriServ/ LexUriServ.do?uri=CELEX:31995Y1003(01):E N:NOT
9. See note.
10. See 1999 Communications Review; at: europa. eu.int/ISPO/infosoc/telecompolicy/review99/ com2000-239en.pdf (accessed 21 August 2006).

11. For a general introduction of the 2003 regulatory framework see: europa.eu.int/information_society/topics/telecoms/regulatory/new_rf/text_en.htm#introduction (accessed 21 August 2006). The five individual directives that comprise the new framework were: Directive 2002/21/EC of the European Parliament and of the Council of 7 March 2002 on a Common Regulatory Framework for Electronic Communications Networks and Services, *Official Journal* L 108/33,24 April 2002 (aka the 'Framework Directive'); Directive 2002/19/EC of the European Parliament and of the Council of 7 March 2002 on Access to, and Interconnection of, Electronic Communications Networks and Associated Facilities, *Official Journal* L 108/7, 24 April 2002 ('Access Directive'); Directive 2002/20/EC of the European Parliament and of the Council of 7 March 2002 on the Authorization of Electronic Communications Networks and Services, *Official Journal* L 108/21 ('Authorization Directive'); Directive 2002/22/EC of the European Parliament and of the Council of 7 March 2002 on Universal Service and Users' Rights Relating to Electronic Communications Networks and Services, *Official Journal* L 108/51, 24 April 2002 ('Universal Service Directive'); Directive 2002/58/EC of the European Parliament and of the Council of 12 July 2002 Concerning the Processing of Personal Data and the Protection of Privacy in the Electronic Communications Sector ('Data Privacy Directive').

12. Regulation (EC) No. 2887/2000 of the European Parliament and of the Council of 18 December2000 on Unbundled Access to the Local Loop, *Official Journal* L 336/4, 30 December 2000.

13. See FCC decision; at: hraunfoss.fcc.gov/edocs_public/attachmatch/FCC-05-150A1.pdf and accompanying news release, at: hraunfoss.fcc.gov/edocs_public/attachmatch/DOC-260433A1.pdf

14. See note.

15. Tenth Report on European Electronic Communications Regulation and Markets; at: europa.eu/scadplus/leg/en/lvb/124217e.htm (accessed 22 August 2006).

16. Original texts at: www.muniwireless.com/reports/docs/res18.pdf; www.muniwireless.com/reports/docs/res19.pdf; English translation: www.muniwireless.com/municipal/watch/1433

17. The history of the introduction of MCI's service can be found in *MCI Communications Corporation and MCI Telecommunications Corporation* v. *American Telephone and Telegraph Company* 708 F.2d 1081, (7th Cir.) (Cert. denied).

18. At: www.fcc.gov/Bureaus/Common_Carrier/Orders /1996/fcc96325.pdf

19. *AT&T Corporation, ET AL*, v. *Iowa Utilities Board*, 525 US 366, 388 (1999).

20. *Verizon* v. *Trinko*, LLP. 540 US 398 (2004).

21. At: hraunfoss.fccgov/edocs_public/attachmatch/DOC-260433A1.pdf (although this announcement refers to unbundling for the sake of ISP access, by 2005 access by competing local exchange carriers was a moot issue due to growing collusion among long-distance and local operators).

22. 93/C 213/01; at: europa.eu.int/ISPO/infosoc/legreg/docs/93c21301.html

23. 94/C 48/01; at: europe.eu.int/ISPO/infosoc/legreg/docs/94c4801.html

24. See note 7.

25. COM(2000)239 final, Brussels, 26 April 2000.

26. At: europa.eu.int/ISPO/infosoc/telecompolicy/review99/wdunisrv.pdf (accessed 18 August 2006).

27. *Official Journal* L 108/51, 24 April 2002.

28. Article 4(2).

29. COM(2006)68 final, Brussels, 20 February 2006.

30. COM(2006)129 final, Brussels, 20 March 2006.

31. SEC(2006)816, Brussels, 28 June 2006.

32. See notes 1 and 2.

References

Anttiroiko, A. (2001) 'Toward the European Information Society', *Communications of the ACM* 44(1): 31–5.

Bangemann, M. (1994) 'Recommendations to the European Council: Europe and the Global Information Society'; at: europa.eu.int/ISPO/infosoc/backg/bangeman.htm

Bauer, J. (1998) 'Universal Service in the European Union', *Government Information Quarterly* 16(4): 329–43.

Bauer, J. (2003) 'Prospects and Limits of Comparative Research in Communications Policy-Making', paper presented at the 31st Telecommunications Policy Research Conference, Arlington, VA, September.

Bauer, J., M. Berne and C. Maitland (2002) 'Internet Access in the European Union and in the United States', *Telematics and Informatics* 19(2): 117–37.

Bourreau, M. and P. Dogan (2004) 'Service-Based vs Facility-Based Competition in Local Access Networks', *Information Economics and Policy* 16(2): 287–306.

Bushkin, A. and J. Yurow (1980) *The Foundations of the United States Information Policy: A United States Government Submission to the High-Level Conference on Information, Computer, and Communications Policy.* Washington, DC: US Department of Commerce.

Cannon, R. (2005) 'The Legacy of the Federal Communications Commission's Computer Inquiries', *Federal Communications Law Journal* 55(2): 168–206.

Cherry, B. (1999) 'Rate Rebalancing Policy: Institutional Factors Favoring Reform in the European Union over the US', paper presented at the 27th Telecommunications Policy Research Conference, Alexandria, VA, September.

Doyle, C. (2000) local 'Loop Unbundling and Regulatory Risk', *Journal of Network Industries* 1: 33–54.

Frieden, R. (2005) 'Lessons from Broadband Development in Canada, Japan, Korea and the United States', Telecommunications Policy 29(8): 595–613.

Fuke, H. (2003) 'Evaluation of New Regulatory Framework of European Union—from Japanese Perspective', paper presented at the 14th ITS European Regional Conference Helsinki, Finland, 23–24 August.

Garcia-Murillo, M. (2005) 'International Broadband Deployment: The Impact of Unbundling: Unbundling Facing New Challenges', *Communications and Strategies* 57: 83–105.

Garnham, N. (2001) 'Universal Service', pp. 199–204 in W. Melody (ed.) *Telecom Reform: Principles, Policies and Regulatory Practices.* Lyngsby: Technical University of Denmark.

Gideon, C. (2006) 'Technology Policy by Default: Shaping Communications Technology through Regulatory Policy', pp. 256–72 in D. Guston and D. Sarewitz (eds) *Shaping Science and Technology Policy: The Next Generation of Research.* Madison: University of Wisconsin Press.

Hornet, R. (1976) *Politics, Cultures, and Communication: European vs American Approaches to Communications Policymaking.* New York: Aspen Institute for Humanistic Studies.

Kiessling, T. and Y. Blondeel (1998) 'The EU Regulatory Framework in Telecommunications: A Critical Analysis', *Telecommunications Policy* 22(7): 571–92.

Kim, J., J. Bauer and S. Wildman (2003) 'Broadband Uptake in OECD Countries: Policy Lessons from Comparative Statistical Analysis', paper prepared for presentation at the 31st Research Conference on Communication, Information and Internet Policy, Arlington, VA, 19–21 September; at: tprc.org/papers/2003/203/Kim-Bauer-Wildman.pdf

Kubicek, H., W. Dutton and R. Williams (eds) (2001) *The Social Shaping of Information Superhighways: European and American Roads to the Information Society.* Frankfurt: Campus Verlag/St Martin's Press.

Levy, D. (1999) *Europe's Digital Revolution: Broadcasting Regulation, the EU and the Nation State.* London: Routledge.

Livingstone, S. (2003) 'On the Challenges of Cross National Comparative Research', *European Journal of Communication* 18(4): 477–500.

Marcus, J. (2002) 'The Potential Relevance to the United States of the European Union's Newly Adopted Regulatory Framework for Telecommunications'; at: hraunfoss.fcc.gov/edocs_public/attachmatch/DOC-224213A2.pdf

Marcus, J. (2005) 'Broadband Adoption in Europe', *IEEE Communications Magazine* 18–20; at: www.comsoc.org/cil/Public/2005/apr/

Melody, W. (1999) 'Telecom Reform: Progress and Prospects', *Telecommunications Policy* 23: 7–34.

Michalis, M. (2002) 'The Debate over Universal Service in the European Union: Plus Ça Change, Plus C'est la Meme Chose', *Convergence* 8(2): 80–98.

Mueller, M. (1997) *Universal Service.* Cambridge, MA: MIT Press.

Pool, I. (1983) *Technologies of Freedom.* Cambridge, MA: Belknap Press.

Redford, E. (1969) *The Regulatory Process.* Austin: University of Texas Press.

Sandholtz, W. (1993) 'Institutions and Collective Action: The New Telecommunications in Western Europe', *World Politics* 45: 242–70.

Sandholtz, W. (1996) 'Emergence of a Supranational Telecommunications Regime', Institute on Global Conflict and Cooperation, Columbia International Affairs Online; at: www.ciaonet.org/wps/saw02/index.html (accessed 17 August 2006).

Schement, J. and M. Mueller (1996) 'Universal Service from the Bottom Up: A Study of Telephone Penetration in Camden, New Jersey', *The Information Society* 12(3): 273–92.

Schneider, V. (2001) 'Different Roads to the Information Society? Comparing US and European Approaches from a Public Policy Perspective', pp. 339–58 in H. Kubicek, W. Dutton and R. Williams (eds) *The Social Shaping of Information Superhighways: European and American Roads to the Information Society.* Frankfurt: Campus Verlag/St Martin's Press.

Servaes, J. and J.-C. Burgelman (2000) 'In Search of a European Model for the Information Society', *Telematics and Informatics* 17: 1–7.

Simpson, S. (2004) 'Universal Service Issues in Converging Communications Environments: The Case of the UK', *Telecommunications Policy* 28(3–4): 233–48.

Skogerbø, E. and T. Storsul (2000) 'Prospects for Expanded Universal Service in Europe: The Cases of Denmark, the Netherlands, and Norway', *The Information Society* 16: 135–46.

Spiller, P. and S. Ulset (2003) 'Why Local Loop Unbundling Fails?', paper presented at the Nordic Workshop on Transaction Cost Economics in Business Administration, Bergen, Norway, 20–21 June; at: mora.rente.nhh.no/conferences/TCE-Workshop2003/papers/Ulset_Spiller.pdf

Streeter, T. (1990) 'Beyond Freedom of Speech and the Public Interest: The Relevance of Critical Legal Studies to Communications Policy', *Journal of Communication* 40(2): 43–63.

Van Zon, H. (2005) 'The Variety of Information Society Development Paths in Central Europe', *AI and Society* 19(3): 309–26.

Waverman, L. and E. Sirel (1997) 'European Telecommunications Markets on the Verge of Full Liberalization', *Journal of Economic Perspectives* 11(4): 113–26.

UNIT 14

Wired or Wireless?
The Regulation of Mobile Networks

The detailed discussion of wireline networks should not distract us from the fact that worldwide, as well as in the United States, mobile telephony is becoming the dominant form of person-to-person communications and that mobile telephone markets thus require their own regulatory attention. Indeed, if you ask around your classroom, you will most likely discover that probably none of your peers have a landline while almost all of them have their very own mobile device. But is it really their own? Telecommunications law and policy scholar Rob Frieden's provocative piece outlines the non-competitive nature of the mobile industry and the ways to make it more competitive. At the end of studying this unit's reading and class discussion you should be acquainted with the technological uniqueness of the mobile industry as well as with the exceptional regulatory framework in which it operates.

The Way Forward for Wireless

Rob Frieden

INTRODUCTION

Wireless telecommunications provide opportunities for enhanced productivity and tetherless access to information, communications and entertainment (ICE) services. Increasingly, versatile handsets offer a third screen for accessing Internet-based content, serving as a supplement to, or potentially a partial substitute for, television sets and computer terminals.[1] More and more people rely on wireless telecommunications as their primary medium for telephone service, and next generation networks offer the promise of near ubiquitous access to both basic voice and enhanced information services.

As wireless telecommunications become a more essential part of the ICE marketplace, regulatory safeguards will remain necessary to ensure that competition remains robust and sustainable. Promoting competition requires intelligent regulatory policy that calibrates the scope of government oversight to that level needed to remedy shortcomings in the marketplace, such as insufficient options, discriminatory pricing, unreasonable restrictions on the use of wireless handsets, and other carrier practices that do not serve the public interest. Additionally, the executive branch and Congress need to reexamine how much radio spectrum the government requires with an eye toward achieving more efficient use so that it can share or reassign unused spectrum for private use.

For the last fifteen years, the Federal Communications Commission (FCC), with only limited congressional guidance and oversight, has embarked on a substantial deregulatory campaign based on the assumption that technological innovations can stimulate competition. The FCC has largely eliminated traditional common carrier regulatory requirements for cellular radiotelephone service providers, commonly referred to as commercial mobile radio service (CMRS) providers.[2] The commission has also started to rethink its spectrum management policies to promote more efficient use by opening up some spectrum assignments to competitive bidding, creating secondary markets for leasing spectrum that is not needed by current licensees, and permitting multiple noninterfering uses for the same spectrum allocation.

The FCC has justified reducing or eliminating regulatory safeguards on the grounds that market forces can ensure robust competition among wireless operators, thereby preventing any single carrier or group of carriers from engaging in practices that would not serve the public interest and could harm consumers. It has established policies that support premature deregulation based on an overly generous assessment of current and future competition.

Additionally, it has supported concentration of ownership and control through mergers and acquisitions that have received its stamp of approval, and has abandoned or refused to establish rules that would stimulate facilities-based competition by making spectrum available to market entrants. The FCC even refrains from enforcing rules and regulations that it has not officially repealed.

Over the last several years, the FCC has abandoned rules that limited the amount of radio spectrum a single CMRS operator can control.[3] In addition, the commission has required carriers to make network time available for resale by unaffiliated ventures[4] and to specify in a tariff the terms and conditions under which their services are to be provided. At the same time, it has approved several multibillion dollar mergers[5] that have reduced the number of national CMRS operators to four, the top three controlling more than 77 percent of the market.[6] When it had the opportunity to craft rules that would encourage entry into the market of new ventures that had the capability of creating competing networks using newly available spectrum, the FCC allowed incumbent operators to acquire and possibly "warehouse" additional spectrum.[7] The FCC also concluded that it generally could assert preemptive jurisdiction over wireless policy decisionmaking by state regulatory agencies on such matters as wireless carrier rates and practices. The FCC's claim of primary jurisdiction would foreclose state courts from issuing binding decisions.[8]

The wireless telecommunications market in the United States juxtaposes marketplace success and global best practices in some categories with remarkably inferior results elsewhere. On the one hand, U.S. carriers offer subscribers access to cheap, subsidized handsets and large baskets of network minutes of use. The FCC has also begun to promote flexibility in spectrum use and leasing so that license holders can target and serve different types of users, with some spectrum available on an unlicensed basis for use by low-powered equipment, such as home Wi-Fi networking routers.

On the other hand, the FCC has allowed the wireless market to become dangerously concentrated through mergers and acquisitions,[9] jeopardizing the future of the commission's deregulatory campaign that relies on marketplace competition in lieu of

government oversight. At the same time, it has done nothing to support the flexible use of wireless handsets by subscribers, or to ensure that wireless carriers operate in a nondiscriminatory manner when providing telecommunications, information, or video services.

Most CMRS subscribers agree to a bundled package that combines a subsidized handset with a two-year service agreement at rates that compensate carriers for the handset subsidy and create strong disincentives for consumers to change carriers. Subscribers are forced to pay substantial early termination financial penalties if they change carriers. Because they subsidize subscribers, CMRS carriers control the operational functions of handsets[10] and often disable features that would provide subscribers with greater freedom to access services offered by companies unaffiliated with the carrier.

The United States lags behind many other countries when it comes to mobile phone market penetration, particularly inexpensive prepaid services.[11] With less and less access to pay telephones, low-income Americans do not have many of the inexpensive, nonresidential wireless options available to their counterparts in most other developed and developing nations. U.S. wireless carriers may charge some of the lowest rates per minute of use, but they also manage to generate some of the highest average return per user (ARPU) by creating service tiers with large monthly minutes of use baskets and a commensurately high monthly rate.

They also do not offer most subscribers some of the cutting edge services available in Europe and Asia. While subscribers in the United States typically have handsets capable of just making telephone calls, sending text messages and storing ringtones, photos, and music, wireless subscribers in other countries already use their handsets for inexpensive, high-speed broadband access to the Internet and a variety of electronic commerce, location-based applications, including ones that allow subscribers to query databases that have the capability of mapping nearby commercial options.

Wireless carrier executives and trade associations representing the industry claim that extreme competition and enhanced consumer welfare justify further deregulation. For next-generation video and Internet services, they want carriers to operate as information service providers largely free of any FCC regulation, including still essential public interest, anti-trust, network neutrality,[12] and consumer protection safeguards. In light of market consolidation and considering that probably only a handful of national carriers will dominate the CMRS marketplace, intelligent "light-handed" regulation will continue to be necessary. Moreover, the FCC should consider how wireless telecommunications networks could help achieve universal service goals with possibly cheaper and more widespread access than what wireline technologies offer.

WIDESPREAD CONFUSION OVER THE NATURE AND TYPE OF WIRELESS TELECOMMUNICATIONS REGULATION

It may come as a surprise that CMRS ventures operate as common carriers subject to regulatory forbearance based on legislation enacted in 1993[13] that was designed to promote growth and competition. This means that while CMRS operators do not have to file tariffs and secure FCC authority to begin or stop providing a particular service, these carriers are still subject to numerous legal obligations, including the duty to operate without discrimination, to refrain from engaging in unreasonable practices that would violate their ongoing duty to serve the public interest, and to interconnect their networks with other carriers so that subscribers can use their handsets anywhere to access any wireline or wireless telephone number.

It appears that both the carriers and the FCC seek to downplay the fact that wireless carriers still must comply with most of the conventional telecommunications service regulations. Regardless of the rhetoric about how competitive the wireless market has become, the law requires the FCC to safeguard the public interest by applying traditional telecommunications, common carrier regulation.

The FCC has chosen to emphasize how competitive the CMRS market has become and how wireless carriers now also offer information services[14] when providing broadband Internet access. Because wireless carriers offer many services, a single, one-size-fits-all regulatory classification would not work in this case. Converging markets, the outcome of technological innovation, make it impossible for the FCC to treat wireless carriers solely as common carriers offering telecommunications services, or solely as private carriers offering information services. By concentrating on the new information services that wireless carriers can offer, the FCC appears disinclined to enforce consumer safeguards, or to reject mergers and acquisitions that further concentrate the industry.

The FCC must begin to address the dangers of further concentration of the industry as well as the need to subject wireless carriers to different degrees of regulatory oversight, because the many types of services they offer trigger different degrees of regulatory oversight. For conventional wireless telecommunications services, the FCC should retain streamlined common carrier regulation and calibrate any further deregulation to an increase in sustainable, facilities-based competition.

With regard to information and video services, the FCC should intervene only when necessary to ensure that wireless carriers operate accessible networks. This would not necessitate common carrier regulation, but it would require wireless carriers to establish clear service terms and conditions and to report instances where competitive necessity supports diversification in price and quality of service.

Wireless carriers appear to have exploited confusion about their current regulatory status. Not many of their subscribers understand much about the availability of regulatory safeguards. Instead, subscribers appear to conclude that they have no recourse beyond the limited safeguards available from nonnegotiable, "take it or leave it" service contracts. Indeed, CMRS service agreements—if read by a subscriber—offer little insight into what obligations the carrier has and what remedies subscribers can pursue. Worse yet, most such agreements force subscribers to abandon legal and regulatory agency options in lieu of compulsory and not necessarily unbiased or lawful arbitration.

Recently, the FCC needed to remind CMRS operators of their ongoing common carrier responsibilities. A CMRS operator must provide subscribers with access to any telephone number, including ones that would require the carrier to accept traffic from another carrier or to hand off traffic to another carrier, as is the case when a subscriber seeks to make or receive calls outside the home service territory.[15]

Nonetheless, the FCC has expressed no interest in forcing wireless carriers to specify clearly their service commitments or to offer subscribers compensation and other remedies when the carriers fail to provide adequate service.

Locked Handsets and Locked Out Access to Content

The FCC has never stated explicitly that wireless carriers have to comply with the commission's "Carterfone"[16] policy requiring wireline carriers to separate the delivery of telephone service from the sale of handsets. As a result, most wireless consumers have not fully appreciated the consequences of such an arrangement, should it be enforced. The carriers have successfully touted the benefits to subscribers of using increasingly sophisticated handsets at subsidized sale prices to access a blend of ICE services. But in exchange for accepting a two-year service contract subject to a significant penalty for early termination, subscribers also accept significant limitations on their freedom to exploit the versatility and all the functions available from their handsets.

Even though wireless subscribers own the handsets they use to access network services, carriers control and limit handset freedoms through the following means:

- Locking handsets so that subscribers cannot access competitor networks (by frequency, transmission format, firmware, or software); in the UnitedStates, carriers even lock handsets designed to allow multiple carrier access by changing an easily inserted subscriber identity module (SIM);

- Using firmware "upgrades" to "brick," i.e., to render inoperative, the handset, or alternatively, to disable third party firmware and software;

- Disabling handset functions, e.g., bluetooth, Wi-Fi access, Internet browsers, GPS services, and e-mail clients;

- Specifying formats for accessing memory, e.g., music, ringtones, and photos;

- Creating "walled garden" access to favored video content of affiliates and partners; and

- Using proprietary, nonstandard interfaces that make it difficult for third parties to develop compatible applications and content.

Wireless service subscribers have begun to recognize how carrier-mandated limitations on handsets often have little to do with legitimate network management and customer service objectives. When handsets provided access primarily to voice telephone calls, text messaging, and ringtones, subscribers may have tolerated, or thought little about, limitations that blocked access to more sophisticated functions and to third-party software, applications, or content. Only recently have mobile phone subscribers started to comprehend the harmful ramifications of this decision. For example, a significant percentage of Apple iPhone purchasers have risked loss of warranty coverage and the possibility of "bricking" their handset—turning it into an expensive paperweight—to evade limitations imposed by their mobile operator (AT&T) regarding which wireless carrier, software, applications, and content iPhone subscribers can access.[17]

Almost forty years ago, the FCC established its Carterfone policy, which required all wireline telephone companies to allow subscribers to attach any technically compatible device. This simple policy has saved consumers money, promoted innovation and stimulated more diversified and expanded network use without any financial or operational harm to network operators. The Carterfone decision effectively separated telephone service from the sale or lease of the handset. The FCC initially refused to do this, but later enthusiastically embraced a court mandate to support the rights of consumers to attach any device to a network that is "privately beneficial without being publicly harmful"[18]

Wireless subscribers do contractually relinquish some freedom in exchange for a subsidized handset. But a wireless Carterfone policy would provide subscribers with the option of attaching an unsubsidized handset free of any carrier imposed attachment restrictions. Critics of applying Carterfone to CMRS networks argue that device attachment freedom subverts the legitimate business practices of carriers. But as regulated telecommunications common carriers, CMRS operators have a duty to comply with lawful curbs on unnecessary subscriber restrictions that do not serve the public interest.

Wireless carriers remain regulated common carriers regardless of whether or not they also provide less regulated Internet access and other information services. In other words, the duties of common carriage do not evaporate simply because wireless carriers enjoy some regulatory forbearance when providing conventional telephone service. When wireless carriers also offer access to information and video services, the carriers do not operate as common carriers. Still, they should not be encouraged to favor content supplied by corporate affiliates or ventures that seek to buy preferential treatment.

Overstating the Scope of Competition

By law, the FCC is required to submit an annual report to Congress on the state of the CMRS market.[19] It uses this report and the statistics compiled as the primary source of evidence for supporting deregulation and dismissing concerns about industry ownership consolidation. Like most ICE industries, wireless has become increasingly concentrated as mergers and acquisitions reduce the number of facilities-based competitors. In addition, two of the four major national CMRS operators, AT&T and Verizon, also have dominant market shares in wireline local and long distance telephone service, as well as in broadband Internet access.

The ability to offer a bundled package of service exploits economies of scale and enables price reductions. But companies such as Verizon and AT&T have vast market power that the FCC blithely ignores. Rather than acknowledge statistics that confirm their growing market power, the FCC has opted to emphasize consumer benefits accruing from lower rates and access to large monthly baskets of network minutes of use. Here again, the commission seems unable to recognize the need for ongoing vigilance and instead chooses to emphasize the positive news supporting deregulation, all but ignoring emerging trends that are potentially harmful.

Spectrum Management Reform

Government management of radio spectrum has failed to take into account technological innovations that support greater flexibility in assigning licenses, particularly multiple non-interfering uses of the same frequencies. The traditional model for spectrum management involves a multilateral process, initiated by the International Telecommunication Union (ITU), a specialized agency of the United Nations, and followed up by national regulatory agencies such as the FCC. Both the ITU and the FCC have allocated spectrum in service-specific slivers, often specifying a single use for a particular frequency band. Technological innovations make it increasingly possible for multiple users to utilize the same frequency and for different types of services to share the same frequency band.

The FCC has cautiously supported flexible use and assignment of spectrum in two ways: 1) identifying more than one type of use for the same frequency band; and 2) encouraging the use of new technologies that promote greater efficiencies in the use of spectrum. The federal government has advocated ITU reallocation of wireless spectrum to allow shared use by operators on land, in air, and in international waters. Both the ITU and the FCC used to allocate mutually exclusive spectrum slivers for each category of usage.

A current dispute over such flexibility pits terrestrial commercial broadcasters against a satellite radio operator, Sirius, eager to install terrestrial signal repeaters to enhance reception.[20] Examples of FCC efforts to promote new spectrum conservation technology include allowing licensees to narrow channel bandwidth and to use compression techniques and new transmission formats that reduce the potential for interference.[21]

The executive branch can support the FCC's efforts and contribute to the successful commercial exploitation of spectrum by also embracing new spectrum conservation technologies. The federal government has reserved rights of access to vast amounts of spectrum that it does not use, uses sparingly, or can use more efficiently. When governments make do with less spectrum, it becomes possible to reallocate spectrum to private and commercial uses. CMRS and other wireless operators claim a shortage in available spectrum contributes to dropped calls and less than ideal quality of service. Making more spectrum available, through reallocation of reserved but unused government spectrum, would improve the quality of service available from private and commercial wireless operators. Better yet, more spectrum for next generation wireless services would promote more competition and greater diversity in the nature and type of services being offered to the public. Congress could help the FCC achieve this objective by requiring it to limit some new frequency bands to market entrants instead of incumbents keen on foreclosing additional competition.

CONCLUSIONS AND RECOMMENDATIONS

Wireless technologies can provide users with extraordinarily versatile access to advanced ICE services in addition to telephone calls, short text messages, ringtones, and music storage. Unfortunately, the cutting edge services, such as true broadband access to the Internet, are not widely available in the United States, nor do national carriers regularly display global best practices in the nature, type, and pricing of services they offer. Wireless carriers appear able to delay investment in next generation networks, because the carriers have concentrated on leveraging money to acquire market share and buy out competitors. Nevertheless, the FCC continues moving along a glide patch toward total deregulation without any apparent worry that the CMRS market has become overly concentrated.

Market concentration appears to make it possible for the four major CMRS operators to avoid significant price competition while collectively applying almost identical service terms and conditions. For example, no wireless carrier offers discounted service to existing subscribers who opt not to acquire new, subsidized handsets, or to new subscribers seeking to activate used handsets. While Verizon has shown a willingness to offer a more open network, most wireless carriers continue to impose restrictions that violate the Carterfone policy. Even the much-touted Apple iPhone frustrates users with restrictions imposed by AT&T or Apple. An estimated 25 percent of all Apple iPhone purchasers engage in some sort of unauthorized modification to their handsets, despite the risk of voiding warranties and permanently ruining their handsets.

Wireless networks can provide a much-needed competitive alternative to legacy wireline networks

and also help promote progress in achieving universal service objectives at a lower price. But such progress can be achieved only if the wireless market remains competitive, and not an adjunct or subordinate to the wireline business plans of major incumbent carriers. The executive branch, Congress, and the FCC need to remain on guard against trends that would prevent wireless carriers from providing a competitive alternative to legacy technologies.

The following specific recommendations should help promote robust facilities-based competition between wireless and wire-based technologies:

- The FCC should state that its Carterfone policy applies equally to wireline and wireless technologies. This policy would require wireless carriers to provide service to any compatible handset and to allow subscribers complete freedom to access any content, software, and applications that do not cause technical harm to the CMRS carrier's network as determined by the FCC or an independent laboratory;

- The FCC should recognize that technological and market convergence will result in wireless carriers offering a blend of telecommunications, information, and video services. It should apply different regulatory requirements, based on the amount of competition the wireless carriers actually face. Even for lightly regulated information and video services, the FCC should require wireless carriers to disclose service terms and conditions, particularly when the carrier offers different qualities of service that might violate legitimate concerns about network neutrality;

- The FCC should not continue refraining from telecommunications service regulation of CMRS carriers until additional sustainable, facilities-based competition arises. In the absence of new players in the market, the FCC should not approve transactions that would lead to further market consolidation;

- The FCC should promote wireless technology alternatives to wireline networks when allocating funds that target universal service goals. Together with state public utility commissions, it should use reverse auctions to achieve lowest cost bidding for service to high cost areas subject to quality of service benchmarks. Before using reverse auctions, the FCC should allow wireless carriers to qualify as eligible telecommunications carriers based on the wireless carrier's actual costs instead of the current practice of applying the incumbent wireline carrier's costs;

- In light of the success of Wi-Fi and other wireless services, the FCC should allocate more spectrum for shared, unlicensed wireless services. It should also expedite efforts to identify and reallocate spectrum for wireless services including unused "white spaces" between two high-powered licensed spectrum uses. More broadly, the executive branch should reexamine the government spectrum needs with an eye toward more efficient use and the possible reassignment of unexploited spectrum for private use; and

- In light of lax FCC enforcement of consumer protection rules, Congress should explicitly state that state public utility commissions and state courts can adjudicate disputes that pertain to quality of service and interpretation of service agreements. In the absence of legislation, the FCC should enforce existing truth in billing regulations and require CMRS operators to provide understandable service agreements that clearly specify all charges, fees, taxes, and surcharges. It should also void compulsory arbitration clauses.

NOTES

1. "Convergence in telecommunications gives many consumers access to multiple technologies or platforms that can be used to send and receive voice communications. Consumers are no longer limited to wireline platforms: they can choose from a range of platforms, including wireless and broadband. As wireless and broadband technologies have become more widely available to and used by consumers, they have increasingly become part of the competitive continuum. As more consumers view and use wireless and broadband services as substitutes for wireline services, the extent to which wireline and broadband services are competitive with wireline services will increase." Ed Rosenberg, *Assessing Wireless and Broadband Substitution in Local Telephone Markets*, Publication No. 07-06 (Washington, DC: The National Regulatory Research Institute, 2007), 31; nrri.org/pubs/telecommunications/07-06.pdf (8 June 2008).

2. The Omnibus Budget Reconciliation Act of 1993, Pub. L. No. 103-66, 107 Stat.312, amended section 332 of the Communications Act of 1934, to create the CMRS carrier category. The law defines CMRS as "any mobile service … that is providedfor profit and makes interconnected service available (A) to the public or (B) to such classes of eligible users as to be effectively available to a substantial portion of the public." 47 U.S.C. § 332(d)(l).

3. Federal Communications Commission, 2000 Biennial Regulatory Report, Spectrum Aggregation Limits for Commercial Mobile Radio Services, Report and Order, WT Docket No. 01-14, 16 FCC Rcd 22668 (2001).

4. Petitions for Rule Making Concerning Proposed Changes to the Commission's Cellular Resale Policies, 6 FCC Rcd. 1719 (1991) *aff'd sub nom.,* Cellnet Communication, 965 F.2d 1106 (DC Cir. 1992). See also *Cellnet Communications, Inc. v. Federal Communications Commission*, 149 F.3d 429 (Sixth Cir. 1998) (affirming the FCC's right to eliminate resale provisions, because elimination of such requirement does not upset customers' rights to use their telephones).

5. Applications of Nextel Communications, Inc. and Sprint Corporation For Consent to Transfer Control of Licenses and Authorizations, WT Docket No. 05-63, Memorandum Opinion and Order, 20 FCC Rcd 13967 (2005). Cingular Wireless had been a joint venture of AT&T and BellSouth Corporation ("BellSouth"). On December 29, 2006, AT&T merged with BellSouth. With the BellSouth acquisition, AT&T thereby acquired BellSouth's 40 percent economic interest in AT&T Mobility LLC ("AT&T Mobility"), formerly Cingular Wireless LLC, resulting in 100 percentownership of AT&T Mobility. In 2007, AT&T began rebranding its wireless operationsfrom Cingular to AT&T.

6. Leslie Cauley, "AT&T Eager to Wield Its iWeapon," *USA Today*, 21 May 2007(displaying

statistics compiled by Forrester Research); available at www.usatoday.com/tech/wireless/2007-05-21-at&t-iphone_N.htm (8 June 2008). While this chapter was being prepared Verizon sought to acquire regional wireless carrier Alltel leading to further industry concentration. See Andrew Ross Sorkin and Lauram M. Holson, "Verizon in Talks to Buy Alltel," *New York Times*, 5 June 2008, Technology; available at www.nytimes.com/2008/06/05/technology/05phone.html?_r=l&oref=slogin (1 July 2008).

7. Service Rules for the 698–746,747–762, and 777–792 MHz Bands, Second Reportand Order, FCC 07-132, 2007 WL 2301743 (released 10 August 2007). See also "*Ex Parte* Comments of the Public Interest Spectrum Coalition," *Service Rules for the 698–746, 747–762, and 777–792 Bands*, WT Docket 06-150 (5 April 2007), www.newamerica.net/files/700%20MHz%20NN%20Comments.pdf (8 June 2008).

8. Wireless Consumers Alliance, Inc. Petition for a Declaratory Ruling ConcerningWhether the Provisions of the Communications Act of 1934, as Amended, or the Jurisdiction of the Federal Communications Commission Thereunder, Serve to Preempt State Courts from Awarding Monetary Relief Against Commercial Mobile Radio Service (CMRS) Providers (a) for Violating State Consumer Protection Laws Prohibiting False Advertising and Other Fraudulent Business Practices, and/or (b) in the Context of Contractual Disputes and Tort Actions Adjudicated Under State Contract and Tort Laws, Memorandum Opinion and Order, 15 FCC Rcd. 17021 (2000).

9. "[The U.S.] is the last market in the world that people choose to bring a new wireless product to. Not second or third—the absolute last. Right now the policy of the FCC has been to encourage AT&T and Verizon to become the twin Bells that dominate the wireless business. They're allowed to buy all the spectrum they can find. The antitrust laws are waived and ignored every time they appear to be a problem. The FCC is the only spectrum auction entity in the world that does not carve out spectrum for new entrants. They do it in Mexico, Canada, the UK, China,

and Japan. Only here does the new entrant not get much of a chance. This is the only country in the world where the rule is the big guys can buy all of it. When you consolidate service providers, just like in the old days, when there was not two Bells like today but one, everybody knows what happens. It's very hard for innovators to get into the market, in terms of content or software or hardware." Reed Hundt, "Interview with Ed Gubbins," *Telephony Online*, 28 February 2008; telephonyonline.com/broadband/news/reed-hundt-auction-0228/ (8 June 2008).

10. "A shortsighted and often just plain stupid federal government has allowed itself to be bullied and fooled by a handful of big wireless phone operators for decades now. And the result has been a mobile phone system that is the direct opposite of the PC model. It severely limits consumer choice, stifles innovation, crushes entrepreneurship, and has made the U.S. the laughingstock of the mobile-technology world, just as the cellphone is morphing into a powerful hand-held computer. ... That's why I refer to the big cellphone carriers as the 'Soviet ministries.' Like the old bureaucracies of communism, they sit athwart the market, breaking the link between the producers of goods and services and the people who use them." Walt Mossberg, "Free My Phone," *All Things Digital Blog* (21 October 2007); mossblog.allthingsd.com/20071021/free-my-phone/ (8 June 2008).

11. The Organization for Economic Cooperation and Development ranks theUnited States 28 among OECD nations in terms of wireless market penetration at 72per 100 inhabitants versus 152 in Luxembourg, ranked number one. OECD, *Key ICT Indicators, Mobile subscribers in total/per 100 inhabitants for OECD* (2007) www.oecd.org/dataoecd/19/40/34082594.xls (8 June 2008). The United States has one of the lowest rates of prepaid service penetration.

12. Network neutrality refers to the extent to which a network operators providesaccess on nondiscriminatory terms and conditions both to end users and sources ofcontent delivered via the carrier's network. See Rob Frieden, "A Primer on NetworkNeutrality," *Intereconomics*

Review Of European Economic Policy 43, no. 1 (January/February 2008): 4–15; "Internet 3.0: Identifying Problems and Solutions to the Network Neutrality Debate," *International Journal Of Communications* 1 (2007): 461–92ijoc.org/ojs/index.php/ijoc/article/view/160/86 (8 June 2008); Rob Frieden, "Network Neutrality or Bias?—Handicapping the Odds for a Tiered and Branded Internet" *Hastings Communications And Entertainment Law Journal* 29, no. 2 (2007): 171–216.

13. The Omnibus Budget Reconciliation Act of 1993, Pub. L. No. 103-66, 107Stat. 312. "A person engaged in the provision of a service that is a commercial mobile service shall, insofar as such person is so engaged, be treated as a common carrier for purposes of this chapter, except for such provisions of subchapter II of this chapter as the Commission may specify by regulation as inapplicable to that service or person. In prescribing or amending any such regulation, the Commission may not specify any provision of section 201, 202, or 208 of this title, and may specify any other provision only if the Commission determines that—(i) enforcement of such provision is not necessary in order to ensure that the charges, practices, classifications, or regulations for or in connection with that service are just and reasonable and are not unjustly or unreasonably discriminatory; (ii) enforcement of such provision is not necessary for the protection of consumers; and (iii) specifying such provision is consistent with the public interest." 47 U.S.C. §332(c)(l)(A)i–iii. See also 47 U.S.C. §160(a) (establishing similar forbearance criteria for other telecommunications service providers).

14. See Appropriate Regulatory Treatment for Broadband Access to the Internet Over Wireless Networks, Declaratory Ruling, WT Docket No. 07-53, FCC 07-30 (released 23 March 2007); fjallfoss.fcc.gov/edocs_public/attachmatch/FCC-07-30A1.pdf(8 June 2008).

15. Reexamination of Roaming Obligations of Commercial Mobile Radio Service Providers, Report and Order and Further Notice of Proposed Rulemaking, WT DocketNo. 05-265, FCC 07-143 (released 16 August 2007); www.fcc.gov/Daily_Releases/Daily_Business/2007/db0816/FCC-07-143A1.pdf (8 June 2008).

16. Use of the Carterfone Device in Message Toll Telephone Service, 13 FCC 2d 420(1968), recon. denied, 14 FCC 2d 571 (1968).

17. "Of the 1.4 million iPhones sold so far (of which 1,119,000 were sold in the quarter ending Sept. 30), [Apple Chief Operating Officer Timothy] Cook estimated that 250,000 were sold to people who wanted to unlock them from the AT&T network and use them with another carrier." Saul Hansell, "Apple: $100 Million Spent on Potential iBricks," *New York Times*, 22 October 2007, Technology, Bits Blog Site, bits.blogs.nytimes.com/tag/iphone/ (8 June 2008). "You bought the iPhone, you paid forit, but now Apple is telling you how you have to use it, and if you don't do things the way they say, they're going to lock it. Turn it into a useless 'brick.' Is this any way to treat a customer? Apparently, it's the Steve Jobs way. But some iPhone users are mad as heck, and they're not going to take it anymore." Alexander Wolfe, "Apple Users Talking Class-Action Lawsuit Over iPhone Locking," *Wolfe's Den Blog*, www.informationweek.com/blog/main/archives/2007/09/iphone_users_ta.html (8 June 2008).

18. *Hush-a-Phone v. United States*, 238 F.2d 266, 269 (D.C. Cir. 1956) (reversing theFCC's prohibition on telephone subscriber use of an acoustic attachment not supplied by the telephone company).

19. Implementation of Section 6002(B) of the Omnibus Budget Reconciliation Actof 1993, Annual Report and Analysis of Competitive Market Conditions With Respect to Commercial Mobile Services, WT 07-71, Twelfth Report, 2008 WL 312884 (released 4 February 2008).

20. Amendment of part 27 of the Commission's Rules to Govern the Operationof Wireless Communications Services in the 2.3 GHz Band, WT 07–293, Notice of Proposed Rulemaking and Second Further Notice of Proposed Rulemaking, 2007WL 4440134 (released 18 December 2007); see also Digital Audio Broadcasting Systems and Their Impact on the Terrestrial Radio Broadcast Service, Second Report and Order First Order on

Reconsideration and Second Further Notice of Proposed Rulemaking, 22 FCC Rcd. 10344 (2007).

21. Implementation of Sections 309(j) and 337 of the Communications Act of 1934 as Amended; Promotion of Spectrum Efficient Technologies on Certain Part 90 Frequencies, Third Memorandum Opinion and Order, Third Further Notice of Proposed Rule Making and Order, WT Docket No. 99-87, RM-9332, 19 FCC Rcd25045 (2004); Replacement of Part 90 by Part 88 to Revise the Private Land Mobile Radio Services and Modify the Policies Governing Them, Report and Order and Further Notice of Proposed Rule Making, PR Docket No. 92-235, 10 FCC Rcd 10076,10077 f 1 (1995).

UNIT 15

Telecommunications or Information? The Boundaries of Regulation

Technological developments not only contributed to the creation of alternative telephone networks (such as the mobile) but also to the creation of additional services provided over traditional telephone networks. Of course you are all acquainted with the Internet, but the origins of the regulatory challenge created by the emergence of new services over telephone lines dates back to the introduction of the mainframe computer and to the data services it made possible to be provided over telephone lines. The principles created in the "Computer Inquiries" in the 1970s and 1980s dictate the regulatory framework of the Internet, thus understanding these historical roots is fundamental. Robert Cannon, a communications policy expert and consultant to the FCC, explains the legacy of the "Inquiries" in a clear manner. What you need to be able to articulate at the end of this unit is the difference between the two types of service—"telecommunications" and "information"—the difference between the regulatory remedies utilized in these proceedings; structural separation, functional separation and open network architecture; and the meaning of the regulatory challenges posed by vertically integrated monopolies—cross-subsidization and discrimination.

The Legacy of the Federal Communications Commission's Computer Inquiries

Robert Cannon

INTRODUCTION

In the 1960s, the Federal Communications Commission ("FCC" or "Commission") awoke to the reality of powerful computers running communications networks, and communications networks over which humans interacted with really powerful computers. Computer services were a disruptive technology. They were substitute services for traditional incumbent communication services. They were highly competitive, highly innovative, and had low barriers to entry. They showed every promise of playing a vital role in the United States economy. In addition, these computer network services were dependent upon the underlying communications network. Thus, the unregulated computer services were simultaneously substitute services for the traditional regulated communications networks and also dependent upon them.

Meanwhile, the communication network services were using gigantic mainframe computers ("big iron") to run their networks. During network peaks, mainframe computers were preoccupied with operating the networks. During off-peaks, these computers had excess capacity. The telephone companies knew a good thing when they saw it and wanted to get into the computer services market, taking advantage, in part, of their inexpensive excess off-peak mainframe

capacity. Thus, the telephone companies became simultaneously the supplier of the crucial transmission capacity and a competitor in the computer services market.

The FCC has struggled with the regulatory treatment of computer networks over communications networks ever since. In 1986, the Commission stated:

> The regulatory issues spawned by the technical confluence of regulated communications services and unregulated [computer networks] have been among the most important matters this Commission has dealt with over the past 20 years. Indeed, during this period, we have addressed these issues, in one proceeding or another, on a virtually continuous basis, as we have sought to revise and refine our regulatory approach in light of rapidly changing technological and marketplace developments.[1]

The history of the FCC and the computer networks, particularly the Internet, is now thirty-five years old. To say that the FCC does not regulate the Internet is to miss the lessons of this history. While it is true that computer networks are unregulated, computer networks were very much a part of the Commission's policy. They were the intended direct beneficiaries of the Computer Inquiries. Safeguards were imposed on common carriers for the benefit of computer networks. In addition, this is not a history of technologically biased regulation, segregating one computer from another based on the technology employed. Rather, this is a market policy, segregating competitive markets from noncompetitive markets. Finally, the conceptual framework follows a Layered Model of Regulation. The separate layers permitted, even created, separate markets (i.e., telephone service, Internet service, application service, and content). These separate markets created separate regulatory policy.

The Computer Inquiries have been referred to by some as "wildly successful."[2] They were a necessary precondition for the success of the Internet.

COMPUTER I (1966)

The Setting

A Better Mouse Trap

It is the 1960s. The FCC faces a problem. At this time there exists a communications network that offers basic communications service. This communications network is provided by the incumbent monopoly, Ma Bell, also known as AT&T. This network has been traditionally regulated by the FCC. It was built in a regulatory environment as a sanctioned monopoly with ratepayer fees.[3]

The problem was that someone figured out how to build a better mouse trap. Someone figured out how to use computers with this network. Someone figured out how to enhance the network by adding devices at the ends of the network, layering protocols on top of the network, and achieving data processing using remote terminals. Ultimately these innovations would evolve into computer networks. These enhancements were dependent upon the underlying communications monopoly and came with the marvelous promise of economic expansion, innovation, and competition. These enhancements, however, also threatened to be a substitute for regulated services, and regulated services threatened to be a bottleneck in the way of the growth of these services.

Western Union

In the 1960s, the FCC's common carrier authority covered not merely Ma Bell; Western Union also fell under Title II of the Communications Act of 1934. The Western Union telegram service was, in retrospect, an interesting service. The service took an order for a message from a user. The user provided a destination address and content for the message. The message then was inserted into the Western Union system. However, if the message originated in Baltimore for a destination in Los Angeles, it did not go straight through a wire from Baltimore to Los Angeles. Rather, the operator in Baltimore, not knowing the full path of the transmission to Los Angeles, knew instead the next hop in the general direction of Los Angeles, and forwarded the message to that next hop. At the next hop, which might have been Chicago, an operator received the telegram, read only the header with the address, and then forwarded the message back into the network in the general direction of the destination. In this way, the message worked its way through the network, being stored and then forwarded, hopping from node to node in a best effort, until it reached its final destination and was stored until delivered to the recipient.[4]

In the 1960s, it dawned on users of mainframe computers that they could take advantage of the excess capacity of the mainframes to send messages to each other. Alfred may log onto the mainframe from one remote terminal, and leave a message for Beth. Beth would then log onto the mainframe from another remote terminal, perhaps in another state, and receive the message. Eventually computer message-switching[5] became a commercial service that did not simply store messages on a mainframe, but transmitted messages through computer networks. Alfred would create a message and hit send. The message would go to the first e-mail server, which would read the address, and then send the message on to the next hop in the network. The next hop would read the address and act accordingly. When the message reached its destination computer, the message was stored until accessed by the recipient, Beth.

These two things look very similar to each other. However, one was regulated; the other was not. One was expensive; the other one was cheap, and avoided regulatory fees. One is a substitute service for the other.[6]

There are two things to be taken away from this. First, message-switching was dependent upon a regulated underlying telephone monopoly for transmission. Second, unregulated message-switching was a substitute service for the regulated telegram services of Western Union.[7] What exactly to do with message switching was one of the significant drivers of the Computer I inquiry.[8]

Big Iron and New Networks

This was a moment of major expansion of the American economy. Big iron mainframe computing had taken hold and was becoming big business. Mainframe computing was also evolving with the advent of time sharing and remote terminal access.[9] The role of IBM, computer manufacturers, and data processing services in the economy had grown and promised continued growth.[10] There were in-house computer services, computer service bureaus, and specialized computer services such as stock quotation services.[11] Computers were being used to facilitate President Kennedy's space race, advance the Cold War, run communications networks that replaced human operators, and re-create the way business was conducted.[12] The Internet would not be born until the end of the 1960s.[13] The United States government responded to the 1950s Soviet launch of Sputnik with, among other things, the establishment of the Advanced Research Projects Agency ("ARPA"). ARPA's computer research program, headed by individuals such as J.C.R. Licklider and Larry Roberts, led a team of researchers to develop the ARPANet. On October 25, 1969, ARPANet went online, transmitting its first message between computers at the University of California at Los Angeles and the Stanford Research Institute. Originally, the government-run ARPANet used the Network Control Protocol; it did not migrate to the Internet Protocol ("IP") for 14 years.[14]

The Issue

In the 1960s, the FCC faced a problem of something the Commission referred to as "convergence."[15] There were computers that facilitated the operation of the communications network and there were computers with which humans interacted.[16] What should the Commission make of these computers? How should they be treated and how do they fall within the regulatory scheme? What type of jurisdiction did the FCC have over these computers and should data processing services be regulated under Title II of the Communications Act of 1934? Should the FCC be concerned that some of those regulated communications companies were wandering off and entering into the unregulated data processing markets, at times using the excess capacity of their communications network computers to do data processing? Were the communication networks keeping up with the needs and the demands of the data processing networks?

Thus, the FCC, in order to resolve these problems, launched in 1966 what came to be known as the *Computer I* inquiry.[17] The task before the Commission could be boiled down to two issues:

(a) [t]he nature and extent of the regulatory jurisdiction to be applied to data processing services; and

(b) [w]hether, under what circumstances, and subject to what conditions or safeguards, common carriers should be permitted to engage in data processing.[18]

The Policy

Classification

The year 1970 saw the FCC's first attempt to divide the world. The FCC concluded that the appropriate division would be between those computers that ran the communications network and those computers at the ends of the telephone lines with which people interacted. The division was technological, focused on computer processing, attempting to divine the difference between circuit- or message-switching and data processing.[19]

The Commission attempted to divide the world between "pure communications" and "pure data processing."[20]

Pure communications exist where the content of the message is transmitted over the network transparently with no change in content or form of the message.[21] Pure data processing is the processing that takes place at the end of the telephone line. It is:

[t]he use of a computer for the processing of information as distinguished from circuit or message-switching. 'Processing' involves the use of the computer for operations which include, *inter alia*, the functions of storing, retrieving, sorting, merging and calculating data, according to programmed instructions.[22]

The problem is that there is computer processing in both communications and data communications. What was the FCC to do with things that looked like they were a little bit of each? The Commission was not too sure, so it created a third category known as *hybrids*.[23] This was the gray area and the FCC declared that it would resolve the classification of these gray services on an ad hoc, case-by-case basis.[24] If it was more communications than not, then it was communications; if it was more data processing than not, then it was data processing.[25] This gray area was the exception that subsumed the rule and quickly became the undoing of *Computer I*.

Regulation

These two categories had very different characteristics that led to different policy results. This pivotal theme goes throughout the Computer Inquiries. The Commission made policy decisions about these different computers based not upon the technology, but upon the markets within which the technology existed.

The pure data processing market was viewed as an innovative, competitive market with low barriers to entry and little chance of monopolization. Viewing this market, the FCC concluded that there was no demonstrated need for regulation or safeguards.[26] The FCC became quite apologetic as *Computer I* went on, clarifying that it never had any intention whatsoever at any time of regulating data processing.[27]

The pure communications market, on the other hand, was provisioned by an incumbent monopoly. This monopoly almost always was AT&T but there were a few other players such as GTE and a large handful of small, mainly rural, incumbent carriers. In any given market, these players exercised control through their regulated monopoly. Thus, the FCC articulated four concerns about the incumbent telephone companies:

(a) That the sale of data processing services by carriers should not adversely affect the provision of efficient and economic common carrier services;
(b) That the costs related to the furnishing of such data processing services should not be passed on, directly or indirectly, to the users of common carrier services;
(c) That revenues derived from common carrier services should not be used to subsidize any data processing services; and
(d) That the furnishing of such data processing services by carriers should not inhibit [the competitive computer market].[28]

The telephone companies were acquiring large computers that helped run their networks during peak performance times. These computers were paid for by ratepayers. During the off-peak hours, these computers would have excess capacity that the telephone companies could use to enter the data processing market.[29] Since these services were paid for with telephone revenue, this gave the telephone companies the ability to enter the data processing market at significantly reduced rates.[30] Having entered the market, the carriers would have the incentive and the opportunity for cross-subsidization and other unfair trade practices.[31]

It was not the design of the FCC to bluntly bar carriers from the provision of data processing services;[32] rather the Commission recognized certain benefits if safeguards could be designed to permit carriers to enter into the market.[33] Also, the Commission at this time was concerned that the telephone companies were sufficiently meeting the needs of data processing and computer services.[34] The Computer Inquiries policy had as its explicit goal the promotion of economic growth and innovation in the computer services market.[35] The Commission recognized the dependency of the computer networks on the underlying communications facility:

There is virtually unanimous agreement by all who have commented in response to our Inquiry, as well as by all those who have contributed to the rapidly expanding professional literature in the field, that the data processing industry has become a major force in the

American economy, and that its importance to the economy will increase in both absolute and relative terms in the years ahead. There is similar agreement that there is a close and intimate relationship between data processing and communications services and that this interdependence will continue to increase. In fact, it is clear that data processing cannot survive, much less develop further, except through reliance upon and use of communication facilities and services.[36]

The communications facility was a crucial resource upon which they depended, supplied by a single provider who also had the potential to be a competitor.

Telephone companies had both the ability and the incentive to act in an anticompetitive manner.[37] They sat in an unusual place in the market of being both supplier and competitor to the data processing services.[38] The Commission expressed misgivings about whether permitting telephone companies to enter the data processing market was prudent, questioning whether telephone companies should be permitted into this market at all.[39] If they were so permitted, then the question was on what terms and with what safeguards?[40]

Safeguard: Maximum Separation

In response to the concerns related to the communications facility, the Commission devised its "Maximum Separation" safeguards.[41] Maximum Separation meant that regulated communications carriers could enter the unregulated data processing market, but only through a fully separate subsidiary.[42] The FCC required that a carrier establish a separate data processing corporation, have separate accounting books, have separate officers, have separate personnel, and have separate equipment and facilities.[43] The carrier was also prohibited from promoting the data processing services offered by the separate subsidiary.[44] The carrier could not use its network computers for non-network purposes; the carrier could not use the excess capacity of the network computers during off-peak times to provision data processing services.[45] Finally, the affiliated subsidiary was not itself permitted to own transmission services but had to acquire all such services on a tariff basis.[46]

There is a bit of a curiosity however about to whom this obligation would apply. Maximum Separation applied only to those carriers with annual operating revenues exceeding $1,000,000.[47] It appears that perhaps the only carriers that surpassed the threshold might be AT&T and GTE. AT&T, however, had other problems. The U.S. Department of Justice initiated an antitrust proceeding against AT&T in 1956, the settlement of which prohibited AT&T from offering unregulated services.[48] By declaring data processing to be unregulated, the FCC may also have been declaring that AT&T was barred from providing such services.[49]

Legacy of Computer I

What is the legacy of *Computer I*? The first principles laid down in *Computer I* are consistently followed throughout the entire proceeding. How these first principles are applied and the outcome that is produced may be different, but the Computer Inquiries are consistently concerned about markets. The data processing market is highly competitive and innovative and demonstrates no need for regulation. The data processing market, however, is dependent upon the communications market. The communications companies are both a bottleneck supplier of services and a competitor in the data processing market. Therefore, strict safeguards were put into place in order to restrain the market power of the communications company and for the benefit of the data processing market. These are border regulations between markets where the divisions between the markets can easily be discerned and maintained. These safeguards create an open communications platform available to all users on a nondiscriminatory basis.

There is another important point. Contrary to popular mischaracterization, this is not a history of regulatory restraint. This is not a history of the FCC "not regulating the Internet."[50] Rather, this is a history of the FCC taking affirmative and aggressive regulation of communications networks, specifically for the benefit of the computer networks. The computer networks were clearly the designated beneficiaries of the safeguards.

Finally, the problems addressed by the Commission in the 1960s are parallel to the issues today. It was called "convergence" back then just like today. The "new service" was a substitute for the old service. The new service was unregulated where the old service was entrenched and regulated. The new service was dependent upon the underlying old service. The old service sought to enter the market of the new service. The old service market was highly consolidated (well, OK, it was a monopoly then). These are similar to today's issues.

COMPUTER II (1976)

The Setting

The ink had not dried on the *Computer I* before it had become clear that it had problems. The FCC was inundated with applications concerning hybrid services and forced to make a case-by-case analysis of where these services might fall.[51] Computer processing was involved in both "pure communications" and "data processing."[52]

In the meantime, a curious thing had happened. The relatively dumb terminals that had been used to communicate with the mainframe computers had become smart. The cost of computer processing units ("CPUs") was dropping dramatically. Computer chips were showing up in places other than IBM big iron. Suddenly, microcomputers made their appearance, there was intelligence at both ends of the line, and distributed computing had been born.[53] The Commission took note of the introduction of packet-switched networks such as Telenet.[54] AT&T was building customer premise equipment—telephones—with which one could enter and manipulate text—word processors.[55] IBM showed no hesitation in demonstrating its displeasure about AT&T's entrance into its market.

The stage was set. *Computer I* would have to be scrapped; *Computer II* was initiated in 1976.[56] Meanwhile the Internet continued in its childhood. In 1972, the nation saw the first public demonstration of ARPANet. The InterNetworking Working Group was convened in 1972.[57] Bob Metcalfe completed his Ph.D. thesis in 1973 on the Ethernet. Vint Cerf and Bob Kahn presented a paper in 1974 on the Internet Protocol.[58] In 1983, the U.S. government declared that ARPANet would migrate from the Network Control Protocol to the Internet Protocol TCP/IP.[59]

The Issue

The FCC returned to square one. How should it classify these different sets of computers? The hybrid middle ground had been a source of aggravation. Dumb remote terminals had given way to smart microcomputers or minicomputers.[60] The concept of interactive computers as something that one accesses with remote terminals over the communications network, with all processing taking place at the mainframe, was vanishing. The classifications of pure communications and pure data processing were unsustainable. Now the FCC faced interactive computers forming logical networks overlaying physical networks. The Commission understatedly described its new situation as "more complicated."[61]

Furthermore, the rigid safeguards of "maximum separation" were called into question. Was it really necessary for a small incumbent telephone company in the foothills of the Appalachian Mountains, with less than 1000 subscribers, to set up a separate corporation simply to offer data processing services?

The Resolution

Basic versus Enhanced Service Dichotomy

Out of the analytical turmoil over classification of these services was born the basic versus enhanced services dichotomy. This established a division between "common carrier transmission services from those computer services which depend on common carrier services in the transmission of information."[62] It established a transformation in the conceptual framework, migrating from attempts to determine differences between technologies to an examination of differences between services experienced by edge users. This came to be the foundation of the FCC's Computer Inquiries.

Basic Services

"Basic service is the offering of 'a pure transmission capability over a communications path that is virtually transparent in terms of its interaction with customer supplied information.'"[63] It is the transmission capacity in the physical network for the movement of information.[64] The basic service is limited to this transmission capacity[65] and does not interact with user supplied information. Computer processing, including protocol conversion, security, and memory storage, provisioned in the network for the benefit of the network, and not for the edge user, is a part of the basic service.[66] In other words, processing used "solely to facilitate the movement of information" is a part of the basic service.[67]

> [T]he generic characteristic of the communications function is that the semantic content of information is not changed at the completion of a given process. A message entering a network is intended to arrive at its destination unchanged. Several computer operations, such as message and circuit switching, may be required to permit the message to transit the network. In this process, individual symbols may be processed, as in code conversion and error correction. Or the message may be accompanied by addressing information, such as dial pulses or message headers, which are used by the communications network for centralized message routing. The purpose of these computer operations is, nevertheless, the transmission of an unaltered message through a network and they do not constitute a data processing service.[68]

Note that what is not a part of the definition of the basic service is the telephony application; basic service is the provisioned transmission service "regardless of whether subscribers use it for voice, data, video, facsimile, or other forms of transmission."[69]

The Commission wanted to ensure that carriers were able to use computers within their networks,[70] so it sought "the stimulation of economic activity in the regulated communications sector by removing ambiguities in the existing definitions."[71] By the creation of the basic versus enhanced dichotomy, the Commission sought to create regulatory certainty, permitting carriers to use computers in association with the basic service without fear that such use would be considered enhanced. If the service were enhanced, either AT&T may not be able to offer the unregulated service, or the carrier could offer the service but only through a separate subsidiary.[72] Thus, the Commission concluded that computer processing that "relates to and is for the purpose of providing a communications service or meeting its

own in-house needs" is a basic service and may be provisioned freely by the carrier.[73]

In its tentative decision, the Commission proposed that there would be three categories: voice, basic non-voice, and enhanced non-voice services. Both voice and basic non-voice fell within what is now known as basic services. Voice was "the electronic transmission of the human voice such that one human being can orally converse with another human being."[74] Basic non-voice was an intriguing formulation. It was:

> [T]he transmission of subscriber inputted information or data where the carrier: (a) electronically converts originating messages to signals which are compatible with a transmission medium, (b) routes these signals through the network to the appropriate destination, (c) maintains signal integrity in the presence of noise and other impairments to transmission, (d) corrects transmission errors, and (e) converts the electrical signals to usable form at the destination.[75]

This formulation is noteworthy because it describes the behavior of such things as TCP/IP. Had this formulation been accepted, the regulatory status of the Internet might have been quite different. But the basic non-voice category along with the division of basic service into two parts was rejected.

As with pure communications, basic services are regulated under Title II under the same rationale, with the same concerns for discrimination and anticompetitive behavior.[76] Computers associated with basic service could be used for the provision of basic service alone.[77]

Enhanced Services

After considerable consideration and reformation, enhanced services was defined as:

> [S]ervices, offered over common carrier transmission facilities used in interstate communications, which employ computer processing applications that act on the format, content, code, protocol or similar aspects of the subscriber's transmitted information; provide the subscriber additional, different,

or restructured information; or involve subscriber interaction with stored information.[78]

This generally means that what goes into the network is different than what comes out of the network.

The simplicity of this definition belies the turmoil that was experienced in developing it. Originally the FCC simply envisioned a reformation of the *Computer I* definitions.[79] The types of activity covered by "data processing" were anticipated to be such things as word processing, arithmetic processing, and process control.[80] But the Commission was uncomfortable with the way that the old definition left too much to the hybrid category. Pointing to processing was insufficient as processing could be utilized by either communications or data processing. The Commission therefore transformed the concept so that, instead of trying to segregate processing capabilities, it instead would make the classification dependent on the nature of the activity involved.[81] This transforms the analysis from an examination of the technology to an examination of the service provisioned.[82]

The basic versus enhanced dichotomy was designed as a bright-line test,[83] eliminating the "hybrid" middle ground[84] and case-by-case review.[85] Enhanced services are anything[86] more than[87] the transmission capacity[88] of basic service. The Commission has articulated a three-prong test for enhanced services. It "employs computer processing applications that: (1) act on the format, content, code, protocol or similar aspects of a subscriber's transmitted information; (2) provide the subscriber additional, different, or restructured information; or (3) involve subscriber interaction with stored information."[89] Enhanced services do not facilitate the basic service; they alter the fundamental character of the basic service (instead, while the basic service remains the same, the enhanced service is layered on top, creating a new service for the edge user).[90] Anything that takes the basic service and uses computer processing to alter that service is enhanced. The image the Commission has at this time is of enhanced service providers ("ESPs") acquiring basic services, adding enhanced services, and then selling the bundled service to consumers on a resale basis.[91]

The Commission affirmed its *Computer I* finding that enhanced services should be unregulated on the grounds that the market was competitive.[92] The Commission has found that e-mail,[93] voice mail,[94] the World Wide Web,[95] newsgroups,[96] fax store-and-forward, interactive voice response, gateway, audiotext information services, and protocol processing[97] are enhanced services.

Internet access service takes the basic transmission capacity and transforms it for the benefit of the edge users. An Internet user and an Internet service provider ("ISP") take transmission capacity and add to it in order to enable Internet access. The physical network speaks analog dial tone. The equipment at the edge of the logical network speaks IP. Therefore, the language of the basic service is transformed into a language that the edge users speak. It is the edge computers, and not the transmission capacity, that adds Internet packets (user-supplied information). Those Internet packets are not a necessary component of the basic service; the basic service is already complete and does not need the packets in order to be successful.

Adjunct Services

A challenge for the Commission was what to do with adjunct services. Adjunct services "facilitate the use of traditional telephone service but do not alter the fundamental character of telephone service."[98] The FCC concluded that adjunct services would "be regulated in the same fashion as the underlying service—whether basic or enhanced—with which it is associated in a particular offering."[99] Note that it is never the other way around—the underlying service does not take on the classification of the adjunct service. The existence of the adjunct service does not alter the regulatory classification of the underlying service.[100]

Some examples follow: directory assistance provides a telephone number in order to facilitate the use of the basic telephone network. Therefore, directory assistance takes on the characteristic of the basic service (it does not transform the basic service into an enhanced service).[101] Reverse directory assistance provides a name or an address that is used for something other than the basic telephone service. Because it does not facilitate the use of the network, it is not an adjunct to the network.[102] Services that facilitate use of the basic service by individuals with disabilities are also basic services.[103]

Protocol Processing

The Commission was confronted with how to deal with protocol processing. As much as the Commission strove to eliminate the middle ground of "hybrid" services, protocol processing remained a gray area. The Commission conceded that protocol processing could be either basic or enhanced. It set forth a straightforward analysis in order to determine in which category such processing should fall. This analysis is the same as determining whether an adjunct service is a basic service. Generally, protocol conversion services are enhanced services.[104] Traditionally, however, three things were considered basic:

> [P]rotocol processing: 1) involving communications between an end user and the network itself (e.g., for initiation, routing, and termination of calls) rather than between or among users; 2) in connection with the introduction of a new basic network technology (which requires protocol conversion to maintain compatibility with existing CPE); and 3) involving internetworking (conversions taking place solely within the carrier's network to facilitate provision of a basic network service, that result in no net conversion to the end user).[105]

As with the adjunct services analysis, where protocol conversion is for the benefit and facilitation of the network as opposed to the edge user, it is a basic service.

The Commission concluded that the simple involvement of packet-switching is not sufficient to conclude that a service is enhanced. AT&T came up with a peculiar resolution with its Interspan service. With this offering, AT&T provisioned a packet-switched frame relay service over a high-speed[106] connection, bundling it with enhanced services, and attempted to sell it as a single indivisible service. The Independent Data Communications Manufacturers Association challenged the provisioning, arguing that under *Computer II*, AT&T had to unbundle the basic from the enhanced service and offer the basic service

to other enhanced service providers. This time, however, the basic service was the AT&T packet-switched frame relay service.

AT&T argued that the Interspan offering as a whole was an information service. In the alternative, AT&T argued that contamination theory meant that the provisioning of the information service indicated that the whole offering was an information service.

The Commission rejected this argument. The frame relay service "provides transport of customer data 'transparently' across the AT&T frame relay network."[107] Regardless of whether the service provisioned to the customer comes as an information service, AT&T was required to unbundle the basic from the enhanced service.[108] The Commission noted that it has never applied the contamination theory[109] to facility-based providers.[110]

What do we take away from these decisions? Many things. AT&T frame relay confirmed that the Commission in *Computer II* intended to open up the communications facility over which enhanced services could be provisioned, regardless of the nature of the basic service. The basic service can be packet-switched and it need not involve telephony. It can be broadband and digital. AT&T's Interspan offering was a far cry from POTS;[111] *Computer II* still applied.

The protocol processing issue has an odd history. Originally, the carriers wanted the protocol processing to be categorized as basic services. At that time, the Bell operating companies ("BOCs") either were not permitted to offer unregulated service pursuant to the Modified Final Judgment, or they were permitted, but only through a separate subsidiary. Thus, unless protocol conversion was basic, they could not offer it.[112] By *Computer III*, carriers such as AT&T wanted protocol conversion to be categorized as enhanced services. Those services, which they were then permitted to offer, would not fall under Title II regulation.

The Telecommunications Act of 1996 and "Information Services"

While the year 1996 brought the Telecommunications Act with its new terminology including "telecommunications," "telecommunications service," and "information service," it did not use the terms "basic" or "enhanced services." The Commission concluded[113] that Congress codified the basic versus enhanced dichotomy using the new terms of "telecommunications" and "information services."[114] The FCC concluded that all enhanced services are information services, although not all information services are necessarily enhanced services. The explanation for this conclusion is rooted in the physical network. Enhanced services are provisioned over *common carriers'*, information services are provisioned over *telecommunications* (not necessarily telecommunications services). While some entities that provision telecommunications are telecommunications services ("common carriers"), not all are. Otherwise, the Commission concluded that the term "information services" should be "interpreted to extend to the same functions" and understood in a consistent manner of enhanced services.[115]

Safeguards

Maximum Separation to Structural Separation

The problem of the bottleneck communications facility remained present on the Commission's mind:

> The importance of the control of local facilities, as well as their location and number, cannot be overstate[d]. As we evolve into more of an information society, the access/bottleneck nature of the telephone local loop will take on greater significance. Although technological trends suggest that hard-wire access provided by a telephone company will not be the only alternative, its existing ubiquity and the amount of underlying investment suggest that whatever changes do occur will be implemented gradually.[116]

The Commission continued to be concerned that communications services adequately met the needs of computer processing technology.[117] The Commission affirmed its recognition of the value to individuals and in the economy of these new innovative services.[118] It also affirmed its concern that the communications facility be maintained as an open platform available to all and that cross-subsidization be prevented.[119]

However, the Commission's theme concerning the inefficiency of structural separation began to grow. The Commission developed the opinion that it was not necessary to impose structural separation on all carriers, but only on those with sufficient market size to be able to abuse their position. Those carriers with insufficient size and market position do not have the same incentives and thus do not require the same level of safeguards:

> Moreover the monopoly rent that a company can extract from such bottleneck facilities is likely to bear some relation to the number of subscribers served. It is probable that many of the new information services that will be offered over telephone lines will incur developmental expenses that will require large customer bases. As we observed, many of them are likely to be national in scope. A telephone company serving a relatively small proportion of the nation's homes and businesses is perhaps less likely to pursue such activities independently. For the most part, long-term profitable entry into the enhanced services field will probably require penetration of the market on a national scale, and it is unlikely that such a national operation could be effectively subsidized from a small pool of monopoly revenues, or that it could gain any significant competitive advantage by restricting the access of its competitors to a very limited network of underlying facilities. The effectiveness of other regulatory tools available to this Commission and other authorities is also considerably improved when they are applied to smaller telephone carriers.[120]

Therefore structural safeguards requiring separate subsidiaries, formerly known as maximum separation, continued to be applied only to the large carriers: AT&T and GTE.[121] Other carriers merely had to comply with the unbundling rules discussed *infra*.[122] In 1984, AT&T begot the BOCs and the BOCs found themselves under the structural separation of *Computer II*.[123] The *Computer II* structural separation safeguards were consistent with *Computer I's* maximum separation, requiring a high degree of separation, independence, and visibility.[124]

Unbundling

Smaller carriers, as stated *infra*, lacked the resources from the regulated side with which to subsidize their unregulated side. They had fewer customers and less ability to discriminate, turning away paying consumers. In light of the reduced incentive in the smaller markets and the reduced resources smaller carriers might have to administer a separate subsidiary, the relative cost of "maximum separation" did not justify the requirement on smaller carriers.

Nevertheless, the small carriers remained in a bottleneck position in the market as the sole supplier of the essential communications service. They still had the incentive and opportunity to take advantage of their monopoly control of the transmission capacity, and to act in anticompetitive ways. In order to ensure that this bottleneck did not hinder the enhanced services market, the Commission required that all facilities-based common carriers who desire to provide enhanced services must unbundle the basic from the enhanced services. They also had to provide the basic service to all other enhanced services on the same terms and conditions.[125] The carrier could provide the service on a bundled basis, but had to make the unbundled offering to unaffiliated ESPs.[126]

Computer I never mentioned CPE because there was no thought that the CPE would get smart enough be a part of the unregulated service. As a result, the Commission promulgated as a part of *Computer II*'s unbundling rules a prohibition against carriers bundling CPE with the provision of telecommunications service.[127] This prohibition was eliminated in 2001.[128]

Layers

With this new conceptual framework, the Computer Inquiries, albeit not necessarily overtly, adopted a layered model of regulation. The Layered Model of Regulation generally divides communications policy into (1) a physical network layer,[129] (2) a logical network layer, (3) applications and services layer, and (4) a content layer.[130] These layers emanate from the first principal concern for markets. These differing layers demarcate natural boundaries between markets. These market boundaries permit communications regulation, where necessary, to be particularly successful.[131] By conceptualizing the policy as layers, the analyst is capable of grouping and segregating issues. Issues related to the physical network layer (i.e., common carrier regulation, spectrum policy, cable franchises) are different from those of the logical layer (i.e., open access, peering) and are different from those in the content layer (i.e., intellectual property, gambling, taxation, libel). Thus, by conceptualizing the policy as layers, the analyst is enabled to identify markets, clarify issues, create boundary regulations that are effective, and, in so doing, target solutions where issues reside without interfering with other industries and opportunities. The Layered Model is a market policy mapped onto a technical conception.

The Layered Model of Regulation is not the same as the OSI ("Open Systems Interconnection") reference model[132] or the IP stack.[133] However, it could be said the Layered Model of Regulation takes its inspiration from and is enabled by these technical reference models. These reference models layer different protocols which enable the provisioning of different services. Each layer is separate from the one above and the one below. The degree of separation is sufficiently complete so that the service provisioned at one layer can be provisioned by one provider while the service provisioned at another layer can be serviced by another provider.[134]

A prime example is the Internet. The Internet protocol is designed as a thin protocol in the middle of the layers. It is agnostic as to applications above or physical networks below.[135] By design, physical networks need only be compatible with or optimized for IP; if IP over the physical network is successful, then the physical network is indifferent to and need not be optimized for any particular application or service. Conversely, applications and services are designed to operate over IP; they are indifferent to and need not be optimized for any particular physical network. This creates a great deal of separation between physical networks, logical (IP) networks, and applications and services.

The result is the robustness and flexibility of the Internet. Any application over IP can be provisioned over any network. An edge user can, for example, download a variety of applications to a laptop. In one moment the laptop can be connected using a dial-up connection. In the next moment it might be connected using a Wi-Fi wireless card. Finally, it might be connected over a corporate local access network ("LAN"). At any moment, the edge user is fully capable of using any application in any of these settings (assuming sufficient bandwidth). The logical network is not optimized for any particular application or any particular physical network.

The FCC implicitly identified that within the different layers are different markets and different regulatory concerns:

- The physical network (layers 1 and 2 of the OSI reference model) is "basic services" provisioned by telephone carriers regulated under Title II.

- The logical network (layers 3 and 4) is TCP/IP or Internet access provisioned by ISPs, directly and intentionally benefiting from the Computer Inquiry safeguards.

- Above the logical layer are services, applications, and content provisioned by applications service providers, content providers, and a host of other players, all generally removed from communication regulation.

The Commission recognized that the communications facility and the enhanced service are separate and identifiable elements of the service provisioned to the consumer.[136] "The underlying carrier's transmission facilities become the basic building block upon which computer facilities can be added to perform myriad combinations and permutations of processing activities."[137] By conceiving it as one network service layered on top of another, the underlying layer is made into an open communication platform available to all:

> The isolation of the transmission component enables any carrier to provide an enhanced … service on the same basis, without threat of unfair competitive advantage accruing to a given carrier by virtue of its control over the underlying transmission facilities. The transmission facility would be common to all entities and removed as a competitive element of the service.[138]

An entity, in a given moment, is either provisioning physical network transmission capacity, or logical network Internet access services. This is a "mutually exclusive" situation described by the Commission.[139]

A service provider in a given moment is provisioning one or the other, but not both simultaneously. For example, the SS7 switch provisions physical network telephone services, not logical network layer Internet services. The IP router provisions Internet access service; it does not provision physical network transmission capacity. A provider can provide both such services, but the services themselves remain distinct.[140]

This layered approach to the Computer Inquiries means clear segregation between basic and enhanced services. Basic is never enhanced; enhanced is never basic. The enhanced service is what is done over the basic transmission facility; it is never the transmission facility. The basic is always the passing of content back and forth; it is never enhanced processing of that content. Enhanced services provisioning always means a basic service plus an enhanced service (an enhanced service cannot exist without an underlying transmission service). Identifying something as an enhanced service does not alter the underlying transmission capacity as basic.[141]

This layered model approach is followed by the FCC throughout *Computer II* and *Computer III*.

Legacy of Computer II

Computer II brought a radical revision in framework. The rationale and the policy goals, however, remained the same. As with *Computer I*, the enhanced services market was viewed as dynamic, innovative, and competitive, while the basic services were viewed as having both the incentive and the opportunity to act anticompetitively.[142]

The premier legacy of *Computer II* is the establishment of the basic versus enhanced dichotomy. This layered approach to regulation becomes the bedrock of the Computer Inquiries success, and distinguishes it from other international schemes. It established a bright-line test and amplified the separation of the communications facility from the enhancement.

This is a "dichotomy." These are things that are opposed to each other. It is a competitive market as opposed to a noncompetitive market. It is an essential service as opposed to innovation built on top. It is a physical network as opposed to a logical network. It is a regulated service as opposed to an unregulated service.

The dichotomy is a bottom-up analysis. First, the basic telecom service is identified. This is the policy concern. This is the restrained market. This is the essential service. Anything more is more. Anything more is competitive. Anything more is not the essential service but the innovation. Anything more is therefore unregulated.

The next significant legacy of *Computer II* is a cost-benefit analysis of structural separation. This theme will lead into *Computer III*, resulting in further drastic revisions to the Computer Inquiry safeguards.

Finally, *Computer II* continued to make clear that, while enhanced services themselves were not regulated, they were the clearly intended beneficiaries of the safeguards.

COMPUTER III (1985)

The Setting

This time the Commission managed to have four years pass without reopening its proceeding. It is 1985. The Domain Name System had just been introduced the previous year. The first commercial ISP had yet to be established.[143] The National Science Foundation Network ("NSFNET") would come online in 1986. And the Internet Engineering Task Force ("IETF") had not yet had its first meeting.[144]

In 1984, AT&T had gone through divestiture forming the BOCs.[145] The BOCs for their part received official blessing from Judge Greene, permitting them to begin to enter the enhanced services market in 1987 and to fully enter the market in 1991.[146] In 1985, the Commission launched *Computer III*,[147] initiating the last phase of the regulatory proceeding that would have so many implications for the deployment of the Internet before the commercial Internet truly broke.

The Issue

The conceptual framework of the Computer Inquiries had been settled in *Computer II* with the establishment of the basic versus enhanced service dichotomy. The policy objectives remain the same. What changes is implementation.

Driving *Computer III* was the perception that the separate subsidiary requirements of *Computer II*

"impose significant costs on the public in decreased efficiency and innovation that substantially outweight [*sic*] their benefits in limiting the ability of AT&T and the BOCS to make unfair use of their regulated operations for the benefit of their unregulated, enhanced services activities."[148] Believing that it could achieve appropriate safeguards, perhaps develop a new and more progressive framework, and also eliminate the cost of the separate subsidiary, the Commission sought to migrate from structural safeguards to non-structural safeguards. In order to do so, the Commission had to establish a scheme that would satisfy its original concerns regarding anticompetitive behavior and continue to make available an open communications platform. The Commission's solution was, in the short term, Comparatively Efficient Interconnection ("CEI") and, in the long term, Open Network Architecture ("ONA").

The Resolution

Comparatively Efficient Interconnection

CEI was seen as an interim solution while BOCs create ONA plans. Under CEI, BOCs would be permitted to enter into enhanced services markets on a non-structurally separated basis (a separate subsidiary was no longer needed; the ESP could be integrated into the BOC) on the condition that they make available[149] CEI plans. These CEI plans were intended to detail what the BOC was provisioning to its affiliated ESP; BOCs would be required to make these provisions available to all other non-affiliated ESPs on the same terms and conditions.[150]

Open Network Architecture

The next step was the move toward Open Network Architecture. This was a radical approach to the issue. While the Commission was in retreat on the notion and value of separate subsidiaries, ONA imposed a progressive vision of the network. ONA required BOCs to break their networks down into basic building blocks, and to make those building blocks available to ESPs to build new services.[151] Although not identical to unbundled network elements,[152] the BOCs would be required to break apart the basic service offering for the benefit of the ESP market. These BOC building blocks would be divided among Basic Service Elements (i.e., Calling Number Identification), Basic Serving Arrangements (fundamental tariffed switching and transport services), Complimentary Network Services (i.e., stutter dial tone, call waiting, call forwarding, call forwarding on busy, hunting), and Ancillary Network Services (i.e., billing services, collection, protocol processing).[153]

BOCs were required to file ONA plans regardless of whether they entered the ESP market.[154] Having successfully filed an ONA plan with the Commission, BOCs would then be permitted to provide integrated ESP services without filing a CEI plan.[155] There was also guidance on how ESPs could request the provision of new services.[156]

The *Computer III* proceeding also set forth a set of other safeguards that fell upon different entities: annual ONA reporting,[157] network information disclosure,[158] cross-subsidization prohibitions,[159] accounting safeguards,[160] and customer proprietary network information.[161]

Litigation

Things did not go quite as planned. In *California III*, the Ninth Circuit reviewed the Commission's move from structural to non-structural safeguards and:

> found that, in granting full structural relief based on the BOC ONA plans, the Commission had not adequately explained its apparent "retreat" from requiring "fundamental unbundling" of BOC networks as a component of ONA and a condition for lifting structural separation. The court was therefore concerned that ONA unbundling, as implemented, failed to prevent the BOCs from engaging in discrimination against competing ESPs in providing access to basic services.[162]

The Court therefore vacated and remanded the proceeding back to the FCC.

On remand, the Commission concluded that the court in *California III* vacated only the Commission's ONA rules, not the CEI rules. Therefore, the Commission issued the Interim Waiver Order that permitted BOCs to provide enhanced services if they complied with the CEI rules.[163] In addition, BOCs must comply with procedures set forth in the ONA plans that they had already filed with and had been approved by the Commission.[164] The Commission also released a Further Notice of Proposed Rulemaking in order to resolve the issues raised in *California III*.[165] This rulemaking, pursuant to the remand, is still pending. In 2002, the Commission released the Broadband Notice of Proposed Rulemaking, which subsumed the *Computer III* proceeding and is currently pending.[166]

In sum, currently under *Computer III*, CEI is an ongoing obligation where BOCs choose to provide enhanced services and the ONA plans that were filed remain binding.

Enforcement

The Commercial Internet eXchange ("CIX") objected to the movement to non-structural safeguards, arguing that this created a problem with enforcement. Recognizing validity to the CIX objection, the Commission stated:

> We believe that competitive ISPs will themselves monitor CEI compliance vigilantly, and will call the Commission's attention to any failure by a BOC to follow through on its CEI responsibilities. … The Commission will not hesitate to use its enforcement authority, including the Accelerated Docket or revised complaint procedures, to review and adjudicate allegations that a BOC is falling short of fulfilling any of its CEI obligations.[167]

Note, however, that this does create certain structural oddities. First, an unregulated industry, with little knowledge of the FCC, is asked to watch a regulated industry. Second, small companies are asked to watch the largest corporations in the United States. Third, ISPs are placed in a position of filing complaints against their sole supplier of a crucial facility. Fourth, contrary to normal jurisprudence, the party that lacks the information has the burden of moving (normally, all things being equal, the party with the information has the burden of moving—in this case, the burden is on the ISPs, because the information is held by the BOCs).

Legacy of Computer III

The legacy of *Computer III* was first and foremost an affirmation of the policy goals set forth in *Computer I* and *Computer II*. *Computer III* does not alter the fundamental philosophy of the Computer Inquiries. Concern for anticompetitive behavior and maintaining an open communications platform is retained. Likewise, the conceptual framework of the basic versus enhanced dichotomy that tracks the technical layers of the network is affirmed.

Computer III alters implementation by initiating new, novel, and even progressive experiments in opening up the communications bottleneck for the benefit of enhanced services. This marks a migration away from structural safeguards. It also signifies renewed emphasis on opening up the facilities network for the benefit of the enhanced service or computer network operating on top of the physical network. It affirms that while enhanced services remain unregulated, the Computer Inquiry policy is designed for the direct benefit of those enhanced services.

The transition from *Computer I* to *Computer II* marked a radical evolution of the conceptual framework, with implementation remaining fundamentally the same. The transition from *Computer II* to *Computer III* marked a radical evolution in the implementation, with the conceptual framework remaining the same.

CONCLUSION

The *Computer III* Final Order was released in 1986. The first commercial ISP was established in 1989. The Commercial Internet eXchange was set up in 1991 as the first exchange point for traffic between commercial Internet backbones (such traffic was not permitted on the NSFNET). The World Wide Web was unleashed in 1991. The White House came online in 1993 and Congress was placed online in 1994. The mid-1990s saw the explosive growth of Internet users.[168] In 1998, Boardwatch magazine reported, at its peak, that there were more than 7,000 ISPs in North America.[169]

Was the success of the Internet attributable to the actions of the Commission? Did the Commission "invent the Internet?" The success of the Internet was clearly the result of the confluence of forces. For the Commission's part, it had established the policy of the Computer Inquiries, deregulated the Customer Premise Equipment market (i.e., modems), and promoted ubiquitous and affordable flat-rate telephone lines (i.e., universal service).[170] All of these were necessary precursors to the success of the Internet.

There is also little new under the sun. The problem that the Commission described itself as facing in 1966 was "convergence." The problems were ones of substitutability, asymmetric regulation between functionally equivalent services, the restricted supply of communications services to a highly competitive enhanced services market, and the desire of the communications services dominant players who wanted to enter the highly competitive enhanced services market. The Commission faces similar issues today.

There is a tendency of regulators to automatically impose legacy regulation on new services that appear similar to, substitutes of, or threats to traditional services. The policymaker must always ask why. Why impose legacy regulation on the new service? By framing the question properly, the policymaker can gain better answers. By framing the question in terms of the layered model, that is, in terms of identifiable markets within communications industries, it helps avoid a mushed view of communications where the difference between applications and the physical network cannot be perceived. If, for example, telephony is uncoupled from the physical network and the old monopoly market, and is now provisioned in the highly competitive applications market, what implications does that have for policy?

The Computer Inquiries have been wildly successful. They followed a layered model of regulation and sought to constrain anticompetitive behavior where it occurred. The potential bottleneck in the physical network layer was identified; the competitive market and potential for growth and innovation for enhanced services was identified. A policy was created which promoted economic and technological expansion.[171] In so doing, the Commission avoided imposing legacy common carrier regulation on new services. It created open communications platforms where innovation could occur, independent of dominant communications players.

NOTES

1. Amendment of Sections 64.702 of the Comm'ns Rules and Regs. (Third Computer Inquiry), *Report and Order*, 104 F.C.C.2d 958, para. 9, 60 Rad. Reg.2d (P & F) 603 (1986) [hereinafter *Computer III Report and Order*].

2. Jonathan Weinberg, *The Internet and "Telecommunications Services," Universal Service Mechanisms, Access Charges, and Other Flotsam of the Regulatory System*, 16 YALE J. ON REG. 211, 222 (1999) ("That approach was wildly successful in spurring innovation and competition in the enhanced-services marketplace: Government maintained its control of the underlying transport, sold primarily by regulated monopolies, while eschewing any control over the new-fangled, competitive 'enhancements.'").

3. Inquiry Concerning the Deployment of Advanced Telecomms. Capability to All Americans in a Reasonable and Timely Fashion, and Possible Steps to Accelerate Such Deployment Pursuant to Section 706 of the Telecomms. Act of 1996, *Report*, 14 F.C.C.R. 2398, para. 45, 14 Comm. Reg. (P & F) 1292 (1999).

4. Delbert D. Smith, *The Interdependence of Computer and Communications Services and Facilities: A Question of Federal Regulation*, 117 U. PA. L. REV. 829 (1969).

5. *See* Computer and Comm. Indus. Ass'n v. FCC, 693 F.2d 198, 203 n.6 (D.C. Cir. 1982) ("'Message-switching' was defined as '[t]he computer-controlled transmission of messages, between two or more points, via communications facilities, wherein the content of the message remains unaltered.'"); Reg. and Policy Problems Presented by the Interdependence of Computer and Comm. Servs., *Tentative Decision*, 28 F.C.C.2d 291, para. 15, 18 Rad. Reg.2d (P & F) 1713 (1970) [hereinafter *Computer I Tentative Decision*].

6. The Author wishes to acknowledge Prof. Dale Hatfield for this point.

7. *See* Smith, *supra* note 4, at 831, 836 (recounting historical context of *Computer I* actions and issues presented).

8. *Id.* at 852.

9. Reg. and Policy Problems Presented by the Interdependence of Computer and Comm. Servs., *Notice of Inquiry*, 1 F.C.C.2d 11, para. 16, 8 Rad. Reg.2d (P & F) 1567 (1966) [hereinafter *Computer I Notice of Inquiry*].

10. Pursuant to the 1956 Consent Decree, IBM was prohibited from entering the computer service bureau market and could only act as a supplier of equipment. Smith, *supra* note 4, at 834.

11. *Computer I Notice of Inquiry*, *supra* note 9, paras. 3-9; Smith, *supra* note 4, at 831, 836 (recounting the historical context of *Computer I* actions and issues presented).

12. Triumph of the Nerds: A History of the Computer: Electronics (1996), *at* http://www.pbs.org/nerds/timeline/elec.html (last visited Nov. 17, 2002); Computer History Museum, Timeline of Computer History, *at* http://www.computerhistory.org/timeline/index.page (last visited Nov. 17, 2002).

13. This paper focuses on the Internet as a primary example of the FCC's Computer Inquiry policy. The Internet is but one example, perhaps a paradigm, among a multitude of what would come to be known as enhanced services.

14. Robert X. Cringely, *PBS Nerds 2.0.1 Timeline* (1998), *at* http://www.pbs.org/opb/nerds2.0.1/timeline/; Richard T Griffiths, *The Origins and Growth of the Internet and the World Wide Web* (Oct. 2001), *at* http://www.let.leidenunivnl/history/ivh/chapl.htm; Computer History Museum, *Internet History and Microprocessor Timeline* 1962–1992, at http://computerhistory.org/exhibits/internet_history (last visited Nov. 17, 2002).

15. *Computer I Notice of Inquiry*, *supra* note 9, para. 13; *see also* Second Computer Inquiry, *Final Decision*, 11 F.C.C.2d 384, para. 19, 47 Rad. Reg.2d (P & F) 669 (1980) [hereinafter *Computer II Final Decision*] ("The *First Computer Inquiry* was a vehicle for identification and better understanding of problems spawned by the confluence of computer and communications technologies taking place at that time.").

16. *Computer I Notice of Inquiry*, *supra* note 9, paras. 10–16 (discussing the migration of common carriers to the use of computers to run networks).

17. See generally *id.*

18. *Computer I Tentative Decision, supra* note 5, para. 14.

19. *Computer II Final Decision, supra* note 15, para. 17.

20. Computer and Comm. Indus. Ass'n v. FCC, 693 F.2d 198, 203 (D.C. Cir. 1982).

21. *Id.* at 203 n.6; *Computer I Tentative Decision, supra* note 5, para. 15.

22. *Computer I Tentative Decision, supra* note 5, para. 15.

23. *Id.* ("Hybrid Service—an offering of service which combines Remote Access data processing and message-switching to form a single integrated service.").

24. Reg. and Policy Problems presented by the Interdependence of Computer and Comm. Servs., *Final Decision and Order*, 28 F.C.C.2d 267, paras. 27, 31–38, 21 Rad. Reg.2d (P & F) 1591 (1971) [hereinafter *Computer I Final Decision*]; *Computer I Tentative Decision, supra* note 5, paras. 39–45.

25. Amendment of Section 64.702 of the Comm'n's Rules and Regs. (Second Computer Inquiry), *Tentative Decision and Further Notice of Inquiry and Rulemaking*, 72 F.C.C.2d 358, paras. 6–7, 17, 45 Rad. Reg.2d (P & F) 1485 (1979) [hereinafter *Computer II Tentative Decision*]; *Computer II Final Decision, supra* note 15, paras. 13–14; Amendment of Section 64.702 of the Comm'n's Rules and Regs., *Notice of Inquiry and Proposed Rulemaking*, 61 F.C.C.2d 103, paras. 13–14 (1976) [hereinafter *Computer II Notice of Inquiry*].

26. *Computer I Tentative Decision, supra* note 5, paras. 19–23: Applying these standards to the record before us we conclude that the offering of data processing services is essentially competitive and that, except to the limited extent hereinafter set forth, there is no public interest requirement for regulation by government of such activities. Thus, there is ample evidence that data processing services of all kinds are becoming available in larger volume and that there are no natural or economic barriers to free entry into the market for these services. The number of data processing bureaus, time sharing systems, and specialized

information services is steadily increasing and there are no indications that any of these markets are threatened with monopolization. *Id.* para. 20. *See also Computer II Final Decision, supra* note 15, para. 127 (reviewing *Computer I* history); *Computer II Tentative Decision, supra* note 25, paras. 16–17 (reviewing *Computer I* history).

27. The Commission stated:

It should be made clear that we are not seeking to regulate data processing as such, nor are we attempting to regulate the substance of any carrier's offerings of data processing. Rather, we are limiting regulation to requirements respecting the framework in which a carrier may publicly offer particular non-regulated services, the nature and characteristics of which require separation before predictable abuses are given opportunity to arise.

Computer I Final Decision, supra note 24, para. 30.

28. *Id.* para. 9. *See also Computer II Tentative Decision, supra* note 25, para. 124 (reviewing history of maximum separation).

29. *Computer I Final Decision, supra* note 24, para. 7; *Computer I Notice of Inquiry, supra* note 9, para. 10–16.

30. *See also Computer II Notice of Inquiry, supra* note 25, para. 3:

First, a major regulatory concern of the Commission was the appropriateness of a carrier utilizing part of its communications switching plant to offer a data processing service. Further, there was the issue of whether communication common carriers should be permitted to sell data processing services and, if so, what safeguards should be imposed to insure that the carriers would not engage in anti-competitive or discriminatory practices. There was also concern as to the extent to which data processing organizations should be permitted to sell communications as part of a data processing package not subject to regulation. *Id.*

31. *Computer I Final Decision, supra* note 24, paras. 21–22; *see also Computer II Notice of Inquiry, supra* note 25, para. 5 ("[W]e were concerned

about the possibility that common carriers might favor their own data processing activities by discriminatory services, cross subsidization, improper pricing of common carrier services, and related anticompetitive practices and activities which could result in burdening or impairing the carrier's provision of its other regulated services."); *Computer I Tentative Decision, supra* note 5, para. 25.

32. *See Computer I Final Decision, supra* note 24, para. 11 (discussing and rejecting parties' views that there should be an outright ban on carrier provision of data processing services).

33. *Computer I Tentative Decision, supra* note 5, paras. 30–33.

34. *Computer I Notice of Inquiry, supra* note 9, para. 21:

   This, then, is another area of concern. Are the service offerings of the common carriers, as well as their tariffs and practices, keeping pace with the quickened developments in digital technology? Does a gap exist between computer industry needs and requirements, on the one side, and communications technology and tariff rates and practices on the other?

   Id. See also Computer I Tentative Decision, supra note 5, paras. 6–11 (resolving the issue of whether common carrier offerings are meeting the needs of the computer industry); *Computer II Final Decision, supra* note 15, para. 14; *Computer II Tentative Decision, supra* note 25, para. 2.

35. *Computer II Tentative Decision, supra* note 25, para. 59.

36. *Computer I Final Decision, supra* note 24, para. 7; *see also Computer I Notice of Inquiry, supra* note 9, para. 1 ("Effective use of the computer is, therefore, becoming increasingly dependent upon communication common carrier facilities and services by which the computers and the user are given instantaneous access to each other.").

37. In 1987, the Federal District Court for Washington, D.C. stated:

That the ability for abuse exists as does the incentive, of that there can also be no doubt. As stated above, information services are fragile, and because of their fragility, time-sensitivity, and their negative reactions to even small degradations in transmission quality and speed, they are most easily subject to destruction by those who control their transmission. Among the more obvious means of anticompetitive action in this regard are increases in the rates for those switched and private line services upon which Regional Company competitors depend while lower rates are maintained for Regional Company network services; manipulation of the quality of access lines; impairment of the speed, quality, and efficiency of dedicated private lines used by competitors; development of new information services to take advantage of planned, but not yet publicly known, changes in the underlying network; and use for Regional Company benefit of the knowledge of the design, nature, geographic coverage, and traffic patterns of competitive information service providers. United States v. W. Elec. Co., 673 F. Supp. 525, 566 (D.D.C. 1987).

38. *Computer I Notice of Inquiry, supra* note 9, para. 15 ("As a consequence, common carriers, in offering these services, are, or will be, in many instances, competitive with services sold by computer manufacturers and service bureau firms. At the same time, such firms will be dependent upon common carriers for reasonably priced communication facilities and services.").

39. *Computer II Tentative Decision, supra* note 25, para. 15.

40. *Id.* para. 3.

41. *Computer I Final Decision, supra* note 24, para. 10; *Computer I Tentative Decision, supra* note 5, paras. 34–35:

Because of the increasing involvement of interstate communications facilities and services in the provision of data transmission, the need for such separation is apparent and urgent. This need exists whether or not at the present time the carrier is engaged in the sale of local or remote access data processing. In either instance, there is a potential for abuse in the form of a commingling of costs associated with the rendition of communication and data processing services, which can give rise to the above-discussed problems of cross-subsidization and other unfair competitive practices in the pricing of regulated and non-regulated services. Also, such commingling of operations and related costs will unduly complicate the task of effective regulation of the communication rates and services of common carriers. It will tend to obscure, if not defeat, the ready identification and allocation for accounting and ratemaking purposes of the costs associated with each activity.

Id. para. 35. *See Computer II Final Decision, supra* note 15, para. 18; *Computer II Tentative Decision, supra* note 25, paras. 4, 123.

42. *See Computer I Tentative Decision, supra* note 5, paras. 36–38.

43. *See id.* para. 36.

44. *Computer I Final Decision, supra* note 24, paras. 18, 21:

"[W]e have decided to modify our rules to prohibit a data affiliate from using the name of its related common carrier in its promotions and, further, to prohibit such affiliate from using, in its corporate name, any words or symbols contained in the name of its affiliated carrier." *Id.* para. 18.

45. *Id.* paras. 13–15, 24. Carriers could use their own computers to meet their own data processing needs and the needs of independent telephone companies, so long as those needs were incidental to the provision of communications services. *Id.* para. 40. The carrier was otherwise, however, prohibited from acquiring the services of its data processing affiliate.

46. *Id.* para. 20.

47. *See Computer II Final Decision, supra* note 15, para. 229.

48. *Computer I Final Decision, supra* note 24, para. 23. *See Computer I Tentative*

49. *Decision, supra* note 5, para. 36.

50. United States v. AT&T, 552 F. Supp. 131 (D.D.C. 1982), *aff'd sub nom.* Maryland

v. United States, 460 U.S. 1001 (1983), *vacated sub nom.* United States v. W. Elec. Co., 2Comm. Reg. (P & F) 1388 (D.D.C. 1996). *See* Accounting Safeguards Under the Telecomms. Act of 1996, *Report and Order,* 11 F.C.C.R. 17539, para. 3 n.5, 5 Comm. Reg. (P & F) 861 (1996) [hereinafter *Accounting Safeguards*]. The Modified Final Judgment ("MFJ") originally prohibited the BOCs from providing information services, providing interLATA services, or manufacturing and selling telecommunications equipment or manufacturing customer premises equipment. The theory behind this prohibition in the MFJ was that the BOCs could leverage their market power in the local market to impede competition in the interLATA services, manufacturing, and information services markets. The information services restriction was modified in 1987 to allow BOCs to provide voice messaging services and to transmit information services generated by others. *Id.* (internal citations omitted); *Computer I Tentative Decision, supra* note 5, para. 24 (stating AT&T "cannot furnish data processing services"). *Cf. Computer II Final Decision, supra* note 15, paras. 277–81 (suggesting that it was not clear what AT&T was and was not permitted to do with regard to enhanced services and customer-premises equipment ("CPE")); *Computer II Tentative Decision, supra* note 25, paras. 135–48 (noting that AT&T was foreclosed from offering data processing services under *Computer I,* but further concluding that AT&T would be permitted into the CPE and enhanced services market).

51. *See* Ann E. Rendahl, *California v. FCC: A Victory for the States,* 13 Hastings Comm. & Ent. L.J. 233, 238–39 (1991):

The FCC determined that it was only necessary to apply this maximum separation policy to common carriers earning over one million dollars a year, but only the American

Telephone & Telegraph Co. (AT&T) fell into this category. However, such line drawing was irrelevant since AT&T and the Bell Operating Companies (BOCs) were already prohibited from providing competitive, non-common carrier services under a 1956 consent decree. …

Id. at 239. *See also* Amendment of Sections 64.702 of the Comm'n's Rules and Regs. (Third Computer Inquiry), *Report and Order*, 104 F.C.C.2d 958, paras. 24–26, 60 Rad. Reg.2d (P & F) 603 (1986) [hereinafter *Computer III Report and Order*] (describing debate concerning whether AT&T would be permitted into the "information services" market).

52. *Compare* Jason Oxman, *The FCC And The Unregulation Of The Internet* (Office of Plans and Policy, Federal Communications Commission, Working Paper No. 31, 1999) *available at* http://www.fcc.gov/Bureaus/OPP/ working_papers/oppwp31.pdf (reviewing FCC precedent from the perspective of how the FCC elected not to regulate information services). *See also* Press Release, Federal Communications Commission, Internet Prospers With "Hands-Off Unregulation;" FCC Paper Rejects Need For Precipitous Action (July 19, 1999) *available at* http://www.fcc.gov/Bureaus/OPP/News_ Releases/ 1999/nrop9004.html (stating "the paper examines the FCC's thirty-year history of not regulating the data services market, and how that tradition of 'unregulation' was a crucial factor in the successful growth of the Internet"); Fcc, *Connecting The Globe, A Regulator's Guide To Building A Global Information Community* Ix–3 (1999), available at http://www.fcc.gov/ connectglobe/ (stating "[t]he Internet has evolved at an unprecedented pace, in large part due to the absence of government regulation"); FCC Chairman William E. Kennard, Address before the Federal Communications Bar Northern California Chapter, San Francisco, CA, "The Unregulation of the Internet: Laying a Competitive Course for the Future" (July 20,

1999) (transcription available at http://www.fcc. gov/Speeches/Kennard/spwek924.html).

53. *See Computer II Tentative Decision*, *supra* note 25, para. 86 ("We recognize the inadequacy of the hybrid service definitions in the existing rule."); *Computer III Report and Order*, *supra* note 49, para. 10 ("After *Computer I* took effect, technological and competitive developments in the telecommunications and computer industries exposed shortcomings in its definitional structure, and in particular its *ad hoc* approach to evaluating the 'hybrid' category.").

54. Amendments of Section 64.702 of the Comm'n's Rules and Regs. (Computer Inquiry), *Supplemental Notice of Inquiry and Enlargement of Proposed Rulemaking*, 64 F.C.C.2d 771, para. 8 (1977) [hereinafter *Computer II Supplemental Notice of Inquiry*].

55. *Computer II Final Decision*, *supra* note 15, paras. 19, 23. *See also Computer II Tentative Decision*, *supra* note 25, paras. 8–11; *Computer II Supplemental Notice of Inquiry*, *supra* note 52, paras. 3–7; *Computer II Notice of Inquiry*, *supra* note 25, paras. 8–10.

56. *Computer II Notice of Inquiry*, *supra* note 25, paras. 10, 12 (describing packet switching networks as "radically new").

57. *Computer II Final Decision*, *supra* note 15, paras. 19, 23. *See also Computer II Supplemental Notice of Inquiry*, *supra* note 52, para. 4 ("In our new Computer Inquiry, we noted that peripheral devices are now capable of duplicating many of the data-manipulative capabilities which were previously available only at centralized locations housing large scale general purpose computers."); *Computer II Notice of Inquiry*, *supra* note 25, para. 10 (noting the ability of network processing, as opposed to CPE, to achieve call forwarding, abbreviated dialing, and other functionality that would come to be incorporated into the public telephone network switches).

58. *Computer II Notice of Inquiry*, *supra* note 25.

59. Cringely, *supra* note 14; Computer History Museum, *supra* note 14.

60. Cringely, *supra* note 14.

61. *Id.*; Computer History Museum, *supra* note 14.

62. *Computer II Supplemental Notice of Inquiry, supra* note 52, para. 7 ("The new technology may also have rendered meaningless any real distinction between 'terminals' and computers.").

63. *Computer II Final Decision, supra* note 15, para. 83.

64. *Id.* para. 86.

65. Computer and Comm. Indus. Ass'n v. FCC, 693 F.2d 198, 205 n.18 (D.C. Cir. 1982); *Computer II Final Decision, supra* note 15, para. 96.

66. *Computer II Final Decision, supra* note 15, para. 93.

67. *Id.* para. 95.

68. *See* Independent Data Comm. Mfrs. Ass'n, Inc., *Memorandum Opinion and Order*, 10 F.C.C.R. 13717, para. 11, 1 Comm. Reg. (P & F) 409 (1995) [hereinafter *Frame Relay Order*] ("The use of packet switching and error control techniques 'that facilitate the economical, reliable movement of [such] information [do] not alter the nature of the basic service.'"); *Computer III Report and Order, supra* note 49, para. 10 ("Data processing, computer memory or storage, and switching techniques can be components of a basic service if they are used solely to facilitate the movement of information."); *Computer II Final Decision, supra* note 15, paras. 95, 98: Use internal to the carrier's facility of companding techniques, bandwidth compression techniques, circuit switching, message or packet switching, error control techniques, etc. that facilitate economical, reliable movement of information does not alter the nature of the basic service. In the provision of a basic transmission service, memory or storage within the network is used only to facilitate the transmission of the information from the origination to its destination, and the carrier's basic transmission network is not used as an information storage system. Thus, in a basic service, once information is given to the communication facility, its progress towards the destination is subject to only those delays caused by congestion within the network or transmission priorities given by the originator. *Id.* para. 95.

69. *Computer III Report and Order, supra* note 49, para. 10.

70. *Computer II Notice of Inquiry, supra* note 25, para. 18.

71. *Computer II Final Decision, supra* note 15, para. 94 (thus we see the initial uncoupling of the telephony application from the transmission facility).

72. *Id.* para. 97. *Computer II Tentative Decision, supra* note 25, para. 12 ("It was stated that by defining data processing positively a carrier would be able to use computers for any purpose which is not data processing."); *Computer II Supplemental Notice of Inquiry, supra* note 52, para. 10.

73. *Computer II Notice of Inquiry, supra* note 25, para. 16.

74. *Computer II Tentative Decision, supra* note 25, paras. 70–71. "[C]omputer processing applications employed within a carrier's network in conjunction with 'voice' and 'basic non-voice' services can be performed without restriction on the use of data processing applications utilized within the framework of these two services." *Id.* para. 70.

75. *Id.* para. 87.

76. *Id.* para. 69.

77. *Id.*

78. *Id.* para. 125 ("The objectives of the maximum separation policy are still valid today.").

79. *Id.* para. 71.

80. Miscellaneous Rules Relating to Common Carriers, 47 C.F.R. § 64.702(a) (2002).

81. The definition was originally proposed as a reformation of "data processing." In the 1976 Supplemental Notice, the definition of data processing proposed was as follows:

"'Data processing' is the electronically automated processing of information wherein: (a) the information content, or meaning, of the input information is in any way transformed, or (b) where the output information constitutes a programmed response to input information."

Computer II Tentative Decision, supra note 25, para. 12 (citations omitted).

82. *Id.* para. 13; *Computer II Supplemental Notice of Inquiry, supra* note 52, para. 9;
Computer II Notice of Inquiry, supra note 25, paras. 17–18.

83. *Computer II Final Decision, supra* note 15, para. 131 ("We have tried to draw the line in a manner which distinguishes wholly traditional common carrier activities, regulable under Title II of the Act, from historically and functionally competitive activities not congruent with the Act's traditional forms."); *Computer II Tentative Decision, supra* note 25, para. 15 ("Under the new definition the determination as to whether a communications or data processing service is being offered would depend on the nature of the processing activity involved.").

84. According to the Commission:

Based on this record, the mandate of this Commission in a rapidly changing technological environment, the market developments resulting from the confluence of technologies, the impossibility of defining at the enhanced level a clear and stable point at which "communications" becomes "data processing," the ever increasing dependence upon common carrier transmission facilities in the movement of information, the need to tailor services to individual user requirements, and the potential for unwarranted expansion of regulation, we conclude that the public interest would not be served by any classification scheme that attempts to distinguish enhanced services based on the communications or data processing nature of the computer processing activity performed. Accordingly, we conclude that all enhanced computer services should be accorded the same regulatory treatment and that no regulatory scheme could be adopted which would rationally distinguish and classify enhanced services as either communications or data processing.

Computer II Final Decision, supra note 15, para. 113. *See Computer II Tentative Decision, supra* note 25, paras. 61–63, 68, 78 ("The regulatory focus should be upon the service

being offered and not merely upon performance of a message switching function.").

85. *Computer II Final Decision, supra* note 15, para. 97 ("[T]he regulatory demarcation between basic and enhanced services becomes relatively clear-cut.").

86. *Computer II Tentative Decision, supra* note 25, paras. 15, 87; *Computer II Supplemental Notice of Inquiry, supra* note 52, para. 14.

87. Computer and Comm. Indus. Ass'n v. FCC, 693 F.2d 198, 209 (D.C. Cir. 1982).

88. *Id.* at 205 ("Enhanced service is any service other than basic service.") (emphasis added).

89. *See, e.g.*, Establishment of a Funding Mechanism for Interstate Operator Servs. for the Deaf, *Memorandum Opinion and Order*, 11 F.C.C.R. 6808, para. 16, 2 Comm. Reg. (P & F) 744 (1996) [hereinafter *Section 255 Order*]; Bell Atl. Tel. Cos., Offer of Comparably Efficient Interconnection to Providers of Video Dialtone-Related Enhanced Servs., *Order*, 11 F.C.C.R. 985, para. 2 n.5 (1995) ("'Enhanced services' use the telephone network to deliver unregulated services that provide *more than* a basic voice transmission offering.") (emphasis added); Bell Operating Cos.' Joint Petition for Waiver of *Computer II* Rules, *Memorandum Order and Opinion*, 10 F.C.C.R. 1724, para. 1 n.3 , 76 Rad. Reg.2d (P & F) 1536 (1995) [hereinafter *BOC's Joint Petition*]; *Computer II Tentative Decision, supra* note 25, para. 69. ("An 'enhanced non-voice service' is any non-voice service which is more than the 'basic' service, where computer processing applications are used to act on the form, content, code, protocol, etc., of the inputted information.").

90. *Computer II Final Decision, supra* note 15, para. 95 (stating "we believe that a basic transmission service should be limited to the offering of transmission capacity between two or more points suitable for a user's transmission needs").

91. *Section 255 Order, supra* note 87, para. 16.

92. *Id. Compare with Computer II Tentative Decision, supra* note 25, para. 77 ("Of the three categories of services that we have established—'voice,'

'basic non-voice,' and 'enhanced non-voice'— 'voice' and 'basic non-voice' services may employ any computer processing applications as long as they do not change the nature of the service." (punctuation altered)).

93. *Computer II Tentative Decision, supra* note 25, para. 73.

94. *Computer II Final Decision, supra* note 15, paras. 7, 127–132. "The market is truly competitive. Experience gained from the competitive evolution of varied market applications of computer technology offered since the *First Computer Inquiry* compels us to conclude that regulation of enhanced services is simply unwarranted." *Id.* para. 128. Computer and Comm. Indus. Ass'n v. FCC, 693 F.2d 198, 207 (D.C. Cir. 1982); Policy and Rules Concerning the Interstate, Interexchange Marketplace, *Report and Order*, 16 F.C.C.R. 7418, para. 3, 23 Comm. Reg. (P & F) 641 (2001) [hereinafter *CPE Order*] (describing market as truly competitive); Access Charge Reform, *Notice of Proposed Rulemaking, Third Report and Order, and Notice of Inquiry*, 11 F.C.C.R. 21354, para. 285, 5 Comm. Reg. (P & F) 604 (1996) ("The Internet access market is also highly competitive and dynamic, with over 2,000 companies offering Internet access as of mid–1996.").

95. *See* Federal-State Joint Board on Universal Serv., Report to Congress, 13 F.C.C.R. 11501, para. 78, 11 Comm. Reg. (P & F) 1312 (1998) [hereinafter *Stevens Report*].

96. *CPE Order, supra* note 92, para. 2.

97. *See Stevens Report, supra* note 93, para. 76.

98. *Id.* para. 77.

99. *CPE Order, supra* note 92, para. 2; 1998 Biennial Reg. Review—Review of Customer Premises Equip, and Enhanced Servs. Unbundling Rules in the Interexchange, Exch. Access and Local Exch. Mkts., *Further Notice of Proposed Rulemaking*, 13 F.C.C.R. 21531, para. 1 n.2 (1998) [hereinafter *CPE Further Notice*].

100. US West Comm., Inc., Petition for Computer III Waiver, *Order*, 11 F.C.C.R. 1195, para. 2 n.5, 1 Comm. Reg. (P & F) 1261 (1995) [hereinafter *US West Petition*].

101. *Computer III* Report and Order, *supra* note 49, para. 7.

102. *US West Petition, supra* note 98, para. 2 n.5.

103. *Section 255 Order, supra* note 87, paras. 17–18.

104. *US West Petition, supra* note 98, para. 26.

105. *Section 255 Order, supra* note 87, paras. 17–18.

106. *Computer III Report and Order, supra* note 49, paras. 20–23; *Computer II Final Decision supra* note 15, para. 99; *Frame Relay Order, supra* note 66, paras. 17–18.

107. Implementation of the Non-Accounting Safeguards of Sections 271 and 272 of the Comm. Act of 1934, as Amended, *Order on Reconsideration*, 12 F.C.C.R. 2297, para. 2, 6 Comm. Reg. (P & F) 972 (1997) [hereinafter *Non-Accounting Safeguards Order on Reconsideration*]. *See also Frame Relay Order, supra* note 66, paras. 14–16.

108. *Frame Relay Order, supra* note 66, para. 6.

109. *Id.* para. 40.

110. *Id.* para. 41.

111. Contamination theory is the argument that when an enhanced service provider acquires telecommunications services, combines it with enhanced services, and then sells to consumers, the enhanced service "contaminates" the basic service, making the service as a whole an enhanced service. The enhanced service provider, by "reselling" telecommunications service, does not thereby become a carrier. *Id.* para. 18.

112. *Id.* paras. 42–45.

113. POTS, a basic term in the communications field, means "plain old telephone service."

114. *Computer III Report and Order, supra* note 49, paras. 33–35.

115. *CPE Order, supra* note 92, para. 2 n.6. ("The Commission has concluded that Congress sought to maintain the basic/enhanced distinction in its definition of 'telecommunications services' and 'information services,' and that 'enhanced services' and 'information services' should be interpreted to extend to the same functions."); *CPE Further Notice, supra* note 97, para. 1 n.2.

116. According to the Telecommunications Act of 1996:

The term "information service" means the offering of a capability for generating, acquiring, storing, transforming, processing, retrieving, utilizing, or making available information via telecommunications, and includes electronic publishing, but does not include any use of any such capability for the management, control, or operation of a telecommunications system or the management of a telecommunications service.

47 U.S.C. § 153(20) (2000).

117. *CPE Order, supra* note 92, para. 2 n.6; *see also* CPE Further Notice, *supra* note 97, para. 1 n.2; *Non-Accounting Safeguards Order on Reconsideration, supra* note 105; *Computer III* Further Remand Proceedings: Bell Operating Co. Provision of Enhanced Servs., *Further Notice of Proposed Rulemaking*, 13 F.C.C.R. 6040, para. 40 (1998).

118. *Computer II Final Decision, supra* note 15, para. 219.

119. *Id.* paras. 100–01; *Computer II Tentative Decision, supra* note 25, para. 66 ("A regulatory structure must be established which adequately addresses present and foreseeable market applications of computer processing technology.").

120. *Computer II Tentative Decision, supra* note 25, para. 66.

121. *Id.* paras. 71–73 (seeking to "insure the availability of transparent common carrier transmission facilities to all on an equal basis.").

122. *Computer II Final Decision, supra* note 15, para. 219.

123. *Computer III Report and Order, supra* note 49, para. 14 (AT&T established AT&T Information Systems, Inc. as its separate subsidiary). *See also* Amendment of Section 64.702 of the Comm'n's Rules and Regs. (Second Computer Inquiry), *Memorandum Opinion and Order*, 79 F.C.C.2d 953, para. 5 (1980).

124. *Computer II Final Decision, supra* note 15, paras. 12, 215–28. "There is little need to subject carriers to the resale structure if such entities lack significant potential to cross-subsidize or to engage in other anticompetitive conduct." *Id.* para. 12.

125. *US West Petition, supra* note 98, para. 2; BOCs Joint Petition, *supra* note 87, para. 3; *Computer III* Further Remand Proceedings: Bell Operating Co. Provision of Enhanced Servs., Notice of Proposed Rulemaking, 10 F.C.C.R. 8360, paras. 3–4 (1995) [hereinafter *Computer III Remand 1995*].

126. *See* 47 C.F.R. § 64.702 (2002).

127. *Computer II Final Decision, supra* note 15, para. 231. *See, e.g., CPE Order, supra* note 92, para. 4; *CPE Further Notice, supra* note 97, para. 33; *Frame Relay Order, supra* note 66, para. 59.

128. *CPE Order, supra* note 92, para. 39.

129. 47 C.F.R. § 64.702(e) (2002); *Computer II Final Decision, supra* note 15, paras. 8–10; *see, e.g., CPE Further Notice, supra* note 97, para. 2.

130. *CPE Order, supra* note 92, para. 1.

131. Note that physical networks include wireless networks. Although it may initially sound confusing, the wireless spectrum is as physical as copper wires, fiber, or coaxial cable.

132. *See* Kevin Werbach, A Layered Model for Internet Policy, presented at Telecommunications Policy Research Conference (Sept. 2000), *available at* http://www.edventure.com/conversation/article.cfm?counter=2414930; Robert M. Entman, Transition to an IP Environment, The Aspen Institute (2001); Michael L. Katz, *Thoughts on the Implications of Technological Change for Telecommunications Policy*, The Aspen Institute (2001); Douglas C. Sicker, Further Defining a Layered Model for Telecommunications Policy, presented at Telecommunications Policy Research Conference 2002 (Sept. 1, 2002), *available at* http://intel.si.umich.edu/tprc/papers/2002/95/TPRC_L_model.pdf; Douglas C. Sicker, Further Defining a Layered Model for Telecommunications Policy (Oct. 3, 2002), *available at* http://intel.si.umich.edu/tprc/papers/2002/95/LayeredTelecomPolicy.pdf; Computer Science And Telecommunications Board, National Research Council, Broadband: Bringing Home The Bits 182 (2002), *available at* http://www.nap.edu/html/

broadband/notice.html (calling for logical layer unbundling).

133. *See* Gerald R. Faulhaber, *Policy-Induced Competition: The Telecommunications Experiments*, Aug. 26, 2001, at http://rider.wharton.upenn.edu/~faulhabe/Policy-Induced%20Competition.pdf (to be published in Information Economics And Policy).

134. OSI Reference Model at http://searchnetworking.techtarget.com/sDefinition/0,,sid7_gci523729,00.html (last visited Nov. 18, 2002).

135. *See, e.g.,* DARPA Internet Program Protocol Specifications (Jon Postel ed., 1981), RFC 791, *at* http://www.ietf.org/rfc/rfc0791.txt (last visited Oct. 10, 2002); Shvetima Gulati, *The Internet Protocol, Part One: The Foundations*, ACM Crossroads Student Magazine, July 2000, at http://www.acm.org/crossroads/columns/connector/july2000.html (last visited Nov. 18, 2002).

136. Physical network services are provisioned by telephone, cable, and wireless companies. Logical network services are provisioned by ISPs and other computer networks. Applications may be provisioned by service providers (i.e., Web hosters, e-mail servers, or USENET servers) or the applications may be used by the edge user on the edge user's computer. Content may be created by the edge user chatting in a chat room or posting Web pages, or it might be created by an information service such as an online news service or a streamed radio station. These are different services provisioned at different layers by different equipment and different companies.

137. This is in contrast to, for example, the telephone network which is a physical transmission network optimized for a single application, telephony.

138. *Computer II Tentative Decision, supra* note 25, para. 73 ("The common carrier transmission facility necessary for the provision of an 'enhanced' service becomes a separate part of the service which must be acquired pursuant to applicable tariff. ...").

139. *Id.* para. 75.

140. *Id.* para. 73.

141. *Stevens Report, supra* note 93, para. 57. *Computer II Tentative Decision, supra* note 25, para. 15; *Computer II Supplemental Notice of Inquiry, supra* note 52, para. 14 ("Under this proposed standard it would be inconsistent to talk in terms of a communications service having non-separable data processing functions, since communications and data processing now would be considered mutually exclusive activities.").

142. *Stevens Report, supra* note 93, para. 57 ("[W]e find strong support in the text and legislative history of the 1996 Act for the view that Congress intended 'telecommunications service' and 'information service' to refer to separate categories of services."). This is true in the broadband context as well. Deployment of Wireline Servs. Offering Advanced Telecomms. Capability, *Memorandum Opinion and Order, and Notice of Proposed Rulemaking*, 13 F.C.C.R. 24011, para. 36, 13 Comm. Reg. (P & F) 1 (1998): An end-user may utilize a telecommunications service together with an information service, as in the case of Internet access. In such a case, however, we treat the two services separately: the first service is a telecommunications service (*e.g.*, the xDSL-enabled transmission path), and the second service is an information service, in this case Internet access. *Id.*

143. Compare this to the Contamination Theory. *See infra* note 109. The underlying transmission service even in Contamination Theory remains a basic service. Contamination Theory merely recognizes that the supply of the transmission facility is the carrier; regulations appropriate to the basic service are appropriate for the carrier and need not be applied to an enhanced service provider who is taking that facility, enhancing it, and selling it to consumers.

144. *Computer II Tentative Decision, supra* note 25, para. 125 ("The objectives of the maximum separation policy are still valid today.").

145. The World's Homepage, *at* http://www.theworld.com/ (last modified Nov. 1, 2002) (established in 1989).

146. Gingery, *supra* note 14; Computer History Museum, *supra* note 14.

147. *Computer III Report and Order, supra* note 49, para. 24.

148. United States v. W. Elec. Co., 673 F.Supp. 525 (D.D.C. 1987), *aff'd in part, rev'd in part*, 900 F.2d 283 (D.C. Cir. 1990), *cert denied* MCI Comm. Corp. v. United States, 498 U.S. 911 (1990); Filing and Review of Open Network Architecture Plans, *Memorandum Opinion and Order*, 4 F.C.C.R. 2449, para. 29, 65 Rad. Reg.2d 1361 (P & F) (1988) [hereinafter *ONA Review*]', *Accounting Safeguards, supra* note 48, para. 3 n.5 ("The information services restriction was modified in 1987 to allow BOCs to provide voice messaging services and to transmit information services generated by others. In 1991, the restriction on BOC ownership of content-based information services was lifted." (citations omitted)).

149. Third Computer Inquiry, *Proposed Rule*, 50 Fed. Reg. 33,581 (Aug. 20, 1985).

150. *See Computer III Report and Order, supra* note 1, para. 3. *See also* Computer III Further Remand Proceedings: Bell Operating Co. Provision of Enhanced Servs., *Report and Order*, 14 F.C.C.R. 4289, para. 7, 15 Comm. Reg. (P & F) 149 (1999) [hereinafter *Computer III Order 1999*]: In *Computer III*, after reexamining the telecommunications marketplace and the effects of structural separation during the six years since *Computer II*, the Commission determined that the costs of structural separation out-weighed the benefits, and that nonstructural safeguards could protect competitive ESPs from improper cost allocation and discrimination by the BOCs while avoiding the inefficiencies associated with structural separation. *Id.*

151. Under current rules, CEI Plans need not be submitted to the FCC but must be posted to BOC Web sites. *Id.* paras. 4, 11–12; Computer III Further Remand Proceedings: Bell Operating Co. Provision of Enhanced Servs., Order, 14 F.C.C.R. 21628, para. 6, 18 Comm. Reg. (P & F) 1344 (1999) [hereinafter *Computer III Order on Reconsideration 1999*].

152. A CEI plan must include information on interface functionality, unbundling of basic services, resale, technical characteristics, installation, maintenance and repair, end-user access, CEI availability, minimization of transport costs, and recipients of CEI. Computer III Further Remand Proceedings: Bell Operating Co. Provision of Enhanced Servs., *Further Notice of Proposed Rulemaking*, 13 F.C.C.R. 6040, para. 4, 15 Comm. Reg. (P & F) 2017 (1998) [hereinafter *Computer III Further Notice 1998*]; *BOC's Joint Petition, supra* note 87, para. 3. See also Ameritech's Comparably Efficient Interconnection Plan for Electronic Vaulting Serv., *Order*, 13 F.C.C.R. 80, para. 16 (1997) [hereinafter *Ameritech's CEI Plan*] ("The CEI requirements are designed to give ESPs equal and efficient access to the basic services that the BOCs use to provide their own enhanced services.").

153. *Computer III Order 1999, supra* note 148, para. 8 n.17: ONA is the overall design of a carrier's basic network services to permit all users of the basic network, including the information services operations of the carrier and its competitors, to interconnect to specific basic network functions and interfaces on an unbundled and equal-access basis. The BOCs and GTE through ONA must unbundle key components, or elements, of their basic services and make them available under tariff, regardless of whether their information services operations utilize the unbundled components. Such unbundling ensures that competitors of the carrier's information services operations can develop information services that utilize the carrier's network on an economical and efficient basis. *Id. See also Computer III Remand 1995, supra* note 123, paras. 15–16.

154. *See* 47 U.S.C. §251(2000).

155. *Computer III Further Notice 1998, supra* note 150, para. 26. *See also ONA Review, supra* note 146, para. 56.

156. *Ameritech's CEI Plan, supra* note 150, para. 7, n.18. *See also* Bell Operating Cos. Joint Petition for Waiver of *Computer II* Rules, *Order*, 10

F.C.C.R. 13758, para. 26, 1 Comm. Reg. (P & F) 690 (1995).

157. *BOC's Joint Petition, supra* note 87, para. 3.

158. *Computer III Further Notice 1998, supra* note 150, paras. 81–84.

159. *Id.* para. 103.

160. 47 C.F.R. § 64.702(d)(2) (2001).

161. 47 U.S.C. § 254(k) (2000); 47 C.F.R. § 64.901 (c) (2001).

162. 47 C.F.R. § 64 (2001).

163. 47 U.S.C. § 222 (2000).

164. *Computer III Further Notice 1998, supra* note 150, para. 15 (footnotes omitted). *See* California v. FCC, 39 F.3d 919 (9th Cir.), *cert. denied*, 514 U.S. 1050 (1994).

165. *See Computer III Further Notice 1998, supra* note 150, para. 16.

166. *Ameritech's CEI Plan, supra* note 150, para. 6; BOCs Joint Petition, *supra* note 87, para. 22; Bell Atl. Tel. Cos. Offer of Comparably Efficient Interconnection to Providers of Video Dialtone-Enhanced Servs., *Order*, 11 F.C.C.R. 985, para. 4 (1995); *Computer III Remand 1995, supra* note 123, paras. 9–12.

167. *Computer III Remand 1995, supra* note 123; see also *Computer III Further Notice 1998, supra* note 150; *Computer III Order 1999, supra* note 148, para. 4 (eliminating the requirement that BOCs receive approval of CEI plans from FCC; and permitting BOCs to simply post plans on Web sites and provide notice to FCC); *Computer III Order on Reconsideration 1999, supra* note 149, para. 4 (denying CIX's petition for reconsideration).

168. Appropriate Framework for Broadband Access to the Internet over Wireline Facilities, *Notice of Proposed Rulemaking*, 17 F.C.C.R. 3019 (2002).

169. *Computer III Order 1999, supra* note 148, para. 15.

170. *Cringeley, supra* note 14; Computer History Museum, *supra* note 14.

171. Bill McCarthy, *Introduction* to Boardwatch Magazine's Directory Of Internet Service Providers 4 (12th ed., Penton Media 2000).

172. Kevin Werbach, *Digital Tornado: The Internet and Telecommunications Policy*, Office of Plans and Policy, FCC, at http://www.fcc.gov/ Bureaus/OPP/working_papers/oppwp29pdf. html (1997); Barbara Esbin, *Internet Over Cable: Defining the Future in Terms of the Past*, Office of Plans and Policy, FCC, at http:// www.fcc.gov/Bureaus/OPP/working__papers/ oppwp30.pdf (1998); Jason Oxman, *The FCC and the Unregulation of the Internet*, Office of Plans and Policy, Federal Communications Commission, at http://www.fcc.gov/Bureaus/ OPP/working_papers/oppwp31.pdf (1999).

173. In 1996, Congress declared that "[i]t is the policy of the United States—(1) to promote the continued development of the Internet and other interactive computer services and other interactive media; (2) to preserve the vibrant and competitive free market that presently exists for the Internet and other interactive computer services, unfettered by Federal or State regulation." 47 U.S.C. § 230(b)(l)-(2) (2000).

UNIT 16
Circuit Switched or Packet Switched?
Regulation of the Internet

Indeed, Internet regulation followed on the heels of the legacy of the "Computer Inquiries," but its unique technological attributes need to be understood before a full-fledged discussion of their regulation can take place. In class discussion we will draw the Internet's "layered model" in order to further understand why it is both similar to and different from its technological predecessors. Angele Gilroy's Congressional Research Service discussion of the debate surrounding the issue of "Network Neutrality" will focus the debate of Internet regulation on its most contemporary challenge. Services over the Internet provide us with what similar services have provided us beforehand: content services resemble those provided by newspapers, broadcasters and cable operators, and voice over Internet Protocol is to the user the same as any other voice service previously provided over circuit-switched networks. The debate on "Network Neutrality" draws the picture for future battles over control of the telecommunications industry and thus serves to illustrate how the principles, institutions and values with which we began the course still affect the regulation of technologies of the future.

Access to Broadband Networks

The Net Neutrality Debate

Angele A. Gilroy

INTRODUCTION

As congressional policymakers continue to debate telecommunications reform, a major point of contention is the question of whether action is needed to ensure unfettered access to the Internet. The move to place restrictions on the owners of the networks that compose and provide access to the Internet, to ensure equal access and non-discriminatory treatment, is referred to as "net neutrality." There is no single accepted definition of "net neutrality." However, most agree that any such definition should include the general principles that owners of the networks that compose and provide access to the Internet should not control how consumers lawfully use that network, and they should not be able to discriminate against content provider access to that network.

What, if any, action should be taken to ensure "net neutrality" has become a major focal point in the debate over broadband regulation. As the marketplace for broadband continues to evolve, some contend that no new regulations are needed, and if enacted will slow deployment of and access to the Internet, as well as limit innovation. Others, however, contend that the consolidation and diversification of broadband providers into content providers has the potential to lead to discriminatory behaviors which conflict with net neutrality principles. The two potential behaviors most often cited are the network providers' ability to control access to and the pricing of broadband facilities, and the incentive to favor network-owned content, thereby placing unaffiliated content providers at a competitive disadvantage.[1]

FEDERAL COMMUNICATIONS COMMISSION ACTIVITY

The Information Services Designation

In 2005 two major actions dramatically changed the regulatory landscape as it applied to broadband services, further fueling the net neutrality debate. In both cases these actions led to the classification of broadband Internet access services as Title I information services, thereby subjecting them to a less rigorous regulatory framework than those services classified as telecommunications services. In the first action, the U.S. Supreme Court, in a June 2005 decision (*National Cable & Telecommunications Association v. Brand X Internet Services*), upheld the Federal Communications Commission's (FCC) 2002 ruling that the provision of cable modem service (i.e., cable television broadband Internet) is an interstate information service and is therefore subject to the less stringent regulatory regime under Title I of the Communications Act of 1934.[2] In a second action, the FCC, in an August 5, 2005 decision, extended the same regulatory relief to telephone company Internet access services (i.e., wireline broadband Internet access, or DSL), thereby also defining such services as information services subject to Title I regulation.[3] As a result neither telephone companies nor cable companies, when providing broadband services, are required to adhere to the more stringent regulatory regime for telecommunications services found under Title II (common carrier) of the 1934 Act.[4] However, classification as an information service does not free the service from regulation. The FCC continues to have regulatory authority over information services under its Title I, ancillary jurisdiction.[5]

The Internet Policy Statement

Simultaneous to the issuing of its August 2005 information services classification order, the FCC also adopted a policy statement (Internet Policy Statement) outlining four principles to "encourage broadband deployment and preserve and promote the open and interconnected nature of [the] public Internet." The four principles are: (1) consumers are entitled to access the lawful Internet content of their choice; (2) consumers are entitled to run applications and services of their choice (subject to the needs of law enforcement); (3) consumers are entitled to connect their choice of legal devices that do not harm the network; and (4) consumers are entitled to competition among network providers, application and service providers, and content providers. Then-FCC Chairman Martin did not call for their codification. However, he stated that they will be incorporated into the policymaking activities of the Commission.[6] For example, one of the agreed upon conditions for the October 2005 approval of both the Verizon/MCI and the SBC/AT&T mergers was an agreement made by the involved parties to commit, for two years, "... to conduct business in a way that comports with the Commission's (2005) Internet policy statement. ..."[7] In a further action AT&T included in its concessions to gain FCC approval of its merger to BellSouth to adhering, for two years, to significant net neutrality requirements. Under terms of the merger agreement, which was approved on December 29, 2006, AT&T agreed to not only uphold, for 30 months, the FCC's Internet policy statement principles, but

also committed, for two years (expired December 2008), to stringent requirements to "... maintain a neutral network and neutral routing in its wireline broadband Internet access service."[8]

The Comcast Decision

In perhaps one of its most significant actions relating to its Internet Policy Statement to date, the FCC, on August 1, 2008, ruled that Comcast Corp., a provider of Internet access over cable lines, violated the FCC's policy statement when it selectively blocked peer-to-peer connections in an attempt to manage its traffic.[9] This practice, the FCC concluded, "... unduly interfered with Internet users' rights to access the lawful Internet content and to use the applications of their choice." Although no monetary penalties were imposed, Comcast was required to stop these practices by the end of 2008. Comcast complied with the order, and developed a new system to manage network congestion. Comcast no longer manages congestion by focusing on specific applications (such as peer-to-peer), nor by focusing on online activities, or protocols, but identifies individual users within congested neighborhoods that are using large amounts of bandwidth in real time and slows them down, by placing them in a lower priority category, for short periods.[10] This new system complies with the FCC Internet principles in that it is application agnostic; that is, it does not discriminate against or favor one application over another but manages congestion based on the amount of a user's real-time bandwidth usage. Despite this compliance, however, Comcast filed an appeal, which is still pending, in the U.S. DC Court of Appeals claiming that the FCC does not have the authority to enforce its Internet policy statement, therefore making the order invalid.[11]

The American Recovery and Reinvestment Act

The FCC has also been called upon to address net neutrality principles within the context of the implementation of the American Recovery and Reinvestment Act of 2009 (ARRA, P.L. 111-5). Provisions require the National Telecommunications and Information Administration (NTIA), in consultation with the FCC, to establish "...

nondiscrimination and network interconnection obligations" as a requirement for grant participants in the Broadband Technology Opportunities Program (BTOP). It is anticipated that the NTIA will release these rules by summer 2009.

The ARRA also requires the FCC to submit a report, containing a national broadband plan, to both the House and Senate Commerce Committees by February 2010. The FCC adopted, on April 8, 2009, a Notice of Inquiry (NOI) to seek input from stakeholders as it begins to develop this plan.[12] Included among the issues under discussion in the NOI is the question of the role of "open networks." More specifically the FCC is seeking comment "on the value of open networks as an effective and efficient mechanism for ensuring broadband access for all Americans" and how the term "open" should be defined. Additional comment is sought regarding the possible adoption of a fifth "nondiscrimination" principle to its August 2005 Internet Policy Statement including whether one is needed and, if so, how "nondiscrimination" should be defined.[13] Comments are due June 8, 2009, and replies July 7, 2009.

Additional Activity

Separately, in an April 2007 action, the FCC released a notice of inquiry (WC Docket No. 07-52), which is still pending, on broadband industry practices seeking comment on a wide range of issues including whether the August 2005 Internet policy statement should be amended to incorporate a new principle of nondiscrimination and if so, what form it should take.[14] On January 14, 2008, the FCC issued three public notices seeking comment on issues related to network management (including the now-completed Comcast ruling, discussed above) and held two (February 25 and April 17, 2008) public hearings specific to broadband network management practices.

NETWORK MANAGEMENT

As consumers expand their use of the Internet and new multimedia and voice services become more commonplace, control over network quality and pricing is an issue. The ability of data bits to travel the network in a nondiscriminatory manner, as well as the pricing structure established by broadband

service providers for consumer access to that data, have become significant issues in the debate.

Prioritization

In the past, Internet traffic has been delivered on a "best efforts" basis. The quality of service needed for the delivery of the most popular uses, such as e-mail or surfing the Web, is not as dependent on guaranteed quality. However, as Internet use expands to include video, online gaming, and voice service, the need for uninterrupted streams of data becomes important. As the demand for such services continues to expand, network broadband operators are moving to prioritize network traffic to ensure the quality of these services. Prioritization may benefit consumers by ensuring faster delivery and quality of service and may be necessary to ensure the proper functioning of expanded service options. However, the move on the part of network operators to establish prioritized networks, although embraced by some, has led to a number of policy concerns.

There is concern that the ability of network providers to prioritize traffic may give them too much power over the operation of and access to the Internet. If a multi-tiered Internet develops where content providers pay for different service levels, the potential to limit competition exists if smaller, less financially secure content providers are unable to afford to pay for a higher level of access. Also, if network providers have control over who is given priority access, the ability to discriminate among who gets such access is also present. If such a scenario were to develop, the potential benefits to consumers of a prioritized network would be lessened by a decrease in consumer choice and/or increased costs, if the fees charged for premium access are passed on to the consumer. The potential for these abuses, however, is significantly decreased in a marketplace where multiple, competing broadband providers exist. If a network broadband provider blocks access to content or charges unreasonable fees, in a competitive market, content providers and consumers could obtain their access from other network providers. As consumers and content providers migrate to these competitors, market share and profits of the offending network provider will decrease, leading to corrective action or failure. However, this scenario assumes that every market will have a number of equally competitive broadband options from which to choose, and all competitors will have equal access to, if not identical, at least comparable content.

Deep Packet Inspection

The use of one management tool, deep packet inspection (DPI), illustrates the complexity of the net neutrality debate. DPI refers to a network management technique that enables network operators to inspect, in real time, both the header and the data field of the packets.[15] As a result DPI can allow network operators to not only identify the origin and destination points of the data packet but also enables the network operator to determine the application used and content of that packet. The information that DPI provides enables the network operator to differentiate, or discriminate, among the packets travelling over its network. The ability to discriminate among packets enables the network operator to treat packets differently. This ability itself is not necessarily viewed in a negative light. Network managers use DPI to assist them in performing various functions that are necessary for network management and that contribute to a positive user experience. For example, DPI technology is used in filters and firewalls to detect and prevent spam, viruses, worms, and malware. DPI is also used to gain information to help plan network capacity and diagnostics, as well as to respond to law enforcement requests.[16] However, the ability to discriminate based on the information gained via DPI also has the potential to be misused.[17] It is the potential negative impact that DPI use can have on consumers and suppliers that raises concern for policymakers. For example, the information gained could be used to discriminate against a competing service causing harm to both the competitor and consumer choice. This could be accomplished by routing a network operator's own, or other preferred content, along a faster priority path, or selectively slowing down competitor's traffic. DPI also has the potential to extract personal information about the data that it inspects, generating concerns about consumer privacy.[18]

Therefore it is not the management tool itself that is under scrutiny, but how it is applied. The DPI technology, in itself, is not what is of concern. It is the behavior that potentially may occur as a result of the information that DPI provides. How to develop a policy that permits some types of discrimination (i.e., "good" discrimination) that may be beneficial to network operation and improve the user experience, while protecting against what would be considered "harmful" or anticompetitive discrimination becomes the crux of the policy debate.

Metered/Consumption-Based Billing

The move by some network broadband operators towards the use of metered or consumption-based billing has caused considerable controversy. Under such a plan, users subscribe to a set monthly bandwidth cap, for an established fee, and are charged additional fees if that usage level is exceeded. Although still not the industry norm in the United States, the use of such billing practices, on both a trial and permanent basis, is becoming more commonplace. For example, in 2008, Time Warner Cable established a usage trial in Beaumont, Texas, that offers a range of service tiers. Similarly, AT&T is currently conducting usage-based trials in Reno, Nevada, and Beaumont, Texas. The move by Time Warner Cable to expand these trials to four additional locations[19] caused considerable controversy and has since been deferred.[20] Some network broadband providers, most notably Time Warner Cable and AT&T, have stressed that these are not permanent pricing structures, but trials established to gain more insight into how consumers use their Internet services and subsequently how best to manage their networks. However, other providers, particularly smaller more regional providers, have stated that such pricing models are already being used and will be necessary in the future as the demand for high bandwidth applications increases.[21] For example, one provider, Sunflower Broadband, located in Kansas, has used such a pricing model for four years. Sunflower offers a range of service levels with a $2 per Gigabyte overcharge which is levied only after a second over usage.[22] Supporters of such billing models state that a small percentage of users consume a disproportionately high percentage of bandwidth and that some form of usage-based pricing may benefit the majority of subscribers, particularly those who are light users.[23] Furthermore, they state that offering a range of service tiers at varying prices offers consumers more choice and control over their usage and subsequent costs. The major growth in bandwidth usage, they also claim, places financial pressure on existing networks for both maintenance and expansion, and establishing a pricing system which charges high bandwidth users is more equitable.

Opponents to such billing plans claim that such practices will stifle innovation in high bandwidth applications and are likely to discourage the experimentation with and adoption of new applications and services. Some concerns have also been expressed that a move to metered/consumption-based pricing will help to protect the market share for video services, offered in packaged bundles by network broadband service providers, that compete with new applications. The move to usage-based pricing, they state, will unfairly disadvantage competing online video services and stifle a nascent market since video applications are more bandwidth-intensive. Opponents have also questioned the specific usage limits and overage fees established in specific trials, stating that the former seem to be "arbitrarily low" and the latter "arbitrarily high."[24] Citing the generally falling costs of network equipment and the stability of profit margins, they also question the claims of network broadband operators that increased revenues streams are needed to supply the necessary capital to invest in new infrastructure to meet the growing demand for high bandwidth applications.[25]

THE POLICY DEBATE

Despite the FCC's ability to regulate broadband services under its Title I ancillary authority and the issuing of its broadband principles, some policymakers feel that more specific regulatory guidelines may be necessary to protect the marketplace from potential abuses; a consensus on what these should specifically entail, however, has yet to form. Others feel that existing laws and FCC policies regarding competitive behavior are sufficient to deal with potential anti-competitive behavior and that no action is needed and, if enacted at this time, could result in harm.

The issue of net neutrality, and whether legislation is needed to ensure access to broadband networks and services, has become a major focal point in the debate over telecommunications reform.[26] Those opposed to the enactment of legislation to impose specific Internet network access or "net neutrality" mandates claim that such action goes against the long standing policy to keep the Internet as free as possible from regulation. They have claimed that the imposition of such requirements is not only unnecessary, but would have negative consequences for the deployment and advancement of broadband facilities. For example, further expansion of networks by existing providers and the entrance of new network providers would be discouraged, they claim, as investors would be less willing to finance networks that may be operating under mandatory build-out and/or access requirements. Application innovation could also be discouraged, they contend, if, for example, network providers are restricted in the way they manage their networks or are limited in their ability to offer new service packages or formats. Such legislation is not needed, they claim, as major Internet access providers have stated publicly that they are committed to upholding the FCC's four policy principles.[27] Opponents also state that advocates of regulation cannot point to any widespread behavior that justifies the need to establish such regulations and note that competition between telephone and cable system providers, as well as the growing presence of new technologies (e.g., satellite, wireless, and power lines) will serve to counteract any potential anti-discriminatory behavior. Furthermore, opponents claim, even if such a violation should occur, the FCC already has the needed authority to pursue violators. They note that the FCC has not requested further authority[28] and has successfully used its existing authority in the August 1, 2008 Comcast decision (see above) as well as in a March 3, 2005 action against Madison River Communications. In the latter case, the FCC intervened and resolved, through a consent decree, an alleged case of port blocking by Madison River Communications, a local exchange (telephone) company.[29] The full force of antitrust law is also available, they claim, in cases of discriminatory behavior.

Proponents of net neutrality legislation, however, feel that absent some regulation, Internet access providers will become gatekeepers and use their market power to the disadvantage of Internet users and competing content and application providers. They cite concerns that the Internet could develop into a two-tiered system favoring large, established businesses or those with ties to broadband network providers. While market forces should be a deterrent to such anti-competitive behavior, they point out that today's market for residential broadband delivery is largely dominated by only two providers, the telephone and cable television companies, and that, at a minimum, a strong third player is needed to ensure that the benefits of competition will prevail.[30] The need to formulate a national policy to clarify expectations and ensure the "openness" of the Internet is important to protect the benefits and promote the further expansion of broadband, they claim. The adoption of a single, coherent, regulatory framework to prevent discrimination, supporters claim, would be a positive step for further development of the Internet, by providing the marketplace stability needed to encourage investment and foster the growth of new services and applications. Furthermore, relying on current laws and case-by-case anti-trust-like enforcement, they claim, is too cumbersome, slow, and expensive, particularly for small start-up enterprises.[31]

CONGRESSIONAL ACTIVITY IN THE 111TH CONGRESS

A consensus on this issue has not yet formed, and no stand-alone measures addressing net neutrality have been introduced in the 111th Congress, to date. House Communications, Technology, and the Internet Subcommittee Chairman Boucher has stated that he continues to work with broadband providers and content providers to seek common ground on network management practices, and at this time, is pursuing this approach.[32]

However, the net neutrality issue has been narrowly addressed within the context of the American Recovery and Reinvestment Act of 2009 (ARRA, P.L. 111-5). The ARRA contains provisions that require the National Telecommunications and Information Administration (NTIA), in consultation with the FCC, to establish "… nondiscrimination and network interconnection obligations" as a requirement

for grant participants in the Broadband Technology Opportunities Program (BTOP). The law further directs that the FCC's four broadband policy principles, issued in August 2005, are the minimum obligations to be imposed.[33] It is anticipated that the NTIA will release these rules by summer 2009.

Notes

1. The practice of charging of different rates to subscribers based on access speed is not the concern.
2. 47 U.S.C. 151 et seq. For a full discussion of the Brand X decision see CRS Report RL32985, *Defining Cable Broadband Internet Access Service: Background and Analysis of the Supreme Court's Brand X Decision*, by Angie A. Welborn and Charles B. Goldfarb.
3. See http://hraunfoss.fcc.gov/edocs_public/attach match/DOC-260433A2.pdf for a copy of former FCC Chairman Martin's statement. For a summary of the final rule see Appropriate Framework for Broadband Access to the Internet Over Wireline Facilities. *Federal Register*, Vol. 70, No. 199, October 17, 2005, p. 60222.
4. For example, Title II regulations impose rigorous anti-discrimination, interconnection and access requirements. For a further discussion of Title I versus Title II regulatory authority see CRS Report RL32985, cited above.
5. Title I of the 1934 Communications Act gives the FCC such authority if assertion of jurisdiction is "reasonably ancillary to the effective performance of [its] various responsibilities." The FCC in its order cites consumer protection, network reliability, or national security obligations as examples of cases where such authority would apply (see paragraph 36 of the final rule summarized in the *Federal Register* cite in footnote 3, above).
6. See http://www.fcc.gov/headlines2005.html. August 5, 2005. *FCC Adopts Policy Statement on Broadband Internet Access*.
7. See http://hraunfoss.FCC.gov/edocs_public/attach match/DOC-261936A1.pdf. It should be noted that applicants offered certain voluntary commitments, of which this was one.
8. See http://hraunfoss.fcc.gov/edocs_public/attach match/DOC-269275A1 .pdf.

9. See http://hraunfoss.fcc.gov/edocs_public/attach match/FCC-08-183A1.pdf.

10. Comcast, *Frequently Asked Questions and Network Management*. Available at http://help.comcast.net/content/faq/Frequently-Asked-Questions-about-Network-Management.

11. For a legal discussion of the FCC's Comcast decision see CRS Report R40234, *Net Neutrality: The Federal Communications Commission's Authority to Enforce Its Network Management Principles*, by Kathleen Ann Ruane.

12. *In the Matter of A National Broadband Plan for Our Future*, GN Docket No. 09-51. Notice of Inquiry, released April 8, 2009. Available at http://hraunfoss.fcc.gov/edocs_public/attach-match/FCC-09-31A1.pdf.

13. For the specific discussion on open networks see paragraphs 47 and 48 of *In the Matter of A National Broadband Plan for Our Future*, cited above.

14. *Broadband Industry Practices*, WC Docket No. 07–52, Notice of Inquiry, 22 FCC Record 7894 (2007).

15. The header contains the processing information which includes the source and destination addresses, and the data field includes the message content and the identity of the source application.

16. For a further discussion of the positive uses, by network operators, of DPI technologies see testimony of Kyle McSlarrow, President and CEO National Cable and Telecommunications Association, hearings on "Communications Networks and Consumer Privacy: Recent Developments," House Committee on Energy and Commerce, Subcommittee on Communications, Technology, and the Internet, April 23, 2009. Available at http://energycommercehouse.gov/Press_111/20090423/testimony_mcslarrow.pdf.

17. For a further discussion of the potential abuses associated with DPI technology see testimony of Ben Scott, Policy Director, Free Press, hearings on "Communications Networks and Consumer Privacy: Recent Developments," House Committee on Energy and Commerce, Subcommittee on Communications,

Technology, and the Internet, April 23, 2009. Available at http://energycommercehouse.gov/Press_111/20090423/testimony_scott.pdf.

18. For example, concern that information can be gathered, without permission, based on consumer use of the Internet to develop user profiles to provide targeted online advertising, also known as "behavioral advertising," has raised privacy issues. For an examination of this issue see testimony from hearings "Communications Networks and Consumer Privacy: Recent Developments," held April 23, 2009, by the House Energy and Commerce Subcommittee on Communications, Technology, and the Internet. Available at http://energycommerce.house.gov/.

19. Time Warner Cable announced, on April 9, 2009, plans to implement usage-based billing trials in Rochester, New York and Greensboro, North Carolina, in August 2009, and Austin and San Antonio, Texas, in October, 2009. See *Statement from Landel Hobbs, Chief Operating Officer, Time Warner Cable Re: Consumption based billing trials*, April 9, 2009. Available at http://www.timewarnercable.com/corporate/announcements/cbb.html.

20. Citing "misunderstanding about our trials," Time Warner Cable announced plans to deferred implementation of usage-based billing trials in Rochester, New York, Greensboro, North Carolina, and Austin and San Antonio, Texas, to enable "consultation with our customers and other interested parties." See *Time Warner Cable Charts a New Course on Consumption Based Billing Measurement Tools to be Made Available*, April 16, 2009. Available at http://www.time-warnercable.com/Corporate/announcements/cbb.html.

21. For example see *ACA: Metered Bandwidth Pricing is Coming*, available at http://www.broadcast-ingcable.com/article/print/210247-ACA_Metered_Bandwidth_Pricing_Is_Coming.php.

22. For additional information on Sunflower Broadband bandwidth management see http://www.sunflowerbroadband.com/bandwidth.

23. For example, Time Warner states that the top 25% of its users consume 100 times more bandwidth than the bottom 25% and 30% of its

high speed Internet service (i.e., Road Runner) customers use less than 1 GB (Gigabyte) per month. See *Consumption Based Billing FAQs*. Available at http://www.timewarnercable.com/corporate/announcements/cbb_faq.html.

24. See Free Press letter to House Energy and Commerce Committee, April 22, 2009. Available at http://www.Freepress.net/files/FP_metering_letter.pdf.

25. *As Costs Fall, Companies Push to Raise Internet Price*, New York Times, April 20, 2009. Available at http://www.nytimes.com/2009/04/20/business/20isp.html.

26. For a more lengthy discussion regarding proponents' and opponents' views see, for example, testimony from Senate Commerce Committee hearings on Net Neutrality, February 7, 2006. Available at http://commerce.senate.gov/public/index.cfm?FuseAction=Hearings.Hearing&Hearing_ID=1708.

27. See testimony of Kyle McSlarrow, President and CEO of the National Cable and Telecommunications Association, and Walter McCormick, President and CEO of the United States Telecom Association, hearing on Net Neutrality before the Senate Commerce Committee, February 7, 2006, cited above.

28. Former FCC Chairman Martin indicated that the FCC has the necessary tools to uphold the FCC's stated policy principles and did not requested additional authority. Furthermore, former Chairman Martin stated that he was "… confident that the marketplace will continue to ensure that these principles are maintained" and is "… confident therefore, that regulation is not, nor will be, required." See former *Chairman Kevin J. Martin Comments on Commission Policy Statement*, at http://hraunfoss.fcc.gov/edocs_public/attachmatch/DOC-260435A2.pdf. However, FCC Commissioner Copps, in an April 3, 2006 speech, did express concerns over the concentration in broadband facilities providers and their "… ability, and possibly even the incentive, to act as Internet gatekeepers …"

and called for a "national policy" on "… issues regarding consumer rights, Internet openess, and broadband deployment." See http://hraunfoss.fcc.gov/edocs_public/attachmatch/DOC-264765A1.pdf, for a copy of Commissioner Copps' speech.

29. The FCC entered into a consent decree with Madison River Communications to settle charges that the company had deliberately blocked the ports on its network that were used by Vonage Corp. to provide voice over Internet protocol (VoIP) service. Under terms of the decree Madison River agreed to pay a $15,000 fine and not block ports used for VoIP applications. See http://hraunfoss.fcc.gov/edocs_public/attachmatch/DA-05-543A2.pdf. for a copy of the consent decree.

30. For FCC market share data for high-speed connections see *High-Speed Services for Internet Access: Status as of December 31, 2007*, Federal Communications Commission, Industry Analysis and Technology Division, Wireline Competition Bureau, released January 2009. View report at http://hraunfoss.fcc.gov/edocs_public/attachmatch/DOC-287962A1.pdf.

31. For example, see testimony of Vint Cerf, VP Google, Earl Comstock, President and CEO of CompTel, and Jeffrey Citron, Chairman and CEO Vonage, hearing on Net Neutrality, before the Senate Commerce Committee, February 7, 2006, cited above.

32. *Boucher Opts For Talks, Not Legislation, On Net Neutrality*, National Journal, Congress Daily, February 26, 2009. *Boucher, Stakeholders Working On Network Management Issues*, Telecommunications Reports, March 15, 2009, p.19.

33. For a further more detailed discussion of the broadband infrastructure programs contained in P.L. 111-5 see CRS Report R40436, *Broadband Infrastructure Programs in the American Recovery and Reinvestment Act*, by Lennard G. Kruger.

9 781609 279936